NICOLE ROUTHIER'S
FRUIT
COOKBOOK

NICOLE ROUTHIER'S

400 SWEET & SAVORY

FRUIT

FRUIT-FILLED RECIPES

COOKBOOK

SOUPS TO DESSERTS

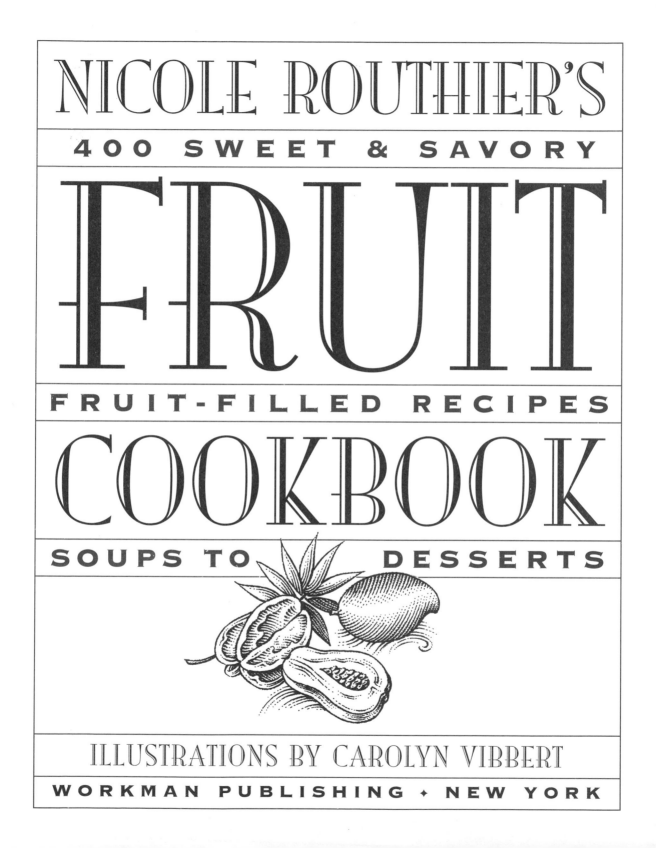

ILLUSTRATIONS BY CAROLYN VIBBERT

WORKMAN PUBLISHING ◆ NEW YORK

This book is dedicated with love to my husband, Anthony Laudin, a meat-and-potatoes guy who cheerfully endured a steady diet of fruits and vegetables.

Library of Congress Cataloging-in-Publication Data

Routhier, Nicole
[Fruit cookbook]
Nichole Routhier's fruit cookbook: 400 sweet & savory, fruit-filled recipes, soups to desserts.
p. cm.
Includes index.
ISBN 0-7611-0506-9 (hardcover: alk. paper). — ISBN 1-56305-565-1
(pbk.: alk. paper)
1. Cookery (Fruit) I. Title.
TX811.R68 1996
641.6'4—dc20
96-10214
CIP

Cover design by Lisa Hollander
Cover illustration by Linda DeVito
Book design by Lisa Hollander and Lori S. Malkin
Book illustrations by Carolyn Vibbert

Workman books are available at special discounts when purchased in bulk
for premium and sales promotions as well as for fund-raising or educational use.
Special editions or book excerpts can also be created to specification.
For details, contact the Special Sales Director at the address below.

Workman Publishing Company, Inc.
708 Broadway
New York, NY 10003-9555

First printing May 1996
10 9 8 7 6 5 4 3 2 1

ACKNOWLEDGMENTS

I'd like to give special thanks to all the people whose help and talents made this book possible:

Judith Weber, my agent, who was the first person to be seduced by my proposal for a fruit cookbook.

Suzanne Rafer, my editor, for her great enthusiasm and faith in this project, and who was such a help in fine-tuning this manuscript. Thanks to her, my initial concept of a "small" fruit dessert cookbook turned into a substantial work.

Anne Magruder, assistant to the editor, whose diligent work is very much appreciated; Isabel Vita, for her meticulous and invaluable proofreading; and Kristen Carr, for trying the recipes.

Lisa Hollander, Lori Malkin, and assistant Natsumi Uda, who gave the book its very seductive look; and Carolyn Vibbert, for her homey, delightful illustrations.

Andrea Glickson and Deborah DeLosa, for their vigorous promotional efforts.

The whole sales department, especially Bert Snyder and Janet Harris, for their enthusiasm and hard work.

Peter Workman, for his cheerful support. When I described some of my fruit recipes to Peter, he exclaimed: "That's something I would love to eat!" From that moment on, I knew I was in very good company.

Marcel Desaulniers, Bharti Kirschner, and Jennifer Millar, generous friends who shared their delicious recipes with me.

My students, whom I relied on for testing and tasting many of my recipes.

All the fruit and vegetable farmers, for the bountiful harvest they provide for us yearlong.

And last but not least, my mom and nanny, who instilled in me a love for good food and fine cooking.

CONTENTS

Introduction: Fruit, Glorious Fruit

Fruitful Beginnings: Dips, Appetizers & Hors d'Oeuvres

Easy to prepare, light, lovely ways to start a meal or kick off a party with flair. Choose from a Strawberry Salsa, Rosy Baba Ghanoush, Roasted Pepper and Apple Dip with Steamed Shrimp, and a host of other possibilities.

Aromatic Soups

Heavenly bowlfuls—steaming hot or cool and refreshing, depending on the season and the mood. Selections include Mexican Lime Soup, Watercress Soup with Asian Pear, Caribbean Vichyssoise, and Piña Colada Soup.

Salads with Fruit Accents

Glorious salad concoctions starring fresh and dried fruits with an innovative twist. Tender Greens with Passion Fruit Vinaigrette, Bistro Salad with Pears and Cheese, Black Bean and Tree Melon Salad, and Chicken Salad with Apricot Chutney—just to mention a few.

Pasta & Grains

The mild flavors of pasta and grains make a perfect base for the seductive flavors of fruit. An international repertoire of sweet and savory dishes include Bangkok Noodles, Fruited Noodle Pudding, Wild Mushroom Risotto with Apples, and Couscous with Dried Fruit.

Sophisticated Seafood

Marrying fruits of the sea with fruits of the land results in dishes that delight and surprise. Selections range from luscious Fillet of Sole with Gooseberries to hearty Trout with Potato and Plantain Salad to sweet Catfish Venice Style to spicy Scallop Curry with Thai Flavors.

The Bird Range

Roasted Chicken Breasts with Glazed Kumquats, Fried Chicken with Orange Cream Gravy, Duck Breasts Montmorency, and Quail in Currant Sauce highlight a wealth of wonderful poultry recipes.

Magnificent Meat

Roasted, braised, stewed, or pan sautéed, meat dishes emerge brighter, lighter, and more enticing with the addition of fruit. Serve up Pepper Steak with Plum Ketchup, Orange Beef with Peanuts, Pork Kabobs with Grilled Peaches, and Glazed Lamb Chops.

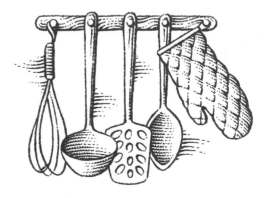

Sweet & Savory Sides

Accent favorite entrées with something different—fruits perk up overworked vegetables with glorious results. Included are Three Fruit Haroset, Sautéed Spinach Catalan, Mashed Potatoes with Roasted Pears, and Okra with Asian Flavors.

From the Pantry:
Chutneys, Pickles, Fruit Butters, Jams, Relishes, Sauces, and Vinegars

Capture the fresh vivid flavor of fruit at the peak of seasonal perfection. Fill your shelves with these exciting pantry favorites: Peach Butter, Ruby Red Raspberry Jam, Sassy Banana Chutney, Pickled Grapes, Spirited Plum Sauce, and Blueberry Vinegar.

Breads, Quick and Slow

Freshly baked and fragrant with fruits— breads, biscuits, and muffins, still warm from the oven are one of the home cook's greatest rewards. Enjoy Fig, Prosciutto, and Pepper Bread, Tuscan Grape Bread, Hot Strawberry Biscuits, and a Persimmon-Almond Loaf.

Festive Breakfasts

As delicious as the classic breakfast fruit dishes are, when the day calls for a special start, serve up Granola Baked Apples, Cranberry-Pumpkin Waffles, Sausage and Orange Marmalade omelets, or a Skillet Apple Frittata.

Smoothies & Spirits

Quick pick-me-ups, thirst-quenchers, frosty floats, and sophisticated cocktails—fruits figure in a wide range of imaginative concoctions. Try a Papaya Smoothie, Litchee-Pineapple Bing, Watermelon Spritzer, Peach Margaritas, and Hot Spiced Wine Punch.

Sorbet & Ice Cream

An array of fruity frozen favorites to cool off the hottest summer days and nights include Tangerine Sorbet, Kiwi Snow, Watermelon Ice, Apple Granita, and an unusual Mango Tea and Litchee Honey Ice Cream.

Soothing Fruit Desserts

A delicous collection of fast, easy, fruit desserts that range from fresh fruit salads to comforting puddings, crumbles, and crisps. Favorite finales include Marinated Pomegranates, Poached Summer Fruits,

English Summer Pudding, Chilled Cherimoya Custard, Apricot Fool, and Bumbleberry Crunch.

Tarts, Pies, Cakes & Cookies

When only a rich indulgence will do—the perfect ending to a perfect meal might include a Napoleon of Nectarines with Caramel Sauce, or a Raspberry-Rhubarb Pie, Spiced Apple Cake, Cosmic Chocolate Cake, or Triple Strawberry Shortcakes. Then, too, you won't go wrong with a plateful of Heavenly Raspberry Brownies or Banana-Chocolate Chip Cookies.

FRUIT, GLORIOUS FRUIT

This cookbook is the product of my long love affair with fruit. For me, fruit always triggers sensual memories, many of which are linked to my childhood experiences in the hot tropical sun of Southeast Asia. I can't remember a time growing up when the scent of fruit wasn't in the air and a huge bowl of fresh fruit wasn't displayed on our kitchen table.

My fascination with fruit started when I was about four years old. In 1960, my mother sent my older sister and me from Vietnam to live with Bau, our Vietnamese-born nanny, in Vientiane, Laos. Her house had a large backyard with a small fish pond, some chicken coops, a half-dozen banana trees, and a papaya tree. Out front there were two small guava trees. In the summer, when the guavas ripened, my sister and I raided the trees. Although such activity, if discovered, was sure to yield swift punishment, we were undeterred. The siren call of those bright yellow fruits dangling from the branches proved too irresistible. Of course, in our joyful harvesting and eating, our faces, hands, and clothes usually got deeply stained with sap, which made our nanny really angry.

As we grew a little older, we developed a knack for sneaking unripe mangoes and tamarinds from our neighbors' trees. We weren't really being bad. We did it partly for the challenge and partly for the pleasure derived from anticipation of the feast to come. The illicit fruits were green and hard and made our lips pucker up, but we ate them anyhow. We would dip them in salt and cayenne pepper and savor them with gusto. In our youthful impatience and excitement, we always seemed to forget that such binges would inevitably cause painful stomachaches!

When I was about ten, my mother started her own restaurant in Vientiane, and we moved to live with her. It was around that time that food became the central interest of my life. Being in the kitchen with my mom was more important to me than jumping rope with my playmates. To me, helping prepare our meals never felt like a chore. The tantalizing smells and incredible tastes of her food made a lifelong impression on me.

It's hard for me to imagine my mother's cooking without limes, mangoes, pineapples, or coconuts. Often, a meal would consist of soup, a big delicious bowl of warm salad, with chunks of fresh fruits. Whether by experience or by instinct, she used fruit as she did other piquant seasonings: to balance savory with sweet and tart tastes and, along with complementary herbs and spices, to bring out the flavor of meats and fish.

My mother remarried when I was in my early teens, and our family moved to the south of France. While living in Cannes and Nice, I was introduced to entirely new and wonderful fruits. Although it seems inconceivable to me now, I had never seen peaches, nectarines, cherries, figs, Italian plums, and raspberries until then. I loved to wander through the open-air markets, where the stalls were piled high with a magnificent harvest of fruits and vegetables at the peak of ripeness and maturity. I remember being overwhelmed by the sweet fragrance of strawberries and the intoxicating aroma of wild lavender, rosemary, and thyme.

THE FRUITED PLAINS

When I came to the United States in the late 1970s, I was shocked to discover that open-air markets were not a universal way of life. I realized that in many parts of the country, shopping for food meant going to a supermarket where fruits, vegetables, and especially meats and fish came bagged or shrink-wrapped in plastic and where, more often than not, the produce was of poor quality and uninviting. Selections were limited to constants like parched citrus fruits, unripened bananas, mealy apples, and rock-hard pears.

Fortunately, things have improved tremendously. Today, at least where I live, farmers' markets and greengrocers are becoming the norm rather than the exception, and even supermarkets are apt to offer more exotic fruits like papayas, plantains, persimmons, and mangoes. Once considered foreign, these fruits are becoming a staple part of the American food experience. Even though breadfruit, guava, and passion fruit are far from being fixtures here, people are not surprised anymore to find pretty slices of star fruit adorning their meats, or a sprinkling of bright pomegranate seeds over a salad. As our country becomes more aware of other cultures and their foods, we are more willing to try and even embrace new, vivid cooking styles and flavors.

SEDUCTIVE FRUIT

Fruit has been an important part of my culinary experience through the years, on three different continents. This timely cookbook is my heartfelt attempt to introduce you to this seductive world. It is a universe filled with vibrant and irresistible flavors, a world in which scents, smells, and tastes merge to give us a pleasurable, sensuous eating experience.

If you have ever tried cooking with fruit, you know that it can perform magic on any given dish. While contributing unexpected depth of flavor, fruit will also make the food taste cleaner and fresher. Fruit is ideally suited to today's concept of lighter, more flavorful, and healthier eating. Because it is naturally sweet, flavorful, and full of texture, fruit enriches a dish; thus it provides a great alternative to cream and butter. This is not a diet book, but I do offer creative ways for you to incorporate fruit into your daily cooking and baking with the most flavor impact and without loading up on fat. With many of us watching our diet, and dietitians stressing the eating of lots of fresh fruits and vegetables, I can't think of a better way to achieve these goals.

From the hundreds of recipes that I tested, I have selected those that I thought were the most pleasing to the palate and the eye. Also, I wanted them to be easy to prepare, so you will be tempted to make them frequently. I have included traditional or updated favorites from many lands, personal little surprises from my own experimentation, and recipes from other cooks and friends, to demonstrate how fruit is universally used and how it can be easily adapted to suit almost any style of cooking.

I hope this cookbook will enable you to capture the magical pleasures that fruit can bring to your table. Have a fruitful time!

FRUITFUL BEGINNINGS

DIPS, APPETIZERS & HORS D'OEUVRES

The urge to have friends over for cocktails and hors d'oeuvres can easily be dulled by the prospect of all the preparation even a small party requires. One of the easiest ways around this predicament is to center the menu on fruit, which is very much in tune with today's lighter approach to food. What could be simpler than setting out a platter of colorful fresh fruits and a bowl of dip for guests to nibble on? How about succulent grilled fruit brochettes or delicate cheese-filled strawberries and grapes?

Occasionally, when I feel extravagant, I serve hors d'oeuvres or finger foods with a little flash. A cold dish, such as Tex-Mex Mussels, topped with a spicy pineapple-tomato salsa, or Fruity Bruschetta, or a hot dish like raspberry-glazed Victory Wings, sets a festive tone for an evening. Chopped Liver Pâté, laced with silky, sweet apricot chutney, is downright luxurious.

For a dinner party, keep in mind that the hors d'oeuvre or appetizer is the prelude to the courses that follow. And since a goal for any meal should be balance, it begins with the first bite: If your entrée is very light and simple, the first course should be something hearty, such as Brazilian Bean Dip, or the sophisticated Crisp-Fried Oysters with Spicy Papaya Salsa. On the other hand, if you plan to serve a substantial main course, something like the simple yet elegant Chilled Melon with Prosciutto might be offered to start. In general, the recipes in this chapter can be made partially or completely ahead. And most are surprisingly simple to prepare.

BRAZILIAN BEAN DIP

YIELD: 4 CUPS

Serve this sweet-spicy South American treat with frosty margaritas or daiquiris to get the party going! You can make the tortilla chips in advance and reheat them in a low oven while you prepare the dip. If you are too busy to make your own corn chips, go ahead and use store bought. The joy of eating this tropical dip won't be diminished.

½ pound spicy Italian sausages, casings removed
1 cup chopped scallions (white and green parts)
½ cup finely chopped green bell pepper
½ cup finely chopped red bell pepper
½ cup finely chopped onion
1 tablespoon minced garlic
½ teaspoon minced fresh Scotch bonnet pepper or 2 fresh hot red chile peppers or jalapeño peppers, minced
1 cup tomato sauce, preferably homemade (page 102)
½ cup chicken broth, preferably homemade (page 30)
1 can (19 ounces) white kidney beans, drained
3 ripe but firm bananas
Salt
Fresh cilantro sprigs, for garnish
Tortilla Chips (recipe follows)

1. Crumble the sausage into a large skillet. Cook over medium heat, breaking up the lumps with a fork until no traces of pink remain, about 5 minutes.

2. Add the scallions, bell peppers, onion, garlic, and Scotch bonnet pepper. Sauté until the vegetables are tender, about 3 minutes.

GREAT MATCHES

BANANAS AND PLANTAINS

Bananas and plantains match up beautifully with both hard and soft cheeses, cured meats, and chocolate. Other compatible ingredients to keep in mind when cooking with bananas or plantains are all herbs and spices, La Grande Passion (Armagnac and passion fruit liqueur), orange liqueur, vinegars of all kinds, and sweet potatoes.

3. Add the tomato sauce, chicken broth, and beans. Reduce the heat to low and simmer for 5 minutes.

4. Peel and slice the bananas. Stir them into the sausage mixture and continue to simmer for 3 to 5 minutes longer. Season to taste with salt.

5. Mash the bananas with a potato masher, then transfer the dip to a serving bowl. Garnish with cilantro sprigs and serve immediately with Tortilla Chips.

Tortilla Chips

YIELD: 6 TO 8 SERVINGS

Vegetable oil
24 corn tortillas (6-inch rounds), cut into 6
    wedges each
Salt (optional)

1. Line 2 baking sheets with several layers of paper towels.

2. Pour oil to a depth of 2 inches into a large, deep, heavy skillet or deep fryer and heat over medium heat to 365°F. Add the tortilla wedges in batches of 12 and fry, turning with a slotted spoon, until crisp, about 1½ minutes. Use the spoon to transfer the chips to the prepared baking sheets. Keep warm in a low oven as you fry the remaining chips.

3. Season with salt, if desired, transfer to a basket, and serve warm.

STRAWBERRY SALSA

YIELD: ABOUT 2½ CUPS

This sweet summery salsa can accompany anything from toasted pita triangles to a cut of grilled fish, shrimp, or chicken. You can transform the flavor and color of this salsa by substituting fresh blueberries or blackberries for the strawberries.

½ medium red onion, thinly sliced

1 jalapeño pepper, minced

½ red bell pepper, stemmed, seeded, and
    julienned

½ yellow bell pepper, stemmed, seeded,
    and julienned

½ green bell pepper, stemmed, seeded,
    and julienned

¼ cup finely shredded fresh cilantro
    leaves (for shredding instructions, see
    page 34)

½ pint (1 cup) fresh strawberries, hulled
    and sliced

¼ cup fresh orange juice

2 tablespoons fresh lime juice

2 tablespoons extra-virgin olive oil

Salt and freshly ground black pepper

Place all the ingredients in a large mixing bowl, and toss to combine. Cover and refrigerate at least 2 hours or up to 4 hours. Fifteen minutes before serving, remove the salsa from the refrigerator, so it loses some of its chill.

SALPICON OF BEEF

YIELD: 6 SERVINGS

Salpicon is a French term for cooked diced fruit, meat, or vegetables bound with a syrup or sauce and usually used as a garnish or as stuffing for pastry. This refreshing minced meat dip, moistened with orange juice, is very popular in Guatemala. The citrus gives it a pleasing clean quality, and pepper and mint add bite. In Guatemala, this salpicon is served with corn chips, but it's equally good with crisp pita triangles or crackers.

4 whole cloves

2 bay leaves

½ medium onion

1 pound lean boneless chuck, cut into
    1-inch cubes

1½ teaspoons salt

⅓ cup fresh orange juice

1 teaspoon grated orange zest

2 tablespoons fresh lime juice

½ cup minced red onion

¼ cup finely shredded fresh mint leaves
    (for shredding instructions, see
    page 34)

½ teaspoon ground cumin

½ teaspoon freshly ground black pepper

½ cup diced orange

Tortilla chips, preferably homemade
    (page 3), pita triangles, and/or crackers
    for dipping

1. Use the cloves to pin the bay leaves to the cut surface of the onion. Place the studded onion, meat, and 1 teaspoon of the salt in a medium-size saucepan and cover with water. Bring to a boil over medium-high heat, skimming the froth as it rises to the surface. Reduce the heat to low, partially cover, and simmer until the beef is very tender, 40 to 45 minutes. Remove from the heat and let the beef cool in the broth, uncovered.

2. With a slotted spoon, transfer the beef to a food processor. (Do not discard the broth.) Pulse until finely chopped. Do not overprocess.

3. In a medium-size mixing bowl, combine the beef, orange juice, orange zest, lime juice, ¼ cup of the reserved broth, the red onion, mint, cumin, remaining ½ teaspoon salt, and the pepper. Finally, fold in the diced orange.

4. Transfer the mixture to a serving bowl and serve surrounded with the corn chips.

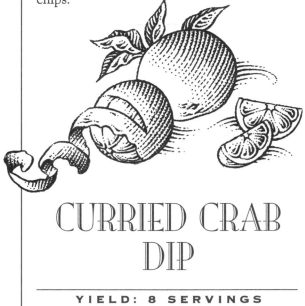

CURRIED CRAB DIP

YIELD: 8 SERVINGS

When two such luxuriantly sweet foods as pears and crabmeat are combined, there's bound to be delicious chemistry. Add curry powder, and you've got an exotic, equatorial taste sensation in which the cooling pear tames the heat of the spices with a surprising twist. Have toast points made from baguettes or pita ready to scoop into this delicious dip.

> 1½ teaspoons unsalted butter
> ¼ cup finely chopped onion
> ¼ cup finely chopped green bell pepper
> ¼ cup finely chopped celery
> ¼ cup thinly sliced scallions (green part only)
> 1 teaspoon minced garlic
> 1 large ripe pear, peeled, cored, and diced
> ½ pound fresh lump crabmeat, picked over
> 1 small egg, lightly beaten
> 6 tablespoons good-quality mayonnaise
> 2 teaspoons Dijon mustard
> 1½ teaspoons curry powder, preferably
>   Madras brand
> ¼ teaspoon Tabasco sauce
> ¼ teaspoon freshly ground black pepper
> ⅛ teaspoon salt
> 2 tablespoons heavy (or whipping) cream
> Paprika

1. Preheat the oven to 375°F. Lightly butter a 1-quart gratin dish.

2. Melt the butter in a nonstick skillet over medium-low heat. Add the onion, green pepper, celery, scallions, and garlic and sauté until tender, about 3 minutes. Remove the pan from the heat and stir in the pear and crabmeat. Let the mixture cool.

3. Whisk together the beaten egg, 3 tablespoons of the mayonnaise, the mustard, curry powder, Tabasco sauce, black pepper, and salt in a small bowl. Add to the crabmeat mixture, stir well to combine, and spoon into the prepared gratin dish.

4. Blend the cream with the remaining 3 tablespoons mayonnaise and spread it over the top. Lightly sprinkle with paprika. (This can be made a day ahead, covered, and refrigerated. Bring to room temperature before baking.)

5. Bake until the dip is hot and bubbling, about 20 minutes. Serve hot.

ROSY BABA GHANOUSH

YIELD: ABOUT 3 CUPS

Eggplant is delicious in any form. However, when roasted and mixed with garlic, tahini, and fresh lemon juice, as in this Middle Eastern dip, it can be dangerously addictive. Pomegranate juice adds an appetizing pink tint to the dip, and the seeds add crunch and a burst of fresh flavor.

2 large eggplants (about 2 pounds total)
1 large pomegranate (see Note)
3 tablespoons tahini sesame paste
4 teaspoons (or more) fresh lemon
    juice
4 large cloves garlic, minced
1/2 teaspoon salt
2 tablespoons chopped fresh flat-leaf
    parsley leaves
Extra-virgin olive oil, to drizzle over
    the dip (optional)
16 pita breads (4-inch rounds), warmed,
    each cut into 4 triangles

1. Prick the eggplants all over with a fork. Roast the eggplants either over coals or gas burners (1 per burner) set at medium heat. Turn frequently until the flesh is soft and the skin completely charred, 8 to 10 minutes. (Or bake the eggplants in a preheated 450°F oven until soft, 25 to 30 minutes). Place in a covered bowl to steam 5 minutes (this helps loosen the skin). When the eggplants are cool enough to handle, remove the skin, and coarsely chop the pulp.

2. Peel the pomegranate and remove the seeds. Place two-thirds of the seeds in a sieve, and press out the juice with your hand. (Be careful: Pomegranate juice stains.) You should have about 1/4 cup of juice. Reserve the rest of the seeds.

3. On a cutting board, mash the garlic and salt with the flat side of a knife until they form a paste.

4. In a large glass bowl, combine the

eggplant with the pomegranate juice, tahini, 4 teaspoons lemon juice, and the mashed garlic. Mix well. Add more salt and lemon juice, if needed.

5. Transfer the dip to a serving bowl. Sprinkle with the chopped parsley and the reserved pomegranate seeds. Drizzle with a little olive oil, if desired. Serve with warm pita triangles.

NOTE: If you want to make this dip when pomegranates are out of season, simply substitute Pomegranate Molasses (see Index) for the fresh juice. Dilute 2 tablespoons Pomegranate Molasses with 3 tablespoons warm water. The dip will taste just as good, although it will lack the crunch of the seeds.

ROASTED PEPPER AND APPLE DIP WITH STEAMED SHRIMP

YIELD: ABOUT 45 HORS D'OEUVRES

A sauce of roasted bell peppers makes a superb dip for chilled shrimp, which are skewered on toothpicks with small chunks of crisp, tart apple. The contrast of cold, sweet,

spicy, and smoky flavors is just wonderful. The dip will keep up to one week in the refrigerator.

2 pounds large shrimp (21 to 25 per pound), shelled and deveined, with tails intact
8 tablespoons extra-virgin olive oil, plus extra for garnish
4 teaspoons minced garlic
2 teaspoons dried red pepper flakes
2 pounds red bell peppers (about 4 large), roasted (for roasting instructions, see page 8) and coarsely chopped
1/2 cup toasted blanched almonds (for toasting instructions, see page 64)
1/4 cup red wine vinegar
1 teaspoon sugar
1/2 Granny Smith apple, peeled, cored, and chopped, plus 1 whole Granny Smith apple
Salt and freshly ground black pepper

1. Arrange the shrimp in a single layer in a steamer basket. Place the basket over boiling water and cover tightly. Steam until the shrimp turn pink, 1 1/2 to 2 minutes. Do not overcook. Remove the shrimp from the steamer and cool. Refrigerate until well chilled.

2. Heat 2 tablespoons of the olive oil in a small skillet over medium heat. Add the garlic and red pepper flakes and sauté until fragrant and lightly golden, 1 minute. Remove the pan from the heat.

3. Place the chopped bell peppers in a food processor or a blender. Add the sautéed garlic mixture, the remaining 6 tablespoons

HOW TO ROAST A BELL PEPPER

Roasting a bell pepper makes it easy to remove the skin and imparts a rich, smoky flavor; it also intensifies the pepper's sweetness. If you are going to roast a pepper, choose one with thick flesh and straight sides.

OVER HOT COALS OR A GAS OR ELECTRIC BURNER: *Place a bell pepper directly on a gas or electric burner at medium heat. Roast the pepper, turning it with tongs, as the flesh becomes soft and the skin charred and blistered over the entire surface, about 10 minutes. (The peppers can be roasted the same way outdoors on the grill.) Place the roasted pepper in a bowl, cover it with a plate, and let sit until cool. Hold the pepper under cold running water and rub the skin off. Pat dry, then core. Cut the pepper in half and scrape out the seeds with a knife.*

WITH A BROILER: *Preheat the broiler. Cut the peppers in half lengthwise. Place them skin side up on a broiler pan 4 inches from the heat, and broil until the skin is blackened and blistered, about 5 minutes. Cool before peeling, coring, and seeding, as described above.*

---

olive oil, the toasted almonds, vinegar, and sugar and process to a purée. Add the chopped apple and process to a purée. (If your blender isn't large enough to hold all the ingredients at once, process in 2 batches and then stir to blend thoroughly.)

4. Transfer the dip to a bowl and season to taste with salt and pepper. Cover and refrigerate until well chilled.

5. When ready to serve, peel and core the remaining apple. Cut it into 8 wedges then crosswise into $^1/_2$-inch-thick pieces. Skewer a shrimp and a piece of apple on each toothpick, and serve with the dip on the side. For a slightly richer dip, pour a thin layer of olive oil over the top.

CREAMY RASPBERRY DIP

YIELD: 1 CUP

*S*erve crisp wedges of apple or pear with this tasty dip, which can also be turned into a dressing for fresh fruit salads. Blackberries can stand in for the raspberries.

6 ounces cream cheese or Neufchâtel
1 tablespoon (firmly packed) light brown sugar
$^1/_4$ teaspoon ground ginger
$1^1/_2$ tablespoons raspberry vinegar, preferably homemade (page 286)
$^1/_2$ cup fresh or thawed frozen raspberries, slightly crushed

*O*ften *a berry seems too huge and perfect to drop in the bucket for some*
indeterminate future. It must be eaten then and there—
a mouthful of dark, winy sweetness.

—KATHRYN STEWART, BLACKBERRYING

Combine the cream cheese, brown sugar, and ginger in a small bowl and blend with an electric mixer until smooth. Add the vinegar and raspberries and mix until blended. Cover and chill before using.

VARIATION

CREAMY RASPBERRY DRESSING: Thin out the dip with ¼ cup fresh orange juice. Serve over fresh fruit salad.

PLANTAIN CHIPS

YIELD: 8 TO 10 SERVINGS

In South America and the Caribbean, green plantains are often sliced wafer-thin and fried to make chips. I find green plantain chips somewhat bland; instead I use a slightly riper fruit because it provides extra flavor and a creamier texture. These melt-in-your-mouth treats are delicious by themselves, but they taste even better when dipped

in a garlicky, pineapple dipping sauce, which eliminates any oily taste. They're also good with any of the salsas in this chapter (see Index for recipes). You may also serve these irresistible chips as snacks, or as an accompaniment to almost any pork, beef, chicken, or fish entrée.

4 ripe but firm (greenish-yellow) plantains,
    peeled (page 10)
Vegetable oil
Salt and freshly ground black pepper
Spicy Pineapple Dip (page 156, Steps 1 and
    2), optional

1. Cut the plantains on the diagonal into slices slightly thicker than ¼ inch. Line a baking sheet with paper towels.

2. Pour oil to a depth of 2 inches into a large, deep, heavy skillet or deep fryer and heat over medium heat to 375°F. Carefully add a handful of plantains, and fry, turning occasionally, until they are golden brown, 2 to 3 minutes. Use a slotted spoon to transfer the chips to the prepared baking sheet. Keep

PLANTAINS

Plantains belong to the same family as common bananas but are larger, starchier, and harder to peel. Although they look like big bananas, the raw fruits never develop much sweetness or flavor; hence they are cooked much like a vegetable in tropical zones around the world.

At whatever stage of ripeness, from green to greenish yellow, to yellow and finally to black, a plantain is always suitable for cooking and extremely versatile. It can be baked, grilled, sautéed, deep-fried, braised, boiled, and even mashed like a potato. Green plantains contain the most starch and are almost tasteless; they are often compared with potatoes and are cooked in similar ways. Experienced cooks often pound green plantains to soften them before cooking. Sliced wafer-thin, green plantain also makes great fried chips. When half- or fully ripe, it becomes sweeter and tastes like a sweet potato. If ripe plantain is unavailable, substitute a very green banana.

COOKING PLANTAINS

If possible, buy several green plantains at a time, and keep them at room temperature. A green plantain can take anywhere from 7 to 10 days to ripen. Cook a couple when they are still green, wait a few days, and cook some more when they are riper. When the plantains have fully ripened to black, bake one in its skin in a preheated 375 °F oven until creamy-tender, 45 to 50 minutes. Peel and serve it whole with a dab of butter and a sprinkling of salt. Or mash it with a little chicken broth, butter, and minced garlic. You might also sauté it in unsalted butter, with brown sugar and a dash of lime juice for a sweet snack or side dish. Unlike bananas, ripe plantains hold their shape quite well in cooking.

PEELING PLANTAINS

To peel a plantain, first trim the pointy ends. If long slices are needed, halve it; if not, cut it into chunks. Using a paring knife, cut slits along the length of each of the ribs, then unwrap the peel around the fruit rather than zipping it straight down. To keep your hands from becoming discolored, peel green plantains under running water.

---

warm in a low oven as you fry the remaining plantains.

3. Season generously with salt and pepper. Serve the chips immediately, passing the Spicy Pineapple Dip on the side, if desired.

FRUITY BRUSCHETTA

YIELD: 16 BRUSCHETTA

A bruschetta is a thick slice of country bread that is brushed with garlic-flavored olive oil, grilled, then covered with a luscious tomato topping. In this variation, peach is added to the traditional Italian "salsa" of tomatoes, red onion, and basil, making for a tasty and beautiful melange. I like to serve bruschetta for lunch, or as an hors d'oeuvre when I have company. For the best flavor, the topping should be at room temperature, and prepared no more than 30 minutes before eating. Assemble just before serving. Instead of peach, you may use cantaloupe, papaya, or mango.

> 4 ripe plum tomatoes (about 1 pound), cut into ¼-inch dice
> 1 cup diced peaches (¼ inch dice)
> ½ cup finely diced red onion
> 16 large fresh basil leaves, finely shredded (for shredding instructions, see page 34)
> 4 teaspoons balsamic vinegar
> ¼ cup plus ⅓ cup extra-virgin olive oil
> Salt and freshly ground black pepper
> 1½ teaspoons minced garlic
> 1 large round loaf country bread
> Kosher salt

1. Preheat the broiler. (If your grill is already on, then skip the broiler—bruschetta prepared on the grill tastes even better.)

2. In a large bowl, gently toss together the tomatoes, peach, red onion, basil, and vinegar with ¼ cup of the olive oil and salt and pepper. Let the mixture sit at room temperature while you make the garlic toasts.

3. Mix the remaining ⅓ cup oil with the garlic in a small bowl. Cut the bread into 8 long slices, about ½ inch thick, and brush with the garlic oil.

4. Toast (or grill) the bread slices until golden brown on both sides. Cut each slice in half and place the halves on a serving platter. Top each piece with a generous spoonful of the salsa, sprinkle with kosher salt, and serve immediately.

GRILLED FIGS WRAPPED IN PROSCIUTTO

YIELD: 16 HORS D'OEUVRES

The trick to this simple and tasty hors d'oeuvre is to use paper-thin, top-quality prosciutto, preferably imported, which is less salty than the domestic kind. Be sure to cook these tidbits very briefly, just until the fig inside is barely warm. Peeled, sliced fresh peach or mango is an excellent substitute for the fig.

> 4 medium fresh black figs (about 2 ounces each), quartered lengthwise
> 16 large fresh basil leaves
> 8 thin slices imported prosciutto (about ¼ pound), each halved crosswise
> Olive oil

1. Place a fig quarter and a basil leaf on each slice of prosciutto and roll up the

prosciutto. Cover and refrigerate until just before serving, up to 6 hours.

2. Prepare coals for grilling or preheat a stovetop grill over medium-low heat.

3. Brush the rolls very lightly with olive oil and grill until the prosciutto is barely browned at the edges and the fig is just warmed through, about 30 seconds per side. Do not overcook or the prosciutto will become too salty. Serve immediately.

INDOOR GRILLING

Even if you don't have a backyard, you can still enjoy grilled foods. A grill pan, which sits directly over a gas or electric burner (larger models fit over two burners), lets you cook exactly as you would over hot coals—lending superb flavor and appealing grill marks. An added benefit of cooking with grill pans is that since foods are cooked on raised ridges, fat drains away, resulting in more healthful dishes.

CHILLED MELON AND PROSCIUTTO

YIELD: 4 SERVINGS

This refreshing and versatile appetizer is often taken for granted—even by me—and I almost left it out of this book. But because the classic combi-nation of sweet melon and salty pro-sciutto is so wonderful, I had to include it. For an unusual twist, the prosciutto can be wrapped around fresh papaya or mango instead of melon. As another sea-sonal variation, peel and split fresh figs, then serve them alongside the prosciutto. This dish becomes a light meal when served with plenty of semolina bread and sweet butter.

1 small ripe honeydew melon or cantaloupe
8 thin slices prosciutto (about ¼ pound),
*   preferably imported*
1 teaspoon cracked black peppercorns
4 lime wedges

1. Halve and seed the melon. Cut each half into 4 wedges and remove the peel.

2. Wrap each wedge of melon wedges in a slice of prosciutto. Cover and refrigerate until ready to serve.

3. Place 2 melon wedges on each appe-tizer plate. Sprinkle with cracked pepper-corns and garnish with a wedge of lime. Squeeze the lime over the melon before eating.

VARIATION

PROSCIUTTO WITH MACERATED APPLES: Arrange 2 slices prosciutto on each of 4 small plates. Peel, core, and finely dice 2 tart apples and place them in a small bowl. Toss with 3 tablespoons muscatel or another sweet, fruity wine, and let sit several minutes, or until the fruit has almost absorbed the wine. With a slotted spoon, spoon the fruit over the prosciutto. Sprinkle with freshly ground black pepper and serve immediately.

LEMON-THYME STRAWBERRIES

YIELD: 8 HORS D'OEUVRES

An impressive offering at any cocktail party, these elegant morsels are especially appropriate for special occasions, such as a bridal shower or special anniversary celebration. Use your prettiest serving dish to complement the colorful strawberries.

> 48 large, beautiful strawberries, with stems attached
> 10 ounces (1⅓ cups) fresh goat cheese, such as Montrachet
> 3 tablespoons freshly grated Parmesan cheese
> 3 tablespoons confectioners' sugar
> 1½ teaspoons finely chopped fresh thyme leaves
> 1 teaspoon finely grated lemon zest

1. Rinse the strawberries and blot them dry with paper towels. Slice off a tiny piece from a side of each berry so that it lies flat on a cutting board; reserve the sliced-off pieces. With a small melon baller, remove a round chunk from the side opposite the cut. Finely chop the centers and reserved strawberry pieces and set aside. You should have about 1 cup of chopped strawberries.

2. Using a fork, mix the cheeses with the confectioners' sugar, thyme, and lemon zest until well combined. Fold in the chopped strawberries.

3. Stuff each strawberry with 1 teaspoon of the cheese mixture. Arrange on serving platters, cover, and refrigerate until needed, up to 2 hours.

GORGONZOLA-STUFFED GRAPES

YIELD: 60 HORS D'OEUVRES

This is not a recipe per se, but rather an idea for a quick, attractive, and delicious snack. You can use any combination of grapes—I've suggested my favorites—but of course it's easier with very large grapes. Or instead of stuffing individual grapes, you can double the amount of cheese filling to make a dip, sprinkle the top with pomegranate seeds, and serve it with an assortment of fresh seasonal fruits.

¼ pound Gorgonzola cheese

2 ounces farmer cheese

1 teaspoon dry gin or vodka

2 tablespoons finely chopped toasted
    pecans (for toasting instructions, see
    page 64)

Salt and freshly ground black pepper

30 large Muscat grapes, halved lengthwise
    and seeded

30 large Thompson seedless or red
    globe grapes, halved lengthwise
    and seeded

1. With a fork, mix the two cheeses with the gin until well blended. Stir in the pecans. Season to taste with salt and pepper.

2. Sandwich a generous ½ teaspoon of the cheese mixture between two grape halves. Secure the stuffed grape with a toothpick. Repeat with the remaining grapes and cheese. Cover and refrigerate until ready to serve, for up to 4 hours.

GRIDDLE-BAKED QUESADILLAS

YIELD: 32 HORS D'OEUVRES

A variation on everyday grilled cheese sandwiches, these refreshing hors d'oeuvres, filled with ripe, juicy pear and Fontina are ideal to serve with margaritas. Fresh mozzarella, Cheddar, or goat cheese may substitute for the Fontina, and Red or Golden Delicious apple for the pear.

1 large ripe pear, preferably Bartlett

8 flour tortillas (8-inch rounds)

4 tablespoons (½ stick) unsalted butter,
    melted

½ pound Fontina cheese, thinly sliced

1. Peel, quarter, and core the pear. Thinly slice each quarter lengthwise, but do not separate the slices. (This will keep them from turning brown too quickly.)

2. Place a tortilla on a work surface and brush the top with melted butter. Place one-eighth of the cheese on the buttered tortilla, leaving a 1-inch border around the edges. Spread one-quarter of the sliced pear over the cheese. Top with a few more slices of cheese.

3. Butter one side of a second tortilla and place it over the filling, buttered side down. Pin the tortillas together at the edges with a few toothpicks. Repeat with the remaining ingredients. (The assembled quesadillas can be covered and left at room temperature for up to 4 hours before cooking.)

4. Heat a large griddle or 2 large nonstick skillets over low heat. Brush 2 quesadillas with melted butter and place them, buttered side down, on the griddle (or in the skillets). Cook the quesadillas until they are lightly browned and crisp on the bottom, about 2 minutes.

5. Brush the top of the quesadillas with melted butter. Using a wide spatula, turn each quesadilla and cook for another 2 minutes. Transfer the quesadillas to a baking sheet and keep them warm in a low oven while you cook the others.

6. Cut each quesadilla into 8 wedges, arrange them on a large platter, and serve immediately.

SMOKED TURKEY, APPLE, AND CHEESE FINGER SANDWICHES

YIELD: 16 HORS D'OEUVRES OR 4 LUNCH SERVINGS

These tiny grilled sandwiches are terrific to nibble on with a glass of chilled fruity white wine, such as a Riesling or Muscat. You can substitute low-sodium boiled ham or paper-thin slices of prosciutto for the smoked turkey and pear for the apple. The sandwiches can be cooked in an electric sandwich grill or a waffle iron, if you have one.

2 teaspoons Dijon mustard
4 tablespoons (½ stick) unsalted butter, softened
8 slices white sandwich bread
1 Granny Smith apple
8 slices (1 ounce each) Muenster, Gruyère, or Fontina cheese
4 thin slices smoked turkey breast (about ¼ pound)

1. In a small bowl, cream the mustard and 2 tablespoons of the butter. Spread the mixture on 1 side of each slice of bread.

2. Peel, quarter, and core the apple. Thinly slice each quarter lengthwise.

3. Layer 1 slice of cheese, 1 slice of turkey, one-quarter of the sliced apple, and another slice of cheese on the mustard-buttered side of each of 4 slices of bread. Cover each with another slice of bread, buttered side in. Press on the sandwiches to hold in the filling.

4. Lightly spread the outsides of each sandwich with the remaining 2 tablespoons butter.

5. Heat a large griddle or 2 large skillets over low heat. Place the sandwiches on the griddle (or in the skillets) and weight them with a heavy saucer. Cook until the bread is

golden brown and the cheese starts to melt, 3 to 4 minutes per side, turning once.

6. Cut each sandwich into 4 squares and serve hot.

COCONUT CHICKEN WITH STRAWBERRY-MUSTARD SAUCE

YIELD: ABOUT 20 HORS D'OEUVRES OR 4 APPETIZERS

Paul Prudhomme started the rage for deep-fried coconut shrimp served with a sweet and tangy marmalade, Cajun mustard, and horseradish dipping sauce. That dish is delicious, but a bit heavy, so I came up with this lighter version, using chicken breast instead of shrimp and baking it instead of frying. As for the sauce, I use Dijon mustard with the horseradish for an extra kick.

¼ teaspoon cayenne pepper
¼ teaspoon freshly ground black pepper
¼ teaspoon salt
¼ teaspoon garlic powder
¼ teaspoon dried thyme, crumbled
2 boneless, skinless chicken breasts (½ pound each), trimmed of excess fat
1 large egg
2 cups shredded coconut, such as Baker's
Strawberry-Mustard Sauce (recipe follows)

1. Preheat the oven to 400°F. Adjust an oven rack to the middle position. Lightly oil a baking pan.

2. Stir together the cayenne pepper, black pepper, salt, garlic powder, and thyme in a small bowl.

3. Slice each breast crosswise into ½-inch-thick strips. Place the chicken in a medium-size bowl, sprinkle with the mixed spices, and toss well to coat each piece.

4. Break the egg into a small bowl, add 1 teaspoon water, and beat lightly with a fork. Place the shredded coconut in a separate bowl.

5. Dip a chicken strip into the beaten egg, then roll it in the coconut to cover. Place the coated chicken strip on the prepared baking pan. Repeat with the remaining chicken strips. (These can be prepared up to 6 hours ahead of time, covered, and refrigerated. Bring to room temperature before baking.)

6. Bake the chicken strips until golden,

turning once, 10 to 12 minutes. Serve with Strawberry-Mustard Sauce on the side.

Strawberry – Mustard Sauce

YIELD: ABOUT 1 CUP

The unusual combination of strawberry preserves, herbs, and heady spices gives a dangerously addictive taste to this sauce. It goes very well with grilled chicken or with roast pork or duck. Keep the sauce in a covered plastic container or clean covered glass jar in the refrigerator for up to 2 weeks.

½ cup strawberry preserves
2 teaspoons Dijon mustard
2 teaspoons horseradish
½ teaspoon cayenne pepper
¼ teaspoon freshly ground black pepper
¼ teaspoon salt
¼ teaspoon dried thyme, crumbled
2 teaspoons fresh lime juice

Place all the ingredients in a small bowl and stir until well combined.

VICTORY WINGS

YIELD: 24 HORS D'OEUVRES

These raspberry-glazed chicken wings are so delicious that you'll have a very hard time keeping them from disappearing before you even get them out of the kitchen. If you succeed, be sure to serve them warm, so all the flavors come through. Have frosty Asian beer like Tsing-Tao or Kirin on hand to accompany the wings.

12 chicken wings (about 3 pounds),
  broken at the joints and tips
  removed, trimmed of excess fat,
  rinsed well and patted dry
2 teaspoons minced garlic
⅓ cup seedless raspberry preserves
¼ cup raspberry vinegar, preferably
  homemade (page 286), or red wine
  vinegar
¼ cup chicken broth, preferably homemade
  (page 30)
¾ teaspoon dried thyme, crumbled
¾ teaspoon ground coriander
¾ teaspoon ground cumin
¾ teaspoon salt
½ teaspoon freshly ground black pepper
½ teaspoon dried red pepper flakes

1. Preheat the broiler.

2. Place the chicken wings and garlic in a shallow flameproof baking pan large enough to hold them all in one layer.

3. Whisk together the preserves, vinegar, and broth in a medium-size bowl and set aside.

4. Place the thyme, coriander, cumin, salt, black pepper, and red pepper in a small bowl and stir to combine. Sprinkle half of the mixture over the chicken and toss well to coat. Reserve the remaining spice mix.

5. Broil 8 inches from the heat until the chicken pieces are golden brown and crisp, about 10 minutes. Turn the chicken pieces and continue broiling for 10 minutes more. Remove from the broiler and pour off all the fat.

6. Place the pan on top of the stove over medium-high heat. Quickly stir the reserved raspberry mixture and pour it over the chicken. Bring to a boil, turning the chicken pieces frequently to coat with the sauce. Cook until the sauce has thickened and the chicken is glazed, 3 to 4 minutes.

7. Remove from the heat, sprinkle the reserved spice mix over the chicken, and toss well. Serve immediately.

GREAT MATCHES

PINEAPPLE

Pineapple is delicious with all shellfish and cured meats. Other compatible ingredients include coconut, kirsch, citrusy herbs such as lemongrass and lemon verbena, and macadamias and hazelnuts. Serve pineapple chunks with a wedge of imported Gorgonzola for an unusual appetizer.

SHRIMP AND PINEAPPLE SATAY

YIELD: ABOUT 40 HORS D'OEUVRES

Every culture has a favorite snack food, like pretzels, tacos, or pizza. In Southeast Asia, that snack seems to be satay, an Indonesian preparation of skewered thinly sliced meat cooked quickly over hot coals. Although satays are traditionally made with beef, chicken, or pork, I make them with a combination of shrimp and pineapple. They are easy to prepare, and great with a spicy peanut dipping sauce on the side. Add grilled vegetables like summer squash, mushrooms, cherry tomatoes, and peppers and you'll have a complete meal. The sauce may be prepared up to 1 day ahead and the satays assembled 4 hours before serving, but don't cook them until the last minute.

½ cup minced shallots
2 tablespoons minced garlic
¼ cup (firmly packed) light brown sugar
2 teaspoons ground cumin
2 teaspoons ground coriander
¼ cup soy sauce, preferably Kikkoman
1 cup canned unsweetened coconut milk, well stirred
2 pounds large shrimp (21 to 25 per pound), shelled and deveined
1 fresh pineapple, peeled, cored, and cut into bite-size chunks
Vegetable oil
Peanut Dipping Sauce (recipe follows)

1. Place the shallots, garlic, brown sugar, cumin, coriander, soy sauce, and coconut milk in a blender or food processor and purée.

2. Place the shrimp and pineapple chunks in a large mixing bowl and toss with the marinade until all the pieces are well coated. Cover and refrigerate for at least 1 hour, or overnight.

3. Place 40 bamboo skewers in a shallow pan and cover with hot water. Soak for at least 30 minutes.

4. Thread 1 shrimp and 1 chunk of pineapple onto each skewer and place them on a large platter. Lightly brush the skewered shrimp and pineapple on both sides with oil.

5. Prepare coals for grilling or preheat the broiler.

6. Grill or broil the skewers, turning once, until the shrimp turn pink, about 2 minutes. Serve immediately with Peanut Dipping Sauce.

VARIATIONS

BEEF SATAY: Cut a beef sirloin steak (1¼ pounds) into 3 × 1-inch strips, about ⅛ inch thick. Marinate the meat as directed above. Thread a slice of meat and piece of pineapple onto each skewer. (You may need more than 40 skewers.) Grill or broil the skewered meat until browned on both sides, 2 to 3 minutes total cooking time.

PORK SATAY: Proceed in the same manner as for beef satay, using 1½ pounds pork tenderloin. The total cooking time should be 4 to 6 minutes.

CHICKEN SATAY: Cut each of 8 boned and skinned chicken breast halves (2 pounds total) lengthwise into 3 even strips. Lightly pound the chicken strips to ½-inch thick with a meat pounder, or the back of a knife. Halve the strips crosswise before marinating them. Thread each skewer with a slice of chicken and a chunk of pineapple. (You'll need 48 skewers here.) The total cooking time should be 3 to 4 minutes.

Peanut Dipping Sauce

YIELD: ABOUT 1 ½ CUPS

Peanut sauce will keep for several weeks in the refrigerator. It's best when served slightly warm, so reheat it before serving. If it's too thick, thin it with a little chicken broth or water. For a simple and delicious first course for 6, toss this sauce with ¾ pound cooked pasta—either semolina or rice noodles—and chunks of fresh pineapple or Granny Smith apple. Toss well and garnish with sliced scallions. Serve slightly warm or at room temperature. This sauce also makes a great dip for crudités.

1 tablespoon Thai massaman curry
　　paste
1½ cups canned unsweetened coconut
　　milk, well stirred
1 tablespoon Thai fish sauce
½ cup creamy peanut butter
4 teaspoons (firmly packed) light
　　brown sugar

1. Combine all the ingredients in a small saucepan, and whisk to blend. Simmer over low heat, stirring occasionally, until the flavors are well blended, 15 to 20 minutes.

2. Transfer to a bowl and serve warm or at room temperature.

TROPICAL FRUIT BROCHETTES

YIELD: ABOUT 40 HORS D'OEUVRES

For easy, flavorful hors d'oeuvres, try grilled fruit. Feel free to substitute any firm fresh fruit that is in season, such as apples, pineapple, or figs. Be sure to select dried fruits that are plump and moist, not shriveled.

12 pitted prunes or dates
12 dried apricots
⅓ cup dark rum
1 large banana
1 small ripe but firm pear, preferably red
　　Bartlett
1 tablespoon fresh lime juice
1 tablespoon (firmly packed) light brown
　　sugar
16 very thin slices lean bacon

1. Combine the prunes, apricots, and rum in a medium-size bowl. Cover and let sit for 1 hour.

2. Place 12 bamboo skewers in a shallow pan and cover with hot water. Soak for at least 30 minutes.

3. Peel the banana, and cut it crosswise into 12 pieces, each about ¾ inch thick. Peel, quarter, and core the pear. Cut each quarter crosswise into 3 pieces, each about ¾ inch thick. Place the banana and pear in a shallow dish and sprinkle with the lime juice and brown sugar. Toss gently to combine. Cover and let sit for 10 minutes.

4. Preheat the broiler.

5. Slice the bacon crosswise into thirds. Wrap a piece of bacon around each piece of fruit and thread a piece of each fruit onto each bamboo skewer. (This can be prepared up to 2 hours ahead of time, covered, and refrigerated.)

6. Place the skewered fruits on a baking sheet and broil until the bacon is golden brown and crisp, about 2 minutes. Turn and broil 2 minutes longer.

7. Remove the fruits from the skewers and drain on paper towels. Serve warm on toothpicks.

TEX-MEX MUSSELS

YIELD: 24 HORS D'OEUVRES

If you like mussels as much as I do, you're probably always on the lookout for interesting new preparations. Try the clean, vibrant flavors of this excellent appetizer: The unusual sweet and spicy tang of this dish is derived from the Tex-Mex salsa of pineapple, tomato, and jalapeño pepper. These mussels are at their best when served chilled. The salsa is so good, you may even want to serve it as a dip with tortilla chips on the side.

2 tablespoons fresh lime juice
2 tablespoons extra-virgin olive oil
*1 tablespoon plus 1 teaspoon soy sauce,
    preferably Kikkoman*
1½ tablespoons finely chopped shallots
½ teaspoon sugar
⅓ cup diced fresh pineapple
*1 large plum tomato, seeded and diced (about
    ⅓ cup)*
1 fresh jalapeño pepper, minced
*1 tablespoon finely shredded fresh cilantro
    leaves (for shredding instructions, see
    page 34)*
Salt and freshly ground black pepper
24 large, plump mussels (about 1 pound)
24 fresh cilantro leaves, for garnish

1. In a small bowl, whisk together the

lime juice, olive oil, soy sauce, shallots, and sugar. Add the diced pineapple, tomato, jalapeño, and shredded cilantro, and stir to combine with a wooden spoon. Season to taste with salt and pepper. Cover and let stand at room temperature for at least 30 minutes for the flavors to marry.

2. To clean the mussels, start by discarding any that are not tightly closed. Scrub each mussel well under cold running water. Then, pull off and discard the stringy beard that extends from the shell. Drain.

3. Place the mussels in a large pot and add ½ cup water. Cover tightly and bring to a boil. Cook until the mussels open, 4 to 5 minutes. Drain. Discard the cooking liquid and any mussels that haven't opened.

4. Pull the mussels from the shells, saving both the mussels and one-half of each shell. Return 1 mussel to each half-shell and arrange them all on a platter. Spoon an equal portion of salsa over each mussel and garnish with a cilantro leaf. Cover and refrigerate until well chilled, about 2 hours. Serve chilled.

Of all the unknown fruits I had tasted, none pleases my taste as do's the pine."

—GEORGE WASHINGTON

CRISP-FRIED OYSTERS WITH PAPAYA SALSA

YIELD: 16 HORS D'OEUVRES

Fried oysters are divine, but are often served with a boring tartar or ketchup-based sauce. Instead, serve these spicy morsels with a refreshing papaya salsa, to lend a cooling note. Oysters are edible throughout the year, but they are at their best from about October to May. So the old saying that oysters should be eaten only in months whose names contain the letter *r* is close to the truth. Oysters spawn during warm summer months and tend to produce large amounts of glycogen (an animal starch), which gives their meat a mushy texture and a bland taste. Shucked oysters should be plump, with a clear, fresh-smelling liquor. Eastern oysters, such as Malpeque (New England), Bluepoint (Midatlantic states), or Indian River (Florida), are some of the best.

> 1 cup unbleached all-purpose flour
> 1/2 teaspoon salt
> 1/2 teaspoon garlic powder
> 1/2 teaspoon cayenne pepper
> 1/2 teaspoon paprika
> 1/4 teaspoon freshly ground black pepper
> 1/4 teaspoon dried thyme, crumbled
> 1/4 teaspoon dried oregano, crumbled
> 1 large egg
> 1 cup milk
> 1 cup fine yellow cornmeal
> Vegetable oil
> 16 large oysters (about 1 pound in their liquor), drained
> Papaya Salsa (recipe follows)

1. Combine the flour, salt, garlic powder, cayenne, paprika, black pepper, thyme, and oregano in a medium-size bowl.

2. Beat the egg and milk together in another bowl. Put the cornmeal in a third bowl.

3. Pour oil to a depth of 2 inches into a large, deep, heavy skillet or deep fryer and heat over medium-high heat to 350°F. Meanwhile, dredge each oyster in the seasoned flour, dip in the egg mixture, and then dredge in the cornmeal. Place the coated oysters on a platter as you work.

4. Fry the oysters, a few at a time, until golden brown, about 2 minutes. Remove the oysters with a slotted spoon and drain them on paper towels. Keep warm in a low oven as you fry the remaining oysters.

5. Serve the oysters on a platter accompanied by toothpicks and a small bowl of papaya salsa.

Papaya Salsa

YIELD: ABOUT 3/4 CUP

For top flavors, prepare this salsa no more than 2 hours before serving. It's equally delicious with chips, or with grilled fish, chicken, or pork.

> 3/4 cup cubed fresh papaya (1/2-inch pieces)
> 2 tablespoons diced red onion
> 2 tablespoons chopped fresh cilantro leaves
> 1/2 small fresh jalapeño pepper, chopped
> 1 1/2 tablespoons fresh lime juice
> Salt

1. Place the papaya, onion, cilantro, and jalapeño in a food processor and pulse until finely chopped. Do not purée.

2. Transfer the papaya mixture to a small bowl and stir in the lime juice. Season to taste with salt. Cover and refrigerate. Bring to room temperature before serving.

HOLIDAY TURKEY PATE

YIELD: 10 TO 12 SERVINGS

This flavorful pâté, studded with cranberries, makes a wonderful centerpiece for a holiday table. It should be prepared at least 2 days in advance to allow the flavors to develop; it can be refrigerated for up to 1 week. Serve it sliced as an elegant first course or set it out on a buffet table with crackers and French bread. Either way, I suggest you serve this pâté with *cornichons* (French-style pickled gherkins) or Peppered Peaches (see Index) on the side.

½ *cup diced carrots*

½ *cup dried cranberries (3 ounces)*

½ *cup ruby port*

6 *slices bacon (about ¼ pound), cut into ½-inch pieces*

1 *medium onion, peeled and cut into eighths*

3 *large cloves garlic, peeled*

½ *pound chicken livers, trimmed of fat and halved*

2 *large eggs*

⅓ *cup light cream, or half-and-half*

1¼ *pounds lean ground turkey*

1 *tablespoon unbleached all-purpose flour*

2 *teaspoons dried thyme, crushed*

1½ *teaspoons salt*

1 *teaspoon freshly ground white pepper*

½ *teaspoon ground allspice*

1. Place the carrots in a small saucepan with salted water to cover. Bring to a boil and cook until just tender, about 2 minutes. Drain, refresh with cold water, and drain again. Set aside.

2. Combine the cranberries and port in a small saucepan and bring to a simmer. Remove the pan from the heat, cover, and let sit for 15 minutes. Drain the berries, reserving the port (there should be about ⅓ cup). Set aside.

3. Preheat the oven to 325°F.

4. Place the bacon in a food processor and process until finely chopped. With the motor running, add the onion and garlic through the feed tube. Add the livers, eggs, cream, and reserved port. Process until the mixture is liquefied, stopping occasionally to scrape the sides of the bowl with a rubber spatula. Add the turkey, flour, thyme, salt, pepper, and allspice. Blend until the mixture is thoroughly mixed and smooth.

5. Scrape the mixture into a large mixing bowl. With a wooden spoon, stir in the carrots and cranberries.

6. Lightly oil an 8½ × 4½ × 2½-inch loaf pan. Fill the pan with the pâté. Tap the bottom of the pan against the counter to eliminate any air holes in the pâté. Smooth the top, and cover tightly with a double thickness of aluminum foil. (The pâté can be prepared 1 day ahead to this point and refrigerated.)

7. Place the loaf pan in a deep roasting

pan. Add hot water to come half-way up the sides of the loaf pan and bake for 1½ hours. Remove the foil and continue to bake until the top of the pâté is brown, or until an instant-read thermometer inserted in the middle of the pâté registers 150° to 155°F, about 30 minutes longer. Cool the pâté, cover with plastic wrap, and store in the refrigerator.

CHOPPED LIVER PATE WITH CHUTNEY

YIELD: 8 TO 10 SERVINGS

One of the easiest, most delicious, and least expensive appetizers that you can make is chopped liver. This recipe combines a bit of Jewish tradition with a bit of my own. For a real treat, serve this spread with toasted rye bread, crusty baguettes, or water biscuits. You can substitute store-bought mango chutney for the home-made apricot chutney in a pinch.

1 pound chicken livers, trimmed of excess fat
    and halved
¼ cup mild olive oil
2 large white onions (about 1 pound), finely
    chopped
½ cup plus 2 tablespoons Spiced Apricot
    Chutney (page 272)
2 large hard-cooked eggs, chopped
Salt and freshly ground black pepper
Fresh parsley sprigs, for garnish (optional)

1. Preheat the broiler.

2. Lightly grease a broiler pan, then arrange the chicken livers in a single layer in the pan. Broil the livers for 8 to 10 minutes, turning once. Set aside to cool.

3. Heat the oil in a large skillet over medium heat, and sauté the onions, stirring frequently, until golden brown, about 10 minutes. Let cool.

4. Combine the livers and ½ cup of the chutney in a large mixing bowl. Mix with a fork, coarsely mashing the livers. Add the chopped eggs and salt and pepper to taste, and stir to combine. Transfer the pâté to a crock, cover, and refrigerate.

5. To serve, spread the remaining 2 tablespoons chutney over the chopped liver. Garnish with fresh parsley sprigs, if desired.

GLAZED CHICKEN LIVERS WITH KUMQUATS

YIELD: 4 APPETIZER OR 2 ENTREE SERVINGS

One of my favorite ways to serve chicken livers is to stir-fry them briefly in a sizzling-hot pan with a sweet and sour sauce. In this variation, I add thin slices of tart kumquats to provide a refreshing counterpoint to the rich livers. This dish is great as an appetizer, served over a bed of wild greens, or as a main course, served with steamed white rice.

1 tablespoon honey
1 tablespoon soy sauce,
    preferably Kikkoman
1 tablespoon oyster sauce
1 tablespoon dry sherry
1 teaspoon chile sesame oil
2 teaspoons red vinegar
1 tablespoon peanut oil
1 teaspoon minced garlic
½ pound chicken livers, trimmed of excess fat
    and halved
½ cup thinly sliced kumquats (5 or 6 large
    kumquats, about 3 ounces total)
1 tablespoon sliced scallions (white and green
    parts)
Fresh cilantro sprigs, for garnish (optional)

1. Combine the honey, soy sauce, oyster sauce, sherry, chile sesame oil, and vinegar in a small bowl and stir until the honey is dissolved. Set aside.

2. Heat a wok or large skillet over high heat until smoking. Add the peanut oil and carefully swirl it to evenly coat the pan. Add the garlic and chicken livers; sauté until the livers start to become firm and turn brown, about 1 minute. Add the kumquats and stir to coat with oil. Add the honey-soy mixture and cook until the sauce is slightly thickened, about 1 minute. Remove from the heat and stir in the scallions. The livers should still be pink inside.

3. Transfer the livers to a warmed platter and garnish with coriander sprigs, if desired. Serve at once.

SAUTEED FOIE GRAS WITH MANGO COMPOTE

YIELD: 4 SERVINGS

Foie gras, which means "fat liver," is the oversize liver of fattened specially bred geese and ducks. When sautéed until browned and lightly crisped on the outside and delectably

THE FRUIT AND CHEESE BOARD

Almost any fruit—from the mundane apple to the exotic papaya—tastes delicious with one cheese or another. So whether you take your cheese before a meal, with wine, or after a meal, as dessert, try the refreshing twist of fresh fruit. Here are some of my favorite combinations:

RIPE PEARS, TART APPLES, MUSKY MELONS, AND DRIED FRUITS have a strong affinity for assertive, nutty blue-veined cheeses such as Roquefort, Stilton, and Gorgonzola, as well as Camembert (Roucoulon is one of the best), Parmigiano-Reggiano, aged Gouda, Fontina, Brie, and the herb-coated aged chèvre and sheep's milk cheeses, such as Brin d'Amour.

BERRIES, PEACHES, NECTARINES, CHERRIES, FIGS, PINEAPPLE, PAPAYAS, and other soft perfumerey fruits are wonderful with fresh cheeses like ricotta, mascarpone, or mild chèvre, such as Chavrous or Boucheron.

BERRIES, CHERRIES, FIGS, PEACHES, AND PLUMS are lovely with luxurious triple-crème cheeses, such as Explorateur, St. André, and soft-ripening goat cheeses, such as Ste. Maur (my favorite).

MUSCAT OR CONCORD GRAPES AND KIWIS are great with creamy Italian Taleggio and Bel Paese, as well as goat cheeses, such as Boucheron and Banon.

When you serve cheese, offer a good selection, including blue-veined, soft, semi-hard, and hard varieties. Always try to include at least one familiar cheese, like chèvre, Brie, or Camembert. Display your assortment decoratively on a cheese board and surround them with a colorful selection of fresh fruit and plenty of crackers or crusty French bread. Serve cheeses ripe and at room temperature so that their flavor and texture may be fully appreciated.

---

buttery within, foie gras is so good, my theory is that it must be an aphrodisiac! To balance its richness I enjoy serving foie gras with a soft, gingery mango compote. I have also used this delicious fruit compote to accompany pan-fried calf's liver and grilled meat or fish. You may substitute 2 cups of diced papaya, peach, or pear for the mango.

1 tablespoon unsalted butter
1 large ripe mango (about 1 pound), peeled, flesh removed from the seed and diced (2 cups)
½ teaspoon grated peeled fresh ginger
2 tablespoons fresh orange juice
Salt and freshly ground black pepper
4 pieces fresh foie gras (3 to 4 ounces each), cut about ½-inch thick
Kosher (coarse) salt

1. To make the mango compote, melt the butter in a large skillet over medium-low heat. Add the mango and ginger, and stir gently until the fruit is coated with butter, about 1 minute.

I consider the mango...one of the most delectable fruits with which God graced an already bountiful world.

—EUELL GIBBONS, STALKING THE WILD ASPARAGUS

2. Add the orange juice and continue to cook until the mango is soft and creamy, about 2 minutes longer. Remove from the heat, and season to taste with salt and pepper. Cover and keep warm. (This can be prepared ahead, cooled, covered and set aside at cool room temperature for several hours or refrigerated. If the compote has been refrigerated, gently reheat it before serving.)

3. Place a large nonstick skillet over high heat. Using a sharp knife, lightly score each piece of foie gras to prevent curling during cooking. Sprinkle with salt and pepper. When the pan is smoking, add the foie gras, and cook until golden brown and crusty, 40 to 45 seconds per side. Do not overcook. Remove from the heat.

4. Spoon the mango compote onto warmed dinner plates and top with a slice of foie gras. Sprinkle some kosher salt over the foie gras, and serve at once.

AROMATIC SOUPS

W hen I think back on my childhood, some of the most enduring memories are of my mother's cooking. She was particularly fond of soups, and would welcome us to the dinner table by setting a huge bowl in front of us urging "Eat your soup, you'll grow stronger!" Whatever she made–a clear vegetable soup, a hearty noodle soup, a tropical soup of beef and pineapple–her creations tasted fresh and heavenly. I once asked her what made her soups so special. This was her secret: A soup tastes only as good as what goes into it. I have always tried to follow her good advice.

Anyone can make an aromatic, tasty, healthful, appetizing, and colorful soup. Producing a rich, steaming potful on a winter evening, or a cool, refreshing bisque in summer doesn't require the skills of an expert chef. It's the unexpected spices and other ingredients that create magic in these recipes–like chiles, lime juice, vinegar, basil, mint, and especially fruits. And while fruits add flavor, texture, and intrigue, their sweet and tart qualities can also help balance the flavors and smooth out rough spots in soups that are more aggressively seasoned.

The fruit soups that you are about to discover in this chapter will prove to be much more than just the hot weather desserts or starters that you have come to expect. They can be served any which way you like. For instance, you can start the day with a Jolting Fruit Soup. Or, if you want to add an exotic flavor to your brunch menu, you can whip up a cool Piña Colada Soup. Having a fancy dinner party? Kick it off with the Mexican Lime Soup or Chilled Honeydew-Lime Soup. Looking for a light alternative to rich pastries and sweets? Surprise your guests with Pink Grapefruit Soup for dessert. Some soups from other cultures are so popular that they have become international favorites. But when I prepare gazpacho, vichyssoise, or borscht, I cannot help but add my own fruity touch. That's when the fun begins.

MAIN SQUEEZE

*W*hether a fruit soup is savory or sweet, it will almost always be improved by a squeeze of fresh lemon or lime juice toward the end of cooking. This is true even when you're working with fruits that are already somewhat acidic.

CHICKEN BROTH

YIELD: ABOUT 3½ QUARTS

Once you have a good chicken broth, you are almost guaranteed great soups and sauces. Normally, chicken broth is made with chicken bones, but I prepare mine with wings, which are inexpensive but very flavorful and give the broth extra body. To obtain a clear broth, do not stir or disturb it in any way as it cooks.

6 pounds chicken wings, rinsed and patted dry
4 medium turnips, peeled and quartered
2 medium carrots, peeled and quartered
2 large onions, peeled and halved
1 rib celery, rinsed and cut into 2-inch chunks
1 medium leek (white and green parts), trimmed, quartered, and washed
8 large garlic cloves, crushed and peeled
3 bay leaves
1 tablespoon black peppercorns
½ bunch fresh thyme sprigs or 1 tablespoon dried thyme, crumbled
1½ tablespoons salt
Stems from 1 bunch fresh parsley

1. Place the chicken wings and 4½ quarts cold water in an 8- to 10-quart stockpot and bring to a boil over high heat. Boil, skimming all the foam as it comes to the surface, for about 5 minutes.

2. Add all the remaining ingredients and return to a boil. Reduce the heat to medium-low to keep the liquid at a steady simmer. Partially cover the pot and simmer gently, without stirring, for about 2½ hours. When the broth is ready, the wings will be cooked through and falling apart.

3. Remove the pot from the heat and let the broth cool. Carefully strain the liquid through a colander lined with a double layer of dampened cheesecloth into a clean 5-quart soup pot. (You should have about 4 quarts of broth.) Discard the solids.

4. Taste the broth. If it tastes weak at this point, bring it to a boil over high heat and boil it for 10 to 15 minutes to concentrate its flavor.

5. If the broth is to be used immediately, degrease it by skimming all the fat off the surface with a ladle. (Or use a degreaser, if you prefer.) If the broth is to be used later, place the pot in an ice bath and let cool completely without degreasing it. Transfer the broth to a large bowl or gallon plastic container, tightly cover, and refrigerate the stock overnight, or for up to 5 days. Remove the layer of fat that has congealed on top before using.

For longer storage, freeze the chicken broth for up to 2 months. To do so, transfer it to smaller nonreactive containers (plastic or stainless steel) of different sizes, since recipes call for varying amounts of broth. It is also a good idea to freeze some broth in ice cube trays to use in recipes that call for it in small amounts. After the cubes are frozen, transfer them to plastic bags and store in the freezer. Once the broth has thawed, use it immediately. Do not refrigerate or freeze it again.

MOM'S GREEN PAPAYA SOUP

YIELD: 4 SERVINGS

Green papaya soup is the Asian equivalent of Jewish chicken soup. It is believed to possess all kinds of powers, such as curing the common cold or restoring strength to women in childbirth. After my sister and I were born, my mother had a bowl of it every day for a month! But you don't have to give birth to enjoy this delicious soup of green papaya and shiitake mushrooms. If green papaya is unavailable, substitute kohlrabi or chayote (mirliton).

4 cups chicken broth, preferably homemade (facing page)
4 quarter-size slices peeled fresh ginger, crushed
1 small green papaya (about 1 pound), peeled, halved, seeded, and sliced ½ inch thick
2 cups sliced shiitake mushrooms
2 scallions, trimmed and thinly sliced (white and green parts)
Salt and freshly ground black pepper
Dash of dry sherry

G R E E N   P A P A Y A

*I*n most Southeast Asian cuisines, the papaya, as well as the mango, is used as a vegetable when still green and underripe. It can either be cooked or used raw in salads and relishes. Green papaya is rich in papain, a powerful enzyme that tenderizes meat, another reason for its popularity. It has a pale, almost white flesh, which is hard and crisp. While it has little flavor, it is noted for the perfect crunch it gives to salads when raw (see the Index for Vietnamese Pawpaw Salad). When cooked, green papaya has a flavor and texture like kohlrabi, but without the kick (see the Index for Stir-Fried Beef with Green Papaya).

Green papaya is available in Asian, Vietnamese, and Thai groceries. Be sure to pick the firmest, greenest fruit without any bruises.

To prepare a green papaya for eating or cooking, peel it with a vegetable peeler, halve it lengthwise, and remove the tiny, bitter white seeds from the cavities. Slice or shred as indicated in recipes.

To shred green papaya, cut each peeled and seeded half into quarters, then shred the pieces lengthwise on a mandoline or through the medium-coarse holes of a hand grater. A food processor fitted with a fine shredding disk will also do this job.

1. Bring the chicken broth and ginger to a boil in a medium-size saucepan over high heat. Add the papaya, reduce the heat, and simmer, covered, until the papaya is just tender, about 10 minutes.

2. Add the mushrooms and continue to simmer, covered, until the mushrooms are tender, about 5 minutes.

3. Stir in the scallions and remove from the heat. Season to taste with salt and pepper, and stir in the sherry.

MEXICAN LIME SOUP

YIELD: 6 SERVINGS

*N*ot long ago, as I vacationed on a lovely island off Cancún, Mexico, I was struck with a flu that threatened my entire stay. Luckily, the chef at the hotel where I was staying urged me to have his *sopa de lima* at least twice a day to get rid of my cold. I did as I was told and believe I was miraculously healed by the soup's magical powers. I bet that what did it was the large amount of garlic, jalapeño pepper, and lime juice in the soup. The soup itself cannot be simpler to make or more delicious.

1 whole (bone-in) chicken breast (about
    1¼ pounds), skin removed

2 tablespoons mild olive oil

½ cup chopped onion

1 tablespoon minced garlic

2 cups chopped tomatoes

2 teaspoons minced fresh jalapeño pepper

¾ teaspoon sugar

5 cups chicken broth, preferably homemade
    (page 30)

1 teaspoon finely grated lime zest

3 tablespoons (or more) fresh lime juice

2 tablespoons shredded fresh cilantro leaves
    (for shredding instructions, see page 34)

Salt and freshly ground black pepper

1 small lime, sliced paper thin, then quartered,
    for garnish

1. Place the chicken breast in a medium-size saucepan, cover with lightly salted water, and bring to a boil over high heat. Reduce the heat to low and simmer, uncovered, until the juices run clear when the point of a knife is inserted into the thickest part of the chicken breast, about 30 minutes. Let the breast cool in the poaching liquid, then pull off the meat and shred it. Cover and set aside. Discard the poaching liquid.

2. Heat the oil in a large soup pot over low heat. Add the onion and garlic and sauté until tender, about 3 minutes. Stir in the tomatoes, jalapeño, and sugar and cook until the ingredients are just heated through, 1 to 2 minutes.

3. Add the chicken broth and bring to a boil. Stir in the chicken, lime zest, 3 tablespoons lime juice, and the cilantro. Remove from the heat. Season to taste with salt, pepper, and more lime juice, if necessary. The soup should have a nicely balanced citrus taste.

4. Ladle the soup into warmed bowls, garnish with a few lime slices, and serve at once.

MEXICAN SOUP SUPPER

MEXICAN LIME SOUP

♦

GUACAMOLE
TORTILLA CHIPS

♦

FRESH PAPAYA HALVES WITH
LIME WEDGES

LEMONY QUINOA SOUP

YIELD: 4 SERVINGS

There is something exquisitely earthy about this hybrid of two wonderful soups, the Greek egg-lemon soup

SHREDDING HERBS

*T*he way herbs are cut can dramatically affect their flavor and appearance. Vigorously chopping herbs can not only bruise them, turning them dark, but it also imparts an unpleasant bitter taste. Just taste an herb before chopping it and again afterward, and you'll see what I mean.

A gentler approach to fresh herbs, shredding does no damage and makes for a finer and more elegant presentation. Appearance aside, the herbs will also taste the way they should: fresh and clean. Here's how to shred herbs like a pro:

REGULAR-SHAPED HERBS

LARGE-LEAFED HERBS, SUCH AS BASIL, MINT, SAGE, AND LIME LEAVES: *Pluck as many leaves as you need from the stems, rinse well to remove any sand, and dry between 2 paper towels. Arrange*

the leaves in small stacks and roll them up lengthwise. With a sharp knife, slice the stacks crosswise into thin shreds.

You can also use this method to shred any large leafy greens, such as spinach or romaine lettuce.

IRREGULAR-SHAPED HERBS

SMALL-LEAFED HERBS, SUCH AS CILANTRO, PARSLEY, DILL, THYME, TARRAGON, AND OREGANO: *Gather the herbs together into a tight bundle, then cut crosswise into thin shreds with a sharp knife.*

---

avgolemono and the Portuguese *canja*, a chicken soup seasoned with lemon and mint. In it, I use quinoa (KEEN-wah), a surprisingly light, crunchy grain, instead of rice. The lemon and mint add sparkle.

 ½ cup quinoa, rinsed (see Note) or long-grain rice

 4 cups chicken broth, preferably homemade (page 30)

 2 large eggs

 ¼ cup fresh lemon juice

 4 tablespoons shredded fresh mint leaves (for shredding instructions, see above)

 Salt and freshly ground white pepper

 4 paper-thin lemon slices, for garnish (optional)

1. Place the quinoa or rice in a large soup pot, cover with water, and bring to a boil over medium-high heat. Reduce the heat and simmer, uncovered, for 3 to 4 minutes. Drain, rinse off the starch, and drain again.

2. Return the blanched quinoa to the soup pot and add the chicken broth. Simmer the mixture, uncovered, over medium-low heat until the grains are translucent and tender, 5 to 6 minutes (1 minute longer, if using rice). Remove from the heat.

3. Just before serving, beat the eggs with the lemon juice in a small bowl until light and frothy. Gradually beat in 1 cup of the hot soup, then add this mixture to the rest of the soup.

4. Reheat the soup over low heat, stirring constantly, for 2 minutes. Do not let it simmer, or it will curdle. Season to taste with salt and white pepper.

5. Place 1 tablespoon of shredded mint leaves in each of 4 warmed soup bowls and top with soup. Garnish with a slice of lemon and serve at once.

NOTE: Buy quinoa at natural food stores. Quinoa is coated with saponin, a bitter natural substance, and needs to be rinsed before using. To do so, place the quinoa in a large bowl and cover with water. Rub it between your hands and drain in a fine sieve. Repeat. During cooking, this grain expands to almost 4 times its dry volume.

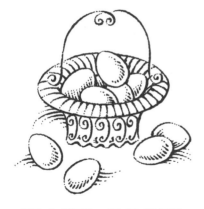

KAKI SOUP

YIELD: 4 SERVINGS

The French call it "kaki," but in Britain, the persimmon is sometimes referred to as a date plum. This appelation seems particularly apt when you taste the

GREAT MATCHES

PERSIMMON

Buttery ripe persimmon goes particularly well with chicken and turkey. It's also nice with herbs and spices of all kinds. Try persimmon with vermouth or Amaretto for a spirited treat.

rich, honeyed sweetness of a perfect specimen. To capture the essence of this delicate fruit, I've developed this light chicken soup featuring slices of fresh persimmon and tiny chicken dumplings.

DUMPLINGS
½ pound lean ground chicken,
    well chilled
1 large egg, lightly beaten
2½ tablespoons cornstarch
2 teaspoons dry sherry
1 teaspoon finely grated peeled fresh ginger
2 teaspoons soy sauce, preferably
    Kikkoman
¼ teaspoon salt

SOUP
5 cups chicken broth, preferably homemade
    (page 30)
4 quarter-size slices peeled fresh ginger,
    crushed
1 tablespoon dry sherry
Salt
2 large ripe persimmons, each peeled
    and cut into 8 wedges
¼ pound button mushrooms, stems
    trimmed, caps thinly sliced
¼ pound snow peas, trimmed
Freshly ground black pepper

PERSIMMON

*E*arly explorers had many negative comments about pessemin (the native American persimmon). They found that the extremely astringent plum-like fruit could "drawe a man's mouth awrie with much torment" if not properly ripe. Americans' interest in the persimmon was aroused only when the sweeter Japanese persimmon was imported into the United States by Commander Matthew C. Perry in 1855. It gradually became popular and was used in beer, breads, pies, puddings, and salads. A native of China, but grown primarily in Japan, the Japanese persimmon is the variety commonly found today in our markets as well as in Mediterranean countries and Chile. The skin color of persimmon can range from yellow to deep, rich orange, depending on the variety.

The heart-shaped Hachiya, the most common variety, should never be eaten until it's very soft. If not fully ripe, it can be quite astringent, due to its high tannin content. Should you have firm persimmons, keep them at room temperature until they are soft, which could take up to a week. To speed ripening, place your persimmons in a bag or plastic container with an apple or a banana, either of which will release ethylene gas, a ripening agent. Sweet, meltingly soft persimmon halves can be enjoyed simply with a wedge of lemon or lime and eaten with a spoon like a melon. The Fuyu variety, shaped somewhat like a small tomato, is tannin-free and ready to eat when only slightly soft, or even when crisp-hard.

Persimmons can have a few seeds or be seedless. Avoid heating them, or they can make your mouth pucker. Added to green or fruit salads, persimmons provide sweetness and luscious texture. When you use them in hot dishes, add slices of peeled persimmon toward the very end of the cooking process. This will help maintain its delicate texture and flavor. For delicious sweet offerings, spoon puréed persimmons over cakes and puddings.

1. Place all the ingredients for the dumplings in a food processor and process to a firm, sticky paste, 30 to 45 seconds, stopping to scrape down the sides of the bowl with a rubber spatula, if necessary. (This mixture may be prepared ahead, covered, and refrigerated overnight.)

2. To make the soup, bring the chicken broth to a simmer in a large soup pot over medium-low heat. Scoop up 1 rounded teaspoon of the chicken mixture and pass it back and forth with a second teaspoon to form a compact dumpling. Drop the dumpling into the simmering broth, and continue making dumplings and dropping them into the broth. To prevent sticking, dip the spoons in cold water before shaping the dumplings.

3. When the dumplings float to the surface, continue cooking 2 to 3 minutes longer. With a slotted spoon, transfer the dumplings to a bowl, and cover. Add the ginger, sherry, and salt to taste to the broth and simmer, uncovered, for 5 minutes.

4. Meanwhile, place 4 persimmon wedges in each of 4 shallow soup bowls.

5. Remove the ginger from the broth and discard. Add the mushrooms, snow peas, chicken dumpling, and the black pepper; cook until the vegetables are crisp-tender and the dumplings are heated through, about 2 minutes. Ladle the soup over the persimmons and serve at once.

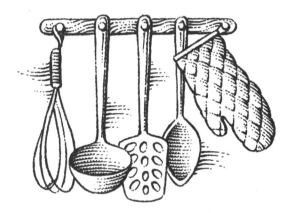

WATERCRESS SOUP WITH ASIAN PEAR

YIELD: 4 TO 6 SERVINGS

Watercress and pear seem made for each other. Not only are they excellent in salads, but they can also serve as the basis for an exquisite soup. For this recipe I use Asian pear for its delicate fragrance and sweetness, but you can use any domestic pear with equally good results. Light and refreshing, this easy-to-prepare soup is also delicious cold.

½ cup chopped onion
4 cups chopped watercress
2 large Asian pears, peeled, cored, and
*   coarsely chopped*
4 cups chicken broth, preferably
*   homemade (page 30)*
1 teaspoon sugar
4 teaspoons unsalted butter, cut into
*   small pieces*
Salt and freshly ground black pepper
Watercress sprigs, for garnish
*   (optional)*
Thin slices of Asian pear, for garnish
*   (optional)*

1. Combine the chopped onion, watercress, and pears with the chicken broth and sugar in a medium-size soup pot. Bring the mixture to a boil, over medium-high heat. Reduce the heat and simmer, uncovered, until the fruit and vegetables are tender, about 5 minutes.

2. Transfer the soup to a blender or food processor in batches and purée it. Return the puréed soup to the soup pot and place it over medium heat. Stir in the butter and season to taste with salt and pepper.

3. Ladle the soup into warmed bowls. Garnish each bowl with a sprig of watercress and a slice of pear, if desired. Serve at once.

ASIAN PEAR

Asian pears are sometimes called Nashi, Chinese pears, or apple pears. They are also known as sand pears, because their skin has a sandy quality. Distantly related to ordinary pears, they come in many different varieties, but in general, they resemble round, firm apples with a pale green, yellow, or brownish skin.

Asian pears are grown in Japan and on the west coast of the United States. They are available beginning in late summer through the fall. Select yellow fruits with the most scent. When perfectly ripe, they acquire a terrific fragrance, like that of the best pears, and their exceedingly juicy flesh has the crisp crunch of apples. The taste of the raw fruit is faintly sweet and acid, but its elusive flavor disappears when mixed with other assertive fruits. It needs no further ripening after purchase and keeps for up to 2 weeks in the refrigerator.

Although an Asian pear is delicious eaten raw—peeled or unpeeled—you can also cook it as you would apples or pears.

BEBE'S CABBAGE SOUP

YIELD: 10 TO 12 SERVINGS

My husband's late grandmother, who was of Russian descent, made the best cabbage soup in the world. Her subtle sweet and sour rendition was full of wonderful bits of cabbage, raisins, and beef brisket that melted in your mouth. It was so good that I always had second helpings. Try it, and you'll see what I mean! If you have a small family, make a whole recipe, serve just what you need, and store the rest in several containers in the freezer for up to 4 months. This way, you'll be able to enjoy the fruits of your labor over a period of time.

1 tablespoon vegetable oil
1 beef brisket (about 2 pounds), rinsed
　　well and patted dry
Salt and freshly ground black pepper
2 medium onions, thinly sliced
1 cabbage (about 1½ pounds), coarsely
　　shredded (about 8 cups)
2 cups canned crushed tomatoes
1 cup golden raisins
½ cup (firmly packed) light brown
　　sugar
¼ cup fresh lemon juice
Chopped fresh flat-leaf parsley leaves,
　　for garnish

1. Heat the oil in a large soup pot or Dutch oven over high heat. Sprinkle the brisket with salt and pepper and brown each side for 3 minutes. Transfer to a platter.

2. Add the onions to the pan, and cook over medium heat, stirring often, until they are tender, about 2 minutes. Then stir in the

cabbage. Add the tomatoes, 1 tablespoon salt, the browned brisket, and 10 cups cold water and bring to a boil. Reduce the heat to low, partially cover, and simmer until the meat is fork-tender, about 1½ hours.

3. Add the raisins and brown sugar, and continue simmering 30 minutes longer.

4. Remove the brisket and place on a cutting board. With two forks, tear the meat apart into fine shreds.

5. Return the shredded meat to the soup and stir in the lemon juice. Adjust the seasoning with salt and pepper, if necessary. The soup should have a well-balanced sweet and sour taste.

6. Ladle the soup into warmed bowls, sprinkle with chopped parsley, and serve.

PINEAPPLE SOUP FROM SAIGON

YIELD: 4 TO 6 SERVINGS

This recipe originally appeared in my first book, *The Foods of Vietnam*. Cooking with fruit is typical in southern Vietnam. Pineapples are abundant there and are used interchangeably as a fruit and a vegetable. In main dishes,

they are often combined with beef, poultry, or seafood. Do not use canned pineapple in this recipe; it does not compare to fresh pineapple in fragrance or delicacy of flavor. Besides tasting wonderful, this unusual soup pairing of pineapple and beef is very dear to me because it was one of the best soups my mother ever made for us.

½ pound beef (chuck or bottom round), sliced against the grain into thin strips

3 tablespoons plus 2 teaspoons Thai fish sauce

1 tablespoon plus ¼ teaspoon sugar

2 cloves garlic, chopped

2 shallots, thinly sliced

Freshly ground black pepper

3 tablespoons vegetable oil

½ medium onion, slivered

1 large ripe tomato, cored, seeded, and cut into wedges

½ fresh ripe pineapple, peeled, cored, and diced (see page 259)

1½ teaspoons salt

1 scallion, trimmed and thinly sliced (white and green parts)

1 tablespoon shredded fresh cilantro leaves (for shredding instructions, see page 34)

1. Combine the beef, 2 teaspoons of the fish sauce, ¼ teaspoon of the sugar, the garlic, shallots, and black pepper to taste in a small bowl. Marinate for 30 minutes.

2. Heat 1 tablespoon of the oil in a large soup pot over high heat. Add the beef and

stir-fry briefly, about 1 minute; the beef strips should still be pink in the center. Transfer the beef to a bowl.

3. Heat the remaining 2 tablespoons oil in the same pot. Add the onion and sauté until lightly browned. Add the tomato, pineapple, and remaining 1 tablespoon sugar and stir-fry over medium heat for about 2 minutes. Add 5 cups water, the salt, and the remaining 3 tablespoons fish sauce and bring to a boil. Reduce the heat to medium and simmer, uncovered, for about 5 minutes.

4. Stir the cooked beef into the soup and remove from the heat. Add the scallion and cilantro, and stir to combine.

5. Transfer the soup to a heated tureen. Sprinkle with black pepper and serve at once.

SOUTH SEAS CLAM CHOWDER

YIELD: 4 SERVINGS

This is a particularly fragrant, succulent, and spicy clam soup. It should be eaten as soon after it's cooked as possible. Since clams are naturally briny, I like to add pineapple juice, coconut milk, and fresh chile, a typical Southeast Asian combination in soups, to balance the flavors. Fresh lime juice and zest are then stirred in at the last minute for an extra kick. You may substitute mussels, shelled shrimp, or bay scallops for the clams. If you do so, cook the seafood for only 2 to 3 minutes.

2 tablespoons mild olive oil
½ cup diced carrot
½ cup diced celery
½ cup chopped onion
1 tablespoon chopped garlic
½ cup tightly packed shredded fresh basil
    leaves (for shredding instructions, see
    page 34)
2 fresh small red chile peppers or 1 fresh
    jalapeño pepper, shredded
2 dozen very fresh clams, preferably
    littlenecks, well scrubbed
½ cup dry white wine
3 cups chicken broth, preferably homemade
    (page 30)
1 cup fresh pineapple juice (for juicing
    instructions, see page 259)
⅓ cup canned unsweetened coconut milk,
    well stirred, or heavy (or whipping)
    cream
3 tablespoons fresh lime juice
Finely grated zest of 1 lime (about
    ½ teaspoon)
Salt and freshly ground black pepper

1. Heat the oil in a large soup pot or Dutch oven over medium-high heat. Add the carrot, celery, onion, garlic, basil, and chile

peppers, and sauté until the vegetables are tender, about 2 minutes.

2. Add the clams and stir to coat. Add the white wine and bring to a boil over high heat. Tightly cover the pot and steam until all the clams have opened, 4 to 5 minutes. Do not overcook. (Discard any clams that don't open.)

3. Add the chicken broth, pineapple juice, and coconut milk and quickly bring to a boil. Remove from the heat and stir in the lime juice and zest.

4. Season to taste with salt and pepper, if necessary. Spoon into warmed soup bowls and serve at once.

APPLE COCONUT CHOWDER

YIELD: 4 SERVINGS

One of my favorite concoctions is this tantalizing apple soup. It's simple to prepare, fresh tasting, and wonderfully infused with lime and coconut flavors, a winning combination! This chowder is chunky. However, you can purée it and serve it cold for a summer lunch or hot in the winter as a light first course. Remove the lime leaves before puréeing.

2 tablespoons unsalted butter
2 cups finely chopped onions
3 Pippin or Granny Smith apples (about 1 pound)
Juice of ½ lemon
4 medium kaffir lime (page 42) or regular lemon leaves or the zest of 1 lime
2½ cups chicken broth, preferably homemade (page 30)
½ cup canned unsweetened coconut milk, well stirred, light cream, or half-and-half
1 tablespoon sugar, or to taste
Salt and freshly ground white pepper

1. Melt the butter in a large soup pot and sauté the onions over medium-low heat, stirring occasionally until soft, about 5 minutes.

2. Meanwhile, peel, core, and slice the apples into eighths. Place in a bowl and toss with the lemon juice to prevent discoloration.

3. Add the apples and lime leaves to the onions, cover, and continue cooking, stirring occasionally, until the fruit is slightly mushy, about 5 minutes.

KAFFIR LIME LEAVES

*W*ild lime leaves, also referred to as kaffir (or keffir) lime leaves, are used by Asian cooks extensively, much like Western cooks use bay leaves, to infuse soups and stews with a unique, heavenly lime scent. But unlike bay leaves, these pretty lime leaves are also edible; they are often sliced into blade-thin shreds to adorn and flavor salads and savory dishes. Wild lime leaves can be identified by their unique shape: They grow in pairs, stem to stem. Look for them in shops specializing in Thai ingredients, where they are sold in small plastic bags and kept either in the refrigerator or the freezer. They may be hard to track down, but it's well worth the effort. If you do manage to find kaffir lime leaves, buy a few bags; well sealed, they will keep for up to a year in the freezer. There's no need to thaw them before using. If lime leaves are unavailable, the closest substitute is fresh lime or lemon leaves (if you happen to live in a warm climate and have a tree in your garden). Another alternative is lime zest: Use the finely grated zest of 1 lime for every 2 lime leaves called for in a recipe. Sprinkle the zest over the dish just before serving, to maintain its delicate perfume. Here are some good mail-order sources for these treasured leaves:

Dewildt Imports, Fox Gap Rd., R.D. 3, Bangor, PA 18013; (800) 338-3433

Nancy's Specialty Market, P.O. Box 327, Wye Mills, MD 21679; (800) 462-6291

Star Market, 3349 North Clark St., Chicago, IL 60657; (312) 472-0599

G.B Ratto & Co., 821 Washington St., Oakland, CA 94607; (800) 325-3483

4. Add the chicken broth, 1 cup water, the coconut milk, and the sugar and bring to a boil. Reduce the heat to low and simmer, partially covered, for 5 minutes, or until the soup is permeated with a lime flavor. Season to taste with salt and white pepper.

5. Ladle the soup into warmed bowls. Garnish with the lime leaves, if desired, and serve hot.

VARIATION

SCALLOP, APPLE, AND COCONUT SOUP: Add ½ pound sliced sea scallops to the soup just before you remove it from the heat: To retain their tender texture, the scallops should be just barely cooked.

CREAM OF FENNEL AND PEAR SOUP

YIELD: 6 SERVINGS

*I*n this soup, the pear brings out the subtle sweetness and licorice taste of the fennel, making for a delicious balance of flavors. I guarantee that one spoonful will immediately soothe and satisfy you. But in addition to tasting wonderful, this soup has a beautiful pale green color. This soup may be prepared a day ahead and reheated before serving. If fennel bulbs are unavailable, you may substitute one bunch of celery, but it won't be quite the same.

> 4 tablespoons (½ stick) unsalted butter
> 2 medium onions, sliced
> 2 large bulbs fennel (1½ pounds total), trimmed (reserving leaves for garnish, if desired), quartered, and thinly sliced
> 3 cups chicken broth, preferably homemade (page 30)
> 2 large ripe pears, preferably Bartlett or Comice, peeled, cored, and sliced
> Salt
> ¼ cup heavy (or whipping) cream, plus extra for garnish
> Freshly ground white pepper

1. Melt the butter in a large soup pot over medium-low heat. Add the onions and stir to coat with butter. Cover, reduce the heat to low, and cook until the onions are translucent, stirring occasionally, about 10 minutes.

2. Add the fennel and stir to coat with butter. Cover and cook until the fennel is just soft, about 15 minutes. Add the chicken broth and bring to a boil. Reduce the heat to low and simmer, covered, until the fennel is very tender, 5 minutes. Stir in the pears and ¾ teaspoon salt. Cover and continue simmering until the pears are tender, about 5 minutes. Remove from the heat and stir in the cream.

3. Ladle the soup into a blender or food processor in batches and purée it. Season with white pepper and salt, if necessary.

4. To serve, ladle the soup into warmed bowls. Drizzle a little cream over the soup in a decorative pattern and garnish with fennel leaves, if desired.

WINTRY QUINCE BISQUE

YIELD: 4 TO 6 SERVINGS

This disarmingly simple soup made with quinces, chicken broth, and crème fraîche is one of my favorites. The slight acidity of the fruit with just a hint of sweetness, makes for a very light, refreshing soup for wintry days. The peel provides a lot of flavor; do not remove it.

> 2 large quinces (about 1½ pounds), unpeeled, quartered, cored, and sliced
> 3 cups chicken broth, preferably homemade (page 30)
> ¾ cup crème fraîche or heavy (or whipping) cream
> ⅛ teaspoon ground cinnamon
> Pinch of freshly grated nutmeg
> Salt and freshly ground white pepper

1. Combine the quinces and chicken broth in a large soup pot and bring to a boil over high heat. Reduce the heat, cover, and simmer until the quinces are very tender, about 10 minutes. Transfer the quinces and broth to a blender or food processor in small batches and purée them.

2. Return the mixture to the soup pot and stir in the crème fraîche, cinnamon, nutmeg, and salt and pepper to taste. Bring to a simmer and serve immediately.

CARIBBEAN VICHYSSOISE

YIELD: 4 TO 6 SERVINGS

You may think of vichyssoise as the ultimate French soup, but it was actually created in America. Louis Diat, the chef at the original New York Ritz Hotel, thought it would perk up flagging appetites during the hot summer months of 1912. Chef Diat's vichyssoise was basically a puréed potato and leek soup served cold. Over time, chefs around the world have come up with many variations on this soup. This one originated on the island of Grenada, where breadfruit is more common than potatoes; the pears are my contribution. Refrigerate the leftover breadfruit and

use it up within a week for other dishes, such as Breadfruit in Vinaigrette (see Index). If breadfruit is unavailable, simply substitute potatoes.

2 tablespoons unsalted butter
½ cup finely chopped, well washed, and dried leek (white part only)
½ cup finely chopped onion
2 cups peeled, cored, and sliced (¼ inch thick) breadfruit, kept in salted water (see box, facing page)
3 cups (or more) chicken broth, preferably homemade (page 30)
2 ripe pears, such as Bartlett or Anjou, peeled, cored, and coarsely chopped
1 cup heavy (or whipping) cream
Salt and freshly ground white pepper
2 tablespoons snipped fresh chives

1. Melt the butter in a large soup pot over medium-low heat. Add the leek and onion and sauté, stirring occasionally, until soft, about 5 minutes.

2. Drain the breadfruit and add it to the pot. Stir to coat with butter.

3. Add the chicken broth and bring to a boil. Reduce the heat to low, cover, and simmer until the breadfruit is very tender, 10 to 15 minutes. Add the pears and remove from the heat.

4. Purée the soup in small batches until smooth in a blender or food processor. Transfer the puréed soup to a large bowl and stir in the cream. If it is too thick, add a bit of chicken broth. Season to taste with salt and

BREADFRUIT

*T*o experience this exotic fruit firsthand, look for *fruita del árbol del pan* in Caribbean or Latin American markets. Breadfruit, or *ulu* (in Hawaiian), is a round or oblong relative of the jackfruit (see page 345) with a tough, prickly green skin. It may measure up to 10 inches in diameter and weigh as much as 10 pounds. The firm flesh is cream-colored and has a starchy texture that is often compared to potato. However, its taste is much closer to that of a Jerusalem artichoke; it may even remind you of a semiripe mango.

One breadfruit weighing around 2 to 3 pounds will yield eight servings. Because of its high starch content, breadfruit is an excellent substitute for potato, taro, rice, beans, or bread crumbs. In Barbados, it is cooked into a paste called breadfruit coo-coo. In Jamaica, it's made into balls and stuffed with saltfish and akee (an egg-shaped fruit of an evergreen tree widely cultivated in Jamaica). Sometimes, breadfruit

is baked whole until tender, the flesh scooped out and combined with a highly seasoned meat or fish mixture and then returned to the shell for serving. In Hawaii, it's incorporated into fish cakes, very much like a sweet potato. In Martinique, it's transformed into a delicious sweet pudding called Pudding au Fruit de Pain. In Grenada, it's used in soup much like the Caribbean Vichyssoise on page 44.

Breadfruit must be cooked before eating. To use, remove the stem and cut the fruit into wedges. Core, peel, and cut ¼-inch thick pieces and keep covered in salted water until you are ready to cook it. It will prevent the breadfruit from turning brown and help bring out its flavor. It can be prepared like a starchy vegetable: boiled, baked, steamed, or fried. To roast, place the stemmed whole breadfruit in a preheated 375 °F oven and cook until the flesh is fork-tender, about 1¼ hours for a 3-pound breadfruit. Cool slightly before peeling.

---

white pepper. Cover and refrigerate until thoroughly chilled.

5. Ladle the soup into chilled bowls and garnish with snipped fresh chives. Serve immediately.

DOWN ISLAND BLACK BEAN SOUP

YIELD: 4 TO 6 SERVINGS

I am very fond of this homey, chunky black bean soup. The plantain and orange are a perfect foil for the smoky sausage and fiery pepper. This is one of those soups that make a perfect one-dish meal on wintry days. Serve it with a loaf of country bread, and maybe finish the meal with refreshing Persimmons in Peppered Vanilla Sauce (See Index).

½ pound dried black beans, rinsed and picked over
4 cups chicken broth, preferably homemade (page 30)
1 cup chopped onions
2 teaspoons minced garlic
⅓ cup diced carrot
¼ cup chopped fresh cilantro, including the stems
2 teaspoons dried oregano, crumbled
2 teaspoons ground cumin
Salt
½ small fresh Scotch bonnet pepper or 1 fresh jalapeño pepper, seeded and finely chopped
½ orange, unpeeled, studded with 6 whole cloves
2 ripe (black) plantains
¼ pound smoked beef sausage, preferably kielbasa, diced
1 cup fresh orange juice
Finely chopped red onion, for garnish

1. Place the beans in a large soup pot or Dutch oven, add 5 cups water, and bring to a boil. Remove from the heat, cover, and soak for 1 hour. Drain the beans, reserving 3 cups of the soaking liquid.

2. Return the beans and the reserved liquid to the pot. Add the chicken broth and bring to a boil. Reduce the heat to low and simmer, uncovered, until the beans are ten-der, 30 to 35 minutes, skimming any foam that rises to the surface.

3. Stir in the chopped onions, garlic, car-rot, cilantro, oregano, cumin, 1 teaspoon salt, the Scotch bonnet pepper, and the studded orange. Raise the heat to medium and bring to a boil. Reduce the heat, cover, and simmer for 30 minutes.

4. Remove and discard the studded orange. Cut the tips off each plantain. Slit the skin lengthwise down the ribs, and unwrap the fruit. Quarter the plantains, then cut them crosswise into ½-inch cubes. Add the plantains and sausage to the beans. Continue simmering, uncovered, until the fruit is ten-der and the sausage is heated through, about 5 minutes longer.

5. Remove from the heat and stir in the orange juice. Adjust the seasoning with salt, if necessary. Ladle the soup into warmed bowls and garnish with chopped red onion. Serve immediately.

CHILLED FRUIT BORSCHT

YIELD: 4 SERVINGS

One day, while making a blueberry tart, I ran out of blueberries. Fortunately for me, I had a few

There's a joke among musicians that if a trumpeter sees someone sucking on a lemon, his lips will pucker up so dramatically that he will be unable to play.

plums sitting in the refrigerator and added them to the blueberries in the tart. The result was so wonderful that I decided to try the combination again, this time in a soup. Light and smooth, this recipe produces just the right balance of sweet and tart flavors, with a boost from the red wine and spices. And the beautiful deep scarlet color will remind you of a beet borscht. You may also serve this soup hot.

1½ *cups sliced Santa Rosa or Italian prune plums (about 4 medium plums)*

1½ *cups fresh or frozen blueberries, picked over, rinsed and drained*

1 *cup dry red wine*

1 *cinnamon stick (3 inches long)*

3 *whole cloves*

⅓ *cup sugar*

Salt (optional)

4 *tablespoons heavy (or whipping) cream, for garnish (optional)*

Lemon slices, for garnish

1. Place the plums, blueberries, wine, cinnamon stick, cloves, and sugar in a soup pot and bring to a boil. Reduce the heat, partially cover, and simmer gently until the fruits are very soft, 10 to 12 minutes.

2. Remove and discard the cinnamon stick and cloves. Ladle the soup into a blender or a food processor in small batches and purée. Strain through a sieve into a bowl, pressing on the solids to extract as much liquid as possible. Adjust the seasoning, if necessary, adding sugar or salt if it's too tart and water if it's too strong. Cover and refrigerate until well chilled, at least 3 hours.

3. Ladle the borscht into 4 chilled bowls, and drizzle each serving with a tablespoon of cream, if using. Garnish each serving with a lemon slice and serve at once.

CHILLED HONEYDEW-LIME SOUP

YIELD: 4 TO 6 SERVINGS

This is a perfect soup to serve after a day at the beach or on the tennis courts. The summery pastel shades of melon and lime will please the eye, and the bubbly wine will add a welcoming sparkle to any summer meal.

> 1 large honeydew melon (about 2 pounds),
>   halved and seeded
> ½ cup thawed frozen limeade concentrate
> 1 cup dry sparkling white wine or
>   Champagne
> Fresh mint sprigs, for garnish

1. With a melonballer, scoop out enough balls from the honeydew to make 1 cup and reserve them for garnish. Peel and cut the remaining flesh into 1-inch cubes. (There should be about 3½ cups.)

2. Place the honeydew cubes and the limeade in a blender or a food processor and purée them. Transfer to a large mixing bowl and stir in the sparkling wine. Cover and chill at least 2 hours before serving.

3. Ladle the soup into chilled bowls. Garnish each serving with honeydew balls and a mint sprig. Serve at once.

JOLTING FRUIT SOUP

YIELD: 4 SERVINGS

Denmark has a popular soup made from dried fruits that goes by the name *rödgröd*. It is customary there to serve this energizing soup after a day of skiing or mushroom hunting. Although I suggest dried sour cherries, you may use dried cranberries or raisins if you wish. The sour cream helps cut the sweetness.

> ½ cup dried apricots, halved
> ½ cup pitted prunes, halved
> ½ cup pitted dried sour cherries
> 6 green cardamom pods,
>   lightly crushed
> ¼ teaspoon whole cloves
> Zest of 1 lemon, removed in strips
>   with a vegetable peeler
> 1 cup sweet vermouth
> ½ teaspoon almond extract
> 2 teaspoons cornstarch
> Sour cream, for garnish
> 2 tablespoons toasted sliced almonds
>   (for toasting instructions, see page 34),
>   for garnish

1. Place the apricots, prunes, and sour cherries in a soup pot with 4 cups water. Bring the mixture to a boil over medium-high heat, remove from the heat, and let the fruits soak, covered, until plumped, 1½ hours.

2. Tie the cardamom pods, cloves, and lemon peel in a small piece of muslin or a double thickness of cheesecloth. Add the spice bag to the fruit mixture, along with the vermouth and the almond extract.

3. Bring the soup to a simmer and cook, partially covered, over low heat until the fruits are very soft, about 25 minutes. Remove and discard the spice bag. Working in batches, ladle the soup into a blender or food processor and purée the fruits.

4. Return the puréed soup to the pot. Mix the cornstarch with ¼ cup water in a small bowl, and add it to the soup. Cook over low heat, stirring, until the soup has thickened slightly, about 2 minutes. If the soup is too thick, dilute it with about ¼ cup hot water.

5. Divide the soup among warmed bowls. Garnish each serving with a dollop of sour cream, sprinkle with toasted almonds, and serve.

TROPICAL GAZPACHO

YIELD: 4 SERVINGS

In Spain, every town has its version of gazpacho, but Seville made the cold vegetable soup famous. Gazpacho is not by any means a new invention; it is mentioned in Greek and Roman literature as a drinkable food, and references to it appear in the Bible. Here, I offer my own version of gazpacho: half fruit and half vegetable. The aroma of this thin soup is similar to that of a Mexican salsa. The bits of chopped pineapple, nectarines, and bell peppers add texture and a most refreshing taste. Unsweetened guava or papaya juice may replace the blended fruit juice.

1½ cups tomato juice

1½ cups unsweetened, blended tropical fruit juices, such as Tropicana's Orange-Kiwi-Passion Fruit

½ cup diced fresh pineapple

½ cup diced fresh nectarine, mango, papaya, or peach

¼ cup diced green bell pepper

¼ cup diced red bell pepper

¼ cup diced yellow bell pepper

2 tablespoons fresh lime juice

2 tablespoons shredded fresh cilantro leaves (for shredding instructions, see page 34)

1 small fresh jalapeño pepper, minced

¼ teaspoon freshly ground black pepper

1. Combine all the ingredients in a medium-size ceramic bowl. Cover and refrigerate until well chilled, at least 4 hours.

2. Serve the soup in chilled bowls placed over crushed ice.

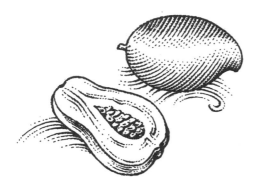

GRAPE GAZPACHO FROM MALAGA

YIELD: 4 TO 6 SERVINGS

Grape gazpacho originated in Málaga, Spain, where it is called *ajo blanco con uvas*. This cold, white soup is made with garlic and grapes and thickened with almonds. Although most recipes call for water, I think the soup gains considerably more character when made with freshly pressed grape juice. For a complete meal, serve this refreshing and flavorful soup with a light salad after a lazy day on the beach.

GREAT MATCHES

GRAPES

Grapes are a natural complement to cheeses like feta and Cheddar. They're also good with pork or prosciutto. Try adding grapes to a green salad tossed with a walnut oil-based vinaigrette.

1½ pounds stemmed seedless green grapes
5 slices white sandwich bread, preferably Pepperidge Farm, crusts removed
½ cup slivered blanched almonds
2 teaspoons minced garlic
2 large hard-cooked egg yolks
½ cup extra-virgin olive oil
3 tablespoons white wine vinegar
1 drop almond extract, or to taste
Salt (optional)
Freshly ground white pepper
24 seedless green grapes, peeled and halved, for garnish
Croutons, preferably homemade (recipe follows), for garnish
1 tablespoon chopped flat-leaf parsley leaves, for garnish

1. Put the 1 ½ pounds of grapes in a blender or food processor and purée. Strain through a sieve into a bowl, pressing on the pulp to extract as much juice as possible. (There should be about 2¼ cups of grape juice.) Discard the solids.

2. Cover the bread with ½ cup water and let sit until very soft, about 5 minutes.

3. Cover the almonds with water in a small saucepan and bring to a boil. Reduce the heat to low and simmer, uncovered, until the almonds are slightly soft, about 3 minutes. Drain.

4. Place the almonds in a blender or food processor and finely chop. Squeeze the excess water from the bread. Add the bread, garlic, and hard-cooked egg yolks to the almonds in the blender and purée. With the motor running, gradually add the olive oil through the feed tube and process until the mixture is thick and smooth.

5. Add the grape juice, 1¼ cups water, the vinegar, and almond extract, and process until smooth. Adjust the seasoning and consistency, if necessary, adding some vinegar or salt if the gazpacho is too sweet and water if it's too thick. Add white pepper to taste.

6. Transfer the soup to a ceramic bowl, cover, and refrigerate until well chilled, at least 4 hours.

7. Serve the soup in chilled bowls placed over crushed ice. Garnish each serving with peeled grapes, croutons, and chopped parsley leaves.

Very Crisp Croutons

ABOUT 4 CUPS

Perfectly made croutons are a great treat. Sprinkled over a soup or salad, they add an interesting crunch and toasty flavor to any dish. And it takes very little effort to make them.

1 baguette

1. Preheat the oven to 350°F.

2. Slice the baguette 1/2 inch thick and cut the slices into cubes. Arrange in a single layer on two 10 x 15-inch baking sheets.

3. Bake until lightly toasted, 10 to 15 minutes, shaking the pans once or twice so the croutons brown evenly. Remove from the oven and cool. Transfer the croutons to a cookie tin and store in the refrigerator for up to 1 month.

VARIATION

Add flavor to croutons by lightly brushing them with olive oil or melted butter just after they come out of the oven. Then sprinkle them with minced garlic, freshly grated Parmesan cheese, chopped fresh or dried herbs, toasted sesame seeds, or cumin seeds. Return the coated croutons to the oven for about 5 minutes to crisp them before cooling and storing.

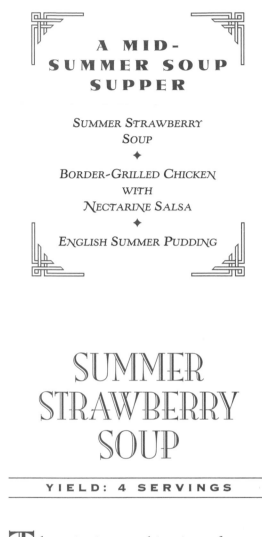

A MID-SUMMER SOUP SUPPER

SUMMER STRAWBERRY SOUP

✦

BORDER-GRILLED CHICKEN WITH NECTARINE SALSA

✦

ENGLISH SUMMER PUDDING

SUMMER STRAWBERRY SOUP

YIELD: 4 SERVINGS

The winning combination of sweet, ripe strawberries and tart balsamic vinegar makes for a delicious summer dessert. I gave this classic Italian pairing a decidedly French twist by puréeing it and calling it a chilled fruit soup. Sparkling fresh mint contributes even more of a summery feel to the soup.

1 pint (2 cups) fresh strawberries, hulled and quartered
⅓ cup sugar
2½ tablespoons balsamic vinegar
3 cups plain low-fat yogurt or buttermilk
2 teaspoons orange liqueur, such as Grand Marnier or Triple Sec
¼ teaspoon finely grated orange zest
¼ teaspoon finely grated lemon zest
1 tablespoon finely shredded fresh mint leaves (for shredding instructions, see page 34)
Thinly sliced strawberries, for garnish

1. Place the quartered strawberries, sugar, and vinegar in a blender and purée. Strain into a large mixing bowl and stir in the yogurt, Grand Marnier, and orange and lemon zests. Refrigerate until well chilled, at least 4 hours or overnight.

2. Just before serving, stir in the mint. Ladle the soup into chilled soup bowls and garnish with sliced strawberries. Serve at once.

PINA COLADA SOUP

YIELD: 4 SERVINGS

It doesn't take much to turn this favorite cocktail into an absolutely delicious soup. If you wish, add small

One of these nuts is a meal for a man, both meat and drink . . .
It is very tasty, as sweet as sugar and as white as milk and it is in the form
of a cup like the surrounding husk. Inside this fruit is enough juice to fill a
phial. The juice is clear and cool and admirably flavored. When a man
has eaten the kernel, he drinks the juice. And so from one nut a man
can have his fill of meat and drink.

— MARCO POLO

chunks of banana, kiwi, papaya, or mango for more color and texture. Serve Piña Colada Soup as a light summer lunch or for dessert.

> *3 cups chopped fresh pineapple*
> *1½ cups canned unsweetened coconut milk, well stirred*
> *¼ cup (or more) sugar*
> *3 tablespoons dark rum*

1. Place all the ingredients in a blender and purée them. Transfer to a large bowl. Add more sugar, if necessary. Cover and refrigerate until the soup is thoroughly chilled, about 4 hours or overnight.

2. Ladle the soup into chilled bowls and place over crushed ice. Serve at once.

PINK GRAPEFRUIT SOUP

YIELD: 4 TO 6 SERVINGS

Although putting tapioca in soup may seem unusual at first, you will be charmed by the way this natural thickener lends body and a pleasing texture. In fact, the tapioca in this recipe is what makes the difference between soup and juice. Wonderfully refreshing, this soup is versatile enough to serve as an appetizer or a dessert in hot or cold weather.

> *8 medium juicy ruby or pink grapefruits*
> *2 tablespoons quick-cooking tapioca*
> *2 tablespoons sugar*
> *2 teaspoons grenadine syrup*

1. Slice off the tops and bottoms of

4 grapefruits. Using a sharp knife with a flexible blade, cut around the fruit in a circular motion to remove the peel and white pith. Working over a colander set in a bowl to collect the juices, cut between the membranes to separate the fruit into sections. Remove any seeds, taking care not to break the segments.

(You should have about 2 cups of grapefruit sections.) Set the fruit sections aside.

2. Juice the remaining 4 grapefruits and combine their juices to the juice collected in the bowl to measure 4 cups.

3. Combine the grapefruit sections, grapefruit juice, tapioca, and sugar in a medium-size saucepan, and bring to a boil over medium heat. Reduce the heat to low and simmer, stirring occasionally, until the tapioca becomes soft and translucent, about 3 minutes. Remove from the heat and stir in the grenadine syrup. Cool slightly before serving.

SALADS

WITH FRUIT ACCENTS

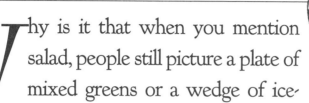

Why is it that when you mention salad, people still picture a plate of mixed greens or a wedge of iceberg lettuce topped with a slice or two of hard pink tomato and perhaps a piece of onion and then doused in an oily, gooey bottled dressing? And why is it when you look for a salad plate in a coffee shop that your choices are usually limited to cottage cheese and fruit, maybe a chef's salad, and of course, the obligatory chicken, tuna, or egg salad?

Luckily, this sorry state of affairs is starting to change: Americans have discovered a whole new world of salad possibilities. One has only to look to California, this country's Garden of Eden, which has taken advantage of its lush bounty of fresh produce to create some of the most exciting salads going. Innovative chefs have been concocting all sorts of interesting combinations to offer not just as side dishes but as appetizers and light main courses.

With the wealth of fresh produce and exotic ingredients showing up in our markets, everyone should now be able to achieve the same excitement at home. Incorporating the varied and wonderful fruits that are available and putting them to best use is the goal of this chapter. Don't expect to see salads with nothing but fruits. In my salad creations, a fruit can be combined with lettuces, vegetables, nuts, and even meats, seafood, grains, and pasta to great advantage.

Fresh fruits are a particularly good addition to salad. They can provide an element of surprise and a sweet flavor dynamic. You may be amazed to find out that some of the fruits you stare at while wondering how to use them, like breadfruit, cherimoya, star fruit, or green papaya, have wondrous, unique tastes and textures.

I equate a salad's distinctive coolness and herbal flavor with summer pleasures. However, I don't see any reason to stop serving them as the first chill arrives. Fall and winter harvests present us with wonderful salad fixings: flavorful cool-weather lettuces, assorted root vegetables, persimmons, pomegranates, and citrus fruits. Even delicious summer fruits, like berries, peaches, and melons shipped from the southern hemisphere, are available at our markets briefly around Christmas.

I also enjoy introducing a fruity flavor to salads by way of the dressing. I keep a few bottles of sweet fruit vinegars in the refrigerator, so I can inject a taste of summer into any salad, especially during winter months, when perfectly ripe and flavorful fruits are sometimes hard to find.

In keeping with the easy-going, informal nature of salads, I don't get annoyed if I can't find a particular ingredient for a salad at a particular time of year. I find it perfectly acceptable to simply leave out the missing component or substitute another. For instance, a salad of romaine lettuce and fresh strawberries with a flavorful lemon dressing is great, but if strawberries aren't available, it's just as fine without the fruit. And in a pinch orange segments or julienned apple can fill in for the strawberries. No matter what I do, I always observe one simple rule: Use the freshest and best-quality produce available.

This section contains light, meatless salads generally intended as appetizers or side dishes, although some can be augmented with meats or seafood to create a substantial meal, such as Black Bean and Tree Melon Salad or Vietnamese Pawpaw Salad.

BLUE AND WHITE SALAD

YIELD: 4 FIRST COURSE OR SIDE DISH SERVINGS

This light luncheon salad is best when blueberries are at their peak in mid-summer, but you can make it anytime of year: Just use frozen blueberries in the vinaigrette and toss the greens with whatever fruit is in season, like apples. Since this dish has both fruit and cheese, you can even serve it at the end of a fancy meal as a salad and dessert in one! For a substantial main-course meal, add strips of roast meat such as lamb, beef, pork, or chicken.

BLUEBERRY VINAIGRETTE

2 tablespoons blueberry vinegar, preferably
    homemade (page 284), or balsamic
    vinegar
1/4 cup chicken broth, preferably homemade
    (page 30)
1 tablespoon peanut oil
1 tablespoon mild olive oil
1/2 teaspoon minced garlic
1 1/2 teaspoons honey
1 teaspoon minced fresh oregano or 1/2
    teaspoon dried oregano, crushed
1/8 teaspoon salt
1/8 teaspoon freshly ground black pepper
2 tablespoons fresh or thawed frozen
    blueberries

SALAD

8 cups torn young mixed salad greens, such
    as mesclun or a mixture of red oakleaf,
    arugula, watercress, and Belgian endive
    or radicchio
1 cup fresh or thawed frozen blueberries
1/4 pound feta cheese, preferably Greek,
    crumbled

1. To make the vinaigrette, place all the
ingredients in a blender and blend until emulsified. (You should have about 1/2 cup.)
Transfer to a jar, cover, and refrigerate until
needed.

2. To make the salad, just before serving,
toss the mixed greens with the vinaigrette in
a large mixing bowl.

3. Divide the salad among chilled dinner
plates. Top with blueberries and crumbled
feta cheese. Serve at once.

TENDER GREENS WITH PASSION FRUIT VINAIGRETTE

YIELD: 4 FIRST COURSE OR SIDE DISH SERVINGS

Be warned: The vinaigrette for this
salad of mixed greens is so volup-
tuous, you may be hooked by its
"passionate" hold on your taste buds.
The fragrant pulp, pleasing tang, and
crunchy seeds of the passion fruit give
this vinaigrette its ambrosial character.
For a more substantial salad, add sweet,
tender cooked shrimp or sea scallops.

PASSION FRUIT VINAIGRETTE

2 passion fruits
1/4 cup mild olive oil
1/2 teaspoon Dijon mustard
1/2 teaspoon soy sauce, preferably Kikkoman
1/8 teaspoon finely grated peeled fresh ginger
1/8 teaspoon freshly ground black pepper
1 tablespoon boiling water
Salt

SALAD

8 cups torn young mixed salad greens, such as
    mesclun or a mixture of red oakleaf,
    arugula, watercress, and Belgian endive
    or radicchio

Parmesan cheese, for garnish (optional)

HOW TO MAKE
PERFECT GREEN SALAD

*E*ven a creation as basic as a salad of fresh greens requires careful preparation. Here are some guidelines for making a sublime salad:

✦ *Use the freshest greens you can find. Cleaned salad greens may be stored for up to 2 days wrapped in paper towels in an unsealed plastic bag in the vegetable drawer of the refrigerator. Remove the greens (along with the vinaigrette and any other salad components) from the refrigerator 10 to 15 minutes before serving so they lose their chill and reveal their true flavors.*

✦ *Be sure that the greens are thoroughly cleaned; nothing ruins a salad like grit. The easiest way to wash greens is to place them in a large bowl or sink full of cold water and swish them around to remove any grit or dirt. Let the greens remain in the water while the grit settles to the bottom of the sink (this will also crisp the greens). Lift the greens gently from the water, so the grit remains behind. Repeat until the water is clear.*

✦ *Dry your greens well. Any water on the greens will dilute the dressing and keep it from coating the greens properly, leaving the greens soggy and the dressing pooled at the bottom of the salad bowl. The easiest way to dry greens is to either roll them up in batches in a clean kitchen towel or whirl them in a salad spinner.*

✦ *Don't overdress. If the greens are well dried, they require very little dressing. Use only enough dressing to lightly coat the salad. Greens and dressing should complement each other, with neither dominating.*

✦ *Serve a green salad the minute it has been dressed. If you don't, the salt in the dressing will draw out moisture from the leaves and result in a sad, soggy mess.*

1. To make the vinaigrette, cut the passion fruits in half over a bowl to catch the juices. Then squeeze each half to dislodge the pulp and seeds. (There should be about 2 tablespoons of passion fruit pulp.)

2. Combine the passion fruit pulp, seeds, olive oil, mustard, soy sauce, ginger, pepper, and boiling water in a small jar. Cover and shake until the vinaigrette is emulsified. Season to taste with salt and shake again. (You should have about ½ cup vinaigrette.) Refrigerate until needed.

3. To make the salad, just before serving, toss the mixed greens with the vinaigrette in a large mixing bowl.

4. Divide the salad among chilled dinner plates. Garnish with shavings of Parmesan cheese, if desired.

STRAWBERRY FIELD SALAD

YIELD: 6 FIRST COURSE OR SIDE DISH SERVINGS

Strawberries, Parmesan cheese, and basil make a perfect flavor marriage in this light, simple romaine salad that is a change from its more pungent counterpart, the classic Caesar salad. For a more substantial salad, add grilled shrimp or strips of grilled chicken breast.

1 head romaine lettuce (about 1 pound)
½ cup firmly packed fresh basil leaves, thoroughly washed
¼ cup freshly grated Parmesan cheese, plus extra, for garnish
1 teaspoon minced garlic
1 tablespoon plus 1 teaspoon Dijon mustard
2 tablespoons red wine vinegar
¼ cup chicken broth, preferably homemade (page 30)
1 tablespoon plus 1 teaspoon extra-virgin olive oil
Salt and freshly ground black pepper
1 pint (2 cups) strawberries, trimmed and quartered
3 tablespoons toasted pine nuts (for toasting instructions, see page 64), for garnish

1. Halve the lettuce lengthwise, then cut each half crosswise into ¼-inch-wide shreds, discarding the core. Wash the lettuce thoroughly, then dry well. Cover and refrigerate until needed.

2. Place the basil, ¼ cup Parmesan, garlic, mustard, vinegar, and broth in a blender and purée. With the motor running, slowly add the oil through the feed tube and process until the dressing is well blended. Season to taste with salt and pepper. (You should have about ¾ cup dressing.) Transfer to a jar, cover, and refrigerate until needed.

3. Just before serving, place the lettuce and strawberries in a large mixing bowl. Add the dressing and toss well.

4. Serve on chilled salad plates, garnished with the toasted pine nuts and grated Parmesan cheese.

STARS AND STRIPES SALAD

YIELD: 4 FIRST COURSE SERVINGS

In this colorful salad, the spicy citrus dressing enhances the delicate flavor of the star fruit without overpowering it. I like to serve it as a light entrée, or as a side dish with fried or grilled foods. For a main course meal, add tender morsels of cooked shrimp or sea scallops. When feijoas, or pineapple guavas, are in season in spring and early summer, use them instead of star fruit for an interesting variation.

1 medium green bell pepper, stemmed,
    seeded, and julienned
1 medium red bell pepper, stemmed, seeded,
    and julienned
1 medium yellow bell pepper, stemmed,
    seeded, and julienned
½ medium jicama, peeled and julienned
    (optional)
½ medium red onion, thinly sliced
2 large star fruits (carambola), sliced
    crosswise ⅛ inch thick
Juice of 2 oranges (about 1 cup)
Juice of 2 limes (about ⅓ cup)
2 tablespoons extra-virgin olive oil
2 fresh hot red chile peppers or jalapeño
    peppers, minced
¼ cup finely shredded fresh cilantro
    leaves (for shredding instructions, see
    page 34)
Salt and freshly ground black pepper
1 ripe but firm avocado

1. Place the bell peppers, jicama, red

onion, and star fruits in a large mixing bowl
and toss to combine.

2. Whisk together the orange juice, lime
juice, olive oil, chile peppers, cilantro, and
salt and pepper to taste in a small bowl. Add
the dressing to the vegetables and toss until
well combined. Cover and refrigerate the
salad for at least 2 hours and up to 4 hours
before serving.

3. Just before serving, drain the salad.
Peel, pit, and cut the avocado into 12 wedges.
Arrange 3 wedges of avocado on each of 4
chilled dinner plates and mound the salad in
the center. Serve at once.

STAR FRUIT

*A*lso known as carambola, star fruit is an oval, waxy yellow fruit, 2 to 6 inches long, with five deep longitudinal ribs. When sliced crosswise, each slice resembles a perfect five-pointed star. Asian in origin (hence its Hindu name, carambola), it is now grown in Hawaii, the Caribbean, Florida, and California. Star fruit is one of those fruits that are not only lovely to look at but are also great for munching. It is succulent and mildly tangy like a grape, and the juicy, translucent flesh is crisp and delicate. One

of my favorite ways of eating this fruit is to slice it up, then dip the crisp, juicy slices in sea salt before popping them into my mouth. The unique star-shaped slices lend an exotic note to salads and fruit plates, or quickly sautéed in butter, they make a delightful garnish for meat and seafood dishes.

Choose fruits that are bruise-free and golden yellow for best flavor. If they are green, keep them at room temperature until they become a deep, golden yellow.

INDIAN SUMMER SALAD

YIELD: 4 FIRST COURSE SERVINGS

In the fall, when persimmons are at their peak, I love to serve this vibrant salad of orange, pink, and green. The best oil for this salad is walnut oil. If you find walnut oil too overpowering (or too extravagant), use a mild olive oil. And if persimmons are not available, substitute kiwis.

GRAPEFRUIT VINAIGRETTE
¼ cup fresh grapefruit juice
¼ cup walnut oil
2 teaspoons Dijon mustard
1 teaspoon minced garlic
Salt and freshly ground black pepper

SALAD
1 large bunch watercress, tough stems removed
4 ripe persimmons, peeled and sliced crosswise ¼ inch thick
2 pink grapefruits, peeled and sectioned (for instructions, see page 318)

Parmesan cheese, for garnish (optional)
Freshly ground black pepper

1. To make the vinaigrette, place all the ingredients in a jar. Cover and shake well. (You should have about ½ cup vinaigrette.) Refrigerate until needed.

2. To make the salad, just before serving, toss the watercress with half the vinaigrette in a mixing bowl.

3. Divide the watercress among chilled salad plates. Arrange the persimmon and grapefruit over the watercress, alternating the fruits. Drizzle the remaining vinaigrette over the salads and garnish with fresh Parmesan shavings, if desired. Sprinkle with black pepper and serve.

SICILIAN ORANGE SALAD

YIELD: 4 TO 6 FIRST COURSE OR SIDE DISH SERVINGS

In Sicily, there is a perfect antidote to a hot, muggy day: a vibrant salad that combines the sweetness of navel orange, the tartness of blood orange, and the sharp tingle of basil and onion, dressed with a drizzle of fruity olive oil. It is sensational with lamb dishes and curry or other dishes that have a spicy seasoning or are rich in butter or oil. If blood oranges are unavailable, increase the navel oranges to 4, and substitute 2 large lemons, sliced paper thin, for the remaining oranges.

3 navel oranges

3 blood oranges

1 medium red onion, sliced into paper-thin
   rings

8 large fresh basil leaves, shredded (for
   shredding instructions, see page 34)

3 tablespoons extra-virgin olive oil

Freshly ground black pepper

1. Peel the oranges, and remove all the pith. Slice into ¼-inch-thick rounds. Arrange the slices on a large, shallow platter.

2. Lay the onion slices on top of the oranges and sprinkle with the shredded basil.

3. Drizzle the olive oil over the salad, and season generously with black pepper.

4. Cover and let stand at room temperature for at least 2 hours before serving for the flavors to marry.

THREE GEMS SALAD

YIELD: 4 TO 6 FIRST COURSE OR SIDE DISH SERVINGS

The intense colors of this simple salad look great on the plate! The sherry vinegar in the dressing blends perfectly with the sweet fruit and peppery arugula. I like to serve this salad as an accompaniment to pasta. If arugula is unavailable, substitute watercress. For a

BLOOD ORANGES

Abundant in the Mediterranean, sweet blood oranges are also grown in California and, to some extent, Florida. Sometimes called sanguine oranges, they are available sporadically at specialty markets from February through May. From the outside, they look much like any other orange, though they are slightly smaller and have a red blush on the skin. When cut open, they reveal a flesh that varies from a light red to an intense scarlet. Around the Mediterranean, blood oranges are prized for their highly aromatic skin and gorgeous burgundy pulp.

Blood orange has an unmistakably rich citrus flavor—a little like grapefruit with a hint of orange and raspberry—and a tartness approaching that of a lemon. In Sicily, its tart, sensational ruby-red juice is often served at elegant breakfasts. When you can get hold of blood oranges, enjoy them as you would any sweet orange. Their vivid, bursting garnet color and juicy qualities are best appreciated in salads (both savory and sweet), sauces, marmalades, and desserts.

snappy cheese course, add pieces of crumbled feta or goat cheese.

1 pound small red beets, scrubbed and
*   trimmed, leaving a 1-inch stem*
2 navel oranges
2 fennel bulbs, trimmed
1/4 cup extra-virgin olive oil
2 tablespoons sherry vinegar
Salt and freshly ground black pepper
4 cups arugula leaves,
*   well rinsed and dried*

1. Place the beets in a saucepan with salted water to cover and bring to a boil over high heat. Reduce the heat to low and simmer, uncovered, until the beets are fork-tender, about 15 minutes. Drain the beets and let cool. Peel and slice 1/4 inch thick, then stack the slices and cut them into 1/4-inch-wide strips. Cover with plastic wrap and refrigerate until just before serving.

2. Peel the oranges with a knife, removing all the pith. Halve lengthwise, then slice into semicircles. Cover and refrigerate until just before serving.

3. Core the fennel and cut it crosswise into paper-thin slices. In a large mixing bowl, toss the fennel with the oil and vinegar and season to taste with salt and pepper. Cover and refrigerate until just before serving.

4. Just before serving, toss the beets and oranges with the fennel and season to taste with salt and pepper. Arrange the arugula on chilled salad plates and mound the fennel salad in the center.

CREAMY SPINACH SALAD WITH APPLES AND WALNUTS

YIELD: 4 FIRST COURSE SERVINGS

As a twist on a typical spinach salad, this composition of fresh spinach, apple, and toasted walnuts laced with lightly whipped cream, cider vinegar, and curry is superb.

1 pound fresh spinach leaves, well rinsed and
*   dried*
1 Red Delicious apple
1 teaspoon lemon juice
1/2 cup heavy (or whipping) cream
1/4 teaspoon curry powder, preferably Madras
*   brand*
2 tablespoons cider vinegar
Salt and freshly ground black pepper
1/2 cup toasted walnut halves (for toasting
*   instructions, see page 64), coarsely*
*   chopped*

1. Remove the stems from the spinach leaves. Tear the leaves into bite-size pieces and place in a large mixing bowl. Without peeling the apple, quarter, core, and slice it as thinly as possible. Sprinkle with lemon juice and add to the mixing bowl.

TOASTING NUTS

*T*oasting nuts greatly enhances their flavor. Toasted nuts become stale more quickly than raw nuts, so toast only as much as you need just before you're going to use them.

To toast, spread shelled nuts in a single layer on a baking sheet and place them in a preheated 350°F oven. Toast until golden brown. Test for doneness by tasting a nut. It should be slightly crunchy, with a pronounced nutty flavor and no burnt aftertaste. Always remember to let toasted nuts cool completely before grinding or chopping, in order to prevent them from becoming pasty or oily.

If you use a toaster oven, cut the suggested toasting time in half.

TYPE OF NUT	APPROXIMATE TOASTING TIME
Almonds, sliced or slivered	10 to 12 minutes
Almonds, whole, blanched or unblanched	12 to 15 minutes
Cashews	12 to 15 minutes
Coconut, shredded	4 to 5 minutes
Hazelnuts	12 to 15 minutes. When the hazelnuts are toasted, remove them from the oven and immediately wrap them in a clean, damp towel. After 5 minutes, remove the skins from the nuts by placing a few at a time inside a dry dish towel and rubbing vigorously with the towel. This should skin most of them. If any skin remains, rub it off with your fingers.
Macadamia Nuts	12 to 15 minutes
Peanuts, unsalted	10 to 12 minutes
Pecans	10 to 12 minutes
Pine Nuts (pignoli)	10 to 12 minutes
Pistachios, shelled, unsalted	10 to 12 minutes. Peel to reveal their lovely pale-green color.
Sesame Seeds	12 to 15 minutes
Walnuts	10 to 12 minutes

2. Lightly beat the cream with the curry powder in a medium-size bowl, and add the vinegar in a slow stream, whisking. Do not overbeat. Season to taste with salt and pepper. Add the dressing to the salad and toss well.

3. Divide the salad among chilled salad plates and sprinkle each portion with toasted walnuts.

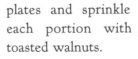

If we compare the small size, hardness and bitter taste of the wild pear with the huge size, sweetness and softness of many of our beautiful fruits, we realize what a marvelous influence cultivation has had. The finest varieties are divided into three classes: pears which 'melt in the mouth'; pears which are crisp but sweet; and pears with firm or crisp flesh and impregnated with an astringent quality which even cooking fails to make disappear completely.

—ALEXANDRE DUMAS PERE IN <u>GRAND DICTIONNAIRE DE CUISINE</u>

BISTRO SALAD WITH PEARS AND CHEESE

YIELD: 4 FIRST COURSE OR SIDE DISH SERVINGS

I enjoy the sharp, tangy, and fruity flavors of this salad combined with the crunch of toasted walnuts. To retain its fresh character, toss the salad only moments before you plan to serve it. Otherwise, the acidity in the dressing will "cook" the greens, making them limp and soggy. When fresh figs are in season, try them as a substitute for the pears.

MUSTARD VINAIGRETTE
4 teaspoons fresh lemon juice
2 teaspoons Dijon mustard
2 tablespoons mild olive oil
2 tablespoons walnut oil
2 tablespoons chicken broth, preferably homemade (page 30)
Pinch of sugar
Salt and freshly ground black pepper

SALAD
2 bunches watercress, picked over and tough stems discarded
2 Belgian endives, sliced crosswise ¼ inch thick
½ pound blue cheese, such as Roquefort, Gorgonzola, Saga, or Danish Blue
2 pears, preferably Red Bartlett, peeled, quartered, cored, and sliced ¼ inch thick
⅔ cup toasted walnut halves (for toasting instructions, see box, facing page), coarsely chopped
Freshly ground black pepper

1. To make the vinaigrette, whisk together the lemon juice, mustard, olive oil, walnut

oil, chicken broth, sugar and salt and pepper to taste in a large mixing bowl. (You should have about ½ cup of vinaigrette.) Cover and set aside.

2. To make the salad, just before serving, toss the watercress and endive with the vinaigrette.

3. Divide the dressed greens among chilled salad plates and crumble the cheese over each serving. Arrange the pears on top and sprinkle with toasted walnuts and pepper. Serve immediately.

THREE-COLOR SALAD WITH GOAT CHEESE

YIELD: 4 TO 6 FIRST COURSE OR SIDE DISH SERVINGS

Take advantage of the festive look of this glorious salad by serving it to your guests around the holidays, when pomegranate is plentiful.

Grapefruit vinaigrette (see step 1, page 61)
2 large bunches watercress, tough stems
    removed
2 large Belgian endives (about ½ pound),
    trimmed and sliced crosswise ¾ inch
    thick
¼ pound mild fresh goat cheese, preferably
    Montrachet
1 large pomegranate, seeded, or about
    1 cup pomegranate seeds
Freshly ground black pepper

1. Prepare the vinaigrette.

2. Just before serving, toss the watercress and Belgian endive with the vinaigrette in a large mixing bowl.

3. Divide the salad among chilled salad plates and crumble the goat cheese over the top. Sprinkle with pomegranate seeds and several grinds of pepper. Serve at once.

SMOKED TROUT AND PEAR SALAD

YIELD: 4 TO 6 FIRST COURSES OR ENTREES

Smoked trout goes wonderfully with pear and watercress. The bite of the greens, the mellow sweetness

VINAIGRETTES

*V*inaigrettes are a treasure to have in the refrigerator for quick salad making. Try to always keep two on hand, perhaps a basic mustard vinaigrette (page 65) and a fruit-flavored one. This way, you'll always be ready to dress your salads in no time at all. Of course, the more quickly you use these vinaigrettes, the fresher they will taste. The vinaigrette recipes in this book make enough for 4 to 6 servings, but they can easily be mutiplied to serve more; any leftovers will keep perfectly in a sealed jar in the refrigerator for up to 1 week.

Before using a vinaigrette, bring it to room temperature and revive it with a quick shake or whisk. As a rule of thumb, figure on using about 2 tablespoons of vinaigrette per serving on salads.

Most vinaigrettes make great marinades for grilled or baked vegetables, meat, poultry, and fish. They are also wonderful drizzled over bread for sandwiches. A light sprinkle of vinaigrette can easily jazz up simple steamed or sautéed dishes. And vinaigrettes make ingenious substitutes for the heavy or complicated sauces that often accompany simply cooked meats, fish, and shellfish. If you use vinaigrette as a sauce, you'll need about 2 or 3 tablespoons to dress the entire dish. Whenever you roast poultry or meat, don't forget to toss a spoonful or so of the rich pan juices into your favorite vinaigrette for depth of flavor.

---

of the pear, and the subtle tang of a grapefruit-based vinaigrette proudly stand up to the robust smoked fish.

> Grapefruit vinaigrette (see step 1, page 61)
> 2 tablespoons fresh lemon juice
> 2 ripe but firm pears, preferably Red Bartlett
> 2 large bunches watercress, tough stems removed
> 2 smoked trouts (about ¾ pound total), skin and bones removed, broken into bite-size pieces
> Freshly ground black pepper

1. Prepare the vinaigrette.

2. Just before serving, fill a medium-size bowl with cold water and add the lemon juice. Quarter and core the pears but do not peel them. Cut each quarter lengthwise into thin wedges and drop the wedges in the water.

3. Toss the watercress with the vinaigrette in a large mixing bowl.

4. Mound the greens on chilled salad plates. Drain the pears and shake off excess water. Arrange the pear slices decoratively around the greens and top with the smoked trout. Sprinkle with pepper and serve.

BIG APPLE WALDORF

YIELD: 4 FIRST COURSE
OR SIDE DISH SERVINGS

Any discussion of fruits and salads would not be complete without the classic Waldorf salad. This dish was created by Oscar Tschirky, the maître d'hôtel of the famed New York Waldorf, for its opening in 1893. All he did was mix raw apples, celery, and walnuts with a good mayonnaise, and a star was born. For a main-course meal, add chunks of cooked chicken or strips of roast pork.

2 large Red Delicious apples
1 large Golden Delicious apple
1 tablespoon fresh lemon juice
3 large ribs celery, sliced ½ inch thick
    (2 cups)
1 cup toasted walnut halves (for
    toasting instructions, see page 64),
    coarsely chopped
½ cup good-quality mayonnaise
2 teaspoons honey
Salt and freshly ground black
    pepper
Boston lettuce leaves

1. Without peeling the apples, core and cut them into ½-inch chunks. Place in a large mixing bowl and toss with the lemon juice. Add the celery and walnuts.

2. In a small bowl, mix the mayonnaise and honey until smooth, then add to the salad. Toss well. Season to taste with salt and pepper.

3. Divide the lettuce leaves among chilled salad plates and top with the apple mixture.

WINTER WHITE SALAD

YIELD: 4 FIRST COURSE
OR SIDE DISH SERVINGS

Celery root (or celeriac) and pear is a classic match. Celery root is a sturdy winter vegetable with a licorice flavor and the texture of a parsnip. In this salad, the pear enhances the natural sweetness of the celery root, and the nuts provide texture and panache. I like to serve this salad as a first course or a light main dish with plenty of good bread and chèvre, like Montrachet, or Edel de Clairon, a mild creamy sheep's milk cheese.

1 tablespoon Dijon mustard

2 tablespoons red wine vinegar

3 tablespoons peanut oil

¾ teaspoon sugar

Salt and freshly ground black pepper

2 medium ripe but firm Bosc or Anjou
pears

3 cups shredded peeled celery root
(about a 1¾-pound celery root,
unpeeled)

3 tablespoons fresh lemon juice

4 leaves red-leaf lettuce

½ cup toasted walnut halves (for toasting
instructions, see page 34), coarsely
chopped

1 tablespoon chopped flat-leaf parsley
leaves

1. To make the dressing, whisk the mustard, vinegar, oil, sugar, and salt and black pepper to taste in a small bowl until emulsified.

2. Peel and quarter the pears. Cut away the cores and cut each quarter lengthwise into 3 slices. Toss in a small bowl with 4 teaspoons of the dressing.

3. Toss the celery root in a medium-size bowl with the lemon juice and the remaining dressing.

4. To assemble the salad, arrange the lettuce leaves on chilled salad plates. Fan the pear slices in a circle on the lettuce. Mound one-fourth of the celery root salad in the center of each plate. Sprinkle with toasted walnuts and chopped parsley before serving.

Don't let the farmer know how good cheese is with pears.

—ITALIAN PROVERB MEANING THAT IF THE
FARMER FINDS OUT, HE WILL HARVEST ALL
THE PEARS FOR HIMSELF AND EAT ALL THE
CHEESE HE PRODUCES

BREADFRUIT IN VINAIGRETTE

YIELD: 4 FIRST COURSE OR SIDE DISH SERVINGS

This delicious breadfruit salad is my twist on German potato salad. It tastes best when eaten warm. Although I steam the breadfruit to preserve its delicate flavor, you can boil it, if you wish. For a heartier dish, you may add cooked diced smoked sausage, such as kielbasa. And if you have any left over, turn the salad into delectable home fries by pan-frying it until lightly brown. Save the remaining breadfruit to make Breadfruit Vichyssoise (see Index). For more on breadfruit, see page 45.

Give me a good working woman and a breadfruit tree, and I need never work again.

—A SAYING (POPULAR AMONG MEN, NO DOUBT) ON ST. VINCENT ISLAND

───────

2 teaspoons Dijon mustard

1 teaspoon minced garlic

½ teaspoon sugar

½ teaspoon freshly ground black pepper

¼ teaspoon ground cumin

2 tablespoons rice vinegar or distilled vinegar

2 tablespoons fresh lime juice

3 tablespoons extra-virgin olive oil

Salt

4 cups peeled, cored, and sliced (¼ inch thick) breadfruit, kept in salted water to cover

½ cup peeled, seeded, and chopped tomatoes

½ cup chopped red onion

2 tablespoons finely shredded fresh cilantro leaves (for shredding instructions, see page 34)

1. Place the mustard, garlic, sugar, pepper, cumin, vinegar, lime juice, olive oil, and salt to taste in a medium-size jar. Cover and shake well. Refrigerate until needed.

2. Pour water to a depth of 1 to 2 inches into a wok or wide shallow pan. Place a snug-fitting steamer rack over the pan. Bring the water to a boil over medium heat. Drain the breadfruit, and put it on the steamer rack. Tightly cover the pot with a lid. Steam until the fruit is fork-tender, about 10 minutes. Cool slightly.

3. Transfer the warm breadfruit to a large mixing bowl. Add the tomato, onion, and cilantro. Shake the dressing, and pour it over the salad. Toss to blend. Let the salad sit for 10 minutes for the flavors to marry. Serve at room temperature.

NICOLE'S CARROT SALAD

YIELD: 4 FIRST COURSE OR SIDE DISH SERVINGS

Every cook in France has a version of carrot salad. Each cook likes to improvise on it by adding bits of fresh herbs or nuts. I like mine moist and creamy but not too sweet or tangy, with plenty of fresh dill. No matter what, the basis of the delicate dressing should be fresh lemon juice.

⅓ cup raisins

Boiling water

1 teaspoon minced garlic

1 tablespoon Dijon mustard

2 tablespoons fresh lemon juice

1 teaspoon honey

⅛ teaspoon salt

⅛ teaspoon freshly ground black pepper

3 tablespoons extra-virgin olive oil

4 cups shredded or grated carrots (1 pound)

2 tablespoons chopped fresh dill

1. Cover the raisins with boiling water and soak for 5 minutes. Drain.

2. For the dressing, whisk together the garlic, mustard, lemon juice, honey, salt, and pepper in a medium-size mixing bowl. Gradually whisk in the oil to make an emulsion.

3. Add the raisins, shredded carrots, and dill to the dressing and toss well. Let stand 10 minutes to tenderize the carrots and allow the flavors to marry before serving.

MOROCCAN CARROT SALAD

YIELD: 4 SIDE DISH SERVINGS

In a Moroccan carrot salad, the carrots are permeated with the flavors of a citrusy marinade fragrant with spices like cinnamon, cumin, and coriander. This salad will definitely perk up your palate and stimulate your appetite. It makes a wonderful first course or an enticing part of mezze platter, a Middle Eastern antipasto, that might include the Minty-Fruity Tabbouleh and Rosy Baba Ghanoush (see Index). It's also a terrific accompaniment to lamb or chicken kabobs.

$\frac{1}{2}$ teaspoon ground cinnamon
$\frac{1}{2}$ teaspoon ground cumin
$\frac{1}{2}$ teaspoon ground coriander
$\frac{1}{2}$ teaspoon salt
1 pound carrots, peeled and sliced $\frac{1}{4}$ inch thick
1 cup fresh orange juice
1 tablespoon honey
2 tablespoons extra-virgin olive oil
3 tablespoons fresh lemon juice
1 teaspoon minced garlic
$\frac{1}{8}$ teaspoon cayenne pepper
$\frac{1}{2}$ cup chopped red onion
1 tablespoon shredded fresh mint leaves (for shredding instructions, see page 34)
1 tablespoon shredded fresh cilantro leaves (page 34)

1. Combine the cinnamon, cumin, coriander, and salt in a small bowl.

2. Combine the carrots, orange juice, honey, and half of the spice mixture in a large saucepan. Bring the mixture to a boil, reduce the heat to medium, and simmer until the carrots are crisp-tender, about 10 minutes. Drain, reserving $\frac{1}{4}$ cup of the cooking liquid.

3. Whisk together the reserved cooking liquid, the olive oil, lemon juice, garlic, cayenne pepper, and the remaining spice mixture in a large mixing bowl. Add the carrots and red onion and toss well. Cover and let stand at room temperature for 1 hour, or refrigerate overnight.

4. Just before serving, toss with the mint and cilantro.

VIETNAMESE PAWPAW SALAD

YIELD: 4 TO 6 SIDE DISH SERVINGS

Mint, cilantro, and green papaya give a refreshing taste to this Vietnamese-style vegetable slaw. Like coleslaw, it goes with almost anything. Don't be discouraged if you cannot find green papaya or fish sauce to make this salad; you can easily substitute shredded white cabbage and a mild soy sauce, such as Kikkoman. If desired, add shredded poached chicken breast for a main-course meal.

2 fresh hot red chile peppers, minced

1 teaspoon minced garlic

2 tablespoons sugar

1 tablespoon rice vinegar or distilled white
   vinegar

3 tablespoons fresh lime juice

3 tablespoons Thai fish sauce

3 tablespoons vegetable oil

Freshly ground black pepper

1 medium green papaya, peeled, seeded,
   and very finely shredded (about 5 cups,
   see page 32)

1 cup finely shredded carrots

1 medium red onion, sliced paper thin

1/2 cup shredded fresh mint leaves (for
   shredding instructions, see page 34)

1/4 cup shredded fresh cilantro leaves (page 34)

1/3 cup unsalted dry-roasted peanuts, coarsely
   ground

1. Whisk together the chiles, garlic, sugar, vinegar, lime juice, fish sauce, oil, and black pepper to taste in a medium-size bowl.

2. Just before serving, combine the papaya, carrots, onion, mint, and cilantro, and half the ground peanuts in a large mixing bowl. Sprinkle the dressing over all and toss well.

3. Transfer the salad to a serving platter and sprinkle with the remaining ground peanuts.

BLACK BEAN AND TREE MELON SALAD

YIELD: 8 SIDE DISHES OR 4 ENTREES

This tropical-style black bean and sweet tree melon (just another name for papaya) salad is extremely refreshing and satisfying. Colorfully displayed in hollowed-out golden papaya shells, it makes a festive presentation on the plate. It can also be served like a salsa and scooped up with chips. For a more substantial meal, add poached shrimp or chicken.

1 cup dried black beans

3 tablespoons extra-virgin olive oil

3 tablespoons fresh lime juice

1 tablespoon plus 1 teaspoon soy sauce, preferably Kikkoman

2 tablespoons chopped red onion

1/2 teaspoon sugar

1 teaspoon ground cumin

1 fresh serrano or jalapeño pepper, minced

4 plum tomatoes, seeded and finely diced

3 ripe papayas, 1 seeded, peeled, and cubed (1/2-inch pieces), and 2 halved and seeded

10 to 12 fresh basil leaves, finely shredded (for shredding instructions, see page 34), plus a few whole basil leaves, for garnish

Salt and freshly ground black pepper

1. Wash and pick over the beans. Place in a large bowl and cover with water. Let soak for at least 4 hours, or overnight.

2. Drain the beans and rinse them under running water. Place in a medium-size saucepan and cover with lightly salted water. Bring to a boil over high heat. Reduce the heat to medium and simmer until the beans are tender but retain their shape, about 30 to 35 minutes. Drain, rinse well with cold water, and drain again.

3. Whisk together the olive oil, lime juice, soy sauce, onion, sugar, cumin, serrano pepper, and tomatoes in a large ceramic bowl. Toss in the black beans, papaya cubes, and shredded basil. Season to taste with salt and pepper.

4. Spoon the salad into the papaya halves. Place on chilled plates and garnish with basil leaves.

PAPAYA

A New World native, papaya is sometimes called tree melon or pawpaw. The papaya was introduced to Asia about a hundred years after Columbus discovered America, and it now grows in tropical climates all over the world. Today, more than fifty varieties of papaya exist. The most common one in our markets is the deep orange-yellow puna variety.

A ripe papaya yields to gentle pressure and has a consistency like that of a ripe cantaloupe. When cut open lengthwise, each cavity reveals a dense nest of translucent black peppercorn-size seeds. It may never have occurred to you to eat the seeds of a fruit, but try sprinkling a small handful of these ebony seeds over a savory or sweet papaya salad; you'll be pleasantly surprised by the crunch and peppery zing they add. With a squeeze of lime juice, papaya makes a sweet and delicious treat. And like melon, papaya goes well with cured ham, especially prosciutto, for a refreshing appetizer.

NAPA SLAW WITH GRAPES

YIELD: 4 TO 6 SIDE DISH SERVINGS

I am partial to salads dressed in oil and vinegar rather than mayonnaise, probably because I never ate mayonnaise as a child. So naturally I prepare my cole slaw with lemon juice, olive oil, sesame oil, and soy sauce. Here, I've added grapes for extra texture and toasted sesame seeds for a nutty flavor. Be sure to serve this slaw just after it's been tossed to preserve the fresh flavors and crunch. The soy vinaigrette can be made well in advance; it will keep for up to a week in the refrigerator. If desired, add shredded poached chicken breast for a main-course meal.

SOY VINAIGRETTE

2 tablespoons soy
    sauce, preferably
    Kikkoman
2 tablespoons fresh
    lemon juice
1/4 cup mild olive oil
3/4 teaspoon Asian sesame oil
1 teaspoon finely grated peeled fresh
    ginger
1 teaspoon sugar
1/4 teaspoon freshly ground black pepper
2 teaspoons boiling water

SALAD

6 cups finely shredded napa cabbage
    (about 1 pound)
1 medium red onion, thinly sliced
1/4 cup finely shredded carrot
1 cup seedless green grapes, halved
2 tablespoons toasted sesame seeds
    (for toasting instructions, see
    page 64)

1. To make the vinaigrette, place all the ingredients in a jar. Cover and shake well. (You should have about 1/2 cup vinaigrette.) Refrigerate until needed.

2. To make the salad, combine the cabbage, onion, carrot, and grapes in a large mixing bowl. Shake the vinaigrette and pour it over the salad. Add the toasted sesame seeds, toss well, and serve.

SWAMP SALAD WITH CHERIMOYA

YIELD: 4 FIRST COURSE SERVINGS

I call this Swamp Salad because it includes hearts of palm and avocado. Still puzzled by the name? Heart of palm, the center shoot of the young Sabal, or Cabbage Palm, is also known as

CHERIMOYA

The cherimoya is the most esteemed of a large family of mostly tropical custardlike fruits of the genus Annona. Sometimes called custard apple, it looks like a large green pinecone covered with thumbprintlike indentations. Its creamy white flesh has been described as having hints of banana, papaya, pineapple, and vanilla, with a touch of the graininess of pears. The fruit contains numerous hard black seeds.

A good cherimoya is the tastiest fruit you'll ever eat, but you have to find one in prime condition and let it ripen properly. Look for one that's firm and light green. If it is dark and smudgy, it may have *been damaged by the cold or by rough handling. Keep the fruit at room temperature for a few days until it yields to gentle pressure like a ripe peach, but don't let it become mushy. Store ripe cherimoyas in the refrigerator for up to 5 days. Strips of cherimoya, with the seeds removed, work well in fruit salads, but the subtle taste of a high-quality cherimoya is best appreciated on its own. You can accent their flavor with a few drops of lime or pineapple juice. Serve it chilled, halved or quartered lengthwise, and eat it with a spoon. Cherimoyas also make exquisite drinks, sorbets, and custard.*

swamp cabbage in its native Florida. The avocado used to be referred to as alligator pear (for its hard and knobby skin) by the first pilgrims, and alligators live in swamps. Hence the name. The soft avocado and cherimoya provide a texture that contrasts nicely with the crunchy carrots and crisp, mellow hearts of palm. The subtle raspberry dressing lets the flavor of each ingredient come through without overpowering any of them. Look for the best-quality canned hearts of palm you can find, as some are preserved with too much brine and lose their delicate flavor. If cherimoya is not in season, substitute a Bosc or Asian pear.

RASPBERRY DRESSING

½ cup plus 1 tablespoon light cream or half-and-half

2 tablespoons raspberry vinegar, preferably homemade (page 286), or red wine vinegar

1 tablespoon Dijon mustard

½ teaspoon sugar

Salt and freshly ground black pepper

3 tablespoons chopped flat-leaf parsley leaves

SALAD

1 can (14 ounces) hearts of palm, drained, julienned

2 medium carrots, peeled and julienned

4 to 6 leaves red-leaf lettuce

1 California (Hass) avocado

1 large ripe cherimoya (about 1 pound)

1. To make the dressing, whisk together the cream, vinegar, mustard, and sugar with salt and pepper to taste in a small bowl until creamy and slightly thickened. Stir in the chopped parsley. (You should have about $2/3$ cup dressing.)

2. To make the salad, toss the hearts of palm and carrots with half the dressing in a medium-size bowl. Cover and let the salad stand at room temperature for the flavors to marry, about 30 minutes.

3. Line a large platter with the lettuce leaves, and top with the marinated hearts of palms and carrots. Peel and pit the avocado, then cut it lengthwise into 16 wedges.

Arrange the avocado wedges around the salad.

4. Quarter the cherimoya. Peel it by running a small spoon between the flesh and skin of each wedge. Break the cherimoya into small chunks and remove the black seeds, taking care not to press the flesh too hard, or it will become mushy. Scatter the cherimoya chunks over the salad.

5. Drizzle the reserved dressing over the avocado and cherimoya, sprinkle with pepper, and serve.

SALAD MEALS

Ever since I was a little girl, salads have been a key part of my diet. Knowing my craving for greens, my mother used to prepare a huge bowl of salad for me at almost every meal, with bits of cold meat or fresh fruit thrown in for good measure. That would always make me enormously happy, and I have carried this passion with me up to this day. In fact, my husband calls me a rabbit because of my love for salads.

My idea of a perfect meal is a bowl of well-dressed tender baby greens with meat, fowl, or fresh or smoked fish. As the crowning glory, I enjoy throwing in colorful, juicy bits of fruit in season, like orange, pineapple, or peach, or wonderful exotics such as mango, papaya, or Asian pear. More often than not, I add a sprinkling of nuts for that pleasing crunch and toasty flavor, or a shaving of Parmesan cheese for added pungency.

The culinary term for this dish, composed salad, was popularized by the great French chef Escoffier. I think the name aptly captures the spirit of these salads: It denotes something carefully made up or lovingly put together, like a work of art. In the salad world, a well-composed salad is a visually appealing plate of greens with great flavors and contrasting colors, shapes, and textures.

Composed salads are also a perfect way to use up leftovers. If I find myself with a portion of last night's roast chicken or pork, I will use it as an easy substitute for fresh-grilled chicken breasts. Leftover lamb is also a fine surrogate for roast beef or other red meat.

Beyond introducing you to new taste combinations and, perhaps, a yet-untried fruit, these recipes should prove, deliciously, that salads are worthy of respect as great change-of-pace entrées. Many salads in this section, such as Shrimp and Endive Salad, Warm Escarole, Raspberry, and Chicken Salad, and Smoked Trout and Pear Salad, also rotate nicely between main course and first course.

SHRIMP AND ENDIVE SALAD

YIELD: 6 FIRST COURSE SERVINGS

I love Belgian endive and this is one of my favorite ways to prepare it. When tossed with a tangy-sweet dressing, this popular winter vegetable mellows, losing some of its bitterness. The marinated shrimp and soft grapefruit provide a nice contrast to the crunchy endive, making for a very tasty salad.

2 tablespoons peanut oil
1 tablespoon mild olive oil
1 tablespoon red wine vinegar
1 tablespoon honey
1 tablespoon soy sauce, preferably
    Kikkoman
1 tablespoon ketchup
½ teaspoon minced garlic
¼ teaspoon ground ginger
¼ teaspoon freshly ground black pepper
Salt
1 pound medium shrimp (26 to 30) in their
    shells
1 large grapefruit
7 large Belgian endives (about 1¾ pounds)

1. Whisk together the peanut and olive oils, vinegar, honey, soy sauce, ketchup, garlic, ginger, and pepper in a small bowl. Set aside.

2. Bring a medium-size saucepan of salted water to a boil. Add the shrimp and boil until they turn pink and float to the surface, 2 to 3 minutes. Drain and refresh the shrimp under cold running water. Set aside to cool. Peel and devein them, discarding the shells.

3. Toss the shrimp with half the dressing in a large mixing bowl. Cover and marinate in the refrigerator for no longer than 30 minutes. Reserve the remaining dressing.

4. In the meantime, peel, section, and seed the grapefruit (see "Sectioning a Citrus Fruit," page 318). Cut each section in half crosswise and place in a small bowl. Set aside.

5. Remove any endive leaves that have darkened. Using a small knife, trim the base of each head slightly. Slice 6 of the endives crosswise ¾ inch thick and add to the shrimp. Separate the leaves of the remaining head and set aside.

6. Drain the grapefruit sections (you can drink the juice) and add them to the shrimp and endive. Drizzle the reserved dressing over the top and toss gently, taking care not to break the fruit sections. Divide the mixture among chilled salad plates or glass compotes, garnish with endive leaves, and serve.

MANGOES AND PAPAYAS

*L*uscious mangoes and papayas are quite compatible with other tropical fruits, like passion fruits and kiwis. But they are equally at home with fresh local berries. On the savory side, try them with almost any kind of meat or fish. Their musky, mysterious qualities are also enhanced by cilantro, basil, mint, chives, and even rosemary.

SHRIMP AND MANGO SALAD

YIELD: 4 ENTREE SERVINGS

In the cuisines of the Pacific Rim, green, unripened mangoes are traditionally used in salads. Inspired by that idea, I developed this shrimp salad using ripe mangoes for their fragrant, juicy, and velvety texture. The distinctive perfume of the mangoes contrasts deliciously with the delicate shrimp and powerful orange-rosemary vinaigrette. And don't worry: Chilling a mango does not diminish its taste but enhances it. You may substitute sliced peaches or papaya or orange sections for the mango.

ORANGE-ROSEMARY VINAIGRETTE

¼ cup mild olive oil
2 tablespoons chicken broth, preferably homemade (page 30)
2 tablespoons red wine vinegar
2 teaspoons Dijon mustard
¼ cup thawed frozen orange juice concentrate
2 cloves garlic, minced
¼ teaspoon salt
½ teaspoon paprika
⅛ teaspoon cayenne pepper
⅛ teaspoon black pepper
1 tablespoon minced fresh rosemary leaves

SHRIMP AND MANGO SALAD

1 medium carrot, peeled and sliced ¼ inch thick
1 small onion, slivered
4 slices lemon
4 small bay leaves
1 tablespoon salt
1 pound large shrimp (21 to 25), shelled and deveined
2 medium ripe mangoes

1. To make the vinaigrette, whisk all the ingredients together in a small bowl, and set aside. (You should have about 1 cup of vinaigrette.) Cover and refrigerate until needed.

2. To make the salad, place 6 cups water, the carrot, onion, lemon, bay leaves, and salt in a large pot and bring to a boil over high heat. Lower the heat to medium and simmer for 30 minutes. Put the shrimp in a colander that fits inside the pot, then place in the sim-

mering liquid. Remove the pot from the heat and let the shrimp sit in the liquid until they are just cooked through, 3 to 4 minutes.

3. Remove the shrimp and refresh under cold water. Drain. Cut each shrimp in half lengthwise, then place in a mixing bowl. Add ½ cup of the vinaigrette to the shrimp. Mix well and let them marinate for 1 hour in the refrigerator.

4. Peel the mangoes and cut them into 1-inch cubes, discarding the pits. Cover and refrigerate until ready to use.

5. Just before serving, add the mango to the marinated shrimp and toss to combine. Divide the salad among chilled dinner plates. Spoon the remaining vinaigrette over the top and serve at once.

SCALLOPS WITH CANTALOUPE AND CUCUMBER

YIELD: 4 ENTREE SERVINGS

The warm scallops, sweet melon, cooling cucumber, and crunchy peanuts make this light, tantalizing dish a welcome meal on hot, humid days. Be sure to select a ripe, perfumy cantaloupe for this recipe.

1 pound jumbo sea scallops (about 16 to 20)
Salt and freshly ground black pepper
1 large egg, lightly beaten
¾ cup dry bread crumbs
¼ cup fresh lime juice
1 teaspoon grated lime zest
¼ cup Thai fish sauce
2 fresh hot red chile peppers or jalapeño peppers, minced
2 tablespoons (firmly packed) light brown sugar
2 teaspoons minced garlic
2 cucumbers, peeled, halved, seeded, and thinly sliced
1 cantaloupe (about 1 pound), halved, seeded, sliced ½ inch thick, and peeled
¼ cup unsalted dry-roasted peanuts, coarsely ground
¼ cup shredded fresh cilantro leaves (for shredding instructions, see page 34)

1. Place 4 bamboo skewers in a shallow pan and cover with hot water. Soak for at least 30 minutes.

2. Rinse the scallops and pat dry. Remove and discard the little muscles on the sides of the scallops. Season with salt and pepper.

3. Thread 4 or 5 scallops onto each skewer, then place the brochettes on a platter. Brush the top of the scallops with some beaten egg and sprinkle with the bread crumbs to coat completely, gently pressing

the bread crumbs onto the scallops. Turn over the brochettes and repeat on the other side. (This can be prepared up to 2 hours ahead, covered, and refrigerated. Bring to room temperature before cooking.)

4. In a medium-size mixing bowl, combine the lime juice and zest, fish sauce, chile peppers, brown sugar, and garlic. Let stand for at least 30 minutes. (This can be prepared ahead, covered, and refrigerated. Bring to room temperature before serving.)

5. Preheat the broiler.

6. Just before serving, broil the brochettes 6 inches from the heat, until the scallops are lightly golden on the outside, and just opaque throughout, about 4 to 5 minutes total, turning the brochettes halfway through cooking.

7. Unthread the scallops. Mound the cucumbers in the center of each dinner plate, then surround them with the cantaloupe slices and scallops. Stir the peanuts and cilantro into the dressing and then spoon over the salad. Serve immediately.

F I S H   S A U C E

It is hard to overstate the importance of fish sauce in the cuisines of Southeast Asia, particularly in Thailand and Vietnam, where it is virtually ubiquitous. Known as nam pla *in Thailand,* nuoc mam *in Vietnam, and* patis *in the Philippines, this clear, amber liquid of fermented anchovies and salt is used in cooking, much like salt in Western cooking. Unimaginatively translated into English as "fish sauce," it is not as frightening as it sounds. While its smell is quite strong, the aroma dissipates during cooking. This condiment acts as an enhancer, adding depth to any food and broadening other flavors without overpowering them. Once you get used to cooking with fish sauce, you can easily become addicted to it. I consider the Thai version, such as Tiparos brand, the best for all-purpose cooking. Fish sauce will keep in your pantry for up to 6 months.*

Because of the increasing popularity of Asian cuisines, fish sauce is showing up in many big-city supermarkets; if you can't find it, try an Asian market. You can also get fish sauce and other hard-to-find ingredients such as coconut milk, curry pastes, chiles, lemongrass, tamarind, kaffir lime leaves, and rice noodles through the mail-order sources listed on page 42.

TROPICAL LOBSTER SALAD

YIELD: 6 APPETIZER OR 4 LUNCH SERVINGS

I'll give anything for a truly delicious lobster salad. When I make my own, I like to complement the sweetness of the seafood with crunch, so I add chunks of juicy apple, pineapple, and celery. Be sure to add the dressing only minutes before you are ready to serve.

½ cup good-quality mayonnaise
¼ cup ketchup
1 tablespoon Cognac
¼ teaspoon Tabasco sauce, or more to taste
3 live lobsters (1 to 1¼ pounds each)
1 apple, such as Red Delicious
1 tablespoon fresh lemon juice
1 cup thinly sliced celery
2 tablespoons small capers
1½ cups cubed fresh pineapple (½-inch pieces)
Soft lettuce leaves, such as Boston or red leaf, for garnish
Salt and freshly ground black pepper
Paprika, for garnish

1. Whisk together the mayonnaise, ketchup, Cognac, and Tabasco sauce until smooth in a small bowl. Cover and refrigerate until needed.

2. Plunge the lobsters into a large heavy pot of boiling salted water. Quickly cover the pot, and bring the water back to a boil. Timing from the moment the water returns to a boil, cook for 10 to 12 minutes longer, depending on the weight of the lobsters. Using tongs, transfer the lobsters to a colander and let sit until cool enough to handle. Remove the rubber bands from the claws.

3. Place the lobsters on a cutting board on their backs. Plunge a large sharp knife right into the middle of the body of a lobster and split it in half from head to tail without going through the back shell. (To hold the lobster in place, and to protect your hands as you do this, use a pot holder, or a folded kitchen towel.) Use both hands to crack the lobster open. Remove the tail meat. Crack the claws open with a meat mallet or hammer and remove the meat. Cut the lobster meat into ¾-inch pieces. (There should be about 4 cups of lobster meat.) If you are not finishing the salad right away, transfer the lobster meat to a bowl, cover, and refrigerate.

4. Peel, core, and cut the apple into ½-inch chunks. Place it in a large bowl and sprinkle with the lemon juice; toss to coat.

5. Toss in the lobster, celery, capers, and pineapple. Cover and refrigerate until ready to serve.

6. Line chilled small glass compote dishes with lettuce. Spoon the mayonnaise mixture into the lobster salad and toss gently to combine all the ingredients. Season to taste with salt and pepper. Divide the lobster salad among the compotes and sprinkle each serving with paprika. Serve chilled.

A LIGHT SUPPER

LEMONY QUINOA SOUP

✦

WARM ESCAROLE, RASPBERRY,
AND
CHICKEN SALAD

✦

CRUSTY BREAD

✦

FRESH FRUITS

WARM ESCAROLE, RASPBERRY, AND CHICKEN SALAD

YIELD: 4 ENTREE SERVINGS

Beautifully dressed in bright red, this salad vibrates with raspberry. I prefer using sturdy escarole, which won't wilt too rapidly on contact with the warm dressing. I've also added corn for extra texture, substance, and color. If you use store-bought raspberry vinegar, use only 2 tablespoons.

RASPBERRY VINAIGRETTE
3 tablespoons mild olive oil
1 medium red onion, thinly sliced
¼ cup raspberry vinegar, preferably
    homemade, (page 286)
    or red wine vinegar
½ pint (1 cup) raspberries
2 tablespoons chicken broth,
    preferably homemade (page 30)
¼ teaspoon sugar
Salt and freshly ground black pepper

CHICKEN SALAD
2 cups fresh or frozen corn kernels
4 skinless, boneless chicken breasts (6 ounces
    each), trimmed of excess fat
Salt and freshly ground black pepper
8 cups (firmly packed) escarole
20 fresh chives, snipped

1. Prepare coals for grilling or preheat the broiler.

2. To make the vinaigrette, heat 1 tablespoon of the olive oil in a large skillet over medium-high heat. Add the onion and sauté until soft, about 1 minute. Add the vinegar and immediately remove the pan from the heat. Stir in the raspberries, crushing them slightly with a fork.

3. Transfer the mixture to a large mixing bowl. Whisk in the remaining 2 tablespoons olive oil, the chicken broth, and sugar. Season with salt and pepper to taste and set aside.

4. To make the salad, drop the corn in a pot of boiling salted water and cook until just tender, about 2 minutes. If you are using

frozen corn kernels, cook them for only 30 seconds. Drain well.

5. Sprinkle the chicken breasts with salt and pepper. Grill or broil 5 to 6 inches from the heat until the juices run clear when pierced with the tip of a small knife, about 8 minutes, turning once. Transfer the chicken breasts to a cutting board. Cut each one in half lengthwise, then crosswise into 1/4-inch slices.

6. Add the escarole, corn, and chicken to the raspberry dressing, and toss until well combined. Divide the salad among dinner plates, sprinkle with fresh chives, and serve at once.

CHICKEN SALAD WITH APRICOT CHUTNEY

YIELD: 4 TO 6 ENTREE SERVINGS

Pickles and fruit chutney add a kick and a touch of complexity to this chicken salad. I believe it is one of the best I've ever made. The fruit chutney, made with apricots and raisins, infuses the salad with sweetness and blends surprisingly well with sour pickles. You may substitute pine nuts for the almonds, if desired.

4 cups cubed cooked chicken
1 cup minced onions
1 cup chopped flat-leaf parsley
2 large sour pickles, minced (about 1/2 cup)
2/3 cup good-quality mayonnaise
1/2 cup Spiced Apricot Chutney (page 272) or store-bought mango chutney
2 teaspoons fresh lemon juice
2 teaspoons dried oregano, crumbled
2 teaspoons dried thyme, crumbled
1/2 teaspoon salt
1/2 teaspoon freshly ground black pepper
Soft lettuce leaves, such as Boston or red leaf, for garnish
1/2 cup toasted sliced almonds (for toasting instructions, see page 64), coarsely chopped

1. Place the chicken, onions, parsley, and pickles in a large mixing bowl, and set aside.

2. Place the mayonnaise, chutney, lemon juice, oregano, thyme, salt, and pepper in a small bowl and stir to combine. Add to the chicken, and stir with a wooden spoon until well blended.

3. Line each dinner plate with lettuce leaves and top with the chicken salad. Sprinkle with toasted almonds and serve.

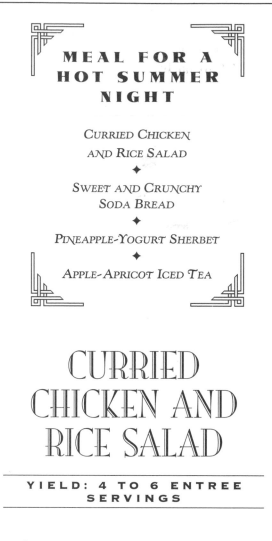

MEAL FOR A HOT SUMMER NIGHT

CURRIED CHICKEN
AND RICE SALAD

◆

SWEET AND CRUNCHY
SODA BREAD

◆

PINEAPPLE-YOGURT SHERBET

◆

APPLE-APRICOT ICED TEA

CURRIED CHICKEN AND RICE SALAD

YIELD: 4 TO 6 ENTREE SERVINGS

At the beginning of my cooking career, I was a chef for a bustling gourmet store in Manhattan. I had a staff of one—myself—and among my daily responsibilities was preparing various soups, roasts, and twenty kinds of salads. It may sound insane, but I loved my job. Having survived those rough days, I'm now very happy to share with you one of the most popular chicken salads that I came up with. If you are using leftover cooked chicken, you will need about 3 cups. You may substitute apples, bananas, feijoas, or fresh pineapple for the pears.

1½ pounds skinless, boneless chicken breast, trimmed of excess fat
3 cups cooked long-grain rice (1 cup raw)
2 ribs celery, cubed (½-inch pieces)
½ cup dried currants or raisins, plumped in hot water for 15 minutes and drained
2 Asian pears
1 cup good-quality light mayonnaise
¾ cup plain yogurt
2 tablespoons honey
1 tablespoon plus 1 teaspoon fresh lemon juice
1 tablespoon plus 1 teaspoon curry powder, preferably Madras brand
¼ teaspoon ground turmeric
2 tablespoons chopped fresh parsley leaves
Salt and freshly ground black pepper
1 head Boston lettuce, leaves separated
½ cup toasted shredded coconut (for toasting instructions, see page 64)
½ cup toasted sliced almonds (or coarsely chopped cashews) (page 64)

1. Place the chicken breasts in a medium-size saucepan and add enough salted water to cover by ½ inch. Bring to a boil over high heat. Reduce the heat to low and simmer until the chicken is tender and the juices run clear when pierced with the tip of a small knife, about 15 minutes. Drain the chicken, discarding the poaching liquid.

2. When the chicken is cool enough to handle, cut it into ¾-inch cubes. Place the cubed chicken, rice, celery, and currants in a

large mixing bowl. Without peeling them, core and cut the Asian pears into ½-inch cubes and add to the bowl. Set aside.

3. Place the mayonnaise, yogurt, honey, lemon juice, curry powder, turmeric, and parsley in a blender or food processor and blend until thoroughly mixed. Season to taste with salt and pepper.

4. Pour the dressing over the chicken-rice mixture. Toss until all the ingredients are thoroughly combined. Season the salad to taste with salt and pepper.

5. Line each chilled dinner plate with lettuce leaves and top with the chicken salad. Sprinkle with the toasted coconut and almonds. Serve at room temperature.

CHICKEN CHAT SALAD

YIELD: 4 TO 6 ENTREE SERVINGS

This refreshing salad is my rendition of a favorite dish called Chicken Chat, which is served in many Indian restaurants. Grilled marinated chicken, boiled potatoes, and sour tamarind dressing make for a nourishing yet subtle winter salad, perfect for lunch or supper. A sprinkling of pomegranate seeds gives the dish a delicious and attractive touch. Begin with a clear soup; and for dessert, serve fruit sorbet and cookies. You can begin marinating the chicken and preparing the dressing the day before.

TAMARIND DRESSING

2 tablespoons tamarind pulp
⅔ cup boiling water
2 tablespoons chicken broth, preferably homemade (page 30)
½ teaspoon salt
4 teaspoons (firmly packed) light brown sugar
1 teaspoon grated peeled fresh ginger
1 teaspoon minced garlic
1 teaspoon ground cumin
½ teaspoon ground coriander
¼ teaspoon cayenne pepper
2 tablespoons chopped fresh mint leaves

CHICKEN AND POTATO SALAD

2 teaspoons garam masala (see Note)
Salt
2 tablespoons mild olive oil
2 pounds skinless, boneless chicken breasts, trimmed of excess fat
2 large baking potatoes (about 1 pound total)
2 tablespoons shredded fresh cilantro leaves (for shredding instructions, see page 34)
Juice of 1 lemon
Soft lettuce leaves, such as Boston or red leaf, for garnish
1 cup pomegranate seeds, for garnish (optional)
Freshly ground black pepper

1. To make the dressing, place the tamarind pulp and boiling water in a small bowl and let stand for 15 minutes to soften. When the mixture is cool enough to handle, give it a stir. Then squeeze the pulp with your fingers to mash it and pull it off the seeds. Strain through a fine sieve, pressing on the solids with the back of a spoon to extract as much juice as possible. Discard the solids. (You should have about $1/3$ cup tamarind juice.)

2. Combine the tamarind juice with the remaining dressing ingredients in a blender or food processor and blend until smooth. Set aside.

3. To make the salad, combine the garam masala, $1/2$ teaspoon salt, and olive oil in a shallow dish. Add the chicken breasts and turn to coat with the oil. Let stand at room temperature for 30 minutes, or refrigerate overnight.

4. Wash the potatoes and cook them in boiling salted water, until fork-tender, about 30 minutes. Drain and let cool. Peel and halve each potato lengthwise; slice each half crosswise $1/4$ inch thick. Place in a large mixing bowl and set aside.

5. Prepare coals for grilling or preheat the broiler.

6. Grill or broil the chicken breasts 5 to 6 inches from the heat until the juices run clear when pierced with the tip of a small knife, about 8 minutes, turning once. Transfer the chicken to a cutting board. Halve each breast lengthwise, and slice each half crosswise $1/4$ inch thick.

7. Add the chicken strips and shredded cilantro to the potatoes. Sprinkle with the tamarind dressing and lemon juice and toss until well combined. Adjust the seasoning until you have a pleasing sweet, sour, and salty balance. (You can make this dish a day ahead. Bring to room temperature before serving.)

8. Line chilled dinner plates with lettuce leaves and top with the chicken salad. Sprinkle with pomegranate seeds, if using, and black pepper and serve.

NOTE: Garam masala, an aromatic spice blend, is available at specialty and Indian food stores. You can make it yourself by combining $1/2$ teaspoon each ground ginger, cardamom, cumin, coriander, curry powder (preferably Madras brand), cinnamon, and black pepper. If you want to intensify the fragrance of the spices, fry them briefly in $1 1/2$ teaspoons heated olive oil, and cool before adding the chicken.

CRACKED WHEAT SALAD WITH CHICKEN, GRAPES, AND PECANS

YIELD: 4 TO 6 ENTREE SERVINGS

My mother-in-law, who is very active in her community, occasionally asks me for menu ideas for her fund-raising luncheons. I came up with this recipe one day when she requested a main-course salad that would be economical and easy to prepare, and most important, would appeal to the majority of the members of her organization. Here's the delicious recipe that I came up with. The flavors of the lemony dressing, sweet, juicy grapes, and toasted pecans make magic with the nutty cracked wheat. It can easily be doubled to feed a crowd. Serve it with your favorite bread; you may also substitute cooked shrimp for the chicken, or 3 cups steamed couscous for the cracked wheat.

1 large skinless, boneless chicken breast half (about 10 ounces)
Salt
¾ cup cracked wheat (bulgur), soaked in warm water for 30 minutes and drained
1½ tablespoons blackberry vinegar, preferably homemade (see box, page 285) or balsamic vinegar
1½ tablespoons fresh lemon juice
1 tablespoon Dijon mustard
⅓ cup mild olive oil
¾ cup seedless green grapes, halved
2 scallions, trimmed, thinly sliced (white and green parts)
½ cup toasted pecan halves (for toasting instructions, see page 64), coarsely chopped
Freshly ground black pepper

1. Place the chicken breast in a medium-size saucepan and add enough water to cover by ½ inch. Add salt and bring to a boil over high heat. Reduce the heat to low, and simmer, uncovered, until the chicken is tender and the juices run clear when pierced with the tip of a small knife, about 15 minutes. Drain, reserving the poaching liquid.

2. Bring 1¼ cups of the poaching liquid to a boil in the same saucepan over medium-high heat. Stir in the drained cracked wheat and cook until half the liquid is absorbed, about 5 minutes. Cover the pan, reduce the heat to low, and continue cooking until the grains are tender and all the liquid is absorbed, about 15 minutes longer. Uncover, fluff with a fork to separate the grains, and let cool.

3. Whisk together the vinegar, lemon juice, mustard, and olive oil in a large mixing bowl. Cut the cooked chicken into ¹/₂-inch cubes. Stir the cracked wheat, chicken, grapes, scallions, and toasted pecans into the vinaigrette and toss until the mixture is well combined. Season to taste with salt and pepper, and serve.

SHOCKINGLY PINK BREAD SALAD

YIELD: 6 ENTREE SERVINGS

What I find most appealing in this pita and vegetable salad is the pleasing crunch of the pomegranate seeds and the appetizing blush of the pomegranate juice in the dressing. This bread salad is so good you should not wait for fall, when fresh pomegranates are available, to serve it. You can also enjoy it at other times of year by simply substituting Pomegranate Molasses (see Index) for the fresh fruit (see Note). The only thing you'll miss is the crunch of the seeds, but the agreeable pomegranate flavor will be there. Be sure to toss the pita wedges into the salad only minutes before you serve it, or you will end up with soggy bread. Serve this salad as a light main course or as an accompaniment to grilled chicken or steak.

1 large cucumber, peeled, seeded, and cubed (¹/₂-inch pieces)
Salt
6 pitas (6 inch rounds), stemmed, halved horizontally, each half cut into 8 thin wedges
1 green bell pepper, stemmed, seeded, and diced
3 cups diced tomatoes
1 cup thinly sliced scallions
1 cup finely chopped flat-leaf parsley
¹/₄ cup finely shredded fresh mint leaves (for shredding instructions, see page 34)

POMEGRANATE VINAIGRETTE
1 large pomegranate (about 1 pound; see Note)
¹/₂ cup extra-virgin olive oil
¹/₃ cup fresh lemon juice
1 tablespoon minced garlic
³/₄ teaspoon ground cumin
³/₄ teaspoon freshly ground black pepper

1. Preheat the oven to 350°F.

2. Meanwhile, place the cucumber in a colander, sprinkle with ¹/₂ teaspoon salt, and drain for 30 minutes.

It was the nightingale, and not the lark,
That pierc'd the fearful hollow of thine ear;
Nightly she sings on yon pomegranate tree:
Believe me, love, it was the nightingale.

—WILLIAM SHAKESPEARE, ROMEO AND JULIET

3. Spread the pita wedges on a baking sheet and bake for 15 minutes, or until crisp. Let the pita cool.

4. Rinse the cucumber well and pat dry. Combine the cucumber, bell pepper, tomatoes, scallions, parsley, and mint in a large mixing bowl. (This can be prepared up to 2 hours in advance. Refrigerate, covered; bring to room temperature before serving.)

5. To make the vinaigrette, cut the pomegranate in half and gently squeeze the seeds and juice into a bowl. (Be careful: Pomegranate juice stains.) Whisk in the olive oil, lemon juice, garlic, cumin, black pepper, and salt to taste. (You should have 1½ cups vinaigrette. This vinaigrette can be made in advance and kept at room temperature until ready to serve.)

6. Toss the pita wedges into the salad. Drizzle the salad with the vinaigrette and toss to combine. Season to taste with salt. Serve immediately.

NOTE: If fresh pomegranate is unavailable, dilute ¼ cup pomegranate molasses with ½ cup warm water and mix with other ingredients for the vinaigrette.

ROAST DUCK SALAD WITH PEACHES

YIELD: 4 ENTREE SERVINGS

I particularly like pairing duck with sweet peaches; it's a natural match. In this fabulous main course salad, the richness of the duck is well balanced by the sweetness of the fruit, the acidity of the vinegar, and the nuttiness of roasted peanuts. For convenience, I buy roast duck from my local Chinese take-out or in Chinatown. These ready-to-serve

*T*he Chinese believe that if they eat enough peaches in their lifetime, their body will be preserved from corruption until the end of the world. To that end, they serve on birthdays a steamed roll in the shape of a peach, called shou-tao, which means "long life peach."

birds are usually quite juicy, tasty, and inexpensive. This salad would be equally tasty with leftover roast beef, pork, veal, or chicken. Papaya, mango, cantaloupe, and blackberries are also good substitutes for the peaches. To complete the meal, serve warm garlic bread.

> 3 tablespoons chopped shallots
> 3 tablespoons sherry vinegar
> 3 tablespoons peanut oil
> 2¹/₂ tablespoons soy sauce
> Pinch (or more) of sugar
> 1 roast duck (2¹/₂ to 3 pounds)
> 2 large ripe peaches
> 8 cups (firmly packed) mixed tender salad
>   greens, such as red oakleaf, arugula,
>   and watercress
> 2 tablespoons fresh thyme leaves
> 4 tablespoons unsalted dry-roasted peanuts,
>   coarsely chopped
> Freshly ground black pepper

1. Whisk together the shallots, vinegar, peanut oil, soy sauce, and sugar in a large mixing bowl and set aside.

2. Remove all the meat from the duck, discarding the bones, fat, and skin. Cut the meat into strips and set it aside.

3. Peel, halve, and pit the peaches, then slice them ¹/₄ inch thick.

4. Just before serving, toss the salad greens, thyme, duck, and peaches in the dressing until well mixed.

5. Mound the salad on dinner plates. Sprinkle with the chopped peanuts and pepper. Serve.

STEAK SALAD WITH BLACKBERRIES

YIELD: 4 ENTREE SERVINGS

*T*his salad is perfect for the summer, when blackberries and currants are plentiful and at their best. You can substitute raspberries for the blackberries. If black currants are unavailable, substitute blueberries. Of course the dish will taste slightly different, but it will be delicious, nevertheless. The marinade may be stored in a jar, refrigerated, and reused once more for marinating meats.

BEEF AND MARINADE

1 top round beef steak, about 1 pound

½ cup soy sauce, preferably Kikkoman

¼ cup dry white wine

2 tablespoons sugar

1 teaspoon minced garlic

1 teaspoon grated peeled fresh ginger or
    ½ teaspoon ground ginger

BLACK CURRANT VINAIGRETTE

1 tablespoon black currants

3 shallots, minced

2 tablespoons black currant vinegar,
    preferably homemade (see box,
    page 285) or red wine vinegar

¼ teaspoon sugar

¼ cup peanut oil or extra-virgin olive oil

2 teaspoons crème de cassis

½ teaspoon soy sauce, preferably
    Kikkoman

SALAD

8 cups (firmly packed) mixed salad greens,
    such as red oakleaf, arugula, watercress,
    and Belgian endive or radicchio

½ pint (1 cup) blackberries

½ cup toasted hazelnuts (for toasting
    instructions, see page 64), coarsely
    ground

1. To marinate the beef, place the meat in a shallow baking dish. In a small saucepan, combine the soy sauce, white wine, sugar,

---

ABOUT SOY SAUCE

*E*ssential to the flavor of Japanese and Chinese dishes, soy sauce is becoming more prevalent in Western-style recipes as well. Americans are certainly familiar with the taste of soy sauce, but most aren't aware that there are many different types. China and Japan are the major producers of authentic soy sauce, and companies in each country make their own very different styles of the condiment. Personally, I'm partial to Japanese soy sauce, because it is mellower and less salty than its Chinese counterpart. My pick for best all-purpose soy sauce is Kikkoman; it is suitable for all types of cooking, because it adds flavor but not color. I use it whenever I need to add a well-rounded, complex flavor with a slightly sweet aftertaste to vinaigrettes, marinades, stir-fries, or soups.

garlic, ginger, and ¼ cup water. Bring to a boil, stirring constantly, until the sugar has dissolved. Remove from the heat and let cool. Pour the marinade over the meat, cover, and let stand at room temperature for 1 hour or in the refrigerator overnight, turning the meat occasionally.

2. To make the vinaigrette, lightly mash the black currants with a fork in a large mixing bowl. Add the shallots, vinegar, sugar, oil,

crème de cassis, and soy sauce and whisk until emulsified. Refrigerate until ready to serve.

3. Preheat the broiler.

4. Remove the steak from the marinade and place it on a rack in a broiler pan. Broil the meat 3 inches from the heat until lightly charred, 4 to 5 minutes per side, for medium-rare. Place the steak on a cutting board.

5. To make the salad, toss the salad greens and blackberries with the vinaigrette in a large mixing bowl. Divide equally among the dinner plates.

6. Slice the meat against the grain in very thin slices and divide it equally among the salads. Sprinkle with ground toasted hazelnuts. Serve immediately.

PASTA & GRAINS

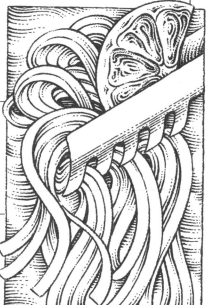

In these days of rush and hurry, a dish of pasta can be made in a short time. Serve it with a simple salad, or maybe cheese and fresh fruit, and you have an exceptionally good meal. I adore pasta for all its varieties, from egg pasta curlicues to flat rice noodles. Like most people, I enjoy a dish of spaghetti with a hearty tomato sauce, quick clam sauce, or glorious pesto sauce. But when I grow bored with these favorites, I take liberties and experiment with sauces that have fruit overtones. To my mind, some of the best pasta and grain dishes are those made with apple, grapes, and lemons. Purists may doubt me on this, but only until they have a taste.

The combination of fruit with pasta and grains may be unusual to many of us, but it is certainly not new. During the Renaissance, sugar, fruits, and spices were often used with great relish in savory courses as a display of wealth. This spirit of pairing sweet and savory flavorings is still alive, as evidenced in a number of Italian pastas as well as the grain and noodle dishes of other ethnic cuisines.

Pasta, grains, and rice all respond favorably to being paired with either dried or fresh fruit. My experience has been that the neutral flavor of these carbohydrates can serve as a perfect base for fruity ingredients and highly seasoned sauces. I've also found that their inherent nuttiness and dense texture can act as a wonderful balance to the seductive flavor of lush fresh fruits. When I experiment with pairing chewy grains such as wild rice, wheat berries, or barley with dried fruit, I'm often happily surprised by how tasty the combinations can be. Adding vegetables, herbs, or nuggets of meat or shellfish to combinations of pasta, grains, and fruits opens up a range of possibilities for salads, side dishes, and even main courses. Many dishes, especially those based on pasta, take on a luxurious quality with the addition of a soupçon of creamy sauce, butter, or cheese.

The recipes in this chapter represent some of my favorite noodle and grain dishes that use dried and fresh fruits with wonderful results. I dug into my international repertoire for ideas and came up with dishes like gnocchi with figs from Italy, curried rice noodles with pineapple from Thailand, sweet noodle puddings from Jewish cookery, and numerous fruited grain dishes of the Mediterranean and the Caribbean.

You will also find a wealth of meatless dishes that make perfect one-course meals, a tribute to the healthy virtues of these indispensable foods. For the sake of our good health, we've been encouraged to add more grains, fruits, and vegetables to our diet, and this is a great way to do it!

SWEET AND SOUR LINGUINE PRIMAVERA

YIELD: 2 TO 4 ENTREE SERVINGS

Italians have been making pasta primavera, a melange of pasta and fresh vegetables, in one form or another for a long time. But it wasn't until the 1970s, when Sirio Maccioni introduced it at Le Cirque in New York City, that it became so trendy. This dish, once so fresh and interesting, has been so widely copied, that it has lost some of its original appeal. So to lift it out of the doldrums, I simply add to the tomato sauce some dried fruits, brown sugar, and lemon juice for a lively sweet and sour taste. Gremolata, an aromatic blend of minced lemon zest and garlic, is stirred in at the end for an unexpected boost. This happy union results in a meatless meal that will satisfy even die-hard meat eaters.

3 tablespoons mild olive oil

¾ cup chopped onion

1 tablespoon plus 1½ teaspoons minced
    garlic

½ teaspoon dried red pepper flakes

1 can (28 ounces) peeled tomatoes,
    including juice

½ cup dry white wine

½ cup golden raisins

¼ cup diced dried apricots

1 tablespoon (firmly packed) light brown
    sugar

1 cube chicken or vegetable bouillon

1½ cups broccoli florets

1 cup cubed zucchini (½-inch pieces)

1 cup cubed yellow squash (½-inch pieces)

2 tablespoons fresh lemon juice

Salt and freshly ground black pepper

½ pound dried linguine

1½ teaspoons grated lemon zest

¼ cup chopped flat-leaf parsley leaves

Freshly grated Parmesan cheese (optional)

1. Heat 1 tablespoon of the olive oil in a large skillet over medium heat. Add the onion, 1 tablespoon of the garlic, and the red pepper flakes, and sauté until soft and fragrant, about 2 minutes.

2. Crush the tomatoes with your fingers, then add them to the skillet, along with the white wine, raisins, apricots, brown sugar, and the bouillon cube. Reduce the heat to low and simmer the mixture for 10 minutes, stirring occasionally.

3. Stir in the broccoli, zucchini, and yellow squash, cover, and simmer until they are tender but not mushy, about 15 minutes.

Remove from the heat and stir in the lemon juice. Season to taste with salt and pepper.

4. Bring a large pot of salted water to a boil. Add the pasta and cook until just tender, 8 to 10 minutes. Drain well.

5. Return the drained pasta to the pot, then add the sauce, along with the lemon zest, the remaining 1½ teaspoons garlic, the parsley, and the remaining 2 tablespoons olive oil. Toss until the pasta is well coated with the sauce. Divide the pasta among warmed shallow bowls. Serve immediately, sprinkled with Parmesan cheese, if desired.

SUMMER PASTA WITH THREE-FRUIT VINAIGRETTE

YIELD: 6 ENTREE SERVINGS

In the summer, I frequently make a main course of chilled pasta. In this refreshing dish, cold angel hair noodles are tossed with fresh tomatoes, pineapple, black olives, and basil laced with lime juice and a healthy dose of extra-virgin olive oil. Instead of angel

O̶f all the gifts of heaven to man, it is next to the most precious. Perhaps it may claim a preference even to bread, because there is such an infinitude of vegetables, which it renders a proper and comfortable nourishment.

—THOMAS JEFFERSON WRITING ON THE OLIVE

hair pasta, you may use vermicelli or thin spaghetti.

½ cup fresh lime juice

½ cup extra-virgin olive oil

¼ cup plus 4 teaspoons soy sauce, preferably Kikkoman

6 tablespoons finely chopped shallots

2 teaspoons sugar

1 cup diced fresh pineapple

1 cup diced seeded plum tomatoes

⅔ cup pitted Kalamata olives, coarsely chopped

2 fresh jalapeño peppers, minced

¼ cup finely shredded fresh basil leaves (for shredding instructions, see page 34)

¼ cup chopped flat-leaf parsley leaves

Salt and freshly ground black pepper

1 pound fresh angel hair pasta

1. Whisk together the lime juice, olive oil, soy sauce, shallots, and sugar in a medium-size bowl. Add the diced pineapple, tomatoes, olives, jalapeño peppers, basil, and parsley, and stir with a wooden spoon to combine. Season to taste with salt and pepper, if necessary. (You should have about 3 cups of sauce.) Cover and let sit at room temperature for at least 30 minutes for the flavors to marry. (You can refrigerate the sauce for up to 2 hours, but bring to room temperature before serving.)

2. Bring a large pot of salted water to a boil over high heat. Add the pasta and cook until just tender, about 2 minutes. Drain the noodles, then run cold water over them until they are no longer warm. Drain well. Using scissors, cut the pasta into shorter strands.

3. Just before serving, toss the pasta with the sauce in a large mixing bowl. Divide the pasta among shallow bowls and serve immediately.

SOUTH OF THE BORDER PASTA

YIELD: 4 TO 6 ENTREE SERVINGS

It's not all that common to find a pasta dish with Mexican flavors, so this dish should be a welcome arrival. Golden strands of vermicelli are crowned with picadillo, a meat sauce similar to spaghetti sauce but made with ground pork and enlivened with raisins, green olives, and red pepper flakes. Delightfully sweet and spicy, it is also delicious over ziti, rotelli, or steamed rice. Also, instead of your standard tomato sauce, try spooning picadillo between layers of lasagna noodles and ricotta cheese for an unexpected twist on an old favorite.

1 tablespoon mild olive oil

¾ cup chopped onion

½ cup chopped green bell pepper

1 tablespoon minced garlic

¾ pound ground pork

1 tablespoon sweet paprika

1 teaspoon ground cloves

1 teaspoon dried oregano, crumbled

½ teaspoon dried red pepper flakes,
    or to taste

2 bay leaves

½ cup golden raisins

2 cups canned peeled tomatoes, including
    juice

1 cup chicken broth, preferably homemade
    (page 30)

⅔ cup dry red wine, preferably a
    Burgundy

1 teaspoon salt, or to taste

½ cup pitted green (Spanish) olives,
    rinsed and halved

1 pound dried vermicelli or spaghetti

¼ cup chopped flat-leaf parsley leaves

Freshly grated Cheddar cheese
    (optional)

1. Heat the olive oil in a large skillet over medium heat. Add the onion, bell pepper, and garlic, and sauté until soft and fragrant, about 2 minutes.

2. Add the ground pork and cook, breaking up the lumps with the back of a wooden spoon, until it is browned, 5 minutes. Add the paprika, cloves, oregano, red pepper flakes, bay leaves, and raisins; stir for 1 minute.

3. Crush the tomatoes with your fingers, then add them to the skillet, along with the chicken broth, red wine, and salt. Reduce the heat to low, cover, and simmer, stirring occasionally, until the meat is tender, about 30 minutes. Stir in the olives and remove from the heat. Adjust the seasoning with salt, if necessary. The sauce is now ready; use it immediately or let it sit for up to 2 hours before serving.

4. Bring a large pot of salted water to a boil. Add the vermicelli, and cook until just tender, 6 to 8 minutes (8 to 10 minutes, if using spaghetti). Drain well. If necessary, reheat the sauce while the pasta is cooking.

5. Return the drained pasta to the pot, then add the sauce. Toss until the pasta is well coated with the sauce. Divide the pasta among warmed shallow bowls and sprinkle with chopped parsley. Serve immediately, topped with Cheddar cheese, if desired.

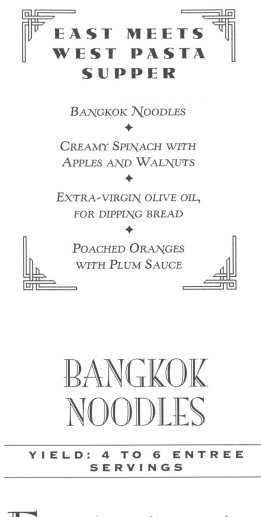

EAST MEETS WEST PASTA SUPPER

Bangkok Noodles

◆

Creamy Spinach with Apples and Walnuts

◆

Extra-virgin olive oil, for dipping bread

◆

Poached Oranges with Plum Sauce

BANGKOK NOODLES

YIELD: 4 TO 6 ENTREE SERVINGS

For pasta lovers who crave a change, this dish is a welcome departure from routine. As proof, I have never found a person who has not slurped up every last length of noodle and spooned up every last drop of sauce from this Thai-inspired curry. Curry is really a style of cooking: Meat, fish, vegetables, noodles, or fruit is cooked in one of myriad combination of ground herbs and spices, to produce a stew-like concoction. Here, in an easy-to-prepare dish, rice noodles and shrimp are laced with a silky sauce of coconut milk flavored with yellow curry paste and basil. Sweet fresh pineapple plays off the heat of the spices. You may substitute cooked linguine for the rice noodles, and small chunks of grilled or sautéed chicken breast for the shrimp.

1½ pounds large shrimp (21 to 25 per pound), shelled and deveined

3 tablespoons plus 2 teaspoons Thai fish sauce

Freshly ground black pepper

1 tablespoon vegetable oil

1 cup chopped onions

1 tablespoon minced garlic

2 teaspoons Thai yellow curry paste

1 tablespoon curry powder, preferably Madras brand

1½ cups canned unsweetened coconut milk, well stirred

1 cup chicken broth, preferably homemade (page 30)

1½ teaspoons sugar

1 pound dried rice noodles (banh pho; ¼ inch wide), soaked in warm water for 30 minutes and drained

1½ cups coarsely chopped fresh pineapple

½ cup finely shredded fresh basil leaves (for shredding instructions, see page 34)

1. Halve the shrimp crosswise, then mix them with 2 teaspoons of the fish sauce and pepper to taste in a small bowl. Cover and refrigerate until ready to use.

2. Bring a large pot of water to a boil.

3. Meanwhile, heat the oil in a large skillet over medium-low heat. Add the onions and garlic, and cook, stirring frequently, until the vegetables are soft, about 2 minutes. Add the curry paste and curry powder. Cook, mashing the curry paste with the back of a spoon, until the mixture is aromatic, about 1 minute. Stir in the coconut milk, chicken broth, sugar, and the remaining 3 tablespoons fish sauce. When the liquid comes to a boil, reduce the heat and gently simmer until the sauce is slightly thickened, 2 to 3 minutes. (The sauce may be prepared to this point up to 2 hours in advance. Gently reheat the sauce while you bring the water for the noodles to a boil.)

4. As the sauce is thickening, turn off the heat under the boiling water, and stir in the noodles. Immediately drain the noodles in a colander. Keep warm.

5. Add the shrimp and pineapple to the simmering sauce, and cook until the shrimp just turn pink, about 2 minutes. Add the noodles. Cook the mixture, tossing to coat the noodles with the sauce, 1 minute longer. Remove the pan from the heat, and stir in the shredded basil.

6. Divide the noodles among warmed shallow bowls and serve immediately.

NOTE: Dried rice noodles, yellow curry paste, fish sauce, and unsweetened coconut milk are available at Southeast Asian grocery stores and at some supermarkets.

LEMON-LIME SPAGHETTINI

YIELD: 4 TO 6 ENTREE SERVINGS

The acidity of the lemon and lime cuts the richness of the cream considerably and imparts a clean taste to this most unusual pasta dish from northern Italy. Serve it as a first course or with fish or grilled meat. Or toss the pasta with some quickly sautéed vegetables, shrimp, or scallops, and make it a main course.

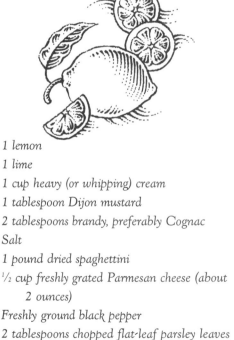

1 lemon
1 lime
1 cup heavy (or whipping) cream
1 tablespoon Dijon mustard
2 tablespoons brandy, preferably Cognac
Salt
1 pound dried spaghettini
1/2 cup freshly grated Parmesan cheese (about 2 ounces)
Freshly ground black pepper
2 tablespoons chopped flat-leaf parsley leaves

1. Using a vegetable peeler, remove half the peel from the lemon and lime. Trim off

any white pith attached to the underside of the peeled strips with a sharp paring knife. Julienne the zest and place it in a small bowl. (You should have about 2 tablespoons.)

2. Slice off the tops and bottoms of the fruits. Using a sharp knife with a flexible blade, cut around the fruit in a circular motion to remove the white pith and remaining peel. Cut between the membranes to separate the pulp into sections. Cut the sections into 1/4-inch dice, removing any seeds. (You should have about 1/2 cup fruit.) Add the pulp to the small bowl with the zest; stir in the cream, mustard, and brandy. Set aside.

3. Bring a large pot of salted water to a boil over high heat. Add the spaghettini and cook until just tender, 6 to 8 minutes. Drain the noodles in a colander.

4. Meanwhile, place the cream mixture in a large heavy skillet and bring to a boil over high heat. Boil until the sauce is slightly thickened, about 2 minutes, and remove from the heat. Add the spaghettini; toss to coat with the sauce. Add the cheese and toss again. Season to taste with salt and pepper. Divide the pasta among warmed plates, sprinkle with chopped parsley, and serve.

LEMONY ORZOTTO

**YIELD: 6 FIRST COURSE OR
4 ENTREE SERVINGS**

When I'm in the mood for risotto but don't want to do all the work, I make it with orzo, a rice-shaped pasta, instead of rice. It takes almost no time to cook, doesn't require any stirring, and emerges every bit as chewy and creamy as the best Arborio rice. In this delightful "orzotto," I coat the pasta in a refreshing, zesty lemon sauce. This simple dish is particularly good for a summer luncheon or a light dinner. Try it!

> 4 3/4 cups chicken broth, preferably
>   homemade (page 30)
> 4 tablespoons (1/2 stick) unsalted
>   butter
> 1 cup chopped onions
> 1 1/2 cups dried orzo
> 3 large egg yolks
> 2 tablespoons fresh lemon juice
> 1/3 cup freshly grated Parmesan cheese,
>   plus extra for serving
> Finely grated zest of 2 lemons
> Salt and freshly ground black pepper
> 2 tablespoons chopped flat-leaf parsley leaves

1. Place 4 1/2 cups of the chicken broth in a medium-size saucepan and bring to a simmer over medium heat. Reduce the heat to low, cover, and keep the broth at a simmer.

*Z*est, *the colored outer layer of the rind of
citrus fruits, is used in cooking and baking
for its flavorful, aromatic oils. You can use a citrus zester, a box grater, or a vegetable peeler to
zest fruit; each tool gives a slightly different effect.
Simply pull the zester from the top of the fruit to
the base so that you end up with long, very thin
strips of zest. Or rub the fruit against a box grater
for grated zest. For wider strips of zest—to steep
in liquid and discard or julienne and add to
recipes calling for coarser pieces of zest—use a
vegetable peeler. Whichever tool you use be sure
that none of the pith (the bitter white underside of
the peel) is included.*

2. Melt 2 tablespoons of the butter in a
large, heavy saucepan over medium heat.
Add the onions and cook until tender, about
3 minutes, stirring frequently. Add the orzo
and stir until the pasta is coated and shiny,
about 1 minute.

3. Add the hot chicken broth (be careful—the mixture will splatter violently).
Reduce the heat to medium-low and gently
simmer until the pasta is tender but firm to
the bite, 8 to 9 minutes. There should still be
some liquid in the pan.

4. Just before removing the pan from the
heat, whisk the egg yolks with the lemon
juice and the remaining 1/4 cup chicken broth
in a small bowl. Remove the pan from the
heat and stir the egg-lemon mixture into the

pasta. Return the pan to the heat and cook,
stirring well, for 1 minute more.

5. Remove the pan from the heat. Stir in
the Parmesan cheese, the lemon zest, and the
remaining 2 tablespoons butter.

6. Season to taste with salt and pepper.
Divide among warmed dinner plates, sprinkle
with chopped parsley,
and serve immediately.
Pass additional grated
Parmesan cheese on
the side, if desired.

GRECIAN PASTA

YIELD: 4 ENTREE SERVINGS

In this dish orzo, a rice-shaped pasta
popular in Greece, is tossed with
tomato sauce, feta cheese, sautéed
greens, and a handful of dried fruits.
When I developed this recipe, I imagined
Greek cooks doing something similar;
hence the title. The saltiness of the soft
feta cheese plays off the aromatic sweetness of the apricots, raisins, and cinnamon, creating a wonderful depth of flavors. You may substitute spinach or escarole for the kale.

2 pounds kale, thick stems removed, leaves
    coarsely chopped, or 2 packages (10
    ounces each) frozen kale, thawed
3 cups chicken broth, preferably homemade
    (page 30)
1 cup dried orzo
2 tablespoons extra-virgin olive oil
1 cup chopped onions
1½ tablespoons minced garlic
¾ cup golden raisins
¾ cup dried apricots, coarsely chopped
1 tablespoon ground cinnamon
¾ teaspoon dried red pepper flakes
Salt
3 cups Quick Tomato Sauce (recipe follows)
¼ pound feta cheese, preferably Greek

1. If using fresh kale, bring a large pot of salted water to a boil. Add the kale in batches, and cook until barely tender, 3 to 5 minutes. (The cooking time will depend on the age of the kale.) Drain in a colander, rinse with cold water, and drain again. Use your hands to squeeze as much liquid from the kale as possible. If using frozen kale, just use your hands to squeeze as much liquid from the thawed leaves as possible. Coarsely chop, if necessary. Set aside.

2. Place the chicken broth in a medium-size saucepan and bring to a boil over medium heat. Stir in the orzo and cook until it is barely tender and most of the chicken broth is absorbed, about 8 minutes. Drain, rinse with cold water, and drain again.

3. Meanwhile, heat the oil in a large skillet over medium heat. Add the onions and garlic and cook until soft, stirring frequently,

about 5 minutes. Stir in the raisins and apricots and sauté for 1 minute. Add the kale, cinnamon, and red pepper flakes, and cook for 3 minutes, stirring frequently. Season to taste with salt.

4. Add the orzo to the skillet. Toss well to coat and reheat the orzo.

5. Divide the orzo among warmed dinner plates, and top with the tomato sauce. Crumble the feta cheese over the top and serve at once.

Quick Tomato Sauce

YIELD: 3 CUPS

Light, sweet, and fresh-tasting, this simple and basic sauce can be made in no time and tossed with pasta, spread on pizza, layered in a lasagna, or used anywhere else you want a meatless sauce. The recipe doubles easily. Stored in a sealed plastic container, the sauce may be frozen for up to 2 months. Reheat before using. If the sauce is too thick, thin it with a bit of water or chicken broth.

FRESH TOMATOES OR CANNED?

If you have ever tasted the intense lushness of a vine-ripe summer tomato, you will never again be satisfied with the woolly, tasteless tomato imperson- ators that invade our supermarkets. If the only fresh tomatoes available to you are pale pink winter toma- toes, you would really be better off using canned tomatoes; that is, if you plan to use them in soups or sauces. Use peeled whole plum or round tomatoes in recipes calling for canned tomatoes in this book. Do not use the crushed or puréed varieties. They lack the clean, light quality of canned whole tomatoes, and they usually include a heavy dose of tomato purée, which exaggerates strong acid flavors.

Fresh, vine-ripened tomatoes should always be used for salads or salsas for the best flavor. If all you can find is semiripe tomatoes from the vine, or color- less tomatoes, do not use them immediately or put them in the refrigerator. Instead, place them in a per- forated paper bag in the company of a very ripe apple, whose tiny breath of ethylene gas will gently ripen them. Or place them in a straw basket in strong, indi- rect sunlight; they will ripen in a few days.

---

2 tablespoons extra-virgin olive oil
1 cup chopped onions
1 tablespoon minced garlic
4 cups finely chopped fresh plum tomatoes
 or 1 can (28 ounces) plum tomatoes,
 including juice
¼ cup shredded fresh basil leaves (for
 shredding instructions, see page 34) or
 1 teaspoon dried basil, crumbled
2 tablespoons shredded flat-leaf parsley
 leaves (for shredding instructions, see
 page 34)
1½ teaspoons sugar, or to taste
1 teaspoon salt, or to taste
Chicken broth (optional)

1. Heat the oil in a large saucepan over low heat. Add the onions and garlic and cook, stirring frequently, until both are very soft and lightly browned, about 10 minutes.

2. Add the tomatoes and juice to the pan (if using canned tomatoes, crush them with your fingers), along with the basil, pars- ley, sugar, and salt. Cook over low heat, uncovered, until slightly thickened, about 8 minutes, stirring occasionally. If the sauce is too thick, thin it with little chicken broth or water. Adjust the seasonings with sugar and salt, if necessary.

3. The sauce is now ready. Use it imme- diately or let it cool, then store in a covered container and refrigerate for up to 1 week. Reheat before serving.

BOW-TIES WITH MELON SALSA

YIELD: 4 TO 6 FIRST COURSE SERVINGS

Sweet, savory, and slightly piquant, this complex pasta salad is very simple to make. All you have to do is toss cooked pasta bow-ties with a colorful, fresh-tasting melon and corn salsa and a sesame vinaigrette. It is a delicious summer dish—satisfying and light. Mixed with just the vinaigrette, the salsa can double as a snack to be scooped up with chips, or pita wedges, or as an exotic sauce over grilled chicken or fish.

CORN-MELON SALSA

2 large ears corn, preferably yellow, husks and
    silks removed
1 cup cubed watermelon (½-inch pieces), seeds
    removed
1 cup cubed honeydew melon (½-inch pieces)
1 cup cubed cantaloupe (½-inch pieces)
1 cup chopped red onions
1 cup shredded fresh cilantro leaves (for
    shredding instructions, see page 34)
¼ cup drained capers

SESAME VINAIGRETTE

3 tablespoons balsamic vinegar
3 tablespoons fresh orange juice
3 tablespoons extra-virgin olive oil
1 tablespoon Asian sesame oil
1 fresh jalapeño pepper, finely chopped,
    or to taste
Finely grated zest of 2 lemons

½ pound dried farfalle (bow-tie pasta)
Salt

1. To make the salsa, cut the corn kernels off of the cobs by running a sharp knife from the tip of the ear straight down to the stem. Avoid tough fibers by not cutting too close to the cob. (You should have about 1½ cups corn kernels.)

2. Bring a large pot of salted water to a boil over medium-high heat. Add the corn kernels and cook for 2 minutes. Drain, rinse under cold water, and drain again. Lightly pat dry with paper towels.

3. Combine the corn, melons, red onions, cilantro, and capers in a large mixing bowl. (This may be covered and refrigerated for up to 4 hours.)

4. To make the vinaigrette, combine all the ingredients in a glass jar. Cover and shake well. Refrigerate until needed.

5. Bring a large pot of salted water to a boil over high heat. Add the bow-ties and cook until just tender, about 10 minutes. Drain, rinse under cold water, and drain again.

6. In large bowl, combine the pasta with the salsa and the vinaigrette. Toss well. Season to taste with salt, if necessary. Serve at once.

GNOCCHI WITH FIGS IN GORGONZOLA SAUCE

YIELD: 4 ENTREE SERVINGS

Fresh figs bring a subtle sweetness and balance to this dish of potato gnocchi glazed with a satiny, thyme-laced Gorgonzola cream sauce. You can find excellent potato gnocchi at your local specialty food store and even in some supermarkets. Just remember not to overcook them. You may replace the Gorgonzola with a similar cheese, such as Roquefort, Saga, or Danish blue, or substitute fettuccine for the gnocchi.

GREAT MATCHES

FIGS

Cheese, cured meats, and balsamic vinegar taste delicious with tender fresh figs. Thyme, basil, and rum are also complementary flavors.

2 teaspoons mild olive oil
2/3 cup chopped scallions (white and green parts)
1/4 cup minced shallots
1/4 cup or more dry white wine
1 cup light cream or half-and-half
1/2 cup crumbled Gorgonzola (1/4 pound)
8 large ripe but firm mission figs, stemmed and quartered
2 tablespoons chopped fresh thyme leaves
2 cups peeled, seeded, and coarsely chopped ripe tomatoes
1 pound fresh potato gnocchi
Salt and freshly ground black pepper
Freshly grated Parmesan cheese, for serving (optional)

1. Bring a large pot of salted water to a boil over high heat.

2. Meanwhile, heat the oil in a large skillet over medium heat. Add the scallions and shallots, and sauté until tender, about 30 seconds. Add the wine, and cook until it is reduced by half, about 30 seconds. Add the cream and cook until it is slightly reduced, about 1 minute. Reduce the heat to low and add the Gorgonzola. Cook, stirring constantly with a wooden spoon, until the cheese is melted. Add the figs, thyme, and 1 1/2 cups of the tomatoes and cook until just heated

PEELING TOMATOES

I don't really mind eating tomato skins, but some cooks pale at the very idea. So, here's the standard method for peeling tomatoes, especially if you have more than a few to prepare:

Bring a large pot of water to a boil. Meanwhile, core the tomatoes, then cut a small X in the bottom of each one. Turn off the heat under the boiling water, and carefully lower the tomatoes into the water. Let sit for 30 seconds. With a slotted spoon, remove the tomatoes and place them in a bowl of cold water. When they are cool enough to handle, peel off the skin with a small paring knife. Cut each tomato in half horizontally, gently squeeze each half to remove the seeds, and then slice or chop as called for in the recipe.

If you have just one or two tomatoes to peel, here's a quick and easy way to do so without having to bring a large pot of water to a boil:

Core the tomato, then cut a small X in the bottom. Pierce the tomato with a long-handled fork and hold it directly over a gas flame. Turn just until the skin begins to crack, about 1 minute. Do not cook any longer, or the tomato will become mushy. Peel off the skin. Seed and chop the tomato as described above.

---

through. Remove the pan from the heat and cover to keep the sauce warm.

3. Drop the gnocchi into the boiling water. Once they rise to the surface, cook 30 seconds more. Drain well in a colander and add the gnocchi to the sauce in the skillet. Season to taste with salt and pepper, and gently toss to combine all the ingredients. If the sauce is too thick, add a little white wine.

4. Divide the gnocchi among warmed dinner plates, and garnish with the remaining chopped tomatoes. Serve immediately, passing freshly grated Parmesan cheese on the side, if desired.

FRUITED NOODLE PUDDING

YIELD: 6 TO 8 SIDE DISH SERVINGS

One of the great specialties of the Jewish kitchen is *lokshen kugel*, a sweet dish of broad noodles baked with fruit and cheese. In fact, when my husband's grandmother—my adopted grandmother then—was still alive, she never failed to have a casserole of this pudding on hand to feed her hungry girlfriends after a good game of bridge. It's also a great side dish for pot roast or roast chicken, or broiled ham steaks, for brunch. This is my version of her kugel, in which I've substituted white wine and beaten egg whites for sour cream. The result is a lighter kugel. Instead of apple, you may use 1 cup fresh pineapple chunks, or any fresh fruit for that matter.

¼ pound (2 cups) broad egg noodles
½ cup dry white wine
1 large apple, such as McIntosh or Granny
        Smith, peeled, cored, and cubed
        (½-inch pieces)
⅓ cup raisins
6 tablespoons sugar
3 tablespoons unsalted butter, at room
        temperature
3 large eggs, separated
1 cup cottage cheese
Finely grated zest of 2 lemons (about
        1½ teaspoons)
1 tablespoon fresh lemon juice
3 tablespoons dry bread crumbs
2 tablespoons unsalted butter, melted

1. Preheat the oven to 350°F. Generously butter an 8-inch baking dish.

2. Bring a large pot of salted water to a boil over high heat. Add the noodles and cook until just tender to the bite, about 5 minutes. Drain, then run cold water over the noodles until they are no longer warm. Drain well.

3. Combine the wine, apple, raisins, and 4 tablespoons of the sugar in a medium-size saucepan. Bring the mixture to a simmer and cook just until the apples begin to soften, about 1 minute. Transfer to a mixing bowl and add the noodles. Toss well and set aside.

4. Cream the 3 tablespoons butter and remaining 2 tablespoons sugar in a medium-size bowl, then stir in the egg yolks, cottage cheese, lemon zest, and lemon juice. Combine the mixture with the noodles.

5. Beat the egg whites until stiff and fold them into the noodles.

6. Transfer the noodles to the prepared baking dish and top with the bread crumbs. Drizzle the crumbs with melted butter.

7. Bake the pudding for 20 minutes. Raise the oven temperature to 400°F, and continue baking until the top is golden brown, 15 minutes more.

GREEN RISOTTO

YIELD: 4 APPETIZER OR 2 ENTREE SERVINGS

I have often served this simple and delicious risotto with watercress and green grapes for a light meal. Besides providing a pleasing green shade, both the watercress and grapes give a surprising nuance of flavor to this rice dish. The best types of Italian rice for making risotto are Arborio, Carnaroli, and Valione Nano. Never rinse this rice, or extra starch will be released during cooking, and you'll end up with a gluey mess.

*4½ cups chicken broth, preferably homemade
    (page 30)*
4 tablespoons (½ stick) unsalted butter
1 cup chopped onions
1 cup Arborio rice
2 cups finely chopped watercress
½ cup dry white wine, preferably Chardonnay
1 cup green seedless grapes, halved
*¼ cup freshly grated Parmesan cheese, plus
    extra for serving*
Salt and freshly ground black pepper
*1 tablespoon finely chopped flat-leaf parsley
    leaves*

1. Place the chicken broth in a medium-size saucepan and bring to a simmer over medium heat. Reduce the heat to low, cover, and keep the broth at a simmer.

2. Melt 2 tablespoons of the butter in a large, heavy saucepan over low heat. Add the onions and cook until tender, about 3 minutes, stirring frequently. Add the rice and stir until the grains are coated and shiny, about 3 minutes. Stir in the watercress.

3. Add the wine (be careful—the mixture will splatter violently) and cook until it is absorbed, stirring frequently. Add ½ cup of the broth and allow it to simmer, stirring well until it is absorbed. Continue adding the broth, ½ cup at a time, stirring constantly, until all the liquid has been added and the rice is slightly creamy and tender, but firm to the bite—*al dente*. The risotto should be slightly runny. Altogether, the rice should cook for 20 to 25 minutes.

4. Just before removing the pan from the heat, stir in the grapes and the remaining 2 tablespoons butter. Remove from the heat and stir in the Parmesan cheese. Season to taste with salt and pepper. Divide among warmed dinner plates, sprinkle with chopped parsley, and serve immediately. Pass additional grated Parmesan cheese on the side, if desired.

VARIATION

RED AND GREEN RISOTTO: Substitute 1 cup pomegranate seeds for the grapes.

WILD MUSHROOM RISOTTO WITH APPLES

**YIELD: 6 APPETIZER OR
4 ENTREE SERVINGS**

Making a perfect risotto—one in which tender but firm pearls of Arborio rice luxuriate in a velvety sauce—requires patience and loving

care. But it's well worth the effort, since all the stirring is what makes the sauce so creamy. In fusing this Italian cooking technique with the Asian practice of combining rice and fruit, I came up with a risotto of sweet apples and earthy mushrooms. Serve it either as a first course, a satisfying main course, or an accompaniment to entrées of meat, fish and poultry.

1 ounce dried porcini mushrooms
4½ cups chicken broth, preferably homemade
    (page 30)
2 Golden Delicious apples
5 tablespoons unsalted butter
Grated zest of 1 lemon
1 cup chopped onions
1 cup Arborio rice
½ cup dry white wine, preferably
    Chardonnay
¼ cup freshly grated Parmesan cheese, plus
    extra for serving
Salt and freshly ground black pepper
1 tablespoon chopped flat-leaf parsley leaves
    (optional)

1. Combine the dried mushrooms with the chicken broth in a medium-size saucepan and bring to a boil over high heat. Reduce the heat to low and simmer until the mushrooms are tender, about 5 minutes. Use a slotted spoon to transfer the mushrooms to a small dish. Place a fine sieve lined with a double layer of cheesecloth over a clean saucepan, and strain the broth into it, leaving behind any grit that has settled at the bottom of the cooking pan. Set the broth aside. Coarsely chop the mushrooms and set aside.

2. Peel and core the apples and cut them into ½-inch cubes. Melt 1 tablespoon of the butter in a large skillet over medium high heat. Add the apples and the lemon zest and sauté until the apples are just tender, about 1 minute. Set aside.

3. Return the broth to low heat, cover, and keep at a simmer.

4. Melt 2 tablespoons of the butter in a large, heavy saucepan over low heat. Add the onions and cook until tender, about 3 minutes, stirring frequently. Add the rice and stir until the grains are coated and shiny, about 3 minutes. Stir in the drained porcini mushrooms.

5. Add the wine (be careful—the mixture will splatter violently) and cook until it is absorbed, stirring frequently. Add ½ cup of the broth and allow it to simmer, stirring well until it is absorbed. Continue adding the broth, ½ cup at a time, stirring constantly, until almost all of it has been added and the rice is slightly creamy and tender, but firm to the bite—al dente. The risotto should be slightly runny. Altogether, the rice should cook for 25 to 30 minutes.

6. Just before removing the pan from the heat, add the remaining 2 tablespoons butter and stir until melted. Remove from the heat and stir in the sautéed apples and Parmesan cheese. Season to taste with salt and pepper. Divide among warmed dinner plates, sprinkle with chopped parsley, if desired, and serve at once. Pass additional grated Parmesan cheese on the side.

RISOTTO WITH PROSCIUTTO AND RAISINS

YIELD: 4 APPETIZER OR 2 ENTREE SERVINGS

Italian cooks are adept at combining rice with a minimum of ingredients to produce a seemingly endless variety of flavorful dishes. This risotto is a perfect example of their remarkable skill. Subtly flavored with salty ham and sweet raisins, this lovely rice dish makes a comforting meal on a fall day.

4½ cups chicken broth, preferably homemade (page 30)
4 tablespoons (½ stick) unsalted butter
1 cup chopped onions
1 cup Arborio rice
½ cup dry white wine, preferably Chardonnay
2 slices prosciutto (about 2 ounces), chopped
½ cup raisins
¼ cup freshly grated Parmesan cheese, plus extra for serving
Salt and freshly ground black pepper
1 tablespoon finely chopped flat-leaf parsley

1. Place the chicken broth in a medium-size saucepan and bring to a simmer over medium heat. Reduce the heat to low, cover, and keep the broth at a simmer.

2. Melt 2 tablespoons of the butter in a large, heavy saucepan over low heat. Add the onions and cook until tender, about 3 minutes, stirring frequently. Add the rice and stir until the grains are coated and shiny, about 3 minutes.

3. Add the wine (be careful—the mixture will splatter violently) and cook until it is absorbed, stirring frequently. Stir in the prosciutto and raisins, then add ½ cup of the broth. Allow the broth to simmer, stirring well until it is absorbed. Continue adding the broth, ½ cup at a time, stirring constantly, until all the liquid has been added and the rice is slightly creamy and tender, but firm to the bite—*al dente.* The risotto should be slightly runny. Altogether, the rice should cook for 20 to 25 minutes.

4. Just before removing the pan from the heat, stir in the remaining 2 tablespoons butter. Remove from the heat and stir in the Parmesan cheese. Season to taste with salt and pepper. Divide among warmed dinner plates, sprinkle with chopped parsley, and serve immediately. Pass additional grated Parmesan cheese on the side, if desired.

FLORENTINE RICE

YIELD: 4 ENTREE OR
6 SIDE DISH SERVINGS

The word *Florentine* usually refers to a dish that contains spinach. Indeed, this one-dish meal, my version of a rice casserole, has a healthy dose of it. Dried fruits, cinnamon, and hot red pepper give this vegetarian casserole a lively Mediterranean touch. And it is a blessing for anyone who works, since it can be made ahead, refrigerated, and reheated at the last minute. For variation, you may substitute 4 cups chopped broccoli for the spinach.

1½ cups chicken broth, preferably homemade
    (see page 30)
1 cup long-grain rice
2 pounds fresh spinach, stemmed, washed, and
    dried, or 2 packages (10 ounces each)
    frozen leaf spinach, thawed
2 tablespoons extra-virgin olive oil
1 cup chopped onions
1½ tablespoons minced garlic
¾ cup raisins
¾ cup dried apricots or figs, coarsely chopped
1½ tablespoons ground cinnamon
1 teaspoon dried red pepper flakes, or
    to taste
Salt
3 cups Quick Tomato Sauce (page 102)
¼ cup freshly grated Parmesan cheese
¾ pound mozzarella cheese, preferably fresh,
    thinly sliced

1. Bring the chicken broth to a boil in a medium-size saucepan over medium-high heat. Stir in the rice and bring to a boil. Reduce the heat to low, cover, and cook until all the liquid is absorbed and the rice is tender, about 18 minutes. Remove from the heat and let sit, covered, for 10 minutes.

2. If using fresh spinach, bring a large pot of salted water to a boil. Add the spinach and cook until just wilted, about 1 minute. Drain the spinach in a colander, rinse with cold water, and drain again. Squeeze as much water out of the spinach as possible. If using thawed spinach, use your hands to squeeze out as much water as possible. Coarsely chop the spinach and set aside.

3. Heat the oil in a large skillet over medium heat. Add the onions and garlic and cook until soft, stirring frequently, about 5 minutes. Stir in the raisins and apricots and sauté for 1 minute. Add the spinach, cinnamon, and red pepper flakes, and cook for 3 minutes, stirring frequently. Remove from the heat and season to taste with salt.

4. Preheat the oven to 350°F. Lightly butter a 9-inch square or round cake pan.

5. Reserve 1½ cups of the tomato sauce for serving, and use the rest to layer the casserole. Spread ½ cup of the tomato sauce evenly in the pan. Spread half the spinach mixture over the sauce and sprinkle with half the Parmesan cheese. Arrange half the mozzarella slices over the sauce. Spread all of the rice evenly over the cheese, then top with 1 cup tomato sauce. Repeat layering with the

remaining spinach mixture and mozzarella, ending with the Parmesan cheese. Tightly cover the pan with aluminum foil. (This can be kept in the refrigerator up to 6 hours before baking, but bring to room temperature before putting it in a hot oven.)

6. Bake the casserole, covered, until the cheese is melted and the rice is heated through, about 30 minutes. Uncover and continue to bake 5 minutes longer.

7. Reheat the reserved tomato sauce. Divide the casserole among warmed dinner plates and spoon the tomato sauce around it. Serve at once.

NEW AGE JAMBALAYA

YIELD: 6 ENTREE SERVINGS

Jambalaya, similar to a Spanish paella, is traditionally made from mixing rice with leftovers to make an entirely new meal. Being of Cajun origin, this dish is usually well seasoned and flavored with combinations of meat, poultry, or seafood; it often contains tomatoes. Jambalaya always bears the signature of it's maker, who brings to it his or her family heritage, personal instincts, and keen eye for what's best in the fridge or in the market. The jambalaya recipe that follows includes tasso (spicy cured ham), smoked sausage, and shrimp. The pineapple, which lends a refreshing and fruity note to this spicy dish, is my touch. Save this for when you entertain; it's a meal in itself. All you will need is mixed greens on the side. If tasso is unavailable, substitute chorizo sausages.

1½ teaspoons dried thyme

1½ teaspoons salt

¾ teaspoon chili powder

½ teaspoon freshly ground black pepper

½ teaspoon freshly ground white pepper

2 tablespoons mild olive oil

10 ounces tasso, cut into ½-inch cubes

6 ounces smoked sausage, such as kielbasa, sliced ½ inch thick

3 tablespoons unbleached all-purpose flour

¾ cup finely chopped onion

¾ cup finely chopped green bell pepper

1 tablespoon minced garlic

2 large bay leaves

1½ cups long-grain rice

⅓ cup dry white wine, preferably Chardonnay

¾ cup canned crushed tomatoes

1½ cup chicken broth, preferably homemade (page 30)

¾ pound fresh medium shrimp (26 to 30 per pound), shelled and deveined

1½ cups cubed fresh pineapple (½ inch pieces)

⅓ cup chopped fresh flat-leaf parsley leaves

½ teaspoon Tabasco sauce, or to taste

PINEAPPLE PRESENTATIONS

*Y*ou can add flair to a savory dish—such as Hong Kong Fried Rice (page 116) or New Age Jambalaya (page 112)—or a fruit dessert that includes pineapple, by serving it in a pineapple shell. Here are a few ways to make lovely presentations with fresh pineapple.

WHOLE PINEAPPLE CONTAINER

Cut the top leaves and cap (the crown) off a pineapple. Set aside.

Insert a grapefruit knife or curved knife into the pineapple as close to the skin and as deep as possible, and cut completely around the circumference in a sawing motion. When you have worked your way around, cut the loosened meat into quarters. Loosen the meat at the bottom of the cut with the tip of the knife and slip out the pieces. Continue cutting down into the pineapple until you have a hollowed-out shell (but make sure you leave a bottom that is a good 1 inch thick).

Trim the core from the flesh and discard. Prepare the pineapple as indicated in the recipe, then fill the shell with the prepared food. Use the crown as a decorative lid.

HALVED PINEAPPLE CONTAINER

Cut an unpeeled pineapple in half lengthwise, cutting through the leafy top. Insert a grapefruit knife or curved knife into the pineapple half, as close to the skin as possible, and cut completely around the edge of the fruit in a sawing motion. Using a paring knife, slice the flesh in half lengthwise. Loosen the flesh at the bottom of the cut with the tip of the knife and slip out the halves.

Prepare the pineapple as indicated above.

PINEAPPLE BOATS

Use this lovely carving technique when you plan to serve fresh pineapple for dessert.

Quarter an unpeeled pineapple lengthwise through the leafy top. Starting from the base of 1 quarter, use a paring knife to separate the flesh from the skin, leaving the end attached to the crown intact. Remove the core. Cut the flesh crosswise into 3/4-inch-thick slices, then stagger the slices across the shell. Repeat with the remaining quarters. Sprinkle the pineapple with rum or kirsch, if desired, and serve well chilled.

1. Preheat the oven to 400°F.

2. Mix the dried thyme, salt, chili powder, and black and white peppers in a small bowl. Set aside.

3. Heat 1 tablespoon of the olive oil in a large, ovenproof skillet over medium-high heat. Lightly dust the tasso and smoked sausage with the flour. Add them to the skillet and brown on both sides, about 2 minutes total. Transfer to a plate with a slotted spoon.

4. Heat the remaining 1 tablespoon olive oil in the skillet. Add the onion, bell

pepper, garlic, and bay leaves, and sauté until the vegetables are tender, about 2 minutes. Add the rice and cook, stirring frequently, until it turns opaque, about 3 minutes. Stir in the spice mixture, then the wine, tomatoes, and chicken broth. Add the tasso and sausages and bring the mixture to a boil.

5. Cover the skillet and place it in the oven. Bake until the rice is tender, 20 to 25 minutes. (The jambalaya may be prepared in advance up to this point.) When ready to serve, reheat the rice in a preheated 350° F oven.)

6. Add the shrimp, pineapple, and parsley to the rice mixture and season to taste with Tabasco sauce. Stir well, cover, and continue to bake 15 minutes longer, or until the shrimp is just cooked through. Serve immediately.

BLACK-EYED RICE

YIELD: 4 TO 6 SIDE DISH SERVINGS

Rice and beans is traditional in many cultures, especially in the southern United States, the Pacific Rim countries, India, and the Caribbean. There are as many variations as there are cooks. My twist on this dish has a definite Southeast Asian flavor. It's made with black-eyed peas, apples, and coconut milk, and seductively scented with ginger and lime zest. The sweet-tart apple and zippy lime zest lend a refreshing note. Serve it as a side dish to roast poultry or use it to stuff vegetables for a meatless entrée. If you use canned black-eyed peas, you'll need 1½ cups, drained. Rinse the beans well before using.

½ cup dried black-eyed peas
½ teaspoon baking soda
1 cup long-grain rice, rinsed
1 cup chicken broth, preferably homemade
    (page 30)
½ cup canned unsweetened coconut milk,
    well stirred
½ teaspoon salt, or to taste
2 teaspoons vegetable oil
1 large Granny Smith apple, peeled, cored,
    and cubed (½-inch pieces)
1 cup chopped onions
1 tablespoon minced garlic
2 fresh hot red chile peppers, finely
    chopped
1 tablespoon finely grated peeled fresh
    ginger
2 teaspoons finely grated lime zest

1. Place the black-eyed peas in a large soup pot and cover with 2½ cups hot water. Bring to a boil over medium-high heat. Boil for 2 minutes, then set aside, covered, for 1 hour.

2. After the peas have soaked, add the baking soda and bring to a simmer over medium heat. Simmer until the peas are just ten-

der, about 10 minutes. Drain; refresh with cold water and drain again.

3. Rinse the pot, then add the peas, rice, chicken broth, coconut milk, and salt. Bring the mixture to a boil over medium-high heat and boil for 1 minute. Reduce the heat to low, cover, and cook until the rice is tender and all the liquid has been absorbed, about 20 minutes. Remove from the heat and let stand, covered, for 10 minutes.

4. Heat the oil in a large skillet over medium-high heat. Add the apple, onions, garlic, chile peppers, and ginger and sauté until soft and fragrant, about 2 minutes.

5. Stir the sautéed vegetables into the rice, along with the grated lime zest. Add salt to taste, if necessary. Serve immediately.

BAYOU DIRTY RICE

YIELD: 4 ENTREE OR 6 SIDE DISH SERVINGS

Some of the most interesting and delicious rice preparations come from Louisiana. This spicy combination of long-grain rice, vegetables, minced pork, and chicken liver is from the Bayou. It doesn't look too pretty (hence the name), but it sure does taste good. In my version, I use lean ground chicken instead of pork and add fresh apples at the last minute to provide a light, refreshing crunch and to temper the heat of the rice. It's such a wonderful mixture of flavors and textures, I find myself serving this dish frequently as a light supper or as a side dish to roast meat.

SPICE MIX
2 teaspoons sweet paprika
1½ teaspoons salt
1½ teaspoons freshly ground black pepper
1 teaspoon ground cumin
1 teaspoon dried thyme, crumbled
1 teaspoon dried oregano, crumbled

RICE
2 tablespoons mild olive oil
5 ounces (½ cup) chicken livers, trimmed of excess fat and coarsely chopped
2¼ cups chicken broth, preferably homemade (page 30)
¼ pound ground chicken
½ cup finely chopped onion
½ cup finely chopped celery
½ cup finely chopped green bell pepper
1 tablespoon minced garlic
2 bay leaves
2 Granny Smith apples, peeled, cored, and cubed (½-inch pieces)
1 cup long-grain rice
½ teaspoon Tabasco sauce, or to taste
1 cup sliced scallions (white and green parts)

1. To make the spice mix, combine all the ingredients in a small bowl and set aside.

2. To make the rice, heat 1 tablespoon of the olive oil in a large skillet over medium-high heat. Add the livers and sauté until browned, about 2 minutes. Place the livers in a small bowl. Set aside.

3. Place the chicken broth in a small saucepan and bring to a simmer over medium heat. Reduce the heat to low, cover, and keep the broth at a simmer.

4. Meanwhile, heat the remaining 1 tablespoon olive oil in the skillet over medium heat. Add the ground chicken and cook, breaking up any lumps with a wooden spoon, until browned, about 2 minutes. Add the onion, celery, bell pepper, garlic, bay leaves, spice mix, and half of the diced apples. Cook until the vegetables are tender, stirring frequently, about 5 minutes.

5. Add the rice to the vegetables and stir until the grains are coated and shiny, about 3 minutes. Stir in the livers. Add the simmering broth (be careful—the mixture will splatter violently) and Tabasco sauce.

Reduce the heat to low, cover the skillet, and cook until the rice is tender and all the liquid has been absorbed, about 20 minutes. Remove from the heat and let sit, covered, for 10 minutes.

6. Remove and discard the bay leaves; stir in the scallions and the reserved apple. Serve immediately.

HONG KONG FRIED RICE

YIELD: 6 ENTREE SERVINGS

Hong Kong chefs are forever reinterpreting traditional Chinese dishes, and variations on this delicious fried rice with pineapple can be found on many of their menus. Here is my version, where fresh pineapple, cooked chicken, and hot bean paste provide a wonderful taste combination, with the sweetness of the fruit balancing the heat of the condiment. When you make fried rice at home in a small wok or skillet, it's best to cook a few ingredients separately, then toss them together for a moment or so to reheat everything. By not overcrowding the wok, you will prevent a drop in cooking temperature; the food will sear quickly and each ingredient will retain its fresh, distinctive flavor.

Shrimp, Chinese sausage, or baked ham can be combined with or substituted for the chicken.

4 cups cooked rice (about 1½ cups raw)
5 tablespoons peanut oil
3 large eggs
Salt
1 large onion, finely diced
2 teaspoons minced garlic
1 teaspoon Szechwan hot bean paste, such as Chef Chow's
1½ cups cubed fresh pineapple (½-inch pieces)
1½ cups cubed cooked chicken (½-inch pieces)
1 tablespoon sugar
1 cup diced celery
Freshly ground black pepper
4 whole scallions, trimmed and sliced into thin diagonal strips
¼ cup soy sauce, preferably Kikkoman
¼ cup chicken broth preferably homemade (page 30)

1. If you are using cold leftover rice, wet your hands and rub the rice to separate the grains. There's no need to do this if you are using just-cooked rice.

2. Place a wok or large skillet over high heat and add 1 tablespoon of the oil. In a bowl, beat the eggs with ¼ teaspoon salt. Add the eggs to the hot oil and cook, stirring, until the eggs are softly set. Remove to a dish and set aside.

3. Swirl 2 tablespoons more oil into the wok. Add the onion, garlic, and bean paste and fry for 30 seconds. Add the pineapple, chicken, and sugar and stir-fry until the ingre-dients are heated through and glazed, about 2 minutes. Add the celery and cook for 1 minute. Season the mixture to taste with salt and pepper and transfer to a bowl. Set aside.

4. Add the remaining 2 tablespoons oil to the wok. Add the scallions and stir quick-ly. Add the rice and stir-fry until heated through, about 2 minutes. Stir in the soy sauce and chicken broth. Stir and toss until the rice is well coated. Add the scrambled eggs and pineapple-chicken mixture and stir until heated through.

5. Transfer the fried rice to a large warmed platter. Sprinkle with black pepper and serve at once.

WEST INDIES RICE PILAF

YIELD: 6 SIDE DISH SERVINGS

Banana, cinnamon, and bay leaves are popular flavorings in Caribbean cuisine. Put the three together and you get a fantastic combina-tion that will lift an ordinary dish to new heights. For instance a once-ordinary rice pilaf, when graced with this aromatic trio, inspires sweet dreams of those islands. Savory with sweet overtones, this rice goes well with almost anything, especially curries and soupy stews. For a more intense flavor, lightly sauté the bananas in melted butter with cinnamon to taste before tossing them into the rice.

3½ cups chicken broth, preferably
*   homemade (page 30)*
½ teaspoon salt
2 tablespoons unsalted butter
½ cup finely chopped onion
1 teaspoon minced garlic
¼ cup finely chopped carrot
2 cups long-grain rice
2 bay leaves
2 firm bananas
Salt and freshly ground black pepper
Ground cinnamon, to taste

1. Place the chicken broth and salt in a small saucepan and bring to a simmer over medium heat. Reduce the heat to low, cover, and keep the broth at a simmer.

2. Melt the butter in a medium-size saucepan over medium-low heat. Add the onion, garlic, and carrot and sauté until just tender, about 2 minutes. Add the rice and bay leaves and stir until the rice turns opaque, about 5 minutes.

3. Add the simmering broth (be careful—the mixture will splatter violently). Quickly stir, and cover the pot with a tight-fitting lid. Reduce the heat to the lowest setting possible and cook until all of the liquid is absorbed and the rice is tender, about 20 minutes.

4. Peel the bananas, quarter them lengthwise, and slice crosswise ¼-inch thick. With 2 forks, toss the banana bits with the hot rice. Season to taste with salt, pepper, and a sprinkling of ground cinnamon. Serve immediately.

WILD RICE WITH WALNUTS AND CURRANTS

YIELD: 4 SIDE DISH SERVINGS

Braising wild rice in chicken broth with vegetables gives it a wonderfully rich taste. With a handful of crunchy walnuts and sweet dried currants, its natural nutty flavor and chewy texture are heightened even further. This is a super side dish with any roast game or pork, and it can also be used as a stuffing for a whole chicken or baked chicken breasts.

1 cup wild rice
2 tablespoons unsalted butter
¼ cup chopped onion
¼ cup diced carrot
3¼ cups chicken broth, preferably homemade (page 30)
2 bay leaves
⅛ teaspoon freshly ground black pepper
½ cup walnut halves
½ cup dried currants
Salt

1. Wash the wild rice in a strainer until the water runs clear. Drain well.

2. Preheat the oven to 350°F.

3. Melt 1 tablespoon of the butter in a medium-size, heavy ovenproof saucepan over medium heat. Add the onion, carrot, and wild rice and sauté to soften the vegetables slightly, about 5 minutes, stirring constantly. Add the broth, bay leaves, and pepper, and bring the mixture to a boil. Cover the pan and place it in the oven. Bake, stirring occasionally, until the rice is tender and the liquid is absorbed, about 1 ½ hours.

4. Melt the remaining 1 tablespoon butter in a skillet over medium heat. Add the

GREAT MATCHES

CURRANTS AND RAISINS

Currants and raisins are delicious accents in cabbage preparations. They also add a delectable sweetness to dark green leafy vegetables like spinach, Swiss chard, kale, and broccoli rabe. Rum, orange-flavored liqueur, and wine are good with these fruits, too.

walnuts and currants and toast until the nuts are fragrant and golden brown, about 3 minutes. Stir into the rice. Season to taste with salt and serve immediately.

COUSCOUS WITH DRIED FRUIT

YIELD: 8 SIDE DISH SERVINGS

Here's one of my favorite side dishes, which does double duty as a stuffing for poultry or crown roasts. It's full of sausage and fruit tidbits, it's quick to prepare, and it's really delicious. If you get the urge to add other dried fruits, like apples or figs, go ahead!

Have fun with the possibilities. Couscous is available in natural food stores and most supermarkets. This dish can be prepared early in the day, covered with aluminum foil, and reheated in the oven. Serve with roast meats or poultry. It's also great with a mixed grill or sword-fish kabob (see Index). If you do serve the couscous with meat, leave out the sausage.

¾ cup dried apricots, diced (½-inch cubes)

½ cup golden raisins

3 tablespoons dry sherry

3 cups chicken broth, preferably homemade (page 30)

4 tablespoons (½ stick) unsalted butter

2 cups couscous

½ pound hot Italian sausage meat (see Note)

2 small fennel bulbs or 3 ribs celery, trimmed and sliced ¼ inch thick (1½ cups)

1½ cups chopped onions

2 tablespoons minced garlic

2 teaspoons dried thyme, crumbled

2 teaspoons dried sage, crumbled

½ cup toasted pine nuts (for toasting instructions, see page 64)

Salt and freshly ground black pepper

1. Combine the apricots, raisins, and sherry in a small bowl. Cover and set aside.

2. Place the chicken broth and butter in a large saucepan and bring to a boil over high heat. Add the couscous in a stream, stirring constantly. Quickly cover the pot and turn off the heat. Let the couscous sit while you prepare the rest of the stuffing.

3. Add the sausage to a large skillet over medium-high heat, and brown, breaking up the lumps with the back of a wooden spoon, about 5 minutes. Add the fennel, onions, and garlic and cook until soft, about 3 minutes. Add the dried fruits, thyme, and sage, and stir for 1 minute. Remove from the heat.

4. Fluff the couscous with a fork to sep-arate the grains. Add the sausage-fruit mix-ture to the couscous. Stir in the pine nuts and mix until all the ingredients are well com-bined. Season to taste with salt and pepper.

NOTE: If you buy sausage links, remove the casings.

CREAMY POLENTA WITH APRICOT-ONION SAUCE

YIELD: 4 ENTREE OR
6 SIDE DISH SERVINGS

Polenta, a staple of northeastern Italy, is a porridge made with coarse cornmeal. I have tried to cook polenta the traditional way, by adding cornmeal in a thin stream to sim-mering liquid while stirring, but the mixture occasionally comes out lumpy. So, I have adopted a simpler method of cooking polenta: I start the cornmeal in cold broth and then cook it slowly until it is thick and smooth. I enjoy serving polenta with a sprightly sauce flavored with anchovies, herbs, and dried apricots. Since I like my polenta with a little texture, I also add fresh corn kernels. This dish is quite filling as a main course followed by a mixed green salad and fresh fruit. It also makes a robust accompaniment to lamb, pork, or game.

APRICOT-ONION SAUCE

1 tablespoon extra-virgin olive oil

1 1/2 cups chopped onions

1 tablespoon minced garlic

1 teaspoon dried oregano, crumbled

1/4 teaspoon dried red pepper flakes, or to taste

8 anchovy fillets, coarsely chopped

1 bay leaf

2 cups canned peeled tomatoes, including juice

1 1/2 cups dry white wine, preferably Chardonnay

1/2 cup diced dried apricots

1 teaspoon salt

1 teaspoon sugar

POLENTA

2 large ears corn, preferably white, husks and silks removed

3 3/4 cups chicken broth, preferably homemade (page 30), at room temperature

3/4 cup stone-ground yellow or white cornmeal

1/3 cup freshly grated Parmesan cheese

1/4 cup chopped flat-leaf parsley leaves, for garnish

Extra-virgin olive oil, for garnish

1. To make the sauce, heat the olive oil in a large, nonstick skillet over medium-high heat. Add the onions, garlic, oregano, red pepper flakes, anchovies, and bay leaf. Sauté, stirring frequently, until the onions are tender, about 3 minutes.

2. Crush the tomatoes with your fingers, then add them to the skillet, along with the wine, apricots, salt, and sugar. Quickly bring to a boil. Reduce the heat to low, and simmer for 15 minutes, stirring occasionally. Season the sauce to taste with salt and sugar, if necessary. (The sauce is now ready; you may use it immediately or let it sit for up to 2 hours before serving.)

3. To make the polenta, cut the corn kernels from the cobs by running a sharp knife from the tip of the ear straight down to the stem. Avoid tough fibers by not cutting too close to the cob. After removing the kernels, scrape the back of the knife down the cob to extract all the remaining meat and "milk." (You should have about 1 1/2 cups corn kernels.)

4. Stir the chicken broth, the cornmeal, and the corn kernels together in a large pot. Cook over low heat, stirring often with a wooden spoon, until the cornmeal no longer feels grainy when you taste it, 5 to 6 minutes. Remove from the heat and stir in the

Parmesan cheese. The mixture should be creamy and slightly runny. If it's too thick, add some hot water.

5. Spoon the polenta into warmed shallow bowls, top with the sauce, and sprinkle with chopped parsley. Drizzle some olive oil over the top. Serve immediately.

VARIATION

GRILLED POLENTA: Prepare the polenta as instructed in the above recipe, but use only 3½ cups chicken broth. Pour the cooked polenta into a well-buttered 9-inch square pan, spreading evenly to smooth out the surface. Cool, cover, then refrigerate until firm, about 2 hours. Cut the polenta into 3-inch squares, then cut the squares in half on the diagonal to make triangles. Brush the polenta pieces with olive oil, then dust lightly with flour. Grill over medium-high heat on a lightly oiled stove top grill or place under a preheated broiler, 6 inches from the heat, until browned, about 2 minutes per side. Serve grilled polenta with Apricot-Onion Sauce or with your favorite tomato sauce.

MINTY-FRUITY TABBOULEH

YIELD: 2 ENTREE OR 4 SIDE DISH SERVINGS

Tabbouleh, one of my favorite salads, is refreshing, filling, healthful, and relatively low in calories. It's great for lunch, dinner, and snacks, and it is a perfect no-wilt summer salad to bring to picnics. In this quick and easy recipe, chewy bulgur wheat, sweet grapes, crisp cucumber, cool mint, and tart vinaigrette produce an unusual but exquisite salad. It makes a perfect side dish to roast meat or chicken. For a more substantial, main dish, add tender cooked shrimp.

¾ cup bulgur (see Note)
1 teaspoon salt
1 cup boiling water
2 tablespoons fresh lemon juice
2 tablespoons extra-virgin olive oil
1 teaspoon minced garlic
⅔ cup diced tomato
½ cup seedless green grapes, halved
½ cup diced cucumber
½ cup sliced scallions (white and green parts)
2 tablespoons shredded mint leaves (for shredding instructions, see page 34)
Freshly ground black pepper

1. Combine the bulgur and salt in a heat-proof salad bowl and pour in the boiling water. Cover tightly and let sit for 30 minutes.

2. Stir in the lemon juice, olive oil, and garlic. Cover and chill the bulgur for 2 hours.

3. Add the tomato, grapes, cucumber, scallions, and mint just before serving and toss to combine. Adjust the seasoning with salt and pepper, if necessary. Serve the tabbouleh cold or at room temperature.

NOTE: Bulgur—precooked and dried cracked wheat—is available in most supermarkets and health food stores.

MEDITERRANEAN BARLEY

YIELD: 4 ENTREES

Combining meat, a starch, and fruit is a Mediterranean tradition. This entrée of spicy sausages, nutritious barley, and sweet grapes, is robust, so save it for cold winter months, when you can serve it as a pleasant change to pasta or rice. Unpeeled wedges of Granny Smith apple make a delicious substitute for the grapes.

3½ cups chicken broth, preferably homemade (page 30)
¼ cup dry sherry
1 tablespoon mild olive oil
1 cup chopped onions
1 tablespoon minced garlic
1 cup sliced button mushrooms
¾ cup pearl barley, rinsed
8 links (about 1¼ pounds) hot Italian sausage
½ shallot, sliced
¼ cup balsamic vinegar
2 cups seedless green grapes
1½ teaspoons ground coriander
Salt and freshly ground black pepper
¼ cup shredded flat-leaf parsley leaves (for shredding instructions, see page 34)

1. Preheat the oven to 350°F.

2. Combine the chicken broth and sherry in a medium-size saucepan and bring to a simmer over medium heat. Reduce the heat to low, cover, and keep at a simmer.

3. Heat the olive oil in a large ovenproof pot over medium heat. Add the onion and garlic and cook until tender, about 5 minutes. Stir in the mushrooms and sauté until they are soft and slightly browned, about 5 minutes. Add the barley and stir until the grains are coated and shiny, about 2 minutes.

4. Add the simmering broth (be careful—the mixture will splatter violently), and bring to a boil. Cover the pot and place it in the oven. Bake until the barley is tender and all the liquid has been absorbed, about 1 hour.

The trees were heavy with fruit, beguiling all the senses—the lustrous cherry, the tender apricot, the fig, white or green, sweeter than sugar, the lemons gold lamps gainst the green.

—SCHEHERAZADE, IN THE ARABIAN NIGHTS

5. Thirty minutes before the barley is ready, prick the sausages all over with a fork and place them in an ovenproof skillet over medium-high heat. Cook until the sausages are golden-brown on both sides, about 6 minutes total. Drain all but 1 teaspoon of the fat from the skillet. Return the skillet with the sausages to the heat and stir in the shallot; cook until fragrant, about 1 minute. Stir in the vinegar, along with the grapes. Place the skillet in the oven and bake, uncovered, until the sausages are cooked through, about 30 minutes, stirring once or twice.

6. Remove the skillet from the oven and stir in the coriander. Season to taste with salt and pepper. Divide the barley among warmed plates and top with the sausages and grapes. Sprinkle with parsley and serve at once.

GOLDEN WHEAT BERRY SALAD

YIELD: 4 ENTREES OR 8 SIDE DISH SERVINGS

Ablaze with golden oranges and flecked with white feta cheese, this elegant salad combines sweet, salty, and citrusy flavors. Fennel adds a refreshing crunch that nicely complements the chewiness of the wheat berries, which are whole unprocessed wheat kernels. For variation, you may substitute 2 cups cooked couscous, quinoa, or red lentils for the wheat berries.

CITRUS VINAIGRETTE

3 tablespoons extra-virgin olive oil

2 tablespoons fresh orange juice

2 teaspoons fresh lemon juice

1 teaspoon finely grated orange zest

1/2 teaspoon finely grated lemon zest

Salt and freshly ground black pepper, to taste

SALAD

1 cup wheat berries, rinsed and picked over
Salt
1 medium fennel bulb (about ¾ pound),
trimmed, halved lengthwise, and thinly
sliced crosswise
3 large oranges, peeled and sectioned (for
instructions, see page 318)
½ cup thinly sliced scallions (white and green
parts)
6 ounces feta cheese, preferably Greek
Freshly ground black pepper

1. To make the vinaigrette, combine all the ingredients in a small jar. Cover and shake until the vinaigrette is well blended. Refrigerate until needed.

2. To make the salad, cover the wheat berries with 4 cups hot water in a large pot. Add salt and bring to a boil over medium-high heat. Boil for 2 minutes. Remove from the heat and let sit, covered, for 30 minutes.

3. Return the wheat berries to a simmer over medium heat. Simmer until the wheat berries are just tender, about 20 minutes. Drain; refresh with cold water and drain again.

4. Toss the wheat berries with half the vinaigrette in a large mixing bowl. Add the fennel, oranges, and scallions, then crumble the feta cheese over the top. Drizzle the remaining vinaigrette over the salad and toss well. Season to taste with salt (keep in mind that feta is quite salty) and pepper. Serve at room temperature.

QUINOA PILAF

YIELD: 2 ENTREE OR 4 SIDE DISH SERVINGS

This light and tasty vegetarian entrée recipe comes from Bharti Kirchner, a noted cookbook author and good friend. She cooks quinoa, a high-protein grain rich in iron and other minerals, pilaf-style with carrots, golden raisins, and a touch of turmeric to tint the tiny grains a pleasant yellow. She then garnishes the dish with hard-cooked egg slices, toasted pine nuts, and dried cranberries, all of which add substance, color, texture, and flavor. This dish is also a good companion to any grilled meat or crown roast.

2 tablespoons vegetable oil
1 cup finely chopped onions
1 tablespoon minced garlic
¼ teaspoon turmeric
1 cup quinoa, thoroughly rinsed (see Note,
page 35)
2 cups hot chicken broth, preferably homemade
(page 30), or water
1 cup cubed carrots (½-inch pieces)
2 tablespoons golden raisins
¾ teaspoon salt
2 hard-cooked eggs, sliced
2 tablespoons dried cranberries or dried
cherries, plumped in hot water for
5 minutes and drained
2 tablespoons pine nuts, toasted (for toasting
instructions, see page 64)

1. Heat the oil in a large skillet or saucepan over medium heat. Add the onions and garlic and sauté until the mixture is aromatic and the onions are lightly browned around the edges, about 5 minutes.

2. Add the turmeric and stir to distribute evenly. Add the quinoa and stir until the grains are coated and shiny, about 1 minute. Add the broth, carrots, raisins, and salt. With the back of a spoon push the quinoa down so that it lies under the surface of the broth.

3. As soon as the mixture comes to a boil, reduce the heat to low, cover, and cook until all the liquid is absorbed and the quinoa is light and fluffy, about 18 minutes.

4. Just before serving, transfer the pilaf to a serving platter. Arrange the egg slices on top. Sprinkle with the plumped cranberries and pine nuts.

SOPHISTICATED SEAFOOD

With growing concerns about improving our diet and reducing fat intake, especially animal fat, it's no wonder that more and more of us are eating fish and shellfish these days. In fact, almost nothing beats seafood for a quick-cooking healthy meal. As part of this trend, many cooks are exploring foreign cuisines, like those of the Mediterranean and Pacific Rim, where "fruits of the sea" are central to the diet. Cooks in these regions have developed some of the freshest, most flavorful, and interesting seafood dishes that exist. Incidentally, many of them include fruit.

The first rule of fish cookery is buy only the freshest seafood. The success of a fish dish depends entirely on the quality of the fish: If it is mediocre, not even the best sauce or the most exotic ingredient will save it. Before I left my childhood home, my mother told me one of the most important facts of life: Know your fishmonger. Taking her advice to heart, I've befriended the Japanese fishmonger in my neighborhood and buy from him regularly to ensure that my seafood is impeccably fresh. We Asians are notoriously finicky about our

CAREFUL COOKING

Many of us have learned that moist fish is infinitely more appealing than dry. Indeed, a cardinal rule in cooking fish is not to overcook it. It doesn't matter whether you're baking, grilling, or steaming; the cooking will be done when the flesh just flakes easily when tested with a fork. The same rules of not overcooking apply to shellfish. They should be cooked just until the flesh loses its translucent character and begins to turn cloudy. Longer cooking will make shrimp, scallops, and the like tough little devils.

seafood. Some of us will even dismiss as inedible a fish that has been caught only a few hours ago. That's why many good Chinese restaurants keep live fish swimming about for their patrons to select just moments before dinner.

Like many other cooks, my attitude toward fish cookery is to keep it simple. But simple cooking doesn't have to be dull. If I'm grilling a piece of fish, I'll toss a few slices of pineapple or a couple bananas on the grill too. Sprinkled with a little brown sugar and cinnamon, the grilled fruit makes a quick, tasty side dish.

Marrying fruit with seafood, if well thought out, can be full of pleasant surprises. Who would expect rosy pieces of steamed salmon topped with a vinaigrette of fresh pineapple and tomatoes? Or pan-fried trout served with a warm, creamy potato and plantain salad? These

combinations may sound odd, but they really work.

In developing the recipes for this chapter, I discovered that combining fruits with fish and shellfish must be done with care. A fruit's flavor, if too strong, can easily overwhelm subtle seafood. Also, fructose, the natural sugar in fruit, is capable of ruining a seafood dish if it is too dominant. Fruits with a high percentage of acidity, like pineapple, grapes, tart apples, tamarind, and especially citrus fruits, blend quite well with most seafood, particularly oily fish like bluefish, salmon, or mackerel. However, sweeter fruits, like mango, papaya, or peach, just need some extra acid to balance the dish, to allow the delicate flavors of fish and shellfish to shine through. Usually, a squeeze of fresh lemon juice or vinegar does the job.

Whatever dish you choose—curried scallops topped with star fruit, perhaps, or broiled bluefish in orange sauce served over a plate of steaming rice—will confirm that seafood, delicately prepared, makes for great dining.

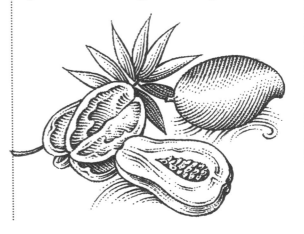

FILLET OF SOLE WITH GOOSEBERRIES

YIELD: 4 ENTREE SERVINGS

Pale green globes, with a thin, papery skin, gooseberries have a flavor similar to that of tart green grapes. Related to currants, gooseberries are a favorite with English cooks, who, besides using them in pies and preserves, commonly pair them with fish, as this recipe deliciously demonstrates. The puckery tartness of the fruit is a perfect foil to the rich tarragon cream sauce that accompanies the delicate sole. If gooseberries are unavailable, leave them out or substitute tart green grapes. In either case, balance the sauce with fresh lime juice. This dish goes particularly well with steamed potatoes or rice.

2 tablespoons unsalted butter
1½ cups well washed and dried, finely chopped leeks (white part only)
½ cup fresh gooseberries, picked over
½ cup clam juice
¼ cup heavy (or whipping) cream
1½ teaspoons chopped fresh tarragon leaves
Salt and freshly ground white pepper
4 fillets of sole (6 ounces each)
4 sprigs fresh tarragon

1. Melt 1 tablespoon of the butter in a small skillet over medium-low heat. Add the leeks, and cook, stirring frequently, until very soft, about 5 minutes.

2. Transfer the leeks to a blender. Add the gooseberries and clam juice. Process to a fine purée. Strain the purée through a fine sieve, pressing on the solids to extract as much liquid as possible. Discard the solids.

3. Return the strained sauce to the skillet over medium-low heat. Add the cream and cook, stirring occasionally, until the sauce is just heated through, about 1 minute. Gently swirl the remaining 1 tablespoon of butter into the sauce. The sauce should look silky and slightly creamy. Do not allow it to boil or it will separate. Stir in the tarragon leaves and remove the pan from the heat. Season to taste with salt and white pepper. The sauce may be kept covered, up to 1 hour, at room temperature.

4. Preheat the broiler.

5. Lightly sprinkle the fillets with salt and white pepper. Place them in a lightly buttered baking dish. Broil 3 inches from the heat until the fillets flake easily when tested with a fork, 2 to 3 minutes, depending on their thickness.

6. Meanwhile, gently reheat the sauce.

7. Using a wide metal spatula, carefully transfer the fillets to warmed dinner plates. Spoon the sauce over the fish and garnish with a sprig of tarragon. Serve at once.

AN ELEGANT LIGHT DINNER

WINTER WHITE SALAD
✦
BAKED HALIBUT IN CIDER BROTH
✦
THREE-FRUIT TERRINE WITH BANANA SAUCE

BAKED HALIBUT IN CIDER BROTH

YIELD: 4 ENTREE SERVINGS

In my adaptation of a favorite Norman dish—sole poached in cider—halibut fillets rest on a tantalizing bed of sweet onions and apples and hearty potatoes. The whole lot is then blanketed in a delicate broth of reduced hard cider and heavy cream. Purpom, a French imported apple cider with a 3.5 percent alcohol content, is available at liquor stores for a very reasonable price. Do not substitute fresh apple cider; it would be too sweet and throw off the delicate balance of this dish. As an excellent accompaniment to this satisfying entrée, serve sliced toasted garlic bread.

> 2 small onions, thinly sliced
> 2 medium red new potatoes (about ½ pound total), boiled for 10 minutes, cooled, and sliced paper thin
> 2 small tart apples, preferably McIntosh or Granny Smith, peeled, cored, and thinly sliced
> Salt and freshly ground black pepper
> 4 halibut fillets (6 ounces each)
> 3 cups hard apple cider, such as Purpom or a good domestic brand
> ½ cup heavy (or whipping) cream
> ¼ cup finely shredded fresh basil leaves (for shredding instructions, see page 34)

1. Preheat the oven to 450°F.

2. Scatter the onion slices over the bottom of a flameproof 13 x 9-inch baking dish. Top with the potato slices, then the apple slices. Season to taste with salt and pepper.

3. Season the fillets with salt and pepper and place them over the vegetable mixture. Add the cider. (This dish can be prepared to this point up to 4 hours ahead, covered, and refrigerated. Bring to room temperature before proceeding.)

4. Place the baking dish over high heat and bring the cider to a boil. Cover the dish

with aluminum foil and transfer it to the oven. Bake until the fish flakes easily when tested with a fork, about 12 minutes.

5. Carefully pour off the cooking liquid into a medium-size saucepan. Cover the fillets and vegetables with foil to keep them warm while you finish the broth. Bring the liquid to a boil over medium-high heat and cook until slightly reduced, about 5 minutes. Add the cream and continue to boil for 1 more minute. Remove the pan from the heat and stir in the basil. Season the broth with salt and pepper, if necessary.

6. Using a wide metal spatula, transfer the fillets and vegetables to warmed shallow bowls. Ladle the hot broth over the fish and serve at once.

STUFFED TROUT, MEDITERRANEAN STYLE

YIELD: 4 ENTREE SERVINGS

Mediterranean cooks are brilliant when it comes to blending savory and sweet elements in a single dish, as demonstrated in this recipe. The stuffing is light and zesty, with a hint of sweetness, and delicate enough not to mask the flavor of the trout. I've also used the stuffing for shrimp and pork with equally delicious results. Stuffed and tied, the trout can be prepared up to 6 hours in advance, covered, and refrigerated. If you would like to serve a sauce with the trout, try my Gingered Citrus Sauce (see Index).

4 dried figs or dates
2 tablespoons mild olive oil
2/3 cup finely chopped onion
2 teaspoons minced garlic
1 teaspoon ground coriander
1/2 teaspoon ground cinnamon
1/2 cup dry bread crumbs
1 tablespoon chopped fresh cilantro leaves
2 tablespoons plus 2 teaspoons fresh lemon
    juice
2 tablespoons toasted pine nuts (for toasting
    instructions, see page 64)
Salt and freshly ground black pepper
4 brook trouts (about 12 ounces each),
    bones and heads removed, tails intact
Lemon wedges, for garnish

1. Preheat the oven to 375°F.

2. Plump the figs in hot water to cover for 15 minutes, drain, and finely chop. Set aside.

3. Heat the oil in a medium-size skillet over medium-low heat. Add the onion and garlic and sauté until aromatic and golden, about 5 minutes. Stir in the figs, coriander, and cinnamon. Remove from the heat and cool slightly.

4. Stir in the bread crumbs, cilantro, lemon juice, and pine nuts. Season to taste with salt and pepper. The filling will be moist and hold together when pressed.

5. Season the inside of the fish with salt and pepper. Fill each one with a quarter of the stuffing (a generous ⅓ cup). Close and secure each trout by tying the body 3 to 4 times with butcher string. (The stuffed trout may be prepared up to this point, in advance, covered, and refrigerated until you are ready to cook them.)

6. Lightly oil a shallow baking dish large enough to hold the fish in a single layer. Place the trout in it, leaving some room around each fish for the heat to circulate.

7. Bake until the fish flakes easily when tested with a fork, about 15 minutes.

8. Transfer the fish to warmed dinner plates and remove the strings. Pour any pan juices over the fish. Garnish with lemon wedges and serve.

TROUT WITH POTATO AND PLANTAIN SALAD

YIELD: 4 ENTREE SERVINGS

Germans like to serve potato salad with almost everything—beef, pork, sausages, even fish. Inspired by that practice, I created just such a salad to go with pan-fried trout, adding my own twist, plantain. The sherry vinegar in the dressing imparts a wonderful tartness to the warm, sweet plantain and creamy potatoes and provides a counterpoint to the rich, delicate trout. This dish can be prepared with any potatoes, but Red Bliss and Yukon Golds are lower in starch and they add a buttery, rich flavor. If trout is unavailable, substitute red snapper, sea bass, or grouper.

SALAD

1 pound Yukon Gold or Red Bliss potatoes

2 tablespoons Dijon mustard

6 tablespoons chicken broth, preferably homemade (page 30)

5 tablespoons sherry vinegar

½ teaspoon salt

½ teaspoon freshly ground black pepper

¼ cup mild olive oil

1 ripe (black) plantain, peeled (page 10) and sliced crosswise ¼ inch thick

½ medium red onion, finely chopped

3 tablespoons chopped flat-leaf parsley leaves

TROUT
1 cup all-purpose flour
4 trout fillets (½ pound each), skin on
Salt and freshly ground black pepper
2 tablespoons mild olive oil

Lemon wedges, for garnish

1. To make the salad, place the potatoes in a medium-size saucepan. Add boiling water to cover. Cook over medium-low heat until fork-tender, 20 to 25 minutes, depending on the size of the potatoes.

2. Meanwhile, make a vinaigrette by whisking together the mustard, chicken broth, vinegar, salt, pepper, and olive oil in a large mixing bowl.

3. Just before draining the potatoes, add the plantain slices to the boiling water. Cook until just heated through, about 30 seconds. Drain and set aside until cool enough to handle.

4. Slice the warm potatoes into rounds, then add them to the vinaigrette along with the plantain slices, red onion, and parsley. Toss the salad gently but thoroughly. Transfer the potato salad to a large platter and set aside.

5. To make the trout, place the flour on a large platter. Sprinkle the fillets lightly with salt and pepper. Dredge each fillet in the flour, shaking off any excess.

6. In a large, heavy skillet, heat the oil over medium-high heat until it is hot but not smoking. Add the trout, skin side down, and cook until the skin is golden brown and crisp, for 2 to 3 minutes. If the fillets warp, use a wide metal spatula to flatten them out. Turn the trout over and cook just until it flakes when tested with a fork, 1 to 2 minutes longer.

7. With a wide metal spatula, transfer the trout, skin side up, to the potato salad on the platter. Serve at once, with lemon wedges to squeeze over the fish, if desired.

BROILED BLUEFISH WITH ORANGE SAUCE

YIELD: 4 ENTREE SERVINGS

You'll be amazed how with just a few ingredients you can make something as wonderfully tasty as this dish. A light orange sauce spiked with heady sesame oil acts as a perfect medium for a truly delicious broiled bluefish. Salmon, grouper, or red snapper fillets can be prepared in a similar way.

2 navel oranges

3 tablespoons soy sauce, preferably Kikkoman

2 teaspoons honey

1 teaspoon Asian sesame oil

1 teaspoon minced garlic

2 scallions, trimmed and thinly sliced
    (white and green parts)

4 skinless bluefish fillets (6 ounces each)

1 tablespoon unsalted butter

Freshly ground black pepper

12 fresh orange segments (for peeling and
    sectioning instructions, see page 318)

1. Using a zester, remove long strips of zest from 1 of the oranges. Set aside. Extract the juice of both oranges. (There should be 1/2 cup of juice.)

2. Combine the orange juice, orange zest, soy sauce, honey, and sesame oil in a shallow flameproof baking dish large enough to hold the fish fillets. Place the dish over low heat, and heat until the marinade is just warmed through. Remove from the heat and stir in the garlic and scallions. Let cool.

3. Add the fish fillets to the cooled marinade. Cover and refrigerate for at least 1 hour, but no longer than 2 hours.

A BLUES STORY

A few summers ago, I was hired to work as a private chef for a family in Bridgehampton, Long Island. What attracted me most to the job was the kitchen: It was brand-new, with marble countertops and a fabulous close-up view of the Atlantic Ocean.

One rainy morning, as I was preparing breakfast in the kitchen, a flock of seagulls suddenly began to scream excitedly at the top of their lungs. I looked up and saw an incredible thing: Dozens of birds were frantically feeding on a giant school of bluefish that had been deposited on the beach by crashing waves. Without any hesitation, a family member, my kitchen assistant, and I ran to the beach as fast as we could, a bucket and fishing pole in hand.

Soon, we were ankle-deep in the water and competing with the gulls for the huge bluefish that were jumping out of the water all around us. As I tried to scoop them up with a bucket, my assistant tried to catch them with her bare hands, and the person with the fishing pole cast his line out into the surf. In a matter of seconds, the commotion was over. The fish and birds retreated to the sea, disappearing as suddenly as they came. Fortunately, we were not left with empty hands.

Exalted, all three of us came back into the kitchen with a beautiful, tremendous bluefish. Each must have weighed between 8 and 10 pounds, and smelled healthily of the sea. To preserve their freshness, I cleaned and dressed the blues within minutes of the catch, then stashed them in the refrigerator. Because fish never comes any fresher than this, I had to quickly decide how I would prepare them to fully take advantage of their unique freshness. I transformed the first blue into a fried treat with sweet and sour sauce. The second was simmered in a Portuguese-style tomato sauce with lots of green olives and potato chunks. And the third was grilled and served with a delicious orange sauce on the side. What a feast that was!

4. Preheat the broiler.

5. Drain the fillets, pouring the marinade into a small saucepan. Place the fillets in a baking dish and broil 4½ inches from the heat until the fish flakes easily when tested with a fork, about 5 minutes.

6. Meanwhile, bring the marinade to a boil over medium-high heat. Cook until the liquid is reduced by one-third, about 5 minutes. Add the butter and stir until completely melted. Remove the sauce from the heat and season to taste with black pepper.

7. Transfer the fish fillets to warmed dinner plates and spoon some of the orange sauce over each one. Top each serving with 3 orange segments. Serve at once.

COD CAKES WITH THAI GREEN APPLE SALSA

YIELD: 4 ENTREE SERVINGS

Fish cakes made with potatoes and cod have been a staple food in the New World for centuries. In New England, it is quite traditional to serve fish cakes at breakfast or brunch, with slices of bacon and, perhaps, some gravy. I know another great way: Pair these fish cakes with a slightly tart salad made with Granny Smith apples, chile peppers, and cilantro for a nutritious but light meal. The refreshing apple salsa neutralizes any fried taste in the cakes. This dish will bring a tropical flavor to your table! Another perfect accompaniment to these fish cakes is Pickled Mango and Cucumbers (see Index).

2 large Idaho potatoes (about 1 pound total),
    peeled and quartered
Salt
2 tablespoons mild olive oil
1 cup chopped onions
1 hake or Atlantic cod fillet (1½ pounds),
    sliced ¼ inch thick
¼ cup chopped flat-leaf parsley leaves
Freshly ground black pepper
2 large eggs, well beaten
1 cup vegetable oil
Thai Green Apple Salsa (recipe follows)

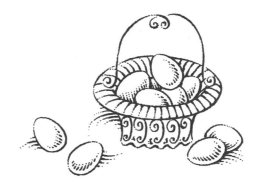

1. Bring a medium-size saucepan of salted water to a boil. Add the potatoes, return the water to a boil, and cook until fork-tender,

10 to 15 minutes. Drain well and return the potatoes to the saucepan. Cover and set aside.

2. Heat the oil in a large skillet over medium-low heat. Add the onions and sauté, stirring frequently, until golden, about 5 minutes. Add the fish and cook, stirring frequently, until it is cooked through and flakes easily when tested with a fork, about 5 minutes. Transfer to a large mixing bowl.

3. Coarsely mash the potatoes. Add the potatoes and parsley to the fish and stir to combine, flaking the fish while you stir. Season to taste with salt and pepper. Stir in the beaten eggs. Cover and refrigerate until well chilled, at least 1 hour, or overnight.

4. Using a ½-cup measure as a scoop, divide the fish-potato mixture into 8 portions. Invert each scoop onto a large plate, briskly tapping a corner of the cup against the plate to release the cake. Gently pat each portion into a round cake.

5. Heat ½ cup oil in each of 2 large skillets over medium heat. Add the fish cakes and fry, turning once, until golden-brown,

about 8 minutes total. Drain the cakes briefly on paper towels. Serve the fish cakes with Thai Green Apple Salsa on the side.

Thai Green Apple Salsa

YIELD: ABOUT 3 CUPS

The salty, sour, and slightly spicy seasonings bring out flavors you never thought green apples had. This salsa complements fried foods primarily, but is also nice with grilled meats, such as chicken and pork.

4 Granny Smith apples, peeled, cored, and thinly sliced
½ teaspoon salt
Juice of 1 large lime
1 small red onion, sliced paper thin
2 small fresh hot red chile peppers or jalapeño peppers, minced
¼ cup shredded fresh cilantro leaves

Stir all the ingredients together in a large mixing bowl. Cover and let sit at room temperature for at least 30 minutes before serving.

TURKISH BAKED SCROD WITH ONION COMPOTE

YIELD: 4 ENTREE SERVINGS

A key ingredient in this easy, delicious dish is pomegranate molasses, which is pomegranate juice and a little sugar cooked down to a thick syrup. It can be found at stores that specialize in Middle Eastern foodstuffs but can easily be made at home from fresh or frozen pomegranate juice. The balance of sweet and tart flavors in the molasses complements the fish, and the crunch of the pomegranate seeds and walnuts is very pleasing. Serve a salad of watercress and steamed rice alongside to round out the meal. You can also enjoy the onion compote (along with the pomegranate seeds, walnuts, and cilantro) spooned over bulgur or rice, as a dip for flatbreads, or as a condiment for grilled and roasted meats.

ONION COMPOTE

2 tablespoons mild olive oil
4 cups finely chopped onions
4 teaspoons pomegranate molasses,
    preferably homemade (recipe follows)
1/4 teaspoon ground cinnamon
2 teaspoons fresh lemon juice
Salt and cayenne pepper

FISH

4 scrod or halibut fillets (6 to 7 ounces each)
2 teaspoons mild olive oil
4 teaspoons fresh lemon juice
Salt and freshly ground black pepper
1/2 cup chopped toasted walnuts (for toasting
    instructions, see page 64)
1/2 cup pomegranate, seeds separated
2 tablespoons chopped fresh cilantro leaves

1. Preheat the oven to 450°F.

2. To make the onion compote, heat the oil in a large nonstick skillet. Add the onions and cook over medium-high heat, stirring frequently, until very tender and golden brown, about 10 minutes.

3. Stir in the pomegranate molasses, cinnamon, and lemon juice and season to taste with salt and cayenne pepper. Remove from the heat.

4. To make the fish, spread the onion compote in a shallow baking pan just large enough to hold all the fish fillets. Arrange the fillets on top and brush them with the olive oil and lemon juice. Sprinkle with salt and pepper.

5. Bake until the fish is cooked through and flakes easily when tested with a fork, 15 to 18 minutes.

6. Using a wide metal spatula, transfer the fillets to warmed dinner plates. Stir the toasted walnuts, pomegranate seeds, and chopped cilantro into the onion mixture. Spoon over the fillets and serve immediately.

*Eat the pomegranate for
it purges the system
of envy and hatred.*

—MUHAMMAD

Pomegranate Molasses

YIELD: 1/2 CUP

This molasses has an intense pomegranate flavor and a sweet-tart taste. Because it is fairly concentrated, a few teaspoonfuls are usually enough to flavor a whole dish. The best time to make this syrup is in the fall, when pomegranates are cheap and plentiful. Any leftover molasses will keep perfectly in a sealed jar in the refrigerator for several months. It is a treasure to have on hand for flavoring Rosy Baba Ghanoush or Shockingly Pink Bread Salad. Or use it to marinate and glaze lamb kabobs (see Index for recipe page numbers). If pomegranates are unavailable, substitute 2 cups cranberry juice.

Pomegranate molasses is also sold in Middle Eastern groceries and some specialty stores; see Note for sources.

> 4 large pomegranates (about 12 ounces to
> 1 pound each)
> 3 tablespoons sugar

1. Firmly knead the pomegranates on a work surface, crushing the seeds inside. Halve crosswise. Using a manual citrus juicer, extract the juice. Strain through a fine sieve placed over a medium-size bowl. (Be careful: Pomegranate juice stains.) Squeeze the seeds with your fingers to extract as much liquid as possible. Discard the seeds and measure 2 cups of juice.

2. In a large saucepan, combine the pomegranate juice and sugar. Cook the mixture over medium-high heat for about 5 minutes, or until the liquid is reduced to about 1/2 cup of dark syrup that resembles black-strap molasses. Remove the pan from the heat and skim any foam from the surface. Cool and use as called for in recipes.

NOTE: Pomegranate molasses is for sale at the Sahadi Importing Company, 187 Atlantic Ave., Brooklyn, NY 11201; (718) 624-4550. It may also be ordered by mail from Dean & DeLuca, 560 Broadway, New York, NY 10012; (800) 221-7714. Knudsen and Cortas are two reliable brands.

CATFISH VENICE STYLE

YIELD: 4 ENTREE SERVINGS

The Venetians have a classic summer dish of fried breaded fillet of sole marinated in a sweet and sour onion sauce that is served either cold or at room temperature. In my version, I use sweet, meaty catfish fillets instead of sole, although almost any type of firm-fleshed fish, like tilefish, tuna, or salmon, is suitable for this dish. Since I prefer serving fish hot, I skip the marinating step without incurring a loss of flavor. Serve mashed potatoes on the side.

2 tablespoons plus 2 teaspoons mild olive oil

2 medium onions, thinly sliced

1/2 small green bell pepper, stemmed, seeded, and thinly sliced

1/2 small red bell pepper, stemmed, seeded, and thinly sliced

2 tablespoons golden raisins, plumped in hot water to cover for 30 minutes and drained

1 teaspoon sugar, or more if needed

3 tablespoons red wine vinegar

1/4 cup dry white wine

1/3 cup chicken broth, preferably homemade (page 30)

Salt and freshly ground black pepper

4 catfish fillets (6 ounces each)

2 tablespoons toasted pine nuts (for toasting instructions, see page 64)

1 tablespoon finely chopped flat-leaf parsley leaves

1. Heat 2 tablespoons of the olive oil in a large skillet over medium-low heat. Add the onions and bell peppers and cook, stirring frequently, until the vegetables are tender and uniformly golden, about 20 minutes.

2. Stir in the raisins, 1 teaspoon sugar, vinegar, and wine. Cook until the liquid is slightly reduced, about 1 minute. Add the broth and heat through. Remove from the heat and season to taste with salt, pepper, and a little more sugar, if necessary. The sauce should have a pleasant balance of sweet and sour. Cover and set aside.

3. Heat the remaining 2 teaspoons olive oil in a large nonstick skillet over high heat. Sprinkle the catfish fillets with salt and pepper. Add them to the skillet and cook until the undersides are well browned, about 3 minutes. Turn and cook for 3 minutes more. The catfish is done when the thickest part is no longer translucent and the flesh flakes easily when tested with a fork.

4. Using a wide metal spatula, transfer the catfish to warmed dinner plates. Briefly reheat the onion sauce and spoon some over the fish. Garnish with toasted pine nuts and chopped parsley. Serve immediately.

GRILLED TUNA STEAKS WITH STRAWBERRY SALSA

YIELD: 4 ENTREE SERVINGS

How often have you been served a dry, grainy, flavorless overcooked tuna steak? Tuna is one of the simplest fish to prepare, provided you follow these guidelines: Buy only the freshest tuna; marinate it before cooking; and allow the fish to cook only 1½ to 2 minutes per side. Once you discover how tender and tasty the tuna comes out, you'll see why overcooking is nothing short of a crime. Borrowing the Southwestern idea of serving fruit salsa with grilled food, I pair grilled tuna steaks with an unusually fresh-tasting strawberry salsa, which looks as colorful as it is luscious.

¼ cup firmly packed fresh basil leaves
⅔ cup mild olive oil
2 tablespoons balsamic vinegar
1 tablespoon soy sauce, preferably Kikkoman
½ teaspoon freshly ground black pepper
¼ teaspoon sugar
¼ teaspoon salt
4 tuna steaks (6 ounces each)
Strawberry Salsa (page 3)
4 sprigs fresh basil

1. Place the basil leaves, olive oil, vinegar, soy sauce, pepper, sugar, salt, and 2 tablespoons hot water in a blender and purée.

2. Arrange the tuna steaks in a baking dish large enough to hold them in a single layer. Pour the marinade over the fish. Cover and marinate for 3 to 4 hours in the refrigerator, turning the steaks occasionally.

3. Prepare coals for grilling or preheat the broiler.

4. Drain the tuna steaks and grill them over medium-hot coals or broil 4 to 5 inches from the heat until charred on the outside but still pink in the center, about 3 minutes, turning the steaks once. Do not overcook. Remove from the heat and place the steaks on warmed dinner plates.

5. Spoon the strawberry salsa over the tuna, garnish each with a sprig of basil, and serve immediately.

VARIATION

GRILLED TUNA WITH SAUTEED TROPICAL FRUITS: Marinate and grill the tuna steaks as directed above. Melt 2 tablespoons butter in a large skillet over medium-high heat. Add to the skillet ½ cup each diced fresh banana, pineapple, mango, and papaya, with 2 tablespoons chopped fresh cilantro leaves, 2 tablespoons fresh lemon juice, and 1 tablespoon sugar. Sauté just until the mixture is heated through, about 30 seconds. Do not overcook. Season to taste with salt and freshly ground black pepper. Spoon the sautéed fruit mixture over the tuna and serve immediately.

TUNA CEVICHE

YIELD: 8 APPETIZER OR 4 ENTREE SERVINGS

Using citrus fruits to flavor and cold-cook fish and shellfish is fundamental to South America's culinary tradition. Zesty with minced hot peppers, red onions, and fresh cilantro, ceviche is a wonderfully refreshing appetizer or a light meal in itself. In Peru, its land of origin, ceviche is always served with lettuce and boiled sweet potatoes. In Ecuador, it is made with the juice of bitter Seville oranges, which unfortunately, are seldom available here. A combination of lime and lemon juices produces a similar result, that even if not quite authentic, is very good. If you have never eaten ceviche before, try this version with fresh tuna. You'll become an instant convert! Because the tuna is barely "cooked" by the acidity of the citrus juices, be sure to buy only the freshest,

top-quality tuna such as yellowfin, from a trusted fishmonger, preferably one who caters to sushi bars. Anything less won't do. The best tuna should feel buttery between your fingers and be of a uniformly rosy color. Avoid tuna that is unevenly gray or brown or that shows any rainbow sheen.

If you are not in the habit of eating half-cooked fish, or are worried about salmonella contamination, you can still enjoy this dish by cooking the tuna slightly before marinating it. Sauté over high heat for no more than 1 minute per side, until it is just browned on the outside, but still slightly raw on the inside. The fish will be cooked further by the citrus juices while marinating.

½ cup fresh lime juice
½ cup fresh lemon juice
1 fresh serrano or jalapeño pepper, minced
2 tablespoons shredded fresh cilantro leaves
  (for shredding instructions, see page 34)
½ small red onion, thinly sliced
1 pound very fresh tuna fillet, cut into
  ¾-inch cubes
½ red bell pepper, stemmed, seeded,
  and julienned
½ green bell pepper, stemmed, seeded,
  and julienned
½ yellow bell pepper, stemmed, seeded,
  and julienned
1 ripe but firm avocado
4 ripe plum tomatoes (about ½ pound total)
¼ cup extra-virgin olive oil
Salt and freshly ground black pepper
12 romaine lettuce leaves, taken from the
  heart

1. Combine the lime juice, lemon juice, serrano pepper, cilantro, and onion in a large ceramic bowl. Add the tuna and toss well.

2. Cover the tuna with the bell peppers, pressing to immerse them in the marinade. Cover and refrigerate for at least 1 hour but no longer than 2 hours.

3. Just before serving, peel, pit, and cut the avocado into ³/₄-inch cubes. Core, seed, and finely dice the tomatoes. Drain the ceviche. Add the avocado, tomatoes, and olive oil and toss gently to combine. Season to taste with salt and pepper.

4. Fan 3 romaine lettuce leaves on each dinner plate and mound some ceviche in the center. Serve immediately.

GLAZED SWORDFISH AND TROPICAL FRUIT KABOBS

YIELD: 4 ENTREE SERVINGS

The delicate sweet and sour peach glaze and the smoky flavor of grilling give these kabobs many dimensions. (An equally delicious glaze can be made with ¹/₂ cup chopped ripe plums or mango.) Any firm-fleshed seafood, such as tuna, monkfish, grouper, scallops, or shrimp, can stand in for the swordfish. Serve these kabobs with steamed white rice or Quinoa Pilaf (see Index).

PEACH GLAZE

3 tablespoons soy sauce, preferably Kikkoman

2 tablespoons hoisin sauce

2 teaspoons rice vinegar or cider vinegar

1 teaspoon sugar

1 teaspoon Asian sesame oil

¹/₂ teaspoon chile paste with garlic

1 teaspoon finely grated peeled fresh ginger

1 large ripe peach, peeled, pitted, and quartered, or ¹/₂ cup thawed frozen peaches

KABOBS

1¹/₂ pounds swordfish steaks or loin, cut into 1-inch cubes

2 large star fruits, sliced crosswise into ¹/₂-inch-thick stars

1 medium pineapple, peeled, cored, and cut into 1-inch cubes

8 cherry tomatoes

2 tablespoons mild olive oil

Salt and freshly ground black pepper

1. Prepare coals for grilling or preheat the broiler.

2. To make the glaze, place all the ingredients in a blender and purée. Set aside.

3. To make the kabobs, thread the swordfish, star fruit, pineapple, and cherry tomatoes

PINEAPPLE PRIMER

Pineapples can ripen only on the plant, having no starch reserves to convert into sugar after they are harvested. However, once picked, a fresh pineapple may lose some of its acidity and therefore taste sweeter. Fragrance is the best indicator of a pineapple's sweetness; it should smell fresh and faintly of pineapple, with no hint of fermentation. Select a firm, plump fruit with a bright green crown. The sooner a fresh pineapple is eaten the better. Cut pineapple keeps best and longest in a plastic bag in the refrigerator.

Cooks should know that raw pineapple contains bromelain, an enzyme with a denaturing effect on the protein in poultry, fish, and meat, which interferes with gelatin's thickening ability. Because of bromelain, dairy products also break down and separate if allowed to stand for more than a few minutes once they're combined with fresh pineapple. To deactivate the enzyme, simmer the fruit for a couple minutes. Or wait until the last minute to fold fresh pineapple into cream cheese or cottage cheese, sour cream, or whipped cream.

A WORD OF CAUTION: Like mango, pineapple skin has resin that produces an itchy rash. Those who are allergic should wear rubber gloves when preparing these fruits.

onto four 14-inch metal skewers or 8 shorter skewers until all the ingredients are used up. Brush lightly with olive oil and sprinkle with salt and pepper.

4. Grill the kabobs over medium-hot coals or broil 4 to 5 inches from the heat, turning once, until the fish is just opaque in the center, about 3 minutes per side. Brush the kabobs lightly with the peach glaze during the last 2 minutes of cooking, turning the kabobs once and taking care to not let the glaze burn (if necessary, move the kabobs to the cooler edges of the grill to finish cooking). Serve immediately.

SALMON WITH PINEAPPLE-TOMATO VINAIGRETTE

YIELD: 4 ENTREE SERVINGS

This is a dish that requires a minimum of fuss but provides a maximum of flavor. Succulent salmon fillets are steamed and then topped with a refreshing vinaigrette infused with fresh basil and sweet, tangy pineapple. You may substitute ½ cup of diced peach, papaya, or green apple for the pineapple.

¼ cup fresh lime juice

¼ cup extra-virgin olive oil

2 tablespoons plus 2 teaspoons soy sauce,
    preferably Kikkoman

3 tablespoons finely chopped shallots

1 teaspoon sugar

½ cup cubed fresh pineapple

2 plum tomatoes, seeded and cubed
    (about ½ cup)

1 fresh jalapeño pepper, minced

2 tablespoons finely shredded fresh basil
    leaves (for shredding instructions, see
    page 34)

Salt and freshly ground black pepper

4 skinless salmon fillets (6 ounces each),
    about ¾ inch thick

1. In a small bowl, whisk together the lime juice, olive oil, soy sauce, shallots, and sugar. Add the diced pineapple, tomatoes, jalapeño, and basil, and stir with a wooden spoon to combine. Season to taste with salt and pepper, if necessary. (There should be about 1½ cups of vinaigrette.) Cover and let sit at room temperature for at least 30 minutes for the flavors to marry.

2. Pour water to a depth of 2 inches into a wok or a wide, shallow pan fitted with a steamer rack or bamboo steamer. Bring the water to a boil over medium heat.

3. Lightly season the salmon fillets with salt and pepper and arrange them on a heatproof plate that fits easily into the steamer. Place the plate of fish on the steamer rack and tightly cover the steamer. Steam the salmon until it is opaque, and the flesh flakes easily when tested with a fork, about 5 to 8 minutes, depending on the thickness of the fish.

4. Using a wide metal spatula, transfer the steamed salmon to warmed dinner plates. Spoon some of the vinaigrette over the top. Serve immediately.

The flesh of the pineapple melts into water and it is so flavorful that one finds in it the aroma of the peach, the apple, the quince, and the Muscat grape. I can with justice call it the king of fruits because it is the most beautiful and the best of all those of the earth. It is doubtless for this reason that the King of Kings has put a crown upon its head, which is like the essential mark of its royalty.

—PERE DU TERTRE, A 16TH-CENTURY FRENCH MISSIONARY/AGRONOMER

SALMON CAKES WITH GINGERED CITRUS SAUCE

YIELD: 8 APPETIZER OR 4 ENTREE SERVINGS

In this unusual twist on conventional fish cakes, I have combined salmon with couscous, a Moroccan pasta, to add body and texture. Crusty on the out-side and moist on the inside, these fish cakes are memorable when paired with a creamy orange sauce flavored with zesty ginger. You can also turn this recipe into shrimp cakes by substituting ½ pound shelled, deveined, and coarsely chopped shrimp for the salmon.

⅔ cup couscous (see Note)
3 tablespoons mild olive oil
2 tablespoons chopped shallots
¼ cup dry white wine, preferably
    Chardonnay
1 skinless salmon fillet (10 ounces), cubed
    (½-inch pieces)
2 large eggs, lightly beaten
2 scallions, trimmed and minced (white and
    green parts)
½ teaspoon salt
1 tablespoon unbleached all-purpose flour, plus
    extra for dusting the salmon cakes
Freshly ground black pepper
Gingered Citrus Sauce (recipe follows)

1. Place the couscous in a medium-size mixing bowl.

2. Heat 1 tablespoon of the olive oil in a small saucepan over medium-low heat. Add the shallots and sauté until tender and translucent, about 1 minute. Add the wine along with ½ cup water and bring to a boil. Remove from the heat and pour over the couscous. Stir with a fork to blend.

3. Add the salmon, beaten eggs, scallions, salt, flour, and black pepper and stir well. It will be dense and cling together.

4. Using a ⅓-cup measure as a scoop, divide the salmon mixture into 8 portions. Gently pat each portion into a 3-inch-round cake.

5. Place the salmon cakes on a lightly floured plate, cover with plastic wrap, and refrigerate until needed.

6. Heat the remaining 2 tablespoons olive oil in a large skillet over medium heat. Sprinkle a little flour over the top of each salmon cake and add the cakes to the skillet. Fry until deep golden, about 2½ minutes per side. Drain on paper towels.

7. Spoon some Gingered Citrus Sauce onto dinner plates and top with the salmon cakes. Serve at once.

NOTE: Couscous is a finely textured, blond Moroccan pasta that resembles a grain. It's made from finely ground durum wheat (semolina), which has been precooked. It's available in most supermarkets and health-food stores.

Gingered Citrus Sauce

YIELD: 1 ½ CUPS

Don't save this creamy sauce just for salmon cakes. It's also marvelous with cold poached salmon, and it makes a great topping for grilled fish, leeks, and roast meats.

8 quarter-size slices peeled fresh ginger
  (1½ ounces total), coarsely chopped
2 large hard-cooked egg yolks
2 teaspoons Dijon mustard
2 teaspoons sugar
¼ teaspoon freshly ground white pepper
¼ teaspoon salt, or to taste
½ cup safflower oil or corn oil
3 tablespoons fresh orange juice
2 teaspoons fresh lemon juice
Dash of Tabasco sauce

1. Place the ginger, cooked egg yolks, mustard, sugar, white pepper, and salt in a blender and process until the ginger is finely puréed. With the motor running, gradually add the oil until it's emulsified, about 30 seconds. Add the orange juice, lemon juice, and a dash of Tabasco sauce and blend just to combine. Adjust the seasoning, if necessary; the sauce should be well balanced, not too spicy, tangy, or sweet.

2. Transfer the sauce to a container, cover, and refrigerate (it will keep for 5 days). Stir before using.

SPICE-RUBBED RED SNAPPER

YIELD: 4 ENTREE SERVINGS

I have crossed elements of Southwestern and Floridian cooking to create this wonderful dish. The combination of smoky, delicate fish with fragrant spices, tart and sweet citrus, and creamy butter is my idea of truly great food. Be sure to leave the skin on the fillets. Once cooked, its crackly-crisp texture will add to your enjoyment. Some steamed asparagus on the side makes for a tasty and elegant meal.

BARBECUE SPICE MIX

1 tablespoon cumin seeds
1 teaspoon coriander seeds
1 tablespoon (firmly packed) light brown sugar
1 teaspoon ground cinnamon
1 teaspoon grated tangerine zest
1/2 teaspoon salt
1/2 teaspoon cayenne pepper
1/2 teaspoon freshly ground black pepper

TANGERINE BUTTER SAUCE

1 cup fresh tangerine juice
8 tablespoons (1 stick) unsalted butter,
  cut into 4 pieces
Salt
4 red snapper or sea bass fillets (6 ounces
  each), skin on
2 tablespoons mild olive oil

1. To make the spice mix, place the cumin and coriander seeds in a small dry skillet. Cook over medium-low heat, until the seeds are lightly toasted and fragrant, about 2 minutes. Let cool. Place the toasted seeds and the remaining ingredients for the spice mix in a spice grinder and blend to a fine powder. (At this point, the spice powder may be sealed in a jar and refrigerated for up to 1 week.)

2. To make the sauce, place the tangerine juice in a medium-size saucepan and bring to a boil over medium heat. Continue cooking until the juice becomes syrupy and reduced to about 1/4 cup, 4 to 5 minutes. Remove from the heat and stir in the butter, 1 piece at a time, until it is completely melted and the sauce is smooth and glossy. Season to taste with salt. (At this point, the sauce may be covered and left at room temperature for up to 2 hours before serving.)

3. Ten minutes before serving, use a sharp knife to lightly score the skin of each fillet to prevent curling during cooking. Rub the fillets on both sides with the barbecue spice mix and set aside.

4. In a large, heavy skillet over medium-high heat, heat the oil until smoking. Carefully add the fillets, skin side down. To prevent the fillets from warping, keep them flat with a wide metal spatula during the first minute of cooking. Cook until the skin is well charred, about 2 minutes. Turn the fillets and cook until the flesh flakes easily when tested with a fork, about 2 minutes more. Remove from the heat, cover, and allow the fillets to sit for about 2 minutes longer before serving.

5. Divide the tangerine sauce among warmed dinner plates and top with the fish fillets. Serve at once.

TAMARIND

Tamarind, the pod of a tropical tree, is eaten like a fruit and used in cooking in Africa, Latin America, India, and Southeast Asia. Much like vinegar, lemon juice, and lime juice, tamarind imparts a complex, fruity, sour taste (like a combination of lime juice and raisins or prunes) to soups, sauces, pickles, chutneys, and drinks. The pods, which are 3 to 4 inches long, resemble fat, broad beans, and have brownish barklike shells when ripe. Inside, the beans are shiny dark brown seeds covered by a reddish-brown, sticky pulp. In Laos, where I used to live, the green, unripe pods were typically pickled, and the ripe pulp sold either plain or spiced with chile and rolled in sugar. Both were eaten as snacks.

Fresh tamarind pods are sporadically available in Latin American markets, and in Asian groceries that feature the foods of Thailand, Vietnam, and India. More widely available is prepackaged tamarind pulp sold in 8-ounce blocks (choose the softest block you can find).

To prepare tamarind for flavoring a dish, soak the pulp in boiling water for 5 to 10 minutes, mash it well with your fingers or a fork to free the pulp from the seeds and fibers, and strain the mixture through a fine sieve, pressing on the solids to extract the juice. Discard the solids. As a rule of thumb, use ⅓ cup boiling water for every 1 tablespoon tamarind pulp. If you use whole tamarind pods, peel them before soaking. Use the ratio of ½ cup boiling water to 2 or 3 pods (the equivalent of 1 tablespoon of packaged tamarind pulp).

Seal any leftover tamarind pulp in a plastic bag, and store it at room temperature where it will keep fresh and soft for several months. Frozen, it will keep indefinitely. Thaw before using.

SEA BASS WITH SPICY TAMARIND SAUCE

YIELD: 4 ENTREE SERVINGS

The pleasure of cooking with tamarind is becoming more accessible with the profusion of Latin and Southeast Asian markets in America, which carry tamarind packaged and fresh. This is my adaptation of a popular Thai specialty in which the sweet and sour tamarind plays off pungent ginger, complementing perfectly the moist sea bass fillets. I've taught this recipe in my cooking classes and students invariably love it. Instead of fish, you may use shrimp, but sauté it for only 2 minutes. Serve with steamed jasmine rice.

2 tablespoons tamarind pulp

²⁄₃ cup boiling water

2 tablespoons Thai fish sauce

2 tablespoons soy sauce, preferably Kikkoman

3 tablespoons (firmly packed) light brown
    sugar

¾ cup unbleached all-purpose flour

4 sea bass or red snapper fillets (6 ounces each)

Freshly ground black pepper

3 tablespoons vegetable oil

1 tablespoon minced garlic

2 quarter-size slices peeled fresh ginger, thinly
    shredded (about 1 tablespoon total)

1½ teaspoons Thai red curry paste

2 scallions, trimmed and thinly sliced (white
    and green parts)

Fresh cilantro sprigs, for garnish

1. Place the tamarind and boiling water in a small bowl and let sit for 5 to 10 minutes. When the tamarind has become quite soft, press the lump and stir with your fingers or a fork to dissolve as much pulp as possible. Strain through a fine sieve, pressing on the solids to extract as much juice as possible. Discard the solids. (You should have about ⅓ cup tamarind juice.) Add the fish sauce, soy sauce, and brown sugar to the tamarind juice and stir until the sugar is dissolved. Set aside.

2. Place the flour on a large platter. Using a sharp knife, lightly score the skin of each fillet to prevent curling during cooking. Pat the fillets dry and sprinkle with pepper. Dredge each fillet in the flour, shaking off any excess.

3. Place a large skillet over high heat for 10 seconds, then add 1½ tablespoons of the oil. When the oil begins to smoke, add the fillets, skin side down. Cover, reduce the heat to medium-high, and cook until the skin is crisp and golden brown and the fish flakes easily when tested with a fork, about 5 minutes. Using a wide metal spatula, transfer the fillets to a platter and cover to keep warm.

4. Wipe the skillet clean and return it to high heat for 30 seconds. Add the remaining 1½ tablespoons oil and stir-fry the garlic, ginger, and curry paste until aromatic, about 30 seconds. Add the tamarind-fish sauce mixture and cook until the sauce is slightly thickened, about 1 minute. Do not reduce the sauce too much, or it will be too salty.

5. Remove from the heat and stir in the scallions. Spoon the sauce over the fillets. Garnish with cilantro sprigs and serve.

A FESTIVE THAI SUPPER

SEA BASS WITH
SPICY TAMARIND SAUCE

✦

THAI GREEN APPLE SALSA

✦

STIR-FRIED SPINACH

✦

STEAMED JASMINE RICE

✦

LITCHEE-PINEAPPLE BING

GRILLED SOFT-SHELL CRABS WITH CITRUS VINAIGRETTE

YIELD: 4 ENTREE SERVINGS

From late May to early June, when blue crabs shed their shells, they are marketed as soft-shell crabs.

Because of their extremely short season, most soft-shell crabs are frozen so they can be marketed all year long. These sweet, tender creatures are considered a true prize, and command hefty prices. Whether they're fresh or frozen, soft-shell crabs are too delicate—and too dear—to smother in a heavy sauce that masks their flavor. Typically they are pan-fried or deep-fried, but I think they are absolutely delicious grilled. A zesty, refreshing citrus vinaigrette is all it takes to bring out their sweet taste. If you don't have an outdoor or stove-top grill,

HOW TO DRESS SOFT-SHELL CRABS

Soft-shell crabs are not especially difficult to dress, or prepare for cooking. Your fishmonger will certainly do it for you, but if you are faced with dressing a soft-shell crab on your own, just follow these simple instructions:

1. Peel back the pointed shell from each side of the front of the crab's body and remove the spongy white gills.

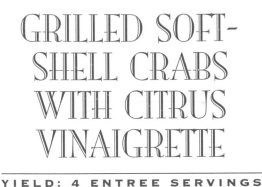

3. Remove the tail flap (apron) by pulling it up and twisting it off.

2. Turn the crab on its back. With a knife or scissors, remove the head by cutting just behind the eyes. Squeeze the cut area gently to force out any green fluid, which has a bitter and unpleasant flavor.

4. Rinse the crab under cold water, and pat dry with paper towels.

you can sauté the crabs in a nonstick pan with 2 teaspoons of oil or broil them. Another good sauce for this dish is Gingered Citrus Sauce (see Index). Serve grilled vegetables on the side.

2 tablespoons mild olive oil
2 tablespoons fresh lemon juice
Salt and freshly ground black pepper
8 soft-shell crabs, dressed (see box, facing page)
Citrus Vinaigrette (recipe follows)

1. Combine the olive oil, lemon juice, and salt and pepper to taste in a shallow dish. Marinate the crabs in this mixture for 10 minutes, turning once.

2. Prepare coals for grilling or preheat the broiler. If using a stove-top grill, place it over medium-high heat until very hot.

3. Grill the crabs (or broil 4 to 5 inches from the heat), basting frequently with the marinade, until the shells are nicely crisp and a deep reddish brown, about 3 minutes per side. Arrange the crabs on warmed dinner plates and spoon the Citrus Vinaigrette over them.

Citrus Vinaigrette

YIELD: ABOUT 2⅔ CUPS

For a vibrant dressing, add the citrus fruits to the vinaigrette just before serving. It goes well with steamed salmon, or grilled chicken breasts too. For instructions on sectioning citrus fruit, see page 318.

½ cup extra-virgin olive oil
3 tablespoons soy sauce, preferably Kikkoman
1 tablespoon plus 1 teaspoon sherry vinegar or balsamic vinegar
1 tablespoon plus 1 teaspoon finely shredded peeled fresh ginger
¼ teaspoon salt
½ teaspoon Tabasco sauce
2 tablespoons boiling water
2 medium oranges, peeled, sectioned, and diced
1 large pink grapefruit, peeled, sectioned, and diced
1 medium lime, peeled, sectioned, and diced
1 medium lemon, peeled, sectioned, and diced
1 teaspoon cracked black peppercorns
2 tablespoons finely shredded fresh basil leaves (for shredding instructions, see page 35)

1. Place the olive oil, soy sauce, vinegar, ginger, salt, Tabasco sauce, and boiling water in a medium-size jar. Cover and shake well. Set the vinaigrette aside.

2. Just before serving, combine the diced fruits in a medium-size non-reactive mixing bowl and pour off any excess juice. Add the cracked pepper, basil, and vinaigrette and toss gently to combine. Serve immediately.

SHRIMP CALYPSO

YIELD: 2 ENTREE SERVINGS

When I got home from a short vacation in the Caribbean, I developed this quick and tasty dish. The vibrant blend of spices, juicy mango, and toasted coconut never fail to transport me back to those sunny isles. If you wish to serve a richer entrée, add ¼ cup heavy cream along with the wine and orange juice when you cook this dish. Serve it over steamed rice or with bread. You may substitute fresh papaya for the mango.

1 pound fresh large shrimp (21 to 25), shelled
  and deveined
¼ teaspoon salt
¼ teaspoon dried oregano, crumbled
¼ teaspoon dried thyme, crumbled
¼ teaspoon ground cumin
¼ teaspoon sweet paprika
⅛ teaspoon cayenne pepper
⅛ teaspoon freshly ground black pepper
1 tablespoon mild olive oil
¼ cup chopped shallots
2 tablespoons dry white wine
2 tablespoons fresh orange juice
½ large mango, peeled, pitted, and sliced
  ⅜ inch thick
1 tablespoon chopped fresh cilantro leaves
¼ cup sweetened shredded coconut, toasted
  (for toasting instructions, see page 64)

1. Place the shrimp in a medium-size bowl. In a separate bowl, combine the salt, oregano, thyme, cumin, paprika, cayenne, and black pepper, and sprinkle the mixture over the shrimp. Toss well, cover, and refrigerate until needed.

2. Heat the oil in a large skillet over high heat. Add the shallots and the shrimp and sauté until the shrimp turn pink, about 2 minutes.

3. Add the wine and orange juice, and cook until almost all the liquid is absorbed. Add the mango, and cook until it is just heated through, 1 minute more.

4. Remove the pan from the heat and stir in the cilantro. Adjust the seasoning if necessary.

5. Transfer the shrimp to warmed dinner plates. Sprinkle with toasted coconut and serve immediately.

A mango is the choicest fruit of India.

—AMIR KHUSRAU

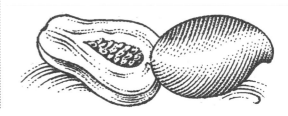

BARBECUED SHRIMP

YIELD: 4 APPETIZER OR 2 ENTREE SERVINGS

Try this dish and you'll agree that shrimp, peach, and rosemary make a great trio. I call this dish barbecued because the seared shrimp are coated with a spicy and sweet peach glaze reminiscent of barbecue sauce. If possible, buy extra large fresh shrimp with the heads attached; that's where all the sweet, juicy roe is. The nutritious bright-orange roe is considered a great delicacy because it is so flavorful.

Since most shrimp is sold without heads, ask your fishmonger to put in a special order for fresh Louisiana shrimp, also known as freshwater shrimp. This unusually sweet variety is typically caught in areas where fresh and salt water meet (lagoons and Mississippi River tributaries in the Gulf of Mexico). Don't worry if whole shrimp are unavailable; this dish is also great with headless everyday shrimp.

CLEANING WHOLE SHRIMP

To clean shrimp with the heads attached, use a pair of small scissors to snip off the top of the head by cutting just below the eyes. Holding the shrimp firmly by the head, insert the tip of the scissors into the shell at the back, where the head and body are joined, and cut the shell down the center to the tail. As you cut, try to barely slit the meat open to expose the vein at the same time. Still holding the shrimp by the head, peel the shell off the body. Remove and discard the black vein that runs along the back. The head will remain attached.

Accompany the shrimp with rice as a main course, or as an appetizer with some good bread to soak up all the delicious sauce. If you make this with whole shrimp be sure to suck the roe before discarding the head.

2 tablespoons unsalted butter
½ cup sliced shallots or onion
1 teaspoon finely chopped fresh rosemary leaves
1 pound extra large fresh shrimp (16 to 20), peeled and deveined and with heads on
Peach glaze (page 142, step 2)

1. Melt the butter in a large skillet over medium-high heat. Add the shallots and rosemary and sauté until they are tender and fragrant, about 1 minute. Add the shrimp and sauté until they start to turn pink, about 1 minute.

2. Stir in the peach glaze and cook until the mixture is thickened and the shrimp are well glazed, 1 minute longer. Serve at once.

CITRUS SHRIMP WITH PROSCIUTTO

YIELD: 4 APPETIZER OR 2 ENTREE SERVINGS

One of my favorite neighborhood Italian restaurants inspired this recipe. Fresh orange juice, orange zest, and Grand Marnier plus a generous helping of salty prosciutto flavor this simple but colorful dish of sautéed shrimp. I often serve these shrimp over pasta for a casual dinner.

8 thin slices imported prosciutto (about ¼ pound), halved crosswise
13 fresh medium shrimp (½ pound), shelled and deveined
Unbleached all-purpose flour
1 tablespoon mild olive oil
2 large shallots, finely chopped
1½ teaspoons minced garlic
1 cup fresh orange juice
¼ cup orange liqueur, such as Grand Marnier or Triple Sec
Finely grated zest of 2 oranges (about 1 teaspoon total)
Freshly ground black pepper

1. Tightly wrap a slice of prosciutto around each shrimp. Dredge the wrapped shrimp in the flour, shaking off any excess.

2. Heat the olive oil in a large skillet over medium-high heat. Add the wrapped shrimp in 1 layer and cook for 1 minute on each side. Transfer the shrimp to a plate.

3. Add the shallots and garlic to the skillet and sauté until they are tender and fragrant, about 1 minute. Stir in the orange juice, orange liqueur, and orange zest. Bring to a boil over high heat and cook until the liquid is reduced by half and beginning to thicken, about 1 minute.

4. Return the shrimp to the pan, and cook, turning, until just heated through. Remove from the heat. Season the sauce to taste with pepper and serve at once.

LOBSTER VERONIQUE

YIELD: 2 ENTREE SERVINGS

In French cuisine, the word *Véronique* indicates that a dish is prepared with green seedless grapes. Typically, fillets of sole are paired with grapes, but lobsters and shrimp also have a great affinity for this fruit. In this easy, tantalizing recipe, the sweet and sour sauce is made from grape and citrus juices, and enriched with a dab of sweet butter at the last minute. Spooned over boiled lobsters, it tastes just wonderful.

¾ pound stemmed seedless green grapes, halved

2 live Maine lobsters (1¼ to 1½ pounds each)

⅓ cup dry white wine, preferably Chardonnay

3 tablespoons (or more) fresh orange juice

1½ tablespoons fresh lemon juice

2 tablespoons finely chopped shallots

½ teaspoon minced garlic

1 tablespoon unsalted butter

Salt and freshly ground black pepper

1. Place all but ½ cup of the halved grapes in a food processor or blender and purée them. Strain the puréed grapes in a fine sieve, pressing on the pulp to extract as much juice as possible. (There should be about ¾ cup grape juice.) Discard the solids. (This can be prepared 1 day ahead and stored, covered, in the refrigerator.)

2. In a pot large enough to easily hold both of the lobsters, bring plenty of salted water to a rolling boil over high heat. Rinse the lobsters briefly under cold running water. Without removing the rubber bands around their claws, plunge the lobsters head-first into the boiling water. Quickly cover the pot and bring the water back to a boil. Timing from the moment the water returns to a boil, cook the lobsters about 12 minutes longer.

3. Meanwhile, make the sauce: Combine the grape juice, wine, orange and lemon juices, shallots, and garlic in a large skillet. Bring the mixture to a boil over high heat, and cook until it's reduced by half and slightly thickened, 2 to 3 minutes. Add the reserved grapes and stir until they are just heated through, about 30 seconds. Remove from the heat, add the butter, and stir until it's completely melted. If the sauce is a bit too thick, thin it with a little orange juice. Season to taste with salt and pepper.

4. Remove the lobsters from the pot with tongs and place them on their backs on a cutting board. Plunge a large knife right into the middle of the body of a lobster and split it in half from head to tail without going through the back shell. (To hold the lobster in place and protect your hands as you do this, use a pot holder or a folded kitchen towel.) Use both hands to crack open the lobster. Remove and discard the dark vein, the sand sac near the head, and any spongy tissue, but leave in the liver (tomalley) and coral (roe), if there is any (see Note, page 162). Pull off the claws and remove the rubber bands. Crack the claws with a mallet or hammer and remove the meat.

5. Place the lobsters, meat side up, on warmed dinner plates. Spoon the sauce over the lobsters and serve at once.

GRILLED LOBSTER, VIETNAMESE STYLE

YIELD: 4 ENTREE SERVINGS

Most of us enjoy picking the meat from a freshly cooked lobster and dipping it, morsel by morsel, into warm clarified butter. It's certainly delicious—if we don't think about the extra calories! Here's an excellent alternative to drawn butter. Once you try lobster dipped in a sweet and spicy pineapple sauce, you may never want to dive into that butter again. This sauce will taste just as delicious with grilled chicken breasts, pork chops, or, for that matter, almost anything. Grilled corn on the cob is a great side dish here.

SPICY PINEAPPLE DIP

1½ teaspoons minced garlic

2 fresh hot red chile peppers or jalapeño
*   peppers, coarsely chopped*

3 tablespoons sugar

¼ cup rice vinegar or distilled white
*   vinegar*

½ cup fresh pineapple juice (for juicing
*   instructions, see page 259)*

¼ cup fresh lime juice

¼ cup plus 1 tablespoon Thai fish
*   sauce*

LOBSTERS

4 live Maine lobsters (1¼ to 1½ pounds each)

1½ tablespoons peanut oil

Salt and freshly ground black pepper

1. Using a mortar and pestle or spice ginder, crush the garlic, chile peppers, and 1 tablespoon of the sugar to a fine paste. Alternatively, you can chop the garlic, chile peppers, and 1 tablespoon of the sugar together and then, with the flat side of a chef's knife, mash the mixture to a fine paste.

2. Transfer the paste to a small bowl and add the remaining 2 tablespoons sugar, vinegar, pineapple and lime juices, and fish sauce. Stir until the sugar is dissolved. Refrigerate, covered, until ready to serve.

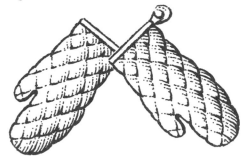

3. In a pot large enough to easily hold the lobsters, bring plenty of salted water to a rolling boil over high heat. Rinse the lobsters briefly under cold running water. Without removing the rubber bands around their claws, plunge the lobsters head first into the boiling water. Quickly cover the pot and bring the water back to a boil. Timing from the moment the water returns to a boil, cook for 5 minutes longer. (The lobster meat will not be fully cooked at this point; it will cook further on the grill.) Remove the lobsters

GRILLING TIPS

Before you begin, scrub the grill rack with a steel brush and soapy water to remove any debris that might cause the food to stick or pick up undesirable flavors. (You could take this measure after a meal, of course, but waiting for the fire to burn out completely so the grill rack is cool enough to handle could mean staying up way past your bedtime. It's fine to wait to clean the grill—as long as you clean it.)

✦ *Remove all old ashes from the grill before you get started, so they don't interfere with air circulation around the fire.*

✦ *Start the fire 30 to 45 minutes before grilling, to give the flames time to subside. Avoid grilling over extremely hot, glowing red coals. Wait until they are covered with whitish-gray ash; at this stage the heat is medium-hot and best for cooking most foods.*

✦ *To test the temperature of the fire, hold your hand 5 to 6 inches above the coals. If you can hold your hand there for just 1 to 2 seconds before it gets too hot, the fire is very hot; 3 to 4 seconds, a hot to medium-hot fire; 5 to 6 seconds, a medium fire; and 7 to 8 seconds, a low fire.*

✦ *Before putting your food on the grill, be sure to rearrange the coals by spreading them out evenly with a long fork. This will also prevent flare-ups during cooking. In case you have flare-ups (a covered grill will not flare up), spray water lightly on the flames.*

✦ *When grilling, always use fireproof mitts and tools with long, heat-resistant handles. Don't wear loose-sleeved or billowy clothing when grilling. Never add lighter fluid to a smoldering fire, and never use kerosene or gasoline.*

---

from the pot with tongs, place in a colander, and cool under cold running water. Remove the rubber bands from the claws.

4. Prepare coals for grilling.

5. Place each lobster on its back on a cutting board. Plunge a large knife right into the middle of the body of a lobster and split it in half from head to tail without going through the back shell. (To hold the lobster in place and to protect your hands as you do this, use a pot holder or a folded kitchen towel.) Use both hands to crack open the lobster. Remove and discard the dark vein, the sand sac near the head, and any spongy tissue, but leave the liver (tomalley) and coral (roe), if there is any (see Note page 158). Pull off the claws and crack them slightly with a mallet or hammer. Lightly rub both sides of the lobsters with peanut oil. Sprinkle the meat with salt and pepper.

6. When the coals are medium-hot place the lobsters, cut side up, on the grill. Cover the grill, and cook just until the lobsters are heated through, 8 to 10 minutes. (Test by inserting a small knife into the flesh and then touching the side of the blade to your lip or tongue; it should feel hot. Or lift a piece of tail meat from its shell, cut through the meat with a small paring knife, and take a peek; it should be firm and opaque throughout.)

7. Place the grilled lobsters on dinner plates and serve with ramekins of the spicy pineapple sauce on the side for dipping.

NOTE: Both the tomalley and coral are delicious to eat as is, but for a special treat, mash them with 1 stick of room-temperature unsalted butter until smooth. Spread the mixture on baguette slices and toast under a preheated broiler until the butter has melted and the bread is golden brown. Serve the delicious toasted bread alongside the lobsters, if desired.

SCALLOP CURRY WITH THAI FLAVORS

YIELD: 4 ENTREE SERVINGS

A plate of steaming jasmine rice topped with an aromatic, spicy seafood and fruit melange is wonderfully tempting. Delicate sweet and tart slices of star fruit tame the heat of the curry, but apple or banana will work well if star fruit is not in season. Instead of scallops, you may use boneless, skinless chicken breasts trimmed of excess fat and sliced ½ inch thick, with delicious results. Green curry paste, unsweetened

GREAT MATCHES

STAR FRUIT (CARAMBOLA)

Tart, clean star fruit is a stellar complement to creamy cheeses like fromage blanc and fresh goat cheese. It's also refreshing with chocolate and nuts, especially hazelnuts and macadamias. Star fruit goes well with most meats, poultry, seafood, and herbs of all kinds.

coconut milk, fish sauce, and kaffir lime leaves are available at Thai markets.

1½ cups canned unsweetened coconut milk, well stirred

4 fresh or frozen kaffir lime leaves or the zest of 1 lime

4 teaspoons Thai green curry paste

1 tablespoon Thai fish sauce, or salt to taste

½ teaspoon sugar

1 heaping tablespoon thawed frozen spinach (see Note)

1 tablespoon vegetable oil

½ cup chopped onion

⅓ cup finely shredded fresh Thai or common basil leaves (for shredding instructions, see page 34)

1½ pounds fresh sea scallops, halved if very large

2 large star fruits, sliced crosswise into ⅛-inch-thick stars

½ cup frozen peas

1 large ripe tomato, peeled, cored, seeded, and diced

Fresh cilantro sprigs, for garnish

1. Place the coconut milk and lime leaves in a small, heavy-bottomed saucepan and bring to a boil over medium heat. Reduce the heat and simmer until the coconut milk is slightly thickened, 8 to 10 minutes, stirring occasionally. Add 2 teaspoons of green curry paste and stir until it dissolves. Continue cooking the mixture until the curry paste is fragrant, 1 to 2 minutes. Remove the pan from the heat.

2. Remove and discard the lime leaves from the coconut milk (or strain, discarding the lime zest). Add the fish sauce (or salt), sugar, and spinach and transfer to a blender. Purée and set aside.

3. Heat the oil in a large skillet over medium-high heat. Add the onion and basil and quickly stir-fry until the onion is soft, about 30 seconds. Add the scallops and the remaining 2 teaspoons curry paste. Stir-fry until the scallops are cooked on the outside but a bit raw on the inside and the pieces are evenly coated with the paste, about 40 seconds. Add the reserved sauce, along with the star fruits and peas. Cook until the star fruits and peas are just heated through, about 1 minute. (If the sauce is too thin, use a slotted spoon to transfer the scallops, fruits, and peas to a serving bowl and continue cooking the sauce until it reaches the consistency of heavy cream, about 5 minutes.)

4. Transfer the curry to a serving bowl, and sprinkle the chopped tomato over the top. Garnish with cilantro sprigs and serve at once.

NOTE: You don't have to thaw a whole box of spinach to get a small amount. Just chop off the amount you need from the frozen brick. Carefully rewrap the remaining spinach and, to prevent melting, quickly return it to the freezer.

ASIAN DINNER PARTY

NAPA SLAW WITH GRAPES

◆

SCALLOP CURRY WITH THAI FLAVORS

◆

HONG KONG FRIED RICE

◆

SAUTEED SNOW PEAS

◆

MANGO TEA AND LITCHEE HONEY ICE CREAM

WINE AND FOOD: SOME CREATIVE PAIRINGS

or me, matching wine and dishes containing fruit is endlessly stimulating and challenging. The possibilities only begin with the conventional wisdom of white wines with fish and fowl, and red wines with meat. But even that commonly accepted principle has many exceptions.

All table wines contain flavors and components that are enhanced or diminished by food. Perhaps most readily identifiable to the untrained palate is sweetness. So many fresh and dried fruit flavors and fragrances are found in wine that fruit is a natural bridge ingredient. Apple, pear, melon, and even tropical fruit flavors are common in Riesling, Chardonnay, Gewürztraminer, Sauvignon Blanc, or Semillon. Ripe fresh berries and cherries dominate many Beaujolais and Pinot Noirs, and even hearty Cabernets can have similar flavors. Dried fruit, like figs, dried cranberries, apricots, and raisins will connect to wines with bright fruit notes, such as Grenache or Gamay. Wines with little or no residual sugar are most easily served and enjoyed with savory, flavorful foods. Sweeter wines, usually called medium or off-dry, work best when poured with a glazed entrée or dessert.

Acids and tannins help offset sweetness in food and can cut richness and cleanse the palate. When oak barrels are used to age wine, certain vanilla flavors are acquired, especially in Chardonnay, which blends superbly with buttery sauces. Also, the often distinctive flavor of the grape from which the wine was made, known as varietal character, make certain matches unforgettable, such as Fumé Blanc and raw oysters.

In deciding which wine to choose, consider the type of dish you are serving, as well as the intensity of the sauce, if any.

For instance, a grilled chicken breast with fresh fruit salsa needs a wine with a direct, refreshing simple taste that can be served cool or cold, such as Soave, a light, Italian wine. Similarly, you would choose an assertive, intensely flavored red wine, such as Cabernet, to complement your venison chili, or a prune-stuffed pork roast. I've also found that young, fresh Zinfandel, Cabernet, Merlot, and even some of the heavier Pinot Noirs stand up beautifully to a rich, heady mix of spices and chiles, especially in those dishes of Southeast Asian origins. I have also paired flowery Gewürztraminers with heavy, non-chile-spiced dishes (for example, a blend of garlic, cumin, turmeric, and star anise) with delicious results.

Generally, I avoid serving red wine with fish or seafood as it contains tannin, which reacts with substances in the flesh of the fish and produces a bitter or metallic flavor in the mouth. Another principle I adhere to religiously is never to serve a dry wine with a sweet food. The sugar in the food will accentuate the acidity in the wine, making the wine taste sour or astringent. Balance is really the key to good matches. I try to make sure that neither the food nor the wine overwhelms the other.

The chart that follows gives some of my recommendations for pairing wine and the fruity dishes showcased in the book. The guidelines I've used aren't always foolproof, so be ready to experiment and have fun in creating new pairings. Let your palate be the judge. And when in doubt, do as I do: Ask your wine merchant for details; he or she should be able to suggest specific bottles or vintages for the particular dish or dishes you have in mind.

IF YOU ARE SERVING . . .	TRY . . .
Salmon Cakes with Ginger Citrus Sauce Citrus Shrimp with Prosciutto Roast Duck with Blueberry Sauce Apricot-Glazed Ham	A rich, full-bodied California Chardonnay, or a similar wine from Burgundy.
Steamed Salmon with Pineapple-Tomato Vinaigrette Grilled Soft-Shell Crabs with Citrus Vinaigrette Baked Halibut in Cider Broth Mom's Chicken Brochettes	Sauvignon Blanc, Pinot Grigio, or a Côtes-de-Provence Rosé (These wines work well with acidic or tomato-based sauces.)

Curried Crab Dip
South Seas Clam Chowder
Cream of Fennel and Pear Soup
Bangkok Noodles
Crown Roast of Pork with Fruited
    Couscous Stuffing
	Fumé Blanc, a light white Graves, or
	    Gewürztraminer

Veal Scallopine with Grapefruit	Muscadet
Broiled Bluefish with Orange Sauce	Pouilly Fumé or Chablis
Grilled Butterflied Leg of Lamb	Italian red wine, such as Nebbiolo or Dolcetto
Wild Mushroom Risotto with Apples Mushroom Ragoût Barbecued Shrimp	Meursault
Green Risotto Lemon-Lime Spaghettini Chopped Liver Pâté with Chutney Stuffed Cornish Hens with Spiced Grape Sauce Roasted Chicken Breasts with Glazed Kumquats Grilled Smoked Turkey, Apple, and Cheese Finger Sandwiches Grilled Banana Pizza	An Alsatian or German Riesling (For smoky meats or cheese and acidic sauces, this wine fits the bill.)
Down Island Black Bean Soup Glazed Lamb Chops	Red Bordeaux (This type of wine is great with hearty meat dishes or stews.)
Quail in Currant Sauce Braised Duck in Orange-Cinnamon Sauce Beef Tenderloin in Cherry Sauce Roast Beef with Black Currant Sauce Swedish Roast Pork Heavenly Raspberry Brownies	Pinot Noir or Cabernet Sauvignon

IF YOU ARE SERVING . . .	TRY . . .
Victory Chicken Wings Fried Chicken with Orange Cream Gravy Chicken and Apple Sausages Stuffed Cornish Hens with Spiced Grape Sauce	Vouvray or Chenin Blanc
Holiday Turkey Pâté Warm Escarole, Raspberry, and Chicken Salad Sweet and Sour Linguine Primavera Calf's Liver with Green Grapes Sesame Duck with Litchees Braised Rabbit with Fresh Figs Orange-Glazed Flank Steaks Sweet and Sour Meatballs Braised Veal Shanks with Dried Cherries Pomegranate Lamb Kabobs	Beaujolais-Village, a light Zinfandel, a California Gamay, or Chianti
New-Age Jambalaya Thai Red Chicken Curry with Pineapple Tea-Smoked Baby Back Ribs with Tangerine Glaze Venison Chili with Papaya	Beer or Cabernet Sauvignon
Shrimp and Pineapple Satay	White Zinfandel
Apple Coconut Chowder	Moselle or a Riesling with some sweetness
Crisp-Fried Oysters with Papaya Salsa Tropical Lobster Salad Sautéed Foie Gras with Mango Compote	Muscadet, Chablis, or Champagne (These wines also tend to go well with salty foods.)
Jennifer's Budino with Warm Plum Compote Gratin of Fresh Strawberries and Rhubarb Simple fresh fruits Orange Rice Pudding with Fresh Apricot Sauce	A sweet dessert wine such as sweet Alsatian or California Gewürztraminer, a light Muscat Canelli, or Vino Santo
Strawberry-Banana Trifle	A late-harvest Riesling

THE BIRD RANGE

Fruit is capable of giving even the most humble dishes an unexpected twist. Whether it's fresh or dried, fruit brings instant appeal to any poultry dish. Because poultry is naturally mild, it presents a perfect canvas for the pure taste of any fruit it's associated with. A bright, fresh fruit salsa makes a piece of grilled chicken more exciting; a sweet-tart blueberry sauce adds unexpected pizzazz to a roast duck; a perfectly ripe banana tucked inside a grilled turkey roll lends a festive feel to a meal.

What is equally fascinating is how the same combination of fruit and poultry can be interpreted so differently in different parts of the world. Take lemon and chicken, for example, and contrast the Chinese preparation of batter-coated chicken in a sweet and shiny lemon sauce with the Moroccan braised chicken with chunks of salty preserved lemons. All these examples just hint at the kinds of matches you will find in this chapter.

In many recipes, I use skinless and boneless chicken or turkey breasts because they are both easy and quick to prepare. To ensure that the breasts cook evenly, I usually put them between two sheets of plastic wrap and use a meat mallet to flatten them to a thickness of about

¼ inch. If they are intended for the grill, I generally marinate them briefly in lemon or lime juice with some seasonings and a bit of olive oil for flavor. The enzyme in the citrus fruit tenderizes the meat and enhances the flavor at the same time.

I prefer using dark meat in braised or stewed dishes such as Thai Red Chicken Curry or Fried Chicken with Orange Cream Gravy, because they are the juiciest parts of a bird. More robust birds such as duck also have a good deal to gain from being cooked slowly in a braising liquid that includes citrus juices or a tart fruit. Again, the acidic quality of the fruit not only tenderizes the meat and balances the gaminess of the bird, it makes the dish taste amazingly good too. I have also cast rabbit in this chapter because its mild-tasting, lean white meat reminds me most of chicken.

So, if you think you've tried everything you can do with poultry, the following recipes will give you a fresh look at the versatile bird range. Fruits make the possibilities for poultry cookery almost endless. In fact, don't think that I ever make precisely the same dish twice: improvisation is half the fun.

PEACHES AND NECTARINES

Sweet, succulent peaches and nectarines are delicious with ricotta and mascarpone cheeses and cured meats. At the height of summer, indulge in luscious sliced ripe peaches and nectarines drizzled with La Grande Passion (Armagnac and passion fruit brandy) or Grand Marnier.

SAUTEED CHICKEN BREASTS WITH PEACHES

YIELD: 4 ENTREE SERVINGS

Starring in this great chicken dish are two of my favorite ingredients: peaches and fresh basil. This quick, light entrée is so good, you may want to try it with mango, nectarines, papaya, or persimmons when they are in season. If you are lucky enough to find a butcher who sells boned and skinned pheasant breasts, which are sweeter and more aromatic than chicken, use them as an elegant substitution for a glamorous meal. Just cook the breasts about 4 minutes per side. Serve this dish with a tart green salad and a few slices of good bread to soak up the delicious sauce.

> 4 skinless, boneless chicken breasts (about 6 ounces each), trimmed of excess fat
> Salt and freshly ground black pepper,
> Unbleached all-purpose flour
> 2 tablespoons unsalted butter
> $^1/_4$ cup thinly sliced shallots
> $^1/_4$ cup balsamic vinegar
> $^1/_4$ cup chicken broth, preferably homemade (page 30)
> $^1/_4$ cup heavy (or whipping) cream
> 2 large ripe but firm peaches (about 1 pound total), cut into $^1/_4$-inch-thick wedges
> 2 tablespoons shredded fresh basil (for shredding instructions, see page 34), or chopped fresh thyme leaves

1. Remove the fillets (the fingersize muscle on the underside of each breast) and set aside. Using the flat end of a meat pounder, lightly flatten each breast.

2. Season the chicken breasts and fillets with salt and pepper, then dredge through the flour, shaking off any excess.

3. Melt 1 tablespoon of the butter in a large skillet over medium-high heat. Add the chicken and sauté until just cooked through, about 2 minutes per side. To test for doneness, cut into the thickest part of the chicken breasts and take a peek. The flesh should be opaque, without a trace of pink. Transfer the chicken to a plate and cover while you make the sauce.

4. Add the remaining 1 tablespoon but-

ter to the skillet. When the butter is hot, add the shallots and sauté until tender, about 30 seconds. Add the vinegar and cook until reduced by half, forming a thick glaze, about 2 minutes. Add the chicken broth and cream, along with any juices collected on the chicken plate. Cook until the sauce is reduced by half and lightly coats the back of a spoon, about 2 minutes. Add the peaches and toss until just warmed through. Do not overcook. Remove from the heat and stir in the basil. Adjust the seasoning with salt and pepper, if necessary.

5. Place the chicken on warmed dinner plates or on a platter. Spoon the sauce and peaches over the chicken and serve immediately.

BORDER-GRILLED CHICKEN WITH NECTARINE-TOMATO SALSA

YIELD: 4 ENTREE SERVINGS

If you yearn for something simple but packed with wonderful flavors, try this Southwestern-style chicken entrée. Grilling chicken breasts keeps the interior of the meat moist and gives the exterior a tantalizing smoky flavor. The sweet, cool taste of a nectarine salsa playing off the warm chicken offers an opulent contrast of flavors with a typical Southwestern spirit.

4 *skinless, boneless chicken breasts (about*
    6 ounces each), trimmed of excess fat
2 *teaspoons fresh lime juice*
2 *teaspoons mild olive oil*
2 *teaspoons minced garlic*
1¹⁄₂ *teaspoons ground cumin*
1 *teaspoon ground coriander*
¹⁄₂ *teaspoon sugar*
Salt and freshly ground black pepper
Nectarine-Tomato Salsa (recipe follows)

1. Place the chicken breasts in a large bowl. In a small bowl, combine the lime juice with the olive oil, garlic, cumin, coriander, sugar, and salt and pepper to taste. Whisk until thoroughly combined. Sprinkle the marinade over the chicken breasts and toss to coat.

2. Place the chicken breasts, one at a time, between 2 sheets of plastic wrap. Flatten each with a meat mallet or the bottom of a skillet. Individually wrap each breast in plastic and refrigerate for 30 minutes.

3. Prepare coals for grilling. Or place a grill pan over medium-high heat.

4. Lightly season the chicken breasts with salt and pepper and grill over medium-hot coals for about 2 minutes per side. Or cook the chicken breasts in a stovetop grill pan over medium-high heat until the juices run clear, about 5 minutes, turning once. To test for doneness, cut into the thickest part of the chicken breasts and take a peek. The flesh should be opaque, without a trace of pink.

5. Place the grilled chicken breasts on warmed dinner plates and top with Nectarine-Tomato Salsa. Serve immediately.

"...A small, richly flavored peach so confused that if you plant its pits you may get nectarines or you may not."
—WAVERLEY ROOT, WRITING OF THE NECTARINE

Nectarine-Tomato Salsa

YIELD: ABOUT 3 CUPS

For top flavors, make this salsa no longer than 30 minutes before serving. It is also great with grilled shrimp or pork. Or you might serve it along side some chips and tortillas as a snack or appetizer.

2 plum tomatoes, finely diced

2 large nectarines (about 1 pound), pitted
    and thinly sliced

1/2 small red onion, thinly sliced

1 jalapeño pepper, minced

1 tablespoon fresh lime juice

1/2 teaspoon sugar

1 tablespoon shredded fresh mint or basil
    leaves (for shredding instructions,
    see page 34)

1 teaspoon mild olive oil

Salt

1/2 teaspoon cracked black peppercorns

Combine all the ingredients in a medium-size mixing bowl. Toss well, cover, and refrigerate until ready to serve.

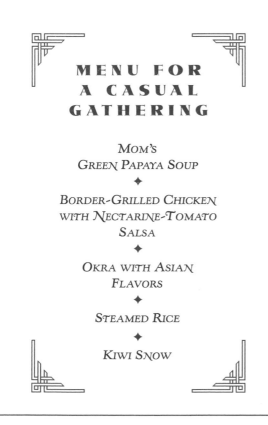

**MENU FOR
A CASUAL
GATHERING**

MOM'S
GREEN PAPAYA SOUP
✦
BORDER-GRILLED CHICKEN
WITH NECTARINE-TOMATO
SALSA
✦
OKRA WITH ASIAN
FLAVORS
✦
STEAMED RICE
✦
KIWI SNOW

MARCEL'S TRELLIS CHICKEN

YIELD: 4 ENTREE SERVINGS

Marcel Desaulniers, a noted restaurateur, cookbook writer, television personality, and friend, contributed this recipe. Having worked in his kitchen at the Trellis restaurant in Williamsburg, Virginia, I know that Marcel is a great practitioner of New American cuisine; he is also skilled at incorporating fruit into his cooking. What I like about this dish is the interplay of the delicate fruits, the bold black peppercorns and crunchy cashew nuts. I also love how pretty it is.

This is a great dish for backyard entertaining, since marinating the meat and onions, and preparing the black pepper butter can be done well in advance, leaving just a quick grilling and warming for the last minute. The recipe can easily be doubled or tripled to feed a crowd. For instructions on sectioning citrus fruit, see page 318.

> 4 skinless, boneless chicken breasts (about 6 ounces each), trimmed of excess fat
> 1/2 cup dry white wine
> 2 tablespoons fresh lemon juice
> Salt and freshly ground black pepper
> 8 tablespoons (1 stick) unsalted butter, at room temperature
> 3 tablespoons minced shallots
> 1 1/2 teaspoons cracked black peppercorns
> Trellis Vinaigrette (recipe follows)
> 2 medium red onions, sliced 1/2 inch thick
> 3 navel oranges, peeled and sectioned
> 1 pink grapefruit, peeled and sectioned
> 1 lime, peeled and sectioned
> 3/4 cup toasted unsalted cashews (for toasting instructions, see page 64), coarsely chopped

1. Place the chicken breasts in a large bowl. In a small bowl, combine 2 tablespoons of the white wine and the lemon juice with salt and pepper to taste. Whisk until thoroughly combined. Sprinkle the marinade over the chicken breasts.

2. Place the chicken breasts, one at a time, between 2 sheets of plastic wrap. Flatten each with the flat side of a meat cleaver or the bottom of a skillet. Individually wrap each breast in plastic and refrigerate for 30 minutes.

3. Melt 1 1/2 teaspoons of the butter in a medium-size nonstick skillet over medium heat. Add the minced shallots, season to taste with salt, and sauté for 1 minute. Add the remaining white wine and bring to a simmer. Reduce the heat to low and simmer until the mixture is almost dry, about 10 minutes.

4. Transfer the shallots to a medium-size bowl and cool to room temperature. Then add the remaining butter and the cracked black peppercorns and stir until thoroughly combined. Cover with plastic wrap and keep at room temperature until needed.

5. Place the Trellis Vinaigrette in a medium-size mixing bowl and whisk to combine. Immerse the onion slices in the vinaigrette, cover with plastic wrap, and refrigerate for at least 1 hour.

6. Prepare coals for grilling.

7. Remove the onion slices from the vinaigrette and season them with salt. Grill over a medium-hot fire for 3 minutes on each side. Place the grilled onion slices on a baking sheet and keep in a low oven while grilling the chicken.

8. Grill the chicken breasts over a medium-hot fire for about 2 minutes on each side. To test for doneness, cut into the thickest part of the chicken breast and take a peek. The flesh should be opaque without a trace of pink. Transfer the chicken to a baking sheet, baste with half of the black-pepper butter, and keep in a low oven while heating the citrus sections.

9. Heat the remaining black pepper butter in a large nonstick skillet over medium heat. When hot, add the citrus sections and cook until warmed through, about 30 seconds.

10. Divide the warmed citrus sections among warmed dinner plates. Place a chicken breast on top of the fruit. Top each chicken breast with grilled onion slices, sprinkle with cashews, and serve immediately.

Trellis Vinaigrette

YIELD: 1 CUP

3 tablespoons cider vinegar

1 1/2 tablespoons fresh lemon juice

2 teaspoons Dijon mustard

1/2 teaspoon salt

1/8 teaspoon freshly ground black pepper

3/4 cup vegetable oil

1. In a medium-size mixing bowl, whisk together the vinegar, lemon juice, mustard, salt, and pepper until thoroughly combined. Gradually whisk in the vegetable oil.

2. Transfer to a glass jar, cover tightly, and refrigerate for at least 1 hour before using.

LEMON CHICKEN

YIELD: 4 ENTREE SERVINGS

This is the kind of dish I like to make when I am on a diet. (Isn't everybody, most of the time?) It's nothing like those batter-fried globs coated with a gluey, cloying lemon sauce that most people come to know from Chinese takeout food. In this dish, lean, tender chicken breasts are bathed in a pleasing light sweet and sour sauce. For an easy but equally flavorful variation, substitute 1 cup fresh pineapple juice for the lemon juice and omit the sugar.

1 cup fresh lemon juice

2 tablespoons julienned lemon zest

1/4 cup sugar

2 cups chicken broth, preferably homemade (page 30)

2 teaspoons arrowroot or 1 teaspoon cornstarch, combined with 1 teaspoon cold water

Salt and freshly ground black pepper

1 tablespoon unsalted butter

4 skinless, boneless chicken breasts (6 ounces each), trimmed of excess fat

4 paper-thin lemon slices , for garnish (optional)

1. Place the lemon juice, lemon zest, and sugar in a medium-size saucepan, and bring to a boil over medium heat. Continue boiling until the liquid is reduced to about 1/4 cup,

6 to 8 minutes. Add the chicken broth and continue to boil until the liquid is reduced by half, about 10 minutes.

2. Stir the arrowroot mixture into the sauce. Reduce the heat to low and simmer, stirring frequently, until the sauce has thickened slightly, about 2 minutes. Remove from the heat and season to taste with salt and pepper, if necessary. Cover and set aside.

3. Melt the butter in a large skillet over medium-high heat. Lightly season the chicken breasts with salt and pepper and sauté until cooked through, about 2 minutes on each side. To test for doneness, cut into the thickest part of the chicken breasts and take a peek. The flesh should be opaque, without a trace of pink. Add the lemon sauce to the pan. Continue to cook for about 30 seconds longer, turning the breasts once or twice to coat with sauce.

4. Transfer the chicken to warmed dinner plates and spoon the sauce over them. Garnish with lemon slices, if desired, and serve.

MOM'S CHICKEN BROCHETTES

YIELD: 8 APPETIZER OR 4 ENTREE SERVINGS

When I think about grilling, I think of these Vietnamese lime-infused chicken brochettes that my mother used to make. Slightly charred with an exquisite balance of sweetness and aromatic lime, they are delicious. They are also a snap to prepare. For best results, try not to let the chicken pieces stand more than 1 hour in the marinade, or the acidity of the lime will over-tenderize it. Serve these brochettes as an appetizer or main course over rice, perhaps with some Peppered Peaches (See Index).

2 shallots, thinly sliced
3 cloves garlic, crushed
1 tablespoon sugar
2 tablespoons fresh lime juice
Finely grated zest of 3 limes (heaping ½ teaspoon)
1 tablespoon Thai fish sauce
1 tablespoon soy sauce, preferably Kikkoman
1 tablespoon peanut oil
¼ teaspoon freshly ground black pepper
1½ pounds skinless, boneless chicken breasts, trimmed of excess fat and cut into 1-inch pieces
1 large onion, peeled and cut into 1-inch squares

1. Using a mortar and pestle or a spice grinder, grind the shallots, garlic, and sugar to a fine paste. Transfer the paste to a medium-size glass mixing bowl, and add the lime juice, lime zest, fish sauce, soy sauce, peanut oil, and black pepper. Stir to blend. Add the chicken pieces. Toss well, cover loosely, and refrigerate for 1 hour.

2. Place 8 bamboo skewers in a shallow pan and cover with hot water. Soak for at least 30 minutes.

3. Prepare coals for grilling or preheat the broiler.

4. Thread the skewers with alternating pieces of chicken and onion using 3 or 4 pieces per skewer.

5. Grill the skewers 3 inches from the coals, turning once, for 6 to 8 minutes. If you are using the broiler, place the skewers on a broiler pan and broil 6 inches from the heat. To test for doneness, cut into a thick chicken piece and take a peek. The flesh should be opaque without a trace of pink. You can also cook the skewered chicken on a hot oiled grill pan on top of the stove. Serve immediately.

ROASTED CHICKEN BREASTS WITH GLAZED KUMQUATS

YIELD: 4 ENTREE SERVINGS

Few things harmonize as well with chicken as the sweet aroma of kumquats and the tart taste of lemon juice, as aptly demonstrated in this dish. Simple to prepare, it should appeal equally to those who watch calories and those

KUMQUATS

In its native Canton, this charming thumb-size winter fruit is lovingly called "golden orange." Indeed, its flavor is reminiscent of orange, with a little tangerine thrown in, but the zestiness is unique. The kumquat is so appreciated in China that miniature fruit-bearing bushes are given at Chinese New Year as a way to wish good luck for the coming year.

A kumquat has a thick, spongy skin that is sur-prisingly sweet, with a hint of the bitterness associated with citrus peel. Its pulp is intensely sour. The whole fruit should be eaten, as the skin and flesh complement each other. It is best to halve kumquats and remove the seeds before using them for cooking.

Fresh kumquats, available from November through February, should be plump and firm. Refrigerated, they will stay fresh for up to 2 weeks.

GREAT MATCHES

KUMQUATS

These tart little fruits are the perfect foil for rich meats, such as liver and sausages. They're also delicious with a range of herbs and spices, including ginger, fennel, star anise, and cilantro. Try them in a dish with hoisin sauce, too.

who want flavorful food with a minimum of fuss. Be sure to use the whole fruit; much of the citrus flavor is concentrated in the sweet, spongy skin. Remove the seeds, if desired.

2 whole bone-in chicken breasts, with skin on (about 3 pounds total), rinsed, and patted dry

Salt and freshly ground black pepper

2 tablespoons mild olive oil

2 large heads garlic, separated into cloves and peeled

$^1/_2$ pound pearl onions, peeled (see Note)

$^1/_2$ cup fresh lemon juice

1 cup chicken broth, preferably homemade (page 30)

2 cups thinly sliced kumquats (20 to 25 large kumquats, about $^3/_4$ pound total)

3 tablespoons sugar

1. Preheat the oven to 450°F.

2. Season the chicken with salt and pepper. Heat the oil in a large, heavy ovenproof skillet over medium-high heat. Add the chicken and brown on both sides, about 30 seconds per side. Push the breasts to the side of the skillet. Add the garlic and onions and cook until lightly browned, about 2 minutes. Stir in the lemon juice and broth. Spread out the chicken evenly in the skillet and transfer the skillet to the oven. Roast until the chicken registers 145°F on an instant-read thermometer inserted in the thickest part of the breast and the vegetables are tender, about 30 minutes.

3. Meanwhile, combine the kumquats, sugar, and $^1/_3$ cup water in a medium-size saucepan and bring to a boil over medium heat. Simmer, uncovered, until the kumquats are translucent and tender, and almost all the syrup has been absorbed, about 15 minutes. Set aside.

4. When the chicken is cooked, transfer it to a cutting board, leaving the sauce in the skillet. Stir the glazed kumquats into the sauce. Bring the mixture to a boil over medium-high heat and cook until slightly thickened and syrupy, about 3 minutes. Season to taste with salt and pepper.

5. Carve each breast in half to obtain 4 boneless halves. Arrange them on warmed dinner plates and top with kumquat sauce.

NOTE: To peel pearl onions, bring a medium-size pot of salted water to a boil. Add the onions, turn off the heat, and let sit for 30 seconds. Drain, refresh with cold water, and drain again. Trim the root end of the onions, and peel them; the peel should slip right off.

FRIED CHICKEN WITH ORANGE CREAM GRAVY

YIELD: 4 ENTREE SERVINGS

Everyone, it seems, enjoys a good piece of fried chicken, even people who avoid fried foods. Once in a while, I, too, crave this old-time favorite. When I make it, I usually marinate drumsticks in fresh orange juice to tenderize them, then coat them with a blend of spices for extra kick. The creamy orange-flavored gravy that accompanies this chicken gives even more appeal. Mashed potatoes are a perfect match for this dish.

8 large chicken drumsticks (about 3 1/2 pounds total), rinsed and patted dry, and skin removed, if desired
1 1/2 cups fresh orange juice
1 1/4 cups unbleached all-purpose flour
1 1/2 teaspoons dried thyme, crumbled
1 1/2 teaspoons ground cinnamon
1 1/2 teaspoons paprika
1 teaspoon salt
1 large egg
3/4 cup buttermilk
Vegetable oil
Orange Cream Gravy (recipe follows)

1. Arrange the drumsticks in a single layer in a shallow dish and add the orange juice. Cover and marinate in the refrigerator for at least 4 hours or overnight, turning the drumsticks once or twice.

2. Combine the flour, thyme, cinnamon, paprika, and salt in a medium-size bowl. Reserve 2 tablespoons of the mixture for the Orange Cream Gravy and set aside.

3. Beat the egg in a small bowl and stir in the buttermilk.

4. Drain the drumsticks, discarding the marinade, then roll them, one at a time, in the flour mixture. Dip into the egg-buttermilk mixture and then into the flour mixture again, firmly pressing the flour with your hands so plenty of it clings to the chicken. Arrange the coated chicken pieces on a platter. (They may be loosely covered with aluminum foil and refrigerated until needed.)

5. Pour oil to a depth of 2 inches into a

large, deep heavy skillet with a tight-fitting lid. Heat over medium-high heat to 375°F. Using tongs, carefully add the chicken pieces and cook until they are evenly browned, about 2 minutes. Cover, reduce the heat to medium-low, and cook, turning frequently until the chicken is tender when tested with the tip of a paring knife, and the juices run clear, about 25 minutes.

6. Drain the chicken on racks or paper towels. Transfer to a warmed platter and serve at once with Orange Cream Gravy.

VARIATION

FRIED CHICKEN WITH SPICY PINEAPPLE DIP: Replace the orange juice in the marinade with fresh pineapple juice. For a lighter sauce, substitute Spicy Pineapple Dip for the Orange Cream Gravy. To make the dip, follow Steps 1 and 2 of the recipe for Grilled Lobster Vietnamese Style (see Index).

Orange Cream Gravy

YIELD: ABOUT 1 1/4 CUPS

This gravy may be prepared while the chicken is frying, or made ahead of time and reheated.

1 tablespoon unsalted butter
2 tablespoons of flour mixture reserved from
    Fried Chicken recipe (above)
1/2 cup thawed frozen orange juice concentrate
3/4 cup chicken broth, preferably homemade
    (page 30)
1/4 cup light cream or half-and-half
1/2 teaspoon ground cinnamon
Salt and freshly ground black pepper

1. Melt the butter in a small saucepan over medium heat. Stir the flour into the butter and cook until golden, about 4 minutes. Then whisk in the remaining ingredients. Cook, stirring frequently, until the sauce is smooth and thick, about 5 minutes.

2. Taste the gravy and adjust the seasoning, if necessary.

RUSTIC CHICKEN STEW

YIELD: 4 ENTREE SERVINGS

In my updated version of a rustic chicken stew, dried apples and white wine are added to round out the old-fashioned flavor of the dish. The dish is baked just long enough for the apples and vegetables to dissolve into a delectable sauce. Like most stews, this one can be made ahead and gently reheated. Mixed dried fruits will work equally well in the dish.

1 tablespoon mild olive oil

1 chicken (3$^1/_2$ to 4 pounds), rinsed, patted
    dry, and cut into serving pieces

1 cup chopped onions

1 tablespoon minced garlic

1 small carrot, cubed ($^1/_2$-inch pieces)

1 small green bell pepper, stemmed, seeded
    and cubed ($^1/_2$-inch pieces)

1 cinnamon stick (3-inches long)

1 large bay leaf

1 teaspoon dried thyme, crumbled

1$^1/_4$ cups dry white wine, preferably Chardonnay

1$^1/_4$ cups chicken broth, preferably homemade
    (page 30)

1 cup dried apples (about $^1/_4$ pound),
    coarsely chopped

2 tablespoons raisins

Salt and freshly ground black pepper

$^1/_3$ cup light cream or half-and-half
    (optional)

1. Preheat the oven to 350°F.

2. Heat the oil in a large ovenproof skillet with a tight-fitting lid or a Dutch oven over medium-high heat. Add the chicken pieces and cook on both sides until evenly browned, about 10 minutes. Transfer the chicken to a plate and set aside.

3. Pour off the fat, leaving 1 tablespoon in the pan. Add the onions, garlic, carrot, bell pepper, cinnamon stick, bay leaf, and thyme. Using a wooden spoon, stir, scraping up any browned bits from the bottom of the pan, until the vegetables are tender, about 5 minutes. Stir in the wine, chicken broth, apples, and raisins, and season to taste with salt and

pepper. Return the chicken pieces to the pan, submerging them into the liquid.

4. Bake, covered, until the chicken is fork-tender, about 50 minutes.

5. When the chicken is done, remove it from the sauce and place on a warmed platter. Bring the sauce to a simmer over medium heat, and quickly stir in the cream, if desired. Remove and discard the cinnamon stick and bay leaf. Ladle the sauce over the chicken, and serve at once.

THAI RED CHICKEN CURRY WITH PINEAPPLE

YIELD: 4 ENTREE SERVINGS

Fiery curry paste, sweet coconut milk, and aromatic herbs are the classic base of Thai curries Fresh fruits are often added as well. I love Thai curries and have always had a particular weakness for this irresistible stew of chicken, potatoes, green beans, and pineapple. Like most stews, this one tastes even better reheated the next day. Noodles, rice, or bread all go well with this curry. For an even more luxurious flavor, substitute duck legs for the chicken, and apple for the pineapple.

An Indian legend goes that during a pilgrimage, a devout Hindu collapsed from hunger and exhaustion in a jungle. A coconut from a nearby tree fell, cracked in half, and woke him up. After eating the coconut, he regained his energy and resumed the journey. For that reason, the coconut tree is now honored as "the tree of life."

1 can (14 ounces) unsweetened coconut milk, well stirred

½ cup chicken broth, preferably homemade (page 30)

1½ teaspoons Thai red curry paste

3 fresh or frozen kaffir lime leaves or 1 teaspoon finely grated lime zest

2 quarter-size slices fresh or frozen galangal or 1 quarter-size slice peeled fresh ginger, crushed

1 stalk fresh lemongrass, crushed and cut into 3-inch lengths

2 teaspoons vegetable oil

4 whole chicken legs (about 3 pounds total), each cut in half at the joints

1 cup finely chopped onions

½ cup firmly packed fresh basil leaves

1 tablespoon minced garlic

1 tablespoon sweet paprika

2 tablespoons Thai fish sauce

1 tablespoon firmly packed light brown sugar

1 cup trimmed and halved green beans

1 large Idaho potato, peeled and cut into 1-inch cubes

1 cup fresh pineapple chunks (1-inch pieces)

1. Combine the coconut milk, chicken broth, curry paste, lime leaves, galangal, and lemongrass in a medium-size saucepan. With the back of a spoon, mash the curry paste against the side of the pan, and stir to dissolve it. Bring to a simmer over low heat and cook until aromatic, about 15 minutes. Remove from the heat and set aside.

2. Heat the oil in a large nonstick skillet over medium-high heat. Add the chicken pieces, skin side down, and brown them on all sides, 10 minutes. Transfer the chicken pieces to a plate.

3. Pour off the fat, leaving 1 tablespoon in the skillet. Return to medium-high heat and add the onions, basil, garlic, and paprika. Cook, stirring until the vegetables are tender, about 2 minutes. Using a wooden spoon, stir in the coconut milk mixture, fish sauce, and brown sugar, scraping up any browned bits from the bottom of the pan. Remove and discard the skin from the chicken pieces, then return them to the skillet, along with any juices collected on the plate.

4. Bring the mixture to a boil. Reduce the heat to low, cover, and simmer for 20 minutes, turning the chicken pieces once or twice.

5. Remove and discard the lime leaves, galangal, and lemongrass. Add the green

beans and potatoes to the sauce, and continue to simmer for another 10 minutes.

6. Add the pineapple and simmer, uncovered, until all the vegetables are tender, 10 minutes longer. Serve the curry at once.

SPANISH ROAST CHICKEN

YIELD: 4 ENTREE SERVINGS

This juicy roast chicken is infused with two of the most widely used flavorings in the Spanish kitchen: orange and sherry vinegar. The marvelous thing about it is that it practically makes its own sauce. To round out the meal, start with Cream of Fennel and Pear Soup, and serve Quinoa Pilaf on the side (see Index).

2 large navel oranges

1 chicken (3$\frac{1}{2}$ to 4 pounds), rinsed and
    patted dry

$\frac{1}{2}$ teaspoon salt

$\frac{1}{4}$ teaspoon freshly ground black pepper

2 teaspoons minced garlic

4 tablespoons ($\frac{1}{2}$ stick) unsalted butter, at
    room temperature

1 large bay leaf

$\frac{1}{2}$ cup chicken broth, preferably homemade
    (page 30)

1 tablespoon sherry vinegar

1. Using a zester, remove the zest from the oranges and set aside. Halve the oranges and juice them; strain the juice into a bowl and set aside. (You should have about 1 cup of juice.)

2. Preheat the oven to 400°F. Lightly brush the rack of a flameproof roasting pan with olive oil.

3. Rub the chicken with the salt and pepper. In a small bowl, combine the garlic, butter, and half the orange zest and stir until it forms a soft paste. Rub the chicken inside and out with the orange butter. Place the bay leaf inside the cavity. Truss the chicken (see page 178).

4. Place the chicken on the prepared rack in the pan and roast for 35 minutes. Baste the chicken with half the orange juice, then reduce the oven temperature to 350°F. Continue roasting the chicken, basting every 15 minutes with the pan juices, until the bird is golden brown and the juices run clear when a thigh is pierced with a fork, 1 hour more.

5. Transfer the chicken to a platter, draining any liquid from its cavity back into the roasting pan. Cover with aluminum foil to keep it warm. Skim the fat from the pan juices.

6. Place the roasting pan, with the pan juices, over medium heat. Using a wooden spoon, stir in the remaining ¹/₂ cup orange juice, scraping up any browned bits from the bottom of the pan. Add the chicken broth, remaining orange zest, and vinegar and bring to a boil. Reduce the heat to medium-low and simmer until the sauce is slightly thickened and syrupy, about 5 minutes.

7. Quarter the chicken and place the pieces on warmed dinner plates. Spoon the sauce over the chicken and serve at once.

TRUSSING A BIRD

Trussing or tying up a bird before roasting helps it cook more evenly. It also helps the bird keep its plump shape, enhancing its appearance. Here's a simple and easy method I use for trussing a chicken or any other bird.

1. *Place the bird on its back on a work surface, with the legs facing away from you. Cut and remove the wing tips.*

3. *Slide the crossed string under the drumstick tips, and tightly pull both ends of the string toward you; one on each side along the legs and breast, pinning the wings to the side of the bird. Cross the ends of the string over the neck, then lift the neck up and loop each end around the neck.*

2. *Cut a piece of kitchen string four times the length of the bird. Slide it under the back of the bird, with its center near the tail. Lift the string on both sides and cross it over the tips of the drumsticks.*

4. *Tie a tight double knot in the string. The bird is now compactly tied.*

CHICKEN CARIBE

YIELD: 4 ENTREE SERVINGS

Don't be put off by the length of this recipe; there's really nothing difficult about it. It may be a little time-consuming, but the result will be well worth your efforts. The inspiration for the dish is a Haitian roast chicken that is customarily filled with two different stuffings, one under the skin and one in the cavity. In this version, I butterfly a chicken and stuff a highly fragrant mixture of dry bread crumbs, raisins, and nutmeg under the skin before roasting. Instead of the traditional mashed banana stuffing in the cavity of the chicken, I simply sauté split bananas in rum to make a quick, tasty accompaniment to the bird.

4 tablespoons (½ stick) unsalted butter

1 cup chopped onions

1½ tablespoons minced garlic

½ cup raisins, plumped in hot water to cover for
    5 minutes, drained, and coarsely chopped

¾ cup dry bread crumbs

1¾ teaspoons freshly grated nutmeg

4 tablespoons fresh lime juice

Salt and freshly ground black pepper

1 chicken (3¾ to 4 pounds), rinsed and
    patted dry

3 tablespoons dark rum

1 tablespoon unsalted butter, melted

4 medium bananas

¾ cup chicken broth, preferably homemade
    (page 30)

1. Melt the butter in a large skillet over medium-low heat. Add the onions and garlic and sauté until golden and aromatic, about 5 minutes, stirring frequently.

2. Stir in the raisins. Remove from the heat and let the mixture cool slightly. Add the bread crumbs, nutmeg, and 3 tablespoons of the lime juice and stir to combine. Season to taste with salt and pepper. The filling should have a balanced sweet and sour taste. It should also be moist enough to hold together. Set aside.

3. Preheat the oven to 400°F.

4. With poultry shears, cut along both sides of the backbone; remove the bone and reserve it for stock. Trim any excess fat from the chicken. Without cutting all the way through, make an incision at the joints where the thighs and drumsticks meet. (This helps the bird cook evenly; this thick part of the leg would otherwise take longer to cook.) Turn the chicken over, breast side up, on a cutting board. With the heel of your hand, firmly press on the wishbone to flatten the bird. Loosen the skin on the breast and legs of the chicken by gently pushing your fingers through the opening at the neck and running them between skin and meat to create a loose pocket. Take care not to tear the skin. Rub both sides of the chicken and the meat under the skin with 2 tablespoons of the rum and the remaining 1 tablespoon lime juice. Season with salt and pepper. Tuck the wings under the chicken.

5. Place the butterflied chicken breast

side up on a rack in a flameproof roasting pan. Place the stuffing under the loosened skin, pushing it down toward the legs and thighs with your fingers, being careful not to poke holes in the skin. Brush the chicken all over with the melted butter.

6. Roast the chicken, basting it frequently with pan juices, until an instant-read thermometer registers 150°F when inserted into the thickest part of the breast, 45 to 50 minutes. Transfer the chicken to a cutting board. Leave the oven on.

7. Skim the fat from the pan juices. Peel and quarter the bananas. Add the bananas and the remaining 1 tablespoon rum to the roasting pan, turning the fruit to coat with rum. Bake just until the bananas are heated through, about 2 minutes. Turn off the oven. Transfer the bananas to a serving platter and keep them warm in the oven while you finish the sauce.

8. Add the chicken broth to the roasting pan. Bring to a boil over medium-high heat, scraping up any browned bits from the bottom of the pan with a wooden spoon. Remove from the heat. Season to taste with salt and pepper and set aside.

9. Quarter the chicken and arrange the pieces on the platter with the bananas. Spoon the sauce over the top and serve at once.

EXOTIC CHICKEN

YIELD: 4 ENTREE SERVINGS

Meat and fruit is a popular combination in Middle Eastern cuisine. In this adaptation of the Moroccan dish *djaj m'kalli*, a whole chicken is slowly cooked in a subtly spiced broth, then finished with the addition of cured olives and pickled lemons, making it thoroughly exotic. If you choose to pickle your own lemons, prepare them at least 1 week before you plan to use them. They are also available at East Indian and African markets and some specialty foods shops. Steamed couscous is an excellent accompaniment to this stew. Dessert can be a cool, refreshing fruit salad or sorbet.

2 cups chopped onions
2 tablespoons minced garlic
1 tablespoon grated peeled fresh ginger
1 cinnamon stick (3-inches long)
$\frac{1}{2}$ cup chopped cilantro leaves
$\frac{1}{4}$ teaspoon saffron threads, crumbled
1 chicken (3 $\frac{1}{2}$ to 4 pounds), rinsed,
    patted dry, and trussed (page 178)
1 tablespoon fresh lemon juice
$\frac{1}{3}$ cup extra-virgin olive oil
Salt and freshly ground black pepper
$\frac{1}{2}$ cup black Mediterranean olives, such as
    Niçoise, Gaeta, or Kalamata
4 slices pickled lemon, preferably homemade,
    coarsely chopped
Fresh cilantro sprigs, for garnish (optional)

1. Preheat the oven to 400°F.

2. Combine the onions, garlic, ginger, cinnamon stick, chopped cilantro, saffron, and 1 cup water in a Dutch oven or large ovenproof soup pot with a tight-fitting lid. Place the trussed chicken on top of the mixture. Pour the lemon juice and olive oil over the chicken and season lightly with salt and pepper.

3. Cover the pot and bake for 1 hour, or until the chicken is tender and its juices run clear when the thickest part of a thigh is pierced with the tip of a sharp knife.

4. Remove the chicken from the pot, draining any liquid from its cavity back into the pot, and transfer to a cutting board.

5. Meanwhile, skim most of the fat from the liquid. Add the olives and pickled lemon. Bring to a boil over high heat and cook, stirring occasionally, until the sauce is slightly thickened, 3 to 5 minutes. Reduce the heat to low and let simmer.

6. Remove and discard the skin from the chicken. Cut the chicken into quarters, removing the rib cage. Return the chicken pieces to the sauce and simmer until they are just heated through.

7. Remove and discard the cinnamon stick. Transfer the chicken to a serving platter and ladle the sauce over it. Garnish with cilantro sprigs, if desired and serve.

CHICKEN AND APPLE SAUSAGES

YIELD: 14 SAUSAGES (5 INCHES LONG)

If you can take or leave those run-of-the mill links found in every supermarket, try these lean, tasty apple and chicken sausages. They can be grilled or added to a tomato sauce for pasta and pizza. You may also form the meat mixture into little patties, quickly brown them in a skillet, and serve them with hot biscuits and scrambled eggs for a fabulous brunch. If you do not plan to use all the sausages at once, they can be frozen (uncooked) for up to 1 month.

1 Golden Delicious apple (about $^1/_2$ pound), peeled, cored, and finely diced
$^1/_2$ cup thawed frozen apple juice concentrate
$^1/_2$ cup chicken broth, preferably homemade (page 30)
$^1/_2$ cup chopped shallots
$2^1/_2$ pounds ground chicken, well chilled
$2^1/_4$ teaspoons salt
1 tablespoon dried thyme, crumbled
1 teaspoon dried sage
$^1/_2$ teaspoon cayenne pepper
$^1/_2$ teaspoon freshly ground white pepper
2 feet sausage casings (optional; see Note)
Mild olive oil

1. Combine the diced apple, apple juice concentrate, chicken broth, and shallots in a medium-size saucepan and bring to a boil

over high heat. Reduce the heat to low, cover the pan, and simmer until the apples are very tender, about 5 minutes.

2. Drain the apples, reserving the cooking liquid, and set aside. Return the liquid to the pan and cook, uncovered, over high heat until it's syrupy and reduced to about $1/2$ cup, 5 to 6 minutes. Remove from the heat. Combine the apples and the reduced juices and place, covered, in the refrigerator until chilled.

3. Place the ground chicken in a large mixing bowl. Sprinkle the salt, thyme, sage, and cayenne and white peppers over the chicken. Add the chilled apples and juice. Using a wooden spoon, stir until all the ingredients are thoroughly combined. Fry a small patty of the mixture as a test and adjust the seasoning, if necessary.

4. If you are making sausage links, attach the stuffing horn to the grinder on a standing mixer according to the manufacturer's instructions. (Or you can use a pastry bag fitted with a $1/2$-inch plain tip to stuff the sausages. There's no need to grind the mixture.) Fit one end of the casing onto the horn. Gradually gather all the casing onto the horn, up to the knotted end. With one hand, feed the sausage mixture into the grinder. Meanwhile, anchor the casing gathered on the horn with your other hand, allowing the casing to unroll as the mixture extrudes. Stop occasionally to mold the filled casing. Do not pack the casing too full or the sausages will burst during cooking. Pierce any air bubbles with a needle. When the casing has been filled, make a knot at the end to secure the filling. To form links, tie the sausage at 5-inch intervals with 3-inch pieces of string. Alternatively, just shape the meat mixture into 10 to 12 patties, each about $3^1/_2$ inches in diameter.

5. Prepare coals for grilling or preheat the broiler.

6. If the sausages are in links, prick them in several places with a thin wooden skewer and brush with olive oil. Grill or broil (4 inches from the heat) the sausages 5 to 6 minutes on each side until cooked through. For patties, brush with a little oil and grill about 5 minutes on each side or fry in an oiled skillet over medium-high heat.

NOTE: Sausage casings are available from most butchers. They are often frozen and packed in salt. To prepare for stuffing, soak the casings in warm water until soft, about 1 hour. Drain. Run cold water through the casing to check for any holes; cut off at the spot where there's a hole. Make a knot at one end of the casing(s). Soak in fresh cold water until ready to use. Drain and pat the casings dry before using.

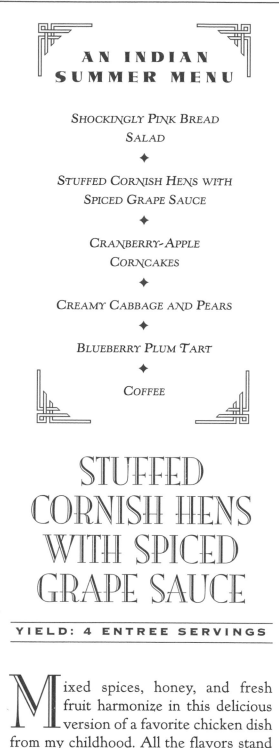

STUFFED CORNISH HENS WITH SPICED GRAPE SAUCE

YIELD: 4 ENTREE SERVINGS

Mixed spices, honey, and fresh fruit harmonize in this delicious version of a favorite chicken dish from my childhood. All the flavors stand

out and the meat is perfectly moist. For this recipe, I use small, young birds, such as Cornish hens, because they have less fat (and fewer calories) than their more mature cousins. Savor the gravy over mashed potatoes.

SPICE MIXTURE
1 teaspoon ground coriander
$1/4$ teaspoon ground cloves
$1/4$ teaspoon ground cinnamon
$1/4$ teaspoon ground nutmeg
$1/4$ teaspoon ground ginger
$1/4$ teaspoon freshly ground white pepper

CORNISH HENS
1 Granny Smith apple, peeled, cored, and
    cubed ($1/2$-inch pieces)
$1/2$ teaspoon cracked black peppercorns
$1/2$ teaspoon salt
5 tablespoons honey
2 Cornish hens (about $1 1/4$ pounds each),
    rinsed and patted dry
3 tablespoons cider vinegar
1 tablespoon unsalted butter
1 tablespoon mild olive oil
$1/2$ cup chicken broth, preferably homemade
    (page 30)
2 tablespoons soy sauce, preferably Kikkoman
$1/4$ pound seedless green grapes, preferably
    Muscat, halved

1. To make the spice mixture, place all the ingredients in a small bowl and stir to blend well.

2. To prepare the hens, combine the apple, cracked peppercorns, $1/4$ teaspoon of the salt, 1 tablespoon of the honey, and

¹/₄ teaspoon of the spice mixture in a small mixing bowl and toss well to coat the apples. Set aside the remaining spice mixture.

3. Stuff the hens with the apples, then secure the openings with toothpicks. Combine 1 tablespoon each of the honey and vinegar, with the remaining ¹/₄ teaspoon salt in a small bowl and stir until the honey is blended with the vinegar. Rub the hens with this mixture.

4. Heat the butter and oil in a Dutch oven or a large, heavy skillet with a tight-fitting lid over medium-high heat. Add the hens and brown them on each side for about 2 minutes. In a small bowl, combine the chicken broth, soy sauce, reserved spice mixture, remaining 3 tablespoons honey and 2 tablespoons cider vinegar. Stir until the honey is blended with the vinegar and pour over the hens. Cover and cook over low heat, turning and basting with pan juices every 10 minutes, until the juices run clear when the thickest part of a thigh is pricked with the tip of a paring knife, about 35 minutes. Five minutes before the hens are done, stir in the grapes.

5. To serve, split each hen in half and place 1 half and some stuffing on each warmed dinner plate. Ladle some grape sauce over each portion. Serve at once.

VARIATION

BRAISED STUFFED PHEASANT: Substitute 2 trimmed pheasants (about 2 pounds each), for the Cornish hens, and cook them 15 to 20 minutes longer.

STUFFED CORNISH HENS WITH QUINCE AND SHIITAKES

YIELD: 4 ENTREE SERVINGS

The soft and creamy filling stuffed under their skin makes the hens look plump and appetizing. It also adds superb flavor. This dish is great for entertaining since the stuffed hens can be prepared a day in advance, covered, and refrigerated. Before roasting, bring them to room temperature. You may substitute 2 cups coarsely grated Golden Delicious apples for the quince. Serve this elegant dish with small new potatoes and snow peas.

2 tablespoons plus 2 teaspoons mild olive oil

¹/₄ cup thinly sliced shallots

1 teaspoon minced garlic

¹/₄ pound shiitake mushrooms, stemmed and
   thinly sliced

1 medium quince, peeled, cored, and coarsely
   grated (about 2 cups grated quince)

Salt and freshly ground black pepper

1 large egg, lightly beaten

³/₄ cup ricotta cheese

¹/₂ cup freshly grated Parmesan cheese

2 teaspoons chopped fresh thyme leaves or
   1 teaspoon dried thyme, crumbled

2 Cornish hens (about 1 ³/₄ pounds each),
   rinsed and patted dry

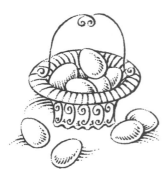

1. Heat 2 tablespoons of the olive oil in a large skillet. Add the shallots and garlic and sauté over medium heat until tender, about 30 seconds. Add the mushrooms and stir constantly until they are wilted and start to release some moisture, about 1 minute. Add the quince and sauté until it has softened, 1 minute more. Remove from the heat and season lightly with salt and pepper. Set aside to cool throughly.

2. Combine the cooled mushroom-quince mixture with the beaten egg, ricotta and Parmesan cheeses, and 1 teaspoon of the

fresh thyme (or ¹/₂ teaspoon of the dried thyme) in a medium-size mixing bowl. The stuffing should be firm. If not, cover and refrigerate until firm but spreadable, about 1 hour.

3. Place a hen on its breast on a cutting board. With poultry shears, cut along both sides of the backbone; remove the bone and reserve it for stock. Using both hands, pull the chicken wide open to expose the interior of the hen; trim all excess fat. Without cutting all the way through, make an incision at the joints where the thighs and the drumsticks meet. (This helps the bird cook evenly; this thick part of the legs would otherwise take longer to cook.) Turn over the butterflied hen, breast side up. With the heel of your hand, firmly press on the wishbone to flatten the bird. Butterfly the second hen in the same manner.

4. Loosen the skin on the breast and legs of each hen by gently pushing your fingers through the opening at the neck, and running them between the skin and meat to create a loose pocket, taking care not to tear the skin. Rub the hens all over with salt and pepper.

5. Preheat the oven to 450°F. Lightly oil a rack and place it in a roasting pan.

6. Spoon one-quarter of the filling under the loosened skin of each hen. With your hand, push the filling toward the leg areas. Fill the breasts areas with the remaining filling. Lightly pat the stuffed hens to distribute the filling evenly. (Or transfer the filling to a

pastry bag fitted with a plain $1/2$-inch tip. Insert the tip under the loosened skin and pipe in the filling, starting at the legs and ending at the breasts.) Combine the remaining 2 teaspoons olive oil and 1 teaspoon fresh thyme ($1/2$ teaspoon dried) and rub the mixture over the hens. Place the stuffed birds, breast side up, in the prepared roasting pan.

7. Roast the hens for 15 minutes, then reduce the oven temperature to 400°F. Continue roasting for 35 minutes until the skin is crisp and golden, basting with the pan juices every 10 minutes. To test for doneness, cut into the thickest part of a thigh and take a peek. The flesh should be opaque, without a trace of pink.

8. With poultry shears, halve the hens lengthwise and carefully transfer each half to a warmed dinner plate. Skim the fat from the pan juices and spoon the juices over the hens. Serve at once.

SESAME DUCK WITH LITCHEES

YIELD: 2 TO 4 ENTREE SERVINGS

Here's an uncomplicated duck recipe with an Asian twist. Five-spice powder, honey, sesame oil, and litchees make for a delicious and very unusual sauce that complements the pan-roasted duck, which, with a healthy dose of sweet, aromatic garlic, becomes a highly seductive taste experience. Take care to cook the garlic slowly so that the cloves become soft but do not loose their shape. For an equally simple accompaniment, serve this savory dish with any noodles or pasta you may have on hand.

1 teaspoon Chinese five-spice powder
1 tablespoon honey
1 tablespoon tomato paste
1 tablespoon soy sauce, preferably Kikkoman
1 tablespoon dark sesame oil
$3/4$ cup chicken broth, preferably homemade (page 30)
20 large cloves garlic, peeled and halved lengthwise
2 cups fresh litchees, peeled, pitted, and halved, or 1 can (20 ounces) litchees in light syrup, drained then halved
1 duck ($4 1/2$ to 5 pounds), thawed if frozen
Salt, and freshly ground black pepper

1. Combine the five-spice powder, honey, tomato paste, soy sauce, sesame oil, chicken broth, and garlic in a small saucepan and bring to a boil over medium-high heat. Cover the pan, reduce the heat to low, and simmer until the garlic is very soft but not mushy, about 20 minutes. Add the litchees, remove from the heat, and set aside until needed.

2. Split the duck in half lengthwise, and trim any excess fat. Then cut each half into 4 pieces (thigh, drumstick, breast, and wing). Rinse the duck pieces well and pat dry with

LITCHEES

The litchee, native to Southeast Asia, is a treasured fruit in China. This jewel of the East grows on trees in clusters like cherries. It has the size and look of a baby plum and is covered with a thin, prickly rose or brown shell. When peeled, it reveals a whitish pulp similar in consistency to a grape but firmer. The center of the fruit contains an ovoid, mahogany-like seed. Litchees are deliciously sweet and juicy, with a perfume reminiscent of musk and roses.

If you can get hold of this precious fruit fresh in the summer, indulge in it. Select litchees that are large, thin-skinned, and of the pinkest color. Because its season is very brief, litchees tend to be expensive. Enjoy these gems au naturel or add them to a fresh fruit salad (such as Tropical Fruit Salad, see Index). You may also use litchees as you would grapes in savory poultry or pork dishes by adding them during the last few minutes of cooking.

paper towels. With the tip of a sharp knife, score the skin of the duck breasts and thighs, taking care not to cut through to the meat. Season with salt and pepper.

3. Place a large skillet over medium-high heat. When it's very hot, add the duck pieces, skin side down, and cook until the skin is very dark brown, about 5 minutes. Cover the skillet, reduce the heat to very low, and cook until the juices run clear when a piece of duck is pierced with the tip of a sharp knife, about 30 minutes. (Do not pour off the fat that accumulates in the pan as the duck cooks, since this helps draw away more of the fat from the skin.)

4. Remove the duck pieces from the skillet and pour off all the fat. Return the skillet to the stove and raise the heat to high.

5. Add the sauce to the skillet, and stir, scraping up any browned bits from the bottom of the skillet with a wooden spoon.

Cook until the sauce has thickened slightly, about 2 minutes. Add the duck pieces, turning them to coat with sauce. Remove from the heat.

6. Transfer the duck pieces to warmed dinner plates, spoon the litchee sauce over them, and serve at once.

ROAST DUCK WITH BLUEBERRY SAUCE

YIELD: 2 TO 4 ENTREE SERVINGS

Duck and blueberries may sound surprising, but the combination is delicious and the dish looks stunning. If you love duck but are intimidated

A SPRING GRADUATION PARTY

CHAMPAGNE

◆

STRAWBERRY FIELDS SALAD

◆

ROAST DUCK WITH BLUEBERRY SAUCE

◆

BAKED STUFF PAPAYA

◆

CRUSTY BREAD

◆

APRICOT KUCHEN

◆

COFFEE

by it, try this method: It's as easy as roasting a chicken. I serve this succulent dish with steamed couscous.

1 duck (4½ to 5 pounds), thawed if frozen, including neck and gizzards
Salt and freshly ground black pepper
1 large juice orange
½ medium onion, quartered
⅓ cup dry white wine
¾ cup chicken broth, preferably homemade (page 30)
2 tablespoons sugar
3 tablespoons red wine vinegar
2 cups fresh or thawed frozen blueberries

1. Preheat the oven to 450°F.

2. Rinse the duck, pat it dry, and trim any excess fat around the neck and tail. Sprinkle the duck inside and out with salt and pepper. Juice the orange and set the juice (about ½ cup) aside for the sauce. Stuff the orange rinds and onion into the cavity of the duck. Using a trussing needle, pierce the skin all over, including the thighs, back, and lower breast where the fat is thickest, at ½-inch intervals. Take care not to pierce the meat.

3. Place a rack in a heavy flameproof roasting pan. Place the duck on its side on the rack; put the neck and gizzards in the bottom of the roasting pan. Roast for 15 minutes. Turn the duck and roast on the opposite side for 15 minutes.

4. Reduce the oven temperature to 400°F. Turn the duck breast breast side up, and continue roasting until the juices run slightly pink when a thigh is pierced at the thickest part with the tip of a sharp knife, 40 to 45 minutes more. If the rendered duck fat starts smoking, add a little water to the roasting pan, as needed.

5. Remove the duck and pour the juices from its cavity into a medium-size saucepan. Transfer the duck to a platter, cover loosely with a sheet of aluminum foil, and set aside. Add the neck and gizzard to the juices in the saucepan, and set aside.

6. Degrease the pan juices and place the roasting pan over medium-high heat. Using a wooden spoon, stir in the white wine, chicken broth, and reserved orange juice, scraping up any browned bits from the bottom of the pan.

7. Add the mixture to the juices in the saucepan, and bring to a boil. Reduce the heat to low and simmer until the sauce is reduced to about ³/₄ cup, 15 to 20 minutes. Strain into a small bowl, degrease if necessary, cover, and set aside. (Up to this point, everything can be prepared a day ahead and refrigerated. Bring to room temperature before proceeding with the recipe.)

8. When ready to serve, preheat the broiler.

9. Remove the orange rinds and onion from the duck's cavity, and using poultry shears, cut the bird into quarters. Place the duck pieces, skin side up, on a baking sheet, and broil 4 inches from the heat until the skin is crisp, 5 to 6 minutes.

10. Meanwhile, combine the sugar and vinegar in a large skillet. Cook over medium heat until the mixture is syrupy, 2 minutes. Add the reserved sauce and cook over medium-low heat until smooth and syrupy, about

1 minute. Add the blueberries and cook just until they are heated through, about 1 minute. Remove from the heat and season to taste with salt and pepper.

11. Transfer the duck quarters to a warmed serving platter. Spoon the sauce over the duck and serve immediately.

VARIATIONS

ROAST DUCK WITH PEACH SAUCE: Substitute 2 cups sliced peeled fresh peaches for the blueberries.

ROAST DUCK WITH PINEAPPLE: Substitute four ³/₄-inch-thick rings fresh pineapple for the blueberries.

ROAST DUCK WITH FRESH FIGS: Follow the directions for Roast Duck with Blueberry Sauce through step 9. Melt 1 tablespoon unsalted butter in a skillet over medium heat, add 6 large fresh figs, and cook about 1 minute. Add the reserved sauce and 2 sprigs fresh thyme (or ¹/₂ teaspoon crumbled dried thyme), cover, and simmer over low heat for about 10 minutes. Season to taste with salt and pepper. Arrange the figs around the duck pieces on a warmed serving platter. Spoon the sauce over the meat and serve.

WHAT'S IN A NAME?

In classic French cuisine, the name of a dish usu-ally indicates a specific method of preparation or combination of ingredients, and often designates the region with which it is closely identified. Sometimes chefs would honor loyal customers by naming special creations after them.

Even today, when dining in a French restaurant, you will find specialties like Sole Véronique or Poulet à la Normande on the menu, for example. In Sole Véronique, you can expect the fish fillet to be served with a buttery white sauce that includes white seedless grapes, while Poulet à la Normande generally calls for chicken, apples, a little cider, Calvados (an apple brandy), and/or cream.

If you are intrigued by how some dishes get their names, here are some of the best known fruit-related terms from the French culinary repertoire:

A L'AGENAISE (IN THE STYLE OF AGEN): This term usually signals the presence of prunes and Cognac or Armagnac in a dish.

A L'ANTILLAISE (IN THE WEST INDIES STYLE): This indicates a seafood or poultry dish served with an accompaniment of tomato-laced rice and pineapple or banana. In desserts, the term usually signals a con-coction of exotic fruits and rum or vanilla beans.

A LA CREOLE (IN THE CREOLE STYLE): Savory dishes prepared in this style are almost identical to the West Indies style.

A LA BIGARADE: A light, sweetish sauce for duck made with a bitter orange from the south of France called bigarade. Curaçao (a liqueur made from bigarade orange zest) is sometimes added, along with orange sections. This sauce should not be confused with the

orange sauce that traditionally goes with the canard à l'orange.

A LA MONTMORENCY: Dishes prepared in this fashion are characterized by a sweet and sour sauce made with red wine and sour cherries from the town of Montmorency. In baking, all desserts à la Montmorency feature fresh or candied cherries soaked in kirsch.

GRAND VENEUR: This term indicates game meat, such as venison, served in a peppery brown sauce enriched with red currant jelly and crème fraîche.

SAUCE CUMBERLAND: A sweet cold sauce for game made with port, orange juice, orange zest, and red currant jelly. It is named after a county in north-western England that is famous for its hunting grounds.

SAUCE MALTAISE (MALTESE-STYLE SAUCE): A hot, deeply colored hollandaise sauce flavored with blood orange (or tangerine) juice, and its finely grated zest. There is also a cold version made with mayon-naise, sometimes with an added touch of Curaçao. These sauces are intended for steamed or chilled veg-etables, especially asparagus or broccoli.

SAUCE ROMAINE (ROMAN-STYLE SAUCE): A sweet and sour brown sauce for game with raisins, dried currants, and toasted pine nuts.

SAUCE JUBILEE (JUBILEE SAUCE): Black cherry sauce flavored with Cognac or kirsch, flambéed and spooned over vanilla ice cream.

SOUPE SENEGALAISE (SENEGALESE-STYLE SOUP): This is a puréed soup of chick-en and apple, flavored with curry powder. It is garnished with toasted sliced almonds and served cold.

DUCK BREASTS MONTMORENCY

YIELD: 2 TO 4 ENTREE SERVINGS

Nothing cuts the richness of duck or goose more agreeably than a sauce of tart cherries. Pork chops are also delicious graced by such a sauce. If fresh boneless duck breasts are unavailable in your area, buy two whole ducks, and quarter them according to the instructions in Sesame Duck with Litchees (page 186). Use the duck breasts for this recipe, then freeze the legs for use in Braised Duck in Orange-Cinnamon Sauce, or Thai Red Chicken Curry (see Index) for example. If you use canned sour cherries, finish the sauce with a squeeze of fresh lemon juice; the acid helps revive the natural flavor of the cherries.

4 boneless duck breasts (8 to 10 ounces each),
    trimmed of excess fat, rinsed, and patted
    dry
Salt and freshly cracked black pepper corns
¼ cup dry white wine
2 cups pitted fresh sour cherries or
    canned sour cherries packed in
    water, drained
6 tablespoons red currant jelly
4 teaspoons soy sauce, preferably Kikkoman
Zest of 1 large lemon
2 tablespoons unsalted butter

1. With the tip of a sharp knife, score the skin of the duck breasts, taking care not to cut through to the meat. The slashes should be ¾ inch apart. Sprinkle both sides with salt and pepper.

2. Place a large nonstick skillet over medium-high heat. When it's very hot, add the duck breasts, skin side down, and brown until the skin is crisp, 10 to 12 minutes. (If the skin browns too quickly, reduce the heat.) Reduce the heat to medium-low, turn the breasts over, and cook until the meat is slightly pink inside, 5 minutes more. Transfer the duck breasts to a plate and cover them loosely with aluminum foil to keep them warm, while you make the sauce.

3. Pour off all the fat from the skillet. Return the skillet to the stove and raise the heat to high.

4. Add the white wine, then immediately stir in the sour cherries, jelly, soy sauce, and lemon zest. Bring the mixture to a boil over medium-high heat, scraping up any browned bits from the bottom of the pan with a wooden spoon. Cook, mashing some of the cherries with the back of the spoon, until the jelly is dissolved and the sauce is syrupy, 4 to 5 minutes. Pour any juices collected on the duck

plate into the pan. Season the sauce to taste with salt and pepper, then whisk in the butter. Remove from the heat.

5. Slice the duck breasts against the grain on the diagonal into 1/4-inch-thick slices and fan them out on warmed dinner plates. Spoon the sauce over the duck breasts, and serve at once.

BRAISED DUCK IN ORANGE-CINNAMON SAUCE

YIELD: 4 ENTREE SERVINGS

The idea for this stew is Guatemalan in origin. There, one popular way to serve red-meat birds like duck or goose is to slowly braise them in a sauce scented with orange and cinnamon. I find that the flavor improves when the stew is cooked hours or even a day ahead and gently reheated just before dinner. Serve it with rice or pasta and the Sicilian Orange Salad (see Index). A sorbet or

fruit compote would be the best way to finish the meal.

1 cinnamon stick (3 inches long), broken
    in half
1/2 teaspoon sugar
1/2 teaspoon dried thyme, crumbled
10 whole cloves
Salt and freshly ground black pepper
4 duck legs (about 2 1/2 pounds total)
1 tablespoon canola or vegetable oil
3/4 cup chopped onion
1 tablespoon minced garlic
3/4 cup peeled, seeded, and chopped fresh
    or canned tomatoes
2 large bay leaves
1 cup fresh orange juice
1 cup chicken broth, preferably homemade
    (page 30)
Fresh cilantro sprigs, for garnish (optional)

1. Combine the cinnamon stick, sugar, thyme, and cloves with 1/2 teaspoon each salt and pepper in a small bowl and set aside.

2. Season the duck legs with salt and pepper. Heat the oil in a large skillet with a tight-fitting lid over medium-high heat. Add the duck legs, skin side down, and brown well on both sides, about 2 minutes. Transfer the duck legs to a plate.

3. Pour off the fat, leaving about 1 tablespoon in the skillet. Add the onion and garlic and sauté over medium-low heat until tender, about 1 minute. Add the tomatoes and the spice mixture and cook, stirring occasionally, until a soft paste forms, about 5 minutes. Add the orange juice and broth, and bring to

a boil. Add the duck legs, along with any juices collected on the plate.

4. Cover and simmer over low heat until the duck is tender, and the sauce is slightly thickened, turning the legs once or twice, about 45 to 50 minutes.

5. Remove and discard the cinnamon, bay leaves, and cloves. Transfer the duck legs to a warmed platter and spoon the sauce over them. Garnish with cilantro sprigs, if desired.

FIGGY QUAIL

YIELD: 2 TO 4 ENTREE SERVINGS

When I lived in the south of France, we had a huge fig tree in our backyard. It produced such an abundance of fruit every fall that we ended up giving most of it away to neighbors, while saving a few for ourselves. Most of the time we enjoyed them au naturel, but my stepfather, who was an excellent cook, liked to use them in his cooking as well. This quail dish, one of the tastiest I've ever had, is the result of one of his experiments. A heavenly cream sauce with port and vinegar (raspberry-flavored vinegar is my touch) harmonizes with the sweet quail meat and figs. Serve with plenty of rice or bread to soak up the rich sauce.

MARINADE
2 tablespoons port
2 tablespoons honey
2 tablespoons soy sauce, preferably Kikkoman
2 tablespoons peanut oil
1 teaspoon minced garlic
1/2 teaspoon freshly ground black pepper

QUAIL
4 quail (about 1 1/4 pounds total), butterflied and boned (see Note), rinsed and patted dry
1 cup heavy (or whipping) cream
1 1/2 teaspoons unsalted butter
1/4 cup sliced shallots
1/2 cup port
1/4 cup chicken broth, preferably homemade (page 30)
2 tablespoons raspberry vinegar, preferably homemade (page 286), or red wine vinegar
4 large fresh Calimyrna figs, halved or 8 small fresh Mission figs, left whole
1 teaspoon chopped fresh thyme leaves or 1/2 teaspoon dried thyme, crumbled
Salt and freshly cracked black peppercorns

1. To make the marinade, combine all the ingredients in a small bowl.

2. Arrange the quail in a single layer in a shallow baking dish and pour the marinade over them. Turn each quail to coat thoroughly with the marinade, cover,

and refrigerate for 4 hours, or overnight, turning once or twice.

3. Pour the cream into a small saucepan and simmer, uncovered, over medium-low heat until thickened and reduced by half, about 20 minutes. Cover and set aside until needed.

4. Remove the quail from the marinade and pat dry. Melt the butter in a large non-stick skillet over medium-high heat. Add the quail, skin side down, in a single layer and cook until the skin is deep brown and crisp, about 2 minutes. Turn the quail and cook until just done, about 2 minutes more. The breast meat should still be juicy and pinkish. Transfer the quail to a plate and cover them loosely with aluminum foil to keep them warm while you finish the sauce.

5. Add the shallots to the skillet and sauté over medium-high heat until tender, about 1 minute. Add the port, broth, and vinegar and bring to a boil. Cook until the mixture is reduced by half, about 3 minutes, then add the reduced cream, figs, and thyme. Partially cover, reduce the heat, and simmer until the figs are heated through, 2 to 3 minutes.

6. Remove from the heat and season the sauce to taste with salt and cracked pepper. Arrange the quail and figs on warmed dinner plates, and spoon the sauce over the quail. Serve immediately.

NOTE: Ask your butcher to butterfly and bone the quail for you.

QUAIL IN CURRANT SAUCE

YIELD: 2 ENTREE SERVINGS

After the classic Mediterranean fashion of pairing game meat with wine and dried fruit, I've developed one of the simplest—and best—quail dishes I've ever had. With a sauce as succulent as this one, it seems perfectly proper to clean your plate with a piece of good, crusty bread. You may also try this delicious sauce on grilled steak or pork chops.

CURRANT SAUCE
1/2 cup dried currants or raisins
1/2 cup Madeira or port
1/2 cup chicken broth, preferably homemade
(page 30)
1/8 teaspoon ground cinnamon
Salt and freshly ground black pepper

QUAIL
4 quail (about 1 1/4 pounds total)
butterflied and boned (see Note, this
page), rinsed and patted dry
Salt and freshly ground black pepper
2 teaspoons unsalted butter
2 teaspoons mild olive oil
1 tablespoon chopped flat-leaf parsley

1. To make the sauce, combine the currants with the Madeira in a small saucepan and let sit for 15 minutes.

2. Cook the wine and currants over medium-high heat until the wine is reduced by half, about 3 minutes. Add the chicken broth and reduce by half, about 3 minutes. Add the cinnamon and season to taste with salt and pepper. Cover and set aside until needed.

3. To cook the quail, sprinkle the quail with salt and pepper. Heat the butter and olive oil in a large skillet over medium-high heat. Add the quail, skin side down, in a single layer and cook until the skin is deep brown and crisp, about 2 minutes. Turn the quail and cook until just done, about 2 minutes more. The breast meat should still be juicy and pinkish. Pour off any excess fat. Add the currant sauce to the skillet and cook 30 seconds more, turning the quail to coat with the sauce.

4. Transfer the quail to warmed dinner plates and spoon the currant sauce over the top. Sprinkle with chopped parsley and serve immediately.

SQUABS IN MADEIRA AND STRAWBERRY SAUCE

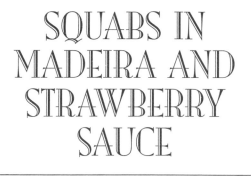

YIELD: 2 TO 4 ENTREE SERVINGS

The combination of slightly acidic strawberries and sweet Madeira produces an intense, fascinating sauce that is especially good with fowl, such as braised squabs. Two 1-pound Cornish hens may be substituted for the squabs. To round out the meal, serve this with a loaf of good onion bread and a mixed green salad tossed with a simple Raspberry Vinaigrette (see Index).

Salt and freshly ground black pepper
2 squabs (about 1 pound each), rinsed and patted dry
1 tablespoon mild olive oil
1 tablespoon unsalted butter
1/2 cup sliced shallots
2 teaspoons chopped fresh thyme leaves, or 1 teaspoon dried thyme, crushed
2 teaspoons chopped fresh rosemary leaves, or 1 teaspoon dried rosemary, crushed
2/3 cup Madeira
2/3 cup chicken broth, preferably homemade (page 30)
1 cup sliced fresh strawberries

1. Combine ½ teaspoon each salt and pepper and rub the mixture on the squabs, inside and out.

2. Heat the oil and butter in a Dutch oven or large, heavy skillet with a tight-fitting lid over medium-high heat. Add the squabs and brown on all sides, about 5 minutes. Reduce the heat to low, add the shallots, thyme, and rosemary, and sauté until the shallots are tender, about 2 minutes. Add the Madeira and broth and bring to a simmer. Tightly cover the pan and cook the squabs, breast side down, until they are just tender, about 30 minutes, turning them once or twice. Transfer the squabs to a warmed platter, and cover them loosely with aluminum foil to keep them warm while you finish the sauce.

3. Bring the sauce to a boil over high heat and cook until it is slightly reduced, about 2 minutes. Skim off any fat.

4. Stir in the strawberries. Add the squabs to the sauce along with any juices collected on the plate. Cover and continue to cook until the berries are just tender and the sauce thickens slightly, 2 minutes longer. Remove the pan from the heat. Season to taste with salt and pepper, if necessary.

5. Transfer the squabs to a cutting board and cut each one in half, using poultry shears. Arrange on a warmed serving platter, spoon the strawberry sauce over them, and serve.

ROAST RABBIT IN POMEGRANATE SAUCE

YIELD: 4 ENTREE SERVINGS

With its lean and mild meat, rabbit has more character than chicken. It is also versatile and relatively inexpensive. I think one of the best ways to prepare rabbit is by marinating and then roasting it. The tart and sweet pomegranate juice in this marinade helps tenderize the meat and flavor it at the same time (note that this recipe calls for a marination time of 1 to 2 days). If pomegranate is not in season, simply substitute cranberry juice.

MARINADE

½ cup fresh pomegranate juice
     (from 1 large pomegranate; for juicing
     instructions, see box, this page)
1 cup Marsala
3 tablespoons mild olive oil
1 teaspoon minced garlic
1 teaspoon minced shallots
1 tablespoon chopped fresh mint, thyme, or
     rosemary leaves

RABBIT

1 fresh rabbit (about 4 pounds), rinsed,
     patted dry, and cut into
     7 or 8 pieces
Salt and freshly ground black pepper
1 teaspoon mild olive oil
1 teaspoon unsalted butter
Seeds from 1 large pomegranate
1 tablespoon chopped flat-leaf parsley leaves

1. To make the marinade, whisk together the marinade ingredients in a mixing bowl. Add the rabbit pieces, cover, and marinate for 1 to 2 days, no longer, in the refrigerator, turning the pieces several times.

2. Preheat the oven to 400°F.

3. To cook the rabbit, drain the rabbit, reserving the marinade. Dry the rabbit with paper towels and sprinkle to taste with salt and pepper.

4. Heat the olive oil and butter in a large, heavy skillet over medium-high heat. Working in 2 batches, add the rabbit and brown on both sides, 7 to 8 minutes per batch.

HOW TO JUICE A POMEGRANATE

Firmly roll and knead a pomegranate on a countertop to crush the seeds and fruit inside. Halve the pomegranate on a plate (so the red juice won't stain the work surface). Using a manual citrus juicer, extract the juice. Strain the juice through a fine sieve placed over a bowl. Gather the seeds left in the strainer and carefully squeeze them with your hand to extract as much liquid as possible. Discard the seeds. Add to the bowl any juices collected on the plate. One large (12-ounce to 1-pound) pomegranate will yield about ½ cup juice.

5. Transfer the rabbit to a roasting pan and roast until the meat is tender and the juices run clear when the meat is pierced with a sharp knife, 15 to 20 minutes.

6. Meanwhile, add the reserved marinade to the skillet. Bring to a boil over high heat, scraping up any browned bits from the bottom of the pan with a wooden spoon. Cook until the sauce is reduced and slightly syrupy, about 10 minutes.

7. Strain any juices that have collected in the roasting pan into the sauce. Strain the sauce through a fine sieve; degrease. Season to taste with salt and pepper.

8. Arrange the rabbit pieces on a warmed serving platter, and spoon the sauce over them. Sprinkle with pomegranate seeds and chopped parsley. Serve immediately.

VARIATION

TURKEY SCALOPPINE IN POMEGRANATE SAUCE: Substitute four thinly pounded turkey cutlets (about 5 to 6 ounces each) for the rabbit. Proceed as directed in the above recipe, but marinate the turkey cutlets for 2 hours instead of 2 days and cook for only 1 minute per side, omitting the roasting step.

BRAISED RABBIT WITH FRESH FIGS

YIELD: 4 ENTREE SERVINGS

The combination of figs and meat is common in Mediterranean dishes. It lends a savory sweetness to many recipes, as this hearty peasant-style stew so deliciously demonstrates. The idea of pairing rabbit, sherry, and figs might sound a bit unusual, but they all go together amazingly well, and the dish is not as heavy as you might suspect. Save this one-dish meal for those cold winter evenings.

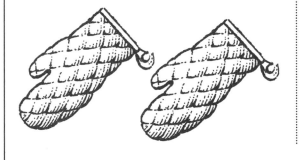

Salt and freshly ground black pepper

1 teaspoon dried thyme, crumbled

1 teaspoon dried sage

1 fresh rabbit (about 4 pounds), rinsed, patted dry, and cut into 7 or 8 pieces

$^1/_2$ cup ($^1/_4$ pound) diced smoked slab bacon

1 teaspoon mild olive oil, if needed

$^2/_3$ cup chopped onion

1 tablespoon minced garlic

1 cup cubed carrots ($^1/_2$-inch pieces)

$^3/_4$ cup dry sherry

$^1/_2$ cup dry white wine, preferably Chardonnay

$^3/_4$ cup chicken broth, preferably homemade (page 30)

2 sprigs fresh thyme

2 bay leaves

8 fresh shiitake mushroom caps, halved

8 fresh Mission figs, halved, or 4 large Calimyrna figs, quartered

1. Combine $^1/_2$ teaspoon salt, 1 teaspoon pepper, the dried thyme, and sage in a small bowl. Rub the mixture all over the rabbit pieces and set aside.

2. Preheat the oven to 375°F. Line a plate with paper towels.

3. Place the slab bacon in a Dutch oven or ovenproof soup pot over medium heat. Cook, stirring often, until the bacon has rendered most of its fat, and is browned and crisp, 5 to 6 minutes. With a slotted spoon, remove the bacon to drain on paper towels. Pour off all but 2 tablespoons of fat from the pan.

4. Raise the heat to high. Add the rabbit pieces and brown on all sides, 5 to 6

FIGS

To eat fresh figs off the tree is a pleasure unknown to most people. Nothing can prepare us for the subtle, honey-sweet succulence of our first fresh fig, especially if we're acquainted only with dried figs, or fig-filled cookies and the like. There are three basic varieties of fig available: Black Mission figs, which are purple, deeply sweet, and rich; Calimyrna figs, which are amber-colored and honey-flavored; and Kadota figs, which are green, fragrant, with a light sweet flavor. Their season lasts from late summer to early fall.

When you select fresh figs for cooking, whether they are big or small, black or green, pick ones that are hard and slightly unripe, then keep them at room temperature until they are soft to the touch. At this stage, they will hold their shape during the cooking process. Once ripe, figs are highly perishable and should be stored in the refrigerator and eaten as soon as possible. If they develop a sour smell, they are overripe. Fresh figs have a delicious nutlike honey flavor that makes them an excellent companion to cheese. Try using sliced fresh figs in sweet or savory salads, in creamed sauces, or paired with rich meats, such as duck or pork. They are also delicious baked, grilled, or in their natural state, with a little bit of heavy cream and sherry or kirsch poured over them.

minutes. Transfer the meat to a plate. If the pot is dry, add 1 teaspoon oil. Add the onion, garlic, and carrots and sauté until the vegetables are tender, about 2 minutes.

5. Add the sherry, wine, and chicken broth to the pot, scraping up any browned bits from the bottom of the pot with a wooden spoon. Add the thyme, bay leaves, bacon, mushrooms, and rabbit pieces. Bring the mixture to a boil, cover, and place in the oven. Bake until the rabbit is fork-tender, about 45 minutes. Transfer the rabbit pieces to a serving platter, and cover loosely with aluminum foil to keep it warm while you finish the sauce.

6. Place the pot over high heat and cook the sauce until it is slightly reduced, about 2 minutes. Add the figs and cook until they are just heated through. Season the sauce to taste with salt and pepper. Spoon the sauce over the rabbit and serve at once.

GRILLED TURKEY-BANANA ROLLS

YIELD: 4 ENTREE SERVINGS

This dish of grilled turkey stuffed with sweet banana and salty prosciutto vibrates with tropical flavors. One bite of it, and you'll be transported to the Caribbean islands. It is also fun to cook.

Besides the Tomato-Peach Chutney called for here, try serving these flavorful smoky turkey rolls with Sassy Banana Chutney or Spiced Apricot Chutney (see Index) for completely different but surprising taste sensations.

2 teaspoons dried thyme, crumbled

1 teaspoon curry powder, preferably Madras brand

1/2 teaspoon salt

1/2 teaspoon freshly ground black pepper

8 turkey cutlets (about 2 pounds)

8 paper-thin slices imported prosciutto (about 1/4 pound)

2 medium bananas, peeled and halved crosswise

12 thin slices bacon

Tomato-Peach Chutney (page 275)

1. Combine the thyme, curry powder, salt, and pepper in a small bowl.

2. Place 2 turkey cutlets, overlapping them slightly, between 2 sheets of plastic wrap. Flatten the cutlets as thinly as possible with a meat pounder or the bottom of a heavy skillet, taking care not to break the meat.

3. Sprinkle the flattened cutlets with one-quarter of the spice mix. Place 2 slices of prosciutto over the meat, then place 1 piece of banana at the base. Fold the sides of the cutlet over the banana then

A CARIBBEAN FEAST

STRAWBERRY DAIQUIRI

◆

TROPICAL LOBSTER SALAD

◆

GRILLED TURKEY-BANANA ROLLS

◆

TOMATO-PEACH CHUTNEY

◆

STEAMED RICE

◆

FLAMED PEACHES AND STRAWBERRIES WITH TEQUILA

roll up to form a neat, fat cylinder. Wrap 3 strips of bacon around the turkey roll. Secure the roll with toothpicks, if necessary. Repeat with the remaining turkey cutlets to make 3 more rolls. Cover and refrigerate until needed.

4. Prepare coals for grilling or heat a stovetop grill pan over medium-low heat. Lightly oil the grill. Grill the turkey rolls, covered, until they are cooked through, about 15 minutes total, turning occasionally to brown on all sides.

5. Remove the bacon, if desired, and cut each turkey roll into 4 slices. Arrange the slices on dinner plates, and serve with Tomato-Peach Chutney.

MAGNIFICENT MEAT

In Laos, where I grew up, pork and poultry were the meats of choice. Beef was also much appreciated, but because it commanded higher prices, we ate it less frequently. Lamb and veal were simply unknown. In fact, it wasn't until we moved to Europe during my early teens that I had my first tastes of lamb, veal, and venison. (I found their flavors exquisite!) Since refrigeration was limited, my mother did her food shopping daily at the main market, and would take me along on weekends, or on days off from school.

This was always an exciting experience for me. I just loved being part of the bustling morning market scene, where smelling and touching the fresh produce and bargaining with the farmers kindled feelings of great pleasure. At the same time, I learned from my mother how to select the best fruits and vegetables, and also took note of which butchers' stalls she favored. We would always stop at the butcher first, to be assured of getting the choicest cuts. Often, the recently butchered meat was so fresh that it was still warm to the touch.

Because beef was expensive, my mother always came up with creative ways to stretch a few ounces to feed us all. She liked to cut it into thin slivers, then marinate and stir-fry it with either fresh chunks of sweet pineapple, sliced star fruit, strips of cabbage, or French-fried potatoes. With tougher cuts of beef, she made hearty soups and stews. On truly special occasions, we would feast on wonderfully juicy steaks, which she had seared in a skillet with a dab of imported French salted butter.

Like beef, veal, pork, lamb, and venison all pair up successfully with fruits. In this chapter you'll find not only the basic steaks and roasts, broiled lamb chops, and meat loaf entrées that are standards for many cooks, you'll also find international favorites such as beef in a cherry sauce. Chinese Tea-Smoked Baby Back Ribs, and Moroccan Lamb Tagine. Fruit adds contrast, textural interest, and intense, complex flavor to a dish, elevating it from just nice to wonderful. Consider roast pork stuffed with Cognac-laced prunes or Pepper Steaks with Plum Ketchup.

Lean cuts of meat benefit especially from an association with fruit. Fruits allow us to make beef, pork, and lamb taste delicious without the burden of additional fat. I use fruity compotes, sauces, and chutneys to replace the butter or cream-laden sauces that often embellish those meats. The dishes emerge lighter and a bit more refined too.

Tart fruits are a natural for rich stews, because they act as a perfect foil for fattier cuts of meats. Take pot roast, for example. My version of this savory dish calls for cooking a beef brisket along with quince and raisins. The fruits add sweetness, and at the same time preserve that intrinsic piquancy often associated with traditional Eastern European cuisine. Veal shank, which the Italians customarily make with carrots, celery, onions, and tomato, can be given a colorful, light twist by cooking it with dried sour cherries and Marsala.

A good many of the dishes that are included in this chapter combine relatively inexpensive cuts of meat with a wide range of fruits and seasonings. They are all fairly simple to prepare. Some employ quick cooking techniques; others require slow cooking but are excellent candidates for plan-ahead meals. No matter what you cook, the key to success to any good food is the same: harmony of ingredients, attention to texture, and visual enticement. Wait until you try the following recipes.

ROAST BEEF WITH BLACK CURRANT SAUCE

YIELD: 4 TO 6 ENTREE SERVINGS

When fresh black currants are abundant in the summer, I like to buy them in quantity, then store them in the freezer. This way, I can enjoy and use these distinctively fragrant berries throughout the year. My favorite way to serve roast beef is with a sauce of pan juices flavored with fresh currants and currant jelly. The berries impart such a subtle sweetness to this dish that you will want to serve it time and again, as I do. If fresh black currants are unavailable, omit them; the pan juices will taste almost as delicious with just the jelly. Red currants are unsuitable for this dish.

2 teaspoons minced garlic
2 teaspoons mild olive oil
Salt and freshly ground black pepper
1 boneless beef shell roast or eye round roast
    (about 2½ pounds)
1 teaspoon dried thyme, crumbled
3 tablespoons brandy, preferably Cognac
¼ cup fresh black currants
2 tablespoons black or red currant jelly
⅓ cup beef broth
1 tablespoon unsalted butter, at room
    temperature

1. Preheat the oven to 500°F.

2. Combine the garlic, oil, and ¼ teaspoon each salt and pepper in a small bowl. Rub the mixture over the roast. Insert a meat thermometer in the thickest part of the roast.

3. Place the meat on a rack in a flameproof roasting pan and roast for 15 minutes. Reduce the oven temperature to 375°F, sprinkle the thyme over the meat, and continue to roast until the internal temperature reaches 145°F (for medium rare), 50 to 55 minutes. (For rare meat, the thermometer should register 125°F.)

ST. PATRICK'S DAY CELEBRATION

DRY SHERRY
♦
SWEET AND CRUNCHY
SODA BREAD
♦
ROAST BEEF WITH BLACK
CURRANT SAUCE
♦
MASHED POTATOES WITH
ROASTED PEARS
♦
CREAMY SPINACH
SALAD WITH APPLES
AND WALNUTS
♦
STEAMED BROCCOLI
♦
ASSORTED ALES AND BEERS
♦
PLUM BREAD PUDDING

4. Transfer the roast to a plate and let it rest for 15 minutes before carving. Reserve the pan drippings to make the sauce.

5. Skim most of the fat from the pan drippings. Place the pan over medium-high heat, add the brandy, and simmer until reduced by half, scraping up any browned bits from the bottom of the pan with a wooden spoon. Add the currants, jelly, and

beef broth, along with any meat juices collected on the plate. Simmer until the currants are soft and the sauce is slightly syrupy, about 3 minutes. Press the berries against the side of the pan with the back of a wooden spoon to crush them slightly. Whisk in the butter, remove the pan from the heat, and season to taste with salt and pepper.

6. Carve the roast into thin slices and serve topped with the black currant sauce.

C H E R R I E S

*T*he *seemingly unusual pairing of cherries and black pepper is in fact quite felicitous, especially in a sauce for beef, pork, or game. Ricotta cheese, mascarpone, and sweet cream all bring out the gentle tartness of ripe cherries. And herbs such as chives, sage, and verbena and nuts such as almonds highlight this fruit's good qualities to great effect.*

BEEF TENDERLOIN IN CHERRY SAUCE

YIELD: 4 ENTREE SERVINGS

I believe that one of the best dishes to come out of France is Boeuf à la Montmorency, or beef in a luscious cherry sauce. Invigorated with port, grenadine, and cherry brandy, the sauce in this recipe is so versatile you can use it on chicken, pork, or game. A loaf of good bread, a jug of wine, and a healthy serving of this dish is the ultimate eating experience. Roasted potatoes and a big salad tossed with freshly grated Parmesan cheese and tomatoes would be fitting accompaniments.

1 can (16 ounces) pitted dark sweet cherries with juice
¼ cup ruby port
½ cup beef broth
1 teaspoon (drained) bottled horseradish
1 teaspoon tomato paste
1 shallot, thinly sliced
1 large bay leaf
½ teaspoon whole black peppercorns
1 teaspoon arrowroot or cornstarch
1 tablespoon mild olive oil
4 beef tenderloin steaks (6 ounces each)
Salt and freshly ground black pepper
¼ cup kirsch (cherry brandy)
1 tablespoon unsalted butter, at room temperature
1 tablespoon grenadine syrup

1. Drain the cherry juice into a large saucepan and set the cherries aside. Add the port, beef broth, horseradish, tomato paste, shallot, bay leaf, and peppercorns. Bring to a boil over medium heat and cook until the mixture is reduced to about ⅔ cup, 12 to 15 minutes. Dissolve the arrowroot in 1 teaspoon water and stir into the sauce. Simmer until the sauce is shiny and slightly thick-

HOW TO FLAMBE

Flambéing, adding brandy or another liquor to a food and igniting it, helps concentrate the flavors of the dish and lends a pleasing note of its own at the same time. It's a simple procedure and when properly done, quite safe: Don't wear loose-sleeved or billowy clothing when preparing a dish that calls for flambéing. And before you begin, clear the cooking area of anything flammable, such as paper, plastic, lighter fluid, hanging herb branches, and the like.

1. Remove the skillet of food that you are flambéing from the heat. Place the liquor in a small saucepan and heat gently over medium heat.

2. Remove the saucepan from the heat. Light the warmed liquor with a long kitchen match and quickly but carefully pour the flaming liquid over the food in the skillet. Using a long metal fork or tongs, turn the ingredients in the flames until the flames subside. This step should take 30 seconds at the most. Once the flame is out, you may return the skillet to the heat.

ened, 1 minute longer. Strain, cover, and set aside. (This can be prepared a few hours ahead. If you refrigerate the sauce, bring it to room temperature before proceeding.)

2. Heat the oil in a large, heavy skillet over high heat. Sprinkle the steaks with salt and pepper and add them to the hot oil. Brown the steaks on both sides and cook until medium-rare (about 6 minutes total) or to your liking. Transfer the steaks to a large platter.

3. Add the cherries and kirsch to the skillet and flambé (carefully following the instructions above). When the flames die out, reduce the heat to low and add the cherry sauce. With a wooden spoon, scrape up any browned bits from the bottom of the pan. Stir in the butter and grenadine syrup.

The sauce should be bright red. Return the beef to the pan and turn to coat with the sauce. Cook until the beef is heated through, about 2 minutes longer. Season the sauce to taste with salt and pepper, if necessary.

4. Transfer the steaks to warmed dinner plates. Spoon the cherry sauce over them and serve at once.

VARIATION

PAN-FRIED CHICKEN IN CHERRY SAUCE: Make the cherry sauce as directed above in step 1. Cut 4 large whole chicken legs (2½ pounds total) at the joints, and season to taste with salt, freshly ground black pepper, and crumbled dried thyme. Brown the chicken pieces in 1 tablespoon mild olive oil over medium-high heat. Cover and cook until the chicken is tender, turning often, 20 minutes.

Transfer the chicken pieces to a warmed platter. Pour off the fat from the pan and finish the sauce as directed in step 3.

PEPPER STEAK WITH PLUM KETCHUP

YIELD: 4 ENTREE SERVINGS

Here is a great way to liven up a simple steak. Treat your family or guests to something special by serving a delicious unexpected fruit ketchup. The robustness of the steaks harmonizes with the delicate plum ketchup to produce a surprisingly flavorful dish. Serve it with French-Fried Plantains (see Index) for a hearty meal.

> 4 well-marbled New York or sirloin beef
>   steaks, ³/₄ to 1 inch thick (1¹/₂ to 2
>   pounds total)
> 1 teaspoon coarsely ground black pepper
> Salt
> 1 tablespoon mild olive oil
> Plum Ketchup (recipe follows)

1. Pat the steaks dry. Press the pepper into the steaks and season with salt.

2. Heat the oil in a large, heavy nonstick skillet over medium-high heat until it begins to smoke. Carefully add the steaks (the oil may splatter) and sauté until brown on both sides and just firm to the touch, 7 to 8 minutes total for medium-rare meat.

3. Transfer the steaks to warmed dinner plates. Pour off the fat from the skillet. With a wooden spoon, stir in 2 tablespoons water over medium-high heat, scraping up any browned bits from the bottom of the pan. Pour the deglazed juices into the Plum Ketchup, and stir until well combined.

4. Top the steaks with some Plum Ketchup and serve. Pass any remaining ketchup at the table.

Plum Ketchup

YIELD: ABOUT 1¼ CUPS

This fruity ketchup is best served warm, so all the flavors can come through. In addition to being delicious on steak, it's great on grilled pork chops. (If you pan-fry the steaks or chops, deglaze the skillet with a couple tablespoons of wine or water and add the juices to the ketchup along with the soy sauce, ginger, and pepper. They will add great depth of flavor.) You may prepare this ketchup a day in advance and reheat it, if you wish. For something different, substitute 1 cup puréed bananas, mangoes, or apricots for the plums.

1 pound Italian plums or red plums
    (about 5 large)
1 tablespoon vegetable oil
½ cup finely chopped shallots
1½ tablespoons minced garlic
½ cup dry red wine, preferably Burgundy
5 teaspoons (firmly packed) light brown sugar
1 teaspoon salt
2 tablespoons soy sauce, preferably Kikkoman
1 teaspoon finely grated peeled fresh ginger
½ teaspoon freshly ground black pepper

1. Bring 3 cups water to a boil in a medium-size saucepan. Score the top and bottom of each plum with a sharp paring knife. Gently lower the plums into the boiling water and cook until very tender, 5 to 8 minutes, depending on their size. Drain.

When cool enough to handle, peel, pit, and mash the plums with a fork to obtain a coarse purée. (There should be about 1 cup.) Set aside.

2. Heat the oil in a medium-size skillet over medium heat. Add the shallots and cook until light golden brown, about 5 minutes, stirring frequently. Add the garlic and sauté for 1 minute. Add the red wine and simmer until it is reduced by half, 3 to 4 minutes. Add the mashed plums, brown sugar, and salt; simmer until the mixture is as thick as ketchup, 4 to 5 minutes. Remove and allow the mixture to cool to room temperature before stirring in the soy sauce, ginger, black pepper, and pan juices, if using. Serve warm.

Gather a peck of tomatoes, pick out the stems, and wash them; put them on the fire without water, sprinkle on a few spoonsful of salt, let them boil steadily an hour, stirring them frequently; strain them through a colander, and then through a sieve; put the liquid on the fire with half a pint of chopped onions, half a quarter of an ounce of mace broke in small pieces; and if not sufficiently salty, add a little more, one table-spoonful of whole black pepper; boil all together until just enough to fill two bottles; cork it tight. Make it in August, in dry weather.

—MARY RANDOLPH'S TOMATO CATSUP IN THE VIRGINIA HOUSEWIFE, 1831

ORANGE BEEF WITH PEANUTS

YIELD: 4 ENTREE SERVINGS

Sweet, *spicy,* and *hot* describe this terrific traditional Thai stir-fry. Orange juice provides a refreshing, delicate flavor as well as relief to the heat of the chile. Enjoy this quick stir-fry with lots of jasmine rice and a bowl of soothing, Chinese-style Watercress and Asian Pear Soup (see Index). As a variation, you may substitute sliced boneless chicken breast or shelled and deveined shrimp for the beef.

3 tablespoons Thai fish sauce

2 tablespoons peanut oil

1 tablespoon cornstarch

1½ teaspoons minced garlic

1 pound lean beef steak, such as sirloin or
   flank, about 1 inch thick, cut across
   the grain into narrow strips about
   2 ½ inches long

Freshly ground black pepper

4 navel oranges

2 teaspoons Sriracha or other hot chile sauce

2 tablespoons (firmly packed) light brown
   sugar

2 teaspoons Worcestershire sauce

4 scallions, trimmed and cut into ½-inch
   pieces (white and green parts)

⅓ cup dry-roasted unsalted peanuts

1. In a medium-size glass bowl, combine 2 tablespoons of the fish sauce, 1 tablespoon of the peanut oil, the cornstarch, and garlic. Add the beef, season to taste with pepper, and toss to coat. Cover and refrigerate until ready to cook.

2. With a zester, remove the zest from the oranges. Finely chop the zest and place in a second medium-size bowl. (There should be 1 tablespoon of chopped zest.) Squeeze the juice from the oranges. (There should be about 1 cup of orange juice.) Add the orange juice, hot sauce, brown sugar, Worcestershire sauce, and remaining 1 tablespoon fish sauce to the zest. Stir until the sugar has dissolved.

3. Heat the remaining 1 tablespoon peanut oil in large skillet over high heat. Add the beef and stir-fry until it is no longer pink, about 1½ minutes. Stir in the orange juice mixture, and bring to a boil. Cook until the sauce thickens and coats the beef, about 2 minutes longer.

4. Remove from the heat, and stir in the scallions and peanuts. Serve immediately.

ORANGE-GLAZED FLANK STEAKS

YIELD: 6 TO 8 ENTREE SERVINGS

Marinating is a practical method of handling large cuts of meat like flank steak, because it helps relax and tenderize the tough muscle fibers. At the same time, the meat is infused with the wonderful fragrance of fresh herbs, spices, wine, or, as in this recipe, fruit juices. Instead of discarding the marinade after the meat has soaked, I reduce it to a thick, flavorful glaze for brushing over the broiled steaks. The herbal aroma of thyme and the sweet tang of orange and lime juices give this dish a most appealing taste.

MARINADE

⅔ cup dry red wine

½ cup fresh orange juice

⅓ cup fresh lime juice

½ cup honey

¼ cup cider vinegar

¼ cup soy sauce, preferably Kikkoman

2 tablespoons mild olive oil

1½ teaspoons minced garlic

1 teaspoon finely grated orange zest

1 teaspoon Tabasco sauce

½ teaspoon ground cumin

½ teaspoon dried thyme, crumbled

¼ teaspoon freshly ground black pepper

2 beef flank steaks (2 pounds each)

1. To make the marinade, combine all the ingredients in a shallow 14-inch glass baking dish and stir until the honey is dissolved. Add the flank steaks and turn to coat with the marinade. Cover and refrigerate overnight.

2. Bring the steaks to room temperature.

3. Prepare coals for grilling or preheat the broiler.

4. Drain the steaks, reserving the marinade. Place the marinade in a large skillet and bring to a boil over high heat. Continue boiling until the liquid is syrupy and mahogany-colored, about 10 minutes. Remove from the heat and let cool. (There should be about 1 cup of glaze.)

5. Brush the glaze on both sides of the steaks. Grill or broil the steaks 4 inches from the heat until nicely glazed, about 5 minutes. Turn and grill or broil 5 minutes longer for medium-rare steaks. Let the meat rest for 5 minutes before carving.

6. Transfer the steaks to a cutting board. If you broiled the steaks, reserve any pan drippings. Holding a sharp knife at a 45-degree angle, cut the steaks across the grain into thin slices. Transfer the meat to a warmed platter, top with the pan drippings, and serve immediately.

VARIATION

GRILLED BUTTERFLIED LEG OF LAMB: Substitute a 6½- to 7½-pound leg of lamb, trimmed, boned, and butterflied (4½ to 5½ pounds boneless). After marinating, grill or broil the lamb for 15 minutes, turning frequently, then baste it with the glaze during the last 15 minutes. Let the lamb rest for 15 minutes before carving.

STIR-FRIED BEEF WITH GREEN PAPAYA

YIELD: 2 TO 3 ENTREE SERVINGS

While green papaya has little flavor of its own, it provides a perfect crunchy foundation for this delightful stir-fry, which contains a small amount of beef to flavor rather than dominate the dish. If green papaya is unavailable, substitute any sturdy vegetable, such as kohlrabi or spaghetti squash. Steamed rice is the best accompaniment to this stir-fry.

½ pound lean beef steak, such as flank steak or sirloin, about 1 inch thick, cut across the grain into narrow strips about 2½ inches long
1 teaspoon minced garlic
1 teaspoon finely grated peeled fresh ginger
1 teaspoon dry sherry
1 teaspoon soy sauce, preferably Kikkoman
6 teaspoons oyster sauce
1 tablespoon plus 2 teaspoons vegetable oil
½ large red bell pepper, stemmed, seeded, and julienned (about ½ cup)
1 medium onion, thinly sliced
2 scallions, trimmed and cut into 1-inch sections (white and green parts)
1 small green papaya (about ¾ pound), peeled, seeded, and finely shredded (for peeling and shredding instructions, see page 32)
2 tablespoons chicken broth, preferably homemade (page 30), or water

1. In a medium-size bowl, combine the beef, garlic, ginger, sherry, soy sauce, and 2 teaspoons of the oyster sauce. Cover and let sit for 30 minutes.

2. Heat 2 teaspoons of the oil in a wok or a large skillet over high heat. Add the beef and stir-fry until just medium-rare, about 30 seconds. Transfer the beef to a bowl.

3. Heat the remaining 1 tablespoon oil. Add the bell pepper, onion, scallions, and papaya and stir-fry just until tender, 3 to 4 minutes. Stir in the broth and the remaining 4 teaspoons oyster sauce, and cook until all the vegetables are tender and well coated with the sauce, about 2 minutes longer.

4. Add the beef, and stir quickly just to reheat. Serve immediately.

VARIATION

STIR-FRIED BEEF WITH PINEAPPLE: Substitute 2 cups diced fresh pineapple for the green papaya. Sprinkle 1 teaspoon sugar over the fruit to offset its acidity, and stir-fry for only 2 minutes.

POT ROAST WITH TZIMMES

YIELD: 6 TO 8 ENTREE SERVINGS

My husband's grandmother Bebe used to make one of the best pot roasts I have ever tasted. She would almost always serve it on Rosh Hashanah, the Jewish New Year. She combined her pot roast with tzimmes, a mixture of carrots, sweet potatoes, and dried fruits. In improvising on her recipe, I have replaced the dried fruit with quinces and added fresh ginger, cinnamon, and cloves for a thoroughly flavorful dish. Save this special dish for winter entertaining; it tastes best when cooked 1 day ahead, and reheated.

1 first-cut beef brisket (about 5 pounds)
Salt and freshly ground black pepper
2 tablespoons mild olive oil
2 medium onions, thinly sliced
1 tablespoon minced garlic
1 tablespoon grated peeled fresh ginger
1 cup dry red wine, preferably Burgundy
1 cup chicken broth, preferably homemade (page 30)
2 teaspoons ground cinnamon
1/2 teaspoon ground cloves
6 medium carrots, peeled and sliced 1/2 inch thick
2 medium sweet potatoes (about 1 pound), quartered lengthwise and sliced 3/4 inch thick (keep in cold water until ready to use to prevent discoloration)
2 large quinces (or 4 tart green apples, such as Granny Smith), peeled, cored, and sliced 3/4 inch thick
1/2 cup raisins, plumped in hot water to cover for 5 minutes and drained
1/4 cup honey

1. Preheat the oven to 350°F.

2. Rub the brisket with salt and pepper to taste.

3. Heat the oil in a large soup pot or Dutch oven over high heat. Carefully add the brisket and brown well, 2 minutes per side. Transfer the brisket to a platter. Add the onions, garlic, and ginger to the pot and cook over medium heat until tender and

golden brown, about 5 minutes, stirring frequently. Add the red wine and bring the mixture to a boil, scraping up any browned bits from the bottom of the pan with a wooden spoon. Cook until the wine is reduced by half, 2 to 3 minutes. Return the brisket to the pot, along with the chicken broth, cinnamon, and cloves. Return to a boil, cover, and place in the oven. Bake for 1½ hours.

4. Add all the vegetables and fruits to the pot. Drizzle with the honey. Gently shake the pan to coat all the ingredients with the cooking liquid. Cover and continue baking for 1½ hours more. Remove the cover for the last 45 minutes to brown the vegetables.

5. Transfer the brisket to a cutting board; it should be fork-tender but still firm. Cover with aluminum foil and let it rest for 30 minutes for easier slicing. If necessary, adjust seasoning of the vegetables and cooking liquid with salt and pepper.

6. With a sharp knife, slice the meat ½ inch thick. You may serve the roast at once with the vegetables and cooking liquid, or, return the meat to the pot, cover, and refrigerate overnight.

7. Reheat the brisket and vegetables in a 350°F oven for about 30 minutes and serve with the vegetables and cooking liquid.

STUFFED CABBAGE IN FRUITED TOMATO SAUCE

YIELD: 6 ENTREE SERVINGS

A delicious way to prepare stuffed cabbage is to braise it in a tomato sauce richly flavored with dried fruits. This recipe, one of my favorites, yields individual meat-stuffed cabbage rolls in a tantalizing sweet-and-sour sauce. These cabbage rolls will taste even better reheated the next day. Have a loaf of fresh crusty bread to sop up all the goodness of the sauce. Rice or mashed potatoes would be good with this dish too.

TOMATO SAUCE
2 tablespoons mild olive oil
1 cup chopped onions
2 teaspoons minced garlic
1 can (28 ounces) crushed tomatoes
1 cup tomato sauce, preferably Quick Tomato Sauce (page 102)
¼ cup (firmly packed) light brown sugar
Salt and freshly ground black pepper

STUFFED CABBAGE

1 white cabbage (about 2 pounds)

1¼ pounds lean ground beef

½ cup minced onion

1 teaspoon minced garlic

2 large eggs, lightly beaten

3 tablespoons ketchup

¼ cup chopped fresh dill

½ teaspoon salt

¼ teaspoon freshly ground black pepper

4 slices white bread, crusts removed

TO FINISH

½ pound dried apricots, plumped in hot water
to cover for 30 minutes and drained

⅓ cup raisins, soaked in hot water to cover for
30 minutes and drained

2 tablespoons fresh lemon juice

¼ cup chopped fresh dill

1. To make the sauce, heat the oil in a large soup pot or Dutch oven over medium heat. Add the onions and garlic and cook, stirring often, until soft, about 5 minutes. Add the crushed tomatoes, tomato sauce, 1½ cups water, and the brown sugar. Season to taste with salt and pepper and stir to blend. Reduce the heat to low, cover the pot, and simmer gently for about 30 minutes.

2. Meanwhile, make the cabbage rolls: Bring a large, deep pot of salted water to a boil over medium-high heat. Remove and discard the core of the cabbage, and place the cabbage, cored end up, in the boiling water. Cook for 5 to 6 minutes. As the large outer leaves become limp, use a fork to peel them off the head one by one, being careful not to tear them. Carefully drain the cabbage

leaves in a colander set in the sink. Refresh under cold running water. Choose the 12 best-shaped, largest leaves. Trim the ribs on the underside so that they are the same thickness as the leaves and can be bent with ease. Drain the leaves on paper towels.

3. Place the beef, onion, garlic, eggs, ketchup, the dill, salt, and pepper in a large mixing bowl. Dip the bread slices in a bowl of water to soften, then squeeze to remove excess water. Add the bread to the mixing bowl. Blend all the ingredients thoroughly with your hands.

4. Place a cabbage leaf smooth side up, with the stem end toward you, on a work surface. Place about ⅓ cup of the filling near the stem end of the leaf. Shape the filling into a log across the base of the leaf with your hands. Fold the sides of the leaf over the filling, then fold over the bottom end of the leaf and roll up to make a neat, compact package. There is no need to tie the roll with string; the leaf will adhere to itself naturally. Assemble the remaining rolls in the same fashion.

5. Place the cabbage rolls, seam side down in a single layer, in the tomato sauce. Add the apricots and raisins and sprinkle with the lemon juice. Cover the pot and cook over low heat until the cabbage rolls and fruits are very tender, about 1 hour.

6. Transfer the cabbage rolls to warmed shallow bowls. Taste the sauce and adjust the seasoning with salt and pepper, if necessary. Stir in the dill. Ladle the fruit sauce over the rolls, and serve at once.

APPLESAUCED MEAT LOAF

YIELD: 6 TO 8 ENTREE SERVINGS

My husband reaches for a jar of applesauce whenever I serve meat loaf, even if it comes with a gravy. He once told me, half-joking, that Jewish tradition dictates it, and implied that I should try it myself. Taking his advice to heart, I did, and developed this meat loaf with applesauce on it! It turned out to be one of the most delicious meat loaves we have ever had, hot or cold. Here's the recipe.

1 pound lean ground beef

1 pound ground pork

½ cup dry bread crumbs

¾ cup minced onion

1 tablespoon minced garlic

2 large eggs

½ cup cold milk

½ cup ketchup

1½ teaspoons salt

1½ teaspoons freshly ground black pepper

1½ teaspoons ground allspice

1½ teaspoons dried thyme, crumbled

1 cup Gingered Applesauce (recipe follows) or store-bought applesauce

3 tablespoons apple cider or apple juice

2 tablespoons (firmly packed) light brown sugar

1 tablespoon Dijon mustard

1. Preheat the oven to 375°F. Lightly butter a roasting pan.

2. Combine the beef, pork, bread crumbs, onion, and garlic in a large mixing bowl. In a separate bowl, lightly beat the eggs. Beat in the milk, ketchup, and seasonings and add to the meat. Mix with your hands just until well combined. Do not overhandle. (A wooden spoon won't do the job as well as your hands.)

3. Shape the meat into an oval loaf in the buttered roasting pan and bake until evenly browned, 50 minutes.

4. Combine the applesauce, apple cider, brown sugar, and mustard in a small saucepan, and heat over medium heat until the sugar is dissolved, about 2 minutes.

5. Pour the applesauce mixture over the meat loaf, covering it well, and continue baking until the top is golden brown, 20 to 25 minutes longer. Remove the meat loaf from the oven and let it rest for 5 minutes before serving.

Gingered Applesauce

YIELD: 2 CUPS

I like my applesauce flavored with fresh ginger for a zingy taste. However, if you prefer yours the traditional way, substitute ¼ teaspoon ground cinnamon for the ginger. Whatever you choose, applesauce is always an excellent companion to grilled or roasted meats.

2 tablespoons fresh lemon juice
4 sweet-tart apples (about 1½ pounds total),
*   such as McIntosh, Cortland, or*
*   Newtown Pippin*
3 tablespoons sugar or more if needed
1½ teaspoons finely grated peeled fresh ginger

1. Place the lemon juice in a large saucepan. Peel, core, and cut each apple into eighths. As you add the apples to the pot, toss them to coat with the lemon juice to prevent discoloration.

2. Add ⅓ cup water, the sugar, and grated ginger and bring to a boil. Reduce the heat to medium-low, cover, and cook until the apples are tender, 4 to 5 minutes. Remove from the heat and mash coarsely with a fork. Taste and add more sugar if necessary. The applesauce should be a bit chunky.

VARIATIONS

APPLE-HORSERADISH SAUCE: Substitute ½ cup of freshly grated peeled horseradish for the ginger. If desired, add 2 cups mayonnaise. It's great with roast beef.

APPLESAUCE WITH FRESH FRUIT: Substitute ½ cup fresh or thawed frozen raspberries, peaches, or blueberries for the ginger, and stir in 2 tablespoons brandy or sake. This is great with game or fowl.

PASSION-APPLESAUCE: Omit the ginger. Just after you remove the pan from the heat, stir the pulp (seeds and all) of 2 passion fruits into the applesauce. This goes well with almost anything, especially grilled sausages, smoked pork chops, and venison.

DESSERT APPLESAUCE: Purée the Gingered Applesauce then thin it with fresh apple cider to the desired consistency. Use it as a topping for ice cream, angel-food cake, or pound cake.

SWEET AND SOUR MEATBALLS

YIELD: 4 TO 6 ENTREE SERVINGS

Say "sweet and sour" and many people hear "gooey Chinese food." This is nothing of the sort. Rather, it's my rendition of Italian meatballs with a Southwestern twist—imagine a succulent and spicy chile sauce dotted with cooling pineapple chunks. Moist and wonderful, the meatballs increase in flavor as they sit overnight. This is the kind of dish you can make well in advance and freeze for busy days. Instead of pineapple, you may use green grapes or canned litchees. Just like their Italian cousins, these meatballs are great with either spaghetti or rice.

SPICE MIX

2 teaspoons ground cumin

1½ teaspoons chile powder

¾ teaspoon ground coriander

¾ teaspoon dried thyme, crumbled

¾ teaspoon dried oregano, crumbled

½ teaspoon freshly ground black pepper

½ teaspoon salt

SAUCE

1 cup tomato sauce, preferably Quick Tomato
    Sauce (page 102)

½ cup chicken broth, preferably homemade
    (page 30)

½ cup ketchup

3 tablespoons (firmly packed) light brown
    sugar

3 tablespoons soy sauce, preferably Kikkoman

1½ tablespoons red wine vinegar

2 pickled jalapeño peppers, minced (optional)

MEATBALLS

¾ pound ground beef

¾ pound ground pork

⅓ cup dry bread crumbs

1 large onion

3 large eggs, lightly beaten

1 tablespoon mild olive oil

2 teaspoons minced garlic

TO FINISH

2½ cups bite-size chunks ripe fresh pineapple

2 tablespoons shredded fresh cilantro or
    flat-leaf parsley leaves (for shredding
    instructions, see page 34)

1. To make the spice mix, combine all
the ingredients in a small bowl and mix well.
Set aside.

2. To make the sauce, combine all the
ingredients in a medium-size bowl. Stir until
the sugar is dissolved. Set aside.

3. To make the meatballs, place the beef,
pork, and bread crumbs in a large mixing
bowl. Grate the onion and add it to the meat.
Add the eggs and half the spice mix. Mix
with your hands until just combined. Do not
overhandle. Shape into 1½-inch balls.

4. Heat the oil in a large skillet (with a
lid) over medium-high heat. Add the meatballs, in batches, and cook until browned on
all sides, about 5 minutes. Using a slotted
spoon, transfer the meatballs, as they are
browned, to a bowl. Add the garlic and
remaining spice mix to the pan, and cook,
stirring, until aromatic, scraping up any
browned bits from the bottom of the pan,
about 30 seconds.

5. Stir the sauce and add it to the pan.
Return the meatballs to the pan, cover and
cook over low heat for 20 minutes, or until
the meatballs are tender.

6. Stir the pineapple into the sauce and
continue to simmer 5 minutes longer.
Sprinkle with shredded cilantro. Serve
immediately.

The cherries from these enormous trees were as big as a small plum, with a deep blackish-red color, and exquisite flavor, and an unforgettable texture, the most delicious fruit one ever sank tooth into, completely and utterly soul-satisfying.

—JAMES BEARD

BRAISED VEAL SHANKS WITH DRIED CHERRIES

YIELD: 4 ENTREE SERVINGS

Inspired by osso buco, the classic Milanese dish of braised veal shanks in tomato sauce, I developed this recipe. Unlike in the classic recipe, these veal shanks are cooked without vegetables or tomatoes. Instead, the sauce is made with Marsala, then subtly flavored with dried cherries. A sprinkling of *gremolata*, a fragrant mélange of minced garlic, lemon zest, and parsley served over the stew provides an inviting spark. As with all veal-shank recipes, try to get the hind shank, which is the meatiest and tenderest part of the shank. The ideal accompaniment for these braised shanks is buttered noodles. Start the meal with a Sicilian Orange Salad (see Index).

4 veal shanks (about 3 pounds total),
     cut about 1½ inches thick
Salt and freshly ground black pepper
¾ cup unbleached all-purpose flour
2 tablespoons mild olive oil
⅓ cup chopped shallots
1 cup chicken broth, preferably homemade
     (page 30)
½ cup Marsala, preferably imported
½ cup dried sour cherries or cranberries,
     plumped in hot water to cover for
     15 minutes and drained
1 teaspoon minced garlic
1 tablespoon grated lemon zest
3 tablespoons finely chopped flat-leaf
     parsley leaves
1 tablespoon unsalted butter

1. Preheat the oven to 400°F.

2. Season the veal shanks with salt and pepper. Place the flour on a platter. Dredge the veal in flour, shaking off any excess.

3. In an ovenproof skillet with a tight-

fitting lid or a Dutch oven large enough to accommodate the shanks in a single layer, heat the oil over medium-high heat. Add the veal shanks and brown on both sides, 2½ to 3 minutes per side. Stir in the shallots and cook until they are soft and aromatic, about 1 minute. Add the chicken broth and Marsala. The liquid should come halfway up the sides of the meat. If necessary, add more Marsala. Bring the mixture to a boil.

4. Cover the skillet and bake 30 to 35 minutes.

5. Turn over the shanks, add the cherries, and continue to bake until the veal is tender, another 30 to 35 minutes.

6. While the veal is cooking, combine the garlic, lemon zest, and chopped parsley in a small bowl and set aside.

7. Turn off the oven. Transfer the shanks to a platter and cover loosely with aluminum foil. Keep them warm in the oven while you finish the sauce.

8. During baking, the liquid in the skil-

let should have reduced by half and thickened slightly. If not, boil the cooking liquid over high heat until slightly thickened, 2 to 3 minutes.

9. Remove the pan from the heat and stir in the butter. Season to taste with salt and pepper.

10. Spoon the sauce over the shanks and sprinkle with the parsley mixture. Serve immediately.

VEAL SCALOPPINE WITH GRAPEFRUIT

YIELD: 2 ENTREE SERVINGS

My mom used to make delicious veal brochettes with chunks of grapefruit on them. Ever since, I have really enjoyed searching out new ways to use this unusual but refreshing combination. Here, it is served as light and flavorful scaloppine, or veal birds— as some people call them—made of thin cutlets dressed up in a wonderful citrus sauce dotted with grapefruit sections. It's a flash to prepare in a pan, but it's no flash in the pan, for it is a dish that will

GREAT MATCHES

GRAPEFRUIT

Tart and bitter grapefruit is an ideal consort for delicate, sweet crabmeat. Grapefruit is also exquisite coupled with veal, chicken, and turkey; cilantro and watercress; and walnut oil.

be long lasting in your repertoire. Thinly pounded chicken, pork, or turkey cutlets are equally good prepared this way.

  2 boneless veal cutlets (about 5 ounces each)
  Salt and freshly ground black pepper
  ³/₄ cup unbleached all-purpose flour
  2 teaspoons mild olive oil
  ¹/₃ cup dry white wine, preferably a Chardonnay
  1 tablespoon unsalted butter
  1 large pink grapefruit, peeled and sectioned
      (for sectioning instructions, see page 318)

1. Lay the veal cutlets between 2 large sheets of waxed paper. Using the flat end of a meat pounder, pound the cutlets until very thin. Sprinkle with salt and pepper. Spread the flour on a platter. Dredge the veal scallops in flour, shaking off any excess.

2. Heat the olive oil in a large nonstick skillet over medium-high heat. When it is very hot, add the veal. Cook until lightly browned, about 1 minute on each side. Transfer the veal to a platter and cover loosely with aluminum foil to keep warm.

3. Add the wine to the skillet and reduce by half, scraping up any browned bits from the bottom of the pan with a wooden spoon. Add the butter and grapefruit

sections. Stir until the butter is melted and the grapefruit is heated through.

4. Season the sauce to taste with salt and pepper and spoon it over the veal. Serve immediately.

CALF'S LIVER WITH GREEN GRAPES

YIELD: 2 ENTREE SERVINGS

Nothing could agree more with the rich taste of liver than the tang of green grapes and the subtle sweetness of balsamic vinegar. This happy alliance is further enhanced by sautéed onions. The result is a truly splendid dish, which tastes even better when it rests on a bed of rice or mashed potatoes.

  2 slices choice calf's liver (about 6 ounces
      each) cut ¹/₂ inch thick
  Salt and freshly ground black pepper
  ³/₄ cup unbleached all-purpose flour
  3 tablespoons mild olive oil
  1 medium onion, thinly sliced
  ¹/₂ pound green seedless grapes, halved
      lengthwise
  2 tablespoons balsamic vinegar
  1 tablespoon unsalted butter
  2 teaspoons snipped fresh chives

1. If some of the thin, stiff membrane is still on the liver, remove it. Also remove any large, white gristly tubes. Rinse the liver and pat dry. Season with salt and pepper. Spread the flour on a platter. Dredge the slices in flour, shaking off any excess.

2. Heat 1½ tablespoons of the olive oil in a large skillet over medium heat. Add the liver and cook until golden brown, about 3 minutes per side. The liver should be a moist pink inside. Test by cutting into a slice while cooking. Transfer the livers to a plate and set aside.

3. Heat the remaining 1½ tablespoons olive oil in the skillet and cook the onion over medium heat until tender, stirring frequently to prevent burning, about 2 minutes. Add the grapes, and sauté until they are heated through, about 1 minute. Add the vinegar and cook until the grapes are soft and render some juice, scraping up any browned bits from the bottom of the pan with a wooden spoon, about 1 minute. Season to taste with salt and pepper. Add the butter and stir just until it melts and the sauce thickens slightly.

4. Return the liver to the skillet, and reheat the slices by turning briefly in the sauce.

5. Transfer the liver to warmed dinner plates and spoon the grape sauce over the top. Sprinkle with chives, and serve immediately.

VARIATIONS

Calf's Liver with Sauteed Apples and Caramelized Onions: Follow the directions for Calf's Liver with Green Grapes, replacing the grape sauce with Sautéed Apples and Caramelized Onions (page 242).

Calf's Liver with Currant Sauce: Cook the calf's liver as directed above, and substitute Currant Sauce (page 194) for the grape sauce. Just before you remove the liver from the skillet in step 2, add the currant sauce to the skillet, turn the liver to coat, and cook just until the sauce is heated through, about 30 seconds.

SWEDISH ROAST PORK

YIELD: 4 ENTREE SERVINGS

There's no denying that Swedish cooks know a great deal about pairing meat and fruit, as this recipe for succulent roast pork stuffed with sweet prunes attests. I've found that after soaking overnight in brandy, the prunes really enhance the pork's natural flavor. Be sure not to let the fruits macerate longer than overnight, or they will develop too strong a taste.

1 boneless loin of pork (1½ pounds)
10 Drunken Prunes (page 392), pitted
Salt and freshly ground black pepper
1 teaspoon mild olive oil
2 teaspoons unsalted butter, at room
*   temperature*
2 baking potatoes
1 teaspoon unbleached all-purpose flour
2 tablespoons sliced shallots
¾ cup chicken broth, preferably homemade
*   (page 30)*
2 tablespoons brandy

1. Preheat the oven to 350°F.

2. Starting from one end of the pork loin, insert a long, narrow, sharp knife through the center of the loin to make a 1½-inch slit. Repeat the process at the other end of the loin. Using your fingers, push the prunes through each end into the pocket to stuff the loin completely.

3. Tie the roast at 2-inch intervals with kitchen string and rub it all over with salt and pepper.

4. Heat the oil and the 1 teaspoon of butter in a large ovenproof skillet or Dutch oven over medium-high heat. Add the roast and brown it on all sides, about 4 minutes total. Transfer the skillet to the oven and roast the meat for 20 minutes.

5. Meanwhile, peel the potatoes and cut them into eighths. Add the potatoes to the skillet, tossing to coat with oil, and continue to roast until the loin registers 150°F on an instant-read thermometer, about 30 minutes longer.

6. Carefully remove the skillet from the oven. Transfer the roast and potatoes to a serving platter. Cover loosely with aluminum foil while you make the sauce.

7. In a small bowl, stir together the remaining 1 teaspoon butter and the flour to make a beurre manié. Set aside.

8. Pour off all but 1 teaspoon of the fat from the skillet. Sauté the shallots in the fat over medium-high heat until fragrant and tender. Deglaze the pan with the chicken broth and brandy, scraping up any browned bits from the bottom of the pan with a wooden spoon. Allow the liquid to boil briefly to cook off the alcohol in the brandy. Whisk in the beurre manié, and remove the sauce from the heat; it should be slightly thickened. Season to taste with salt and pepper.

9. Carve the roast into ¼-inch-thick slices and spoon the sauce over the top.

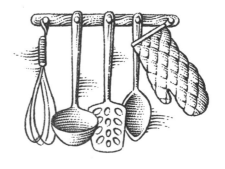

CROWN ROAST OF PORK WITH COUSCOUS STUFFING

YIELD: 6 ENTREE SERVINGS

Stuffed with couscous, spicy sausage, sweet dried fruits, and fennel, this crown roast makes a most impressive centerpiece for a buffet or holiday table. Ask your butcher to put the crown roast together for you; allow 2 ribs per guest. Cook the roast and the Couscous with Dried Fruit (the stuffing) separately. Roasting the crown by itself allows you to cook it upside down without having to cover the bones to prevent them from burning. Without the stuffing, the roast will also take less time to cook. By searing the roast at a high temperature for the first 30 minutes, you'll end up with a richer, browner exterior that's pleasantly crisp. Although this dish is a meal in itself, you may serve Gingered Applesauce as well as Orange Roasted Fennel and Brussels Sprouts (see Index) on the side.

> Juice of 1 lemon
> 2 teaspoons finely chopped garlic
> 1¼ teaspoons salt
> 1 teaspoon ground ginger
> ¼ teaspoon freshly ground black
>   pepper
> 1 crown roast of pork (about 6 pounds),
>   12 to 14 ribs
> ½ cup apple juice
> ½ cup dry white wine
> Couscous with Dried Fruit (page 119)
> 12 to 14 Pickled Lady Apples (page 277)

1. Preheat the oven to 500°F.

2. Mix the lemon juice, garlic, salt, ginger, and pepper in a small bowl. Rub the mixture all over the crown roast.

CROWN ROAST

A crown roast is formed from center-cut loin sections of beef, pork, or lamb, with anywhere from 6 to 12 ribs each tied together in the shape of a crown or circle. When planning a crown roast dinner, ask your butcher to prepare the meat for you, so all you'll have to do is cook it. He should be happy to oblige, if you give him at least one day's notice. To put the crown roast together, the butcher will trim the loins, then makes slits in the chine between the ribs so that the loins can be bent into a circle. Then, with a large needle threaded with twine, he will attach the 2 frenched loins tightly together end to end, with the meat on the inside, and the rib bones pointing upwards, forming a crown.

3. Place the roast, rib end down, in a roasting pan without the rack (the roast will rest on the bones). Add the apple juice and white wine to the roasting pan. Roast, uncovered, for 30 minutes.

4. Reduce the oven temperature to 350° F. Continue to roast until an instant-read meat thermometer inserted through the thickest part of the meat (between 2 ribs) registers 165°F to 170°F, about 2 hours (allow 20 minutes a pound). Baste every 30 minutes with the pan juices.

5. Meanwhile, prepare the Couscous with Dried Fruit. If necessary, reheat it, covered, in the oven during the last 30 minutes of the crown's roasting time.

6. When the roast is done, turn it over onto a serving platter. Fill the cavity with the couscous stuffing, and cover each rib end with a pickled lady apple. Transfer to a serving dish any stuffing that doesn't fit into the crown.

7. To carve the chops, steady the roast with a carving fork and cut downward between the ribs. Serve at once.

PORK TENDERLOIN WITH STRAWBERRY-LOQUAT SAUCE

YIELD: 4 ENTREE SERVINGS

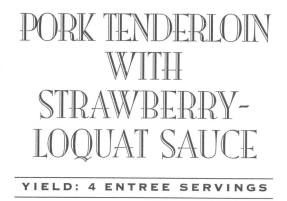

Loquat, a delicate and exquisite fruit of early spring, tastes like apricot, plum, and pineapple all at once, with floral overtones. Because it is seasonal, somewhat expensive, and not widely available commercially, be sure to treat yourself if you happen to find it at your produce market! Here's a quick and delicious recipe that employs the glorious loquat and the lovely strawberry to enliven a pork roast. Madeira sets off the sweet, tart flavors of this fruit duo. If you can't find loquats, don't despair; the dish won't suffer a bit if you use 1 cup of fresh strawberries.

1 pork tenderloin (about 1 pound), trimmed of excess fat
Salt and freshly ground black pepper
1 1/2 teaspoons mild olive oil
1 1/2 tablespoons unsalted butter
1/2 cup loquats, seeded, peeled, and quartered
1/2 cup fresh strawberries, hulled and quartered
1 teaspoon sugar
1/4 cup Madeira

1. Cut the tenderloin in half so that it

fits in a medium-size skillet and season the pieces with salt and pepper.

2. Heat the olive oil and ¹/₂ tablespoon of the butter in a medium-size skillet over high heat. Add the tenderloin and brown it on all sides, about 2 minutes total. Cover the pan, reduce the heat to low, and cook until the pork registers 150°F on an instant-read thermometer, about 15 minutes. Transfer the tenderloin to a plate and cover to keep warm.

3. Pour off the fat in the pan. Add the loquats, strawberries, and sugar to the pan, and sauté until the fruits are just soft, 30 seconds. Stir in the Madeira with a wooden spoon, scraping up any browned bits from the bottom of the pan. Add any meat juices collected on the plate to the pan. Simmer until the sauce thickens slightly, about 1 minute. Stir in the remaining 1 tablespoon butter until it is completely melted. Remove from the heat. Season the sauce to taste with salt and pepper.

4. Slice the tenderloin ¹/₄ inch thick and place on a warmed serving platter. Spoon the fruit sauce over the meat, and serve at once.

PORK WITH CHUTNEYED APRICOT SAUCE

YIELD: 4 ENTREE SERVINGS

Quick to prepare, this dish gives me the perfect opportunity to use my homemade apricot chutney (or any other fruit chutney for that matter). Although the sauce benefits from the light cream, the dish will be equally tasty if you omit it. To save some time, you can also make a perfectly delicious version of this dish using store-bought mango or banana chutney.

PORK SCALOPPINE
1 pork tenderloin (about 1 pound)
Salt and freshly ground black pepper
³/₄ cup unbleached all-purpose flour

APRICOT SAUCE
²/₃ cup Spiced Apricot Chutney (page 272)
³/₄ cup fresh orange juice
3 tablespoons fresh lime juice
1 teaspoon Dijon mustard
1 tablespoon unsalted butter
¹/₃ cup dry white wine, preferably Chardonnay
¹/₂ cup light cream or half-and-half
2 tablespoons sliced scallions

1. To make the scaloppine, cut the tenderloin crosswise into 8 slices, each ¹/₄ inch thick. Lay the slices between 2 large sheets

PORK SAFETY

*S*ome cooks, fearing trichinosis (a disease caused by parasites sometimes present in raw pork), routinely cook their pork until the internal temperature reaches 160°F. Such a long cooking period will certainly kill any parasites, but it will also deaden most of the meat's desirable qualities, like moistness, tenderness, and flavor. Now that pork is so lean, not overcooking it is more crucial than ever. Tests have shown that the trichinae are killed at 138°F. Thus, I recommend cooking pork to between 145°F and 150°F, at which point it will be moist, juicy, and safe. However, whole loins or crown roasts, should be cooked to an internal temperature of 170° because they are thick cuts with large bones and more protective fat covering. To determine when the meat of a crown roast is done, insert an instant-read thermometer between the ribs so that it doesn't touch any bone, which could skew the reading.

of waxed paper. Using the flat side of a meat pounder, lightly flatten the slices.

2. Lightly sprinkle the slices with salt and pepper. Spread the flour on a platter. Dredge the pork in the flour, shaking off any excess.

3. To make the sauce, in a small bowl, combine the chutney, orange juice, lime juice, and mustard.

4. Melt the butter in a large nonstick skillet over medium-high heat. When the foam subsides, add the pork slices and brown them quickly, about 1 minute per side in 2 batches, if necessary. Carefully add the white wine. Quickly turn the pork. Cover the pan and cook until almost all the liquid has evaporated, about 1 minute.

5. Stir the apricot sauce and add it to the pan. Bring to a boil and continue boiling for 1 minute. Add the cream, return to a boil, and cook until the sauce thickens slightly and coats the back of a spoon, 2 to 3 minutes. Sprinkle with the scallions. Remove from the heat.

6. Transfer the pork to warmed platter and top with the sauce. Serve at once.

PORK KABOBS WITH GRILLED PEACHES

YIELD: 4 ENTREE SERVINGS

*T*he sweetness in this dish comes from the American South in the form of peaches and brown sugar, and the peach-flavored vinegar in which the pork is marinated adds a jolt of tartness. To round out the meal, serve a simple watercress and tomato salad dressed with just a light splash of balsamic vinegar and olive oil.

> $^1/_3$ cup peach vinegar, preferably homemade (page 287), or $^1/_4$ cup cider vinegar
>
> $1^1/_2$ tablespoons soy sauce, preferably Kikkoman
>
> 3 tablespoons (firmly packed) light brown sugar
>
> 3 tablespoons mild olive oil
>
> 2 teaspoons finely grated peeled fresh ginger
>
> $1^1/_2$ pounds boneless pork shoulder, trimmed of excess fat and cut into $1^1/_2$-inch cubes
>
> 2 large peaches, peeled, halved, and pitted
>
> 1 tablespoon fresh lime juice
>
> 4 thin slices pancetta (about $^1/_4$ pound)
>
> 1 large onion, cut into 8 wedges, layers separated

1. Stir together the vinegar, soy sauce, 2 tablespoons of the brown sugar, 2 tablespoons of the olive oil, and the ginger in a medium bowl. Add the pork and toss to combine. Cover and marinate in the refrigerator for at least 2 hours or overnight.

2. Place 8 bamboo skewers in a shallow pan and cover with hot water. Soak for at least 30 minutes.

3. Place the peaches in a pie pan and sprinkle with the lime juice and remaining 1 tablespoon brown sugar. Wrap a slice of pancetta around each peach half and set aside.

4. Drain the pork cubes and thread them, alternating with onion pieces, onto the skewers. Lightly brush the kabobs with the remaining 1 tablespoon olive oil.

5. Prepare coals for grilling or preheat the broiler.

6. Grill or broil the kabobs 4 inches from the heat until the pork is no longer pink in the center, 4 to 5 minutes per side. Grill or broil the peaches until the pancetta is crisp and the peaches are just warmed through, about 2 minutes. Serve at once.

VARIATION

POMEGRANATE LAMB KABOBS: Replace the vinegar and brown sugar in the marinade with 2 tablespoons Pomegranate Molasses (page 138) diluted in $^1/_4$ cup water. Substitute lamb for pork, and proceed as for the above recipe. Dilute an additional 2 tablespoons pomegranate molasses with 1 tablespoon water, and brush the mixture over the grilled kabobs before serving.

ROASTED PORK CHOPS IN GRAPE SAUCE

YIELD: 4 ENTREE SERVINGS

These flavorful roasted pork chops may be your answer to a soul-warming dinner when you have a hankering for something humble yet appealing. In this recipe, the chops are roasted on a bed of balsamic-doused grapes. As the grapes cook, they release their juices, which blend with the vinegar to produce a delicious sweet and sour sauce. These chops may be best enjoyed with baked or mashed potatoes flavored with garlic.

4 center-cut pork chops (about 2 pounds total), 1 inch thick
Salt and freshly ground black pepper
1 tablespoon mild olive oil
½ cup balsamic vinegar
2½ pounds red or green seedless grapes, stems removed (about 6 cups total)
3 tablespoons unsalted butter, chilled and cut into 3 pieces

1. Preheat the oven to 500°F.

2. Pat the chops dry and season well with salt and pepper.

3. Heat the oil in a large, ovenproof skillet over medium-high heat. Add the chops and brown them for about 1 minute on each side. Transfer the chops to a platter. Pour off any fat from the skillet and return it to the heat. Stir in the vinegar with a wooden spoon, scraping up any browned bits from the bottom of the skillet, and reduce slightly, about 30 seconds. Add the grapes and toss to coat with the vinegar. Return the chops to the skillet, pushing them under the grapes, so the meat will be basted with the juices as it cooks.

4. Roast, uncovered, turning the chops once, until the grapes are soft and the meat is tender and juicy, about 20 minutes. Season to taste with salt and pepper.

5. With a slotted spoon, remove the chops and grapes and transfer them to a warmed serving platter.

6. Stir the butter, 1 tablespoon at a time, into the sauce until well blended, slightly thickened, and glossy.

7. Pour the sauce over the pork chops and grapes and serve immediately.

BRAISED CRANBERRY PORK CHOPS

YIELD: 4 ENTREE SERVINGS

Although cranberries will probably always be associated with Pilgrims and winter holidays, they are gaining in popularity and are no longer confined to the traditional sauce that goes with the turkey. Whether cooked in stews or baked with chicken, these marble-size berries are extremely versatile and can transform an everyday meal. This dish of braised pork chops is a perfect example. The happy alliance of cranberry and pork is further enhanced by earthy mushrooms and fragrant fresh dill. The results are truly luxuriant chops.

¼ cup unbleached all-purpose flour

½ teaspoon salt

½ teaspoon freshly ground black pepper

4 pork loin chops (about 2 pounds total), 1 inch thick

1 tablespoon mild olive oil

2 teaspoons minced garlic

1 cup chopped onions

1 cup sliced fresh mushrooms

1 cup fresh or frozen cranberries, coarsely chopped

1 cup peeled, seeded, and chopped tomatoes

½ cup dry white wine

1 cup chicken broth, preferably homemade (page 30)

¼ cup soy sauce, preferably Kikkoman

1 teaspoon sugar

¼ cup chopped fresh dill

1. Combine the flour, salt, and pepper in a shallow dish. Coat the chops with the flour mixture, shaking off any excess.

2. Heat the oil in a large skillet over medium heat. Add the pork chops and brown them on both sides, about 5 minutes total. Transfer the chops to a plate.

3. Add the garlic, onions, mushrooms, cranberries, and tomatoes to the skillet and sauté until the mushrooms start to render some moisture, about 2 minutes. Add the white wine, chicken broth, soy sauce, and sugar. As soon as the mixture comes to a boil, reduce the heat to low. Add the chops along with any juices collected on the plate. Cover the pan and cook for 30 minutes. Turn the chops in the sauce and continue to cook, covered, until the meat is fork-tender, 30 minutes more.

4. Stir in the dill and serve at once.

TEA-SMOKED BABY BACK RIBS WITH TANGERINE GLAZE

YIELD: 4 ENTREE SERVINGS

I am a great fan of barbecued spareribs, and these Chinese-style, tangerine-glazed, baby back ribs are the best I've ever savored. What makes them so succulent and memorable is the final smoking over a bed of sweetly fragrant tea leaves, tangerine peels, and brown sugar. You may serve this dish as a main course with steamed rice and sautéed vegetables or cut the ribs into individual portions and serve them for cocktails. They are sure to prove so popular that you will find yourself making them again and again.

CRANBERRIES

These bright scarlet pellets, which the Native Americans taught Pilgrim women to use, provide a tangy and colorful note to winter meals. Their name is derived from the Dutch cranbeere (literally "craneberry"), which they were called because cranes living in the New England bogs ate them.

Native to New England, cranberries grow on vines in marshes or bogs. In spring, the vines bloom with pink flowers. By summer, the petals are gone, leaving behind a tiny green node that will become a ripe cranberry around September.

There are two main methods of harvesting the fruit. In dry harvesting, the berries are combed from the vine with a machine to ensure that the fruit is handled gently so that it remains intact. Since this method is expensive and labor-intensive, many growers allot only a small portion of their total crop to it, and as a result, few fresh cranberries come to market,

pushing up the price. Most fresh cranberries sold during the holidays are harvested in this manner.

The wet harvesting method involves flooding the cranberry bogs, then loosening the berries with giant "egg beaters." Once the berries float to the surface, they are skimmed off with a machine. This rough method is very efficient for the grower but leaves few berries undamaged. The damaged cranberries are either dried or quickly processed into jellies, juices, and sauces. Ninety percent of the country's cranberry crops are harvested in this manner.

Avoid a last-minute search for cranberries by purchasing them ahead of time whenever you find them, then store them in the refrigerator. They will keep for about 2 weeks. If you don't plan on using them within that time, freeze the berries in plastic bags when you get home. It isn't necessary to defrost the berries before use.

MARINADE AND MEAT

2 medium tangerines
1 tablespoon minced garlic
1 tablespoon grated peeled fresh ginger
1/2 cup hoisin sauce
1/4 cup honey
1/4 cup soy sauce, preferably Kikkoman
1/4 cup ketchup
2 tablespoons dry sherry
1 teaspoon Szechwan hot bean paste
1/2 teaspoon liquid smoke, preferably Haddon House
1/2 teaspoon garlic powder
1/4 teaspoon freshly ground black pepper
1/4 teaspoon freshly ground white pepper
3 1/2 pounds pork baby back ribs or lean pork spareribs

FOR SMOKING

1/2 cup black tea leaves, such as Lapsang Souchong, Earl Grey, or Jasmine
1/4 cup (firmly packed) light brown sugar

1. To make the marinade, peel the tangerines. Reserve the peels for the final smoking, then cut the tangerines in half horizontally. Using a manual citrus juicer, extract the juice from the tangerines. (You should have about 1/2 cup juice.)

2. Combine the tangerine juice and all the remaining marinade ingredients through the white pepper in a large roasting pan. Stir until well blended.

GREAT MATCHES

TANGERINES AND ORANGES

Like other citrus fruits, oranges and tangerines are very agreeable and tend to get along with most kinds of foods. More unusual partners might include prosciutto, mussels, beets, wild rice, olives, and feta cheese.

3. Using a sharp knife, cut halfway down between each rib to separate them slightly. Add the ribs to the marinade, turning to coat. Cover and refrigerate at least 4 hours, or overnight, turning the ribs over occasionally.

4. Preheat the oven to 375°F.

5. Drain the ribs, reserving the marinade. Pour hot water to a depth of ½ inch into a large roasting pan. Place a rack in the roasting pan, making sure the rack clears the water. Arrange the ribs on the rack. Bake until the ribs are well browned, turning them twice and basting every 10 minutes with some of the marinade, about 50 minutes. Remove the pan from the oven. Increase the oven temperature to 500°F.

6. Remove the rack and the ribs from the pan. Pour off the water from the pan. Line the bottom of the pan with a triple layer of thick aluminum foil. Sprinkle the tea leaves, brown sugar, and reserved tangerine peels over the foil and replace the rack and

ribs. Continue baking, uncovered, until the ribs are crisp, about 15 minutes longer.

7. Transfer the reserved marinade to a small saucepan and bring to a boil. Reduce the heat and simmer, covered, for 5 minutes. Brush the ribs with this sauce and cut into individual portions, if desired. Serve hot.

APRICOT-GLAZED HAM

YIELD: 16 TO 18 ENTREE SERVINGS

There are countless recipes for glazed ham, but here's the best. It was given to me by my friend Danielle, who owns La Fromagerie, a French gourmet store in New York City. The key to this recipe is the ham. I use Lundy's, an excellent brand, but it is sometimes hard to find. You may use your favorite brand, or ask your butcher to recommend a good one for you. You should use a bone-in, fully cooked brine-cured ham, as opposed to the stronger, saltier Smithfield type. This baked ham tastes delicious either warm or cold—and it's ideal for entertaining, since it will feed a crowd. Any leftovers will freeze beautifully and you can turn them into creative sandwiches, omelets, and salads.

½ pound dried apricots
¾ cup Madeira
1 smoked and fully cooked bone-in ham
    (18 to 20 pounds)
2 tablespoons Dijon mustard
2 cups fresh apple cider
1½ cups (firmly packed) light brown sugar
¼ cup apricot preserves

1. Preheat the oven to 375°F.

2. Place the apricots in a small saucepan. Add the Madeira, cover, and set aside.

3. Remove and discard the rind on the surface of the ham. Trim the fat to ⅛ inch thick. Place the ham, fat side up, in a shallow roasting pan. Spread the mustard over the ham.

4. Mix the cider and the brown sugar in a bowl, and pour the mixture over the ham.

5. Insert a meat thermometer into the thickest part of the ham, being sure that it does not touch the bone. Bake the ham for 1 hour, basting frequently with the cider from the pan.

6. Add the apricot preserves to the apricots soaking in the saucepan and bring the mixture to a boil. Remove from the heat.

7. Spread the glaze over the ham and continue to bake 30 minutes longer, basting often with the glaze.

8. Reduce the oven temperature to 325°F and bake 30 minutes more, or until the glaze has caramelized, and the thermometer registers 160°F, basting the ham with the glaze every 5 minutes. (Total baking time should be 2 hours.)

9. Remove the ham to a carving board to cool for 30 minutes before slicing. Skim off any fat from the pan juices. Serve the ham hot, passing the pan juices alongside in a gravy boat.

HAM AND BANANA ROLLS WITH MOZZARELLA

YIELD: 4 ENTREE SERVINGS

When I'm too busy to cook anything elaborate, I make these banana-stuffed ham rolls, which take almost no time to prepare. To embellish the rolls a bit, I add wine-scented mushrooms and mozzarella cheese before broiling them. Voilà! A flavor-packed meal within 30 minutes. Serve with bread or steamed rice and a green salad.

2 tablespoons unsalted butter

1 cup chopped onions

4 cups (about ¹⁄₂ pound) sliced mushrooms

*2 teaspoons chopped fresh thyme
    leaves*

1 cup dry white wine

Salt and freshly ground black pepper

4 ripe but firm bananas

Juice of 1 lemon

*8 slices boiled ham (about 1 pound total),
    cut about ¹⁄₈ inch thick*

*8 slices fresh mozzarella cheese (about
    ¹⁄₂ pound)*

1. Melt the butter in a large skillet over medium-high heat. Add the onions and sauté until tender, about 1 minute. Add the mushrooms and sauté until they become limp and render some liquid, about 2 minutes. Stir in the thyme. Add the wine and cook until it has been absorbed by the vegetables. Season to taste with salt and pepper. Scrape the mixture into a gratin dish.

2. Peel and halve the bananas crosswise. Put the banana pieces in a shallow dish and pour the lemon juice over them. Turn to coat with the lemon juice.

3. Preheat the broiler.

4. Wrap a slice of ham around a piece of banana, then place it, seam side down, over the mushrooms in the gratin dish. Repeat with the remaining ham and bananas. Top the ham rolls with mozzarella.

5. Broil the ham rolls 8 inches from the heat just until the cheese melts and browns

slightly, and the bananas are heated through, 3 to 5 minutes. Serve immediately.

KNACKWURST WITH SAUERKRAUT AND APPLES

**YIELD: 4 ENTREE
SERVINGS**

Pork, apples, and sauerkraut are old friends and have always been a tasty part of the Oktoberfest tradition. The recipe that follows captures that spirit. In keeping with the German theme, round out the meal with steamed or boiled potatoes and a fresh loaf of rye bread. Don't forget to have plenty of spicy brown mustard and beer on hand for the occasion! If you prefer, substitute 4 bratwurst or smoked pork chops for the knackwurst.

1 tablespoon mild olive oil

8 knackwurst (about 1½ pounds total),
 pricked with a fork in several
 places

1 medium onion, chopped

2 tart apples, such as Granny Smith,
 peeled, cored, and cubed (½-inch
 pieces)

1 pound fresh or bagged sauerkraut,
 rinsed well and squeezed dry
 (see Note)

1 cup chicken broth, preferably homemade
 (page 30)

⅔ cup dark beer

2 tablespoons red wine vinegar

1 tablespoon plus 1 teaspoon (firmly
 packed) light brown sugar

2 bay leaves

1 teaspoon dried juniper berries

12 whole cloves

1 teaspoon caraway seeds

¼ teaspoon freshly ground black pepper

Salt

1. Heat the oil in a large skillet over medium heat. Add the knackwurst and brown on all sides, about 5 minutes. Transfer the sausages to a platter and cover to keep them warm.

2. Add the onion and apples to the oil left in the skillet and sauté until they are tender, about 5 minutes. Add the sauerkraut, and stir until it's heated through, 2 minutes. Add the broth, beer, vinegar, brown sugar, bay leaves, juniper berries, and cloves, and bring the mixture to a boil. Reduce the heat to low, cover the pan, and simmer the mixture for 5 minutes.

3. Stir in the caraway seeds and black pepper, and season to taste with salt. Add the knackwurst, cover, and simmer 5 minutes longer to heat the sausages thoroughly.

4. Remove and discard the bay leaves and cloves and serve at once.

NOTE: Do not substitute canned sauerkraut; it has an unpleasant metallic taste that is not destroyed by cooking.

PORK AND LAMB SAUSAGES WITH APRICOTS

YIELD: 2 TO 4 ENTREE SERVINGS

These fresh sausage patties incorporate wonderful Mediterranean spices that make your mouth tingle: cinnamon, coriander, cumin, red pepper flakes, and cayenne pepper. Apricots and orange zest add a bit of sweetness to complement the heat. Serve them as an entrée or part of a brunch. You can turn them into burgers by making larger patties and placing them on buns. Pear and Yogurt Raita (see Index), a cooling side dish, would be an excellent accompaniment to these patties.

¼ cup coarsely chopped dried apricots

½ pound ground pork

½ pound ground lamb

1 tablespoon minced garlic

1½ teaspoons finely grated orange
    zest

1½ teaspoons ground cinnamon

1½ teaspoons ground coriander

1½ teaspoons ground cumin

½ teaspoon dried red pepper flakes

¼ teaspoon freshly ground black pepper

¼ teaspoon cayenne pepper

1 teaspoon salt

2 tablespoons chopped fresh cilantro
    leaves

Mild olive oil

1. Place the apricots in a small bowl and cover with the boiling water. Soak for 15 minutes and drain, reserving the liquid.

2. Prepare the coals for grilling or pre-heat the broiler. Or, heat a stove top grill over medium-high heat.

3. In a medium-size mixing bowl, combine the pork and lamb with all the remaining ingredients except the oil. Add the drained apricots and 1 tablespoon of the reserved liquid. Mix until just combined, taking care not to overmix.

4. Divide the mixture into eight portions, then form each portion into a patty about 2½ inches in diameter.

5. Brush the patties with oil and grill or broil until they are cooked through, 2 to 3 minutes per side. Serve hot.

GLAZED LAMB CHOPS

YIELD: 4 ENTREE SERVINGS

The simplest preparations are often the best. It would be hard to find anything easier to make or more delicious than these broiled chops, which are coated with a glaze of sweet currant jelly and zesty Dijon mustard. I think they go perfectly with sautéed string beans or steamed fresh asparagus. You can substitute center-cut pork chops for the lamb, but allow the meat to cook 5 to 6 minutes per side.

⅓ cup red currant jelly

⅔ cup Dijon mustard

8 loin lamb chops, about ¾ inch thick
    (2 pounds total)

1. In a medium-size saucepan, combine the jelly and mustard. Bring to a boil over medium-high heat, stirring to mix well with a wooden spoon. Simmer over low heat until

all the jelly has melted and the mixture has thickened, about 5 minutes. Let cool.

2. Pat the lamb chops dry and rub them with the glaze. Marinate in the refrigerator for at least 2 hours or overnight.

3. Preheat the broiler.

4. Place the lamb chops on a rack in a roasting pan and broil 6 inches from the heat until they are nicely glazed, about 3 minutes per side for medium-rare.

LAMB STEAKS WITH PEAR SAUCE

YIELD: 4 ENTREE SERVINGS

An excellent way to dress up lean lamb steaks is to quickly sear them in a skillet and then make a light sauce of puréed pear in the same pan. Port and dry sherry are added to complement the lamb's robust flavor. This fruit sauce is also well suited for pork or veal chops. If you are lucky enough to get hold of musky tree-ripened guavas, substitute them for the pear making sure to scoop out and discard the seeds before you use the fruits. Quince and apple also make good substitutes.

1 large pear, peeled, quartered, and cored
3/4 cup chicken broth, preferably homemade (page 30)
2 teaspoons mild olive oil
4 lamb steaks (about 2 pounds total), cut 1/2 inch thick
Salt and freshly ground black pepper
1/4 cup chopped shallots
1/4 cup ruby port
1/4 cup dry sherry
1 tablespoon snipped fresh chives

1. Combine the pear with 1/2 cup of the chicken broth in a small saucepan and bring to a boil over high heat. Cover, reduce the heat to low, and simmer until the pear is fork-tender, about 5 to 8 minutes (10 minutes if using quince). Remove from the heat. Transfer the pear and its cooking liquid to a blender and purée until smooth. The purée may be prepared well in advance, covered, and refrigerated until ready to use.

2. Heat the olive oil in a large nonstick skillet over high heat. Season the lamb steaks with salt and pepper and add them to the skillet. Cook until well browned, without overcooking, about 1 1/2 minutes per side for medium-rare steaks. Transfer the steaks to a platter and cover loosely with aluminum foil to keep warm.

3. Pour off the fat from the pan. Add the shallots and cook over medium heat until soft, about 30 seconds. Add the port and sherry and cook until the liquid is reduced by half, scraping up any browned bits from the bottom of the pan with a wooden spoon, about 1 minute. Stir in the remaining 1/4 cup

chicken broth and the pear purée. Cook until the sauce is slightly thickened and smooth, about 30 seconds. Stir in any lamb juices collected on the platter. Remove from the heat.

4. Season the sauce to taste with salt and pepper, then spoon it over the lamb steaks. Sprinkle with chives and serve at once.

MOROCCAN LAMB TAGINE

YIELD: 4 ENTREE SERVINGS

The English term *stew* does little justice to this uniquely Moroccan soul food known as a *tagine*. Tagines incorporate the fruits and vegetables of the season with meat, fish, or fowl and are cooked by simmering at length over a fire. A tagine may include tender pieces of beef or lamb simmered in a honey sauce redolent of cinnamon and ginger, or chicken baked in a saffron-scented broth fragrant with cilantro and lemon. The word *tagine* also refers to the cooking and serving vessel, a special earthenware dish topped with a conical lid. This piece of equipment is designed to prevent the steam from escaping, thus keeping the food moist. A Dutch oven is all you will need to prepare this glorious stew. The following recipe for lamb with prunes and its unusual blend of spices and herbs. It is one of my favorites, especially served on a bed of couscous.

4 small lamb shanks (about 1 pound each), rinsed and patted dry
Salt and freshly ground black pepper
2 tablespoons mild olive oil
3 medium onions (about 1 pound total), coarsely chopped
2 tablespoons minced garlic
2 teaspoons grated peeled fresh ginger
1/2 teaspoon ground turmeric
9 cardamom pods, shells removed and seeds finely ground, or 3/4 teaspoon ground cardamom
1 teaspoon ground cinnamon
2 cups chicken broth, preferably homemade (page 30)
1/2 bunch cilantro, rinsed and tied together with string
1 cup pitted prunes
5 teaspoons fresh lemon juice
1/4 cup chopped flat-leaf parsley leaves
1/2 cup toasted sliced blanched almonds (for toasting instructions, see page 64)

1. Season the lamb shanks well with salt and pepper.

2. In a large Dutch oven or soup pot, heat the oil over medium-high heat until it is hot but not smoking. Carefully add the lamb shanks (in 2 batches if necessary), and sear the meat on all sides until it is golden, about 5 minutes. Transfer the shanks to a platter.

3. In the fat remaining in the pan, cook the onions, garlic, and ginger over medium-

low heat, stirring frequently, until they are fragrant and tender, about 5 minutes. Add the turmeric, cardamom, cinnamon, and chicken broth. Bring the liquid to a boil, and add cilantro and the lamb shanks, along with any juices that have accumulated on the platter. Simmer the mixture, covered, until the meat is fork-tender, about 1 hour and 15 minutes. Add the prunes and continue to simmer for 15 more minutes.

4. With a slotted spoon, transfer the lamb and prunes to a serving platter, and cover loosely with aluminum foil to keep them warm. Discard the cilantro. Bring the cooking liquid to a boil over medium-high heat, and cook until it is thickened and reduced to about 1 cup, 2 to 3 minutes. Season the sauce to taste with lemon juice, salt, and pepper.

5. Ladle the sauce over the lamb and prunes. Sprinkle with chopped parsley and toasted almonds before serving.

VENISON CHILI WITH PAPAYA

YIELD: 4 TO 6 ENTREE SERVINGS

I think chili is fun to cook, because it allows for lots of leeway. The two basic components are the seasonings and the meat. The rest is really up to you. You can use ground or cubed meat, add or leave out tomatoes, make it with or without beans, on a bed or rice or accompanied by bread. My version calls for spicy Italian sausage and gamy venison in the stew. Venison has the same fat and calorie content as skinless chicken and a dense, beeflike texture and mild flavor, like that of lean lamb. This chunky chili, fragrant with spices, is sure to sate any appetite on a wintry day.

½ pound dried black beans, rinsed, and picked over
1½ pounds venison stewing meat, cubed (½-inch pieces)
2 tablespoons medium-hot chili powder, preferably Grandma's brand
3 tablespoons mild olive oil
½ pound hot Italian sausages, casings removed
2 cups chopped onions
2 tablespoons minced garlic
2 teaspoons dried oregano, crumbled
2 teaspoons ground cumin
1½ teaspoons salt
1½ teaspoons freshly ground black pepper
1½ teaspoons sugar
1 can (1 pound) Italian plum tomatoes, including the juices
¾ cup dry red wine
1 cup beef broth
3 tablespoons tomato paste
2 tablespoons red wine vinegar
Sour cream
2 medium ripe papayas, peeled, seeded, and cubed (½-inch pieces)
1 cup sliced scallions, green part only

1. Place the beans and 1 quart water in a large, heavy saucepan and soak overnight. Combine the meat with the chili powder and 2 tablespoons of the olive oil in a bowl. Cover and refrigerate overnight.

2. Heat the remaining 1 tablespoon olive oil in a Dutch oven or soup pot over medium-high heat. Working in batches, brown the venison on all sides, about 5 minutes per batch. With a slotted spoon, transfer the meat to a bowl. Crumble the sausage into the pan. Cook, breaking up the lumps with a fork, until the meat is no longer pink, about 3 minutes.

3. Stir in the onions and garlic, and cook for 5 minutes. Reduce the heat to medium. Stir in the oregano, cumin, salt, black pepper, and sugar and cook until aromatic, 2 minutes.

4. Stir in the venison, tomatoes, red wine, beef broth, and tomato paste. Bring the mixture to a boil. Reduce the heat to low, cover, and simmer until the meat is very tender, stirring occasionally, about 1½ hours.

5. Meanwhile, bring the beans to a boil over high heat. Reduce the heat to low and simmer until the beans are tender but not mushy, about 1 hour, adding more water if necessary to keep the beans covered. Drain well.

6. Degrease the chili, then stir in the beans and vinegar. Simmer 5 minutes. Adjust the seasoning, if necessary. The chili should be thick, but can be thinned with broth, if necessary.

7. Ladle the chili into large bowls. Top with sour cream, papayas, and scallions. Serve at once.

SWEET & SAVORY SIDES

In my home, not a meal goes by without the presence of some sort of vegetable. So, I'm always looking for new ways to make them as flavorful as possible, and to present them at their glorious best.

There's nothing like fruit to perk up popular but overworked vegetables. Cranberries or raisins added to leafy greens gives them a brand new twist. Carrots and turnips slowly roasted with dried fruits take on a rich caramel sweetness. When served alongside a plain turkey breast, it will seem like a holiday meal. And the next time you're making stuffing as a side dish, prepare it from quinces and cranberries—scrumptious! And it only takes a little more time and

effort than any packaged variety you can find on the supermarket shelves.

On occasion, I employ the tropical technique of using fruits as vegetables. For instance, I'll stuff a mellow papaya with fresh herbs and bread crumbs and bake it to melting perfection, or I'll sauté chunks of golden apples with onions to supreme succulence. I've even substituted plantains for potatoes when making French fries! The recipes included here will show you that even the simplest touches, such as a splash of fruit juice or a sprinkling of fruit-flavored oil can work magic.

Served next to any entrée, all these vamped-up side dishes will lend a magical touch, and at the same time balance an otherwise banal main dish.

HAROSET

YIELD: 4 CUPS

One of the symbolic foods of the Jewish Passover holiday is haroset, a fruit and nut sweetmeat. I learned that it represents the mortar used by Jewish slaves in Egypt when they were forced to build pyramids for Pharaoh. During the Passover meal, haroset is eaten in a matzoh (flatbread) sandwich with horseradish. Haroset can be refrigerated, covered, for up to 6 hours before serving and eaten chilled or at room temperature. Substitute pecan halves or slivered almonds for the walnuts, if you wish. Traditionally, haroset is eaten with matzohs and horseradish, but it makes a tasty side dish to meat stews, especially pot roast.

2 large apples, such as Granny Smith or
McIntosh, peeled, cored, and cut into
¼-inch dice
1½ cups toasted walnut halves (for toasting
instructions, see page 64), coarsely
chopped
¼ cup sweet red wine, such as Manischewitz,
port, or Marsala
4 teaspoons honey
1 teaspoon ground cinnamon

Combine the apples and walnuts in a mixing bowl. Stir in the red wine, honey, and cinnamon. Serve chilled or at room temperature.

THREE FRUIT HAROSET

YIELD: 4 CUPS

For an exquisite variation, try this fruitier version of haroset which also includes dates and oranges. Just be sure to use a thin-skinned orange, or the bitter oils in the skin will overwhelm the other ingredients. It, too, goes well with matzoh and horseradish or as a succulent side dish to roast meats.

2 tart apples, such as
Granny Smith or
McIntosh, peeled, cored, and diced
1 small juice orange (unpeeled), diced
and seeded
⅔ cup pitted dates
1½ cups toasted pecan halves (for toasting
instructions, see page 64), coarsely
chopped
⅓ cup sweet wine, such as Manischewitz,
Marsala, or port
1 teaspoon ground cinnamon
½ teaspoon ground ginger

Combine the apples, orange, dates, and pecans in a mixing bowl. Stir in the wine, cinnamon, and ginger. Cover and refrigerate for at least 30 minutes and up to 4 hours for the flavors to marry. Serve chilled or at room temperature.

A QUICK APPLE PRIMER

Whoever coined the proverbial "an apple a day keeps the doctor away" must have known a thing or two about this virtuous fruit, once called "the fruit of immortality." Although I cannot really attest to its alleged virtues, there is a host of reasons that the apple is America's queen of fruits (the banana being king). Take, for example, my favorite apple, the Fuji (a Japanese cross of little-known Rolls Janet and the popular Red Delicious). With its exotic red striping on a pink background, it is not only pretty to look at but also a joy to eat. A bite into its crisp, fragrant flesh releases a spurt of juice that is honey-sweet and lemony tart. Besides providing satisfying bulk with few calories (a medium apple only contains 80 calories or so), this fruit also has a high acid content, which acts as a natural mouth freshener. That's maybe why so many people, including myself, love eating apples out of hand.

Another appealing aspect of this fruit is its year-round availability. Although apples are synonymous with autumn and most often bring to mind sweet desserts such as pies and cakes, their superb texture and flavor can also be used to great effect in savory dishes. In fact, of all fruits, there may be none better suited to complementing other foods. This may explain why apples are so often paired with meat, fowl, and sausage dishes. Grated, sliced, or cubed, an apple adds instant zip to a dish and never overwhelms other ingredients.

When cooking with apples, it's handy to know that:

✦ Apple juice and apple cider can be used interchangeably in recipes.

✦ 3 medium apples equal 1 pound.

✦ 1 pound of unpeeled apples yields about 3 cups of peeled and sliced or diced fruit.

✦ Overripe apples, once the bruises are removed, make excellent applesauce.

✦ Cortland apples are favored for making salads and fruit cups, because their white flesh resists browning. They are also good for all-purpose cooking.

✦ Golden Delicious apples (the second best-selling apples, after Red Delicious, to which they bear no relation) are particularly desirable for snacks, fresh desserts, and salads. They are also good for all-purpose cooking.

✦ Good substitutes for tart crisp apples such as Granny Smiths are Cortland, McIntosh, Puritan, Twenty One, Rhode Island Greening, Newtown Pippin, and Jerseymac. Underripe apples may also be used.

✦ Rome Beauties are very good for baking, because they retain their shape and flavor.

✦ Underripe apples can be chopped, diced, sliced, and grated for sautéing with vegetables or adding to cakes, muffins, pies, and other savory dishes.

✦ Sliced or cut apples will stay white longer if tossed with some fresh lemon juice. Cortland and Golden Delicious do not discolor as quickly as other varieties.

PEAR AND YOGURT RAITA

YIELD: 2 CUPS

Speedy to prepare, this refreshing Indian-style salsa made with yogurt and sour cream goes well with highly seasoned food such as sausages and grilled meat. The warm, powerful flavors of cumin, black pepper, and ginger accent the cool, smooth yogurt. For a lighter raita, replace the sour cream with yogurt. You may substitute 2 cups diced peaches, nectarines, mango, or papaya for the pears.

2 teaspoons whole black peppercorns

¹/₂ teaspoon cumin seeds

²/₃ cup plain yogurt

¹/₃ cup sour cream

¹/₂ teaspoon ground ginger

¹/₈ teaspoon freshly grated nutmeg

2 medium ripe pears, such as Anjou or Bartlett, peeled, cored, and cubed (¹/₂-inch pieces)

1 tablespoon chopped fresh cilantro leaves

1. Place the peppercorns and cumin seeds in a skillet and toast over medium heat, shaking the pan frequently, until the spices are aromatic but not burned, about 2 minutes. Coarsely grind the spice mixture in a spice grinder.

2. Combine the yogurt and sour cream with the spice mixture, ginger, and nutmeg in a medium-size bowl and stir until smooth. Fold in the pears and cilantro. Either serve or cover and refrigerate for up to 1 day.

One must sit up at night to eat a pear.

—ENGLISH PROVERB SUGGESTING THAT PEARS MUST BE EATEN AT THE MOMENT OF ABSOLUTE RIPENESS.

SAUTEED APPLES AND CARAMELIZED ONIONS

YIELD: 4 TO 6 SIDE DISH SERVINGS

I frequently serve this dish with robust meats such as grilled sausage, pork, duck, or calf's liver instead of sauces or green vegetables. The fruity tang of the apples and the deep, sweet flavor of caramelized onions are also a perfect foil for game. You can also flavor the apples with tarragon instead of thyme.

2 tablespoons unsalted butter

4 medium onions, thinly sliced

4 apples, preferably McIntosh or Granny
    Smith

4 teaspoons fresh lemon juice

2 teaspoons sugar

1 tablespoon chopped fresh thyme
    or 1½ teaspoons dried thyme,
    crushed

2 tablespoons Calvados
    or applejack

Salt and freshly ground
    black pepper

1. Melt 1 tablespoon of the butter in a large nonstick skillet. Add the onions and sauté over medium-low heat, stirring frequently to prevent burning, until very soft and lightly caramelized, about 10 minutes. Transfer the onions to a bowl.

2. Meanwhile, peel, core, and cut each apple into 16 wedges. As you cut them, place the apples in a mixing bowl, and toss with the lemon juice to prevent discoloration.

3. Melt the remaining 1 tablespoon of butter in the same skillet and sauté the apples, sugar, and thyme over high heat until just tender, about 2 minutes. Flambé the apples with the Calvados (see flambéing box, page 205).

4. When the flames die out, return the onions to the skillet. Sauté until the onions are just heated through and the mixture is well combined. Remove the pan from the heat.

5. Season to taste with salt and pepper and serve immediately.

BANANA CARIOCA

YIELD: 4 TO 6 SIDE DISH SERVINGS

South Americans are infinitely imaginative in their use of bananas. This Brazilian treatment is one of the many "little dishes" that are served with or before an entrée. It is not only quick and easy to prepare, it is also loaded with flavor, most notably from the caramelization of the sugar in the bananas. This dish will perform magic next to pork or chicken.

2 tablespoons peanut oil or unsalted butter

4 large ripe bananas, peeled and sliced
    ½ inch thick

1 medium onion, finely chopped (about
    ½ cup)

½ cup chopped green bell pepper

½ cup chopped red bell pepper

½ cup chopped celery

2 scallions, trimmed and sliced (white and
    green parts)

2 teaspoons minced garlic

½ small fresh Scotch bonnet pepper
    or 1 jalapeño pepper, minced

Salt

1. Heat 1 tablespoon of the oil in a large skillet over high heat. Add the bananas and sauté until they are golden brown, turning frequently. Transfer to a plate and set aside.

2. Heat the remaining 1 tablespoon oil over medium heat. Add the onion, bell peppers, celery, scallions, and garlic and sauté until soft, about 2 minutes.

3. Add the bananas and chile pepper to the skillet. Cook gently for 2 to 3 minutes over low heat, stirring frequently. Season to taste with salt and serve at once.

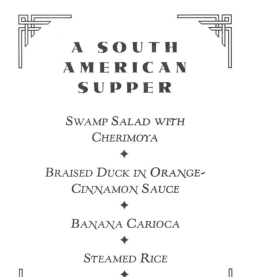

A SOUTH AMERICAN SUPPER

Swamp Salad with Cherimoya

◆

Braised Duck in Orange-Cinnamon Sauce

◆

Banana Carioca

◆

Steamed Rice

◆

Tropical Fruit Salad

SAUTEED SPINACH CATALAN

YIELD: 4 SIDE DISH SERVINGS

In Mediterranean cooking, dried fruits often find their way into vegetable dishes. A good example is this delicate sauté of spinach with raisins and pine nuts from northeastern Spain. It's best served warm or at room temperature. In place of spinach, you can use kale, Swiss chard, or broccoli rabe (rapini).

> 2 pounds young, tender spinach, well rinsed, tough stems and thick ribs removed
> 2 tablespoons extra-virgin olive oil
> 2 teaspoons minced garlic
> 1/3 cup raisins, plumped in hot water for 15 minutes and drained
> 1/3 cup pine nuts, lightly toasted (for toasting instructions, see page 64)
> Salt and freshly ground black pepper

1. Bring a large pot of salted water to a boil, add the spinach, and cook just until it is wilted and tender, about 1 minute. Drain thoroughly and set aside.

2. Heat the oil in a large skillet over medium-high heat. Add the garlic and cook until golden, about 30 seconds. Do not let it brown. Reduce the heat to medium.

3. Add the raisins and pine nuts and stir to coat with the oil, about 30 seconds. Add the spinach, season to taste with salt and pepper, and sauté until the spinach is heated through, 1 to 2 minutes. Serve warm or at room temperature.

VEGETABLES IN TANGERINE SAUCE

YIELD: 4 SIDE DISH SERVINGS

As a change of pace from plain-old steamed or boiled vegetables, serve this quick stir-fry of broccoli and carrots lightly coated with a Chinese-style sweet-and-spicy tangerine sauce.

> 5 medium carrots, peeled and cut on the
>   diagonal $^3/_8$ inch thick
> 5 cups broccoli florets (about 2 heads)
> 2 large tangerines
> 2 tablespoons peanut oil
> 2 teaspoons minced garlic
> $^1/_4$ teaspoon Szechwan hot bean paste
> 2 tablespoons dry sherry
> 1 tablespoon Asian sesame oil
> 1 tablespoon plus 1 teaspoon oyster sauce
> 2 teaspoons soy sauce, preferably Kikkoman
> $1^1/_2$ tablespoons unsalted butter

1. Bring a large pot of salted water to a boil. Add the carrots and cook until they are just tender, about 3 minutes. Using a slotted spoon, remove the carrots and drain in a colander. When the water returns to a boil, add the broccoli florets and cook until they are just tender, about $1^1/_2$ minutes. Drain in the colander. Refresh the vegetables under cold running water. Drain well.

2. Using a zester, remove long strips of zest from the tangerines and set aside. Juice the tangerines. (There should be about $^1/_2$ cup of juice.)

3. Combine the tangerine zest, peanut oil, garlic, and hot bean paste in a small bowl and set aside.

4. Combine the sherry, sesame oil, oyster sauce, and soy sauce in another bowl and set aside.

5. Heat a large skillet over high heat. Add the tangerine zest mixture. Cook until fragrant, about 15 seconds, then add the sherry mixture. Cook until the sauce is reduced by half and forms a glaze, about 1 minute. Stir in the butter, then add the vegetables. Stir until the vegetables are heated through and glazed with the sauce. Serve at once.

BRAISED RED CABBAGE

YIELD: 8 TO 10 SIDE DISH
SERVINGS

A traditional accompaniment for Christmas duck and goose, this sweet and sour cabbage dish is equally good with calf's liver, pork, or sausages. It is excellent when prepared a day in advance and reheated.

1 medium red cabbage (about 2 pounds)
4 tablespoons (½ stick) unsalted butter
2 tablespoons (firmly packed) light brown
    sugar
2 cups minced onions
4 tart apples, such as Granny Smith, peeled,
    cored, and sliced ½ inch thick
½ cup raspberry vinegar, preferably homemade
    (page 286)
1 cup chicken broth, preferably homemade
    (page 30)
1¼ teaspoons salt
½ cup apple jelly

1. Preheat the oven to 350°F

2. Remove and discard the outer leaves from the cabbage. Core, wash, and shred the cabbage.

3. Melt the butter in a Dutch oven or ovenproof soup pot over medium heat and stir in the brown sugar. Add the onions and

apples and cook until just tender, about 2 minutes. Stir in the cabbage, add the vinegar, cover, and cook over low heat for 10 minutes.

4. Add the broth and salt. Cover and bake until the cabbage is very soft, about 1 hour, stirring occasionally.

5. Stir in the jelly and adjust the seasoning with salt, if necessary. Serve immediately.

CREAMY CABBAGE AND PEARS

YIELD: 4 TO 6 SIDE DISH
SERVINGS

Exquisite and easy to prepare, this creamy side dish tastes a bit like fresh sauerkraut with a hint of sweetness coming from the pears. Sometimes I serve it with nothing more than a loaf of my favorite bread and a green salad, but most of the time, I serve it as an accompaniment to game or fowl.

1 small savoy or napa cabbage (about
   1 pound)
3½ tablespoons unsalted butter
2 medium ripe but firm Bosc or Anjou pears
1 tablespoon fresh lemon juice
½ teaspoon sugar
Salt and freshly ground black pepper

1. Remove and discard the outer leaves from the cabbage. Core, wash, and finely shred the cabbage.

2. Melt 1 tablespoon of the butter in a large saucepan over low heat. Add the cabbage and toss well to coat with butter. Cover and simmer, stirring occasionally, until the cabbage is just tender, about 10 minutes. Stir in 2 more tablespoons of the butter, cover, and remove from the heat.

3. Peel, halve, core, and thinly slice the pears. Toss with the lemon juice in a small bowl. Melt the remaining ½ tablespoon butter in a skillet over high heat. Add the pears and sugar and sauté until just heated through, about 30 seconds.

4. Stir the pears into the cabbage. Season to taste with salt and pepper and serve.

ORANGE-ROASTED FENNEL AND BRUSSELS SPROUTS

YIELD: 4 TO 6 SIDE DISH SERVINGS

Fennel and Brussels sprouts are two of my favorite cold-weather vegetables. When they are both in season, from late fall through the winter, toss them together in an aromatic blend of mashed garlic, peppercorns, anise seeds, and orange zest, and juice and bake. The result is superb roasted vegetables packed with wonderful flavors.

1 orange
1 teaspoon minced garlic
½ teaspoon whole black peppercorns
½ teaspoon anise seeds
1 tablespoon fresh orange juice
¼ cup extra-virgin olive oil
1 pound fennel (2 medium bulbs), stalks
   trimmed to 1 inch
1 pound fresh Brussels sprouts
Salt

1. Preheat the oven to 400°F.

2. Make the orange oil: Using a zester, remove the zest from the orange in long strips. Pound the garlic, black peppercorns,

anise seeds, and orange zest to a fine paste with a mortar and pestle. Scrape the paste into a small bowl and stir in the orange juice and olive oil. Set aside.

3. Halve the fennel bulbs lengthwise, then slice them lengthwise into ½-inch-thick pieces, without cutting through the core. You want each half to retain a fan shape.

4. Remove and discard the outer leaves of the Brussels sprouts. With a sharp paring knife, cut a deep X in the cores to allow for even cooking.

FRUITS ON THE GRILL

Grilled fruits are delicious and add pleasure to a simple meal. They can easily replace a sauce, condiment, or even a vegetable side dish. Although most people don't usually consider giving fruits this treatment, I've tried grilling just about every fruit except berries and grapes. During grilling, a fruit's flavor and sweetness intensify, and it picks up an appetizing smoky taste. If you enjoy grilled fruit as much as I do, you may consider investing in a grill basket, which secures small pieces of fruits between two wire racks, facilitating turning, or a stovetop grill pan if you don't have an outdoor grill.

All grilled fruits, whether cut or whole, should be brushed lightly with mild olive oil or other vegetable oil to prevent them from sticking to the grill and drying out. Not all fruits need to be peeled (see below). Once the fruits are removed from the fire, revive their vibrancy by brushing them again with a bit of olive oil or softened butter. By doing so, you will not only add extra flavor but also give them a glorious look. Depending on how sweet you want the fruit, you can also brush them with a little molasses, honey, or hoisin sauce.

What follows is a quick guide to grilling specific fruits. The cooking times are approximate and will vary depending on how hot the fire is and the degree of doneness you prefer.

BANANAS OR RIPE PLANTAINS: *Halve the unpeeled fruit lengthwise. Grill the banana halves, cut side down, until they are golden in color, about 2 minutes. Flip them and grill 2 minutes longer.*

FRUIT HALVES *(soft fruits such as apricots, figs, guavas, mangoes, nectarines, kiwis, peaches, pears, and plums): Grill the fruit cut side down to start, turning once, and continue to grill until the fruit is soft but not mushy. Test for doneness after grilling for 2 to 3 minutes per side. If the fruits are tiny, or if you are grilling a large amount of fruit, use a grill basket.*

MELONS *(cantaloupe, honeydew, and casaba, and also papaya): Halve, peel, and remove the seeds from the fruit. Cut each half into ¾-inch-thick wedges. Grill until the pieces are soft but not mushy, about 2 minutes per side.*

ORANGES *(or grapefruit): Peel, then slice the oranges ½ inch thick. Remove the seeds. Grill until the orange slices are soft but not mushy, about 2 minutes per side.*

PINEAPPLE: *Peel, then slice a whole fresh pineapple into ½-inch-thick rings. Grill until the pineapple slices are light golden, about 2 minutes per side.*

STAR FRUIT: *Slice the fruit crosswise ½ inch thick. Grill until the slices are light golden, about 2 minutes per side.*

5. Toss the vegetables with the orange oil in a large baking dish, and season to taste with salt. Bake until the vegetables are just tender, about 20 minutes. Serve at once.

MUSHROOM RAGOUT

YIELD: 4 SIDE DISH SERVINGS

Brimming with earthy flavors, this distinctive mushroom stew makes an excellent accompaniment to grilled meats and grilled fish like tuna or swordfish.

½ pound shiitake or button mushrooms
2 slices smoked bacon (about 2 ounces),
*   thinly sliced*
1 tablespoon unsalted butter
½ cup chopped onion
1 tablespoon minced garlic
1 Golden Delicious apple, peeled, cored,
*   and sliced*
¼ cup heavy (or whipping) cream
1 tablespoon chopped fresh thyme leaves,
*   or 1½ teaspoons dried thyme,*
*   crumbled*
Salt and freshly ground black pepper

1. Prepare the mushrooms: Remove and discard the stems. If the mushrooms need cleaning, simply wipe the caps with a damp paper towel. If they are small, leave them whole. If large, quarter them.

2. Fry the bacon in a large skillet over medium heat. When it begins to turn crisp, add the butter, onion, and garlic. Cook until the onion is tender, about 1 minute.

3. Add the mushrooms and sliced apple and sauté until they are tender and the mushrooms render some liquid, about 5 minutes. Add the cream and thyme, and simmer until the cream has thickened, 2 minutes longer.

4. Remove the pan from the heat. Season the ragoût to taste with salt and pepper and serve at once.

OKRA WITH ASIAN FLAVORS

YIELD: 4 SIDE DISH SERVINGS

Although okra—stewed or fried—is usually associated with Southern cooking, other cultures serve this vegetable in any number of delightful ways. In Southeast Asia, okra is simply blanched and bathed in a sauce vibrating with fresh pineapple, lime, chile, and basil. For the highest-quality okra, select bright green pods no longer than 3 inches. Old, big pods are fibrous, and darken when exposed to air.

1 teaspoon minced garlic

2 fresh hot red chile peppers, coarsely chopped

1 tablespoon plus 1½ teaspoons sugar

2 tablespoons rice vinegar or distilled white
     vinegar

¼ cup fresh pineapple juice

2 tablespoons fresh lime juice

2 tablespoons plus 1½ teaspoons Thai fish
     sauce

1 pound fresh okra, trimmed

2 tablespoons shredded fresh basil leaves (for
     shredding instructions, see page 34)

1. Make the sauce by crushing the garlic, chiles, and 1½ teaspoons of the sugar to a fine paste with a mortar and pestle.

2. Transfer the paste to a small bowl and add the remaining 1 tablespoon sugar, vinegar, pineapple juice, lime juice, and fish sauce. Stir until the sugar is dissolved and set aside.

3. Bring a large pot of salted water to a boil. Add the okra and cook over medium-high heat until just tender, 3 minutes. (Longer cooking will result in slimy okra.) Drain.

4. Transfer the hot okra to a serving platter and immediately top with the sauce. Sprinkle with the shredded basil and serve at once.

MASHED POTATOES WITH ROASTED PEARS

YIELD: 4 SIDE DISH SERVINGS

The unexpected addition of pear to mashed potatoes sends this comfort food into a league of its own. Both the potatoes and pears are roasted to eliminate moisture and at the same time concentrate their flavors. Since the pears are still moist after roasting, milk is not needed. All you need is a dab of butter to bring out all the goodness of these two compatible ingredients. This purée makes a wonderful accompaniment to game, smoked meat, or sausages. The mashed potatoes may be prepared up to 4 hours in advance, covered, and refrigerated. Reheat in the microwave or over a double boiler before serving.

3 large baking potatoes (about 1½ pounds
     total), pricked with a fork in several
     places

3 ripe but firm pears, preferably Bartlett or
     Bosc (about 1½ pounds total)

1½ tablespoons unsalted butter

Salt and freshly ground white pepper

1. Preheat the oven to 450°F.

2. Place the potatoes on a baking sheet

and roast until they are barely soft, about 50 minutes.

3. Peel, quarter, and core the pears. Place the pears on the baking sheet with the potatoes and roast until the potatoes and the pears are soft, about 20 minutes more.

4. Place the pears a medium-size mixing bowl and mash with a fork or potato masher. Using oven mitts to protect your hands, cut the potatoes in half lengthwise and scoop the flesh into the pear purée. Add the butter and mash together the potatoes and pears. Be sure not to overmash; there should still be small chunks of pear and potato left in the mixture. Season to taste with salt and white pepper. Serve hot.

POTATO PANCAKES WITH GINGERED APPLESAUCE

YIELD: ABOUT 4 DOZEN POTATO PANCAKES

I was first introduced to potato pancakes with applesauce by my husband's family during a celebration of Hanukkah. The potato pancakes (or latkes) are a symbolic reminder of the significance of this holiday. In 176 B.C., after

GREAT MATCHES

PEARS

The mellow sweetness of a velvety ripe pear is a wonderful counterpoint to the saltiness of Gorgonzola and other blue cheeses, feta cheese, and cured meats like bacon, ham, prosciutto. Cloves, cinnamon, ginger also bring out a pear's gentle splendor.

a hard-won victory over the Roman army, the Jews returned to Jerusalem to reassess the damages done to their cherished temple. They spent many days cleaning and repairing it. For the rededication ceremony, they lit a gold menorah with a tiny amount of oil they found at the site. Although the oil seemed just enough to last for one day, it miraculously kept the menorah lit for eight days. To recall the miracle of the burning oil, foods fried in oil became traditional Hanukkah fare.

Traditionally, latkes are made by grating raw potatoes. This produces lots of moisture, which inhibits the pancakes from getting really crisp when fried. I have found a most satisfactory method for turning out extra-crisp pancakes. I parboil the potatoes before shredding and frying them. These pancakes are some of the best you'll ever taste!

4 large boiling potatoes (about 2¼ pounds total), scrubbed
Salt and freshly ground black pepper
½ cup chicken fat or vegetable oil
Gingered Applesauce (page 214)

1. Place the potatoes in a large pot with salted water to cover, and bring to a boil over medium-high heat. Reduce the heat to medium and boil until the potatoes are barely tender, not cooked through, about 12 minutes. Drain and cool.

2. Peel and shred the potatoes, using the medium holes of a box grater or a food processor fitted with a coarse shredding disk.

3. Transfer the shredded potatoes to a large, well-oiled baking sheet and toss them with salt and pepper to taste. Press the potatoes together with the bottom of a wide metal spatula to form a compact rectangle, with an even thickness of about 1/4 inch.

4. Dip a 2-inch round cookie cutter into flour, then use it to make pancakes. After making as many pancakes as possible, gather the potato scraps, press them together to form another thin rectangle and cut out more pancakes. Repeat until all the potatoes are used up. Return the pancakes to the baking sheet with a metal spatula. Cover with plastic wrap. (You can refrigerate these overnight.)

5. Line a baking sheet with several layers of paper towels.

6. Divide the oil between 2 large cast-iron skillets and heat over medium-high heat until it begins to smoke. Add the potato pancakes without crowding, and cook until brown and crusty, about 4 to 6 minutes, turning once. With a slotted spoon, transfer the

pancakes to the prepared baking sheet. Keep them warm in a low oven while you cook the remaining pancakes.

7. Transfer the potato pancakes to a large warmed platter. Serve immediately with Gingered Applesauce.

FRENCH-FRIED PLANTAINS

YIELD: 4 TO 6 SIDE DISH SERVINGS

Since plantains have the same starchy and creamy texture as potatoes, I developed this recipe in which plantain sticks the size of large French fries are breaded and deep-fried. The results are crunchy morsels that come very close in texture to French fries but are even more addictive in taste. Be sure to make plenty, as they will quickly disappear!

4 ripe (black) plantains
2 large eggs
1 1/2 cups seasoned (Italian-style) dry bread crumbs
Vegetable oil, for deep frying
Salt

1. Cut the tips off each plantain. Slit the skin lengthwise and peel it off the fruit.

Halve each plantain crosswise and cut each half into 6 long sticks about ¹/₂ inch thick.

2. Break the eggs into a small, shallow bowl and beat lightly. Place the bread crumbs in a shallow dish. Dip a plantain stick into the beaten eggs to coat evenly, then quickly and lightly roll it in the bread crumbs, making sure that every bit of it is covered. Place the breaded plantain on a large platter. Repeat with the remaining plantain sticks.

3. Line a baking sheet with several layers paper towels.

4. Pour oil to a depth of 2 inches into a large, deep, heavy skillet (if using an electric fryer, pour oil to a depth of 3¹/₂ inches). Over medium heat, slowly heat to 350°F. Working in batches, add several breaded plantains, and fry, turning occasionally, until crisp and golden brown, about 1 minute. Use a slotted spoon to transfer the fried plantains to the prepared baking sheet. Keep them warm in a low oven while you fry the remaining plantains. Sprinkle with salt and serve immediately.

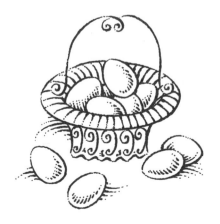

SOUFFLEED SWEET POTATOES

YIELD: 8 SIDE DISH SERVINGS

Both adults and children adore this unusually succulent side dish in which the sweet potatoes, somewhat bland on their own, pick up the fruity aroma of bananas. For variation, substitute 3¹/₂ cups puréed squash or pumpkin for the sweet potatoes.

3 large sweet potatoes (2 pounds total)
4 tablespoons (¹/₂ stick) unsalted butter
¹/₃ cup milk
2 ripe but firm bananas, peeled and mashed
*   until smooth (about 1 cup)*
2 large egg yolks
¹/₂ teaspoon freshly grated nutmeg
Salt and freshly ground black pepper
5 large egg whites, at room temperature

1. Place the potatoes in a large saucepan, cover with cold water, and bring to a boil. Reduce the heat to medium, and cook until the potatoes are fork-tender, about 30 minutes. Drain, rinse under cold running water, and let cool.

2. Preheat the oven to 475°F. Butter a 1- or 1¹/₂-quart shallow baking dish.

3. Peel the sweet potatoes and mash them in a mixing bowl.

4. Combine the butter and milk in a small saucepan and cook over medium-low heat until the butter is melted. Stir the hot milk into the mashed potatoes. Add the bananas. Add the egg yolks, one at a time, and beat with a wooden spoon until the mixture is light. Add the nutmeg and salt and pepper, to taste. (This dish can be made up to this point, covered, and refrigerated overnight.)

5. Add a pinch of salt to the egg whites and beat with a whisk or an electric mixer until they hold stiff peaks. Gently fold the beaten egg whites into the potato mixture.

6. Transfer the mixture to the prepared dish, and bake until the potatoes are puffed and lightly browned, about 20 minutes. Serve at once.

SCALLOPED YAMS WITH APPLES, PRUNES, AND LEMON

YIELD: 8 TO 10 SIDE DISH SERVINGS

Because true yams are rarely seen outside of Latin markets, the "yams" or "Louisiana yams" you see at your local supermarket are probably sweet potatoes. Although a yam is definitely not a sweet potato, the two resemble one another, taste alike, and can be used interchangeably. Yams come in all colors, from pale orange to purple. The darker the skin, the deeper and sweeter the flesh. Since the flavor of yams improves greatly when paired with other sweet ingredients, I've combined them with apples, prunes, and a lemon-scented syrup. The bread crumb topping adds extra crunch.

8 medium yams (about 5 pounds total),
    rinsed well
1 tablespoon minced garlic
3 Granny Smith apples
1 cup pitted prunes, coarsely chopped
½ cup dry sherry
½ cup (firmly packed) light brown sugar
2 teaspoons finely grated lemon zest
¾ teaspoon freshly grated nutmeg
¼ teaspoon salt
¼ teaspoon freshly ground black pepper
6 tablespoons (¾ stick) unsalted butter,
    melted
3 tablespoons fresh lemon juice
½ cup dry bread crumbs

1. Place the yams in a large pot, cover with cold water, and bring to a boil. Reduce the heat to medium, and cook until the yams are fork-tender, 25 to 30 minutes. Drain, rinse under cold running water, and let cool.

2. Preheat the oven to 375°F. Butter an 11½- x 9- x 2½-inch-deep casserole dish and sprinkle 1 teaspoon of the minced garlic over the bottom.

3. Peel the yams and slice them ½ inch thick. Core and thinly slice the apples. Layer one-third of the yams in the prepared dish. Cover the yams with half the apple slices. Scatter half of the prunes over the apples. Repeat the layers, starting with the garlic, and ending with the yams.

4. In a small saucepan, combine the sherry, brown sugar, lemon zest, nutmeg, salt, pepper, and 4 tablespoons of the melted butter. Heat, stirring, until the mixture is hot, and the sugar has dissolved. Stir in the lemon juice and pour the syrup evenly over the yams.

5. In a small bowl, mix the bread crumbs thoroughly with the remaining 2 tablespoons melted butter and sprinkle over the yams.

6. Bake for 1 hour, or until bubbling. Serve hot.

BAKED ACORN SQUASH WITH PEACH BUTTER

YIELD: 4 SIDE DISH SERVINGS

Instead of loading your baked squash with lots of the traditional combination of brown sugar and butter or bacon fat, perk it up instead with fruit butter. Although I suggest using homemade peach butter here, commercial peach butter, available in health food stores and some supermarkets, will do in a pinch. And you don't have to stick with peach; vary it by using apple, pear, or banana butter.

2 acorn squash (about 1½ pounds each), halved lengthwise and seeded
½ cup peach butter, preferably homemade (page 263)
2 tablespoons unsalted butter
Freshly grated nutmeg
Salt and freshly ground black pepper

1. Preheat the oven to 400°F.

2. Fill each squash half with 2 tablespoons of the peach butter and ½ tablespoon of the butter. Arrange the squash, cut side up, in a baking dish, cover the dish with aluminum foil, and bake until tender, 40 to 45 minutes.

3. Sprinkle each squash with nutmeg, salt, and pepper. Serve at once.

BAKED STUFFED PAPAYA

YIELD: 4 SIDE DISH SERVINGS

If you have never tried papaya as a vegetable, this delicious preparation is a fine introduction. Simplicity in itself, it consists of baked papaya halves stuffed with a fragrant mixture of bread crumbs and herbs. It's an excellent accompaniment to roast meat, grilled steaks, and fish. The fruit can be stuffed ahead and baked just before serving.

½ cup dry bread crumbs
¼ cup finely chopped flat-leaf parsley
*   leaves*
¼ cup finely chopped shallots
2 teaspoons minced garlic
2 tablespoons extra-virgin olive oil
2 tablespoons fresh lime juice
Salt and freshly ground black pepper
2 ripe but firm papayas (about 1¼
*   pounds each), halved lengthwise,*
*   seeds removed*
4 lime wedges (optional)

1. Preheat the oven to 400°F. Lightly oil a baking sheet.

2. In a medium-size bowl, stir the bread crumbs, parsley, shallots, garlic, olive oil, and lime juice until well combined. Season to taste with salt and pepper. Spoon the mixture into each papaya half.

3. Place the papaya halves on the prepared baking sheet and bake until the fruit is warm and the filling is lightly browned on top, about 20 minutes. Serve the baked papaya with a squeeze of fresh lime juice, if desired.

QUINCE AND CRANBERRY STUFFING

YIELD: 12 SIDE DISH SERVINGS

When roasting turkey or goose, baking the stuffing separately usually makes more sense. The bird's cooking time is reduced, and it's unnecessary to remove all stuffing immediately after roasting. In this delicious fruit and vegetable stuffing, the subtle tang of the quinces and cranberries is a perfect foil for the richness of a bird. It can be prepared early in the day, covered with aluminum foil, and refrigerated until ready to bake. Start baking the stuffing 45 minutes before the bird is done.

4 large quinces (about 3 pounds total)

3 tablespoons fresh lemon juice

6 tablespoons (¾ stick) unsalted butter

1½ cups chopped onions

4 cups sliced mushrooms (about 1 pound)

1 cup fresh cranberries

½ cup chicken broth, preferably homemade
    (page 30)

4 teaspoons sugar

Salt and freshly ground black pepper

4 large eggs, well beaten

1 cup chopped pecans

8 slices white bread, preferably French, cubed
    (½-inch pieces)

2 tablespoons chopped flat-leaf parsley leaves

1. Peel, quarter, and core the quinces. Slice them ¼ inch thick, place in a mixing bowl, and toss with the lemon juice. Set aside.

2. Melt the butter in a large skillet over medium heat. Add the onions, mushrooms, and quinces, and cook, stirring frequently, until the quinces are crisp-tender, about 5 minutes. Stir in the cranberries, broth, and sugar. Immediately remove from the heat and transfer to a large mixing bowl. Season to taste with salt and pepper, and let cool.

3. Preheat the oven to 325°F. Butter a large glass casserole dish.

4. Add the beaten eggs, pecans, and bread cubes to the quince-cranberry mixture. Toss until well combined.

5. Turn the stuffing into the prepared casserole. Place the casserole in a large roast-ing pan and add enough hot water to the roasting pan to come halfway up the outside of the casserole. Bake until the stuffing is lightly browned on top, 40 to 45 minutes. Garnish with chopped parsley and serve hot.

ROASTED VEGETABLES, SICILIAN STYLE

YIELD: 4 SIDE DISH
SERVINGS

Sicilian cooks have an affinity for things sweet-and-sour. Nowhere is this love affair more apparent than in their treatment of vegetables. In my spin on this Italian theme, I have paired carrots, turnips, and pearl onions with brown sugar and balsamic vinegar. The mixture is then roasted until it's perfectly caramelized. As soon as the vegetables come out of the oven, they are tossed with a handful of dried cranberries, currants, toasted pine nuts, and fresh basil. Like so many Italian vegetable preparations, this cheerful dish—which goes well with roast chicken, turkey, or pork—is best eaten at room temperature so that all the distinctive flavors can come through. You may substitute dried cherries for the cranberries.

1 pint (2 cups) pearl onions

2 tablespoons extra-virgin olive oil

2 tablespoons balsamic vinegar

2 tablespoons (firmly packed) light brown sugar

3 large carrots, sliced ½ inch thick

3 medium turnips, peeled, and sliced into
    ½-inch-thick wedges

Salt and freshly ground black pepper

⅓ cup dried cranberries, plumped in hot water
    for 30 minutes and drained

2 tablespoons dried currants

2 tablespoons toasted pine nuts (for toasting
    instructions, see page 64)

2 tablespoons shredded fresh basil leaves (for
    shredding instructions, see page 34)

1. Preheat the oven to 450°F.

2. Bring a large pot of salted water to a boil. Add the pearl onions. Quickly drain the onions, and refresh them under cold running water. Peel the onions.

3. Combine the olive oil, vinegar, and brown sugar in a large baking dish. Add the carrots, turnips, and onions and toss to coat with the seasoning. Season to taste with salt and pepper.

4. Bake, stirring occasionally, until the vegetables are crisp-tender and caramelized, about 25 minutes.

5. Remove the dish from the oven, and stir in the plumped cranberries, currants, toasted pine nuts, and basil. Serve warm or at room temperature.

BARBECUED BAKED BEANS

YIELD: 4 TO 6 SIDE DISH SERVINGS

Most people think that because I am a professional chef, I must cook and eat fancy meals all the time. Nothing could be further from the truth! My husband enjoys hot dogs and canned baked beans, and this recipe is a good example of what I do to perk up the beans a bit, without undue fuss. I usually serve them with Boston Brown Bread (see Index), so I always keep a loaf or two in my freezer for impromptu meals.

2 cans (16 ounces each) baked pork and beans,
    drained

1 Granny Smith apple, peeled, cored, and
    finely diced

¾ cup bottled thick, spicy barbecue sauce, such
    as Master Choice or President's Choice

1 tablespoon (firmly packed) light brown sugar

1 tablespoon cider vinegar

½ cup finely chopped onion

½ teaspoon ground cumin

Salt and freshly ground black pepper

HOW TO PEEL, CUT, AND JUICE A PINEAPPLE

1. Cut off the top and bottom of the pineapple with a sharp knife.

2. Stand the fruit on one of its surfaces on a cutting board. Following the contour of the fruit, carefully and evenly cut away the rind, a strip at a time, from top to bottom. Be careful not to cut too deep into the meat.

3. Look at the cut pineapple. You'll see that the eyes are lined up like spirals. Working row by row, remove the eyes, 3 to 4 at a time, by cutting out V-shaped wedges and slicing them off the fruit.

FOR RINGS: Lay the pineapple on its side and slice it about ½ to ¾ inch thick. With a small knife, remove the tough inner core from each slice, and discard.

FOR WEDGES: Cut the fruit lengthwise into eighths. Trim and discard the core from each wedge.

FOR CHUNKS: Make wedges and cut each crosswise into bite-size pieces.

FOR JUICE: Start with a small, fairly ripe pineapple. Peel, core, and cut it into small chunks. Finely purée the fruit in a blender or food processor. Pour the purée into a bowl through a fine sieve lined with a triple layer of dampened cheesecloth. Gather the edges of the cheesecloth together and wring out as much liquid as possible. (You should have about 1½ cups of juice.) The juice may be stored in a covered jar and refrigerated for up to 3 days.

Combine the beans, apple, barbecue sauce, brown sugar, vinegar, onion, and cumin in a large saucepan and season to taste with salt and pepper. Cook over low heat, stirring frequently, until the apple and onions are just tender, about 15 minutes. Serve as an accompaniment to hot dogs.

BOMBAY LENTILS

YIELD: 6 TO 8 SIDE DISH SERVINGS

This is my version of a hearty Indian stew. The fresh pineapple not only lightens up the stew, but it also tames the heat and makes the lentils pulse with sweetness. You can use any type of lentils in this recipe, but if you do make it with one of the smaller, more exotic varieties—like green, yellow, red, or black lentils—cut the cooking time in half. You can make this stew well in advance of serving; it will thicken slightly as it cools, so add a little hot water before reheating.

1 cup (½ pound) brown lentils, rinsed and
    picked over
2 bay leaves
4 large cloves garlic, crushed, plus 2 teaspoons
    minced garlic
Salt
2 tablespoons unsalted butter
1 medium onion, finely chopped (about ½ cup)
1 fresh green serrano or jalapeño pepper,
    minced
2 teaspoons minced peeled fresh ginger
1 large Idaho potato (about ½ pound), peeled
    and cubed (½-inch pieces)
1 cup finely chopped fresh pineapple
2 large ripe tomatoes, peeled, seeded, and
    finely chopped
5 cardamom pods, crushed
1 cinnamon stick (3 inches)
Freshly ground black pepper

1. Place the lentils, bay leaves, crushed garlic, and 2 teaspoons salt in a medium-size saucepan with 4 cups cold water. Bring to a boil over high heat, then reduce the heat to medium. Simmer, uncovered, until the lentils are tender but retain their shape, about 15 minutes. Drain, reserving 1 cup of the cooking liquid. Remove the bay leaves and garlic.

2. Melt the butter in a large skillet over medium heat. Sauté the onion, minced garlic, serrano pepper, and ginger until tender, about 2 minutes. Stir in the potato and cook until golden, about 5 minutes.

3. Stir in the pineapple, tomatoes, cardamom, and cinnamon stick. Add ½ cup of the reserved liquid, cover the skillet, and simmer, over low heat for 10 minutes, stirring occasionally.

4. Add the lentils, ½ teaspoon salt, and remaining ½ cup liquid. Continue to simmer, covered, until almost all the liquid has been absorbed, about 10 minutes longer, stirring occasionally. Remove from the heat and adjust the seasoning with salt and pepper, if necessary. Serve at once.

FROM THE PANTRY

CHUTNEYS, PICKLES, FRUIT BUTTERS, JAMS, RELISHES, SAUCES, AND VINEGARS

The fruits of summer—berries, cherries, nectarines, peaches, and plums—are at their glorious peak for just a few weeks. And once gone, they don't return for a whole year. The best way to take full advantage of a fruit's elusive perfection—besides picking it early on a sultry summer day and popping your prize right into your mouth—is to capture it in a jar, so it can be stashed away in the pantry to be savored later in the year.

You're probably so used to buying ready-made jams, chutneys, pickles, and vinegars that it may seem pointless to make your own. After all, delicious condiments are widely available. But preserving at home offers unlimited variety, the chance to customize your canned goods, and the satisfaction of producing

A WORD ON FRUIT SPREADS

*T*here is very little difference in the various spreads we know as jellies, jams, conserves, preserves, marmalades, and butters. They are all made of fruit and sugar and are jellied to varying degrees; they differ mostly in consistency.

Try not to use fruits that are overripe when making fruit spreads, because they will have lost a lot of their pectin, a natural substance that causes jelling. I try to avoid commercial pectins (even though they are mostly concentrated natural pectin, usually from apples) when I make preserves because a lot of sugar is required to activate them. You may need to cook fruits with low concentrations of pectin longer, but the end result will taste more like fruit than sugar.

If a jam or marmalade won't jell after you have bottled it, rescue it by returning it to the pot (pour it out of the jars) and cooking it until the jelly stage (220°F) is reached. If you still doubt you have sufficient pectin, throw in a couple of peeled, chopped apples. You'll end up with a fruit blend, of sorts, but the apples shouldn't affect the flavor of the dominant fruit. You will have to sterilize the jars again, and use fresh lids.

For best results, don't double your batches, and always use a jelly or candy thermometer to determine when a preserve has reached the jellying stage.

FRUIT BUTTER

Fruit butters are made from fruit pulp, slowly cooked until the flavor is very concentrated and the texture is velvety smooth and thick. Spices may be added according to your taste.

CONSERVE

Conserves are jamlike products made by cooking two or more fruits with sugar until the mixture rounds up in a spoon, like jam. A true conserve contains nuts and raisins, but you can add or omit these ingredients according to your taste.

JAM

Jams are made by cooking crushed or puréed fruits with sugar until the jellying point (220°F) is reached, or until the mixture rounds up in a spoon. Commercial pectin may be added to help further jellying if a specific fruit lacks natural pectin.

JELLY

The objective in making jelly is to obtain a clear, transparent product. Therefore, just the strained juice from fruit is used to make jelly. It is gelatinized enough to make it firm and capable of holding its own shape, yet it is soft enough to spread. Unsweetened canned or frozen fruit juices are excellent for making quick jellies.

MARMALADE

Marmalades are made from fruit juice and pieces of fruit. Thus, marmalades stand somewhere between a jelly and a preserve. Citrus fruits such as orange, grapefruit, and lemon are ideal for making marmalades, for their white pith contains most of the pectin found in these fruits.

PRESERVES

Preserves are similar to jams, but usually made with whole pieces of fruit, which are cooked in sugar syrup so that the fruit retains its shape. They are clear and shiny, with a tender and plump consistency. The word preserves has come to mean jams, jellies, and other types of preserved fruits in general.

healthful, delicious foods with surprising ease. I make my own preserves and relishes because they taste better, have less sugar and salt, and usually cost less than most commercial brands. I also get great pleasure from admiring the jars of golden peach butter, chunky banana chutney, and bright fruit jam that line my pantry shelves.

A fully stocked pantry also makes gift giving a cinch: Fat little tubs of vividly colored jams and relishes and slender graceful bottles of pale fruited vinegars are always on hand for a last-minute gift during the holidays or a friend's house warming. Those who enjoy good food always appreciate this thoughtful gesture.

PEACH BUTTER

YIELD: 4 TO 5 HALF-PINT JARS

This homemade fruit butter highlights the wonderful flavor of the fruit, not the sugar. Silky smooth and delicately sweet with peach flavors, this butter provides the "taste of summer" throughout the year. You may substitute mangoes or nectarines for the peaches. To spice up this fruit butter, add ½ teaspoon each of ground ginger and nutmeg

to the pulp during the second stage of cooking.

5 pounds fresh peaches
¼ cup fresh lemon juice
1½ cups sugar

1. Follow the steps on page 268 to sterilize five 8-ounce canning jars. Sterilize the lids according to the manufacturer's instructions.

2. Bring a large pot of water to a boil. Score X on both ends of each peach, then drop it into the boiling water. Use a slotted spoon to transfer the peaches to a bowl of cold water after 30 seconds. When they are cool enough to handle, peel, pit, and slice the peaches. (You should have about 10 cups of sliced fruit.)

3. Combine the sliced peaches, lemon juice, and ½ cup water in a large saucepan. Cook over medium-high heat, stirring often, until the fruit is quite soft, 15 to 20 minutes. Cool the fruit slightly and then purée it in a food processor. You should have about 6½ cups of purée.

4. Return the purée to the saucepan and add the sugar. Cook over medium heat, stirring frequently to prevent scorching, until the mixture is thick and creamy, or until a spoon drawn through the mixture leaves a clean line at the bottom of the pan, 25 to 30 minutes.

5. Pack and process the peach butter according to the instructions on page 274.

PRUNE BUTTER

YIELD: TWO 12-OUNCE JARS

Since prunes are available year-round, you can make this smooth, high-fiber spread any time you wish. Lemon zest adds interest without overwhelming the flavor of the prunes. Dried apricots, dates, and figs, can be used in the same fashion.

1 pound pitted prunes
½ cup sugar
Finely grated zest of
    1 lemon

1. Place the prunes in a mixing bowl and cover with 3½ cups water. Let sit overnight in the refrigerator.

2. Follow the steps on page 268 to sterilize two 12-ounce canning jars. Sterilize the lids according to the manufacturer's instructions.

3. Transfer the prunes and their soaking liquid to a medium-size sauce pan and cook over medium heat until the prunes are tender, about 5 minutes.

4. Cool the fruit slightly. Transfer the mixture to a blender or food processor and purée. Strain the purée through a fine sieve into a bowl, pressing on the solids to extract as much pulp as possible. There should be about 3½ cups of purée.

5. Return the purée to the pan with the sugar and lemon zest. Cook over low heat, stirring frequently to prevent scorching, until the mixture thickens, about 20 minutes. Remove from the heat.

6. Pack and process the prune butter according to the instructions on page 274.

QUINCE BUTTER

YIELD: 2 HALF-PINT JARS

Quince is an aromatic fruit, reminiscent of pear and apple combined. Unlike most fruits, quince requires cooking to be palatable. Its hard, dry flesh makes it perfect for butters, since it has very little moisture and doesn't cook down as much as most other fruits. The longer you cook quince butter, the thicker it becomes. I like mine when it reaches the spreading consistency of a thick pumpkin purée. You may substitute pears or apples for the quince. Spread this fragrant butter over freshly baked breads, bagels, muffins, and scones. Or use it to fill an omelet, along with some Cheddar cheese.

2 pounds fragrant quinces, unpeeled
½ cup (firmly packed) light brown sugar or
    pure maple syrup, or more to taste
¼ teaspoon ground cinnamon
Freshly grated nutmeg

You can go to tiny shops in Paris that put up their jams in beautiful little pots. But there is nothing like good homemade jam. It is hard to pin down exactly what is so wonderful about it, but it is wonderful.

—LAURIE COLWIN

1. Follow the steps on page 268 to sterilize two 8-ounce canning jars. Sterilize the lids according to the manufacturer's instructions.

2. Quarter, core, and seed the quinces. Cut each quarter lengthwise into 4 slices and place them in a large soup pot with 1 cup water. Partially cover and cook over low heat until the fruit is very soft and the water has almost evaporated, 30 to 35 minutes. Cool the fruit slightly. Transfer it to a blender or food processor and purée.

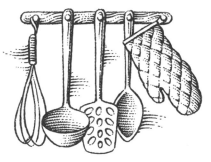

3. Return the purée to the pot. Cook over low heat, stirring frequently to prevent scorching, until the mixture is thick and creamy, or until a spoon drawn through the mixture leaves a clean line at the bottom of the pot, 30 to 35 minutes. Remove from the heat.

4. Pack and process the quince butter according to the instructions on page 274.

STRAWBERRY-RHUBARB JAM

YIELD: 4 HALF-PINT JARS

Tart rhubarb goes so well with sweet strawberries that the twosome have been a favorite dessert combination for generations. Not only are rhubarb and strawberries great baked in pies, they also make marvelous jams, as exemplified in this recipe. The jam is flavorful and not too sweet, and is well complemented by the aromatic lemon zest. In fact, it is so wonderful you might consider putting up more than just a few jars. You'll find it hard to resist this treat on a warm toasted scone or atop a scoop of vanilla ice cream.

*3 pints (6 cups) fresh strawberries, hulled
    and quartered
1³/₄ pounds rhubarb, trimmed and sliced
    ¹/₂ inch thick (about 5 cups total; see Note)
2 cups sugar
¹/₂ teaspoon salt
Finely grated zest of 3 large lemons (about
    1¹/₂ teaspoons)*

1. Follow the steps on page 268 to sterilize four 8-ounce canning jars. Sterilize the lids according to the manufacturer's instructions.

2. Place the strawberries, rhubarb, sugar, salt, and lemon zest in a large saucepan and bring to a boil over high heat. Reduce the heat to low and continue to simmer, uncovered, stirring frequently, until the mixture is thick and bubbling, 25 to 30 minutes. Skim the foam as it rises to the top. Test the jam: It's ready when a spoonful dropped on a cold plate holds its shape. If the jam is not ready, continue cooking for 5 to 10 minutes and test again. Remove from the heat.

3. Pack and process the jam according to the steps on page 274.

NOTE: When you use rhubarb, be sure to discard the leaves, since they can be very toxic; only the red stalks are edible.

CHERRY JAM

YIELD: 3 HALF-PINT JARS

To me, the cherry season is one of the most pleasurable, a time to enjoy cherries in every possible way, like in this pure and simple jam. If you find the jam too sugary, cut the sweetness with more lemon juice.

10 cups pitted fresh cherries (about
    4 pounds before pitting)
1 cup sugar
⅓ cup fresh lemon juice
1 cinnamon stick (3 inches)

1. Follow the steps on page 268 to sterilize three 8-ounce canning jars. Sterilize the lids according to the manufacturer's instructions.

2. Purée half the cherries in a blender or food processor. Coarsely chop the remainder.

3. Place the puréed cherries, chopped cherries, sugar, lemon juice, and cinnamon stick in a large saucepan and bring to a boil over high heat. Reduce the heat to medium and boil, stirring frequently, until the mixture has thickened, about 15 minutes. Skim the foam as it rises to the top. Test the jam: It's ready when a spoonful dropped onto a cold plate holds its shape. If the jam is not ready, continue cooking for 5 to 10 minutes and test again. Remove fom the heat.

4. Pack and process the jam according to the instructions on page 274.

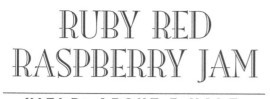

RUBY RED RASPBERRY JAM

YIELD: ABOUT 5 HALF-PINT JARS

It takes almost no effort to produce a big batch of raspberry jam at home for a fraction of the cost of a store-bought product, plus you have all the fun of making it. I think the seeds give raspberry jam its unique character, but if you prefer seedless jam, heat the crushed berries until soft, then pass them through a sieve or food mill before combining them with the sugar. Since raspberries contain very little pectin, it will be necessary to add liquid pectin to help the jelling process.

4½ pints (9 cups) fresh raspberries
5 cups sugar
1 pouch or ½ bottle (3 ounces) liquid pectin,
    such as Certo

1. Follow the steps on page 268 to sterilize five 8-ounce canning jars. Sterilize the lids according to the manufacturer's instructions.

2. Place the raspberries in a large soup pot, and crush them with a potato masher.

3. Stir the sugar into the crushed raspberries. Slowly bring the mixture to a boil over medium-low heat and cook, stirring constantly, until the sugar dissolves. Raise the heat to high and bring the mixture to a full, rolling boil.

4. Quickly stir in the liquid pectin. Return to a rolling boil, and boil hard for 2 minutes, stirring constantly. Remove from the heat. Do not overcook, or the pectin may not gel.

5. Pack and process the jam following the instructions on page 274.

BLUEBERRY-APPLE PRESERVES

YIELD: FIVE 12-OUNCE JARS

I've added apples to these blueberry preserves to provide the pectin necessary for jelling. The apples do not add a noticeable flavor, but do provide a pleasant chunky texture.

4 pints (8 cups) ripe blueberries, stemmed
3 large tart apples, such as Granny Smith
    (about 1½ pounds total), peeled,
    cored, and finely chopped
Grated zest of 2 oranges (about
    1 tablespoon)
Juice of 2 oranges (about ¾ cup)
2 cups sugar
2 tablespoons fresh lemon juice

1. Follow the steps below to sterilize five 12-ounce canning jars. Sterilize the lids according to manufacturer's instructions.

2. Place the berries in a large soup pot and crush them slightly with a potato masher. Stir in the remaining ingredients.

3. Bring the mixture to a full, rolling boil over high heat and boil, stirring occasionally, until the sugar dissolves. Reduce the heat to medium-high and cook, stirring frequently, until the mixture is slightly thick, about 20 minutes. Skim the foam as it rises to the top. Test the preserves: It's ready when a spoonful dropped onto a cold plate holds its shape.

If the jam is not ready, continue cooking for 5 to 10 minutes and test again. Remove from the heat.

4. Pack and process the preserves according to the instructions on page 274.

STERILIZING JARS AND LIDS FOR CANNING

I use standard home canning (Mason) jars with self-sealing lids (the type with rubber-edged flat lids and separate ring bands); they are available at most hardware stores and many supermarkets. These lids seal automatically as the contents of the jars cool, forming an airtight vacuum so that bacteria cannot contaminate the contents. It's a good idea to get the canning jars in different sizes, based on your needs. I find the half-pint (8-ounce) and three-quarter-pint (12-ounce) sizes most convenient for canning. However, if you have pint or quart jars on hand, use them. Canning jars can be reused, but do not reuse a lid that has been processed before; it will not seal the jar properly the second time around.

All canning materials must be sterilized before use. First wash the jars, lids, and utensils in warm, soapy water, then rinse thoroughly. Sterilize them by following these steps:

1. Choose a large, wide pot that can be fitted with a rack or an inverted plate to prevent the jars from touching the hot bottom of the pot and cracking. The pot should also be deep enough to fill with enough water to cover the jars.

2. Place the rack or plate in the pot. Place the jars upright on the rack and fill each with hot (not boiling) water. Fill the pan with hot water until the jars are completely covered by water. Bring to a boil and continue to boil gently for 10 minutes. (You can also sterilize jars and other utensils in your dishwasher if it has a sterilizing cycle.)

3. In a separate pot of simmering water, boil the lids and ring bands according to the manufacturer's instructions.

DAMSON PLUM JAM

YIELD: TWO 12-OUNCE JARS

Autumn is an ideal season to make plum jam, so you can enjoy it throughout the winter months. In addition to being delicious and economical to prepare, this jam is as deeply rich as it is colorful.

> 5 cups coarsely chopped pitted Damson plums
>   (about 2¼ pounds before pitting)
> 2 cups sugar
> 3 tablespoons fresh lemon juice

1. Follow the steps on the facing page to sterilize two 12-ounce canning jars. Sterilize the lids according to the manufacturer's instructions.

2. Combine all the ingredients with ¾ cup water in a large soup pot. Bring the mixture to a full, rolling boil over high heat and boil, stirring occasionally, until the sugar dissolves. Reduce the heat to medium-high and cook, stirring frequently, until the mixture is thick and glossy, about 20 minutes. Test the jam: It's ready when a spoonful dropped onto a cold plate holds its shape. If the jam is not ready, continue cooking for 5 to 10 minutes and test again. Remove from the heat.

3. Pack and process the jam according to the instructions on page 274.

GOLDEN MARMALADE

YIELD: 6 HALF-PINT JARS

When you make marmalade, don't double the recipe. It will take hours to reach the jellying stage, and even worse, you risk destroying the natural pectin in the fruit by overcooking, thus guaranteeing that the mixture will never jell. The extra step of soaking the fruit overnight helps to tenderize the citrus pith and rind and release their pectin. There are four different fruits in this marmalade, but the predominant flavor is that of apricots and oranges, with a pleasant bitterness.

> 3 blood oranges or navel oranges
> 2 lemons
> 1½ cups coarsely chopped fresh
>   pineapple
> ¾ cup dried apricots, coarsely chopped
> About 3⅓ cups sugar

1. Scrub the oranges and lemons well. Quarter each fruit, then cut crosswise into thin slices, removing the seeds. Place the sliced fruits in a large soup pot.

2. Place the pineapple in a food processor or blender and process until puréed. (There should be about 1 cup of purée.) Add the puréed pineapple, apricots, and 8 cups water to the pot.

3. Bring the mixture to a boil over high heat. Reduce the heat to low and simmer the fruits for 5 minutes. Cover and let stand for at least 10 hours, or overnight, at cool room temperature.

4. Follow the steps on page 268 to sterilize six 8-ounce canning jars. Sterilize the lids according to manufacturer's instructions.

5. Measure the fruit and liquid and return to the pot; you should have 10 cups. Add ¹⁄₃ cup sugar for each cup of fruit mixture.

6. Bring the mixture to a full, rolling boil over high heat, stirring to dissolve the sugar. Reduce the heat to medium high, and cook, uncovered, stirring frequently to prevent scorching, until the jelly stage is reached, about 40 minutes. Test the marmalade: It's ready when a spoonful dropped onto a cold plate holds its shape. If the marmalade is not ready, continue cooking for 5 to 10 minutes and test again. Remove from the heat.

7. Pack and process the marmalade according to the instructions on page 274.

FESTIVE CACTUS PEAR AND WINE JELLY

YIELD: ABOUT 7 HALF-PINT JARS

Even though I am usually not a fan of either cactus pears or jellies, I think this is one instance when two wrongs make a right! In this recipe, I use the sweet-tart juice of prickly pears, but you may substitute fresh apple, grapefruit, or pineapple juice. This jelly is a most appropriate condiment for grilled lamb chops, roast duck, venison, or pork. Ruby-red in color, with a delicate wine taste, cactus pear jelly is also great for glazing fruit tarts.

5 large ripe cactus pears, peeled and quartered

1 cup Muscat, Sauternes, or other sweet dessert wine

2 cups sugar

1 pouch or ½ bottle (3 ounces) liquid pectin, such as Certo

1. Follow the steps on page 268 to sterilize seven 8-ounce canning jars. Sterilize the lids according to the manufacturer's instructions.

2. Place the cactus pear pieces in a food processor and purée. Strain through a fine sieve, pressing on the pulp to extract as much

CACTUS PEARS

*S*haped like a large egg, the cactus pear (also known as prickly pear, Indian pear, Indian fig, or Barbary fig) comes from the nopal or opuntia cactus plant. At first glance, a cactus pear may look like a small, pinkish-green hand grenade covered with fuzzy black dots. A closer look at these dots will reveal short, pointy needles. Be careful when handling cactus pears, because these prickly spines can easily irritate your skin if you don't protect your hands.

The cactus pear is actually a berry, with a multitude of tiny, hard black seeds in its soft, spongy flesh. This unusual fruit, which is very popular in tropical climes, yields a gorgeous ruby-red pulp. Tastewise, its juicy meat will remind you somewhat of a ripe watermelon with a hint of perfume. Before using, rub each fruit with a paper towel to get rid of the spines, then remove the peel with a paring knife to expose the meat. If you don't mind the seeds, you can enjoy cactus pear the same way you would watermelon: Eat it raw or add it to fruit salads. Just be sure to spit out the hard seeds, as they can scratch your throat or cause indigestion! When puréed and strained, the pulp provides a juice that can be enjoyed straight or with the addition of a little sugar and liquor, can be used to make refreshing ices and dessert sauces. Cactus pears are available in the fall, winter, and spring.

juice as possible. (There should be 1 cup of juice.)

3. Combine the cactus pear juice, wine, and sugar in a medium-size, heavy saucepan. Cook over medium-low heat, stirring constantly, just until bubbles appear around the edge of the pan and the sugar is dissolved, 5 to 6 minutes.

4. Stir in the pectin, and cook 1 minute longer. Remove from the heat, and skim the foam.

5. Pack and process the jelly according to the instructions on page 274.

SASSY BANANA CHUTNEY

YIELD: ABOUT 3 CUPS

*T*his Caribbean chutney is so succulent you might be tempted to eat it right out of the pot! It tastes great with roasted or grilled lean meat, such as pork and lamb chops, chicken, quail, or duck, but I like it best with curried dishes. The luscious body of this chutney comes from the onion mixture; be sure to allow it to cook slowly and long enough to form almost a thick paste. Try to use a Scotch bonnet pepper in this chutney; its floral scent will enhance the flavor of the bananas. If you wish, you may preserve this chutney while it's still hot in hot sterilized jars according to the instructions on pages 268 and 274.

> 1 tablespoon unsalted butter
>
> 1½ cups chopped onions
>
> 1 tablespoon minced garlic
>
> 1 tablespoon grated peeled fresh ginger
>
> ½ cup apple cider
>
> ½ cup malt vinegar or red wine vinegar
>
> ½ cup (firmly packed) light brown sugar
>
> 4 large almost-ripe bananas, peeled, and cut into 1-inch rounds
>
> ¼ cup raisins
>
> 1¼ teaspoons salt
>
> ⅛ teaspoon ground cloves
>
> ⅛ teaspoon grated nutmeg
>
> ⅛ teaspoon ground cinnamon
>
> ½ small fresh Scotch bonnet pepper, minced (about ½ teaspoon), or 1 teaspoon minced fresh jalapeño pepper

1. Melt the butter in a large skillet over medium heat. Add the onions, garlic, and ginger, and cook, stirring frequently with a wooden spoon, until the vegetables are very soft and golden brown, about 10 minutes. The mixture will look pasty.

2. Add the cider, vinegar, and brown sugar and bring to a simmer, scraping up any browned bits from the bottom of the pan with a wooden spoon, about 30 seconds. Reduce the heat to low, add the bananas, raisins, salt, cloves, nutmeg, and cinnamon and cook until the mixture is almost as thick as ketchup, about 10 minutes. The banana pieces should still hold their shape. Remove from the heat and stir in the Scotch bonnet

pepper. This chutney gets better with age and will keep, covered and refrigerated, for about 1 month.

SPICED APRICOT CHUTNEY

YIELD: 4 HALF-PINT JARS

With its melt-in-your mouth quality, this chutney is wonderfully infused with orange and ginger. It's particularly well suited to chicken and spicy foods, such as lamb curries. For quick, satisfying cocktail nibbles, serve dollops of this chutney on cream cheese and crackers. A similar chutney can be made with peach or mango.

> 2 pounds fresh apricots
>
> 1 small orange
>
> 1 piece fresh ginger (2 inches long), peeled
>
> 10 cloves garlic
>
> 1 cup golden raisins
>
> 1 cup cider vinegar
>
> ½ cup (firmly packed) light brown sugar
>
> ½ teaspoon cayenne pepper
>
> ½ teaspoon salt
>
> ¼ teaspoon ground cinnamon

PICKLES, RELISHES, AND CHUTNEYS

*P*ickling is among the oldest known methods of preserving food, dating back to Biblical times. Although most people think of pickles as cucumbers, they can be any fruit, vegetable, or even meat, including a wide variety of relishes. Pickled products are soaked in either a salt or vinegar solution anywhere from a few hours to several weeks, to preserve the food and develop a sour taste.

FRUIT PICKLES *are usually prepared from whole fruits packed in spicy, sweet, and sour syrup. Pickled fruits are great companions for sandwiches and grilled or roasted meat.*

RELISHES *are prepared from fruits or vegetables (or a combination of the two) that have been chopped and cooked to a soft consistency in a spicy vinegar solution, often with added sugar, hot peppers, and other spices. As such, chutney is also considered a relish.*

CHUTNEY *is derived from the Hindi* chatni, *which refers to licking one's fingertips. Although most of us associate chutneys with bottled varieties like Major Grey, to true food aficionados, the major is an imposter, since it bears no resemblance to traditional Indian recipes. Thanks to today's adventurous chefs, chutneys of all kinds are rapidly gaining popularity, not only on restaurant menus but also in our kitchens. By incorporating a little chutney here and there, we can add a new dimension to soups, vegetables, and entrées.*

I think chutneys are great with just about anything roasted or stewed. They are especially delicious alongside grilled pork chops or chicken just off the barbecue! When a dish seems boring to me, like plain rice or chopped liver, I stir in a little fruit chutney for a magical sweet and sour note. As a healthy alternative to butter, I've also taken to spreading fruit chutney on breads.

1. Follow the steps on page 268 to sterilize four 8-ounce canning jars. Sterilize the lids according to the manufacturer's instructions.

2. Blanch the apricots by immersing them in boiling water for 30 seconds. Peel and pit them. Coarsely chop in a food processor. Do not overprocess. Transfer the apricots to a large, nonreactive saucepan.

3. With a zester, remove the zest from the orange in long strands, and add to the saucepan. Remove and discard the white pith from the orange. Chop the orange, removing any seeds, and add the fruit to the saucepan.

4. Place the ginger and garlic in the food processor and mince them.

5. Add the ginger-garlic mixture and all the remaining ingredients to the saucepan. Bring to the boil, then simmer, partially covered, until all of the liquid has evaporated and the chutney has thickened, 45 to 50 minutes. Stir frequently with a wooden spoon to prevent scorching. Remove from the heat.

6. Pack and process the chutney according to the instructions on page 274.

PACKING AND PROCESSING

When canning fruit, it's important to assemble the necessary equipment before you begin. This organization not only makes the work easier but also saves time during the crucial stages of packing and sealing the jars. Besides canning jars and lids, a few other pieces of equipment are necessary: a large, heavy-bottomed pot, for even cooking; a large, deep, wide pot, for sterilizing and processing the jars; a jar lifter, to move the hot jars in and out of boiling water; a long wooden spoon; a ladle; a candy thermometer; and a small, narrow, flat-bladed metal spatula to release air bubbles in the filled jars. To prevent hot, sticky jam from burning my hands or messing up the jars and countertop, I like to fill the jars with a Pyrex measuring cup with a pouring lip. Another easy way is to use a widemouthed canning funnel. A timer is also necessary for accurately measuring the processing times.

For safety in preserving foods, the United States Department of Agriculture recommends processing the just-filled jars for 10 minutes in a boiling water bath. This step ensures that the food inside the jars reaches a temperature of 240°F, at which point potentially dangerous bacteria and enzymes are destroyed. If you follow the directions and precautions outlined in this chapter, you can safely jar and enjoy your preserves without worry.

As you prepare your food for canning, sterilize enough jars to accommodate your recipe following the directions on page 268. Once your food is ready to be packed, follow these steps:

1. Work with one jar at a time. Use tongs or a jar lifter to remove a sterilized jar from the boiling water bath (or dishwasher). Pour any water back into the pot (do not discard the boiling water; you'll need it for processing once all the jars are sealed). Invert the jar on a paper towel for 2 seconds to let any excess water drip out. Fill and pack the food in the hot ster-ilized jar, leaving ¼-inch headspace for butters, jams, jellies, and marmalades and ½ inch for relishes, chutneys, and pickles.

2. Run a spatula around the inside wall of the filled jar to release any air bubbles. Wipe the rim of the jar with a clean wet towel to remove any food particles or stickiness.

3. Place a sterilized lid on the mouth of the jar and screw the band down just until it feels tight. If you fasten the band too tightly, the jar may crack during processing.

4. Repeat filling the remaining jars in the same manner. If you end up with less than full jar, just put it aside for immediate use and enjoyment.

5. Using tongs or a jar lifter, carefully place the sealed jars on a rack (or inverted plate) in a large pot with boiling water (this can be the same pot you used for sterilizing the jars). Make sure the water covers the jars completely. Start timing the processing from the moment the water returns to a steady boil. Boil for 10 minutes.

6. Turn off the heat and use the tongs to transfer the jars to a rack or towel. Let the jars cool, undisturbed, to room temperature. At this point the preserves are ready to be put away.

7. Label and date the jars, then store them in a dark, dry, cool area like the cellar, a pantry, or the refrigerator. They should keep for up to 1 year.

NOTE: After opening, refrigerate preserves, and use them quickly, preferably within a couple weeks. As an extra safety precaution, always check for mold. If the food looks fuzzy or moldy, discard it.

Thank goodness someone finally had the courage to eat one of those little golden-red globes and proclaim it for its delicious acidity and wondrous texture.

—JAMES BEARD WRITING ON THE TOMATO IN BEARD ON FOOD

TOMATO-PEACH CHUTNEY

YIELD: 2 CUPS

Although the canyons of New York City aren't home to many gardens—or any orchards—the produce markets in my neighborhood provide delicious fruits and vegetables all year long. In the summer, when tomatoes and peaches are at their peak of flavor and lowest prices, I use them in as many ways as I can. This robust peach and tomato chutney has red wine, bal-

samic vinegar, and raisins to balance all the flavors, while toasted walnuts add an interesting crunch. Serve this luxuriant relish as an accompaniment to game, or spoon it over toasted garlic bread for tasty little snacks or hors d'oeuvres. A mango can easily stand in for the peaches.

1 tablespoon unsalted butter
$\frac{1}{2}$ cup chopped onion
1 tablespoon finely chopped peeled fresh ginger
2 teaspoons sugar
$\frac{1}{4}$ cup chicken broth, preferably homemade (page 30)
1 tablespoon dry red wine, preferably Pinot Noir
1 tablespoon balsamic vinegar
2 medium ripe but firm peaches (about $\frac{3}{4}$ pound total), pitted and cubed ($\frac{1}{2}$-inch pieces)
$\frac{1}{4}$ cup golden raisins, plumped in hot water for 5 minutes and drained
3 plum tomatoes (about $\frac{3}{4}$ pound total), cored, seeded, and finely diced
Salt and freshly ground black pepper
$\frac{1}{2}$ cup toasted walnuts (for toasting instructions, see page 34), coarsely chopped

1. Melt the butter in a large skillet over medium heat. Add the onion and ginger and sauté until aromatic and tender, 2 minutes.

2. Stir in the sugar, broth, red wine, and vinegar. When the mixture comes to a simmer, stir in the peaches, raisins, and tomatoes. Cook until the chutney is slightly thickened, the fruit tender, and most of the liquid has evaporated, about 5 minutes. Season to taste

with salt and pepper. The mixture should have a pleasing balance of sweet and sour. Remove from the heat, and let cool.

3. Stir in the walnuts and serve at room temperature. Store any leftover chutney in a covered jar. It keeps well in the refrigerator for up to 1 month.

CRANBERRY-ORANGE RELISH

YIELD: ABOUT THREE 12-OUNCE JARS

Here's a classic American relish that's an important part of Thanksgiving tradition. There can be many variations on cranberry relish, but I find this one so appealing because it is laden with bitter oranges, sweet raisins, and crunchy walnuts. When you prepare this relish, do not cook the berries much longer after they pop or they will turn bitter. Without canning, the relish can safely be refrigerated for 2 weeks.

2 small navel oranges
1 bag (12 ounces) fresh or frozen
  cranberries, picked over
1½ cups cranberry juice cocktail
1¼ cups sugar
½ cup raisins or chopped dates
⅓ cup chopped walnuts

1. Follow the steps on page 268 to sterilize four 8-ounce canning jars. Sterilize the lids according to the manufacturer's instructions.

2. Without peeling the oranges, finely chop them.

3. Combine the oranges, cranberries, cranberry juice, sugar, and raisins in a medium-size saucepan. Bring the mixture to a boil, then reduce the heat to medium-low and cook until the cranberries have popped, about 5 minutes.

4. Reduce the heat to low and simmer, stirring frequently, until the mixture is thick, about 10 minutes. Remove from the heat and stir in the walnuts.

5. Pack and process the relish according to the instructions on page 274.

VARIATION

GINGERED CRANBERRY-RAISIN RELISH: Combine 1 bag (12 ounces) fresh or frozen cranberries, 1 cup raisins, 1 cup (firmly packed) light brown sugar, 1½ cups apple cider, and 2 tablespoons finely grated peeled ginger in a medium-size saucepan. Bring the mixture to a boil, then cook over medium heat, stirring often, until the berries pop, about 5 minutes. Makes 4 cups.

PICKLED GRAPES

YIELD: 4 ½ CUPS

If you find traditional vegetable pickles too boring, try this light and refreshing alternative. Pickling grapes in a tangy, spicy brine creates an exciting new taste. I particularly enjoy this mixture of red and green grapes; it makes for quite a colorful combination, attractive enough to give as a gift. Allow the grapes to marinate at least overnight so that the flavors will develop. Serve these pickled grapes with grilled or roasted meats. They will keep up to 4 months in the refrigerator.

1½ cups seedless green grapes, stemmed
1½ cups seedless red grapes, stemmed
8 medium cloves garlic, halved lengthwise
1½ cups rice vinegar or distilled white vinegar
1 cup sugar
1 teaspoon salt
6 quarter-size slices peeled fresh ginger
1 teaspoon ground coriander
½ teaspoon dried red pepper flakes

1. Pack the grapes and garlic in a glass bowl or jar.

2. Combine the vinegar, sugar, and salt in a medium-size saucepan and bring to a boil over medium-high heat, stirring occasionally, until the sugar is dissolved, about 3 minutes.

3. Remove from the heat and stir in the ginger, coriander, and pepper flakes. Pour the mixture over the grapes. Cover tightly with plastic wrap or a lid and allow the grapes to stand at least 2 hours or overnight at room temperature. Drain before serving.

PICKLED LADY APPLES

YIELD: 4 PINTS

Crab apples, those lovely pinkish miniature fruits, are also known as lady apples. Lovers of sweet and sour food will find these tiny pickles most delightful. Be sure to choose firm, ripe fruits that are free of blemishes. Serve pickled lady apples as a condiment with roast meats, especially pork. Seckel pears can also be pickled by following this recipe. These precious-looking pickles also make wonderful holiday gifts. For a festive look, don't peel, core, or remove the stems from the apples. I also like to leave the spices floating in the syrup for extra flavor and eye-

2. Let the apples cool in the syrup. Pack the fruit into 4 pint jars and fill with the syrup, leaving ¼ inch headspace. Seal. Store the jars in the refrigerator.

PICKLED LEMONS

YIELD: 1 QUART

VOODOO MARY MIX

Combining the pulp and juice of pickled lemons with the traditional ingredients for a bloody mary mix lends a depth of flavor and a subtle mystery. To make 1 quart, take 6 pieces of pickled lemons and scrape their pulp into a large glass pitcher. Return the rind to the brine for other uses. Add 3 cups tomato juice, ½ cup packing brine from the pickled lemons, ⅓ cup Worcestershire sauce, 1 tablespoon bottled horseradish, 1 teaspoon Tabasco sauce (or more to taste), and 1 teaspoon freshly ground black pepper. Stir until well blended. Serve as is over ice, or add vodka to taste. Voilà, you've got yourself a delicious voodoo drink!

appeal. If you like, you may preserve the hot lady apples in hot, sterilized jars according to the instructions on pages 268 and 274.

> 4 cups cider vinegar
> 2 cups fresh apple cider
> 2⅔ cups sugar
> 2 sticks cinnamon (3 inches long each)
> 2 teaspoons whole cloves
> 2 teaspoons cracked black peppercorns
> 2 pounds lady apples

1. In a large soup pot, combine the vinegar, apple cider, sugar, and spices. Bring the mixture to a boil over medium heat and cook until syrupy, about 5 minutes. Add the apples and return to a boil. Reduce the heat to low and simmer until the apples are fork-tender, 15 to 20 minutes, depending on their size.

Pickled lemons (also known as preserved lemons) are a staple Moroccan condiment. They usually take up to 3 weeks to age, by which time the lemons are soft, mellow, and not at all bitter. Added to various foods, they impart a tangy brininess similar to that of olives but with the unique perfume of lemon. In most Moroccan dishes, only the pickled peel is used, the pulp being scraped away and discarded. I have found, however, that the pulp makes a delicious addition to bloody marys and to salad dressings whenever a salty, sour taste is welcome. You can also use pickled lemons to stuff a bird before roasting; or add them, chopped, to a curry or seafood salad. Substitute the juice and pulp for vinegar in salad dressings or add it to a sugar syrup to make Zesty Lemon Drink (see Index).

FREEZE NOW, COOK LATER

It can't replace fresh fruit, but frozen fruit is great for baking and making cooked sauces, jams, and purées. Seasonal fruits need to be frozen at their peak of ripeness for top flavor. They should be sealed in airtight, leakproof plastic containers. Always label and date the containers and store them no longer than 9 to 10 months. The method you select for freezing is really determined by the size, softness, and ripeness of the fruit you are working with and its intended use. After sorting, rinsing, and draining the fruits, prepare them for the freezer by either dry packing or sugar packing them as follows:

DRY PACKING

Raspberries, strawberries, blackberries, blueberries, cranberries, cherries, figs, and hard fruits like apples can be frozen successfully in this manner. This is a quick, general-purpose method for preserving fruits that will remain suitable for baking and cooking. Spread whole berries, figs, or cherries (with pits and stems intact) on baking sheets and place them in the freezer for 3 to 4 hours, or until the fruits are hard. Apples should be peeled, cored, and sliced first, then tossed with fresh lemon juice to prevent darkening. Once the fruits have frozen, seal them in heavy plastic bags or plastic containers. The advantage of this method is that the fruit slices or berries are individually frozen, which allows you to remove a handful of fruit from the package when you need only a small quantity.

SUGAR PACKING

This method of freezing seems most satisfactory with soft, juicy fruits like plums, nectarines, mangoes, peaches, and apricots. Plums and nectarines should be halved, pitted, and sliced. Mangoes should be peeled, the flesh cut from their pit, and sliced. Peaches and apricots must be immersed in boiling water for about 30 seconds to loosen their skins, then peeled, halved, pitted, and sliced. To prevent any of the fruits from darkening, the slices should be tossed with some fresh lemon juice. Spread the sliced fruit in a shallow nonreactive pan and sprinkle with sugar (I use the ratio of ½ cup sugar to 4 cups fresh fruit). With a spatula, carefully stir the fruit until it is well coated with the sugar. Immediately pack the fruit into containers or freezer bags, leaving ½ to 1 inch of headspace, and freeze before the sugar draws juices from the fruit. The amount of sugar you add should be adjusted according to the natural sweetness of the fruit and your own taste, so don't be afraid to experiment with the sweetening.

4 thin-skinned lemons, scrubbed and quartered
¼ cup kosher salt
Juice of 8 or 9 lemons (about 1½ cups)

1. In a 1-quart widemouthed jar, combine the lemons and the salt. Add the lemon juice to cover the lemons by ½ inch.

2. Cover and store at room temperature, shaking the jar twice a week for 2 to 3 weeks. The lemons are ready when the rind is soft. Discard any skin that might develop on the surface of the jar.

NOTE: If you wish to speed up the pickling process, gently heat the quartered lemons before packing them in lemon juice and salt. To heat, arrange the lemon wedges in a single layer in a microwave-safe dish. Cover the dish with plastic wrap, and microwave on high for 30 seconds, or until the lemons are warm to the touch. Proceed as directed in the recipe. With this short-cut method, the lemons will be pickled and ready for use in just 4 or 5 days instead of 2 or 3 weeks.

PICKLED MANGO AND CUCUMBER

YIELD: 4 CUPS

This simple pickle features the flavors of Thailand. The tantalizing combination of sweet mango, crunchy cucumber, and cool mint make this condiment a perfect accompaniment to grilled meat or fish. I personally like it with hamburgers. It is best served the same day you make it. Many mango aficionados, including myself, consider gnawing on the pit the best part of eating the fruit. So don't just throw the pit away—the meat that surrounds it is the sweetest.

½ cup rice vinegar or distilled white vinegar
2 tablespoons sugar
½ teaspoon salt
2 tablespoons Thai fish sauce
½ teaspoon dried red pepper flakes
1 ripe but firm mango
1 medium Kirby cucumber, halved
    lengthwise, then cut crosswise into
    thin slices
½ small red onion, sliced paper thin
2 tablespoons shredded fresh cilantro leaves
    (for shredding instructions, see page 34)
2 tablespoons finely shredded mint leaves
    (page 34)

1. Combine the vinegar, sugar, and salt with ½ cup hot water in a small saucepan and stir until the sugar is dissolved. Bring the mixture to a boil over medium-high heat. Immediately remove from the heat and pour into a large mixing bowl. Stir in the fish sauce and red pepper flakes and let cool.

2. Cut off a small slice across the stem end of the mango. Stabilize the fruit by standing the sliced end on a cutting board. Following the contour of the fruit, carefully and evenly cut away the skin, a strip at a time, from top to bottom. Working from top to bottom, slice each "cheek" of the mango away from the large, flat pit, ending up with 2 thick pieces. Halve each cheek lengthwise, then cut crosswise into pieces about ¼ inch thick. Add the mango slices to the bowl.

3. Add the cucumber, onion, and cilanto and gently stir with a fork to combine. Cover and let the mixture marinate at room temperature for at least 1 hour, or refrigerate up to 4 hours.

HOW TO SELECT A MANGO

Whether you intend to cook a mango or use it raw, it is essential to choose a good one. Select a ripe but firm fruit with unblemished skin and an intense, musky perfume at the stem end. The fruit should feel heavy for its size, and show some yellow and red blush on the skin. Do not refrigerate a mango, but keep it in a cool place (55 °F) in your kitchen for up to 2 days. If exposed to low temperatures (as in the refrigerator), its fragrance gets somewhat muted and the flavor will be affected. If you do get a mango that has been refrigerated, be sure to let it come to room temperature before serving, so its flavors are revived.

To ripen mangoes, put them in a bag with an apple or banana, and leave them at room temperature.

The natural gas (ethylene) exuded by apples or bananas will hasten the ripening of the mangoes. Check their progress each day. When ripe, the mangoes will become more fragrant, develop a blush on their skin, and yield gently to the touch. Be careful not to let them get too soft or develop a fermented smell; if they do, they are past their prime.

For cooking and eating, I like to use the Haden mango that is imported from Mexico. Plump, almost fiber-free, and red-blush skinned, this roundish variety has a wonderful tangy-sweet flavor and is meatier than its cousins, the Haitian Madame Francis and the Floridian Van Dyke. These are typically long, oval shaped, and golden, with flesh that is honey-sweet but fibrous.

4. Drain the pickles, discarding the marinade. Add the mint and toss gently to combine.

PEPPERED PEACHES

YIELD: 2 PINTS

Peaches pickled in lemon juice, sugar, and cracked black pepper make one of the most delicious condiments you can imagine for grilled meats or sausages. The pickling process takes 6 to 7 days. During this time, the peaches will release their own juices to produce a spicy yet sweet pickle. For the crunch, be sure to choose slightly underripe peaches. These pickled fruits also go well with sandwiches and pâtés.

¾ cup fresh lemon juice
2 tablespoons sugar
1 tablespoon cracked black peppercorns
4 medium slightly underripe peaches (about
    1½ pounds total)

1. Combine the lemon juice, sugar, and cracked pepper in a small bowl and stir until the sugar is dissolved.

Six pounds of cantaloupe cut as nearly one size as possible, 4 quarts water, 1 ounce alum; bring to boiling point, drop in your fruit, cook 15 minutes, lift and drain a short while. Then take 1 quart of vinegar, 3 pounds white sugar, 3 tsps. yellow mustard seed, 1 tsp. black mustard seed, 1 tsp. whole mace, 8-inch stick of cinnamon, 9 whole cloves, about a dozen whole allspices. Place the fruit in it and slowly cook until clear; requires about 2 hours.

—AN OLD PENNSYLVANIA RECIPE FOR SPICED CANTALOUPE

2. Pack the peaches into 2 pint jars, then add the lemon juice mixture to come three-quarters of the way up the fruits.

3. Cover the jars and refrigerate. Shake the jars once a day to redistribute the juices. The pickled peaches should be ready within 6 or 7 days. Once pickled, the peaches will keep for up to 2 weeks in the refrigerator. Drain the fruits before serving.

CUMBERLAND SAUCE

YIELD: ABOUT 1¼ CUPS

Cumberland sauce was originally invented by English cooks as a condiment to serve with cold game. This is my new spin on an age-old favorite. I think you will find it good with any cold meat, especially pâtés, and with grilled meats or baked ham. The sauce will keep, covered in a jar, for several months in the refrigerator.

½ cup dried currants
½ cup red currant jelly
½ cup port
½ cup thawed frozen orange juice concentrate
2 large shallots, thinly sliced
Grated zest of 1 small lemon, and its juice
Grated zest of 1 small orange, and its juice
1 bay leaf
1 tablespoon cider vinegar
2 teaspoons English-style dry mustard
1 tablespoon grenadine syrup (optional), preferably homemade (page 343)
Salt to season

1. Combine the currants, jelly, port, orange juice concentrate, shallots, citrus zests and juices, and bay leaf in a medium-size saucepan and bring to a boil. Reduce the heat to medium and boil until the mixture is reduced by one-third. Remove from the heat. Let the mixture cool and discard the bay leaf.

2. Combine the vinegar and mustard in a small bowl and stir to form a paste. Add to the sauce. Transfer the sauce to a food processor or blender and pulse just until the mixture is coarsely puréed. Stir in the grenadine syrup, if using, and season to taste with salt. Let the sauce cool to room temperature before serving. Store any leftover sauce, covered, in the refrigerator for up to 2 months.

FRESH PLUM SAUCE

YIELD: ¾ CUP

Bright crimson in color, this savory, chunky plum sauce is redolent of ginger. It's a perfect match for roast game and fowl, such as duck, pheasant, Guinea hen, or goose. The sauce will keep in a covered container for up to 1 week in the refrigerator. Reheat it slightly before serving.

8 small Italian prune plums (about ½ pound total), pitted and quartered
3 quarter-size slices peeled fresh ginger
1 tablespoon (firmly packed) light brown sugar or more if needed
¼ teaspoon salt or more if needed
½ teaspoon cornstarch

1. Combine the plums, ginger, brown sugar, and salt with ¼ cup water in a small saucepan. Bring to boil, stirring frequently, to dissolve the sugar. Reduce the heat to low, cover, and simmer until the plums are very soft, about 10 minutes.

2. Remove and discard the ginger. Dilute the cornstarch with 2 tablespoons cold water and stir into the plum mixture. Cook over low heat until the sauce is slightly thickened and coats the back of a spoon, about 1 minute. Remove from the heat and adjust the seasonings with sugar and salt, if necessary. The sauce should taste sweet and sour but well balanced.

SPIRITED PLUM SAUCE

YIELD: 1 CUP

This sauce is complex and robust because it's made with red wine and Madeira. You can use it to baste grilled meats, or simply serve it with roasted poultry. It will keep in a covered container for up to 1 month in the refrigerator. If fresh plums are unavailable, use 1 cup canned plums (well drained) and add 2 tablespoons red wine vinegar to offset the sweetness of the packing syrup. Omit the sugar, unless you need some to balance flavors. For more on flavored vinegars, see the box above.

8 small Italian prune plums (about ½ pound total), pitted and quartered
½ cup dry red wine, preferably Cabernet or Pinot Noir
½ cup Madeira
1 teaspoon tomato paste
⅓ cup chicken broth, preferably homemade (page 30)
1 tablespoon sugar, or more if needed
1 tablespoon soy sauce, preferably Kikkoman, or more if needed

1. Combine the plums, red wine, and Madeira in a medium-size saucepan. Bring to a boil over medium heat and cook until syrupy and reduced by two-thirds, about 15 minutes.

2. Place in a blender, add the tomato paste, and blend until puréed.

3. Return the purée to the saucepan. Add the chicken broth, sugar, and soy sauce and simmer over low heat until the sauce is thickened slightly and coats the back of a spoon, about 10 minutes.

4. Strain the sauce through a fine sieve, pressing on the fruit to extract as much of the juice as possible. Adjust the sauce with sugar and soy sauce, if necessary. The sauce should taste sweet, sour, and salty, but well balanced.

BLUEBERRY VINEGAR

YIELD: ABOUT 3 CUPS

Twenty minutes is all it takes to make this unique violet-colored vinegar with a mild and sweet flavor. Since

FRUIT-FLAVORED VINEGARS

*H*aving a variety of fruit-flavored vinegars on hand lets you create unusual salad dressings or sauces, which add magic to any recipe that calls for vinegar. They make marvelous marinades, memorable mayonnaises, and zesty chutneys. Brush them over grilled fish or chicken for a delicious gloss. Drizzled over fresh fruit, shortcakes, ice cream, even fish and chips, they are divine. Diluted with crushed ice and a little seltzer, they make delectable apéritifs.

In most store-bought fruit-flavored vinegars, the harsh taste of vinegar usually dominates the fruit. Making fruit vinegar at home will allow you to taste the distinctive flavor of the fruit, especially if you use only the best sun-ripened varieties fresh from the farmstand. The fruit-flavored vinegars in this section are velvety and rich, yet light and naturally fat-free. Since these vinegars are brightly colored, you may want to store them in bottles with unusual shapes and shades. You can also use canning bottles with self-sealing corks, which are available at hardware stores.

As described in the vinegar recipes, the method I use for making fruit vinegars combines luscious fruit purées with just enough rice vinegar and sugar to make them mild and richly palatable. I prefer to use unseasoned Japanese rice vinegar because it is milder and less acidic than other wine vinegars and because its neutral but pleasing flavor marries well with a variety of fruits. My method also has the advantage of allowing you to enjoy the vinegar at once, instead of having to wait for days before using it, as you would with the old-fashioned kind.

For those die-hard traditionalists, here's how to quickly infuse fruit vinegars the old-fashioned way: Simply combine 1 pint (2 cups) berries or 1 pound sliced peaches, pears, or plums with 2 cups good-quality rice or red- or white-wine vinegar plus 3 tablespoons sugar in a glass container. Stir with a wooden spoon, bruising but not mashing the fruit. Cover and steep at room temperature for 3 to 5 days. Transfer the mixture to an enameled or stainless-steel saucepan and heat just to the boiling point. Do not fully boil. Remove from the heat and strain through a cheesecloth into a 16-ounce sterilized jar (page 268). Cork or seal the bottle. Stored in a cool place, it will keep almost indefinitely.

blueberries are also available frozen, it can be made anytime during the year, whenever the mood strikes. You can substitute black currants, cranberries, or sliced plums for the blueberries. For more on flavored vinegars, see the box above.

2 cups fresh or frozen (thawed and drained) blueberries

2 cups Japanese brewed rice vinegar, or a good distilled white vinegar with an acid content between 4 and 5 percent

½ cup sugar

A PRETTY GIFT

T̶o make wonderfully clear, decorative vinegars for gifts, I often put colorful assortments of ingredients like slices of fresh kumquat, tiny Chinese red dates, fresh red or black currants, lemongrass, sprigs of fresh chives, hot red chile peppers, and a variety of whole peppercorns (black, white, green, and pink) in a quart jar and fill it with rice vinegar. Then, I let the vinegar steep for at least 2 weeks before offering it to appreciative friends.

1. Follow the steps on page 268 to sterilize two 12-ounce bottles (or three 8-ounce canning jars). Sterilize the caps (or lids) according to the manufacturer's instructions, or have ready 2 clean corks.

2. Combine the blueberries, rice vinegar, sugar, and 1 cup water in a medium-size saucepan. Bring the mixture to a boil over high heat, then reduce the heat to medium-low and simmer until the liquid has reduced to about 3 cups, 10 to 12 minutes.

3. Remove from the heat and let the vinegar cool. Transfer the mixture to a blender or food processor, and purée in batches. Skim the foam, then strain the vinegar mixture twice through a fine sieve into a bowl. Discard the solids.

4. Drain the bottles, then fill with the strained vinegar. Seal with a clean cork (or sterilized lid). Store in a cool, dry place or refrigerate.

RASPBERRY VINEGAR

YIELD: ABOUT 2 CUPS

With a vivid red color, this vinegar is also rich in raspberry flavor. It is delicious in vinaigrettes or added to pan drippings to make a quick, light, and flavorful sauce for meats and poultry. A variation on this vinegar can be made by using fresh strawberries or blackberries instead of the raspberries.

3 cups raspberries thawed and drained, if frozen

1 cup Japanese brewed rice vinegar, or a good distilled white vinegar with an acid content between 4 and 5 percent

¼ cup sugar

1. Follow the steps on page 268 to sterilize a 16-ounce bottle (or two 8-ounce canning jars). Sterilize the caps (or lids) according to the manufacturer's instructions, or have ready a clean cork.

2. Purée the berries in a food processor, then pour the purée into a medium-size bowl.

3. Combine the vinegar, sugar, and ½ cup water in a medium-size saucepan. Bring to a boil over high heat, then reduce the heat to medium-low and simmer until slightly syrupy, 4 to 5 minutes. Pour the vinegar mixture into the raspberry purée and stir to combine. Let cool.

4. Skim the foam, if there is any, then strain the vinegar mixture through a fine sieve, pressing on the solids to extract as much juice as possible. Discard the seeds. Drain the bottle, then fill with the strained vinegar. Seal with a clean cork (or sterilized lid). Store in a cool, dry place, or refrigerate.

PEACH VINEGAR

YIELD: ABOUT 2 CUPS

Besides salad dressings, this mild, summery peach vinegar will add zip to any grilled foods either in a glaze or a marinade. You may substitute nectarines or mangoes for the peaches, if you wish.

2 ripe peaches (about 12 ounces total), peeled, pitted, and chopped
1 cup Japanese brewed rice vinegar, or a good distilled white vinegar with an acid content between 4 and 5 percent
3 tablespoons sugar

1. Purée the peaches in a food processor, then pour the purée into a medium-size bowl. (There should be 1 cup of peach purée.)

2. Combine the vinegar, sugar, and ½ cup water in a medium-size saucepan. Bring to a boil over high heat, then reduce the heat to medium-low and simmer until slightly syrupy, 4 to 5 minutes. Stir the vinegar mixture into the peach purée. Let cool.

3. Follow the steps on page 268 to sterilize a 16-ounce bottle (or two 8-ounce canning jars). Sterilize the cap (or lid) according to the manufacturer's instructions or have ready a clean cork.

4. Skim the foam, if there is any, then strain the vinegar mixture through a fine

sieve, pressing on the solids to extract as much juice as possible. Discard the solids. Drain the bottle, then fill with the strained vinegar. Seal with a clean cork (or sterilized lid). Store in a cool, dry place or refrigerate.

VARIATION

MANGO–PASSION FRUIT VINEGAR: For the peaches, substitute ¾ cup mango purée plus the strained pulp of 1 large passion fruit (about ¼ cup). Proceed with the recipe.

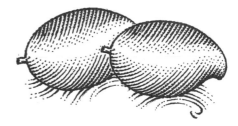

BREADS,
QUICK AND SLOW

Many people experience baking bread as therapeutic or Zenlike, falling into a mystical reverie of sorts during the gentle, repetitive process of kneading. Other types may think of it more as a scientific experiment, or even mastery of the elements. Certainly, bread is one of the few foods that requires so much control from its creator from start to finish. Whatever your bent, it is easy to understand the anticipation and pride anyone feels upon catching the scent of baking bread wafting through the kitchen.

The recipes in this chapter, whether savory or sweet, are unique; apart from a few of the tea breads, you would probably not be able to buy these foods anywhere. But after trying out such recipes as Fig, Prosciutto, and Pepper Bread, Grilled Banana Pizza, and Apple-Cinnamon Bread, you're sure to enjoy a tremendous sense of achievement. And eating the fruits of your labor will be the most delicious reward yet.

GRILLED BANANA PIZZA

YIELD: 4 APPETIZER OR
2 ENTREE SERVINGS

Banana pizza anyone? Inspired by the excellent wood-grilled pizzas that are so popular these days, I wanted to develop an unusual version with some kind of fruit. After several tests, banana won thumbs up. Grilling the dough instead of baking it yields crunchy and smoky pizzas. The smoky quality is further enhanced by the sweet, spicy, and salty flavors of sautéed bananas, prosciutto, basil, and mozzarella. You don't even need an outdoor grill; a stovetop grill pan will give excellent results.

2 tablespoons extra-virgin olive oil, plus extra for grilling

4 ripe bananas, peeled and cut into ½-inch rounds

2 large onions (about ½ pound total), peeled and cut into thin slivers

Salt and freshly ground black pepper

Pinch of cayenne pepper, or to taste

2 teaspoons fresh lemon juice

⅓ recipe Pizza Dough (recipe follows)

4 thin slices of prosciutto, cut into strips

16 large fresh basil leaves

½ pound fresh mozzarella cheese, thinly sliced

1. Heat 1 tablespoon of the olive oil in a large nonstick skillet over high heat. Add the bananas and sauté until they are golden brown, about 3 minutes. Transfer the bananas to a bowl and set aside.

2. Heat the remaining 1 tablespoon oil in the same skillet. Add the onions and sauté over medium-low heat until tender and golden brown, about 5 minutes. Add the sautéed bananas and stir to combine. Season to taste with salt, black pepper, and cayenne pepper. Remove from the heat and stir in the lemon juice. Cover and set aside.

3. Invert a large baking sheet and coat with olive oil. Use your fingers to press the pizza dough into a 14 x 10 ½-inch rectangle, slightly more than ⅛ inch thick. Make sure that the dough has an even thickness. With a sharp knife, halve the dough crosswise. Brush each half with olive oil.

4. Heat 2 stovetop grill pans over medium-high heat (or prepare an outdoor grill). When the griddles are hot, lift the dough rectangles by the corners of their short sides, and lay them flat on the griddles. Grill until the dough puffs slightly, the underside stiffens, and dark grill marks appear, about 3 minutes.

5. Using tongs, turn the dough over. Reduce the heat to medium. Quickly brush the grilled surfaces with olive oil and spread half the banana-onion mixture over each crust. Top each pizza with 2 slices prosciutto, 8 basil leaves, and half the mozzarella. Cook until the cheese has melted, 6 to 7 minutes, making sure that the underside is not burning.

6. Serve the pizza at once with olive oil drizzled over the top, if desired.

VARIATION

CHAMPAGNE GRAPE AND PROSCIUTTO PIZZA: Instead of the banana-onion mixture, scatter ½ cup stemmed Champagne grapes (or halved seedless red grapes) over each crust. Substitute sliced Fontina cheese for the mozzarella and sprinkle each pizza with 2 tablespoons freshly grated Parmesan cheese. Grill until the cheese melts.

Pizza Dough

YIELD: ENOUGH DOUGH FOR 6 LARGE PIZZAS

This dough makes a great base for any savory pizza topping: Try it with grilled assorted vegetables or sliced ripe tomatoes and crumbled fresh goat cheese. For delicious flatbreads, brush the dough with some extra-virgin olive oil and sprinkle with chopped fresh rosemary, sautéed onions, grated or shaved fresh Parmesan cheese, and kosher salt before grilling.

> 1 package active dry yeast
> Pinch of sugar
> 1 cup warm water (105 °F to 115 °F)
> 2¼ teaspoons kosher salt
> ¼ cup fine white cornmeal or semolina flour
> 1 tablespoon extra-virgin olive oil, plus 1 teaspoon
> 2⅔ cups unbleached all-purpose flour, plus extra for kneading

1. Dissolve the yeast and sugar in the warm water in a large mixing bowl. Cover and let sit until the yeast starts foaming, about 5 minutes.

2. Stir in the salt, cornmeal, ¼ cup of the flour, and 1 tablespoon of the oil.

3. Gradually add the remaining flour, stirring with a wooden spoon until the dough is stiff. Knead the dough once or twice in the bowl to form a rough mass.

4. Turn out the dough onto a lightly floured board and knead until it is smooth and shiny, about 5 minutes, adding only enough extra flour to keep the dough from sticking. Shape the dough into a ball.

5. Place the remaining 1 teaspoon olive oil in a large bowl, add the dough, and turn it to coat well with the oil. Cover the bowl with plastic wrap and let the dough rise in a warm, draft-free place until doubled in size, 2 to 3 hours.

6. Punch down the dough and knead it once more, for about 5 minutes. Return the dough to the bowl, cover with plastic wrap, and let it rise again for about 45 minutes.

7. Punch down the dough, then divide it into 3 portions. Shape each piece into a ball. If you don't plan to use the dough right away, wrap each portion in plastic and then in a freezer bag. Refrigerate it for up to 2 days (bring to room temperature before using, but do not let it rise again) or freeze it for up to 2 months. If the dough is frozen, thaw it overnight in the refrigerator and then bring to room temperature, without letting it rise again) before using. Each portion will yield 2 large pizzas.

FIG, PROSCIUTTO, AND PEPPER BREAD

YIELD: 2 LOAVES

This splendidly flavorful bread makes wonderful eating straight from the oven. It needs no spread; just dip it in extra-virgin olive oil at the table, if you wish. If you are lucky enough to have any leftovers, freeze the bread for busy days.

> 1 package active dry yeast
> 1 cup warm water (110 °F to 115 °F)
> 1 tablespoon plus 1½ teaspoons
>   sugar
> 2 tablespoons extra-virgin olive oil
> 1½ cups unbleached all-purpose flour,
>   plus extra for kneading
> 1 cup semolina flour
> ¾ cup bread flour
> ½ teaspoon salt
> ½ cup diced dried figs (¼-inch cubes)
> ½ cup diced prosciutto (¼-inch cubes)
> 1 tablespoon cracked black peppercorns
> 1 tablespoon fine yellow cornmeal
> 1 large egg yolk

1. Combine the yeast, warm water, and 1½ teaspoons of the sugar in a small bowl. Cover and let sit until the yeast starts foaming, 5 to 10 minutes. Stir in 2 tablespoons of olive oil.

2. Place 1 cup of the all-purpose flour and the semolina flour, the bread flour, the remaining 1 tablespoon sugar, and the salt in a large mixing bowl. Stir until well combined. Add half the liquid mixture to the flour. Mix with your hands to moisten the flour as much as possible. Add the remaining liquid to the dough and mix until the flour is thoroughly incorporated.

3. Transfer the dough to a lightly floured board and knead until smooth and elastic to the touch, about 15 minutes, gradually adding ¼ cup of the remaining all-purpose flour. If the dough feels sticky, add 1 or 2 tablespoons flour.

4. Rub the dough all over with olive oil then place it into a large mixing bowl. Cover tightly with plastic wrap and let the dough rise in a warm, draft-free place until doubled in size, about 1 hour. (Move to a slightly warmer place if the dough hasn't doubled in 1 hour.)

5. In a medium-size bowl, toss the figs with the prosciutto and cracked pepper.

6. Turn the dough out onto a lightly floured surface. Without punching it down, cut the dough into 2 portions. Pat 1 portion of dough evenly into a large oval, about

DRIED FRUITS VERSUS FRESH FRUITS

If you really enjoy eating dried fruit, such as raisins, prunes, figs, and apricots and are wondering how they compare nutritionally to fresh fruit, here are some facts:

♦ *Because dried fruit has very little moisture, it contains more nutrients than an equal amount of fresh fruit. In addition to higher amounts of minerals such as iron and potassium, dried fruit also has more fiber. On the downside, it is higher in calories because the*

fruit sugars become concentrated as moisture is removed. For example, ½ cup grapes has about 50 calories and ½ gram of fiber; the same amount of raisins contains 230 calories and 4 grams of fiber. Furthermore, most of the water-soluble vitamin C is lost when fruit is dried.

♦ *In its updated food pyramid, the U.S. Department of Agriculture considers ¼ cup dried fruit 1 serving and ½ cup diced fresh fruit, 1 serving.*

---

12 inches long. Sprinkle ¼ cup of the fig-prosciutto mixture over the dough. Roll up the dough lengthwise. Pat the dough into an oval again and sprinkle evenly with ¼ cup of the fig mixture; roll it up again. Pinch the ends to seal the roll. Sprinkle the cornmeal onto a baking sheet. Place the loaf, seam side down, on the baking sheet.

7. Repeat with the remaining portion of dough. Cover the loaves with a dish towel, and let rise in a warm place until almost doubled in size, about 30 minutes.

8. Adjust an oven rack to the middle shelf and preheat the oven to 425°F.

9. Beat together the egg yolk and 2 teaspoons water and brush it onto the loaves once they have risen. Slash the tops of the loaves with a sharp knife, making diagonal cuts.

10. Place the baking sheet in the middle of the oven and reduce the heat to 375°F. Bake until the loaves are brown and a bamboo skewer or toothpick inserted in the center comes out clean, about 30 minutes.

11. Cool the bread slightly on a rack before serving.

TUSCAN GRAPE BREAD

YIELD: 1 LOAF

This great recipe for the Florentine sweet bread *schiacciata al'uva* comes from Sheila Lukins, cook extraordinaire, co-author of the best-selling *Silver Palate* and *New Basics* cookbooks, and author of the *All Around the World Cook-*

book. Traditionally, this half-brioche, half-pizza bread with red grapes, sugar, herbs, and anise seed is served during the grape harvest. Sheila prefers using Concord grapes (seeds and all), for the crunch and tartness they provide and for the attractive crimson that bleeds into the bread. If you prefer, use seedless grapes, such as Thompson Red Flame. I've slightly modified the texture and flavor of the dough by adding some bread flour and using less sugar and more grapes. This bread is simply too delicious to limit to grapes; so try it with other fruits in season, like plums, sour cherries, or blueberries. It's a good accompaniment to roasts and a delight when toasted.

SPONGE

³⁄₄ cup unbleached all-purpose flour

2 teaspoons sugar

1 package active dry yeast

¹⁄₂ cup warm water (105 °F to 115 °F)

BREAD

¹⁄₂ cup raisins

¹⁄₄ cup Strega liqueur or kirsch (cherry brandy)

¹⁄₄ cup extra-virgin olive oil

2 tablespoons fresh rosemary leaves

1 teaspoon anise seeds, crushed

2 cups Concord grapes (with seeds), stemmed

1¹⁄₂ cups unbleached all-purpose flour

¹⁄₂ cup bread flour

4 tablespoons sugar

¹⁄₂ teaspoon salt

*1 large egg, lightly
        beaten*

*Freshly ground
        black pepper*

1. To make the sponge, stir together the flour, sugar, yeast, and warm water in a bowl until smooth. Cover and let stand in a warm place until doubled in bulk, 30 to 45 minutes.

2. While the sponge is rising, start the bread: Combine the raisins and liqueur in a small bowl, cover, and set aside.

3. Heat the olive oil in a small skillet over low heat, and add the rosemary and anise seeds. Cook until the mixture is fragrant, about 5 minutes. Cool slightly.

4. In a medium-size bowl, toss the grapes with 2 tablespoons of the flavored oil, and set aside.

5. Place the all-purpose flour, bread flour, 2 tablespoons of the sugar, the salt, and the egg in a food processor. Add the sponge, 1¹⁄₂ tablespoons water, and the remaining 2 tablespoons herb oil. Pulse the processor until the mixture forms a cohesive mass. Then process until the dough rides with the blades, 40 to 45 seconds. The dough should be soft and just slightly sticky.

6. Transfer the dough to a lightly floured board and knead until smooth, about 2 minutes. Drain the raisins and work them into the dough; knead 1 minute. Let the dough rest in a warm, draft-free place for 10 minutes.

7. Roll the dough out on a lightly floured board to form a rectangle that will fit snugly into a 13 x 9 inch baking pan. Lightly oil the baking pan. Place the dough in the

YEAST BREAD TIPS

*T*o ensure success when making yeast bread, it helps to know these facts:

✦ *Too much heat will kill yeast (the liquid you proof it in should be between 105 °F to 115 °F), and cool temperatures slow it down. Proofed yeast should bubble within 5 or 10 minutes; if not, the yeast may be too old. Your best bet is to restart the process, using a fresher package of yeast.*

✦ *Dough containing heavy elements (like fresh fruit, dried fruit, nuts, or ham) should have a higher gluten content in the flour. It is accomplished by mixing bread flour, which has a high gluten content (15 to 20 percent protein) with unbleached all-purpose flour. This will strengthen the dough and prevent heavy ingredients from falling to the bottom of the loaf.*

✦ *Once you have mixed your dough, you can interrupt and retard the rising process at any point by covering and refrigerating it for up to 24 hours; this gives you a lot of leeway.*

✦ *When yeast bread is in its final rising, if you stop the process before the dough reaches its maximum* volume, your oven will contribute the last part of the loaf's bulk. Bakers call this "oven push," and it prevents the bread from becoming too airy.

✦ *To test a bread for doneness, remove the loaf from the oven and give the bottom a good tap with your knuckles. It should sound resonant and hollow. If there's any sign of wetness or heaviness, or any steam coming from the bottom of the loaf, more baking time is needed.*

✦ *If the crust seems too crisp and heavy when the bread comes from the oven, wrap the loaf in a towel and briefly leave it to cool. The loaf will be trapped in its own steam and the crust will soften.*

✦ *Serve breads warm; warmth intensifies all flavors.*

✦ *To preserve their freshness, wrap the cooled loaves securely in plastic then aluminum foil and store in a breadbox for 2 days. Frozen, the bread will keep for up to 3 months.*

pan, and make a lip all around the edges of the dough. Distribute the grapes and their oil over the dough. Sprinkle with pepper and the remaining 2 tablespoons sugar. Cover the dough loosely, and let it rise in a warm, draft-free place until doubled in size, about 1 hour.

8. Adjust an oven rack to the middle shelf and preheat the oven to 400°F.

9. Transfer the baking pan to the oven, and bake until the loaf is puffed and deep golden, about 25 minutes. Cool slightly before serving.

APPLE-CINNAMON BREAD

YIELD: 1 LOAF

*E*njoy this spongy, light-as-a-feather bread fresh from the oven or toasted, well coated with some good preserves and a strong cup of coffee. Apple Butter or Lemon and Honey Butter (see Index) complement it best. Sealed in plastic bags, it will stay moist for up to 3 days. It also makes great French toast for brunch. For a special treat, use it to make Upside-Down French Toast with Apples and Bananas (see Index).

3³⁄₄ cups unbleached all-purpose flour

2 packages active dry yeast

1 cup milk

8 tablespoons (1 stick) unsalted butter,
*   cut into 8 pieces*

¹⁄₂ cup sugar

2 teaspoons salt

1¹⁄₂ teaspoons vanilla extract

3 large eggs, lightly beaten

3 Granny Smith apples

1 tablespoon ground cinnamon

1. Sift the flour into a large mixing bowl. Sprinkle the yeast over the flour. Make a well in the center.

2. Place the milk, butter, and sugar in a medium-size, heavy saucepan over medium-low heat, and stir until the butter is melted and the sugar dissolved. Remove from the heat and add ¹⁄₄ cup water, the salt, and the vanilla. Cool until warm (120°F to 130°F).

3. Add the warm milk and beaten eggs to the well in the flour. With a large wooden spoon, draw the flour into the liquid and mix until the dough is well blended, soft, and sticky, about 2 minutes.

4. Cover the bowl with plastic wrap and let the dough rise in a warm, draft-free place until doubled in size, about 3 hours (the dough will be very soft and sticky).

5. Adjust an oven rack to the lowest shelf and preheat the oven to 350°F. Butter and flour a 10-inch tube pan or a 12-cup Bundt pan.

6. Peel, core, and cut each apple into eighths. Cut the wedges across into thin slices and toss with the cinnamon.

7. Stir down the dough, then mix in the apples. Transfer the dough to the prepared pan. Bake until the top side is golden or until a bamboo skewer inserted in the center of the bread comes out clean, 55 to 60 minutes.

8. Cool in the pan on a rack for 20 minutes. Turn out the bread onto a serving platter, and serve warm.

BOSTON BROWN BREAD

YIELD: 2 LOAVES

Brown bread is a staple of New England's culinary tradition, where it is more closely associated with baked beans than frankfurters are.

QUICK BREADS

*O*n the baking spectrum, quick breads—corn-bread, muffins, biscuits, scones, doughnuts, and tea bread—fall somewhere between cakes and yeast breads. Leavened with baking powder, baking soda, or both, quick breads are much faster to prepare than breads made with yeast, since they don't have to rise before baking.

Making good quick breads is easy—the trick is not to overmix the batter. Gently stir the wet and dry ingredients together with a wooden spoon until the flour is just incorporated into the batter; the batter should look lumpy and drop easily from the spoon. If mixed longer, the flour will develop gluten and the bread will be tough, dry, and full of air holes. Also, be sure to use only fresh baking powder or baking soda. (Test by stirring 1 teaspoon baking powder or soda into ⅓ cup hot water; if the mixture doesn't bubble vigorously, your powder or soda is not fresh.) If your leavening agent is stale, your breads and cakes may not rise properly.

The revamped traditional quick breads in this chapter are all delicious for breakfast or lunch, or at any time of the day.

Unlike most breads, this one is cooked by steam to produce a fairly moist, dense loaf. Hearty and wholesome, this dark bread is a bit on the sweet side because of the molasses and dried currants. Although dried fruits are not typically found in a Boston Brown bread, the currants add interest as well as textural contrast. If dried currants are hard to find, simply substitute dark raisins. Slice only as much of this bread as you will need for a meal, then tightly wrap the remainder in aluminum foil, seal in a plastic bag, and freeze it. To serve, reheat it in the foil for about 20 minutes in a preheated 350°F oven, (or steam it). You can also slice the bread and toast it, which brings out its distinctive flavor. It's delicious with Barbecued Baked Beans (see Index) or simply with butter and jam.

1 cup rye flour
1 cup whole wheat flour
1 cup fine yellow cornmeal
1 cup dried currants or raisins
2 teaspoons baking soda
1 teaspoon salt
2¼ cups buttermilk
⅔ cup dark molasses

1. Generously butter two 1-pound coffee cans. Set aside.

2. Combine the rye flour, wheat flour, cornmeal, currants, baking soda, and salt in a large mixing bowl.

3. Mix the buttermilk with the molasses in a separate bowl. Gradually stir the liquid ingredients into the flour mixture, and stir just until the flour is moistened.

4. Divide the batter between the 2 coffee cans. The mixture should fill the cans about two-thirds full. Cover the cans with a double layer of aluminum foil. Secure the foil tightly with string, or packing tape, being careful not to puncture it.

5. Place the cans inside a large Dutch oven or soup pot, and add enough boiling water to come halfway up the outsides of cans. Bring the water to a full, rolling boil over high heat. Tightly cover the pan, reduce the heat to low, and steam until a bamboo skewer or toothpick inserted in the center of the loaf comes out clean, about 2 hours.

6. Remove the foil and allow the bread to cool for 5 minutes before unmolding. To unmold, invert the cans and ease out the loaves. Cut the bread into ³/₄-inch slices while it is still hot and serve at once.

SWEET AND CRUNCHY SODA BREAD

YIELD: 1 LOAF

Moistened with buttermilk, this tasty soda bread is also loaded with sweet prunes and crunchy walnuts. Soda bread tastes best straight from the oven. Do not keep it longer than necessary, as it tends to dry out and lose its tender texture. Serve it as an accompaniment to savory dishes, for breakfast, or as part of an afternoon tea with friends. For variation, you may substitute plumped dried cherries, golden raisins, or dates for the prunes.

3 cups unbleached all-purpose flour
¹/₃ cup sugar
1 tablespoon salt
1 teaspoon baking soda
1 teaspoon baking powder
¹/₂ cup coarsely chopped prunes
¹/₂ cup coarsely chopped walnuts
2 large eggs
1³/₄ cups buttermilk
2 tablespoons unsalted butter,
*   melted and cooled*
2 tablespoons unsalted butter, at
*   room temperature*

1. Adjust an oven rack to the lowest shelf and preheat the oven to 375°F. Generously butter an 8-inch round cake pan.

2. Sift together the flour, sugar, salt, baking soda, and baking powder into a large mixing bowl. Add the prunes and walnuts, and stir until well combined.

3. Lightly beat the eggs in a separate bowl, then stir in the buttermilk and melted butter. Add this liquid mixture to the dry ingredients, and stir with a wooden spoon just until blended. The mixture should be soft, similar to biscuit dough. Do not overmix.

4. Turn the dough into the prepared pan, then dot the top with softened butter. Bake until the bread is puffed and golden brown or until a bamboo skewer or toothpick inserted into the center comes out clean, 45 to 50 minutes.

5. Cool in the pan on a rack for 10 minutes. Turn out the bread onto a serving platter and cut into wedges. Serve warm.

SAVORY PLANTAIN CORNBREAD

YIELD: 8 SERVINGS

The soft, sweet plantain in this moist cornbread contrasts nicely with the crusty cornmeal and spicy jalapeño peppers. If you have any leftover cornbread, crumble it to make a great stuffing for roast turkey or chicken. Although this cornbread is best straight from the oven, you may bake it up to 4 hours ahead of time and reheat it before serving.

4 slices smoked bacon (about ¼ pound), sliced crosswise into thin strips
4 scallions, trimmed and thinly sliced (white and green parts)
1 cup fine yellow cornmeal, preferably stone-ground
¼ cup unbleached all-purpose flour
1 tablespoon sugar
2 teaspoons baking powder
¾ teaspoon salt
½ teaspoon baking soda
1 cup buttermilk
1 large egg, lightly beaten
3 tablespoons unsalted butter, melted and cooled
2 tablespoons minced pickled jalapeño peppers (about 4)
1 ripe (black) plantain, peeled, quartered lengthwise, then sliced crosswise ¼ inch thick

1. Place the bacon in an 8-inch cast-iron skillet. Cook over medium-high heat, stirring with a wooden spoon, until the bacon is crisp and the fat rendered, about 5 minutes. Add the scallions and quickly stir until they are just wilted, about 30 seconds. Drain the mixture into a small colander placed over a

bowl. Set the bacon and scallions aside. Pour 2 tablespoons of the bacon fat back into the skillet.

2. Place the skillet in the oven and preheat the oven to 425°F.

3. Meanwhile, combine the cornmeal, flour, sugar, baking powder, salt, and baking soda in a medium-size mixing bowl. Mix well.

4. In another bowl, combine the buttermilk, egg, melted butter, and jalapeño peppers. Mix well. Add to the dry ingredients, along with the plantain and bacon-scallion mixture. Stir with a wooden spoon just until the dry ingredients are moistened. Do not overmix.

5. Carefully pour the batter into the smoking-hot skillet and bake until the top is golden brown and a toothpick or a knife

point inserted in the center comes out clean, 20 to 25 minutes. Cool slightly before cutting into wedges.

APPLE AND CHEDDAR CHEESE BISCUITS

YIELD: ABOUT 14 BISCUITS

If you want something quick and tasty to accompany a plain bowl of soup or a wintry stew, you will not be disappointed with these moist and tasty biscuits. They contain apple and Cheddar cheese, a natural marriage of flavors.

BISCUIT AND SCONE TIPS

For tender, flaky biscuits and scones, try to handle the dough as little as possible. This will prevent excessive development of gluten, which would toughen the baked product.

✦ Knead the moistened dough briefly, just 2 or 3 times, until it holds together, and pat it (do not roll) 5 or 6 times into a sheet ½ inch to ¾ inch thick.

✦ A very good way to prevent excess working of the dough is to pat it directly into a skillet or round baking pan, cut it into wedges, and bake at once.

✦ If you'd rather make round biscuits or scones, dip a 3-inch cookie cutter into flour to prevent sticking, and push it straight down through the dough (do not twist the cutter; this would produce lopsided biscuits). Pull the cutter straight up and out. Place the biscuits on an ungreased baking sheet, with space between them. Gather the dough scraps and repeat kneading, patting, and cutting one more time. From start to finish, this whole process should take you only 5 minutes.

✦ Serve biscuits and scones warm; warmth intensifies all flavors.

1¼ cups cake flour

1¼ cups unbleached all-purpose flour

1 teaspoon baking soda

¾ teaspoon salt

1½ tablespoons sugar

1 cup grated aged Cheddar cheese

1½ cups peeled, cored, and diced tart
    apples, such as Granny Smith

1¼ cups light cream, half-and-half, or plain
    yogurt

3 tablespoons unsalted butter, melted

1. Adjust an oven rack to the lowest
shelf and preheat the oven to 375°F.

2. Sift together the flours, baking soda,
salt, and sugar into a mixing bowl. Add the
Cheddar cheese and apple and stir until thoroughly combined.

3. Add the cream slowly and mix with
a wooden spoon until just blended. The mixture should be soft and tender, similar to biscuit dough. Do not overmix.

4. Turn out the dough onto a well-
floured board. Gather the dough and gently
knead 2 or 3 times until it is well formed. Do
not overwork it. Pat the dough, 5 or 6 times,
into a circle about ½ inch thick. Dip a 3-inch
round cookie cutter in flour and cut out as
many circles as possible. Gather the dough
scraps, pat them into a ½-inch-thick circle,
and cut out more biscuits.

5. Place the biscuits on an ungreased
baking sheet and brush the tops with melted
butter. Bake until the biscuits are light gold-
en, 12 to 15 minutes. Serve hot.

HOT STRAWBERRY BISCUITS

YIELD: ABOUT 14 BISCUITS

Subtly flavored with rosemary and
lemon and chock-full of strawberries, breakfast biscuits don't come
any better than these. To make these biscuits even more special, try spreading
some Strawberry Butter or Lemon
Honey Butter on them. These wonderful
biscuits are also the foundation for
Triple Strawberry Shortcakes (see Index
for page numbers).

BISCUITS

2 cups sifted unbleached all-purpose flour

¼ cup sugar

1 tablespoon baking powder

¼ teaspoon baking soda

½ teaspoon salt

2 teaspoons minced fresh rosemary leaves,
    or dried rosemary, crumbled

1 teaspoon finely grated lemon zest

6 tablespoons vegetable shortening,
    chilled

1 large egg

⅔ cup buttermilk

1 cup diced (¼-inch cubes) fresh strawberries

GLAZE

3 tablespoons unsalted butter, melted

1½ tablespoons sugar

2 teaspoons fresh lemon juice

1. Adjust an oven rack to the middle shelf and preheat the oven to 400°F. Lightly butter a baking sheet.

2. To make the biscuits, sift together the flour, sugar, baking powder, baking soda, and salt into a large mixing bowl. Add the rosemary and lemon zest, and mix until well combined. With a pastry blender, fork, or your fingers, cut in the shortening until the mixture resembles coarse meal. Make a well in the center.

3. In a separate bowl, lightly beat the egg, then stir in the buttermilk. Add this liquid and the strawberries to the well, and mix with a wooden spoon just until blended. The mixture should be soft and tender. Do not overmix.

4. Turn out the dough onto a well-floured board. Gather the dough and gently knead 2 or 3 times until it is well formed. Do not overwork it. Pat the dough, 5 or 6 times, into a circle about ½ inch thick. Dip a 3-inch round cookie cutter in flour and cut out as many circles as possible. Gather the dough scraps, pat them into a ½-inch-thick circle, and cut out more biscuits.

5. Place the biscuits on the prepared sheet and bake until they are golden, about 20 minutes. Transfer the biscuits to a rack to cool slightly.

6. To make the glaze, combine the melted butter, sugar, and lemon juice in a small bowl. Brush the glaze over the warm biscuits. Serve hot.

WHOLE WHEAT PEAR SCONES

YIELD: 8 SCONES

Scones are simple little cakes. They are a fine treat not only for breakfast but also for tea time. These scones are light, crisp, and deliciously spiced. Traditionally, the dough is cut into individual rounds with a cookie cutter, but I find it more practical if the dough is cut and baked in the same pan. This way, you will not be tempted to overwork the dough, which will produce hard-as-rock scones. Experiment with other fruits, particularly raisins, apples, or blueberries. Scones may be made earlier in the day and reheated in a 400°F oven for 5 minutes before serving.

¾ cup unbleached all-purpose flour

¾ cup whole wheat flour

½ teaspoon ground cinnamon

½ teaspoon ground ginger

1 teaspoon baking powder

½ teaspoon baking soda

½ teaspoon salt

¼ cup (firmly packed) light brown sugar

4 tablespoons (½ stick) unsalted butter, chilled and cut into pieces

2 medium, ripe pears, preferably Bosc or Anjou

1 large egg

¼ cup plain yogurt

2 tablespoons unsalted butter, melted

1. Adjust an oven rack to the middle shelf and preheat the oven to 375°F. Lightly butter an 8-inch round cake pan.

2. Sift together the flours, cinnamon, ginger, baking powder, baking soda, and salt into a medium-size bowl and add the brown sugar. Mix well. Using a pastry blender, cut in the chilled butter until it's the size of small peas.

3. Peel, core, and finely chop the pears. Stir the pears into the flour mixture, then make a well in the center.

4. In another small bowl, beat the egg and yogurt together lightly. Pour the liquid mixture into the center of the dry ingredients. Using a fork, gradually stir the dry ingredients into the wet ingredients to form a moist dough. Do not overwork the dough.

5. Transfer the dough to the buttered pan, patting it lightly into an even circle. Using a large, sharp knife, cut through the dough, dividing it into 8 equal wedges. Brush the top of the dough with melted butter.

6. Bake until the scones are golden brown, 12 to 15 minutes. Serve hot.

CRANBERRY-RAISIN SCONES

YIELD: 12 SCONES

These scones, splitting at the seams with dried cranberries and raisins, are just perfect when topped with a little butter and jam. Their texture is especially soft, and they taste faintly sweet and tart. Although scones are best while they are still hot, they're still good if you serve them at room temperature. Dried sour cherries can be substituted for the cranberries.

1³/₄ cups self-rising cake flour
¹/₂ teaspoon baking soda
¹/₂ teaspoon salt
3 tablespoons sugar
4 tablespoons (¹/₂ stick) unsalted butter, chilled and cut into pieces
¹/₂ cup golden raisins
¹/₂ cup dried cranberries
²/₃ cup heavy (or whipping) cream
2 tablespoons unsalted butter, melted

1. Adjust an oven rack to the middle shelf and preheat the oven to 375°F. Lightly butter an 8-inch round cake pan.

2. Sift together the flour, baking soda, and salt into a medium-size bowl and add the sugar. Mix well. Using a pastry blender or 2 knives, cut in the chilled butter until it's the size of small peas.

3. Stir the raisins and cranberries into the flour mixture.

4. Using a fork, gradually stir in the cream to form a soft dough. Do not over-work the dough or you will have hard scones.

5. Transfer the dough to the buttered pan, patting it lightly into an even circle. Using a large, sharp knife, cut the dough into 8 equal wedges. Brush the top of the dough with melted butter.

6. Bake until the scones turn golden, 12 to 15 minutes. Serve hot.

BANANA DOUGHNUTS

YIELD: 16 DOUGHNUTS

If you've never known the pleasures of fresh homemade doughnuts, with their crisp outsides and rich crumb interiors, give this recipe a try. Light, tender, and full of cinnamon sugar, these doughnuts are packed with wonderful flavors. Be sure to fry the holes along with the doughnuts. Watch out; they are so scrumptious, they will disappear in a blink!

2³⁄₄ cups unbleached all-purpose flour
1¹⁄₂ teaspoons baking powder
1 teaspoon baking soda
3 teaspoons ground cinnamon
3 tablespoons unsalted butter, at room temperature
1¹⁄₂ cups plus 2 tablespoons sugar
2 large eggs
¹⁄₄ cup milk
¹⁄₄ cup orange, pineapple, or apple juice
1 teaspoon vanilla extract
2 medium, ripe bananas, diced (¹⁄₄-inch cubes)
Vegetable oil, for deep frying

1. Sift together the flour, baking powder, baking soda, and 1 teaspoon of the cinnamon into a large bowl. Make a well in the center.

2. Cream the butter and ¹⁄₂ cup plus 2 tablespoons of the sugar in a small bowl. Beat in the eggs. Stir in the milk, fruit juice, vanilla, and bananas. Pour this mixture into the center of the dry ingredients, and stir with a wooden spoon just until blended. The dough should be very soft but not sticky. Do not overmix.

3. Cover and chill the dough for 1 hour.

4. Place half the dough on a well-floured board, knead lightly, and pat it into a circle approximately ³⁄₄ inch thick. Cut with a floured 2¹⁄₂-inch doughnut cutter. Gather the dough scraps, knead briefly, pat into a ³⁄₄-inch-thick circle, and cut out more doughnuts. Continue until all the dough is used up. Place the doughnuts on a lightly floured baking sheet while you work with the remaining half of the dough.

5. Pour oil to a depth of 2 inches into a large, heavy skillet (if using a deep-fryer, add oil to a depth of 3½ inches). Slowly heat the oil to 350°F over medium heat. Fry the doughnuts, in batches, until golden brown on both sides, about 2 minutes. Do not overcrowd the skillet. Drain on paper towels. Keep warm in a low oven as you fry the remaining doughnuts. Be sure the oil returns to 350°F before you fry the next batch.

6. Mix the remaining 1 cup sugar and remaining 2 teaspoons cinnamon in a medium-size bowl. Roll the warm doughnuts in the sugar mixture and serve at once.

BLUEBERRY-BANANA MUFFINS

YIELD: 12 MUFFINS

One of the joys of making your own muffins is that you can vary their flavors by adding practically any kind of fruit that strikes your fancy. Personally, I enjoy my muffins dense in texture, packed with fruit, and served straight from the oven. Here is my favorite recipe for delicious blueberry and banana muffins, followed by a wealth of variations. All muffins freeze well, so make plenty for busy days. To reheat, pop the frozen muffins into a preheated 350°F oven and bake for 10 minutes. Or, wrap them in a barely damp paper towel and microwave on high power for 20 to 30 seconds.

2 cups unbleached all-purpose flour
¼ cup granulated sugar
5 teaspoons baking powder
½ teaspoon salt
1 large egg, lightly beaten
1 cup buttermilk
2 teaspoons vanilla extract
1 teaspoon grated lemon zest
4 tablespoons (½ stick) unsalted butter,
    melted and cooled slightly
1 large ripe banana
¾ cup fresh or thawed frozen blueberries
½ cup chopped walnuts or pecans or
    slivered almonds
¼ cup (firmly packed) light brown sugar

1. Adjust an oven rack to the lowest shelf and preheat the oven to 375°F. Lightly butter a standard (12-cup) muffin tin. Set aside.

2. Sift together the flour, sugar, baking powder, and salt into a medium-size mixing bowl. Make a well in the center

3. In a small bowl, stir together the egg, buttermilk, vanilla, lemon zest, and melted butter. Pour the wet ingredients into the

flour well. Stir with a wooden spoon just until moistened. The batter should look lumpy with no flour showing and fall easily from the spoon. Do not beat the batter until smooth; overmixing it will result in tough and dry muffins.

4. Peel the banana and quarter it lengthwise, then slice crosswise 1/2-inch thick. Fold the banana and blueberries into the batter and spoon the mixture into the muffin tin, filling each cup about two-thirds full. Stir together the walnuts and the brown sugar, then sprinkle the mixture over each muffin.

5. Bake until the muffins are well browned, or until a bamboo skewer or toothpick inserted in the center of a muffin comes out clean, about 30 minutes. Cool slightly in the tin on a rack before unmolding. Serve immediately.

VARIATIONS

APPLE MUFFINS: Substitute 2 large Golden or Red Delicious apples, peeled and chopped, for the banana and blueberries. Add 1/4 teaspoon each ground cinnamon and nutmeg to the flour mixture. Reduce the buttermilk to 3/4 cup and add 1/4 cup thawed frozen apple juice concentrate or fresh cider.

BLUEBERRY-APPLE MUFFINS: Substitute 1/2 cup chopped apple for the banana.

BANANA MUFFINS: Use 2 large ripe bananas. Omit the blueberries.

BLUEBERRY MUFFINS: Use 1 1/2 cups fresh or frozen blueberries. Omit the bananas.

CRANBERRY-ORANGE MUFFINS: Increase the granulated sugar to 1/2 cup. Substitute 1 1/2 cups chopped fresh, frozen, or dried cranberries for the banana and blueberries, and substitute 2 teaspoons grated orange zest for the lemon zest. Reduce the buttermilk to 1/2 cup and add 1/2 cup fresh orange juice.

PEAR MUFFINS: Add 1/4 teaspoon each ground ginger and allspice to the flour mixture. Substitute 2 large peeled, cored, and chopped Anjou, Bosc, or Bartlett pears for the banana and blueberries.

PINEAPPLE MUFFINS: Add 1/8 teaspoon each ground cinnamon, ginger, and nutmeg to the flour mixture. Reduce the buttermilk to 3/4 cup and add 1/4 cup fresh pineapple juice. Substitute 1 1/2 cups chopped fresh pineapple or canned crushed pineapple (well drained) for the banana and blueberries.

RASPBERRY MUFFINS: Add 1/2 teaspoon ground cinnamon to the flour mixture, and increase the granulated sugar to 1/3 cup. Substitute 1 1/2 cups fresh raspberries for the banana and blueberries. Omit the nut-brown sugar topping.

STRAWBERRY MUFFINS: Increase the granulated sugar to 1/3 cup. Substitute 1 1/2 cups chopped fresh strawberries for the bananas and blueberries. Omit the nut-brown sugar topping.

DRYING FRUITS

*S*un drying, an extremely popular method of food preservation, has been practiced by people in hot, dry climates for centuries. For the modern cook, the simplest and most economical place to dry fruits is in an oven. All you have to do is set it to very low, put in the halved or sliced fruit, and go about your business. Another option, if you plan to dry fruit frequently, is to invest in a small dehydrator.

Basically, any fruit can be oven-dried. Dates, figs, apples, peaches, pears, plums, apricots, currants, pineapples, grapes, cherries, blueberries, strawberries, and cranberries are the fruits most frequently dried. Tropical fruits like mangoes, bananas, persimmons, and star fruits lend themselves equally well to this process. As with anything else, the better the fruit, the better the final product. Out-of-season fruits, which often arrive in the supermarket not fully ripe, may benefit the most because the drying process helps intensify their flavor. All dried fruits should be stored in tightly covered jars and refrigerated. Properly stored, they will remain flavorful for up to 6 months.

Removing the moisture from a fruit greatly changes its character. The water disappears, and the flesh and skin darken. The natural sweetness and flavor of the fruit becomes concentrated, giving it more depth. Hence, dried fruits are much higher in calories, nutrients, fiber, and sugar than fresh fruits.

The degree to which fruit is dried is a matter of personal preference. As a rule of thumb, the fruit should be wrinkled and shrunk to about three-quarters of its original size but still somewhat juicy inside and with only a slight change in color.

Dried fruits make wonderful snacks and are great for baking and cooking. They add flavor to the simplest of recipes, like muffins, nut breads, pancakes, or cookies. Toss them into breakfast cereal, add to stuffing, or sprinkle over ice cream. They can also be plumped in hot water, fruit juices, wine, brandy, Cognac, rum, port, or Marsala.

TO OVEN-DRY FRUITS

✦ Choose firm, not-so-juicy, bruise-free fruits. Wash the fruit if you plan to leave the skin on; otherwise, peel, core, and cut in half or slice into 1/4-inch-thick pieces.

✦ Arrange the fruit, cut side up, in single layers on baking sheets. In a dehydrator or a regular oven, dry at temperatures between 120 °F and 140 °F (the warm setting on your oven). At 140 °F (higher temperatures will bake the slices), it will take approximately 6 hours for the slices to dry thoroughly. If you want to dry the fruit overnight, set the temperature at 120 °F. For evenly dried slices, turn them occasionally on the sheets.

✦ After the initial drying, leave the fruits to dry completely in the open air for a couple more days. When the fruits are dried to your liking, arrange them in containers, taking care to separate the layers with parchment paper. Store in the refrigerator.

✦ For great, fat-free apple chips, cut 3 whole Red Delicious apples into thin slices, about 1/8 inch thick. Coat the slices with fresh lemon juice. Spray several baking sheets with cooking oil, then spread out the apple slices in a single layer. Leave the fruit to dry in a 200 °F oven until crisp, 3 to 4 hours. Pack the chips in a container and store in a cool, dry place. Makes about 4 ounces.

RAISIN-ORANGE MUFFINS

YIELD: 12 MUFFINS

These are what I call perfect breakfast muffins; moist and delicate, with a special citrus flavor. Since they are not overly sweet, they make superb companions to salads too. Personally, I find them most irresistible when topped with thin slices of smoked meat and a dab of chutney.

1 large navel orange
1 1/2 cups unbleached all-purpose flour
1/2 cup sugar
1 teaspoon baking powder
1 teaspoon baking soda
3/4 teaspoon salt
4 tablespoons (1/2 stick) unsalted butter, at room temperature
1/2 cup raisins
1/3 cup orange juice
1 large egg, lightly beaten

1. Adjust an oven rack to the lowest shelf and preheat the oven to 400°F. Butter a standard (12-cup) muffin tin.

2. Using a zester, remove long strips of zest from the orange. Set the zest aside. With a sharp paring knife, remove and discard the white pith from the orange.

MUFFIN TIPS

✦ When a muffin recipe calls for fresh fruit, be sure to use ripe or even slightly overripe fruit for the very best flavor.

✦ If you prefer, you can grease the tins with a vegetable oil spray instead of melted butter.

✦ Use the batter promptly. Use a spoon or 1/4-cup measure to scoop up the batter to fill the muffin tin. A general rule is to fill the cups two-thirds full, but individual recipes can vary. Don't worry about leveling the tops.

✦ If any cups remain unfilled, fill them with water to keep them from scorching.

✦ If you want to serve hot, freshly baked muffins first thing in the morning but have little time to cook, do this: The night before, mix the dry ingredients in a bowl, cover it with plastic wrap and let it sit at room temperature overnight. Combine the wet ingredients (eggs, milk, fruit juice) in a separate bowl, cover, and refrigerate. In the morning, preheat the oven and grease the pans. Quickly combine the wet and dry ingredients and finish the recipe. Voilà! The muffins can bake while you shower or get dressed.

✦ Muffins are best fresh but may be stored in an airtight container for a day or two. Wrapped in aluminum foil (when they are cool but still fresh) and sealed in a freezer bag, they will keep in the freezer for up to 3 months.

Coarsely chop the orange. (There should be about 1 cup of orange pulp.)

3. Sift together the flour, sugar, baking powder, baking soda, and salt, into a large mixing bowl. Make a well in the center.

4. Place the softened butter, raisins, and orange zest in a food processor. Process until the raisins are finely chopped. Add the chopped orange, orange juice, and beaten egg. Process until the mixture is well blended, then pour it into the flour well. Stir with a wooden spoon just until the ingredients are moistened. Do not overmix.

5. Divide the batter evenly among the prepared muffin cups. Bake until the muffins are golden brown, or until a bamboo skewer or toothpick inserted in the center of a muffin comes out clean, about 20 minutes. Cool slightly in the tin on a rack before unmolding. Serve immediately.

JAMAICAN BANANA TEA BREAD

YIELD: 1 LOAF

If you think all banana breads are the same, wait until you try this one! What makes it so special is the delicate balance of flavors. Just follow the measurements and steps in this recipe very carefully, and you'll see what I mean.

> 2 1/4 cups unbleached all-purpose flour
> 1 1/4 teaspoons baking soda
> 1/2 teaspoon salt
> 8 tablespoons (1 stick) unsalted butter,
>   at room temperature
> 1/2 cup (firmly packed) light brown sugar
> 2 large eggs
> 1/3 cup sour cream
> 2 tablespoons dark rum
> 2 tablespoons fresh lime juice
> 1 1/2 teaspoons finely grated lime zest
> 1 1/3 cups mashed ripe banana (about
>   3 large)
> 1/2 cup sweetened shredded coconut,
>   toasted lightly and cooled (for
>   toasting instructions, see page 64)

1. Adjust an oven rack to the middle shelf and preheat the oven to 350°F. Lightly butter an 8 1/2 x 4 1/2 x 2 1/2 -inch loaf pan.

2. Sift together the flour, baking soda, and salt into a small bowl.

3. Cream the butter and brown sugar in a large mixing bowl with an electric mixer at medium speed. Beat in the eggs, 1 at a time, followed by the sour cream, rum, lime juice, lime zest, and the banana, mixing until just combined after each addition. The mixture will look curdled.

4. Reduce the speed to low and gradually add the flour mixture, beating until

TEA BREAD TIPS

Made of a thick batter leavened with baking powder, tea breads are typically flavored with mashed, puréed, or chopped fresh fruit and nuts. Here are a few hints on how to successfully produce moist and tender tea breads with a cakelike interior:

◆ *If dried fruits are to be rehydrated, soak them in warm fruit juice or liquor until they get plump. Use the liquid in the recipe, too. Drain and dry the fruits well with paper towels.*

◆ *Coating solid, dry ingredients (like dried fruits, fresh cranberries, and nuts) by mixing them with the dry ingredients prevents them from sinking to the bottom of the bread during baking.*

◆ *Fold fresh, moist fruits (like soft berries, peaches,*

plums) into the batter at the very end, just before you pour it into the pan.

◆ *Combine the wet and dry ingredients in a sequence that does not require persistent beating of the flour, which develops gluten and makes the bread tough.*

◆ *Never open the oven door before the appointed time, as the bread, disturbed by the cold air wafting through the oven, will not rise properly, or worse, will sink in the middle.*

◆ *To preserve a tea bread's freshness, wrap it securely in plastic, then aluminum foil and store in a breadbox or refrigerator for 2 days at the most. Frozen, it will keep for up to 3 months.*

◆ *Serve them warm; warmth intensifies all flavors.*

---

smooth. Add the toasted coconut, and fold until well incorporated.

5. Scrape the batter into the prepared loaf pan. Bake until the bread is nicely browned on top and a bamboo skewer or toothpick inserted in the center comes out clean, about 1 hour and 10 minutes.

6. Cool in the pan on a rack for 10 to 15 minutes before unmolding. Serve warm.

CRANBERRY-ORANGE BREAD

YIELD: 1 LOAF

One of the most popular uses for cranberries is cranberry bread. After several experiments, I came up with this recipe, which has a very moist texture and just the right balance of sweet and tart flavors. I prefer it without nuts, but if you wish, add ½ cup chopped walnuts or macadamias to the flour mixture along with the raisins or cranberries.

2 cups unbleached all-purpose flour

1 tablespoon baking powder

1 teaspoon baking soda

$\frac{1}{2}$ teaspoon salt

$1\frac{1}{4}$ cups fresh or frozen whole cranberries

$\frac{1}{2}$ cup dark raisins

2 large eggs

$\frac{1}{2}$ cup sugar

$\frac{2}{3}$ cup fresh orange juice

2 tablespoons thawed frozen orange juice
concentrate

2 teaspoons finely grated orange zest

4 tablespoons ($\frac{1}{2}$ stick) unsalted butter,
melted and cooled

1. Adjust an oven rack to the middle shelf and preheat the oven to 350°F. Lightly butter an $8\frac{1}{2}$ x $4\frac{1}{2}$ x $2\frac{1}{2}$-inch loaf pan.

2. Sift together the flour, baking powder, baking soda, and salt into a large mixing bowl. Add the cranberries and raisins. Stir until well combined.

3. Lightly beat the eggs with the sugar in another bowl, then stir in the orange juice, orange juice concentrate, orange zest, and melted butter.

4. Make a well in the middle of the dry ingredients and add the liquid mixture. Stir with a wooden spoon just until the dry ingredients are well moistened. Do not overmix. The batter will be fairly thick.

5. Scrape the batter into the prepared loaf pan. Bake until the bread is browned and a bamboo skewer or toothpick inserted in the center comes out clean, about 1 hour.

6. Cool in the pan on a rack for 10 to 15 minutes before unmolding. Serve warm.

STRAWBERRY-LEMON BREAD

YIELD: 1 LOAF

Besides being quick and easy to prepare, this fruity tea bread also tastes delicious, especially when it's still slightly warm. To use up any leftovers, slice the bread and toast it. It's great for breakfast, lunch, or a snack.

BREAD

2 cups unbleached all-purpose flour

1 teaspoon baking soda

$\frac{1}{4}$ teaspoon salt

$\frac{1}{2}$ cup chopped walnuts

2 large eggs

$\frac{1}{2}$ cup sugar

8 tablespoons (1 stick) unsalted butter,
melted and cooled

$\frac{1}{4}$ cup milk

1 tablespoon grated lemon zest

2 cups fresh strawberries, hulled and cut
into $\frac{1}{2}$-inch pieces

GLAZE

$\frac{1}{4}$ cup fresh lemon juice

3 tablespoons sugar

This berry is the wonder of all the Fruits growing naturally in those parts...The Indians bruise them in a Morter, and mixe them with meale and make Strawberry bread.

—ROGER WILLIAMS, WRITING OF THE RHODE ISLAND STRAWBERRY

1. Adjust an oven rack to the middle shelf and preheat the oven to 350°F. Lightly butter an 8½ x 4½ x 2½-inch loaf pan.

2. To make the bread, sift together the flour, baking soda, and salt into a large mixing bowl. Add the walnuts and stir to combine.

3. Lightly beat the eggs with the sugar in another bowl, then mix in the melted butter, milk, lemon zest, and strawberries.

4. Make a well in the middle of the dry ingredients and add the liquid mixture. Stir with a wooden spoon just until the dry ingredients are moistened. Do not overmix. The batter will be fairly thick.

5. Scrape the batter into the prepared loaf pan. Bake until the bread is nicely browned and a bamboo skewer or toothpick inserted in the center comes out clean, about 1 hour and 5 minutes.

6. Cool in the pan on a rack for 10 to 15 minutes.

7. Meanwhile, make the glaze: Place the lemon juice and sugar in a small, heavy saucepan and stir to dissolve the sugar. Place over medium heat and simmer until the mix-

ture is syrupy and reduced by half, about 3 minutes. Do not let it burn. Remove the pan from the heat.

8. Remove the bread from the pan. Pour the warm lemon glaze over the top of the loaf. Cool completely on the rack before serving.

VARIATION

BLUEBERRY-ORANGE BREAD: Substitute 2 cups fresh or frozen blueberries for the strawberries, and orange zest and juice for the lemon.

PERSIMMON-ALMOND LOAF

YIELD: 1 LOAF

Fragrant and fruity, this persimmon loaf is my variation on an old-fashioned date tea bread. With its sweet and nutty flavors, it is a favorite of both children and adults for brunch or for lunch with chicken salad. Orange glaze makes a perfect topping for this quick bread, but if you like to experiment, try Date Spread (see Index).

2 cups unbleached all-purpose flour

1½ teaspoons baking soda

1 teaspoon baking powder

1 teaspoon ground cinnamon

½ teaspoon salt

¼ teaspoon freshly ground nutmeg

2 large ripe persimmons (about 1 pound)

8 tablespoons (1 stick) unsalted butter, at room temperature

½ cup sugar

1 large egg

¼ cup sour cream

2 teaspoons almond extract

1 cup dried apricots or peaches, chopped

½ cup toasted sliced almonds (for toasting instructions, see page 64)

Orange Glaze (recipe follows), optional

1. Adjust an oven rack to the middle shelf and preheat the oven to 350°F. Lightly butter an 8½ x 4½ x 2½-inch loaf pan.

2. Sift together the flour, baking soda, baking powder, cinnamon, salt, and nutmeg into a mixing bowl. Set aside.

3. Peel the persimmon and scoop the flesh into a medium-size mixing bowl. Mash with a fork. (There should be about 1 cup mashed pulp.) Set aside.

4. Using an electric mixer, beat the butter and sugar at medium-high speed until light and fluffy. Add the egg and beat until thoroughly combined. Add the persimmon pulp, sour cream, and almond extract. Blend at low speed to combine the ingredients. The mixture will look curdled.

5. Add the sifted flour mixture, ½ cup at a time, and beat at low speed until the batter is smooth, stopping occasionally to scrape down the sides of the work bowl with a spatula. Fold in the chopped apricots and toasted almonds. The batter will be very dense and sticky.

6. Scrape the batter into the prepared loaf pan. Bake until a bamboo skewer or toothpick inserted in the center of the loaf comes out clean, about 1 hour.

7. Cool the bread in the pan on a rack for about 20 minutes before unmolding. Then unmold and spread with Orange Glaze, if desired.

Orange Glaze

YIELD: 1 CUP

2 teaspoons cornstarch

½ cup fresh orange juice

½ cup thawed frozen orange juice concentrate

1½ tablespoons unsalted butter

2 tablespoons confectioners' sugar (optional)

½ teaspoon almond extract

1. In a small saucepan, mix the cornstarch with the orange juice, and stir until the cornstarch is dissolved.

2. Cook over low heat, stirring constantly with a wooden spoon, until thick and smooth, 2 to 3 minutes.

3. Stir in the orange juice concentrate and the butter. Remove from the heat. For a sweeter glaze, beat in the confectioners' sugar.

4. Cool slightly before adding the almond extract.

FESTIVE BREAKFASTS

The sweet charms of fruit are frequently called to the breakfast table. A glass of freshly squeezed orange juice or cereal topped with sliced bananas is a morning must for some people. As delicious and energizing as the classics are, with the variety of fruit that is available to us throughout the year, it would be a pity to stick slavishly to them. Instead of a chilled grapefruit half, why not try a seductive eye-opener liked mixed fruits of the season, a baked apple, or granola with yogurt and fresh berries?

Breakfast really comes into its own on weekend mornings, when time and inclination permit indulging in a substantial meal rather than rushing out the door and grabbing a doughnut on the way to work. There's something wonderfully comforting and luxurious about beginning the day with a leisurely breakfast. But even if you can't linger over a towering stack of hotcakes and a bottomless cup of coffee, breakfast can still feel special.

Most of the recipes in this chapter are perfect for a weekend brunch, especially if you are entertaining. Included are some ideas for delicious fruit butters, syrups, and sauces to accompany them. All are homey, easy to prepare, and should get your day off to a great start.

And remember, when looking for new breakfast ideas, don't limit yourself just to the recipes in this chapter. Why not begin with a fruity breakfast shake (see Smoothies and Spirits, page 341) followed by pancakes or eggs? And if you still think breakfast isn't breakfast without bread, go ahead and serve some won-

derful fruited muffins or quick tea breads (see Breads Quick and Slow, page 289) alongside. If you are diet conscious, or time is in short supply, consider serving just a light fruit soup like Pink Grapefruit Soup (page 53).

QUICK BREAKFAST IDEAS

If a fruit eaten out of hand is not exactly what you had in mind for a quick breakfast, here are some suggestions for delicious alternatives:

✦ *Spread some cream cheese on toast or crackers and top with banana slices and crumbled bacon.*

✦ *Try peanut butter (or cream cheese) with raisins or chopped dates on toast or crackers.*

✦ *Smear Date Spread (page 339) over rice cakes, muffins, scones, or toast.*

✦ *Mix muesli or granola with fruit yogurt and mixed fresh fruits.*

✦ *Toss sliced fresh pineapple, kiwi, papaya, pear, banana, and strawberries with a bit of orange juice. Serve in wide bowls with a choice of cream, yogurt, granola, and raisins for topping.*

✦ *Top cooked oatmeal with dried raisins, sliced bananas, strawberries, and toasted sliced almonds.*

✦ *Arrange sections of grapefruit and oranges in a ring on a small plate. Top with a scoop of yogurt, then sprinkle with your favorite granola and garnish with fresh strawberries.*

✦ *Arrange slices of pineapple and persimmon in a crown pattern on a small, ovenproof plate. Spread some ginger marmalade over the fruits and broil to form a glaze. Top with a small scoop of pineapple sorbet or frozen yogurt.*

✦ *Heat up some Gingered Applesauce (page 214) or any applesauce you have on hand. Stir in sliced strawberries or peaches just as the apples finish cooking. Drizzle with cream and serve warm.*

✦ *Arrange peeled and cored pear or apple wedges on a small, ovenproof plate. Sprinkle with brown sugar, lemon juice, maple syrup, and butter. Brown under the broiler.*

✦ *Arrange banana halves in a microwave-safe baking dish. Sprinkle with lime juice, brown sugar, and a dash of rum. Cover with plastic wrap and cook on high power in a microwave oven for 1 minute, or until the fruit is soft.*

WARM FRUIT MEDLEY

YIELD: 2 SERVINGS

On a cold day, a warm assortment of fruits is a welcome alternative to the usual fruit cup. This simple medley is heated just long enough to remove the chill from the fruits.

1 large pink grapefruit, peeled and
*   sectioned (for instructions,*
*   see page 318)*
1 pear, preferably Comice, Anjou,
*   or Bartlett*
1 banana
3 tablespoons raisins, preferably
*   golden raisins*
¼ cup fresh orange juice
1 tablespoon honey
Ground ginger

1. Place the grapefruit segments in a medium-size saucepan.

2. Peel, core, and cut the pear into ½-inch pieces. Add to the saucepan. Peel the banana and slice it ½ inch thick. Add them to the saucepan, along with the raisins, orange juice, and honey. Season the mixture to taste with ground ginger.

3. Cook over low heat until warm, about 2 minutes. Serve warm.

STEWED FRUIT

YIELD: 6 SERVINGS

Stews made from dried fruit are a German and Austrian classic, used more as an accompaniment to meat dishes than a dessert. The popularity of compotes dates from when dried fruits were a welcome change from the monotonous winter diet of cabbage and turnips. Today fruit stews are usually served at breakfast or as an ending to a meal. This one is delicious spooned over hot oatmeal or served at a brunch buffet alongside smoked meats. And, for a wonderful contrast of hot and cold sensations, top the warm fruit with a scoop of tart fruit sorbet such as Tangerine Sorbet (see Index), or frozen yogurt. To sweeten this compote, I use a hard apple cider (3.5 to 4 percent alcohol), such as Purpom, which is available at liquor stores. Do not substitute fresh apple cider; it would make the compote too sweet.

1 pound dried fruits, such as apples, apricots,
*   peaches, pears, prunes, and cherries*
1 bottle (750 ml) hard apple cider,
*   such as Purpom*
1 stick cinnamon (3 inches)
Zest of 1 lemon
Pinch of salt
2 tablespoons fresh
*   lemon juice*

SECTIONING A CITRUS FRUIT

There are two reasons to section citrus fruits: First, to remove all the peel, bitter pith, and fibrous membranes; second, to obtain neat, elegant looking segments of fruit that will embellish a dish, especially salads and desserts. Here is how I section grapefruits, oranges, tangerines, limes, and lemons:

1. Slice off the top and bottom of the fruit with a sharp knife.

2. Stand the fruit on one of its cut surfaces on a cutting board. Following the contour of the fruit, carefully and evenly cut away the rind and the white pith, a strip at a time, from top to bottom, exposing the fruit. Cut off any small pieces of pith or membrane you may have missed.

3. Working over a bowl to catch the juices, cut between the membranes and the meat to separate the fruit into sections. Squeeze the membranes before discarding them to extract any juice. Remove any seeds, taking care not to break the fruit segments. Use the collected juices to add to a vinaigrette or sauce, or just drink it, if you like, for a quick vitamin-rich pick-me-up.

---

1. Place the dried fruits, cider, cinnamon stick, lemon zest, and salt in a large saucepan and bring to a boil over high heat. Reduce the heat to low and simmer until the fruit is tender, stirring occasionally, about 15 minutes. Remove the pan from the heat, and stir in the lemon juice. Let cool.

2. Serve the fruit warm or at room temperature. (It can be prepared 1 day ahead, covered, and refrigerated. Reheat before serving.)

GRANOLA BAKED APPLES

YIELD: 4 SERVINGS

One forgets how good a baked apple can be in the morning. Earthy and mellow, this one is filled with nutlike nuggets of oats, which add texture and taste. Use your favorite granola mix for the crispy sweet filling here. I like one that includes raisins. For an even more seductive breakfast, serve these baked apples with Blueberry Sauce or Sour Cherry Compote (see Index) instead of yogurt or light cream.

> 4 firm apples, such as Rome Beauty
> ¾ cup granola
> 2 tablespoons (firmly packed) light brown sugar
> ¼ cup apple cider or apple juice
> Plain yogurt or light cream or half-and-half (optional)

1. Preheat the oven to 350°F.

2. Cut a thin slice off the top of each apple and discard. Core the apples, being careful not to cut all the way through the bottoms. Cut out and reserve the center of the apples, leaving a ½-inch-thick shell. Chop enough of the reserved apple to measure ½ cup and set aside. With a vegetable peeler, remove a ½-inch-wide strip of peel around the top of each apple.

3. Mix the granola with the reserved ½ cup chopped apple and the brown sugar. Use the mixture to fill the scooped-out apples.

4. Place the apples upright in a shallow baking dish and pour the cider around them. Cover the dish with aluminum

foil and bake until the apples can be easily pierced with the tip of a knife, 30 to 35 minutes. Serve at once, topped with yogurt, if desired.

OVEN-PUFFED PANCAKES

YIELD: 2 SERVINGS

These glorious creations are nothing more than giant popovers, topped with sautéed fresh fruit. They are very easy to prepare, impressive-looking, light, and crispy. I serve these pancakes with fresh peaches, but you can use any fruit in season, such as apples, nectarines, plums, or strawberries.

> 3 large eggs
> 2 tablespoons plus ½ teaspoon granulated sugar
> ¼ teaspoon freshly grated nutmeg
> ¼ teaspoon salt
> ½ cup unbleached all-purpose flour
> ½ cup milk
> 3 tablespoons unsalted butter
> 2 medium peaches, unpeeled, thinly sliced
> Confectioners' sugar
> Maple syrup

1. Adjust the oven rack to the middle position, and preheat the oven to 425°F.

BREAKFAST FOR 4

Macerated Nectarines
and Berries

◆

Oven-Puffed Pancakes

◆

Grilled Breakfast
Sausages

◆

Coffee and Tea

2. In a large bowl, whisk the eggs with 2 tablespoons of the granulated sugar and the nutmeg until well blended. Add the flour and whisk until smooth, about 1 minute. Add the milk and whisk until smooth.

3. Heat 2 ovenproof 6-inch skillets or baking pans (you can use small pie pans or cake pans) until very hot. Melt 1 tablespoon of butter in each skillet and divide the batter between the pans.

4. Bake in the middle of the oven until the pancakes are puffed, golden brown, and crusty around the edges, about 20 minutes. Do not open the oven door during the first 5 minutes, or the pancakes will not rise properly.

5. Just before the pancakes are ready, melt the remaining 1 tablespoon butter in a small skillet over medium-high heat. Add the peaches and the remaining ½ teaspoon

granulated sugar and sauté until soft, about 2 minutes.

6. Using a wide metal spatula, transfer the pancakes to warmed plates and top with the sautéed peaches. Dust with confectioners' sugar. Serve hot.

I made my supper of huckleberries and blueberries on fair Haven Hill, and laid up a store for several days.

—**HENRY DAVID THOREAU**

HUCKLEBERRY PANCAKES

YIELD: 4 SERVINGS

The smell of pancakes cooking on a griddle is certainly enticing. And the sight of a towering stack of pancakes lavished with whipped butter, fresh fruit, and warm syrup, is irresistible. This is my favorite recipe. Although it's for huckleberry pancakes, you can substitute any berry that's in season. Serve them piled high with Raspberry Butter or Lemon and Honey Butter (see Index).

HUCKLEBERRIES

Often confused with wild blueberries, huckleberries are smaller, more tart, and have an intense blueberry flavor. Tiny edible seeds make these berries crunchy when fresh. Huckleberries must be gathered from the wild. They are available from mid-June through Labor Day.

3/4 cup plus 1 tablespoon unbleached
    all-purpose flour
1/2 teaspoon baking soda
1/2 teaspoon salt
1 large egg
2 tablespoons sugar
1 cup buttermilk
1 teaspoon vanilla extract
4 tablespoons (1/2 stick) unsalted butter,
    melted and cooled
1 1/2 cups huckleberries
2 cups sliced fresh strawberries, for garnish
Confectioners' sugar
Warm maple syrup

1. Sift together the flour, baking soda, and salt into a medium-size mixing bowl.

2. In a small bowl, lightly beat the egg with the sugar, then stir in the buttermilk, vanilla, and 2 tablespoons of the melted butter.

3. Add the liquid ingredients to the flour mixture and stir until just moistened. The batter should have the consistency of thick cream with some lumps. Do not overmix.

4. Heat a large griddle or 2 large non-stick skillets over medium-high heat, then brush each lightly with some of the remaining melted butter. Gently drop the batter into the skillets by heaping tablespoonfuls, 2 inches apart. Press a few huckleberries into each pancake and cook until the undersides are golden brown and bubbles are breaking on top, about 1 1/2 minutes. Turn and cook 1 1/2 minutes longer on the other side. Keep the pancakes warm in a low oven as you cook the rest of the batter.

5. Divide the pancakes among warmed plates and top with the strawberries. Sprinkle with confectioners' sugar and serve with warm maple syrup.

APPLESAUCE GRIDDLE CAKES

YIELD: 4 SERVINGS

Save this superb version of pancakes with applesauce for colder days, when fresh berries are in short supply. For an extra treat, spread the pancakes with Apple Butter (see Index) and top them with maple syrup. Or spoon a large dollop of warm Gingered Applesauce (see Index) over the top and omit the bananas.

*¾ cup plus 1 tablespoon unbleached
    all-purpose flour*
½ teaspoon baking soda
½ teaspoon salt
1 large egg
2 tablespoons sugar
½ cup plain yogurt
½ cup smooth applesauce
1 teaspoon vanilla extract
*4 tablespoons (½ stick) unsalted butter,
    melted and cooled*
2 cups sliced bananas, for garnish
Confectioners' sugar
*Warm maple
    syrup*

1. Sift together the flour, baking soda, and salt into a medium-size mixing bowl.

2. In a small bowl, lightly beat the egg with the sugar, then stir in the yogurt, applesauce, vanilla, and 2 tablespoons of the melted butter.

3. Add the liquid ingredients to the flour mixture and stir until just moistened. The batter should have the consistency of thick cream with some lumps. Do not overmix.

4. Heat a large griddle or 2 large non-stick skillets over medium-high heat, then brush lightly with some of the remaining melted butter. Gently drop the batter into the skillets by heaping tablespoonfuls, 2 inches apart. Cook until the undersides are golden brown and bubbles are breaking on top, about 1½ minutes. Turn and cook 1½ minutes longer on the other side. Keep the pancakes warm in a low oven as you cook the rest of the batter.

5. Divide the pancakes among warmed plates and top with the bananas. Sprinkle with confectioners' sugar and serve with warm maple syrup.

BANANA PANCAKES

YIELD: 4 SERVINGS

Intensely flavorful and satisfying, these banana pancakes, strewn with crunchy roasted peanuts, remind me of a wonderful breakfast I had in Hawaii. Serve them with sliced bananas and Lemon and Honey Butter (see Index) to your kids; they will adore them. Another marvelous topping is Gingered Pineapple Syrup (see Index). Be sure to use ripe to slightly overripe bananas in your pancakes for the best flavor. You may substitute toasted pecans, walnuts, or macadamias for the peanuts.

3 medium, ripe bananas

1 tablespoon fresh lemon juice

1¼ cups unbleached all-purpose flour

2 tablespoons sugar

4 teaspoons baking powder

¾ teaspoon salt

2 large eggs

1 cup milk

6 tablespoons (¾ stick) unsalted butter,
    melted and cooled

1 teaspoon vanilla extract

⅓ cup roasted unsalted peanuts,
    coarsely chopped

Confectioners' sugar

Warm maple syrup

1. Peel 2 of the bananas, halve them lengthwise, and slice crosswise ¼-inch thick. (There should be about 1 cup of banana.) In a small bowl, toss the banana slices with the lemon juice and set aside.

2. Sift together the flour, sugar, baking powder, and salt into a medium-size mixing bowl.

3. In another medium-size bowl, lightly beat the eggs, then stir in the milk, 2 tablespoons of the melted butter, the vanilla, peanuts, and bananas.

4. Add the banana mixture to the flour mixture and stir until just moistened. The batter should have the consistency of thick cream with some lumps. Do not overmix.

5. Heat a large griddle or 2 large non-stick skillets over medium-high heat, then brush lightly with some of the remaining melted butter. Drop 2 tablespoons of batter onto the griddle for each pancake, 2 inches apart. Cook until the undersides are golden brown and bubbles are breaking on top, about 1½ minutes. Turn and cook 1½ minutes longer on the other side. Keep warm in a low oven as you cook the rest of the batter.

6. Slice the remaining banana. Divide the pancakes among warmed plates and top with the sliced banana. Sprinkle with confectioners' sugar and serve with maple syrup.

VARIATION

CRISPY BANANA-PEANUT WAFFLES: Make the waffle batter as for the pancakes, but increase the flour to 1½ cups, and substitute ⅓ cup melted solid vegetable shortening (such as Crisco) for the melted butter. Pour about ½ cup of batter into a very hot buttered waffle iron. Bake until the waffles are golden and crisp. Makes 6 waffles.

By buying them ripe and letting them rot just a little, bananas are sheer heaven . . .

—COLETTE

HOW TO PICK A MELON

A ripe melon wedge accompanied by a slice of lemon makes a perfect breakfast starter. When buying a melon (other than watermelon), pick it up and sniff the stem end. If it doesn't smell sweet and perfumy, it isn't. The stem end should give to gentle pressure.

If your market is selling cut melon in addition to whole, inspect the cut ones first (look for deeply colored and crisp, juicy flesh), as the cut melons that were chosen for display were most likely culled from

the same batch as the whole ones.

If you can't find a ripe specimen, don't despair. Take the fruit home and keep it in a warm spot out of the sunlight (in an unlit oven, for example) for 2 to 3 days. The underripe fruit will gradually soften and develop fragrance, and the flesh inside will become juicy. Be patient: Don't cut into the fruit unless you are satisfied with its degree of ripeness. Once cut, the fruit will stop ripening.

LEMON CHEESE BLINTZES

YIELD: 5 SERVINGS

Blintzes are delicate egg-rich Eastern European pancakes rolled around a plain cheese filling and lightly fried. They are usually topped with some kind of fruit sauce, and maybe a dollop or two of sour cream. They are perfect at the brunch table, where they are at their glorious best with a steaming cup of coffee. The nice thing about blintzes is that you can leisurely assemble them during the weekend, wrap them individually in plastic, and store them in the freezer, where they will keep for months. When your mood strikes, just thaw and then cook a few. Even though I suggest a sour cherry compote as an

accompaniment, you may substitute Blueberry Sauce or Quince Butter (see Index) if you prefer it.

FILLING
$\frac{1}{2}$ *pound farmer cheese or pot cheese*
2 ounces cream cheese, at room temperature
1 egg, lightly beaten
1$\frac{1}{2}$ teaspoons finely grated lemon zest
1 teaspoon sugar
$\frac{1}{4}$ teaspoon vanilla extract

BLINTZ PANCAKES
2 eggs
1 cup milk
$\frac{2}{3}$ cup unbleached all-purpose flour
4 tablespoons ($\frac{1}{2}$ stick) unsalted butter, melted and cooled

COOKING AND SERVING
2 tablespoons unsalted butter
Sour Cherry Compote (page 338)
$\frac{3}{4}$ cup sour cream
Confectioners' sugar

1. To make the filling, place both types of cheese in a large mixing bowl and, using an electric mixer at medium speed, blend until they are smooth. Add the beaten egg, lemon zest, sugar, and vanilla to the cheese and blend until well combined. Cover and refrigerate until you are ready to assemble the blintzes.

2. To make the blintz pancakes, combine the eggs, milk, 3 tablespoons water, and the flour in a blender or food processor. Blend until the batter is well mixed, scraping down the sides of the bowl as necessary. Transfer the batter to a medium-size bowl. Stir in 2 tablespoons of the melted butter. Cover and let sit for 1 hour.

3. Heat a 6-inch nonstick omelet or crêpe pan over medium heat. Brush the pan lightly with some of the remaining melted butter and heat until the butter is hot but not smoking. Stir the batter and fill a ⅓-cup measure two-thirds full with batter. Lift the pan and add the batter. Quickly tip and rotate the pan to cover the bottom evenly with the batter. Return the pan to the heat and cook the pancake for about 45 seconds. Loosen the edges of the pancake with the tip of a knife, then slide the pancake onto a clean kitchen towel laid out on the counter.

4. Continue making the pancakes, taking care to stir the batter thoroughly each time before adding it to the pan. Stack and cover the cooled pancakes. Set aside at room temperature until ready to assemble.

5. To assemble the blintzes, place a pancake, browned side up, on a flat surface. Place 2 tablespoons of the filling in the center of the pancake. With the back of a spoon shape the filling into a 3-inch-long log across the pancake. Fold up the bottom of the pancake to cover the filling. Fold in the sides over the filling, then roll up the blintz to seal. Place the blintz on a large plate lined with waxed paper. Continue to assemble the remaining blintzes in the same manner.

6. To cook the blintzes, place 1 tablespoon of butter in each of 2 large skillets over medium-low heat. When the butter is hot, add 5 blintzes to each pan and pan-fry until the bottom of the blintzes are golden brown, about 2 minutes. Carefully turn the blintzes over and continue frying for 2 minutes longer.

7. Divide the blintzes among warmed plates. Spoon some Sour Cherry Compote over the blintzes and top with some sour cream. Lightly dust with confectioners' sugar and serve immediately.

CRANBERRY-PUMPKIN WAFFLES

YIELD: 4 SERVINGS

Two Native American foods blend in these thick, moist waffles that are just right for brisk autumn mornings. Indulge yourself by topping these waffles with a scoop of sour cream and a generous sprinkling of toasted sunflower seeds, raisins, and confectioners' sugar. Or simply serve them with Stewed Fruit or Orange-Flavored Honey (see Index). Slightly thinned with milk, this batter can be used for making pancakes as well.

2 cups unbleached all-purpose flour

2 tablespoons sugar

4 teaspoons baking powder

1 teaspoon salt

1 teaspoon ground cinnamon

1 teaspoon ground ginger

1½ cups milk

4 tablespoons (½ stick) unsalted butter

¼ cup solid vegetable shortening, preferably Crisco

2 large eggs

1 cup canned, puréed pumpkin

½ cup dried cranberries, plumped in hot water to cover for 10 minutes and drained

Melted butter, for buttering the waffle iron

1. Place the flour, sugar, baking powder, salt, and spices in a large mixing bowl and stir with a fork until blended.

2. Place the milk, butter, and shortening in a small saucepan and heat over low heat until the butter and shortening have melted. Cool slightly.

3. In a separate bowl, beat the eggs with the pumpkin purée. Stir in the cooled milk and shortening. Add to the dry ingredients and stir with a wooden spoon until well combined. Stir in the cranberries.

4. Preheat the waffle iron; this should take about 10 minutes.

5. Butter the preheated waffle iron and add about ½ cup batter. (It takes from ½ to ⅔ cup batter to make 1 waffle, depending on the size of your waffle iron.) Bake the waffles until they are golden and crisp. Serve hot.

ORANGE WAFFLES

YIELD: 4 SERVINGS

Incredibly moist and delicious, these orange-flavored waffles are fabulous for any breakfast or brunch. For breakfast, you can even add crumbled bacon to the batter, if you wish. To top these waffles off, serve them with Orange-Flavored Butter (see Index), warm maple syrup, and perhaps a pile of mixed fresh fruit. Topped with chocolate ice cream, they make an unusual and lovely dessert!

2¼ cups unbleached all-purpose
    flour
2 tablespoons sugar
4 teaspoons baking powder
1 teaspoon salt
1½ cups milk
6 tablespoons (¾ stick) unsalted butter
2 large eggs
2 tablespoons thawed frozen orange juice
    concentrate
1 tablespoon grated orange zest
Melted butter, for buttering the waffle
    iron

1. Place the flour, sugar, baking powder, and salt in a large mixing bowl and stir with a fork until blended.

2. Place the milk and butter in a small saucepan and heat over low heat until the butter has melted. Cool slightly.

3. In a separate bowl, beat the eggs with the orange juice concentrate and zest. Stir in the cooled milk and butter. Add to the dry ingredients, and stir with a wooden spoon until well combined.

4. Preheat the waffle iron; this should take about 10 minutes.

5. Butter the preheated waffle iron and add about ½ cup batter. (It takes from ½ to

¾ cup batter to make 1 waffle, depending on the size of your waffle iron.) Bake the waffles until they are golden and crisp. Serve hot.

UPSIDE-DOWN FRENCH TOAST WITH APPLE AND BANANA

YIELD: 8 SERVINGS

This French toast may remind you of a perfectly caramelized *tarte Tatin*, the luscious French upside-down apple tart. I like the idea of preparing the toast in advance by layering all the ingredients in one pan. When I'm ready to cook, all I have to do is pop the pan into the oven. This mode of advance preparation is ideal if you have a crowd over for brunch. The French toast will come out moist, succulent, and adorned with a fragrant mélange of apple and banana. Just serve it as is, without any additional fruit, butter, or syrup. For a super treat, use Apple-Cinnamon Bread (see Index) instead of challah, when you make this or any French toast.

APPLES

*C*risp sweet apples are wonderful with cheese, especially Gouda, Gruyère, and Cheddar. They hold their own against assertive foods, like game, smoked meat and fish, horseradish, cabbage, and wild mushrooms. But they can also be subtle enough to let delicacies such as scallops, shrimp, blueberries, and cream take center stage.

4 tart apples, such as McIntosh or
   Granny Smith

5 tablespoons fresh lemon juice

6 large ripe bananas

1 teaspoon ground cinnamon

1 teaspoon ground ginger

1/2 teaspoon ground cloves

1/2 teaspoon freshly grated nutmeg

6 tablespoons (3/4 stick) unsalted butter

1 cup (firmly packed) light brown sugar

2 tablespoons maple syrup

4 large eggs

1 cup milk

1 teaspoon vanilla extract

8 to 10 slices challah bread (1 inch thick)

1. Peel, core, and cut each apple into 3/4-inch-thick wedges. Place the apple wedges in a large mixing bowl and toss gently with the lemon juice to prevent discoloration. Peel the bananas, and slice them crosswise 3/4 inch thick. Add the bananas to the apples and toss to coat evenly with lemon juice. Sprinkle the cinnamon, ginger, cloves, and nutmeg over the fruits, and toss well to combine.

2. Melt 4 tablespoons of the butter in a large skillet over medium-high heat. Add the fruit and sauté until tender, about 30 seconds. Add the brown sugar and maple syrup and cook until the sugar is dissolved, 30 seconds longer. Remove from the heat.

3. Pour the contents into a lightly buttered 13 x 9-inch baking pan. In a medium-size bowl, beat the eggs, then stir in the milk and vanilla. Dip the bread slices into the egg mixture just to moisten (both sides), then place them over the fruit in a single layer in the pan, making sure to cover the fruit entirely. Pour any leftover egg mixture over the bread. Dot the bread with the remaining 2 tablespoons butter. Let the mixture sit for 10 minutes. (This can be prepared up to this point in advance, covered, and refrigerated overnight.)

4. Preheat the oven to 375°F.

5. Bake the French toast, uncovered, until the top is golden, 30 to 35 minutes. Cool for 5 minutes. Place a serving tray over the pan, and carefully turn them over to unmold the French toast. Spoon any syrup or fruit left in the pan over the bread, and serve at once.

BLUEBERRY ROLL

YIELD: 8 TO 10 SERVINGS

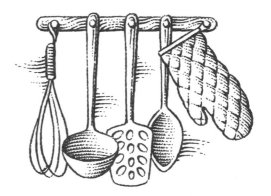

This moist, tender rolled biscuit, luxuriously filled with sweet berries, is easy and quick. Raspberries, blackberries, or thinly sliced plums are perfect substitutes for the blueberries. The fruit roll may be prepared a few hours in advance—or even the night before—and reheated in a 350°F oven for 10 minutes before serving. If you like, you can even serve blueberry roll for dessert with some thick cream.

2 cups fresh or thawed frozen blueberries

¼ cup plus 3 tablespoons granulated sugar

1 teaspoon fresh lemon juice

3½ cups unbleached all-purpose flour, or more if needed

2 teaspoons baking powder

2 teaspoons salt

½ cup solid vegetable shortening, preferably Crisco, chilled

1½ cups milk

4 tablespoons (½ stick) unsalted butter, melted

½ teaspoon ground cinnamon

1 tablespoon (firmly packed) light brown sugar

1. Preheat the oven to 425°F. Generously butter a 14 x 10-inch baking sheet.

2. Gently mix the blueberries with ¼ cup of the granulated sugar and the lemon juice. Set aside.

3. In a separate bowl, combine the flour, baking powder, salt, and the remaining 3 tablespoons granulated sugar. With a fork or pastry blender, cut in the shortening until the mixture resembles coarse meal. Add the milk and mix well with a fork until the dough is soft but not sticky. If the dough is too sticky, add a little flour, but no more than a tablespoon.

4. Turn out the dough onto a well-floured board and pat it into a rough rectangle. Gently roll it into a long rectangle (11 x 15 inches) about ⅜ inch thick. Brush the dough with half the melted butter and sprinkle with cinnamon. Spread the blueberries over the dough, leaving a 1½-inch border all around. Starting from a long side, roll up the dough like a jelly roll. Tuck the ends of the dough under the roll to prevent the filling from leaking out.

5. Transfer the blueberry roll to the prepared pan. Brush the roll with the remaining melted butter, and sprinkle with brown sugar. Bake for 35 minutes, or until golden brown. Garnish the roll with any blueberry drippings and serve warm.

LUXURIOUS SOFT SCRAMBLED EGGS

YIELD: 4 SERVINGS

Smoked trout and pear have an affinity for each other, and the combination is just delicious in scrambled eggs. Cream cheese lends a creamy, smooth consistency to this egg dish. If you prefer, substitute smoked salmon or fresh lump crabmeat for the trout and apple for the pear.

12 large eggs

2 tablespoons heavy (or whipping) cream

1/3 cup sliced scallions (white and green parts)

2 tablespoons unsalted butter

1 large pear, peeled, cored, and cubed (1/2-inch pieces)

6 ounces cream cheese, cubed (1/2-inch pieces), at room temperature

1/4 pound smoked trout, skin and bones removed, cut into small pieces

Salt and freshly ground black pepper

1. Combine the eggs, heavy cream, and sliced scallions in a large mixing bowl. Using a fork or wire whisk, beat the mixture until well blended.

2. Melt 1 teaspoon of the butter in a large nonstick skillet over medium-high heat. Add the pear and sauté until slightly soft, about 30 seconds. Transfer the pear to a plate.

3. Add the remaining butter to the pan and reduce the heat to medium-low. When the butter has melted, pour in the egg mixture. Cook, stirring gently with a rubber spatula, until the eggs are softly set but not runny, 3 to 4 minutes. Do not overcook. Scatter the cream cheese pieces evenly over the eggs, then immediately remove the pan from the heat.

4. Quickly fold in the sautéed pear and smoked trout, taking care not to break up the cream cheese too much. Season to taste with salt and pepper and serve at once.

SAUSAGE AND ORANGE MARMALADE OMELETS

YIELD: 2 SERVINGS

Brimming with cooked sausage and marmalade, these scrumptious omelets offer a pleasing contrast of savory and sweet flavors. You can use a good store-bought marmalade, but if you use Golden Marmalade your omelet will taste even better. For an easy variation, substitute ¼ cup of julienned ham (boiled or baked) or prosciutto for the cooked sausage.

¼ pound sausage meat or sweet Italian sausages, casings removed and meat crumbled

3 scallions, trimmed and sliced (white and green parts)

6 large eggs

Salt

Tabasco sauce

2 tablespoons unsalted butter

4 tablespoons Golden Marmalade (page 269) or orange marmalade

1. Heat a small nonstick skillet over medium-high heat. Add the sausage meat and cook until browned, 5 to 8 minutes. Drain off most of the fat. Stir in the scallions and cook until wilted, about 30 seconds. Remove from the heat and cover to keep the filling warm.

2. In a medium-size mixing bowl, beat the eggs with 2 tablespoons water, a pinch of salt, and a few drops of Tabasco sauce.

3. Heat a 6-inch nonstick omelet pan over medium heat. Quickly add 1 tablespoon butter and swirl it to coat the bottom and sides of the pan. Pour half of the beaten eggs into the pan. With a rubber spatula, stir the eggs in a circular motion as you shake the pan with the other hand to keep the uncooked eggs moving.

4. After a couple minutes, the eggs should be set on the bottom and the top should be creamy. Remove from the heat and spoon half the warm sausage filling onto one side of the eggs. Top the filling with 2 tablespoons of the marmalade.

5. Fold the other half of the eggs over the filling and slide the omelet onto a warmed plate. Keep in a low oven as you make a second omelet with the remaining ingredients. Serve immediately.

VARIATION

APPLE AND CHEESE OMELET: Substitute ¼ cup each applesauce (or sautéed diced apples) and grated cheese (Cheddar, Gruyère, smoked Gouda, or mozzarella) for the sausage and marmalade filling.

SKILLET APPLE FRITTATA

YIELD: 4 SERVINGS

A frittata is an Italian omelet, traditionally made with ham and cheese and baked. My version of the frittata is flavored with apple, and it

A TUSCAN BRUNCH

BELLINI COCKTAIL

✦

ASSORTED FRUIT MUFFINS
OR
TUSCAN GRAPE BREAD

✦

SKILLET APPLE FRITTATA

✦

CAPPUCCINO OR ESPRESSO

doesn't require any baking. Practically everything is combined in the skillet and cooked over the stove. And the leftovers (if you are lucky enough to have any) make great sandwiches!

8 large eggs
Salt and freshly ground black pepper
2 tablespoons unsalted butter
1 cup diced peeled apple (¼-inch cubes),
　　preferably Granny Smith
½ cup diced onion (¼-inch cubes)
½ cup diced green bell pepper (¼-inch cubes)
½ cup diced cooked ham (¼-inch cubes)
2 teaspoons minced garlic
1 cup diced mozzarella cheese (½-inch cubes)
¼ cup freshly grated Parmesan cheese

1. Beat the eggs with 2 tablespoons water and salt and pepper to taste. Set aside.

2. Heat a large nonstick skillet over medium-high heat. Quickly add the butter and swirl it around to coat the bottom and sides of the pan. Add the apple, onion, bell pepper, ham, and garlic. Cook, stirring often, until the vegetables are just tender, about 2 minutes. Season the mixture to taste with salt and pepper.

3. Pour the beaten eggs over the vegetables. Scatter the mozzarella over the eggs, and sprinkle with the Parmesan.

4. Cover the pan and cook over very low heat until the eggs are set and the cheese has melted, about 12 minutes. (If desired, pop the frittata under a preheated broiler until the top is golden brown, about 2 minutes.) Cut the frittata into wedges and serve at once.

CRANBERRY-APPLE CORNCAKES

YIELD: 4 SERVINGS

On cold mornings, I enjoy serving these savory corncakes with sausage. If you like making your own sausage, try the Pork and Lamb Sausages with Apricots (see Index; they're well worth the effort!) Cranberry-Apple Corncakes are also a good side dish with pork or poultry dishes. Leftovers can be crumbled and used to stuff Cornish hens or chickens.

2½ tablespoons unsalted butter, plus extra
    for serving
½ large Granny Smith apple, peeled, cored,
    and diced (¼-inch cubes)
¼ cup fresh or frozen cranberries, coarsely
    chopped
⅓ cup chopped onion
3 teaspoons sugar
¾ cup fine yellow cornmeal
¼ cup unbleached all-purpose flour
½ teaspoon baking powder
½ teaspoon baking soda
¼ teaspoon ground ginger
1 large egg
¾ cup milk
½ cup grated Cheddar cheese

1. Melt 1½ tablespoons of the butter in a medium-size skillet over medium heat. Add the apple, cranberries, and onion and sauté until soft, about 2 minutes. Stir in 1 teaspoon of the sugar and set aside to cool.

2. Combine the cornmeal, flour, baking powder, baking soda, ginger, and remaining 2 teaspoons sugar in a large bowl. Make a well in the center.

3. In a small bowl, beat the egg, then stir in the milk, cheese, and the cooled sautéed fruits. Add this mixture to the dry ingredients and stir with a fork until just moistened.

4. Melt the remaining 1 tablespoon butter and use it to lightly butter a hot griddle or the bottom of a hot skillet. Drop the batter by heaping tablespoonfuls onto the griddle. Cook the corncakes over medium heat until the undersides are golden, about 2 minutes. Turn them gently, then cook until the other side is golden. Serve immediately with butter or keep warm in a low oven until serving.

RASPBERRY BUTTER

YIELD: ½ CUP

Preserves and softened butter are all you need to make a delightful fruit-flavored butter that will instantly glorify warm toast, waffles, biscuits, or muffins. If you wish to vary the flavoring, substitute another favorite fruit preserve. This butter can be stored, covered, in the refrigerator for up to 1 week or frozen for up to 3 months.

8 tablespoons (1 stick) unsalted butter,
    at room temperature
2 tablespoons raspberry preserves, preferably
    seedless
Pinch of salt
1 tablespoon framboise (raspberry brandy)
    or crème de cassis (optional)

Combine the butter and preserves in a mixing bowl and beat with a wooden spoon until light and fluffy. Then slowly beat in the salt and brandy until smooth. Transfer to a crock and serve immediately or refrigerate until ready to use. (If refrigerated or frozen, bring the raspberry butter to room temperature and lighten it up by beating it with an electric mixer just before serving.)

CALVADOS BUTTER

YIELD: ½ CUP

The homey perfumes of the apples and cinnamon in this lush butter are almost like the autumns of childhood distilled. Enjoy this spread as it melts over a stack of steaming-hot pancakes. Calvados Butter can be stored, covered, in the refrigerator for up to 1 week or in the freezer for up to 3 months.

8 tablespoons (1 stick) unsalted butter, at
    room temperature
1 tablespoon thawed frozen apple juice
    concentrate
1 tablespoon Calvados or other apple brandy
½ teaspoon ground cinnamon
Pinch of salt

Place the butter in a mixing bowl and beat with a wooden spoon until light and fluffy. Slowly beat in the apple juice concentrate, Calvados, cinnamon, and salt and con-

tinue beating until smooth. Transfer to a crock and serve immediately or refrigerate until ready to use. (If refrigerated or frozen, bring the butter to room temperature and lighten it up by beating with an electric mixer just before serving.)

LEMON AND HONEY BUTTER

YIELD: ½ CUP

To wake up your taste buds, try this zingy butter over your toasted muffins or scones. Store the butter, covered, in the refrigerator for up to 1 week, or freeze it for up to 3 months.

8 tablespoons (1 stick) unsalted butter, at
    room temperature
¼ cup honey
1½ teaspoons finely grated lemon zest
2 tablespoons fresh lemon juice
Pinch of salt

Combine the butter, honey, and lemon zest in a mixing bowl and beat with a wooden spoon until light and fluffy. Slowly beat in the lemon juice and salt until smooth. Transfer to a crock and serve immediately or refrigerate until ready to use. (If refrigerated or frozen, bring the butter to room temperature and lighten it up by beating it with an electric mixer just before serving.)

IDEAS FOR BREAKFAST TOASTS

APPLE-CHEDDAR TOAST: *Top half a bagel or a slice of rye bread with thin slices of apple, tomato, and Cheddar cheese. Pop the bagel under a preheated broiler. Broil until the cheese melts.*

NECTARINE-RICOTTA TOAST: *Blend ½ cup ricotta cheese, 1 tablespoon toasted sliced almonds, 1 tablespoon honey, and a pinch of freshly grated nutmeg. Spread the cheese mixture on slices of toast, then top with fresh nectarine (or peach) slices .*

MAPLE-GLAZED BANANA ON RAISIN TOAST: *Heat 1 tablespoon each butter and maple syrup in a small sauté pan. Add 1 sliced banana and cook over low heat until it is glazed with the syrup. Spread slices of raisin toast with cream cheese, then top with the glazed bananas. Sprinkle with toasted chopped pecans.*

ORANGE-FLAVORED HONEY

YIELD: ½ CUP

Enticingly fragrant with orange flavors, this quickly made honey is a welcome variation on flavored butters. It tastes great drizzled over plain yogurt and crunchy granola. You can even warm it up and serve it as a topping for your favorite waffles or pancakes. Orange-blossom honey is available in health-food stores and gourmet shops.

½ cup orange-blossom honey
1 teaspoon finely grated orange zest
Pinch of salt

Place the honey, orange zest, and salt in a small bowl and whisk until thoroughly blended. Transfer to a crock and serve.

GINGERED PINEAPPLE SYRUP

YIELD: 1 CUP

Gingered Pineapple Syrup is a light, smooth topping with a mild ginger flavor. It is outstanding drizzled over waffles, pancakes, or ice cream. It may be kept in the refrigerator for up to 1 month and reheated as needed. Feel free to substitute pear for the pineapple or light corn syrup for the maple syrup.

   1 cup chopped fresh pineapple
   1 cup maple syrup
   2 teaspoons finely grated peeled fresh ginger

1. Place the pineapple, maple syrup, and grated ginger in a blender. Process until the mixture is finely puréed.

2. Pour the mixture into a small saucepan. Simmer over low heat until the syrup is infused with the ginger and aromatic, 2 to 3 minutes.

3. Strain the syrup, pressing on the pulp to extract as much liquid as possible. Discard the pulp and serve the syrup at once or refrigerate and reheat before serving.

VARIATIONS

GINGERED LEMON SYRUP: Substitute 1 cup fresh lemon juice for the chopped pineapple and ³/₄ cup sugar for the maple syrup.

LIME SYRUP: Substitute 1 cup fresh lime juice for the chopped pineapple, 1 cup sugar for the maple syrup, and 2 teaspoons finely grated lime zest for the ginger.

BLUEBERRY SYRUP

YIELD: 2 PINTS

Dousing French toast, waffles, or pancakes in deep-purple blueberry syrup on a cold January morning seems an ideal way to invoke memories of summer Sundays. This flavored syrup is also a good base for milkshakes and sodas. Fresh or frozen raspberries, blackberries, or strawberries make good substitutes for the blueberries.

   4 cups fresh or frozen blueberries
   1¹/₂ cups sugar

1. Follow the steps on page 268 to sterilize 2 pint canning bottles. Sterilize the lids according to the manufacturer's instructions.

2. Combine the berries with 2 cups water in a large saucepan. Bring the mixture to a full, rolling boil over high heat. Boil, stirring constantly, for 10 minutes.

3. Strain the mixture through a chinois or a sieve lined with a double layer of cheesecloth into a bowl. Pour an additional ¹/₂ cup water over the berries in the sieve and press on the berries to extract as much liquid as possible. Discard the solids.

4. Return the liquid to a clean saucepan. Add the sugar and bring the liquid to a full

boil. Reduce the heat to low and simmer, stirring constantly, until the syrup begins to thicken, 10 to 12 minutes. Do not overcook or the mixture will jell. Skim the foam, if necessary.

5. Pour the syrup into the hot sterilized bottles and seal. This syrup will keep for up to 1 month in the refrigerator.

BLUEBERRY SAUCE

YIELD: ABOUT 1 ½ CUPS

Here's a delectable topping for cheese blintzes, pancakes, waffles, or any breakfast treat that would benefit from a fruity sauce—even fresh fruit salad.

1¾ cups fresh or frozen blueberries
¼ cup granulated sugar
3 tablespoons confectioners'
sugar
1 tablespoon fresh
lemon juice

1. Combine all the ingredients in a small saucepan. (If the berries are frozen, add 1 tablespoon water.)

2. Bring the berries to a boil over medium-high heat, stirring frequently. Reduce the heat to low and cook for 2 minutes, crushing some of the berries with a fork. Remove the pan from the heat and let cool slightly. Serve warm.

FRUIT BUTTERS, SYRUPS, AND OTHER TOPPINGS

With breakfast, I always try to serve fruit butters, spreads, syrups, compotes, and the like. In my opinion, they are essential. Warm muffins, pancakes, and waffles just wouldn't taste the same without the sweet and lovely finishing touch fruit toppings provide.

The recipes included here are but the tip of the topping iceberg. They are based on fruit in one form or another, and the results are sweet elixirs packed with the very essence of fruit. They also make perfect toppings for ice cream, cake, and other desserts.

The procedures are adaptable to almost any fruit. Don't be reluctant to experiment. You will, I'm sure, find even more ways to use these excellent "sweet seasonings."

SOUR CHERRY COMPOTE

YIELD: 2 CUPS

Although you could use fresh sour cherries to make this topping, I normally don't. They have a high acid content and require quite a bit of sugar to balance their tartness. Less assertive (and more convenient), canned pitted sour cherries are more appropriate. Be sure to use the water-packed variety. If sour cherries packed in syrup are all you can find, halve the amount of sugar in the recipe. Try it over ice cream, pound cake, or poached apples or pears.

1 can (16 ounces) pitted sour cherries
    in water
2/3 cup plus 1 tablespoon confectioners'
    sugar
1 1/2 teaspoons cornstarch
1/4 teaspoon ground cinnamon

1. Drain the cherries, reserving the packing liquid (or syrup).

2. Combine the confectioners' sugar, cornstarch, and cinnamon in a small saucepan, and stir in the cherry liquid, mix-

ing well. Bring the mixture to a boil over medium-high heat and add the cherries. Reduce the heat to low and simmer, stirring often, until the mixture thickens, about 2 minutes. Serve warm.

BLUEBERRY-WALNUT SPREAD

YIELD: 1 1/2 CUPS

Neufchâtel cheese, with its mild flavor and smooth, creamy texture, is similar to cream cheese. But neufchâtel has a third less fat. This slightly sweet spread is wonderful on crackers, bagels, scones, toasted pita, and even raw fruits and vegetables. Chopped dried apricots, cranberries, or cherries can easily substitute for the blueberries.

1/2 cup dried blueberries
1/4 cup port
1/4 cup white grape juice
1 package (1/2 pound) Neufchâtel cheese,
    at room temperature
1/4 cup chopped toasted walnuts or pecans
    (for toasting instructions, see page 64)
1 teaspoon grated lemon zest
Pinch of salt

1. Bring the blueberries, port, and grape juice to a boil in a small saucepan over high heat. Reduce the heat to low and simmer

until the berries are plump and the liquid has reduced to about 1 tablespoon, about 5 minutes. Remove the pan from the heat, and let the mixture cool.

2. With a wooden spoon or fork, stir together the cheese, nuts, lemon zest, and salt in a medium-size bowl. Add the berries and mix until the spread is well combined. Serve at room temperature.

DATE SPREAD

YIELD: 1 ½ CUPS

This spread is a pleasing merger of sweet and tart tastes with a hint of sunny rum. It makes an outstanding spread on rice cakes, toasted bagels, muffins, or scones. Also, try using it as a frosting for fruit breads or cakes. Stored in a jar or plastic container, it will keep for at least 2 weeks in the refrigerator. You may substitute prunes for the dates, and 1 teaspoon ground cinnamon for the rum.

¼ pound pitted dates
1 tablespoon dark rum
2 teaspoons fresh lime juice
1 package (½ pound) Neufchâtel cheese,
    at room temperature

1. Combine the dates with ½ cup water in a small saucepan and bring to a boil.

Reduce the heat to low and simmer until the dates are very soft and the mixture thickens, about 4 minutes. Remove from the heat and cool slightly.

2. Purée the dates with the rum and lime juice in a food processor. Add the cheese and blend until the mixture is smooth and fluffy, stopping occasionally to scrape the sides of the bowl with a rubber spatula. Transfer the spread to a plastic container, cover, and refrigerate until ready to use. Bring to room temperature before serving.

VARIATION

FRUITED CREAM CHEESE: Mix ½ pound Neufchâtel cheese with 1 small grated apple, ¼ cup chopped raisins, ¼ cup chopped walnuts, and 2 tablespoons honey. Balance the sweetness of the spread with a few drops of fresh lemon juice, if desired.

PASSION-FRUIT FROSTING

YIELD: ¾ CUP

Frosting made from passion fruit is sublime. Enjoy it spread over warm muffins and scones, or as a terrific icing on Spiced Apple Cake (see Index). Refrigerated, the frosting keeps for up to 1 month. Bring it to room temperature before using.

2 passion fruits

4 tablespoons (½ stick) unsalted butter, at
   room temperature

¾ cup confectioners' sugar

1. Place a sieve over a small bowl. Cut each passion fruit in half while holding it over the bowl to catch the juices. Scoop the flesh into the sieve. Work the seeds against the sieve with the back of a wooden spoon to extract as much juice as possible. (There should be about 4 teaspoons of passion fruit juice.)

2. In a separate bowl, beat the butter and the confectioners' sugar until smooth and creamy. Gradually beat in the passion fruit juice. Use the frosting at once or cover and refrigerate. (If refrigerated, bring to room temperature and beat with an electric mixer to lighten, just before serving.)

PASSION FRUIT

With a delightful fragrance suggesting guava, lemon, and pineapple, passion fruit must be one of the most heavenly fruits on this planet. And true to its sensuous name, its intense, musky fragrance is apt to stir passion in anyone who sniffs it (it has that effect on me, anyhow).

The fruit is native to Brazil and grows on vines in subtropical zones around the world. If you live in Hawaii, chances are you'll find this fruit (called lilikoi there) hanging in your own (or your neighbor's) back-yard. Another likely place is Florida, where it is often sold by its Portuguese name, maracujá. According to one story, this fruit got its exotic name from early Jesuit missionaries in South America who saw in the parts of its beautiful flower the hammer and nails used in the crucifixion. Another story says that St. Francis of Assisi dubbed it passion fruit because he saw visions of its flowering vine growing on the cross.

Although passion fruit is finally showing up in American markets, it is still sporadic and pricey, since most of it is flown in from distant places. Egg sized, it can be identified by its leathery blackish-purple (or yellowish in certain varieties) skin. If a fruit looks wrinkled, it's a good sign that it's fully ripe. Choose the largest fruits you can and shake each piece to find out whether it contains a lot of juice (you should be able to hear it slosh around). If they haven't yet developed wrinkles, store the fruits at room temperature until they are wrinkly all over and fragrant. After that, they can be refrigerated up to 10 days. You can freeze the whole fruits in plastic bags. Defrost before opening the fruits.

The best way to eat a passion fruit is to slice it in half while holding it over a small bowl to catch the juices. When cut into, it reveals a juicy, vibrant yellow pulp thick with black edible teardrop-shaped seeds. Its wonderful tart-sweet flesh will remind you of the flavors of lime juice and honey combined, while the crunchy seeds add a pleasing textural counterpoint. Scoop out the flesh, and eat it with a spoon, seeds and all. If you don't enjoy the seeds, just press the pulp through a sieve to extract the juice. Strained frozen fruit purée is also available at very reasonable prices in Hispanic markets and some gourmet shops.

One passion fruit yields about 1 tablespoon of intensely flavored pulp. The pulp of one or two of these small fruits is often enough to endow a dish with a hint of the tropics. Use passion fruit as you would citrus fruits: in vinaigrettes, syrups, sauces, beverages, sorbets, mousses, and the like.

SMOOTHIES & SPIRITS

Fruits figure in all kinds of drinks, and just as in cooking, they really allow us to create imaginative concoctions. The complexities and nuances of taste that we have come to expect in food are just as important in beverages. Any one-dimensional taste, such as pure sweetness is boring. Adding a little acidity, perhaps a squeeze of fresh lime or lemon juice, and a sweet drink suddenly perks up. Add sliced or puréed fruit or fizzy carbonated water, and it takes on a whole new personality.

In this chapter, you'll find basic drinks and not-so-ordinary sippers. From great eye-openers (fruit juices) to rich indulgences (smoothies and shakes) to sophisticated cocktails and punches, I've included drinks to please every palate and every mood. Looking for the ultimate beverage thirst quencher? Try a pitcher of Ginger Lemonade or Tamarind Nectar. Or, warm your body and spirit with mugs of Hot Lemon Rumba or Hot Apple Pie Drink. Most of these drinks are alcohol-free. All are delicious to sip whether on a lazy summer afternoon or in the chill of a winter evening. Cheers!

BREAKFAST ENERGIZERS

Besides the usual orange or grapefruit juice, a whole range of other fruit drinks can boost your energy level, which makes them especially suited for breakfast. Following are some recipes for fruit juices, shakes, smoothies, and the like.

TWO FLOWERS JUICE

YIELD: 2 SERVINGS

Combining fruit and vegetable juices may sound peculiar, but the results are truly refreshing. I've enjoyed many variations: carrot and orange juice, beet and pineapple juice, and even carrot, beet, and orange juice. Get out your juicer and try this pairing of carrot and pineapple juices. It'll get your juices going in the morning. You may substitute apple juice for pineapple juice.

1 cup pineapple juice
1 cup carrot juice
Crushed ice
2 thin slices peeled fresh ginger (optional)

1. Combine the carrot and pineapple juices in a small pitcher, stirring well.

2. Fill 2 tall glasses with crushed ice, and add the juice. Garnish with ginger, if desired. Serve at once.

FOUR FRUIT SMOOTHIE

YIELD: 1 ½ QUARTS, OR 6 TO 8 SERVINGS

This delicious drink, made with four different types of fruits, has a distinctive floral overtone. It is full-bodied, and has a beautiful pink hue with tiny black dots floating in it. If kiwi is unavailable, substitute fresh strawberries. The juice will keep for a couple of days in the refrigerator; reblend it before serving.

1 cup chopped fresh pineapple, partially frozen

2 ripe bananas, peeled and cut into ½-inch pieces, partially frozen

3 kiwi, peeled and quartered, partially frozen

1 cup well-chilled, fresh orange juice

½ cup well-chilled Simple Syrup (see recipe page 348)

3 tablespoons grenadine syrup, preferably homemade (see box, this page)

1½ cups ice water

6 to 8 whole fresh strawberries, for garnish

6 to 8 slices kiwi, for garnish

1. Working in 2 batches, combine the frozen pineapple, banana, kiwis, and orange juice in a blender. Blend at high speed until smooth.

2. Transfer the puréed fruit mixture to a large pitcher and stir in the simple syrup, grenadine syrup, and water.

3. Pour the smoothie into champagne or balloon wine glasses. Garnish the rim of each glass with a whole strawberry and kiwi slice, if desired.

GRENADINE SYRUP

*Y*ou can make a very flavorful pomegranate syrup by combining ½ cup each pomegranate juice and sugar in a small saucepan and simmering the mixture, stirring until the sugar is dissolved, for 5 minutes. Cool then seal in a glass jar. The syrup will keep indefinitely in the refrigerator. It comes in handy for flavoring and coloring drinks and sauces.

SMOOTHIE BLUES

YIELD: 4 CUPS, OR 4 SERVINGS

I have dubbed this drink *smoothie blues*, not because it cheers me up when I'm down in the dumps—although it probably would—but because of its bluish hue and because its flavors remind me of the tropics. Guava nectar is available fresh at health food stores or canned in supermarkets.

⅔ cup frozen blueberries

1 banana, peeled, coarsely chopped and partially frozen

6 large fresh strawberries, coarsely chopped and partially frozen

2 cups well-chilled guava nectar

4 whole fresh strawberries, for garnish

1. Working in 2 batches, combine all

the ingredients in a blender. Process on high speed until smooth.

2. Pour the smoothie into champagne or balloon wine glasses. Garnish the rim of each glass with a whole strawberry, if desired.

TIPS FOR PERFECT SHAKES

✦ For maximum nutritional benefit, use fresh fruit and fresh juice whenever possible.

✦ To get more juice from citrus fruits, leave them at room temperature for 30 minutes before juicing.

✦ Freezing chunks of fruit and using them in place of ice cubes is a good way to keep shakes cold without diluting them.

✦ It's usually better to crush ice cubes a bit before putting them in the blender.

✦ Smoothies and other fruit shakes will separate, especially if a dairy base has been added, so serve them immediately or plan to reblend before serving.

JACKFRUIT DELIGHT

YIELD: ABOUT 3 CUPS, OR 3 TO 4 SERVINGS

Jackfruit lends a wonderfully sweet and fragrant flavor to this refreshing drink. If you prefer, you can substitute canned litchees or 1½ cups chopped fresh (peeled) peaches or cantaloupe for the jackfruit.

1 can (20 ounces) jackfruit in light syrup, drained and partially frozen
1½ cups white grape juice, partially frozen
⅔ cup well-chilled grapefruit juice
½ cup well-chilled orange juice
3 tablespoons honey
Fresh mint sprigs, for garnish (optional)

1. Working in 2 batches, combine the jackfruit, fruit juices, and honey in a blender. Blend at high speed until smooth.

2. Pour into parfait glasses or short-stemmed cocktail glasses. Garnish with fresh mint sprigs, and serve with a straw.

JACKFRUIT

One of the world's largest tropical fruits, jackfruit is closely related to the breadfruit. Huge and rather strange-looking, a jackfruit can weigh up to 100 pounds. It has a tough, rough, green rind that is covered with pointy nubs. The flesh has an inimitable aromatic flavor. It is yellow and juicy and divided into numerous sections, with pods containing white seeds that look like giant beans. Chunks of jackfruit are sold by street vendors in Thailand as snacks. Only available in this country canned and packed in syrup, jackfruit can be found in stores carrying Indian, Southeast Asian, or Latin American products. In Asia, both the ripe and unripe fruit is used in cooking. When underripe, the pulp and seeds are added to curried dishes or are baked and served as a vegetable. Extremely sweet when ripe, it can be eaten raw or sweetened and used in desserts. As a child, I used to enjoy munching on the dried, roasted seeds; they taste just like chestnuts.

BLENDER BREAKFAST

YIELD: 4 SERVINGS

This light, delicious drink is like a milkshake, but is nutritious enough for a lunch substitute on busy days. As a bonus, it provides lots of energy without a lot of calories.

½ pint (1 cup) fresh strawberries, hulled, coarsely chopped, and partially frozen

1 banana, peeled, coarsely chopped, and partially frozen

1 cup unsweetened pineapple juice, frozen

2 cups well-chilled milk

2 tablespoons honey

2 fresh pineapple rings, halved, for garnish

4 whole fresh strawberries, for garnish

1. Working in 2 batches, combine the strawberries, banana, pineapple juice, cold milk, and honey in a blender. Blend at high speed until smooth.

2. Pour into chilled tall glasses and garnish each serving with half a pineapple ring and a whole strawberry.

APPLE-BANANA LASSI

YIELD: ABOUT 3 ½ CUPS, OR 2 TO 3 SERVINGS

Lassi is a thin, cooling yogurt drink served throughout India—and in Indian restaurants all over the world. It can be seasoned with just salt and pepper and served as an appetizer or sweetened with sugar and chunks of fresh fruit. Easy to make at home, this recipe for lassi uses a delicious combination of apple and banana. Tonic water adds extra fizz and produces a frothy, creamy drink. Ripe mango, peach, guava, or persimmon are also excellent for making lassi.

½ cup well-chilled plain low-fat
     yogurt
2 cups well-chilled tonic water
2 tablespoons honey
1 medium apple, such as Golden Delicious,
     peeled, cored, and cut into small
     chunks
½ ripe banana, peeled and cut into
     small chunks
⅛ teaspoon ground cinnamon, plus extra,
     for garnish (optional)
Ice, for serving

1. Working in 2 batches, combine the ingredients through the cinnamon in a blender. Blend at high speed until smooth.

2. Fill tall glasses with ice, and add the lassi. Garnish with a sprinkling of ground cinnamon, if desired. Serve immediately.

PAPAYA SMOOTHIE

YIELD: 3 CUPS, OR 2 TO 3 SERVINGS

There is a hot dog stand around the corner from one of my neighborhood movie houses that is known citywide for the delicious papaya shakes it serves. Sipping one after the movies is one of my cherished habits. Inspired by that drink, I developed this exotic papaya smoothie. Light and soothing, this fruit drink has a pleasing pale orange color. It can also be served as an unusual dessert after a light meal.

1 small papaya, peeled, seeded, and coarsely
     chopped
½ cup well-chilled milk
⅔ cup well-chilled Simple Syrup (recipe
     follows)
2 tablespoons fresh lime juice
1 cup crushed ice
Fresh mint sprigs, for garnish (optional)

1. Working in 2 batches, combine all of the ingredients through the ice in a blender. Blend at high speed until smooth.

2. Pour into milkshake glasses, garnish with fresh mint, and serve with a straw.

POPULAR THIRST QUENCHERS AROUND THE GLOBE

AGUAS FRESCAS: (Mexico and other Latin American countries) Refreshing, sweet, water-based drinks flavored with tamarind, hibiscus buds, strawberries, melon, or other fresh tropical fruits.

ARAK: (Lebanon) A water-based thirst quencher flavored with pomegranate molasses.

BATIDOS: (Cuba, Mexico, and some Caribbean Islands) Light versions of milkshakes made with a selection of fresh tropical fruits such as mango, papaya, passion fruit, or soursop and ice.

BINGS: (China) Fruit shakes made with sugar syrup, ice cream (or coconut milk), and chopped fresh fruit served over crushed ice.

BUKO: (Philippines) A cooler made by freezing a mixture of the clear water from a green coconut (one that's not fully mature and still in its shell) with the jellylike flesh lining the shell, water, and sugar. The frozen mixture is then shaved into tall glasses and served with a spoon and straw.

CITRON PRESSE: (France) Freshly squeezed lemon juice (or blood orange juice in Sicily) with sugar and mineral water (or sparkling water) served on the side.

COMPOTES: (Ukraine) Made from cooked cherries and grapes and served chilled. Cold borscht made from beets, is thinned with orange juice and topped with sour cream.

GARAPINA: (Latin America) Made from pineapple peelings covered with hot water, soaked for a day, then strained. It's sweetened and zipped up with a bit of lime or lemon juice, and served chilled.

GUYBANO: (Philippines) Soursop meat blended until smooth with water and sugar.

HALO-HALO: (Philippines) A sundae-like concoction layered with strands of purple yam, white beans, jackfruit, cubes of coconut gelatin, bits of plantain, condensed milk, shaved ice, and a scoop of ice cream.

HOSAF: (Turkey) Whole grapes or chunks of fresh fruit mixed with iced water and sugar. Served with a spoon and straw.

LASSI: (India) Cold sweetened yogurt drink, similar to a milkshake, made with fresh fruit purées. Also popular are refreshing drinks made with pomegranate juice mixed with mango, guava, coconut, and pineapple juices.

MORISONANDO: (The Dominican Republic) Sweetened orange juice blended with cold milk.

NAM MANOA: (Thailand) A cool, refreshing lime drink made with salt, served over ice.

NUOC XI MUOI: (Vietnam) Crushed salted preserved plums mixed with sugar syrup, then served over crushed ice.

PLANTER'S PUNCH: (The Caribbean) Popular rum and fruit juice drink.

SHORBA DIL MANDARINE: (Morocco) Clementine juice with sparkling mineral water.

VITAMINAS: (Brazil) The Brazilian version of smoothies, made with cold milk and fresh tropical fruit such as mango, cherimoya, or even avocado blended together until liquefied and frothy.

Friends are like melons.
Shall I tell you why?
To find one good,
You must a hundred try.

—CLAUDE MERMET

Simple Syrup

YIELD: 4 CUPS

Keep a batch of this syrup in your refrigerator to use for sweetening fruit-based drinks, iced teas, and sorbets. It will also come in handy for poaching, macerating fruits, and moistening cakes. Refrigerated, it will keep indefinitely.

2½ cups sugar
2½ cups warm water

1. Combine the sugar and water in a medium-size saucepan; stir until the sugar has dissolved. Bring the mixture to a boil over high heat, and continue boiling, uncovered, for 2 minutes. Remove from the heat and let cool.

2. Pour into a clean glass jar or bottle. Store, tightly covered, in the refrigerator.

CHERIMOYA VITAMINA

YIELD: ABOUT 3 CUPS, OR 3 TO 4 SERVINGS

Brazilians call their milk shakes *vitaminas* for a good reason: These beverages are packed with vitamins from fruits and dairy ingredients. Made of cherimoya and yogurt, this smooth and nourishing concoction is a very pleasurable way to get your vitamins. Feel free to substitute milk or other fresh fruits, such as mango or peach, or a combination of pear and banana.

1 large ripe cherimoya (about 1 pound)
½ cup well-chilled plain low-fat yogurt
⅓ cup well-chilled fresh orange juice
2 tablespoons honey
½ cup crushed ice
Tonic water, for thinning (optional)
Fresh mint sprigs, for garnish (optional)

1. Peel the cherimoya and break it up into small chunks, removing all the seeds. (There should be about 1½ cups of cherimoya pulp.)

2. Working in 2 batches, put the cheri-

moya, yogurt, orange juice, honey, and crushed ice in a blender. Blend at high speed until smooth. Add a little tonic water, if desired, to obtain your preferred consistency.

3. Pour into tall glasses, garnish with fresh mint, and serve with a straw.

VARIATION

FRESH FRUIT PARFAIT: Purée mango or peach with the yogurt, orange juice, and honey. In a parfait glass, layer the mixture with cubed mango (or peeled peaches) and blackberries. Top with your favorite granola mix.

SUMMER COOLERS

Icy cold summertime beverages are a refreshing way to endure the heat. The following thirst quenchers are quick and easy to make, and appropriate to serve any time of the day. Prepare a glass for yourself or have a pitcher ready to enjoy with family and friends.

PASSION FRUIT COLADA

YIELD: 1 QUART, OR 4 TO 6 SERVINGS

Here is my nonalcoholic version of piña colada. For a different tropical flavor, I use passion fruit sorbet, which is readily available at my local supermarket. If you prefer to use canned

sweetened coconut cream (like Coco Lopez) instead of the unsweetened variety, omit the simple syrup and add ¼ cup water to the beverage. This shake should be made just before serving as it loses volume and froth if allowed to stand.

2 cups passion fruit sorbet

1⅓ cups well-chilled canned unsweetened coconut milk, well stirred

½ cup well-chilled Simple Syrup (facing page)

3 tablespoons fresh lime juice

1 cup ice water

Crushed ice, for serving

1. Working in 2 batches, combine the sorbet, coconut milk, syrup, lime juice, and water in a blender. Blend at high speed until smooth.

2. Fill 4 to 6 cocktail glasses ³⁄₄ full with crushed ice and pour in the drink. Serve with a straw.

MANGO-PASSION FRUIT FLOAT

YIELD: 2 SERVINGS

A familiar milk shake, spritzer, or lemonade may not lead to fantasizing, but add an exotic ingredient or two and suddenly you're transported to a sunny island, complete with white sand beaches and colorful sunsets. Sip this festive and delicious drink and you'll see what I mean. Vary the flavors by substituting other fruits, juices, and sorbets.

> ¹⁄₂ cup chopped fresh mango
> ¹⁄₂ cup well-chilled pineapple juice or a
>   tropical juice blend
> 1 cup well-chilled plain low-fat yogurt or
>   buttermilk
> ¹⁄₂ cup passion fruit sorbet
> Fresh mint sprigs, for garnish (optional)

1. Combine the mango, pineapple juice,

and yogurt in a blender. Blend thoroughly until smooth.

2. Pour the beverage into 2 chilled tall glasses. Top each serving with ¹⁄₄ cup passion fruit sorbet. Garnish with mint sprigs, if desired. Stir before serving.

ORANGE SODA

YIELD: 4 SERVINGS

Similar to a float, this cooling orange drink will make you forget about the heat. A richer soda may be made with vanilla ice cream instead of orange sherbet.

> ¹⁄₂ can (6 ounces) thawed frozen orange juice
>   concentrate
> ¹⁄₄ cup fresh lime juice
> ¹⁄₄ cup sugar
> 1 well-chilled can (12 ounces) ginger ale
>   or 7-Up
> ¹⁄₂ pint orange sherbet
> Orange slices, for garnish (optional)

1. Combine the orange juice concentrate, lime juice, and sugar with 2 cups water

LONGAN

Native to India and China, the longan is a cherry-size fruit related to the litchee, but it is less perfumey, with a thin, brownish shell. When you crack open the pod between your teeth or with your fingernails, it reveals a juicy, pearly white flesh that's quite firm and sweet, with a shiny brown pit lodged in the center. Nicknamed dragon's eye by the Chinese (because of an ovoid, white eye shaped mark on the pit), longan is one of the most prized fruits in Asia. It is rarely seen outside the tropics, since it is extremely vulnerable to the cold. However, I've frequently found and purchased fresh longans in New York's Chinatown during the late summer months. Like litchees, they fetch steep prices but are well worth the money. Fortunately, for those of us who cannot wait until summer for this delicious fruit, it is available year-round in canned and frozen forms at more affordable prices (though not to be compared with the fresh fruit in flavor). Use them as you would litchees or pitted cherries in dessert soups, sweet-and-sour dishes, fruit salads, and smoothies, or as a garnish for cocktail drinks.

in a large pitcher, and stir until the sugar dissolves. Chill.

2. Just before serving, add the ginger ale. Place ¼ cup of orange sherbet in each of 4 tall glasses, and pour the soda into each. Garnish with a slice of orange, if desired. Serve immediately with a straw. Stir before serving.

LITCHEE-PINEAPPLE BING

YIELD: 4 TO 5 SERVINGS

Growing up in Southeast Asia, I especially enjoyed *bing*, a very popular refresher that is half-liquid and half-solid. Typically, it includes sugar syrup and ice cream, sometimes coconut milk, and chopped fresh fruit. Poured over crushed ice, the mixture makes a cooling and delicious concoction to satisfy anyone's thirst on hot, humid days. Litchee and pineapple is one of my favorite combinations, but you can use almost any fruit that is juicy and has a wonderful fragrance, such as honeydew, peach, pear, mango, guava, cherimoya, or jackfruit.

½ cup sugar
2 cans (16 ounces each) litchees
    or longans in heavy syrup
2 cups chopped fresh pineapple
½ cup vanilla ice cream
About 8 cups crushed ice

1. Combine the sugar with 1½ cups water in a heavy saucepan and bring to a boil over high heat. Reduce the heat to medium

The pineapple is of such excellence that the gods might luxuriate upon it and that it should only be gathered by the hand of a Venus.

—JEAN DE LERY

and cook, uncovered, until you have a light syrup, about 5 minutes. Remove the pan from the heat and let the syrup cool.

2. Drain the litchees, reserving the syrup from 1 can only.

3. Working in 2 batches, place the pineapple, half of the litchees, the reserved litchee syrup, the vanilla ice cream, and the syrup in a blender. Process until the mixture is liquefied and foamy.

4. Fill 4 or 5 sundae glasses all the way to the top with crushed ice. Pour in the *bing*, then top each drink with ¼ cup of the remaining litchees. Serve immediately with a straw and a spoon.

HOW TO CHOOSE A WATERMELON

To find a ripe whole watermelon, follow these guidelines:

✦ *Look for a melon that is heavy, with a healthy sheen. Check the underside (the side that has rested on the ground) for a yellowish cast; rinds of unripe watermelons are white.*

✦ *Another way to determine the ripeness of a watermelon is the "thump" method. Tap the melon gently with your knuckles; ripe ones sound hollow.*

✦ *If your market is selling cut watermelon in addition to whole, inspect the cut ones first (look for deeply colored and crisp, juicy flesh with dark seeds), as the whole and cut melons were probably culled from the same crop.*

WATERMELON SPRITZER

YIELD: 1 QUART, OR 4 SERVINGS

Street vendors hawking bright red watermelon wedges piled in huge pyramids over ice were a familiar scene during the hot, sticky summers of my childhood. I can still remember the great feeling of biting into the fruit's refreshing, juicy flesh. One of the many ways we enjoyed it was sprinkled with salt and chile pepper. The balance of sweet, salty, and spicy seemed like heaven to me. Another less exotic but equally cooling way to serve it is in this easy liquid form.

3 cups chopped seeded watermelon

2 tablespoons sugar

2 tablespoons fresh lime juice

1 cup well-chilled citrus-flavored seltzer
    or tonic water

Ice cubes

4 small wedges watermelon, for garnish

1. Working in 2 batches, place the watermelon, sugar, lime juice, and seltzer in a blender. Blend the mixture until finely pureéd.

2. Fill 4 tall glasses with ice cubes, and pour the drink into each. Garnish with watermelon wedges, and serve at once.

VARIATION

CRANBERRY SPRITZER: Fill 4 tall glasses with ice cubes. Fill each with ½ cup cranberry juice cocktail and ½ cup club soda or sparkling mineral water.

RASPBERRY COOLER

YIELD: 3 QUARTS, OR 12 SERVINGS

A crowd pleaser for summer barbecues, this alcohol-free punch can also be made with frozen raspberries. Combine the juices a day ahead and store in a gallon jug in the refrigerator. As the guests arrive, pour the fruit-juice base into a punch bowl and add club soda.

2 pints (4 cups) fresh raspberries

⅓ cup sugar

1 cup boiling water

3½ cups orange juice

3½ cups pineapple juice

1 quart well-chilled club soda

Whole fresh raspberries or Raspberry
    Ice Ring (page 361), for garnish
    (optional)

1. Place the berries and sugar in a medium-size bowl, and crush with a wooden spoon. Add the boiling water. Strain the mixture through a sieve, pressing on the solids to extract as much pulp as possible.

2. Combine the raspberry pulp with the orange and pineapple juices, stirring to blend. Cover and refrigerate until well chilled.

3. Just before serving, add the club soda. Serve in a punch bowl, garnished with fresh whole raspberries.

FRUIT SHRUB

YIELD: ABOUT 1 QUART

Popular during our grandmothers' time, shrubs are classic summer coolers that derive from the heritage of Colonial America. In the days before refrigeration, people stored bottles of fruit vinegar in their cellars, ready to be mixed with sugar and cold water (or alcohol) and enjoyed by afternoon guests on the verandah. The word *shrub* probably derived from the Arabic *shurb*, meaning drink. But unlike shurbs (which had no alcohol in them), shrubs were usually mixed with rum or brandy. Personally, I enjoy making this alcohol-free version with my own homemade fruit-flavored vinegars, but you can certainly use any good commercial brand. If you do, be sure to halve the amount of vinegar called for in the recipe, since commercial vinegar is much more acidic then homemade. For an Italian-style apéritif, use seltzer instead of water.

1 cup Raspberry Vinegar (page 286),
Blueberry Vinegar (page 284), or
Peach Vinegar (page 287)
1/2 cup well-chilled Simple Syrup (page 348)
Ice cubes, for serving
Fresh mint sprigs, for garnish (optional)

1. Mix the fruit vinegar, syrup, and 2 cups cold water in a pitcher, and fill with ice. Let the ice melt for about 30 minutes.

2. Fill tall glasses with more ice, if desired, and pour in the shrub. Garnish with a sprig of fresh mint, if desired.

GINGER LEMONADE

YIELD: ABOUT 2 QUARTS, OR 8 SERVINGS

Cold lemonade, highly esteemed the world over, may be the ultimate thirst quencher. It is usually all you need to dispel the heat, but I particularly like the refreshing extra kick of fresh ginger. The mineral water will add some effervescence to the lemonade, but regular water will do.

1 piece fresh ginger (3 inches), peeled and
crushed
1 1/2 cups sugar
4 cups cold soda water, seltzer, or sparkling
mineral water
1 1/2 cups fresh lemon juice
Ice, for serving
1 lemon, thinly sliced
Fresh mint sprigs, for garnish (optional)

1. To make the syrup, mix the ginger and sugar with 1 1/2 cups of water in a medium-size saucepan. Bring to a boil over high heat, stirring to dissolve the sugar. Simmer over low heat until the ginger is aromatic

and the liquid is syrupy, about 10 minutes. Let cool. Remove and discard the ginger.

2. Stir in the soda water and lemon juice. Transfer the lemonade to a large pitcher. Add the lemon slices and refrigerate until well chilled.

3. Fill tall glasses with ice, then fill with the lemonade. Garnish with a lemon slice and a sprig of fresh mint, if desired.

VARIATIONS

WATERMELON LEMONADE: Make the syrup as directed above, but omit the ginger. Add 1½ cups puréed watermelon to the lemonade. Garnish with watermelon wedges.

RASPBERRY LEMONADE: Make the syrup but omit the ginger. Add 1½ cups strained puréed raspberries to the lemonade. Garnish with whole raspberries

PINEAPPLE LEMONADE: Proceed as for the above recipe, using ¾ cup fresh lemon juice and ¾ cup pineapple juice.

JUICING LEMONS

Size, thickness of skin, temperature, and softness of the fruit, are all factors that influence the amount of juice you can extract from a lemon. Here are a few tips to maximize the amount of juice you can get from a lemon:

◆ *Choose large, ripe lemons that are soft and thin-skinned.*

◆ *If the lemons have been refrigerated, leave them at room temperature for at least 30 minutes before juicing. Warm lemons will yield more juice.*

◆ *Before cutting and squeezing the lemons, firmly knead them on a countertop. The pressure breaks some of the membranes that hold in the juice inside the fruit, thus releasing more juice.*

ZESTY LEMON DRINK

YIELD: 1 SERVING

Salty and sour, this beverage is the Southeast Asian version of lemonade. A perfect antidote to hot summer weather; try it!

2 pieces Pickled Lemons (page 278)
2 tablespoons of brine from Pickled Lemons
2 tablespoons well-chilled Simple Syrup (page 348)
Ice, for serving
Cold club soda or seltzer

A wise man will accustom himself to the pure and fine water, or to the excellent lemonade.

—FRANÇOIS BERNIER

1. Place the pieces of pickled lemon into a tall glass, and finely crush them, peel and all, with a fork. Add the brine and Simple Syrup.

2. Fill the glass with ice, then add club soda to reach the top of the glass. Stir before serving.

TAMARIND NECTAR

YIELD: 2 QUARTS, OR 8 SERVINGS

Asians enjoy a wide range of fruit-flavored drinks. My favorite has to be tamarind juice, which is similar in taste to lemonade. In the summer, I always have a freshly made jug of it in the

refrigerator. Its tart, tangy flavor makes it another great thirst quencher.

> ½ pound tamarind pulp
> 4 cups boiling water
> ½ cup sugar
> 1 lemon, thinly sliced
> Ice, for serving
> 4 cups well-chilled club soda, seltzer, or sparkling mineral water

1. Soak the tamarind in the boiling water in a large bowl for 30 minutes. When the mixture is cool enough to handle, use your fingers or a fork to mash the pulp. Strain through a fine sieve, pressing to extract as much juice as possible. Discard the solids.

2. Stir in the sugar, then add the lemon slices. Mix well, and pour the tamarind juice into a jug. Chill for several hours. Before serving, add ice and the club soda. Drop a slice of lemon into each serving for garnish.

STRAWBERRY ICED TEA

YIELD: 1 QUART, OR 4 SERVINGS

The wonderful berry flavors in this iced tea are provided by natural herbal fruit teas with some added preserves. Although I use strawberry preserves in this recipe, you may also use other types of fragrant preserves, such as apricot, raspberry, or peach, to flavor this beverage.

4 blackberry or raspberry herbal
     tea bags
2 cups boiling water
1 cup strawberry preserves
Ice cubes, for serving
1 lemon, thinly sliced
Fresh mint sprigs, for garnish

1. Place the tea bags in a large heatproof pitcher and cover with the boiling water. Allow the tea to steep for 10 minutes. Squeeze the tea bags and discard.

2. Add the strawberry preserves and stir until dissolved. Stir in the 2 cups water. Chill for several hours. Strain before serving.

3. Fill tall glasses with ice, then pour in the tea. Drop a slice of lemon and a sprig of mint (if desired) into each glass for garnish.

VARIATION
PASSION FRUIT ICED TEA: Instead of strawberry preserves, add to the tea the strained pulp of 2 to 3 large passion

fruits, and sweeten the beverage to taste with Simple Syrup (page 348).

ICED APPLE TEA WITH APRICOTS

YIELD: 1 QUART, OR 4 SERVINGS

This tea is delicately tinged with the flavors of apple, apricot, and cinnamon. Keep a batch in the refrigerator; it's delicious anytime.

4 apple-cinnamon herbal tea bags
1/2 cup firmly packed dried apricot halves
1/2 cup sugar
4 cups boiling water
Ice cubes, for serving
4 slices lemon
Fresh mint sprigs, for garnish

1. Place the tea bags, apricots, and sugar in a large heatproof jar or pitcher, and cover with the boiling water. Let cool. Squeeze the tea bags and discard. Cover and refrigerate the tea for 2 days or longer to allow the apricots to steep.

2. To serve, put a couple of tea-soaked apricot pieces in each of 4 tall glasses, then fill with ice cubes. Pour the tea into each. Garnish with a slice of lemon and a sprig of mint.

DRINKS WITH SPIRIT

Whether entertaining just a few guests or a crowd, fruit-enhanced cocktails and punches are always popular. Summer get togethers invite kirs, bellinis, daiquiris, coladas, sangrias, and margaritas. These cool libations not only make wonderful apéritifs but are also excellent accompaniments throughout a meal.

And for the wintry days, there are steamy hot punches and mulled cider. These brews tend to be a little more potent than their cool counterparts, because they need a little something extra to invigorate and warm our bodies in the chill of winter. Is there anything cozier than curling up on the sofa in front of the fireplace with a mug of hot punch? I doubt it.

BLUSHING PINK COCKTAIL

YIELD: 2 SERVINGS

To give a little panache to an ordinary glass of white wine before dinner, why not try adding a bit of concentrated fruit juice or fruit-flavored liquor? This pink cocktail is delightfully flavored with both cranberry juice and orange liqueur. You will be nicely surprised at how good the drink tastes and how elegant it looks. If you want to treat yourself and a guest to an even more special drink, substitute Champagne for the white wine.

> 4 tablespoons thawed frozen cranberry juice
>   cocktail concentrate
> 3 tablespoons orange liqueur, such as
>   Grand Marnier or Triple Sec
> Chilled sparkling white wine
> 4 whole fresh cranberries, for garnish
> 2 small slices orange

1. Place 2 tablespoons of the cranberry juice concentrate and 1½ tablespoons of the orange liqueur in each of 2 champagne glasses.

2. Fill each glass almost to the top with the wine; stir.

TIPS FOR COCKTAILS

✦ *When you make alcoholic drinks, don't wield a heavy hand, and don't guess. One way to make sure your drinks are neither too strong nor too weak is to measure the liquor with a 1- to 1½-ounce jigger.*

✦ *For the best possible drink, use bottled mineral waters that are subtly flavored with fruit in recipes calling for mineral or carbonated water.*

✦ *Keep punches cold and add a festive and attractive note by floating fruit-filled ice rings in the punch bowl.*

✦ *If you plan to serve more than just a couple frozen daiquiris, margaritas, or piña coladas, it's a good idea to blend these drinks ahead of time in the quantity you need, transfer the mixture to plastic containers, and freeze it. In this case, you can even substitute cold water for the crushed ice called for in various recipes; the alcohol will keep the mixture from freezing solid. Process to a slush just prior to serving.*

---

3. For garnish, thread each of 2 toothpicks with 1 cranberry, a folded orange slice, and another cranberry. Place one atop each glass before serving.

VARIATION

CRIMSON COCKTAIL: Follow the directions for the Blushing Pink Cocktail, but substitute Grenadine Syrup (page 358) for the cranberry juice cocktail concentrate; add a few pomegranate seeds for garnish.

KIR

YIELD: 2 SERVINGS

Here's another splendid cocktail for special occasions. The name Kir was given to this apéritif by the citizens of Dijon, France, in honor of their former mayor and World War II hero-priest, Canon Felix Kir. It was his favorite apéritif. To make a Kir Royale, use a dry Champagne instead of the still wine. As a variation, you may substitute 1 tablespoon each Chambord (black raspberry liquor) and raspberry brandy for the crème de cassis.

2 tablespoons crème de cassis
Chilled dry white wine, such as Chablis
    or Chardonnay
2 strips lemon peel

1. Place 1 tablespoon cassis in each of 2 wine glasses and fill them to almost the top with chilled white wine; stir.

2. Twist a lemon peel over each drink and drop it in. Stir the drinks gently and serve.

BELLINI COCKTAIL

YIELD: 4 SERVINGS

Fresh peach purée adds a shock of color and a boost of flavor to this famous cocktail, which originated at Harry's Bar in Venice, Italy. Fragrant white peaches would make an authentic cocktail, but they're not really necessary. Bellinis can be varied by substituting strawberry, apricot, or mango purée for the peaches.

1 large peach (½ pound), peeled, pitted, and
*   coarsely chopped*
¼ cup well-chilled Simple Syrup (page 348)
2 tablespoons peach brandy
1 tablespoon fresh lemon juice
Chilled dry Champagne
4 small peach wedges, for garnish (optional)
4 springs fresh mint, for garnish (optional)

1. Place the peach in a blender or food processor and process until finely puréed.

2. Put the peach purée, Simple Syrup, brandy, and lemon juice into a cocktail shaker filled with crushed ice. Shake well and strain the mixture into 4 champagne glasses. (Or, combine the purée, syrup, and lemon juice in a small pitcher and refrigerate until well chilled. Just before serving, pour the fruit mixture into the glasses.)

3. Thread a wedge of peach and a sprig of fresh mint onto each of 4 toothpicks. Place the garnish atop each glass, and serve.

FRESH PEACH PUNCH

YIELD: ABOUT 1 GALLON, OR 16 SERVINGS

It is almost worth planning a party just so you can serve this spectacular punch! For an even more flavorful beverage, use white peaches, if you can get them when they are in season. Fresh mangoes, apricots, raspberries, or strawberries may also be used with excellent results. The strawberry ice ring in the punch bowl not only helps keep your beverage constantly cold, it also makes for a striking presentation. Make the ice ring a day ahead.

1 bottle (750 ml) white wine, preferably a
*   Riesling*
1 cup peach brandy
1 cup sugar
1 pound ripe peaches, pitted and thinly sliced
2 bottles (750 ml each) dry Champagne,
*   well chilled*
Strawberry Ice Ring (recipe follows), optional

1. Combine the wine, peach brandy, sugar, and sliced peaches in a punch bowl. Stir until the sugar is dissolved. Cover and refrigerate until well chilled.

2. Just before serving, add the Champagne, then float the Strawberry Ice Ring atop the punch.

STRAWBERRY ICE RING

YIELD: 1 ICE RING

Instead of fresh strawberries, you may use fresh melon balls or any other fruit that will complement a particular punch. You can even make a flower ring by floating edible flowers in the ice, like pansies, lavender, or nasturtiums.

6 cups water
1 pint (2 cups) fresh strawberries, unhulled

Pour 4 cups of the water into a 6- or 8-cup ring mold, and float the strawberries in it. Place in the freezer until completely frozen, about 3 hours. Add the remaining 2 cups water to cover the berries, and freeze until solid, 2 to 3 hours longer.

VARIATION

RASPBERRY ICE RING: Scatter ¹/₂ pint (1 cup) fresh raspberries and a few pretty mint leaves in the bottom of a 6- or 8-cup ring mold. Add 2 cups water. Freeze until solid, about 2 hours. Add the remaining 4 cups water and freeze until solid.

STRAWBERRY DAIQUIRI

YIELD: 2 SERVINGS

Created in Santiago, Cuba, the daiquiri has become quite a popular drink in North America. A daiquiri is a frosty, sweetened fresh fruit purée that is enlivened with lime juice and rum. In addition to strawberry, this delicious drink can be made with banana, peach, or almost any tropical fruit. It goes great with spicy foods such as barbecued ribs. To make a good-looking drink, I usually dip the glass rims into Kosher salt before pouring in the drink.

1 package (10 ounces) frozen strawberries
*   in syrup, partially thawed, or 1 pint*
*   (2 cups) fresh strawberries*
¹/₄ cup light rum, or to taste
¹/₄ cup fresh lime juice
¹/₃ cup confectioners' sugar
2 cups crushed ice
Kosher salt, for the glass rims (optional)
2 whole fresh strawberries, for garnish

1. Place the strawberries, rum, lime juice, and confectioners' sugar in a blender. Cover and blend at medium speed until the mixture is puréed. Gradually add the crushed ice, blending until smooth.

2. If desired, pour some Kosher salt on a small plate. Dip the rims of 2 shallow champagne glasses in water and then in the salt.

3. Pour in the daiquiri. Garnish each with a whole strawberry, and serve at once with a straw.

PEACH MARGARITAS

YIELD: 2 SERVINGS

Similar to a daiquiri, this margarita has a base of sweetened fruit purée, which is invigorated with tequila and Triple Sec. Blueberries, mango, nectarines, honeydew, or cantaloupe can replace the peaches in the purée.

1 package (10 ounces) frozen peaches in syrup, partially thawed, or 2 cups sliced fresh peaches
1/4 cup fresh lime juice
2 tablespoons tequila, preferably Cuervo Gold
2 tablespoons orange liqueur, preferably Triple Sec
1/3 cup confectioners' sugar
2 cups crushed ice
Kosher salt, for the glass rims (optional)
2 wedges fresh peach, for garnish

1. Place the peaches, lime juice, tequila, Triple Sec, and confectioners' sugar into a blender. Cover and blend at medium speed until the mixture is puréed. Gradually add the crushed ice, blending until smooth.

2. If desired, pour some Kosher salt on a small plate. Dip the rims of 2 shallow champagne glasses in water and then in the salt.

3. Add the margarita and garnish each serving with a peach wedge. Serve at once with a straw.

PINA COLADA

YIELD: 2 SERVINGS

Canned sweetened cream of coconut makes it easy to whip up this fresh, creamy tropical drink on your own front porch. Even though a lot of people use pineapple juice alone to make a piña colada, I think it should be made with chunks of fresh pineapple for the most authentic flavor. This frothy beverage is even good enough to sip as a dessert!

1 cup fresh pineapple chunks
½ cup canned cream of coconut, such as
    Coco Lopez
¼ cup light rum, or to taste
2 cups crushed ice
2 slices fresh pineapple, for garnish

1. Place the pineapple, cream of coconut, and rum in a blender. Cover and blend at medium speed until the mixture is puréed. Gradually add the crushed ice, blending until smooth.

2. Pour the piña colada into 2 shallow champagne glasses. Garnish each with a pineapple slice and serve at once with a straw.

SANGRIA

YIELD: 3 QUARTS,
OR 12 SERVINGS

The blood-red sangria is a staple drink in Spain and other Spanish-speaking countries. It is also one of the most cooling summer drinks I know. Sangria is fruity, light, and sparkling on the tongue. It combines citrus juices, red wine, and an assortment of fresh fruit chunks. The carbonation of the soda water added at the end drives the scent of the fruits right up the nose. Sangria doesn't have to be too strong and can be made sweet or dry according to the amount of sugar syrup used. Any fruits at all may be added.

1¼ cups fresh orange juice
1¼ cups fresh pineapple juice
¼ cup fresh lime juice
¼ cup fresh lemon juice
1 bottle (750 ml) red Burgundy or Rioja
1 cup well-chilled Simple Syrup (page 348)
4 ripe peaches or nectarines, pitted and cut
    into thin slices
½ Golden Delicious apple
    (unpeeled), cored and cut
    into thin wedges
1 lime, thinly sliced
1 lemon, thinly sliced
1 small orange, thinly
    sliced
2 cups well-chilled club
    soda, or to taste
Ice cubes, for serving

1. Combine the orange, pineapple, lime, and lemon juices in a large pitcher. Add the red wine, Simple Syrup, peaches, apple, lime, lemon, and orange slices. Let the mixture sit for at least 1 hour, or cover and refrigerate overnight.

2. Just before serving, transfer the beverage, including the fruits, to a punch bowl. Add the club soda and ice cubes. Serve the sangria in tall glasses.

HOT CRANBERRY-LEMON PUNCH

YIELD: 3 QUARTS,
OR 12 SERVINGS

Hot punches are traditional winter drinks that are great for sipping after sleigh rides or caroling or anytime there's a chill in the air. This one certainly justifies braving the elements! Be sure your urn and mugs are warm before adding the punch.

1 bottle (32 ounces) cranberry juice cocktail
2 cans (6 ounces each) thawed frozen
    lemonade concentrate
2/3 cup honey
2 cinnamon sticks (3 inches each)
12 whole cloves
1 small lemon, thinly sliced
2 cups fruity red wine, preferably a Beaujolais
2 tablespoons unsalted butter (optional)
Thinly sliced lemon rounds, for garnish

1. Combine the cranberry juice cocktail, lemonade concentrate, honey, cinnamon, cloves, and lemon slices with 4 cups water in a large saucepan, and bring to a simmer over medium-low heat, stirring until the honey has dissolved.

2. Partially cover and simmer over medium-low heat until the flavor of the spices is infused into the liquid, about 15 minutes.

3. Add the wine. Heat thoroughly, but do not boil. Remove from the heat, and discard the spices. Stir in the butter, if desired.

4. Pour the punch into warm mugs or short-stemmed cocktail glasses. Float a round of lemon on each drink.

HOT LEMON RUMBA

YIELD: 1 ½ QUARTS,
OR 8 SERVINGS

Hot punches are to winter what frosty drinks are to summer. Serve mugs of this jovial blend of lemonade, orange juice, and dark rum as a part of a cool-weather brunch buffet, and you'll get things off to a great start.

2 cans (6 ounces each) thawed frozen
    lemonade concentrate
Juice of 2 large oranges (about
    1 cup)
3/4 cup dark rum
Thinly sliced lemon or orange
    rounds, for garnish

1. Combine the lemonade, orange juice, and rum with 4 cups water in a medium-size saucepan, and heat to just below the boiling point.

2. Pour into warm mugs and garnish with slices of lemon or orange. Serve at once.

HOT MULLED APPLE CIDER

YIELD: 2 QUARTS, OR 8 SERVINGS

One of my favorite hot beverages is mulled apple cider. I enjoy serving it at breakfast, or at any time of day, for that matter. This great drink will most definitely rejuvenate your spirits and warm your soul after a day of mushroom hunting or skiing. You may also try it as a delicious liquid dessert or as an after-dinner drink. A touch of butter makes this drink stand out! Omit the alcohol and Chantilly Cream, if desired, and top each serving with an orange slice.

2 quarts fresh apple cider, unpasteurized
1/3 cup sugar
2 cinnamon sticks (3 inches each)
8 whole cloves
4 star anise or 2 whole allspice berries
Zest of 2 oranges
4 teaspoons unsalted butter (optional)
8 to 12 ounces Calvados or other apple brandy
Chantilly Cream (page 411)

1. Combine the apple cider, sugar, cinnamon, cloves, star anise, and orange peel in a large saucepan and bring to a simmer over medium-low heat. Partially cover and simmer until the flavor of the spices and orange peel are infused into the cider, about 15 minutes. Remove from the heat and stir in the butter, if desired.

2. Pour the cider into warm mugs or short-stemmed cocktail glasses. Add 1 to 1½ ounces Calvados to each serving and stir. Garnish each drink with a spoonful of Chantilly Cream.

HOT SPICED WINE PUNCH

YIELD: ABOUT 1 QUART, OR 4 SERVINGS

Aromatic with oranges and spices, and sweet with port and currants, this uplifting red wine punch is quite effective at warming up your body. It is also the perfect remedy for soothing a sore throat.

1 orange

2 cups red Burgundy

1½ cups fresh orange juice

¼ cup sugar

1 cinnamon stick (3 inches)

6 cloves

2 cardamom pods, crushed

2 quarter-size pieces peeled fresh ginger,
    crushed

½ cup dried currants or seedless raisins

⅓ cup port or Madeira

4 slices orange, for garnish

1. Using a vegetable peeler, remove the zest of the orange in wide strips.

2. Place the orange zest, wine, orange juice, sugar, cinnamon, cloves, cardamom, and ginger into a medium-size sauce pan and bring to a simmer over medium-low heat for 15 minutes. Strain and add the currants and port.

3. Return the mixture to low heat and heat to just below the boiling point.

4. Pour the wine into warm mugs or short-stemmed cocktail glasses. Float a slice of orange on each drink before serving.

SORBET
& ICE CREAM

There's simply no denying ice cream its rightful spot on the throne of American desserts. People even enjoy it in the dead of winter—something I find amazing, having been raised in the tropics. As much as Americans adore ice creams, I love fruit ices even more for their cool, light qualities. I can still taste those wonderful snow cones and shaved fruit ices I savored as a small child during the long, hot summers in Southeast Asia. When I think of those frozen treats, I always feel a sense of well-being.

You might wonder why bother making your own ice creams and sorbets when you can get them at the local ice cream parlor or supermarket. Here again, I maintain that there is still nothing to compare with the reward of preparing something yourself. Plus, you can come up with your own flavors. No special skills are required to make these frozen treats. All you really need is an ice cream maker and a freezer. Now, with the ever-increasing number of faster, simpler, inex-pensive ice cream machines available, there's no excuse for not making your favorite fruit ices, sorbets, and ice creams at home to your heart's content.

I hope the following recipes will inspire you to churn out some wonderful treats for your family and friends. You will also find a few ice cream recipes that call for no more work than opening a container of purchased ice cream, and "doctoring" it up with some fruit for more appealing and satisfying results.

A WORD ON SORBETS, SHERBETS, GRANITAS, AND ICES

*S*ORBET: *The French term sorbet refers to a fat-free frozen fruit or wine-and-syrup mixture. Originally from the Middle East, sorbet (sharbat in Persia and serbet in Turkey) was a cooling sweet drink with a base of fresh fruit, diluted and chilled with snow. To my taste, it's more refreshing than ice cream. It's also far lower in calories, and it's easy and inexpensive to make.*

Most sorbets are fruit-based, and can be made with any fruit imaginable. For a good sorbet, you need to have a perfect balance of acid (usually lemon juice, which brings out the flavor of fruits), sugar, water, and sometimes liquor flavoring. If you use anything alcoholic, be careful not to use too much, since alchohol can prevent the fruit mixture from freezing properly.

When you create your own sorbet, check its density by floating a fresh egg in the mixture. Do the egg test just before chilling the mixture. Since the liquid is naturally sweet, the egg will float. If the exposed part of the eggshell is about the size of a nickel, the proportions of sugar to acid are correct. However, if your mixture is too sweet, too much egg shell will show. In that case you need to adjust the mixture accordingly by adding liquid and acid. For best results, always chill the sorbet (or any ice cream) mixture before you put it in an ice-cream maker. Store and serve sorbet as you would ice cream.

SHERBET: *The American version of a sorbet, sherbet is creamier, with a little milk, light cream, yogurt, or egg white added to the fruit purée to smooth it out.*

GRANITA: *Granita, from the Italian grano meaning "grained" or "grainy," is a type of icy sweet. While a sorbet is smooth, a granita is coarser, more granular in texture. Granitas also contains 30 percent less sugar than sorbets. Of Arabic origins, the first granitas in Italy were probably made in Sicily or Naples, where sweetened lemon juice or coffee was commonly poured over shaved ice.*

Granitas are made differently than sorbets. There are two basic ways to make them, the stirring method and the freezing/chopping method. The stirring method requires patience. It calls for stirring the mixture with a fork every 20 minutes or so for 2 to 3 hours. This method produces a granita with tiny ice crystals. The freezing and chopping method produces a granita with coarser slivers of ice. The mixture is poured no higher than 3/4 inch in a shallow pan, preferably stainless steel, and frozen until solid. The ice is removed from the pan, then chopped into fine pieces with a large stainless steel knife. You can serve it immediately or return it to the pan and refreeze it until serving. No further chopping is necessary. Like sorbets, granitas can include some liquor or fruit brandy. You can also serve them as a refreshing break between seafood and meat courses on a long menu. Likewise, they signal the switch from white wine to red wine.

ICES: *Mixtures of fruit juice, syrup (or sugar), and water frozen in an ice cream maker, fruit ices are a little more watery than sorbets but have a smoother texture than granitas.*

TANGERINE SORBET

YIELD: ABOUT 1 QUART, OR 8 SERVINGS

There is a wonderful clean edge to this tangerine sorbet. It tastes just puckery enough to refresh on hot, sultry days. The sorbet may be stored in the freezer for up to a week. Let it soften for a few minutes before serving if it's too firm.

8 large tangerines
1½ cups sugar
¼ cup fresh lemon juice
Fresh mint sprigs, for garnish (optional)

1. With a zester, remove strips of zest from 4 of the tangerines. Set aside. Extract the juice from all 8 tangerines. (There should be about 3 cups of juice.)

2. Combine the tangerine zest, sugar, and 1 cup water in a medium-size saucepan and bring to a boil over high heat. Reduce the heat to medium-low and simmer until the syrup is reduced to 1 cup, about 20 minutes. Remove from the heat and let cool.

3. Drain the syrup into a large bowl, reserving the candied zest for garnish. Stir the tangerine juice and lemon juice into the syrup. Cover and refrigerate until well chilled (or chill over a bowl of ice water, stirring the mixture occasionally).

4. Freeze the mixture in an ice cream maker according to manufacturer's instructions. If not serving immediately, transfer the sorbet to a plastic container. To prevent ice crystals from forming, place a piece of plastic wrap directly on the surface of the sorbet before putting the lid on the container. Store in the freezer.

5. If not using an ice cream maker, place the chilled mixture in a stainless steel or other metal baking pan, cover with plastic wrap, and freeze until softly set, about 2 hours. Transfer the partially frozen mixture to a food processor and process until smooth and fluffy, about 10 seconds. Return the mixture to the baking pan, freeze until half-set, and repeat the process. After the second blending, transfer it to a plastic container. To prevent ice crystals from forming, place a piece of plastic wrap directly on the surface of the sorbet before putting the lid on the container. Store in the freezer until the sorbet is solid, about 4 hours.

6. Remove the sorbet from the freezer 10 minutes before serving. Serve in chilled stemmed glasses. Garnish each serving with the reserved candied tangerine zest and a mint sprig, if desired.

MANGO COLADA SORBET

YIELD: 6 CUPS, OR 12 SERVINGS

I have turned one of my favorite cocktails, the piña colada, into a frozen treat, but for a deliciously different taste, I use mango instead of pineapple. The sorbet is smooth, rich, colorful, and intensely flavored. Of course, because of the coconut milk, it is not exactly low in fat. Peach or pineapple sorbet can be made the same way by substituting 3 cups chopped peeled peaches or pineapple for the mangoes.

2 large ripe mangoes, peeled and pitted, or
   3 cups drained canned mango
6 tablespoons fresh lime juice
¼ cup dark rum
1 cup canned unsweetened coconut milk,
   well stirred
1½ cups Simple Syrup (see page 361)
Fresh mint sprigs, for garnish (optional)

1. In a blender or food processor, purée the mangoes, lime juice, and rum. Blend well, about 2 minutes, stopping occasionally to scrape down the sides of the bowl with a rubber spatula.

2. Transfer the mango purée to a large mixing bowl and add the coconut milk and syrup. Stir until the mixture is well blended and smooth. Refrigerate the mixture until chilled (or chill over a bowl of ice water, stirring the mixture occasionally).

3. Freeze the mixture in an ice cream maker according to manufacturer's instructions. If not serving immediately, transfer the sorbet to a plastic container. To prevent ice crystals from forming, place a piece of plastic wrap directly on the surface of the sorbet before putting the lid on the container. Store in the freezer.

4. If not using an ice cream maker, place the chilled mixture in a stainless steel or other metal baking pan, cover with plastic wrap, and freeze until softly set, about 2 hours. Transfer the partially frozen mixture to a food processor and process until smooth and fluffy, about 10 seconds. Return the mixture to the baking pan, freeze until half set, and repeat the process. After the second blending, transfer it to a plastic container. To prevent ice crystals from forming, place a piece of plastic wrap directly on the surface of the sorbet before putting the lid on the container. Store in the freezer until the sorbet is solid, about 4 hours.

5. Remove the sorbet from the freezer 10 minutes before serving. Serve the sorbet in chilled stemmed glasses.

The menu meandered gracefully through fish, flesh, fowl, and truffles and finally melted away into sorbets.

**—LONDON DAILY TELEGRAPH,
SEPTEMBER 27, 1864**

PEAR SORBET

YIELD: ABOUT 1 QUART, OR 8 SERVINGS

Pears make my all-time favorite homemade sorbet. Choose fruits that are slightly over the hill; they make the best sorbet because they are at their sweetest and have the best aroma.

> 4 large very ripe Bartlett pears (about 2
>   pounds total), peeled, halved, and cored
> 1 cup sugar
> 1 tablespoon fresh lemon juice
> 3 tablespoons pear brandy, such as Poire
>   Williams

1. In a medium-size saucepan, combine the pears with the sugar, the lemon juice, and ³/₄ cup water. Cook over low heat just until the pears are soft, about 20 minutes.

2. Stir in the liqueur, then let cool. Transfer the mixture to a blender or food processor and purée, stopping occasionally to scrape down the sides of the bowl with a rubber spatula. Cover and refrigerate until well chilled (or chill over a bowl of ice water, stirring the mixture occasionally).

3. Freeze the mixture in an ice cream maker according to the manufacturer's instructions. If not serving immediately, transfer the sorbet to a plastic container. To prevent ice crystals from forming, place a piece of plastic wrap directly on the surface of the sorbet before putting the lid on the container. Store in the freezer.

4. If not using an ice cream maker, place the chilled mixture in a stainless steel or other metal baking pan, cover with plastic wrap, and freeze until softly set, about 2 hours. Transfer the partially frozen mixture to a food processor and process until smooth and fluffy, about 10 seconds. Return the mixture to a baking pan, freeze until half-set, and repeat the process. After the second blending, transfer it to a plastic container. To prevent ice crystals from forming, place a piece of plastic wrap directly on the surface of the sorbet before putting the lid on the container. Store in the freezer until the sorbet is solid, about 4 hours.

5. Remove the sorbet from the freezer 10 minutes before serving. Serve the sorbet in chilled stemmed glasses.

KIWI SNOW

YIELD: 4 SERVINGS

Your guests will think this dessert is a rich mousse, so when you tell them it's fat-free, they'll be surprised and delighted. In this super-easy dessert, frozen kiwi fruit is puréed, then whipped up to a light, creamy consistency with egg whites. The kiwis provide not only color and flavor but also a pleasing crunch from their tiny black seeds. For best results, serve the fruit snow as soon as it's ready. A similar dessert can be made with any soft, juicy fruit, such as cherimoya, berries, peaches, melons, mangoes, apricots, or papayas. Depending on the acidity or sweetness of the fruit you choose, add a couple teaspoons of lemon juice to balance the taste of the snow, which should be on the tart side.

3 ripe kiwis, plus a few kiwi slices, for garnish
2 large egg whites (see Note)
3 tablespoons sugar
Dash of kirsch (cherry brandy; optional)

1. Peel and halve the kiwis. Cut each half into 4 wedges. (There should be about 1 cup of fruit.) Place the wedges on a plate and freeze until hard, about 1 hour.

2. Place the frozen kiwi in the food processor and blend just until powdery, about 30 seconds.

SAFER EGGS

If you are reluctant to use raw egg whites in recipes like the one for Kiwi Snow because of the possible presence of salmonella bacteria, here is an easy solution. Since only heat (160°F), acid (between 3 pH and 3.5 pH), or prolonged freezing can kill salmonella bacteria, an easy way to neutralize raw egg whites is with fresh lemon juice. For this, all you have to do is add the lemon juice to the egg whites (use the ratio of 1 tablespoon lemon juice for every 2 large egg whites), stir gently, and refrigerate the mixture for 48 hours. After this period, the eggs will emerge "sanitized" and ready for safe use. You can also store the acidulated egg mixture in the freezer for up to 3 months for future use (it will come in handy for other desserts, especially meringues, or any dish that calls for raw egg whites.) You can either thaw the eggs in the refrigerator overnight or leave them to thaw at room temperature for no longer than 2 hours. Use as soon as they are thawed.

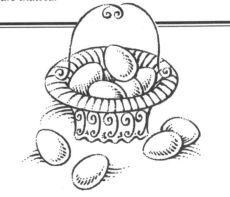

3. Transfer the crushed kiwi pulp to a large mixing bowl, then add the egg whites, and sugar. Using an electric mixer, beat at high speed until the mixture rises and is fluffy, 5 to 6 minutes.

4. Spoon the kiwi snow into individual

ice cream dishes, and garnish with slices of kiwi. Serve immediately.

NOTE: This recipe contains raw egg whites, which can carry the bacteria that cause salmonella. If you are uncertain about the quality of your eggs, you may want to "sanitize" the whites according to the instructions in Safer Eggs (see box, facing page). You'll have to start the process at least 48 hours before you intend to prepare the recipe.

WATERMELON ICE

YIELD: 1 QUART, OR 8 SERVINGS

Fruit ices appeal to me because they capture the very essence of ripe fruits. Watermelon, with its naturally high water content, is ideal for making ice. This lovely watermelon ice is delicate and tastes clearer than the fruit itself. A similar ice can be made with puréed honeydew, cantaloupe, or pink grapefruit juice.

2 cups watermelon, chopped and seeded
1 cup well-chilled Simple Syrup (page 348)
⅓ cup fresh lemon juice

1. Place the watermelon in a blender or food processor and process until finely puréed.

2. In a large mixing bowl, stir together the watermelon purée, syrup, lemon juice, and 1 cup cold water.

3. Freeze the mixture in an ice cream maker according to the manufacturer's instructions. If not serving immediately, transfer the ice to a plastic container. To prevent ice crystals from forming, place a piece of plastic wrap directly on the surface of the ice before putting the lid on the container. Store in the freezer.

4. If not using an ice cream maker, place the chilled mixture in a stainless steel or other metal baking pan, cover with plastic wrap, and freeze until softly set, about 2 hours. Transfer the partially frozen mixture to a food processor and process until smooth and fluffy, about 10 seconds. Return the mixture to a baking pan, freeze until half set, and repeat the process. After the second blending, transfer it to a plastic container. To prevent ice crystals from forming, place a piece of plastic wrap directly on the surface of the ice before putting the lid on the container. Store in the freezer until the ice is solid, about 4 hours.

5. Remove the ice from the freezer 10 minutes before serving. Serve in chilled stemmed glasses.

SUGARED BABIES

*U*se sugared (frosted) fruits to give a dramatic, elegant, and summery look to cakes, tarts, pies, ice creams, and sorbets. Small whole fruits, such as kumquats, lady apples, mandarin segments, strawberries, cranberries, bunches of currants, cherries, and grapes (especially Champagne grapes), are great candidates for sugaring. For special appeal, choose perfect fruits with stems attached, or use your scissors to snip bunches into small clusters. Nasturtium leaves or edible flowers can also be sugared in the same manner as follows:

1. With a fork, lightly beat an egg white (see Safer Eggs, page 372) until slightly frothy. Avoid making too much froth. Holding a fruit by the stem or inserting a fork into the fruit, dip it into the egg white. Let any excess egg white drip off the fruit.

2. Roll the fruit in a bowl of superfine sugar until evenly coated. Transfer the fruit to a plate, and let dry 30 minutes, or until the sugar forms a crisp, dry coating. The fruit may be tightly sealed in a container and kept in the refrigerator for up to 1 week.

APPLE GRANITA

YIELD: 1½ QUARTS, OR 12 SERVINGS

*G*ranita, an Italian icy sweet, can be made with almost any type of flavoring, and may even include fresh fruit. Its characteristic flaky texture and low sugar content set it apart from regular fruit ices. At the end of a meal, no matter how much you have eaten, I guarantee you will find room for this light and intensely apple flavored treat—and perhaps even a few light, crisp cookies. You may also serve it as a cooling intermezzo between courses of a larger meal.

1 cup dry white wine, such as a dry Riesling
   or Chardonnay
3 tablespoons fresh lemon juice
6 large Golden Delicious apples (about
   3 pounds total)
²⁄₃ cup sugar
¹⁄₃ cup Calvados or other apple brandy
Fresh mint sprigs, for garnish (optional)

1. Place a 9-inch square stainless steel or other metal baking pan in the freezer.

2. Combine the white wine, lemon juice, and 1 cup water in a large pot. Peel and core the apples, then cut them into ½-inch cubes, and add to the pot. (As you add the apples to the pot, stir occasionally to coat the fruit with the liquid to prevent the apples from discoloring.) Stir in the sugar and bring the mixture to a boil over high heat. Reduce the heat to low and simmer, uncovered, until the apples are very soft, about 10 minutes.

3. Transfer the mixture to a blender or food processor and purée until smooth. Stop occasionally to scrape down the sides of the bowl with a rubber spatula. Transfer to a mixing bowl, stir in the Calvados, and let cool to room temperature.

4. Pour the mixture into the chilled pan, cover, and freeze until slushy, about 2 hours. Remove from the freezer, stir with a fork, and return to the freezer. Repeat stirring the mixture every 20 minutes until the granita reaches the consistency of shaved ice, 2 to 3 hours longer.

5. Alternately, cover and freeze the mixture until firm, but not frozen solid, about 3 hours. Break the iced mixture into chunks, and with a sharp knife, chop into flaky pieces. Return to the pan and freeze until solid, about 3 hours longer.

6. Allow the mixture to soften slightly, about 5 minutes, before scooping into chilled dessert cups or red-wine glasses. Serve garnished with mint sprigs.

VARIATION
PEACH GRANITA: Fresh peaches also make an excellent granita. Use the ripest ones you can find in order to preserve their full-bodied flavor. Blanch 1½ pounds fresh peaches in boiling water for 1 minute, then peel and pit them before proceeding with the recipe. Instead of Calvados, flavor the granita with peach schnapps or Cognac.

CONCORD GRAPE GRANITA

YIELD: 1 ½ QUARTS, OR 12 SERVINGS

Concord Grapes make one of the loveliest granitas I know. This wonderful granita has a delightful flavor and a shocking purplish color. If you wish, garnish it with a few litchees or star fruit slices and mint. Instead of Concord grapes, you can try almost any other juicy colorful fruits, like blood orange, pink grapefruit, watermelon, or strawberries. Serve with light, crisp cookies, if desired.

1½ pounds Concord grapes, stemmed
½ cup sugar
1 cinnamon stick (3 inches)
Zest of ½ lemon
2 tablespoons port
Fresh mint sprigs, for garnish

1. Place a 9-inch square stainless steel or other metal baking pan in the freezer.

2. Put the grapes in a blender or food processor and blend until puréed. Stop occasionally to scrape down the sides of the bowl with a rubber spatula. Strain through a sieve, pressing on the pulp with the back of a spoon to extract as much liquid as possible. (Be careful: Grape juice stains.) There should be about 2 cups of grape juice. Discard the solids.

3. Combine the grape juice, sugar, cinnamon stick, and lemon zest with 2 cups water in a medium-size saucepan and bring to a boil. Reduce the heat to medium and cook for 5 minutes. Remove the cinnamon stick. Stir in the port and let cool to room temperature.

4. Pour the mixture into the chilled baking pan, cover, and freeze until just set, about 2 hours. Remove from the freezer, stir with a fork, and return to the freezer. Repeat stirring the mixture every 20 minutes until the granita reaches the consistency of shaved ice, about 2 hours longer.

5. Alternately, cover and freeze the mixture until firm but not frozen solid, about 3 hours. Break the iced mixture into chunks, and with a sharp knife, chop into flaky pieces. Return to the pan and freeze until solid, about 3 hours longer.

6. Allow the mixture to soften slightly, about 5 minutes, before scooping into chilled dessert cups or red-wine glasses. Garnish with mint sprigs.

VARIATION

BLOOD ORANGE GRANITA: Combine 2 cups blood orange juice, 2 cups water,

¾ cup sugar, 2 tablespoons Grand Marnier, and 2 tablespoons fresh lemon juice. Stir until the sugar is completely dissolved. Taste and add more sugar, if necessary. Freeze the granita as directed above. Fresh pomegranate juice or cranberry juice cocktail can substitute for blood orange.

PINEAPPLE-YOGURT SHERBET

YIELD: 5 CUPS

Tangy, light, and refreshing, this easy-to-make sherbet has a yogurt base that complements the pineapple perfectly. The yogurt provides some body and a creamy texture, without the extra calories found in heavy cream. For the best flavor, use a very ripe pineapple. A spoonful of crème de menthe over the sorbet makes it even more wonderful.

*4 cups fresh, very ripe pineapple chunks
(about 1½ pounds total)
2 cups well-chilled plain yogurt
1 cup light corn syrup
1 teaspoon fresh lemon juice
½ teaspoon finely grated lemon zest
Pinch of salt*

1. Place the pineapple chunks in a

blender or food processor and process until finely chopped. Stop occasionally to scrape down the sides of the bowl with a rubber spatula.

2. Add the yogurt, corn syrup, lemon juice, lemon zest, and salt. Process until the mixture is well blended and only some very fine bits of pineapple remain.

3. Freeze the mixture in an ice cream maker according to manufacturer's instructions. If not serving immediately, transfer the sherbet to a plastic container. To prevent ice crystals from forming, place a piece of plastic wrap directly on the surface of the sherbet before putting the lid on the container. Store in the freezer.

4. If not using an ice cream maker, place the mixture in a stainless steel or other metal baking pan, cover with plastic wrap, and freeze until softly set, about 2 hours. Transfer the partially frozen mixture to a food processor and process until smooth and fluffy, about 10 seconds. Return the mixture to the baking pan, freeze until half-set, and repeat the process. After the second blending, transfer it to a plastic container. To prevent ice crystals from forming, place a piece of plastic wrap directly on the surface of the sherbet

before putting the lid on the container. Store in the freezer until the sherbet is solid, about 4 hours.

5. Remove the sherbet from the freezer 10 minutes before serving. Serve in chilled stemmed glasses.

GREAT MATCHES

BERRIES

*B*ursting ripe berries of all kinds go with rich heavy cream, sour cream, and creamy cheeses, including chèvre and Gorgonzola. They're also nice flavored with liqueurs, such as crème de cassis, Grand Marnier, and raspberry liqueur, and sweet wines. Try berries—either macerated in wine or plain—with chocolate for a simple, unforgettable dessert.

RASPBERRY ICE CREAM

YIELD: 1 QUART, OR 8 SERVINGS

This very-berry ice cream is what homemade ice cream is all about. Similar fruited ice creams can be made with any other ripe, fragrant fruit, such as strawberries, peaches (peeled), bananas, papayas, or plums. Be sure to toss the fruit with a little fresh lemon

juice or lime juice before crushing it to bring out all its goodness.

> 1 pint (2 cups) fresh raspberries or 1 bag
>   (12 ounces) frozen unsweetened
>   raspberries, thawed and well drained
> 1 cup sugar
> 1 cup heavy (or whipping) cream
> 1 cup light cream or half-and-half
> 6 large egg yolks
> Pinch of salt
> 1 teaspoon vanilla extract

1. Toss the berries with ¼ cup of the sugar in a medium-size bowl. Mash slightly with a fork. Cover and refrigerate until well chilled, 2 to 3 hours.

2. Combine the heavy cream and light cream in a medium-size saucepan and scald over low heat. Remove from the heat.

3. Whisk the egg yolks with the remaining ¾ cup sugar and salt in large bowl until thick and lemon-colored. Gradually whisk in the scalded cream.

4. Return the mixture to the saucepan and cook over low heat, stirring often, until the mixture thickens enough to coat a wooden spoon, 5 to 7 minutes. Do not let the mixture simmer or boil. Strain the custard through a fine sieve into a medium-size bowl. Stir in the vanilla extract and let cool to room temperature.

5. Refrigerate the custard until well chilled, 2 to 3 hours (or chill over a bowl of ice water, stirring the custard occasionally).

6. Stir the crushed raspberries into the custard. Freeze the mixture in an ice cream maker according to the manufacturer's instructions.

7. Transfer the ice cream to a plastic container, cover, and freeze for several hours or overnight, to mellow. Before serving, soften the ice cream slightly in the refrigerator.

CHERRY-CHOCOLATE ICE CREAM TERRINE

YIELD: 6 TO 8 SERVINGS

This frosty fantasy is nothing more than chocolate ice cream pressed into a loaf pan with brandy-soaked cherries. If you have a pretty mold, this would be a nice way to use it. When sliced, the terrine reveals a luscious fruit-packed interior. When strawberries or muscat grapes are in season, substitute them for the cherries. If you do, be sure to hull and halve the strawberries or seed the grapes before using them.

> 1 pound (2 cups) pitted fresh cherries, halved
> ¼ cup dark rum or kirsch (cherry brandy)
> 2 tablespoons confectioners' sugar
> 2 pints dark chocolate ice cream
> Brandied Sour Cherries (page 444), optional

6. To loosen the ice cream, briefly dip the bottom of the pan into a bowl of hot water. Invert the ice cream onto a platter. Garnish with Brandied Cherries, if desired, slice, and serve.

A VERY QUICK ICE-CREAM DESSERT

I always keep a jar of Cognac-soaked prunes (see Drunken Prunes, page 392) on hand, because they come in handy for quick desserts when I have company. All you have to do is scoop a little good-quality coffee and vanilla ice cream into a sundae glass, then spoon a few Drunken Prunes over the top. Instant desserts don't get any easier or more elegant.

1. Toss the fresh cherries with the rum and confectioners' sugar in a medium-size bowl, cover, and chill for at least 2 hours.

2. Remove 1 pint of the ice cream from the freezer and let sit at room temperature until it reaches a spreadable consistency, 10 to 15 minutes.

3. Spread the softened ice cream evenly over the bottom of a 1½-quart loaf pan. Cover with plastic wrap, and freeze until hard, 1 to 2 hours.

4. Remove the remaining pint of ice cream 10 to 15 minutes before you are ready to spread the second layer of ice cream, and let it soften to a spreadable consistency.

5. Drain the fresh cherries, and scatter them over the frozen ice cream layer. Spread with the second pint of softened ice cream. Cover with plastic wrap, and freeze until hard.

MANGO TEA AND LITCHEE HONEY ICE CREAM

YIELD: 1¾ QUARTS, OR 14 SERVINGS

This unusual ice cream is not made with fresh mangoes or litchees but with fragrant infusions of their blossoms. Mango tea is black tea flavored with dried mango flowers, and litchee honey is a delicious elixir produced by bees that feed on litchee blossoms. The delicate twosome is a tremendous hot brew and a fantastic frozen treat. Don't be discouraged if you can't find mango tea or litchee honey. Just substitute a fruit-flavored herbal tea, like strawberry, raspberry, or peach (break open a few bags if you can't find it loose), and orange or

blueberry honey (available in health food stores). For an elegant presentation, I arrange sliced fresh mangoes decoratively around the ice cream before I serve it.

1½ cups milk
3 tablespoons mango tea leaves
6 large egg yolks
1 cup litchee honey
2 cups heavy (or whipping) cream

1. Bring the milk to a boil in a medium-size, heavy saucepan. Remove the pan from the heat and stir in the tea leaves. Cover and let sit for 30 minutes.

2. In a mixing bowl, beat the egg yolks with an electric mixer until pale yellow ribbons form when the beaters are lifted, about 5 minutes. Gradually add the honey. Beat until well combined.

3. Strain the tea-infused milk directly into the egg mixture in the bowl and discard the tea leaves. Mix well and return it to the saucepan over low heat. Stir constantly with a wooden spoon until the mixture thickens enough to coat the spoon, about 10 minutes. Do not let the mixture simmer or boil. Strain the custard through a fine sieve into a large bowl set over ice. Stir constantly until the custard is cool, about 10 minutes. Cover the custard with plastic wrap, and refrigerate until cold, about 1 hour.

4. In a mixing bowl, whip the cream until soft peaks form. Gently fold the chilled custard into the whipped cream. Freeze the custard in an ice cream maker according to the manufacturer's instructions.

5. Transfer the ice cream to a plastic container, cover, and freeze for several hours or overnight, to mellow. Before serving, allow the ice cream to soften slightly in the refrigerator.

SOOTHING FRUIT
DESSERTS

There is no finer way to end a meal than with ripe fresh fruit. Besides eating it alone or accompanied by a morsel of creamy cheese after dinner, I enjoy quick fruit desserts made with just a few other ingredients: chilled fruit compote in summer or roasted pears in the winter. In these simple preparations, I always seek to bring out a fruit's essence—with a dusting of sugar, a sprig of mint, or a splash of Cognac, for example—rather than mask it with overbearing syrups and sauces.

I think of the recipes in this chapter as cooks' desserts (as opposed to pastry chefs' desserts) because they don't take a lot of time or effort. It was hard to limit myself to these few, since an almost infinite variety of combinations is possible and they all taste wonderful to me. What follows is a broad selection of fruit desserts: No-Bake Fruit Desserts, such as fruit salads; Spoon Desserts, such as custards; and Simple Baked Desserts, such as crisps and crumbles.

To make these desserts, look for fragrant fruits that give a little when squeezed gently. Since perfectly ripe fruits are usually loaded with natural sugars, fresh fruit desserts need relatively little sweetening.

NO-BAKE FRUIT
DESSERTS

These recipes call for macerating fruit in wine or liquor, cooking it quickly over a flame, or simply tossing it with a few other ingredients. Be sure to use the best fruit you can get your hands on: In these simple concoctions, there's nothing to disguise a bad apple.

TROPICAL FRUIT SALAD

YIELD: 8 SERVINGS

I frequently serve this fruit salad to my guests when I entertain. It's simple to prepare, light, colorful, and packed with tropical flavors. Although not necessary, a dollop of passion fruit- or orange-flavored whipped cream complements the fruit salad very nicely. Or, if you prefer, top this salad with a scoop

of coconut sorbet. It makes an outstanding dessert for brunch too.

1 medium mango, peeled, pitted, and cut into 1-inch cubes
1 small papaya, peeled, seeded, and cut into 1-inch cubes
2 cups fresh cherries (or any berries in season), pitted and halved
2 cups fresh litchees, peeled, pitted, and halved, or 1 can (20 ounces) litchees in light syrup, drained then halved
1 can (20 ounces) jackfruit in syrup, drained, each section torn in half
2 tablespoons honey
Juice of 2 limes
1/4 cup shredded fresh mint (for shredding instructions, see page 34)
Orange Chantilly or Passion Fruit Chantilly (page 412; optional)
Fresh mint sprigs, for garnish (optional)

1. Combine the mango, papaya, cherries, litchees, and jackfruit in a large mixing bowl.

2. Stir the honey and lime juice together in a small bowl until the honey is dissolved. Add the honey mixture and mint to the fruit, and toss to combine. Cover and refrigerate until well chilled.

3. To serve, spoon the salad into individual fruit cups. Garnish each serving with a dollop of Chantilly and a mint sprig, if desired.

MACERATED NECTARINES AND BERRIES

YIELD: 4 SERVINGS

Literally "strawberries of the woods," *fraises des bois* are wild strawberries that are smaller and more aromatic than regular strawberries. You can purchase them at some farm stands or hunt for them in the woods in late June and early July. If they are unavailable, fresh strawberries can stand in for them. If Moscato di Pantelleria, a perfumey Italian orange Muscat wine is unavailable, substitute another fruity dessert wine, such as Sauternes or spumante, or

½ cup each dry white wine and Triple Sec or Marsala. This dish also makes a good starter for a brunch.

2 nectarines, halved, pitted, and thinly sliced
48 whole *fraises des bois*, or 12 large fresh strawberries, hulled and quartered
½ pint (1 cup) fresh blueberries
2 tablespoons fresh lemon juice
2 tablespoons sugar, or to taste
1 cup well-chilled Muscat wine, preferably Moscato di Pantelleria
Fresh mint sprigs, for garnish

1. Combine the nectarines, *fraises des bois*, blueberries, lemon juice, and sugar in a large nonreactive bowl, adjusting the amount

of sugar as necessary. Toss the mixture well, cover, and refrigerate until a syrup forms, about 1 hour.

2. Just before serving, spoon the macerated fruits and their syrup into champagne glasses or large wine goblets.

3. Pour ¼ cup of the chilled wine into each glass. Garnish with mint sprigs, and serve.

MARINATED POMEGRANATES

YIELD: 4 SERVINGS

Here's the simplest of simple desserts: crunchy pomegranate seeds infused in orange liquor. If you are as much a pomegranate fancier as

POMEGRANATES

Pomegranate is a red, leathery-skinned fruit the size of a large orange graced with a princely crown and edible garnet seeds enclosed in white honeycombed membranes. Prized throughout antiquity as a symbol of fertility and abundance because of its myriad seeds, this fruit has been a source of myth, legend, and inspiration for poets like Chaucer and Shakespeare, both of whom praised its evident charms.

No one knows for sure where this ancient fruit originated, but it is quite popular throughout the Mediterranean, the Middle East, Central America, and South America. People in these regions enjoy pomegranate so much that they routinely incorporate it into almost everything: drinks, dips, salads, soups, and desserts. It is prized for its uniquely sweet and tart seeds, which add a pleasant crunch as well as a refreshing burst of flavor and color to a dish.

Pomegranates are available in our markets from early fall through mid-December. To enjoy the best pomegranates, select large, bright fruits that are heavy for their size, have thin, smooth skins, and show no sign of rot in the calyx. Whole fresh pomegranates will keep for up to 3 months in the refrigerator. For longer storage, seal the seeds (see below for peeling instructions) in plastic bags and freeze them.

To open a pomegranate, gently score the rind with a paring knife from top to bottom in sections (but without cutting through the fruit), then break the pomegranate into segments. With your fingers, dislodge the seeds from the tight membranes. Use these shimmering seeds to add a glamorous touch to almost any dish, sweet or savory: Sprinkle a few over a salad or a roast bird, or marinate them in liquor and spoon them over ice cream. Children love to drink straight from the pomegranate. To loosen the juice from the seeds, firmly roll the whole unpeeled fruit back and forth on a hard surface, pressing on it to crush the juice sacs inside. Puncture a deep hole in the skin (watch out for stains) and quickly suck out the delicious juice, continually squeezing the fruit as you go.

I am, you will love it. Serve the marinated fruit as is, or spoon it over ice cream or yogurt.

3 large pomegranates
Juice of 1 lemon
⅓ cup sugar
¼ cup orange liqueur, such as Grand Marnier or Curaçao

1. Using a paring knife, gently score the leathery skin of each fruit lengthwise in sections, but without cutting through the fruit, then break the pomegranate into segments. With your fingers, dislodge the seeds from the membranes.

2. Combine the pomegranate seeds, lemon juice, sugar, and orange liqueur in a medium-size bowl. Mix well to dissolve the sugar. Cover and refrigerate for 1 hour before serving.

CINNAMON-SUGARED ORANGES

YIELD: 4 SERVINGS

A Parisian girlfriend once served me this highly delicious dessert when she had me over for dinner. The idea behind it is to layer slices of fresh oranges with spices and let them sit in the refrigerator long enough for a syrup to form. It is amazing what just a little sugar, cinnamon, and lemon juice can do to a naked orange. The result is a simple but sophisticated dessert that allows the natural flavor and freshness of the fruit to shine through.

½ cup sugar
1 teaspoon ground cinnamon
4 navel oranges
4 teaspoons fresh lemon juice
4 sprigs fresh mint, for garnish

1. Combine the sugar and cinnamon in a small bowl. Mix well and set aside.

2. Slice off the tops and bottoms of the oranges. Using a sharp knife with a flexible blade, cut away the peel from the oranges by following their contour. Be sure to remove all the white pith as well, to expose the flesh. Slice each orange ¼ inch thick, but keep the slices in the order in which they were cut.

3. In a shallow glass baking dish, "reconstruct" each orange by stacking the slices. As you work, sprinkle each slice with the cinnamon sugar, dividing it evenly among the oranges. Secure the reconstructed orange by inserting a bamboo skewer (trimmed to size) down its center. Repeat sugaring the remaining 3 oranges in the same manner.

4. Sprinkle the oranges with lemon juice. Cover the dish with plastic wrap, and refrigerate until well chilled, about 2 hours.

Baste the oranges 2 or 3 times with the syrup that forms as they macerate.

5. Using a wide spatula, carefully transfer the oranges to 4 dessert plates. Spoon some syrup over the oranges, and remove the skewers. Gently press a sprig of mint onto the top of each orange and serve with a spoon and fork.

POACHED ORANGES WITH PLUM SYRUP

YIELD: 4 SERVINGS

Oranges are delicious when poached and served in a bright, red plum syrup. In the fall, when fresh pomegranates are available, I like to sprinkle a tablespoon of their ruby-red seeds over this dessert for garnish. Try serving this dessert chilled or warm. It would also make a wonderful starter for breakfast or brunch.

4 large navel oranges
3 tablespoons sugar
3 small red plums (about 1/2 pound),
    pitted and quartered
2 tablespoons orange liqueur, such
    as Grand Marnier or
    Curaçao

1. Using a zester, remove the zest from the oranges, and reserve.

2. Remove all the white pith from the oranges with a sharp knife. Slice the oranges 1/2 inch thick. Remove the seeds, if any.

3. Place the orange slices in a medium-size saucepan with the sugar, 1/2 cup water, and the reserved orange zest. Bring the mixture to a simmer and cook for 5 minutes. Using a slotted spoon, transfer the oranges to a bowl, and save the poaching liquid. Cover the oranges and refrigerate until well chilled.

4. To make the syrup, place the plums and the poaching liquid in a blender, and purée until smooth. Pour the purée back into the saucepan, add the orange liqueur, and cook the mixture over medium-high heat until thick and syrupy, about 2 minutes. Strain through a fine sieve, pressing on the solids with the back of a spoon to extract as much liquid as possible. (There should be about 2/3 cup of plum syrup.) Cover and refrigerate until well chilled.

5. Spoon the plum syrup into compote dishes, then top with the chilled poached orange slices. Serve.

POACHING FRESH FRUITS

*W*hen a fruit doesn't seem quite ripe or flavorful enough, it can benefit from poaching in a flavored syrup. Poaching helps soften the fruit's texture as well as improve its flavor. Sometimes, I poach a fruit not because it lacks sugar but to intensify its natural sweetness and at the same time infuse it with an herb or spice.

The most delicious way to poach fruit is by using Simple Syrup (page 348) with fresh lemon juice and maybe a stick of cinnamon, some crushed ginger, or liqueur. I use the ratio of 2 tablespoons fresh lemon juice for every 2 cups syrup. Make sure you use enough to cover the fruit. Pour the syrup along with any flavorings into a large pot or casserole, bring the mixture to a boil, then reduce the heat to low. Peel or halve the fruits as indicated below, then carefully add them to the pot. If necessary, add some more syrup or water to cover the fruits completely. Cook just below simmering until the fruit is fork-tender but not mushy.

When the fruits are just tender, turn off the heat, and let them cool in the syrup to absorb as much flavor as possible. If the fruits seem too soft, remove them immediately from the syrup, and cool them as fast as possible in the refrigerator.

To serve, spoon some of the poaching syrup over the fruit. Both can be either warm or chilled. Or serve the poached fruit with a fruit sauce, if you wish, and save the syrup for future use. It can be reused a few times for poaching. Stored in a jar in the refrigerator, the syrup will keep indefinitely. If it becomes too thick, thin it with water.

What follows is a quick guide to poaching specific fruits. The cooking times are approximate and do not include the cooling in the syrup. The times will also vary depending on how large the fruit is and the degree of softness you prefer.

APPLES OR PEARS: *For apples, select Rome Beauty or Granny Smith. For pears, use Bosc or Comice. With a vegetable peeler, remove the skin from the fruits, starting at the stem ends. Core the fruits through the bottom end with a melon baller. Trim the bottoms flat so the fruits stand upright. As the fruits are peeled, it's a good idea to rub them with some lemon juice, to prevent discoloration. Carefully place the fruits in the syrup. Poach for 15 to 20 minutes.*

APRICOTS OR PLUMS: *Make a lengthwise slit into each fruit and remove the pits. Poach the unpeeled fruits for 5 to 8 minutes.*

MANGOES: *With a sharp knife, peel the mangoes, starting at the stem ends. Cut a thick slice of mango from each side of the pit. Save the pit for yourself and poach the slices for 10 to 15 minutes.*

ORANGES: *With a sharp knife, cut away the peel from the oranges by following their contour. Be sure to remove all the white pith as well, to expose the flesh. Add the peeled oranges to the syrup, along with any juice that may have exuded from the fruits. Poach for 5 to 8 minutes.*

PEACHES: *Peel the peaches, cut them in half, and remove the pits. Poach for 8 to 10 minutes.*

POACHED SUMMER FRUITS

YIELD: 4 TO 6 SERVINGS

Similar to a fruit compote, this light and visually appealing warm dessert is delicious. I'm also fond of the yin-yang effect that it creates when ladled over a scoop of frozen yogurt. If red currants are unavailable, use ½ pint each blackberries and raspberries. Also, try fall fruits like fresh figs, persimmons, tangerines, pears, and plums to make a slightly different but no less wonderful fruit dessert.

2 navel oranges
⅓ cup sugar
½ pound ripe but firm apricots (about 4 medium), halved and pitted
½ pint (1 cup) fresh blackberries
½ pint (1 cup) fresh raspberries
¼ pint (½ cup) red currants
¼ cup crème de cassis
Frozen yogurt (optional)
Fresh mint sprigs, for garnish

1. Slice off the tops and bottoms of the oranges. Using a sharp knife with a flexible blade, cut the peel away from the oranges, following the contour of the fruit. Remove the white pith as well, to expose the flesh. Working over a bowl to collect the juices, cut between the membrane to separate the fruit into segments. Take care not to break the segments.

2. Combine the sugar and 1 cup water in a medium-size saucepan and stir until the sugar is dissolved. Bring to a boil over medium heat, and then simmer until a light syrup forms, about 3 minutes.

3. Add the apricots and simmer until they are just heated through, about 1 minute (if the apricots are very ripe, simmer them for only 30 seconds). With a slotted spoon, transfer them to a serving bowl.

4. Add all the berries to the syrup and simmer until they are just heated through, 15 seconds. With a slotted spoon, transfer them to the bowl with the apricots.

5. Add the orange segments and any juices to the syrup and simmer for 30 seconds. Use a slotted spoon to transfer them to the bowl of fruit.

6. Drain any syrup collected in the fruit bowl into the saucepan. Cook the syrup over medium-high heat until reduced by half. Remove from the heat and stir in the crème de cassis. Pour the syrup over the fruit in the serving bowl.

7. Spoon the warmed poached fruits into individual compote dishes. Top with a scoop of frozen yogurt, if desired. Garnish with fresh mint sprigs.

POACHED FRESH FIGS

YIELD: 4 SERVINGS

My family used to live in the south of France, where we had a huge fig tree in our garden. In season, I loved eating fresh figs off the tree in the very early morning, when their thin skin was still moist with golden dew. Today I find warm figs bathed in a light syrup scented with lemon and fresh thyme even more sublime. If you have access to fresh fig leaves, add a few to the poaching liquid (omitting the thyme) for an aromatic bouquet and peppery kick. Once the syrup has cooled, save the leaves for garnish. Poached figs also make a wonderful starter at breakfast or brunch.

1 cup dry white wine
³/₄ cup sugar
Zest of 2 large lemons
2 sprigs fresh thyme (optional)
8 fresh Calimyrna figs
Sour cream, for garnish (optional)

1. Combine the wine, sugar, 1½ cups water, the lemon zest, and thyme, if using, in a medium-size saucepan and bring to a boil, stirring until the sugar is dissolved. Reduce the heat to medium-low and simmer for 5 minutes.

2. Add the figs to the syrup and continue to simmer until the figs are soft, about 5 minutes. Remove from the heat and let the figs cool slightly in the syrup. Remove and discard the thyme.

3. Divide the figs among 4 stemmed glasses and spoon the warm syrup and lemon zest over the fruits. Serve at once or refrigerate until well chilled, about 3 hours. Top with a dollop of sour cream, if desired.

FRESH PERSIMMONS IN PEPPERED VANILLA SAUCE

YIELD: 4 SERVINGS

On its own, a delicate, perfectly ripe persimmon is special, but a sauce of sweet vanilla and the kick of peach brandy and cracked pepper make it sublime. This super-quick dessert will work equally well with fresh figs, but use sweet vermouth instead of peach brandy.

> 4 large ripe persimmons
> 1 cup melted vanilla ice cream,
>   chilled
> 1/3 cup peach brandy
> 1/2 teaspoon cracked black peppercorns
> Fresh mint sprigs, for garnish
>   (optional)

1. Stem and peel the persimmons. Cut each into 6 wedges. Cover and refrigerate until ready to serve.

2. Just before serving, pour 1/4 cup melted vanilla ice cream on each of 4 dessert plates, and arrange 6 wedges of persimmon on the ice cream.

3. In a small saucepan, heat the brandy and cracked pepper over medium-low heat and flambé according to the instructions on page 205. Spoon the flambéed brandy over the persimmons. Garnish with mint, if desired, and serve immediately.

THREE-FRUIT TERRINE WITH BANANA SAUCE

YIELD: 10 TO 12 SERVINGS

Now that everyone is so aware of problems caused by overdoing the fat and cholesterol, the challenge is to satisfy and dazzle guests with elegant healthful desserts. This French fruit mold, brimming with pears, oranges, and raspberries set in gelatin, is the answer to such a challenge. Not only delicious, when sliced, the terrine reveals colorful alternating layers of luscious fruits. A rum-laced banana sauce adds another flavor dimension. The terrine should be prepared at least a day in advance and may be kept refrigerated for up to 3 days. For variation, you may substitute Raspberry Sauce (see Index) for the banana sauce. Serve with light, crisp cookies, such as tuiles, if desired.

> FRUIT TERRINE
> 4 ripe pears, preferably Bartlett or Bosc
> 7 juice oranges
> Fresh orange juice, if necessary
> 1/3 cup sugar
> 2 tablespoons (2 envelopes) unflavored gelatin
> 3/4 cup very good Sauternes, Muscat, or other
>   sweet white wine
> 1/2 pint (1 cup) fresh raspberries

BANANA SAUCE
½ cup sugar
2 ripe, but firm bananas
Juice of 1 lemon
1 teaspoon dark rum

Fresh mint sprigs, for garnish (optional)

1. To make the terrine, peel, quarter, and core each pear. Place them in a large saucepan and cover with cold water. Bring to a simmer over medium heat, and cook, uncovered, until fork-tender, 5 to 8 minutes, depending on ripeness. Remove the pears and drain on paper towels.

2. Slice off the tops and bottoms of the oranges. Using a sharp knife with a flexible blade, carefully cut away the peel, following the contour of the fruit. Remove all the white pith as well. Working over a colander placed in a bowl to collect the juices, cut between the membrane to separate the fruit into sections. (You should have about 2 cups of orange segments.) Strain the juice, measure it, and add orange juice, if necessary, to measure ¾ cup.

3. Mix the orange juice and sugar in a medium-size saucepan and sprinkle in the gelatin. Set aside and let soften for 5 minutes. Heat the mixture over low heat, stirring with a wooden spoon, until the gelatin and sugar are completely dissolved, about 2 minutes. Remove from the heat and add the Sauternes. This will be your aspic. Set aside to cool but don't refrigerate.

4. Cut each piece of pear lengthwise

into 3 segments. Pour about ¼ cup of the aspic into a 1½ quart loaf pan. Arrange one-third of the pears evenly in the bottom of the pan. Top the pear layer with half the raspberries. Arrange half the orange segments on top of the raspberries. Gently ladle in enough aspic to just cover the fruits. Repeat the layering process until the terrine is filled, ending with the pears. Cover with plastic wrap and refrigerate until set, about 6 hours, or overnight.

5. To make the sauce, mix the sugar and 1½ cups water in a medium-size saucepan and bring to a boil over medium heat. Peel and cut the bananas into 1-inch pieces. Add them to the syrup along with the lemon juice, and cook until the bananas are soft, about 2 minutes.

6. Transfer the banana mixture to a blender or food processor and purée it. Strain the sauce through a fine sieve into a medium-size bowl. Stir in the rum. Transfer the purée to a jar with a lid and refrigerate until ready to serve. Thin with 2 tablespoons water, if necessary. The sauce should be thin but retain the flavor of the bananas.

7. About 1 hour before serving, place the terrine in the freezer. To unmold, briefly dip the pan in hot water and invert the terrine onto a large serving platter. Using a sharp serrated knife dipped in hot water, carefully cut the terrine into slices about ¾ inch thick.

8. Place each slice on a dessert plate and surround it with some banana sauce. Serve, garnished with mint leaves, if desired. Pass any extra banana sauce in a pitcher.

DRUNKEN PRUNES

YIELD: 2 PINTS

Prunes soaked in spirits are one of the most delicious things you could possibly eat. I've done all kinds of wonderful things with them, like wrapping them in bacon and broiling them for lovely appetizers, stuffing them in a roast loin of pork for a delicious entrée (Swedish Roast Pork, see Index), or spooning them over cakes or ice cream for devastatingly good but effortless desserts. Because the brandy acts as a natural preservative, there's really no need to process or refrigerate the jars. The prunes will be ready for use after soaking overnight, and they will keep for up to 1 year. Just like the brandy in which they are packed, the longer the fruit sits, the better it tastes. For best results, use top-quality jumbo pitted prunes. If you don't have brandy, you can soak the fruits in dark rum, whisky, sherry, or port.

1 pound (3 cups) pitted prunes
Boiling water
1½ cups (or more) brandy, preferably Cognac

1. Place the prunes in a large bowl and cover with boiling water. Let sit until the fruits are plumped and soft, about 30 minutes. Drain off the water.

2. Place the prunes in 2 pint jars, and add enough brandy to each jar to completely cover the fruits. Cover and store the jars in your pantry or in the refrigerator, for up to 1 year.

FLAMED PEACHES AND STRAWBERRIES WITH TEQUILA

YIELD: 2 SERVINGS

The intense, pure flavor of peaches and strawberries shines through in this simple dessert. Fresh mango or papaya makes excellent substitutes for the peach.

1 lemon
2 peaches (about ¾ pound total)
½ pint (1 cup) strawberries
1½ tablespoons unsalted butter
1½ tablespoons sugar
2 tablespoons peach brandy
2 tablespoons tequila, such as Cuervo Gold

When peaches are really ripe you can peel them the way Spanish and Portuguese waiters do: Rub each peach with the dull side of a table knife without breaking the skin. This loosens the skin so that, with practice, it can be removed in one piece with a squeeze of the hand, a spectacular trick.

—JAMES BEARD

1. Using a zester, remove enough of the zest from the lemon to measure 1 teaspoon. Do not include any white pith. Juice the lemon and reserve 2 teaspoons of juice. Set aside.

2. Pit the peaches and slice them into ¼-inch-thick slices. Wash, hull, and quarter the strawberries.

3. Melt the butter in a medium size skillet over medium-low heat. Add the lemon zest, peaches, strawberries, sugar, and lemon juice. Sauté until the fruits are slightly softened, about 1 minute. Add the peach brandy and continue to cook over low heat until a light syrup forms, about 1 minute. Remove from the heat.

4. Heat the tequila in a small saucepan over low heat, and use it to flambé the fruits, following the instructions on page 205.

5. As soon as the flames die out, spoon the fruits into dessert plates, and serve at once.

KIWIS IN GINGERED SYRUP

YIELD: 4 SERVINGS

I think kiwis achieve their ultimate glory when served with a light, ginger syrup. They look elegant and taste clean, which makes them an ideal end to a rich meal. For an even more delightful fruit soup, add pitted dark cherries, blackberries, sliced peaches—or star fruit, for its attractive shape.

¼ cup apple or quince jelly

2 tablespoons sugar

6 quarter-size pieces peeled fresh ginger, crushed

Zest of 1 lemon

8 kiwis

¼ cup fresh raspberries

8 fresh mint sprigs, for garnish (optional)

1. Combine the jelly, sugar, ginger, and lemon zest with 1 cup water in a small saucepan. Bring to a simmer over medium heat and stir until the sugar and jelly are dissolved, about 2 minutes.

2. Let cool and strain the syrup into a medium-size bowl. Cover and refrigerate until ready to serve, or until the syrup is well chilled.

3. Peel and slice the kiwis. Arrange 2 kiwis in each of 4 shallow bowls. Spoon the syrup over the kiwi. Garnish with fresh raspberries and mint sprigs, if desired.

LIGHT CHERRY SOUP

YIELD: 4 SERVINGS

This recipe is a lightened-up rendition of a traditional Asian pudding, in which fruit, usually banana, is cooked in a sweet coconut milk mixture thickened with tapioca pearls. It is so tasty and refreshing, you might become addicted to it. I also think this is one of the most delicious and best ways to use up all those height-of-the-summer cherries that you don't quite know what to do with. You can vary the character of this soup by changing the type of fruit you use—for instance, bananas give a creamier texture, apples add a mellow taste. Just remember that this dessert works well only with firm-fleshed types of fruit.

⅓ cup sugar
1 pound fresh sweet black cherries, pitted
2 tablespoons quick-cooking tapioca
¼ cup canned unsweetened coconut milk, well stirred, or light cream (or half-and-half), plus extra for garnish
1 teaspoon vanilla extract

1. Combine the sugar with 2 cups hot water in a medium-size saucepan, and stir until the sugar dissolves. Bring to a boil over medium-high heat.

2. Add the cherries, reduce the heat, and simmer over low heat until they are just tender, about 3 minutes.

3. Stir the tapioca into the coconut milk and add the mixture to the simmering cherries. Continue to simmer until the tapioca is translucent and the mixture thickens slightly, about 7 minutes. Stir occasionally to prevent scorching. Remove from the heat and let cool.

4. Stir in the vanilla extract and transfer the soup to a large bowl. Cover and chill.

5. Serve the soup in individual dessert cups. Top with additional coconut milk, if desired.

ENGLISH SUMMER PUDDING

YIELD: 8 TO 10 SERVINGS

Don't be surprised if you don't see any pudding in this classic old-fashioned English dessert. To the British, the term *pudding* covers a range of dishes that are sweet or savory, hot or cold, including steamed and molded cakes like this one: packed layers of bread and fruit that have been refrigerated overnight. During that time, the bread slowly soaks up all the delicious syrup rendered by the berries. The recipe may be made with raspberries alone, if you wish. Frozen unsweetened raspberries work perfectly, too (you'll need three

12-ounce bags), providing the extra juices necessary to soak up the bread and making for an enticingly moist pudding. Traditionally, slices of day-old bread are spread with butter before they are used to line the mold. I eliminate the butter (and therefore the extra calories) and think that the pudding tastes cleaner. It's just perfect when you serve it with a spoonful of Chantilly Cream. Don't pass it up! For top flavors, plan to prepare this dessert 2 days before serving.

2½ cups fresh raspberries
1½ cups fresh blackberries
1½ cups fresh blueberries
1½ tablespoons orange liqueur, such as Grand Marnier or Triple Sec
⅓ cup plus 2 tablespoons sugar
12 slices firm white sandwich bread, such as Pepperidge Farm
Mixed fresh berries, for garnish (optional)
Fresh mint sprigs, for garnish (optional)
Chantilly Cream (page 411) for serving

1. Combine the berries, Grand Marnier, and ⅓ cup of the sugar in a medium-size saucepan and place over low heat. Cook until the sugar has just melted to form a light syrup and the berries are barely warm, about 2 minutes. Remove the pan from the heat and set it aside.

2. Using a long, sharp knife, trim the crusts sparingly from the bread, keeping the slices as large as possible. Cut 6 of the slices lengthwise in half. Set all the bread aside.

3. Line a 1½-quart loaf pan with plas-

tic wrap, allowing a generous overhang on the sides. Smooth the plastic on the bottom, and around the sides of the pan.

4. Line the bottom of the pan with 2½ slices of bread so that they fit snugly. Line the sides and ends of the pan with additional halved bread slices so they fit snugly.

5. With a slotted spoon, transfer half the berries to the bread-lined pan, spreading them out evenly. Sprinkle 1 tablespoon sugar over the berries, then cover the fruits with 2½ slices of bread. Spoon the remaining berries over the bread, then sprinkle with the remaining 1 tablespoon sugar. Pack the fruits so they are level with the bread lining the sides of the pan. Cover the berries with the remaining 2½ slices of bread. Drizzle the remaining berry syrup evenly over the bread.

6. Fold the plastic overhangs over the

pudding, and cover the pan with plastic wrap. Place a 2-pound can or bottle on top of the pudding to weigh it down. Refrigerate for at least 6 hours, or overnight.

7. Remove the weight. Unfold the plastic wrap that's on the top of the pudding. Place a large platter upside down over the pudding, and invert the pan onto the platter. Gently lift off the pan, then peel off the plastic wrap. Garnish the top of the pudding with fresh berries and mint, if desired.

8. To serve, use a sharp knife to cut the pudding into slices. Pass the Chantilly Cream or sour cream separately.

SPOON DESSERTS

These luscious soft delights are a great way to pamper your loved ones—and yourself. An English-style trifle unites strawberries, bananas, and ladyfingers. And puréed papaya meets coconut in a cooling Asian pudding. Whether light and airy or rich and dense, these are exquisite comfort foods.

MARGARITA MOUSSE WITH BLACKBERRIES

YIELD: 4 SERVINGS

Here is a ravishing parfait in which a mousse flavored with lime, tequila, and Triple Sec is layered in chilled glasses with luscious fresh blackberries. Talk about your frozen margaritas! This simple, very satisfying dessert is good enough to please the sweetest tooth. Prepare the parfaits a few hours before serving so they have a chance to chill properly. Raspberries, blueberries, or lingonberries are excellent substitutes for the blackberries.

3/4 teaspoon unflavored gelatin
2 large eggs, separated (see Note)
4 tablespoons sugar
2 tablespoons fresh lime juice
2 teaspoons tequila, such as Cuervo Gold
1 tablespoon plus 2 teaspoons Triple Sec
1/2 teaspoon finely grated lime zest
Pinch of salt
1/2 cup well-chilled heavy (or whipping) cream
2 1/2 cups fresh blackberries
Fresh mint sprigs, for garnish

1. Put 2 tablespoons cold water in a small saucepan, and sprinkle the gelatin over it. Let sit for 5 minutes to soften the gelatin. Heat the mixture over low heat, swirling gently until the gelatin is completely dissolved and no grains remain, about 2 minutes. Set aside.

2. Bring 2 cups water to a simmer in a medium-size saucepan over low heat. Place the egg yolks, 2 tablespoons of the sugar, the lime juice, tequila, and 2 teaspoons of the Triple Sec in a heatproof bowl and whisk until blended. Place the bowl over the pan (it should not touch the simmering water). Whisking vigorously, cook the yolk mixture until it is thick and pale yellow, 5 minutes.

3. Remove the bowl and stir in the melted gelatin and lime zest. Continue whisking until the egg mixture is cool. Cover the custard and chill it for 30 minutes.

4. Ten minutes before you are ready to serve dessert, place four 10-ounce parfait glasses in the freezer to chill.

5. In a medium-size mixing bowl with clean beaters, beat the egg whites with a pinch of salt until they hold soft peaks, about 2 minutes. Add the remaining 2 tablespoons sugar and continue to beat until the egg whites hold stiff peaks, about 1 minute longer. Add the beaten egg whites to the bowl with the chilled custard but do not fold in yet. In the same bowl used to beat the egg whites, beat the cream with the remaining 1 tablespoon Triple Sec until stiff peaks form, about 2 minutes. Now, fold the whites into the yolk mixture, then fold in the whipped cream.

6. Set aside the 4 largest, most beauti-

ful blackberries. Alternate layers of the mousse and blackberries in the chilled parfait glasses, beginning and ending with the mousse. Top each parfait with a reserved blackberry and a sprig of fresh mint. Cover each glass with plastic wrap and refrigerate until well chilled, at least 4 hours, before serving.

NOTE: This recipe contains raw egg whites, which can carry the bacteria that cause salmonella. If you are uncertain about the quality of your eggs, you may want to "sanitize" the whites according to the instructions in Safer Eggs (page 372). You'll have to start the process at least 48 hours before you intend to prepare the recipe.

BERRIES IN RED WINE SAUCE

YIELD: ABOUT 2 CUPS

When I have friends over for a low-key dinner, I enjoy serving this full-bodied berry sauce over some purchased ice cream for a quick, delicious, but impressive dessert. This sauce is so good, I'm sure you will find other ways of using it, like spooning it over mousse or angel food cake, for

example. And if you thicken the sauce slightly with cornstarch, it makes a great topping for cheesecake as well.

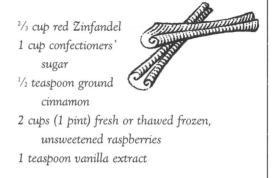

⅔ cup red Zinfandel
1 cup confectioners' sugar
½ teaspoon ground cinnamon
2 cups (1 pint) fresh or thawed frozen, unsweetened raspberries
1 teaspoon vanilla extract

1. Combine the wine, sugar, and cinnamon in a small saucepan, and bring to a boil over high heat. Reduce the heat to low, and simmer until the mixture becomes syrupy, about 5 minutes.

2. Stir in the raspberries and vanilla extract and remove from the heat. Cool the sauce to room temperature, then refrigerate until well chilled.

YIN-YANG PAPAYA DESSERT

YIELD: 4 SERVINGS

In Southeast Asia, during the blazing hot seasons, people often serve this refreshing sweet dessert to cool their bodies and tempers. It is as simple to make as it is pleasing to the eye and the palate. When this dessert is served, the white of the tapioca contrasts sharply with the orange of the papaya purée to create a yin-yang color pattern. Extremely refreshing and not overly sweet, this dessert is an ideal finish to any meal. Ripe melon, mangoes, peaches, pears, plums, or strawberries may be used instead of the papaya.

> 1 cup canned unsweetened coconut milk, well stirred
> ³/₄ cup milk
> 3 tablespoons sugar
> 2 tablespoons quick-cooking tapioca
> ½ teaspoon vanilla extract
> 2 medium ripe papayas (about 1½ pounds)
> Fresh mint sprigs, for garnish

1. Combine the coconut milk, milk, sugar, and tapioca in a medium-size saucepan, and bring to a boil over high heat. Reduce the heat to low and simmer, stirring frequently, until the tapioca is translucent and the mixture is slightly thickened, about 5 minutes. Do not overcook; the mixture will continue to set as it cools. Stir in the vanilla extract.

2. Let the tapioca cool. Cover and refrigerate until it is well chilled, at least 1 hour.

3. Halve the papayas and remove the seeds. With a spoon, scoop out the flesh and place it in a blender or food processor. Process the papaya to a purée. (There should be about 2 cups of purée.) Cover and refrigerate until well chilled, at least 1 hour.

4. To serve, spoon the tapioca pudding into 1 side of each soup bowl, then add the papaya purée on the other side, forming a yin-yang pattern. Garnish with a mint sprig and serve at once.

CHILLED CHERIMOYA CUSTARD

YIELD: 4 SERVINGS

The creamy, slightly granular texture of this light dessert will remind you of a ripe pear. It's the simplest thing in the world to prepare, yet it's so flavorful. This dessert is a favorite with children, who invariably ask for seconds. If cherimoya is unavailable, substitute 1 cup diced ripe mango or pear, and use orange juice instead of pineapple juice.

> ¼ cup pineapple juice
> 1 teaspoon unflavored gelatin
> 1 large ripe cherimoya (about ³/₄ pound)
> ½ cup milk
> 2 tablespoons sugar
> ¼ teaspoon vanilla extract
> 4 thin orange slices, for garnish (optional)

1. Place the pineapple juice in a small saucepan, sprinkle the gelatin over the juice, and let the mixture sit for 2 minutes. Heat

the mixture over low heat until the gelatin is completely dissolved, about 2 minutes. Set aside to cool.

2. Peel the cherimoya and break it into small chunks, removing all the seeds. (There should be about 1 cup of cherimoya pulp.)

3. Place the cherimoya, milk, sugar, and vanilla extract in a blender. Blend at high speed until smooth. With the motor running, add the cooled pineapple juice and gelatin mixture.

4. Pour the mixture into individual compote dishes, cover, and chill. Garnish each dessert with a slice of orange, if desired.

GRAND MARNIER SABAYON OVER CHAMPAGNE GRAPES

YIELD: 4 SERVINGS

Sabayon, from the Italian *zabaglione*, is a luscious egg-based sauce traditionally made with Marsala, a Sicilian fortified wine, and served as a warm dessert in itself. If you don't have or don't care for Marsala, you can readily substitute other wines. When I make this sauce, I usually flavor it with dry white wine and Grand Marnier. I also like to enrich it a bit with whipped cream, then serve it cold over fresh fruit. Spooned over sweet Champagne grapes, tangerine sections, or fresh berries, it is heavenly! Champagne grapes are a variety of red wine grape that grows in miniature clusters. Tiny but crisp and sweet, these delicious seedless grapes should be eaten with their needle-thin stems. Look for these precious fruits from late summer to early fall. And, if you like some extra texture, crumble a couple amaretti cookies over the dessert before serving.

> 4 large egg yolks
> 3 tablespoons dry white wine
> 3 tablespoons orange liqueur, such as Grand Marnier or Triple Sec
> 1/4 cup sugar
> 1 1/2 pounds Champagne grapes, rinsed and drained well
> 1/2 cup well-chilled heavy (or whipping) cream

1. Bring 2 cups water to a simmer in a medium-size saucepan over low heat. Place the egg yolks, white wine, Grand Marnier, and sugar in a heatproof bowl, and whisk to blend. Place the bowl over the pan (it should not touch the water). Whisking vigorously, cook the yolk mixture until it is foamy and thickened, about 5 minutes.

2. Remove the bowl, and continue whisking until the egg mixture is cool. Cover and refrigerate until well chilled.

3. Place a large mixing bowl and the beaters of an electric mixer in the freezer to chill.

4. When you are ready to serve, arrange the grapes in 4 wine goblets or dessert glasses.

5. Whip the cream in the chilled mixing bowl with the chilled beaters until soft peaks form. Fold the whipped cream into the chilled sabayon. Spoon the sauce over the grapes, and serve.

STRAWBERRY-BANANA TRIFLE

YIELD: 8 TO 10 SERVINGS

Trifle, the most venerable of English desserts, can be varied endlessly according to what type of fruits are at their peak when you prepare it. Typically, cake is moistened with syrup, then layered in a deep, clear trifle dish with a thick pudding or lemon curd and fruits in season. The top is covered with whipped cream or clotted cream before serving. This version, with strawberry, banana, and lemon, is one that I have often prepared for my dinner guests, because the flavors work so well together, and the result never fails to impress. What's more, you can make it year-round, substituting frozen strawberries if fresh ones are scarce. Like the English Summer Pudding (see Index), which gains flavor as it sits, this dessert has the virtue of lending itself to advance preparation. Prepare it the day before, cover it tightly with plastic wrap, and refrigerate until serving time. It's sinfully rich, but worth every calorie!

LEMON CURD
3 large eggs
1 large egg yolk
½ cup plus 2 tablespoons confectioners' sugar
¼ cup fresh lemon juice
1 tablespoon finely grated lemon zest
6 tablespoons (¾ stick) unsalted butter, cut into 6 pieces
1 cup sour cream

TRIFLE
2 pints (4 cups) fresh strawberries, washed, hulled, and quartered
¼ cup plus 2 tablespoons granulated sugar
3 tablespoons dark rum
16 to 18 ladyfingers
3 large ripe bananas
1 cup well-chilled heavy (or whipping) cream
2 tablespoons confectioners' sugar
Whole fresh strawberries, for garnish (optional)

1. To make the lemon curd, pour water to a depth of about 1 inch into the bottom of a double boiler and bring to a boil over high heat. Reduce the heat to low to maintain a steady simmer. In the top of the double boiler, off the heat, whisk the eggs, egg yolk, and confectioners' sugar gently until well combined. Stir in 2 tablespoons water, the lemon juice and zest, and the butter.

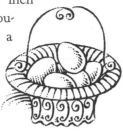

2. Place the top of the double boiler over the simmering water and cook, stirring occasionally, until the butter starts to melt. Then cook, whisking constantly, until the mixture thickens and bubbles in the center, 10 to 12 minutes. The cream should be thick, smooth, and shiny.

3. Remove from the heat and cool the curd quickly by placing the top of the double boiler in a bowl of ice water, stirring the curd occasionally as it cools. When cool, stir in the sour cream. Cover and refrigerate.

4. To make the trifle, place the strawberries and 2 tablespoons of the granulated sugar in a bowl and mash with a fork. Cover and set aside.

5. Combine the remaining ¼ cup granulated sugar with 1 cup water in a small saucepan. Bring to a boil over medium-high heat and continue cooking until syrupy, about 3 minutes. Stir in the rum, and let the syrup cool slightly.

6. To assemble the trifle, dip half the ladyfingers, one by one, into the warm syrup, then arrange them snugly in a single layer onto the bottom of a 10-cup trifle bowl or stemmed compote. Peel and thinly slice 1½ bananas. Arrange the slices over the ladyfingers. Spread half the lemon curd over the bananas. Cover the lemon curd with half the mashed strawberries.

7. Peel and slice the remaining 1½ bananas. Repeat the layering process, ending with the strawberries. Cover and chill for several hours before serving.

DRESSING UP LEMON CURD

*U*se the lemon curd recipe on page 401 to create a whole new dessert with one of these easy-to-fix ideas.

✦ *For tarts, spoon the chilled lemon curd into baked tart shells and top with fresh berries or sliced bananas. Glaze the fruits by lightly brushing them with melted currant or apple jelly.*

✦ *For parfaits, layer the chilled lemon curd and Tropical Fruit Salad (see Index) in chilled parfait glasses.*

✦ *For a delicious sauce, stir some warm milk or water into the lemon curd until it reaches a consistency you like, and spoon over fruit, cake, or vanilla ice cream.*

✦ *For frozen pops, thin lemon curd with warm milk or water and spoon it into 3-ounce paper cups. Cover with aluminum foil, insert wooden sticks, and freeze until firm.*

8. Ten minutes before you are ready to serve the trifle, place a large mixing bowl and the beaters of an electric mixer in the freezer to chill.

9. Whip the cream in the chilled bowl with the chilled beaters at medium-high speed, until it starts to thicken. Add the confectioners' sugar and continue to whip at medium speed until stiff peaks form. Do not overbeat, or it will turn into butter. Pipe the whipped cream decoratively over the top of the trifle. Garnish with whole berries, if desired.

APRICOT FOOL

YIELD: 4 TO 6 SERVINGS

Fools, some of the oldest and simplest of English desserts, are a staple in England and Canada during the spring and summer, when berries of all kinds abound. It's basically a mixture of puréed fruit, sugar, and thick cream. Its name may have come from the French *foulé*, meaning crushed or pressed. As I love apricots, those most delicate, refreshing, and tempting of all summer fruits, I use them to make this delicious fool that vibrates with swirls of orange and white. It is essential that you select fresh, ripe apricots to maximize the fruity-tart flavor of this dessert. Canned apricots will not do. A slice of angel food cake or pound cake would be perfect with this fool.

> $^{1}/_{4}$ cup granulated sugar
> 1 teaspoon fresh lemon juice
> $^{1}/_{2}$ pound ripe apricots, halved and
>   pitted, plus a few apricot slices,
>   for garnish
> $^{1}/_{3}$ cup plus 2 tablespoons confectioners'
>   sugar
> 1$^{3}/_{4}$ cups well-chilled heavy (or whipping)
>   cream
> 3 tablespoons apricot brandy or orange
>   liqueur, such as Grand Marnier
>   or Triple Sec
> Fresh mint sprigs, for garnish
>   (optional)

1. Combine the granulated sugar and lemon juice with 1 cup water in a medium-size saucepan. Bring to a boil over high heat and cook, stirring, until the sugar is dissolved.

2. Add the apricots to the syrup. Reduce the heat so the liquid barely simmers, and cook, uncovered, until the fruit is tender, about 5 minutes. Remove the pan from the heat, cover, and allow the fruit to cool in the syrup. (The poached fruit and syrup may be chilled and served as is.)

3. Drain the apricots, reserving the syrup for another use. Place the apricots with 2 tablespoons of the confectioners' sugar in a blender and purée them. (There should be about 1 cup of purée.) Transfer to a large mixing bowl and set aside to cool.

4. Place a large mixing bowl and the beaters of an electric mixer in the freezer to chill.

5. Whip the heavy cream in the chilled bowl with chilled beaters at medium-high speed, until it starts to thicken. Add the remaining $1/3$ cup of the confectioners' sugar and the brandy, and continue to whip until stiff peaks form.

6. Add the whipped cream to the apricot purée. Using a rubber spatula, partially fold the mixtures together, leaving distinct swirls of orange and white; do not blend thoroughly. Spoon into compote glasses. Cover and chill for several hours. Garnish with apricot slices and mint sprigs.

VARIATION
BERRY FOOL: Replace the apricots with fresh or frozen berries. In a blender or food processor, purée 2 cups fresh strawberries, raspberries, or blackberries (or a mixture of 2 kinds of berries), then press the mixture through a fine sieve. Add confectioners'

sugar to taste (about $1/2$ cup), 2 tablespoons Grand Marnier or crème de cassis, and a few drops of fresh lemon juice. Whip $1^3/_4$ cups heavy (or whipping) cream to stiff peaks, then partly fold the cream into the berry purée.

ORANGE RICE PUDDING WITH FRESH APRICOT SAUCE

YIELD: 4 TO 6 SERVINGS

Rice pudding is one of those simple, can't-miss sweets for home cooks who don't like fancy baking. You will enjoy this creamy rendition; it is packed with wonderfully refreshing flavors. Although it is quite delicious by itself, here's how to turn this sweet creation into an elegant dessert: Serve it in wine goblets with rum-soaked mango and top with apricot sauce and toasted almonds. It's just as good made with cherries, peaches, pears, or mixed berries. Instead of the apricot sauce in the recipe, serve this dessert sometime with the alternative, Kumquat Sauce; it's absolutely divine!

MANGOES IN POLITE COMPANY

There's something fun, in a primal sort of way, about eating a mango right off the pit—getting its fibers stuck between your teeth and making a sticky mess of your face, hands, and clothes in the process. But sometimes it's necessary to be neat. There is a charming tropical method of cutting and serving a mango elegantly. Here's how:

1. Cut a small slice from the stem end of an unpeeled mango. Stabilize the mango by standing it on a cutting board on the flat end. Starting from the top, slice both cheeks of the mango off the large, flat pit, ending up with 2 thick pieces and the pit.

2. With a paring knife, deeply score the flesh (don't cut into the skin) of each mango cheek in a dia-mond pattern. Grasp one of the mango cheeks with both hands, with the flesh side facing up. Gently push up from the skin side to turn the fruit inside out—the scored flesh will stand out attractively and can be removed easily with a spoon at the table. Repeat with the remaining mango cheek. Do not discard the juicy, tasty pit; give it to your child (or save it for yourself) to gnaw on. The sweet flesh that clings to it is the best part of the fruit!

A WORD OF CAUTION: Like pineapple, mango skin has resin that produces an itchy rash in some people. Those who are allergic should wear rub-ber gloves when preparing this fruit.

½ cup basmati or other long-grain rice

1¼ cups milk

¼ teaspoon salt

½ cup thawed frozen orange juice
    concentrate

¼ cup golden raisins, plumped in boiling
    water to cover for 15 minutes and
    drained

1½ cups cubed fresh mango (½-inch pieces)

2 tablespoons dark rum

2 teaspoons fresh lime juice

½ cup well-chilled heavy (or whipping)
    cream

Apricot Sauce (recipe follows) or Kumquat
    Sauce (page 407)

2 tablespoons toasted slivered almonds (for
    toasting instructions, see page 64)

1. Place the rice in a medium-size saucepan and cover with water. Bring to a full boil and continue boiling for 5 minutes. Drain well. (The rice will be partially cooked at this point.)

2. Combine the boiled rice with the milk, ½ cup water, and the salt in a medium-size saucepan over medium-high heat. Bring to a boil. Reduce the heat to low and simmer, uncovered, until the rice is tender and almost all the liquid has been absorbed, about 15 minutes, stirring often. Remove from the heat and stir in the orange juice concentrate and raisins. Cool, then cover and refrigerate until well chilled.

3. Combine the mango, rum, and lime juice in a small bowl. Cover and chill in the refrigerator for at least 30 minutes.

4. Ten minutes before serving, place a

medium-size mixing bowl and the beaters of an electric mixer in the freezer to chill.

5. Whip the cream in the chilled bowl with the chilled beaters at medium-high speed until stiff peaks form. Don't overbeat the cream, or it will turn into butter. Fold the whipped cream, a third at a time, into the rice pudding.

6. Spoon the macerated mango into large wine goblets, then top with the rice pudding. Spoon some Apricot or Kumquat Sauce over the pudding and sprinkle with toasted almonds.

Apricot Sauce

YIELD: ABOUT 1 ¼ CUPS

Spoon this flavorful sauce over rice pudding, poached fruit, angel food cake, or pound cake.

¼ cup granulated sugar
1 teaspoon fresh lemon juice
½ pound ripe apricots, halved and pitted
2 tablespoons confectioners' sugar

1. Combine the granulated sugar and lemon juice with 1 cup water in a medium-size saucepan. Bring to a boil over high heat and cook, stirring, until the sugar is dissolved, about 1 minute.

2. Add the apricots to the syrup. Reduce the heat so the liquid barely simmers, and cook until the fruit is tender, about 5 minutes. Remove the pan from the heat, cover, and allow the fruit to cool in the syrup.

3. Drain the apricots, reserving the syrup. Place the apricots with the confectioners' sugar in a blender and purée them. Add ¼ cup of the reserved syrup and blend until thoroughly incorporated.

4. Strain the sauce through a fine sieve. If the sauce seems too thick, thin it out by adding a couple more tablespoons of syrup. Transfer the sauce to a jar, refrigerate, and use within 1 week.

VARIATIONS

PEACH SAUCE: Follow the directions for Apricot Sauce, substituting 2 large ripe peaches for the apricots.

MANGO SAUCE: Follow the directions for Apricot Sauce, substituting 1 large peeled and pitted ripe mango for the apricots.

A WORD ABOUT MASCARPONE

An Italian version of fresh clotted cream, but less dense, Mascarpone (used in Jennifer's Budino) is a soft, buttery cheese that is sinfully rich (it has close to 80 percent butterfat). Similar in taste to a combination of cream cheese and sour cream, it is an essential ingredient in many Italian desserts, among them the much celebrated tiramisù. It is also superb as is, spooned over fresh berries or other fresh fruit. Mascarpone is sold in fine cheese shops and Italian gourmet specialty shops. Because of its high butterfat content, it can spoil quickly, so refrigerate it as soon as you bring it home and do not plan on keeping it more than a few days.

Kumquat Sauce

YIELD: 1 CUP

As a nice touch, serve this sauce cold or warm over ice cream, angel food cake, or puddings.

½ cup sugar

1½ teaspoons cornstarch

⅓ cup fresh orange juice

¼ cup orange liqueur, such as Grand Marnier or Triple Sec

½ cup thinly sliced kumquats (5 or 6), seeds removed

2 tablespoons unsalted butter (optional)

1. Combine the sugar, cornstarch, orange juice, and Grand Marnier in a small saucepan. Stir to dissolve the sugar and cornstarch. Add the kumquats.

2. Bring the mixture to a boil, reduce the heat to low, and simmer until the sauce has thickened slightly, 5 to 6 minutes. For a richer sauce, whisk in the butter. Serve the sauce warm or chilled.

JENNIFER'S BUDINO WITH WARM PLUM COMPOTE

YIELD: 6 SERVINGS

I am so happy to have a recipe from Jennifer Millar to share with you. Jenny, who was my roommate at the Culinary Institute of America, in Hyde Park, New York, is one of the most talented pastry chefs in San Francisco. "*Budino* is an Italian baked custard," Jennifer says, "and it is a dessert served for the family. This recipe came about when I was experimenting with mascarpone." She added that, to fully enjoy the creaminess of this custard, we should not overbake it. Her *budino*, complemented by a tart plum compote, bursts with flavors and colors. It is simply wonderful! I've used fresh (peeled) peaches instead of plums with good results, too.

BUDINO

1 pound mascarpone, at room temperature
6 large egg yolks
5 tablespoons sugar
1/2 teaspoon vanilla extract

PLUM COMPOTE

4 plums (about 1 pound total), such as Red
*   Beauty, Black Beauty, Santa Rosa, or*
*   Queen Rosa, cut into eighths*
2 tablespoons sugar, or more if needed
1 teaspoon finely grated orange zest
Juice of 1 orange (about 1/2 cup)
1/4 teaspoon vanilla extract
1/4 teaspoon almond extract

1. Preheat the oven to 250°F.

2. To make the *budino*, whisk the mascarpone, egg yolks, sugar, and vanilla extract together in a large mixing bowl. Strain the mixture through a fine sieve.

3. Pour the custard into six 1/2-cup ramekins. Place the ramekins in a shallow baking pan, and pour boiling water into the pan to come halfway up the sides of the ramekins.

4. Bake for 45 minutes. Jiggle a ramekin; the center of the custard should still be very loose. Carefully remove the ramekins from the water bath, and let them cool on racks. Cover and refrigerate until well chilled or overnight.

5. To make the fruit compote, combine the plums, 2 tablespoons sugar, zest, and juice in a small pan. Cook the mixture uncovered over low heat until the plums soften and give up their juice but still retain their shape, about 10 minutes.

6. Add the vanilla and almond extracts, taste, and add more sugar, if necessary. Remove from the heat and set aside.

7. Run a paring knife around the edge of each custard and turn them out onto dessert plates. Spoon the warm compote over the chilled custards and serve.

STEAMED CRANBERRY-APPLE PUDDING

YIELD: 8 SERVINGS

This slightly tart, moist, crimson dessert, evocative of the December holiday season, is the perfect ending to cold-weather festivities. Since it should be served warm, you can prepare it in one of two ways. Either make the batter in advance, then steam the pudding in the oven just before dinner or cook the pudding in advance and quickly reheat it in a microwave oven just before serving. The light cranberry sauce that accompanies the pudding can also be prepared in advance and reheated. For an elegant presentation, I use small ramekins for the pudding, but you can certainly use a 1½-quart loaf pan instead of the ramekins. If you do, bake the pudding for 55 minutes to 1 hour. Fresh red currants make a striking garnish, if you can find them.

> 10 slices firm white sandwich bread, such as
>   Pepperidge Farm, crusts removed
> 1 cup fresh or frozen whole cranberries
> 1 medium apple, preferably Rome Beauty,
>   peeled, cored, and coarsely chopped
> 1 cup sugar
> 1 tablespoon cranberry juice cocktail or
>   water
> 1 tablespoon fresh lemon juice
> 8 tablespoons (1 stick) unsalted butter,
>   cut into small pieces, at room
>   temperature
> 2 large eggs
> Light Cranberry Sauce (recipe follows)
> Fresh red currants, for garnish (optional)
> Fresh mint sprigs, for garnish (optional)

1. Tear the bread and place it in a food processor. Process until finely chopped. (There should be about 3 cups of tightly packed bread crumbs.) Set aside.

2. Combine the cranberries, apple, ¾ cup of the sugar, and the cranberry juice in a medium-size saucepan. Cook the mixture over medium heat until the berries pop and the apple is tender, about 10 minutes. Remove from the heat and stir in the lemon juice. Set aside to cool.

3. Process the butter and remaining ¼ cup sugar in the food processor until light and fluffy. Blend in the eggs, one at a time, followed by the bread crumbs, and the cranberry-apple mixture. Blend thoroughly.

4. Lightly butter eight ½-cup ramekins. Pour the mixture into the ramekins, and firmly tap the molds on the work surface to force out any air bubbles. (The pudding can be prepared to this point 1 day ahead, tightly covered with plastic wrap, and refrigerated. Bring to room temperature and remove the plastic wrap before baking.)

5. Adjust an oven rack to the middle shelf and preheat the oven to 400°F.

6. Place the ramekins in a shallow baking pan and fill the pan with enough boiling water to come halfway up the sides of the ramekins. Cover the pan with aluminum foil, and bake until a bamboo skewer inserted into the center of the pudding comes out clean, 20 to 25 minutes.

7. Allow the puddings to stand for 5 minutes. Run a small paring knife around the

edges of each ramekin, then unmold the warm puddings onto dessert plates. Top each pudding with some Light Cranberry Sauce. Garnish with red currants and mint sprigs, if desired, and serve.

Light Cranberry Sauce

YIELD: ABOUT 1 CUP

Don't limit this tart, luscious ruby sauce to Steamed Cranberry Pudding. Serve it warm over ice cream or chilled over fresh fruit, mousse, cheesecake, or pound cake.

> 1 cup cranberry juice cocktail
> ¼ cup sugar
> 1 tablespoon cornstarch
> 1 cup fresh or frozen whole cranberries
> 2 tablespoons orange liqueur, such as Grand Marnier or Triple Sec
> 2 tablespoons grenadine syrup, preferably homemade (page 343)
> 1 tablespoon unsalted butter

1. Combine the cranberry juice, sugar, and cornstarch in a medium-size saucepan. Stir until the cornstarch is dissolved.

2. Cook the mixture over medium heat, stirring often, until the sauce is translucent and reaches the consistency of maple syrup, 3 to 4 minutes. Add the cranberries, and cook over low heat for 1 minute, or until the berries are just heated through. Do not let them pop. Remove the pan from the heat and stir in the liqueur, grenadine syrup, and butter. Gently swirl the sauce in the pan until the butter has completely melted and the sauce is shiny. If the sauce is too thick, add a little more cranberry juice.

VARIATION

LIGHT POMEGRANATE SAUCE: Follow the directions for Light Cranberry Sauce, but substitute 1 cup fresh pomegranate juice for the cranberry juice and 1 cup pomegranate seeds for the whole cranberries.

PLUM BREAD PUDDING

YIELD: 8 SERVINGS

This bread pudding is a breeze to make, which should appeal to those who enjoy preparing desserts but get edgy when they have to spend time on a complicated production. Unlike many bread puddings, this one is moist, light, and not too cloying. Tart, luscious plums complement the sweetness in this recipe, but other fruits are good too. I have made this pudding with nectarines, cherries, or combinations like peach and blueberry or mango and raspberry, with equally delicious results.

4 large eggs

⅓ cup plus 1 tablespoon sugar

2½ cups milk

4 tablespoons (½ stick) unsalted butter, melted

2 tablespoons dark rum

¼ teaspoon freshly grated nutmeg

⅛ teaspoon ground cloves

1½ pounds fresh purple plums, preferably Empress

1 loaf (1 pound) day-old challah or white bread with crust, cut into 1-inch cubes

¾ cup raisins

Chantilly Cream (recipe follows)

1. Adjust an oven rack to the middle shelf and preheat the oven to 375°F. Lightly butter a 9-inch square baking dish.

2. Beat together the eggs and ⅓ cup of the sugar in a medium-size bowl. Mix in the milk, butter, rum, nutmeg, and cloves. Set aside.

3. Halve, pit, and cut the plums into ¼-inch-thick wedges.

4. Layer the bread with the raisins and one-third of the plums into the buttered baking dish. Pour the egg mixture over the bread. With a fork, press to submerge the bread. Neatly arrange the remaining plum wedges on top of the bread in overlapping rows, then sprinkle with the remaining 1 tablespoon sugar.

5. Place the dish on a baking sheet to catch any drippings, and bake until a bamboo skewer inserted in the center of the bread pudding comes out clean, about 1 hour. Remove the dish from the oven and let it cool slightly.

6. Serve the pudding warm, accompanied by Chantilly Cream.

Chantilly Cream

YIELD: 4 CUPS

We call it whipped cream, but it is known to the French by the elegant name *crème Chantilly*. When you make Chantilly Cream, which is usually flavored with vanilla, brandy, or other flavorings, try to keep everything that comes in contact with the cream cold. The colder the cream and the whipping utensils, the lighter your Chantilly will be. For best results, serve the Chantilly as soon as you whip it. But if you decide to hold it a little longer, be sure to transfer it to a fine sieve placed over a bowl before you refrigerate it. This step will prevent your Chantilly from becoming a soggy mess, as the moisture that separates from the cream will drip directly into the bowl.

EAU-DE-VIE (FRUIT BRANDY)

The clearest and most potent fruit brandies in the world are the eaux-de-vie ("waters of life") of France's Alsace region, Germany, and Switzerland. Unlike "flavored" liqueurs or brandies, which have syrup added to them, are low in alcohol, and are usually deeply colored, eaux-de-vie are crystal-clear, fiery brandies that contain as much as 45 percent alcohol (90 proof). They usually command stiff prices, because it takes a considerable amount of fruit (about 50 pounds) to make each liter. More American-made brands are on the market, but French and German makes still tend to dominate liquor store shelves. Although eaux-de-vie can be made with virtually any fruit, the six most common, most popular flavors are the following:

- ✦ *Apple (France:* Calvados; *U.S.:* Applejack)

- ✦ *Cherry (France:* Kirsch; *Germany:* Kirschwasser)

- ✦ *Raspberry (France:* Framboise; *Germany:* Himbeergeist)

- ✦ *Pear (France:* Poire Williams; *Germany:* Williams Birnenbrand)

- ✦ *Yellow plum (France:* Mirabelle; *Germany:* Mirabellenwasser)

- ✦ *Purple plum (France:* Quetsch; *Germany:* Swetschgenwasser; *Hungary and the Balkans:* Slivovitz)

---

2 cups well-chilled heavy (or whipping) cream
2 tablespoons confectioners' sugar
2 tablespoons vanilla extract, fruit eau-de-vie (see box, this page), rum, or Cognac (optional)

1. About 10 minutes before you are ready to serve dessert, chill a medium-size mixing bowl and whisk in the freezer.

2. Pour the chilled cream into the chilled mixing bowl. With an electric mixer, start beating it on low speed and gradually raise the speed to medium-high. As soon as the cream starts to thicken, add the confectioners' sugar and the vanilla or brandy, if you are using any. Continue to beat until the cream holds stiff peaks. But don't overbeat, or it will turn into butter. Serve immediately.

VARIATIONS

ORANGE CHANTILLY: Substitute 2 tablespoons Grand Marnier or orange flower water (available in health food stores) for the vanilla.

PASSION FRUIT CHANTILLY: Substitute 2 tablespoons strained passion fruit juice for the vanilla.

SPICED CHANTILLY: Substitute 1/2 teaspoon each ground cinnamon and ginger for the vanilla.

GRATIN OF RED AND BLACK BERRIES

YIELD: 4 SERVINGS

I love this dessert because it's delicious, easy to make, attractive, and not overly sweet. The berries must be just warmed through, not cooked, for the sour cream to bring out their full flavors. If blackberries are not available, substitute blueberries. If you have fresh figs, quarter them and add them to the berry mix.

1 pint (2 cups) fresh raspberries
½ pint (1 cup) fresh blackberries
½ cup sour cream
1 tablespoon framboise (raspberry brandy) or orange liqueur, such as Grand Marnier or Triple Sec
4 tablespoons (firmly packed) light brown sugar
Fresh mint sprigs, for garnish (optional)

1. Combine the berries and place them in an 8-inch baking dish or Pyrex pan.

2. Combine the sour cream with the framboise and 2 tablespoons of the brown sugar, and pour over the berries. Cover and refrigerate until the sour cream is well chilled, about 1 hour.

3. Preheat the broiler.

4. Sprinkle the remaining 2 tablespoons brown sugar over the berries. Broil 6 inches from the heat until the sugar is caramelized and hard, and the sauce starts to bubble, about 1½ minutes. Do not overcook, or the berries will become mushy.

5. Spoon the berries into dessert bowls. Garnish with mint sprigs, if desired. Serve at once.

STRAWBERRIES AND RHUBARB BRULEE

YIELD: 6 TO 8 SERVINGS

I believe there must be an infinite number of great ways to combine strawberry and rhubarb. Here's one of my favorite recipes joining these soul mates. This dessert, a sort of quick crème brûlée, is rich and full of contrasting textures. As the brown sugar caramelizes over the cream, it forms a thin, delicious crackly sheet. Be sure to remove all the green leaves from the rhubarb, since they can be very toxic.

1½ pints (3 cups) fresh strawberries, hulled and sliced ¼ inch thick
1 tablespoon fresh lemon juice
1 tablespoon orange liqueur, such as Grand Marnier or Triple Sec
⅓ cup plus 2 tablespoons granulated sugar
1 pound fresh rhubarb, cut into 1-inch sections (about 3 cups total)
1 cup well-chilled heavy (or whipping) cream
⅓ cup (firmly packed) light brown sugar

1. In a large mixing bowl, combine the sliced strawberries, lemon juice, Grand Marnier, and 2 tablespoons of the granulated sugar; mix well. Cover and let stand at room temperature for 30 minutes.

2. Meanwhile, combine the rhubarb with the remaining ⅓ cup granulated sugar in a medium-size saucepan. Cover and cook over low heat until the rhubarb is very soft and shredded, about 15 minutes. Remove from the heat and set aside to cool to room temperature.

3. Transfer the rhubarb to a 1-quart gratin dish or pie pan, then top with the macerated strawberries. Cover with plastic wrap and refrigerate until well chilled, about 2 hours or overnight.

4. About 10 minutes before serving place a large mixing bowl and the beaters of an electric mixer in the freezer to chill.

5. Preheat the broiler.

6. Whip the heavy cream in the chilled bowl with the chilled beaters until stiff peaks form. Do not overbeat, or it will turn to butter. Spread the cream over the fruit mixture. Sift the brown sugar evenly over the cream.

7. Broil 6 inches from the heat, until the sugar has just melted, about 2 minutes. Serve at once.

GRATIN OF CITRUS FRUITS WITH SOFT MERINGUE

YIELD: 6 SERVINGS

To my taste, Curaçao best underlines the delicate citrus in this dessert. Whichever you use, it will be a sheer delight. This gratin is excellent for a dinner party, because most of it can be set up in advance. The custard may be prepared up to 2 days ahead, and the dessert assembled up to 1 hour before serving. The meringue should be whipped up just before broiling. If you like to make spectacular individual desserts, freeze hollowed-out grapefruit halves, then fill them with the chilled custard, top with the meringue, and broil. (Should your custard overheat, it will break and curdle, giving you rather fancy scrambled eggs. If it is just slightly curdled, you can salvage it by whipping it immediately in a blender. It should smooth out perfectly. If large dots of eggs still remain, it has over-curdled. In this case, throw it away and start over.)

6 large eggs, separated, at room temperature
    (see Note)
$\frac{1}{3}$ cup granulated sugar
Juice of 1 pink grapefruit (about $\frac{2}{3}$ cup)
Juice of 2 oranges (about $\frac{1}{2}$ cup)
Juice of 1 lemon (about 2 tablespoons)
1 pink grapefruit
2 navel oranges
2 tablespoons orange liqueur, such
    as Grand Marnier or
    Triple Sec
10 ladyfingers
Pinch of salt
$\frac{1}{2}$ cup confectioners'
    sugar

1. Whisk the egg yolks with the granulated sugar in a large mixing bowl until the mixture is thick and light yellow. Gradually add the grapefruit juice, orange juice, and lemon juice, mixing until well combined.

2. Transfer the yolk mixture to a heavy-bottomed, medium-size saucepan. Place the pan over medium-low heat and cook, whisk-ing constantly, until the mixture is thick enough to coat the back of a spoon, about 10 minutes. Do not let the mixture boil or it will curdle (see above). Pour the cooked custard into a medium-size bowl and place in a bowl of ice water. Stir the custard frequently to cool. Cover and refrigerate until well chilled, at least 4 hours or overnight.

3. Slice off the tops and bottoms of the grapefruit and oranges. Using a sharp knife with a flexible blade, cut away the peel and pith, following the contour of the fruit. Working over a colander placed in a bowl to catch the juices, cut between the membrane to separate the fruit into segments. Set the colander with the fruits aside.

4. Stir together the orange liqueur and 3 tablespoons of the collected fruit juices in a medium-size bowl. Briefly dip each side of the ladyfingers into the mixture and arrange them in a single layer to completely cover the bottom of an 8-inch round baking dish. Pour the chilled custard over the ladyfingers, spreading evenly. Arrange the fruit segments over the custard in concentric circles. Cover and refrigerate until ready to broil.

5. Just before serving, preheat the broiler.

6. Place the egg whites and a pinch of salt in a large mixing bowl and beat until soft peaks form. Gradually add the confectioners' sugar, 2 tablespoons at a time, and continue beating until the meringue holds stiff peaks and looks glossy.

7. With a spatula, spread the meringue evenly over the prepared custard, covering the filling completely. Broil 6 inches from the heat until the meringue is golden brown, about 1 minute. Watch carefully, or the meringue will burn. Spoon into dessert bowls and serve immediately.

NOTE: This recipe contains raw egg whites, which can carry the bacteria that cause salmonella. If you are uncertain about the quality of your eggs, you may want to "sanitize" the whites according to the instructions in Safer Eggs (page 372). You'll have to start the process at least 48 hours before you intend to prepare the recipe.

SIMPLE BAKED DESSERTS

Sliced pears are roasted to tenderness and then topped with a buttery bourbon sauce. A jumble of fresh berries is tucked under a rich dough and baked to luscious perfection. And golden apricot halves are blanketed and baked in an almond-laced cream. As easy as they are to make, you won't be surprised at how wonderful they taste.

ROASTED PEARS WITH BOURBON SAUCE

YIELD: 4 SERVINGS

I have always had a weakness for pears scented with aromatic spices. I think that the flavor of pears treated this way is unmatched. Here, the pears are oven-roasted and basted with one of the most sinfully delicious sauces imaginable. This confection is a good example of how you can turn a modest fruit into a sublime dessert with almost no effort. These

roasted pears are also wonderful over shortcake (see Index) topped with some Chantilly Cream (page 411).

$^1/_3$ cup apricot preserves

$^1/_3$ cup bourbon

3 tablespoons port or Madeira

2 teaspoons fresh lemon juice

$^1/_4$ teaspoon ground cinnamon

$^1/_8$ teaspoon ground cloves

$^1/_8$ teaspoon ground ginger

1 tablespoon unsalted butter

4 large ripe but firm pears, preferably Bartlett or Anjou, with stems on

2 tablespoons heavy (or whipping) cream

1. Preheat the oven to 400°F.

2. Combine the apricot preserves, bourbon, port, lemon juice, cinnamon, cloves, and ginger in a small saucepan and bring to a simmer over medium heat. Cook, stirring often, until the preserves are melted, 2 to 3 minutes. Add the butter, and stir until melted. Remove from the heat.

3. Peel the pears, but leave the stems on. With a corer, remove the core from the base (wide end) of each pear, leaving the stems intact.

4. Stand the pears in a shallow baking dish, and pour the bourbon sauce over them. Roast until the pears are tender and the sauce is caramelized, about 30 minutes, basting the fruits with the sauce every 5 minutes.

5. Divide the roasted pears among dessert plates. Stir the heavy cream into the sauce left in the baking dish and spoon it over the pears. Serve warm.

HARVEST APPLE CRUMBLE

Apple crumbles don't come any better than this. The recipe comes from my sister-in-law, Adrienne Laudin, who made this dessert for Thanksgiving one year. I enjoyed it so much, I asked her for the recipe. Once you taste this apple dessert, you will want to serve it time and again. A crumble is like a crisp but not as rich. I like this confection best when served warm; it just melts in your mouth!

FILLING

6 medium Granny Smith apples (about 1$^1/_2$ pounds total)

$^1/_3$ cup sugar

1 teaspoon ground cinnamon

Juice of $^1/_2$ lemon

TOPPING

$^3/_4$ cup unbleached all-purpose flour

$^1/_4$ cup sugar

4 tablespoons ($^1/_2$ stick) unsalted butter, chilled

1. Preheat the oven to 400°F. Butter a 2-quart baking dish.

2. To make the filling, peel, core, and cut the apples into ½-inch pieces and place them in a large saucepan with the sugar, cinnamon, and lemon juice. Cook over medium heat, stirring occasionally, for 15 minutes, or until the apples are just tender. Spoon into the prepared baking dish.

3. To make the topping, combine the flour and the remaining ¼ cup sugar in a small bowl. With a pastry cutter or 2 table knives, cut in the butter until the mixture is crumbly. Sprinkle over the apples.

4. Bake until the topping is golden brown, about 30 minutes. Transfer to a rack to cool slightly. Serve warm.

PEAR-CRANBERRY CRISP

YIELD: 6 TO 8 SERVINGS

When I bake, I often pair sweet and tart fruits, such as juicy pears and cranberries, to create intriguing tastes. Here, the fruit, combined with pear brandy, bursts with warm flavors from under a mound of crumbly dough. This crisp is on the tart side, but you may add sugar to suit your taste. The unbaked crisp may be assembled well in advance, covered, and refrigerated up to 1 day before baking. Leftover crisps do not keep well, therefore, try to serve this dessert the same day it's baked.

> ¾ cup plus 1 tablespoon unbleached
>   all-purpose flour
> ⅓ cup (firmly packed) light brown sugar
> ⅛ teaspoon salt
> 6 tablespoons (¾ stick) unsalted butter,
>   at room temperature
> ⅓ cup toasted pecan halves (for toasting
>   instructions, see page 64), coarsely
>   chopped
> 5 ripe but firm medium pears (about
>   3 pounds total), preferably Bosc or
>   Bartlett
> 1½ cups fresh or frozen whole cranberries
> 1 tablespoon fresh lemon juice
> ¼ cup granulated sugar
> 2 tablespoons pear brandy, such as Poire
>   Williams
> Spiced Chantilly (page 412)

1. Adjust the oven rack to the middle shelf and preheat the oven to 375°F.

2. To make the topping, in a mixing

bowl, combine $^3/_4$ cup of the flour, the brown sugar, and the salt. Using 2 table knives or a pastry blender, cut 4 tablespoons of the butter into the flour until the mixture resembles coarse meal. Add the pecans and toss the mixture gently.

3. Peel, quarter, and core the pears and slice them lengthwise $^3/_4$ inch thick. In a large mixing bowl, toss the pears and cranberries with the lemon juice, granulated sugar, brandy, and remaining 1 tablespoon flour. Transfer the mixture to a 2-quart baking dish or 9-inch square baking pan, spreading it evenly. Dot the fruits with the remaining 2 tablespoons butter, and cover with the topping mixture.

4. Bake until the topping is crisp and the pears are tender, about 50 minutes.

5. Cool the crisp slightly and serve topped with Spiced Chantilly.

BUMBLEBERRY CRUNCH

YIELD: 8 SERVINGS

Some cooks have a penchant for giving odd names to their dishes, apparently for no other reason than the fun of saying them. I came across a dessert called bumbleberry pie in Springdale, Utah, near Zion National Park, a short while ago. Intrigued by the sound of it, I asked the waitress what went into it. With a smile, she said the chef told her never to reveal his secret ingredients. My curiosity piqued, I ordered a slice of his mysterious pie. After much tasting and analysis, I figured that the pie's filling was a mixture of blackberries, blueberries, and raspberries, accented with cinnamon and nutmeg. Since I really liked the taste, I decided to create this lighter version, which is closer to a crisp than a pie. You may substitute 1 cup raspberries for the blackberries.

FILLING
1 pint (2 cups) fresh or frozen blueberries
$^1/_2$ pint (1 cup) fresh or frozen unsweetened raspberries
$^1/_2$ pint (1 cup) fresh or frozen blackberries
$^1/_3$ cup sugar
$1^1/_2$ teaspoons ground cinnamon
Freshly grated nutmeg, to taste

TOPPING
1 cup unbleached all-purpose flour
$^3/_4$ cup sugar
$^1/_4$ teaspoon salt
6 tablespoons ($^3/_4$ stick) unsalted butter, chilled, cut into 12 pieces

Light cream or half-and-half, for serving (optional)

1. Preheat the oven to 350°F.

2. To make the filling, combine the berries, sugar, cinnamon, and nutmeg in a mixing bowl. Toss well to blend all the ingredients. Pour the mixture into a 10-inch round baking dish.

3. To make the topping, combine the flour, sugar, and salt in a mixing bowl. Work the butter into the flour mixture with your fingertips to form small pellets. Cover the berries with this mixture.

4. Bake until the crust is light golden brown and the berries bubbly, 30 to 35 minutes. Remove and allow to cool slightly before serving. Serve warm topped with light cream, if desired.

BAKED APRICOTS IN ALMOND CREAM

YIELD: 4 TO 6 SERVINGS

When I am not eating fresh apricots out of hand, the second best way for me to enjoy this lovely fruit is by baking it. In this dessert, the hot mingling of apricot, almonds, and butter produce a finale that is hard for anyone to resist.

> 5 tablespoons unsalted butter, at room
>   temperature
> 3 tablespoons sugar
> 2 large egg yolks
> 1 teaspoon almond extract
> ½ teaspoon vanilla extract
> ¼ cup blanched sliced almonds, finely
>   ground
> 8 fresh apricots (about 1 pound total)
> ¼ cup apricot preserves
> 2 tablespoons fresh lemon juice
> Heavy (or whipping) cream (optional)

1. Cream the butter and sugar in a small bowl with a wooden spoon until light and fluffy. Add the egg yolks, one at a time, beating well after each addition. Add the almond extract, vanilla extract, and ground almonds; mix until well combined.

2. Halve and pit each apricot. Arrange the halves, cut side down, in a 10-inch round

GREAT MATCHES

APRICOTS

Apricots go well with spices like curry, ginger, nutmeg, cardamom, and star anise. They also add a nice accent to pork, lamb, veal, poultry, and game dishes. Try them with pistachios or almonds for a real treat.

Pyrex pan or pie plate. Spread the almond cream over the fruit, being sure to cover it completely. (This can be covered and refrigerated overnight, if desired. Bring to room temperature before baking.)

3. Preheat the oven to 500°F.

4. Bake until the almond cream starts to set and the edges are golden, about 8 minutes.

5. Meanwhile, mix the apricot preserves with the lemon juice.

6. Spoon the preserves over the baked apricots and bake until the topping is golden brown and bubbly, about 3 minutes longer. The almond cream should not be completely set. Transfer to a rack to cool. Serve warm in compote dishes, with a bit of cream, if desired.

OLD-FASHIONED PRUNE PUDDING

YIELD: 4 TO 6 SERVINGS

Made with brandy-soaked prunes, this delicious, rustic dessert originates from Brittany, France, where it is known as Far Breton. Its light texture lies somewhere between a flan and a quiche. If you're not a prune fan, any fresh, firm fruit, such as cherries, grapes, pears, or apples would make an admirable substitute. Pair the fruit with an appropriate brandy (for example, cherry brandy, or kirsch, for cherries, pear brandy or rum for pears, Calvados for apples) and increase the sugar to $\frac{1}{3}$ cup. Serve the pudding warmed. If the baked dessert has been refrigerated, bring to room temperature and gently reheat it in a preheated 350°F oven for about 5 minutes.

1 pound dried pitted prunes
2 tablespoons Armagnac, Cognac, or
*   dark rum*
4 large eggs, lightly beaten
$\frac{1}{4}$ cup sugar
2 cups milk
$\frac{2}{3}$ cup unbleached all-purpose flour
$\frac{1}{4}$ teaspoon salt

1. Toss the prunes and Armagnac in a medium-size bowl. Cover and let stand for 30 minutes.

2. Adjust an oven rack to the middle shelf and preheat the oven to 375°F.

3. Place the eggs, sugar, milk, flour, and salt in a food processor or blender, and blend to make a smooth batter.

4. Lightly butter a 1-quart round baking dish. Scatter the prunes and the Armagnac on the bottom of the baking dish. Pour the batter over the prunes.

5. Bake until the top is nicely browned and puffy, and a toothpick inserted in the center comes out dry, 50 to 55 minutes. Let the pudding cool in the dish on a rack. The pudding will flatten slightly as it cools. Serve warm or at room temperature.

TARTS, PIES,
CAKES & COOKIES

When I was 13 years old, my mother installed a brand new stove in our kitchen, our first stove ever, complete with an oven. We became the talk of the neighborhood, and curious neighbors even stopped by our house to admire that modern piece of equipment. At the time, we were living in Laos, where gas and electricity were a luxury, not a necessity. People who were able to afford a refrigerator or a gas stove were deemed prosperous. As such, my mother was a successful citizen, but sadly, the same word cannot be applied to her baking efforts. Although she was a terrific cook, desserts were definitely not her strong point. So, what's a girl to do when her mother doesn't bake? I decided to teach myself.

Before beginning my baking adventures, I looked for sources of inspiration. The only reference available was a small Vietnamese cookbook my mother had. In it, there was a section on French-style desserts. One day, I decided to surprise my mother by making a hot lemon soufflé, hardly a dessert for novices! In the excitement of my first real culinary experiment, I could not restrain myself from opening the oven door (something you should never do when a soufflé is rising) to check on the progress of my creation. What emerged was not a billowy soufflé, but a rather flat omelet. Since I had no way of knowing that it was a royal failure, I thought my dessert was a success because it tasted really *wonderful*. When I presented my mother with the "surprise," I can still remember that puzzled look that came over her face. In any case, she was kind enough to taste my so-called soufflé and compliment me on my efforts. I eagerly took her cue as an encouragement, and have continued baking ever since.

Years later, as a student in Paris, I shared an apartment with my sister and her husband. Part of the deal was that I would cook and bake, and they would do all of the cleaning. Since both of them had cavernous sweet tooths, I received many requests for cakes and tarts, especially on weekends, when friends came to visit, or to take along when we went calling. All that baking didn't bother me a bit, because it was good practice, and it gave me a chance to give other people pleasure.

Although I've given up swapping cakes for chores, I still bake frequently. One of the things that gives me immense pleasure is making beautiful birthday cakes for my family and friends. My husband is sure that he maintains job security by bringing the Christmas cookies I bake to his office each year. For me, baking is a hobby that comforts me, lets me indulge myself and have some fun.

The following recipes are my all-around favorite baked desserts with a fruity touch. Some are culled from my European days (tarts, clafouti, kuchen, and chocolate cake); others are my variations on all-American favorites, such as fruit pies and cheesecakes, upside-down cakes and shortcakes. And, of course, wonderful fruit cookies.

NAPOLEON OF NECTARINES WITH CARAMEL SAUCE

YIELD: 4 SERVINGS

Napoleon is the English name for the traditional French pastry called *mille-feuille* ("thousand layers"), which is made with thin, flaky puff-pastry sheets that are layered with cream or another fruit filling. My version features fragrant and juicy slices of nectarines and whipped cream on puff pastry, topped with a luscious caramel sauce. The result is a dessert to die for. The baked puff pastry, macerated nectarines, and caramel sauce may be prepared up to 4 hours in advance. For the best possible dessert, whip the cream right before serving.

1 sheet (about ½ pound) frozen
    puff pastry, thawed but kept
    chilled
4 large, very ripe nectarines (about
    2 pounds)
2 tablespoons granulated sugar
1 teaspoon fresh lemon juice
1 cup well-chilled heavy (or whipping)
    cream
2 tablespoons orange liqueur, such as
    Grand Marnier or Triple Sec
Confectioners' sugar, for dusting
½ cup Caramel Sauce (recipe follows)

1. Roll out the pastry on a lightly floured surface to form a 12-inch square about ¹⁄₁₆ inch thick. Using a fork, prick the pastry all over, including the edges, then cut the square into twelve 3×4-inch rectangles. Transfer the pastries to a baking sheet, and chill them in the freezer until firm, about 20 minutes.

2. Adjust the oven rack to the middle shelf and preheat the oven to 350°F.

3. Transfer the sheet of pastries to the oven. Bake until the pastries are slightly puffed and browned, about 20 minutes. Cool on the baking sheet on a rack.

4. About 10 minutes before you are ready to serve dessert, place a mixing bowl and the beaters of an electric mixer in the freezer to chill. Halve and pit the unpeeled nectarines, then slice as thinly as possible. Place in a mixing bowl and sprinkle with 1 tablespoon of the granulated sugar and the lemon juice. Toss gently to combine. Cover and refrigerate.

5. Whip the heavy cream in the chilled bowl with the chilled beaters at medium-high speed until it starts to thicken. Add the orange liqueur and the remaining 1 tablespoon granulated sugar and continue to whip until stiff peaks form. Don't overbeat, or it will turn into butter. Gently fold the whipped cream into the nectarines.

6. Place a pastry rectangle, shiny side up, on a dessert plate. Layer with a spoonful of fruit and cream filling. Top with another pastry rectangle and repeat the layers, ending with a pastry rectangle. You should have 3 layers of pastry and 2 of filling. Prepare 3 more Napoleons with the remaining pastries and filling.

7. Dust the pastries with confectioners' sugar. Spoon Caramel Sauce over the Napoleons. Serve at once.

Caramel Sauce

Do not stir the caramel sauce at any point during the caramelization process: The sugar will crystallize on contact with a cold spoon or brush and become a gluey mess. Simply swirl the liquid in the pan, if you must. Once the cream has been added, stir the mixture with a wooden spoon to smooth the sauce. Also, pay attention to the color of the caramelized sugar; do not let it turn too dark, or the sauce will be bitter. Remove the pan as soon as the sugar turns the color of maple syrup. The sauce can be refrigerated for up to 1 week; briefly reheat it before serving. If it has thickened, thin it with 1 or 2 tablespoons hot water. You can use this recipe in any dessert calling for caramel sauce.

- ½ cup sugar
- 3 tablespoons light corn syrup
- ⅔ cup heavy (or whipping) cream, at room temperature
- 2 tablespoons unsalted butter

1. Place the sugar and corn syrup in a medium-size, heavy-bottomed saucepan and cook over low heat until the sugar has dissolved and the mixture begins to change color, about 5 minutes. Bring to a boil over medium-high heat, swirling the pan until the mixture starts to smoke and turn a rich golden brown, about 3 minutes.

2. Remove the pan from the heat and add the cream (be very careful—it may splatter). Return the pan to the heat and cook, stirring with a wooden spoon, until the caramel is smooth, about 1 minute. Add the butter, and remove the pan from the heat. Stir until the butter is melted and the sauce is shiny. Cool slightly before serving.

VARIATION

Tipsy Caramel Sauce: Add 2 tablespoons Kahlúa and 2 tablespoons Triple Sec to the sauce just before removing the pan from the heat. For simple, delicious treats, serve this spirited caramel sauce over crêpes, vanilla ice cream, or as a fondue of sorts, with assorted fresh fruit and angel food cake cubes.

WARM APPLE TART

Besides the occasional sprig of fresh mint in my fruit salads, I never gave much thought to adding fresh herbs to sweet foods until I traveled to England. There, I had the opportunity to sample some of the most delicious desserts pairing fruits and fresh herbs, such as apple tart and tarragon, poached spiced pears with lemon balm, and berry fools with sweet cicely. The assertive flavor of these herbs offers a pleasant surprise, and makes the desserts seem suddenly new. There are dozens of ways to make apple tart, but this one, made with crisp, buttery puff pastry, tart apples, and sparkling tarragon, has become one of my favorites. Serve it right from the oven. If fresh tarragon is unavailable, substitute 1 teaspoon ground cinnamon.

1 sheet (about ½ pound) frozen puff pastry,
    thawed but kept chilled
2 large Granny Smith or McIntosh apples
    (about 1 pound total)
Juice of ½ lemon
2 tablespoons sugar
2 tablespoons unsalted butter
1 tablespoon snipped fresh tarragon
Vanilla ice cream (optional)

1. Roll out the pastry on a lightly floured surface to form an 11-inch square about ⅛ inch thick. Transfer it to a baking sheet. Prick the pastry all over with a fork to prevent it from puffing during baking.

2. Peel, quarter, and core the apples. Rub them with the lemon juice to prevent discoloration, and then cut them lengthwise into paper-thin slices. Arrange the apples in rows, overlapping the slices, and covering the pastry completely. Sprinkle the apples with the sugar, then dot with butter. Chill the tart in the freezer until firm, about 20 minutes.

3. Adjust an oven rack to the lowest shelf and preheat the oven to 450°F.

4. Transfer the baking sheet to the oven. Immediately reduce the temperature to 400°F and bake until the pastry is well cooked, about 25 minutes.

5. Remove the tart from the oven, sprinkle with the tarragon, and return it to the oven. Continue to bake until the apples are slightly caramelized, about 5 minutes longer.

6. Serve the tart immediately, topped with vanilla ice cream, if desired.

*The apple grows
so bright and high,
And ends its days in apple pie.*
—SAMUEL GOODMAN HOFFENSTEIN

BLUEBERRY-PLUM TART

YIELD: 8 TO 10 SERVINGS

The tart pairing of blueberries and plums provides a nice counterpoint to the sweet, intensely flavored almond filling that lines the crust. The unbaked tart shell may be prepared well in advance, wrapped and frozen, then baked when needed. Don't defrost it; just move it directly from the freezer to the oven, but reduce the oven temperature slightly and let it bake a few minutes longer.

TART SHELL

1½ cups unbleached all-purpose flour

1 tablespoon granulated sugar

¼ teaspoon salt

12 tablespoons (1½ sticks) unsalted butter, cut into ½-inch pieces, and frozen

3 to 4 tablespoons ice water

BLUEBERRY-PLUM FILLING

⅓ cup blanched whole almonds (page 449)

5 tablespoons granulated sugar

2 tablespoons unbleached all-purpose flour

½ teaspoon almond extract

4 medium black plums, cut into ½-inch-thick wedges

1½ pints (3 cups) fresh blueberries

1 tablespoon confectioners' sugar

Chantilly Cream (page 411) or vanilla ice cream (optional)

1. To make the tart shell, put the flour, granulated sugar, salt, and butter in a food processor. Pulse until the mixture resembles small pebbles. Uncover and sprinkle 3 tablespoons of the ice water over the flour mixture. Cover and pulse just until the dough holds together, about 10 seconds; do not overprocess. The dough should be soft, not crumbly. If it feels too dry or crumbly, add 1 or 2 teaspoons ice water and pulse until it just holds together. Turn out the dough onto a lightly floured surface and press it together to form a cohesive mass.

2. On a lightly floured board, roll out the dough into a 13-inch circle about ⅛ inch thick. As you roll, lift and turn the dough frequently, dusting the board with flour as necessary to prevent the dough from sticking.

3. Gently fold the dough circle in half, and then in half again. Lift the folded circle and place it in an 11-inch round tart pan, with the point in the center. Unfold the dough to line the pan, leaving the excess dough hanging over the rim. Trim, if necessary, leaving a 1-inch overhang. Fold in the overhang and press it around the edges to reinforce the crust and prevent it from

GREAT MATCHES

PLUMS

*T*he musky perfume of ripe plums blends well with all berries, especially blueberries. Plums are also surprisingly good with potatoes, sweet and white. Try plums with cured meats like bacon, pancetta, and prosciutto for a sweet and salty treat.

shrinking during baking. Using a fork, prick the pastry all over. Freeze the tart shell for at least 2 hours before filling and baking. (At this point, the pastry can be frozen for up to 3 months.)

4. Adjust an oven rack to the lowest shelf and preheat the oven to 425°F.

5. To make the filling, place the almonds, 3 tablespoons of the granulated sugar, and the flour in a food processor. Process until the almonds are finely ground. Add the almond extract and blend well.

6. Spread the almond mixture evenly into the frozen tart shell. Distribute the plums evenly over the almond mixture, and then layer on the blueberries. Sprinkle the berries with the remaining 2 tablespoons granulated sugar.

7. Place the tart in the oven, reduce the oven temperature to 400°F, and bake until the tart crust is golden brown, 45 to 50 minutes. Transfer the tart to a rack and let cool completely.

8. Just before serving, lightly sift the confectioners' sugar over the tart. Cut into wedges and serve with Chantilly Cream or vanilla ice cream, if desired.

ONE-CRUST STRAWBERRY PIE

YIELD: 8 SERVINGS

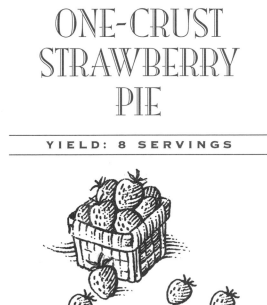

I'm always up for a good strawberry pie, especially when it's filled with fresh fruit. This pie is more like a tart, since it has only a bottom crust. To keep that crust from absorbing the sauce that coats the strawberries and becoming soggy, I coat the baked pie crust with a thin layer of dark chocolate. When the chocolate has set, I arrange whole fresh strawberries in the shell and then cover them with a light sauce made from crushed strawberries. The intense strawberry flavor with a hint of chocolate is pure delight!

CRUST

1 cup plus 2 tablespoons unbleached
    all-purpose flour
1 teaspoon sugar
½ teaspoon salt
8 tablespoons (1 stick) unsalted butter,
    at room temperature
¼ cup sour cream
½ teaspoon vanilla extract

STRAWBERRY FILLING

⅔ cup semisweet chocolate pieces
2 tablespoons unsalted butter
3 pints (6 cups) fresh strawberries, washed
    and hulled
½ cup sugar
2 teaspoons cornstarch
1 tablespoon framboise (raspberry brandy) or
    kirsch (cherry brandy)
Chantilly Cream (page 411); optional

1. To make the crust, place the flour, sugar, salt, and butter in a food processor. Pulse until the mixture resembles coarse meal. Add the sour cream and vanilla extract. Pulse just until the dough is moistened.

2. Turn out the dough onto a large piece of plastic wrap. Gather the dough in the plastic wrap, and press it into a flat, compact disk. Wrap the dough in the plastic and chill for at least 2 hours.

3. Adjust an oven rack to the lowest shelf and preheat the oven to 375°F.

4. On a lightly floured board, roll out the dough into an 11-inch circle about ⅛ inch thick. As you roll, lift and turn the dough frequently, dusting the board with flour as necessary to prevent the dough from sticking.

5. Gently fold the dough in half, and then in half again. Lift the folded circle and place it in a 9-inch pie pan, with the point in the center. Unfold the dough to line the pan, pressing the dough into the bottom and sides. Trim the dough, leaving a 1-inch overhang. Fold the overhang back toward the inside to reinforce the edges and prevent the crust from shrinking during baking. Crimp the edges decoratively.

6. Prick the bottom of the pastry with a fork. Line the pastry with aluminum foil, and fill the plate with pie weights or dried beans.

7. Bake the shell for 15 minutes. Remove the foil and weights, and continue to bake until the shell is golden brown, about 15 minutes longer. Remove the shell from the oven and allow it to cool.

8. To make the filling, combine the chocolate and butter in a metal bowl or the top of a double boiler and place over simmering water. Stir until the chocolate has melted and the mixture is smooth. Brush the warm chocolate into the pie shell, evenly covering the bottom and sides.

9. Place 1 pint of the berries in a blender or food processor and purée them with the sugar and cornstarch. Transfer the purée to a small saucepan. Cook over medium heat, stirring, until the mixture is clear

and thick, about 3 minutes. Remove from the heat and cool. Stir in the framboise.

10. Arrange the remaining 2 pints strawberries, tips up, in the pie shell in concentric circles, working from the outside in, until the bottom is covered. Pour the cooked berry mixture over and chill for several hours before serving with Chantilly Cream, if desired.

Raspberries grow by the way,
With pleasure you may assay.

-ANONYMOUS POET AND CRUSADER

RASPBERRY-RHUBARB PIE

YIELD: 8 TO 10 SERVINGS

If I had to choose just one fruit pie, this would be it. During the months of June and July when both raspberries and rhubarb abound, nothing could beat this sumptuous fruit combination for

making pies. Be sure to remove all the leaves from the rhubarb, as they are quite toxic.

CRUST
2 cups unbleached all-purpose flour
1 teaspoon sugar
1 teaspoon salt
8 tablespoons (1 stick) unsalted butter, cut into small pieces, well chilled
4 tablespoons vegetable shortening, preferably Crisco, cut into small pieces, well chilled
¹⁄₃ cup ice water, or more if needed

RASPBERRY-RHUBARB FILLING
2 large, fat stalks fresh rhubarb (1¹⁄₄ pounds), cut into ¹⁄₂-inch pieces
1 pint (2 cups) fresh raspberries
1¹⁄₄ cups plus 2 teaspoons sugar
²⁄₃ cup unbleached all-purpose flour
1 tablespoon grated lemon zest
Juice of ¹⁄₂ lemon
2 tablespoons unsalted butter, cut into small pieces, well chilled
2 tablespoons heavy (or whipping) cream, for brushing

1. To make the crust, put the flour, sugar, salt, butter, and vegetable shortening in a food processor. Pulse until the mixture resembles small pebbles. Uncover and sprinkle the ice water over the flour mixture. Cover and pulse just until the dough is moistened, about 10 seconds; do not overprocess. The dough should be soft, not crumbly. If it feels too dry or crumbly, add 1 or 2 additional teaspoons ice water and pulse until it just holds together. Turn out the dough onto a lightly floured surface and press it together to form a cohesive mass.

2. Cut the dough into 2 pieces, one twice the size of the other. Shape each portion into a ball, then lightly press each piece into a disk.

3. On a lightly floured board, roll out the large piece of dough into a 12-inch circle about ⅛ inch thick. As you roll, lift and turn the dough frequently, dusting the board with flour as necessary to prevent the dough from sticking.

4. Gently fold the dough in half, and then in half again. Lift the folded circle and place it in a 10-inch pie pan, with the point in the center. Unfold the dough to line the pan, pressing the crust into the bottom and sides. Let the excess pastry hang over and chill.

5. Roll out the remaining piece of dough into a 9-inch circle. With a pastry wheel, cut about six 1¼-inch-wide strips for the lattice top. Place them on a large plate and chill for at least 30 minutes.

6. Adjust an oven rack to the lowest shelf and preheat the oven to 375°F.

7. To make the filling, in a large mixing bowl, toss the rhubarb and raspberries with 1¼ cups of the sugar, flour, lemon zest, and lemon juice until all the fruit is well coated with the flour mixture. Pour the filling into the prepared crust and dot with butter. Arrange the pastry strips over the filling following the instructions in the box below, and fold the overhang from the pie shell over the edge, toward the center of the pie.

8. Brush the lattice and folded edge with heavy cream, then sprinkle with the remaining 2 teaspoons sugar. Put the pie on a baking sheet to catch the drippings as it bakes. Bake until the filling has bubbled and thickened, about 50 minutes. Let the pie cool in the pan on a rack before serving.

HOW TO MAKE A QUICK LATTICE PIE TOP

To make a lattice top for a pie, roll a piece of pastry dough to a circle about ⅛ inch thick, roughly the same diameter as the pie you are making. Using a ruler and a sharp paring knife, cut out strips about 1½ inches wide. Place 1 long strip straight down the middle of the pie, then 1 or 2 shorter strips on either side, about 1½ inches apart. Give the pan a one-sixth turn clockwise (the top of the middle strip should be at 2 o'clock). Place 3 to 5 more strips vertically over the first strips, with a long strip in the center, about 1½ inches apart. This will give your pie crust a beautiful diamond pattern.

STORING CAKES, PIES, AND TARTS

✦ *Most cakes, pies, and tarts taste best the same day they are baked. However, if you decide to keep them for a day or two, wrap them well in foil, then place in plastic bags and store in the refrigerator.*

✦ *All cakes freeze well, too. To store, wrap them well in foil, then seal them in freezer bags. Freeze for up to 6 months.*

✦ *Allow frozen cakes to defrost at room temperature for 1 or 2 hours. Or let them thaw overnight in the refrigerator.*

✦ *Do not freeze pies and tarts. Because of their juicy fillings, they tend to become soggy after thawing. It's better to keep unbaked crusts in the freezer, then fill and bake them anytime you need a pie or a tart.*

SOUR CHERRY PIE

YIELD: 8 SERVINGS

The best way to savor sour cherries is to bake them in a pie. Since fresh sour cherries can be exceedingly juicy, they usually require quite a bit of flour or cornstarch to "tighten" their juices. Some cooks swear by cornstarch, but I find the combination of granulated tapioca and flour more satisfactory, because it produces a filling that's not gluey but just dense enough. The tapioca also adds extra texture and interest. Introduce some lemon and almond extracts, two flavors that seem to harmonize with cherries, and you've got yourself a really fabulous pie. When cut into, it reveals a precious jewel-like interior awash in a rich ruby sauce begging to be tasted!

CRUST

1½ *cups unbleached all-purpose flour*

2 *teaspoons sugar*

½ *teaspoon salt*

3 *tablespoons unsalted butter, cut into small pieces, well chilled*

3 *tablespoons vegetable shortening, preferably Crisco, cut into small pieces, well chilled*

3 *tablespoons ice water, or more if needed*

1 *teaspoon distilled white vinegar*

SOUR CHERRY FILLING

4 *cups pitted sour cherries (or 3 cups pitted sour cherries combined with 1 cup strawberries)*

¾ *cup plus 2 teaspoons sugar*

3 *tablespoons quick-cooking tapioca*

2 *tablespoons unbleached all-purpose flour*

¼ *teaspoon salt*

2 *tablespoons fresh lemon juice*

Finely grated zest of 1 lemon (about 1 teaspoon)

1 *teaspoon almond extract*

2 *tablespoons unsalted butter, cut into small pieces, well chilled*

2 *tablespoons heavy (or whipping) cream*

1. To make the crust, put the flour, sugar, salt, butter, and vegetable shortening in a food processor. Pulse until the mixture resembles small pebbles. Uncover and sprinkle with the ice water and vinegar. Cover and pulse just until the dough is moistened, about 10 seconds; do not overprocess. The dough should be soft, not crumbly. If it feels too dry or crumbly, add 1 or 2 teaspoons more of ice water and pulse until it just holds together. Turn the dough out onto a lightly floured surface and press it together to form a cohesive mass.

2. Cut the dough into 2 pieces, one twice as large as the other. Shape each portion into a ball, then lightly press each piece into a disk.

3. On a lightly floured board, roll out the large piece of dough into an 11-inch circle about $\frac{1}{8}$ inch thick. As you roll, lift and turn the dough frequently, dusting the board with flour as necessary to prevent it from sticking.

4. Gently fold the dough in half, and then in half again. Lift the folded circle and place it in a 9-inch pie pan, with the point in the center. Unfold the dough to line the pan, pressing the crust into the bottom and sides. Let the excess pastry hang over and refrigerate to chill.

5. Roll out the remaining piece of dough into an 8-inch circle. With a pastry wheel, cut about six 1¼-inch-wide strips for the lattice top. Place them on a large plate and chill for at least 30 minutes.

6. Adjust an oven rack to the lowest shelf and preheat the oven to 375°F.

7. To make the filling, in a large bowl, place the cherries with ¾ cup of the sugar, the tapioca, flour, salt, lemon juice, lemon zest, and almond extract and toss until all the fruits are well coated with the flour mixture. Turn the filling into the prepared crust and dot with butter. Arrange the pastry strips over the filling following the instructions in the box on page 432, and fold the overhang from the pie shell over the edge, toward the center of the pie.

8. Brush the lattice and folded edge with heavy cream, then sprinkle with the remaining 2 teaspoons sugar. Put the pie on a baking sheet to catch the drippings as it bakes. Bake until the filling has bubbled and thickened, about 50 minutes. Let the pie cool in the pan on a rack before serving.

PEACH COBBLER

YIELD: 6 TO 8 SERVINGS

One of my fondest food memories since coming to the United States to live is my first taste of a cobbler. I think these deep-dish fruit pies with flaky shortcake topping must be the friendliest of American desserts: They are always warm, tender, and easy on the cook. Wonderfully homey, they can be made with any fresh fruit you choose: sliced peaches, apples, plums, pears, berries, and mangoes, just to name a few. In this version, with Cognac-scented peaches, I use a buttery cookie crust instead of the usual biscuit dough for a crispier texture. If you substitute apples, pears, or any other firm fruit, increase the cooking time by about 5 minutes. For a real treat, serve topped with heavy cream, Chantilly Cream (page 411), or ice cream.

CRUST
1 cup unbleached all-purpose flour

1/2 teaspoon salt

1/3 cup vegetable shortening, preferably Crisco, cut into small pieces, well chilled

2 tablespoons ice water, or more if needed

2 teaspoons granulated sugar

PEACH FILLING
3 pounds peaches

1/3 cup (firmly packed) light brown sugar

2 tablespoons Cognac or peach brandy

1 tablespoon all-purpose flour

Grated zest of 1 large lemon

4 teaspoons fresh lemon juice

1/2 teaspoon ground cinnamon

1/4 teaspoon freshly grated nutmeg

1/8 teaspoon salt

3 tablespoons unsalted butter, cut into small pieces

1. To make the crust, sift together the flour and salt into a medium-size mixing bowl. Using a pastry blender or a fork, blend in the shortening until the mixture resembles coarse crumbs.

2. Sprinkle in the ice water, a tablespoon at a time, mixing lightly after each addition until the pastry just holds together. If the dough feels too dry and crumbly, add 1 additional teaspoon cold water. Gather the dough into a ball and divide it in half. Keep 1 piece of dough refrigerated as you work with the other piece.

3. Roll out 1 piece of the dough out on a lightly floured board to a 1/8-inch-thick rectangle about 9 × 6 inches. Using a ruler as a guide, cut the pastry with a pastry wheel into five 1-inch-wide strips. Roll out and cut the second piece of dough in the same manner. Put the strips of dough on a large plate, sprinkle them with the granulated sugar, then cover and refrigerate.

4. To make the filling, bring a large pot of water to a boil and add the peaches. Turn off the heat, and let the peaches stand for about 30 seconds. Drain the peaches and refresh them under cold running water. Peel and pit the peaches, then slice them 1/2 inch thick.

5. Toss the peaches with the brown sugar, Cognac, flour, lemon zest, lemon juice, cinnamon, nutmeg, and salt in a medium-size bowl. Cover and let stand for 30 minutes.

6. Adjust an oven rack to the lowest shelf and preheat the oven to 350°F.

7. Spoon the peaches and their syrup into a 9½-inch pie pan. Dot with the butter.

8. Arrange half the pastry strips diagonally over the peaches, spacing them 1 inch apart. Arrange the remaining strips over the first ones to form a lattice following the instructions in the box on page 432. Trim the pastry overhangs at the rim.

9. Place the pan on a baking sheet to catch any drippings. Bake until the pastry is golden brown, about 45 to 50 minutes. Remove the cobbler from the oven and cool slightly on a rack. Serve warm.

SPICED APPLE CAKE

YIELD: 10 TO 12 SERVINGS

You don't need be an experienced baker to pull off this homey cake, which can be made quickly. I've added applesauce to the batter, to pro-vide extra moisture, and chunks of fresh apple on top for extra texture. If the flavor of cardamom is not to your liking, substitute nutmeg. This cake is at its best when served warm, with a cup of tea or coffee. Any leftover cake should be wrapped tightly in plastic and stored in the refrigerator for up to 1 week. Reheat the cake lightly in the oven before serving, if you wish.

1½ cups unbleached all-purpose flour
1 teaspoon baking soda
½ teaspoon ground cardamom
½ teaspoon ground cinnamon
½ teaspoon ground cloves
⅛ teaspoon salt
6 tablespoons (¾ stick) unsalted butter, cut
    into small pieces, at room temperature
¾ cup plus 1 tablespoon sugar
1 large egg, lightly beaten
1 cup applesauce
½ cup raisins or coarsely chopped dates
½ cup chopped walnuts
4 medium tart apples, preferably McIntosh

1. Adjust an oven rack to the middle shelf and preheat the oven to 350°F. Butter an 8-inch square baking pan.

2. Sift together the flour, baking soda, cardamom, cinnamon, cloves, and salt into a bowl. Set aside.

3. In a large mixing bowl, beat the butter with a wooden spoon until soft, then stir in ¾ cup of the sugar, a little at a time, beating until smooth. Beat in the egg. Stir in the flour mixture in 3 parts, alternating with the

USEFUL CAKE HINTS

✦ *To measure flour, fill a dry-measure cup by dipping it into the flour or spooning the flour into it, then level it off with the straight edge of a knife.*

✦ *Unless you avoid animal fats, do not substitute shortening, margarine, or other vegetable-fat-based spreads for the butter in cakes. Because these shortenings don't have as fine a taste or texture as butter and do not hold up as well in baking, your cakes will not turn out satisfactorily.*

✦ *Creaming butter requires butter that is at room temperature. To speed up the softening process, cut the butter into smaller pieces and let it stand a while at room temperature, or knead it with your fingers.*

✦ *Fill cake pans no more than two-thirds full to allow room for the batter to rise.*

✦ *After filling a cake pan, tap the bottom of the pan once or twice on the work surface to evenly distribute*

the batter and eliminate any air bubbles trapped inside. Smooth the top of the batter with a rubber spatula, if necessary.

✦ *Allow 10 to 15 minutes for your oven to preheat before baking.*

✦ *To ensure even baking, always bake the cake on the center rack of the oven. Rotate the pan halfway through the baking time.*

✦ *Let cakes cool in their pans on wire racks for 10 to 15 minutes before loosening them. If the cake should stick to the pan, use a metal spatula to loosen it gently.*

✦ *When cooling a layer or loaf cake, place a rack over the cake pan, invert it, and lift off the pan. Place a second rack against the bottom of the cake, invert again, and let the cake cool right side up.*

---

applesauce. The batter should be dense and smooth. Stir in the raisins and nuts.

4. Scrape the batter into the prepared pan, and smooth out the top. Peel, quarter, and core the apples. Cut each quarter lengthwise into ½-inch-thick wedges. Press the apple wedges into the batter in rows. Sprinkle the remaining 1 tablespoon sugar over the apples.

5. Bake until the cake is golden brown and a bamboo skewer inserted in the center comes out clean, about 1 hour. Cool in the pan on a rack. Serve warm.

VARIATION

PASSION FRUIT FROSTED CAKE: Follow the directions for Spiced Apple Cake, but omit the cardamom, cinnamon, and cloves and the apple topping. After the cake has cooled, spread it with Passion Fruit Frosting (see Index), and arrange fresh nectarine, peach, papaya, or mango slices on top of the cake.

CHERRY CLAFOUTI

YIELD: 6 TO 8 SERVINGS

Clafouti is an Italian country cake made with fruit (which the French have adopted as their own but make denser, more like a thick pancake, usually with black cherries). Since I love anything with cherries in it, I have made it a practice to bake this delectable cake (Italian-style) every summer at the height of the cherry season. Don't limit this dessert to cherries. Pears, peaches, nectarines, and even blueberries, raspberries, and strawberries also work quite successfully. If you want to upgrade this dessert a notch, serve it with Raspberry Sauce. Cover any leftover clafouti loosely with aluminum foil and store at room temperature for the first day after baking. For longer storage, refrigerate it for up to four additional days. Reheat before serving in a preheated 350°F oven until slightly warm (about 10 minutes).

1 pound fresh Bing cherries, pitted
½ cup plus 2 teaspoons sugar
¼ cup plus 1 tablespoon kirsch (cherry brandy)
  or Amaretto
8 tablespoons (1 stick) unsalted butter,
  at room temperature
2 large egg yolks
1 large egg
1 teaspoon almond extract
½ cup unbleached all-purpose flour,
  sifted
¼ teaspoon ground cloves
Raspberry Sauce (recipe follows; optional)

1. In a small bowl, toss the pitted cherries with 2 teaspoons of the sugar and 1 tablespoon of the kirsch. Set aside.

2. Adjust an oven rack to the lowest shelf and preheat the oven to 400°F. Butter a 9-inch round Pyrex baking dish.

3. Place the remaining ½ cup sugar and the butter in a small bowl. Using an electric mixer at medium speed, cream the mixture until light and fluffy, about 5 minutes. Beat in the egg yolks and egg, 1 at a time, at 1-minute intervals, scraping the sides of the bowl occasionally. Reduce the speed to low. Blend in the almond extract and the remaining ¼ cup kirsch. The mixture will look curdled.

4. Mix the flour and ground cloves and add all at once, scraping the sides of the bowl again. Increase the speed to medium-low and mix until the batter is smooth, approximately 30 seconds longer. Take care not to overmix. The batter will have the consistency of thick cream.

5. Place three-quarters of the cherries and their juices in the bottom of the baking dish. Spread the batter over the fruit. Arrange the remaining fruit on top.

6. Bake until the cake is golden brown and puffed, and a bamboo skewer inserted in the center comes out clean, 30 to 35 minutes.

7. Remove from the oven. Cool in the baking dish on a rack. Serve warm with Raspberry Sauce, if desired.

Raspberry Sauce

YIELD: ABOUT 1 CUP

 ou can also make this recipe with blackberries.

1 pint (2 cups) fresh raspberries
5 tablespoons confectioners' sugar

1. Combine the raspberries and confectioners' sugar in a small saucepan. Cook over low heat until the berries are soft, 3 to 4 minutes.

2. Transfer the mixture to a food processor or blender and purée it. Strain through a fine sieve into a small bowl and discard the seeds. Stir in 2 tablespoons cold water to thin the sauce.

3. Transfer the sauce to a jar and refrigerate for up to 1 week.

APRICOT KUCHEN

YIELD: 8 TO 10 SERVINGS

Kuchen are the German or Austrian equivalents of our coffee cakes. In German homes, a good hostess always makes sure that she has a kuchen or two on hand to welcome guests over tea or coffee. These simple, homey confections are usually leavened with yeast or baking powder, and may or may not include fresh fruit. Some call for whole eggs, others only yolks; some require ground almonds, others don't. There are dense cakes and lighter ones. I like mine with whole eggs, almond extract, sliced almonds, and fresh apricot halves pressed into the batter. Leavened with baking powder, it's an excellent, feathery-light kuchen in which the tart apricots marry well with the almonds. This cake is particularly delicious when served warm with whipped cream, but it is also perfectly good just as it is. Instead of fresh apricots, you can use fresh plums, pears, mangoes, or peaches. If you do, cut the larger fruits into wedges, then rub them with some fresh lemon juice to prevent discoloration.

1 cup unbleached all-purpose flour

1½ teaspoons baking powder

½ teaspoon salt

8 tablespoons (1 stick) unsalted butter,
    at room temperature

½ cup plus 1 tablespoon granulated
    sugar

3 large eggs

2 teaspoons almond extract

1 teaspoon vanilla extract

8 fresh apricots (about 1 pound total)

½ cup sliced almonds (unblanched)

Confectioners' sugar, for dusting

Chantilly Cream (page 411; optional)

1. Adjust an oven rack to the middle shelf and preheat the oven to 375°F. Butter and flour a 10-inch springform pan.

2. Sift together the flour, baking powder, and salt into a medium-size mixing bowl and set aside.

3. Using an electric mixer at medium speed, cream the butter with ½ cup of the sugar in a large mixing bowl until light and fluffy, about 5 minutes. At low speed, beat in the eggs, one at a time, and continue beating until the eggs are well incorporated and the mixture is fluffy. Blend in the almond and vanilla extracts. At this point, the mixture will look curdled.

4. With the mixer at low, gradually add the flour mixture. Continue beating at low speed until the batter is thick and smooth, about 1 minute, stopping to scrape down the sides of the bowl once or twice. Do not over-mix the batter.

5. Scrape the batter into the prepared pan, spreading evenly. Cut each apricot in half and remove the pits. Gently press the apricots, cut side down, into the batter. Sprinkle the top with sliced almonds and remaining 1 tablespoon sugar.

6. Bake until the top of the kuchen is brown and firm and a bamboo skewer inserted in the center comes out clean, 35 to 40 minutes. Cool in the pan on a rack.

7. To release the cake, run a small, sharp knife around the sides of the pan. Remove the sides of the pan, transfer the kuchen to a platter, and dust with confectioners' sugar. Serve warm with Chantilly Cream, if desired.

TIPS FOR PREPARING CAKE PANS

Follow these simple tips for buttering and flouring your cake pans before baking. They will ensure easy cake removal.

✦ *Use a pastry brush to apply a light film of melted butter on the bottom and sides of the cake pan. Or instead of butter, use a pure vegetable cooking spray to lightly coat the cake pan.*

✦ *Sprinkle a little flour into the pan. Tilt and tap the pan so the flour covers all the buttered surfaces. Tap out the excess flour and discard it.*

BANANA-CRANBERRY UPSIDE-DOWN CAKE

YIELD: 8 SERVINGS

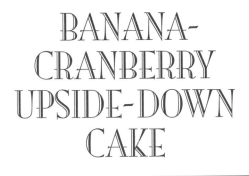

When my mother married an American officer and our family moved to France, my stepfather introduced us to all sorts of cakes and pies. He was a very good cook and baker. As I remember, the very first dessert he made for us was the all-American pineapple upside-down cake. My sister and I loved it so much we devoured the whole cake at one sitting. Ever since, I have always associated upside-down cakes with pineapple—until I came to America. To my delight, I discovered that you can top this cake with almost any fruit that you wish. In turn, I'm now happy to share with you my favorite upside-down cake, with banana and cranberry topping. Be sure to serve this cake warm; that's when it's at its best. You can prepare the cake one day before serving,

then cover and refrigerate it. Gently reheat the cake in a low oven right before serving.

TOPPING

5 tablespoons unsalted butter

$2/3$ cup (firmly packed) light brown sugar

$1/2$ teaspoon ground cinnamon

$1/2$ teaspoon ground cloves

$1/2$ teaspoon ground ginger

2 ripe bananas

1 cup fresh or frozen whole cranberries

CAKE

$1 1/2$ cups unbleached all-purpose flour

2 teaspoons baking powder

$1/2$ teaspoon salt

$2/3$ cup milk

1 teaspoon vanilla extract

$1/2$ teaspoon finely grated lemon zest

8 tablespoons (1 stick) unsalted butter, at room temperature

$1/2$ cup granulated sugar

2 large eggs

Raspberry Sauce (page 439; optional)

1. Adjust an oven rack to the middle shelf and preheat the oven to 350°F.

2. To make the topping, place the butter, brown sugar, cinnamon, cloves, and ginger in a 9- or 10-inch ovenproof skillet and cook over medium heat, stirring, until the butter is melted. Remove from the heat.

3. Cut the bananas on the diagonal into $1/2$-inch-thick slices, and arrange them over the mixture in the skillet. Add the cranber-

ries, pressing them into the spaces between the bananas. Set aside.

4. To make the cake, sift together the flour, baking powder, and salt into a bowl. In a separate bowl, mix the milk with the vanilla extract and lemon zest. Set aside.

5. Using an electric mixer at medium speed, cream the butter with the sugar until light and fluffy. Add the eggs, one at a time, beating well at low speed after each addition. Add the flour mixture in 3 parts, alternating with the milk mixture, beating after each addition until the batter is smooth.

6. Pour the batter over the fruits in the skillet, and bake until a bamboo skewer inserted in the center of the cake comes out clean, 45 to 50 minutes. Let the cake sit in the skillet for 15 minutes. Invert the cake onto a plate, then slide it onto a serving platter. Serve warm with Raspberry Sauce, if desired.

COSMIC CHOCOLATE CAKE

YIELD: 10 TO 12 SERVINGS

The combination of brandied sour cherries and bittersweet chocolate is so enchanting that, to honor the components, I had to include this wonderful rendition of chocolate cake. More complex and delicious than ordinary chocolate cake, this version is dense and very moist, almost fudgelike in the interior. I guarantee this dessert is worth cheating on your diet for! Dried cranberries can stand in for the dried sour cherries in a pinch. Also, plan to prepare the Brandied Sour Cherries at least 1 week in advance for the fruits to mellow.

$\frac{1}{2}$ cup dried sour cherries
$\frac{1}{4}$ cup brandy, preferably Cognac
12 ounces bittersweet chocolate, preferably
     Callebaut or Valrhona, coarsely chopped
12 tablespoons (1$\frac{1}{2}$ sticks) unsalted butter
6 large eggs, at room temperature
6 large egg yolks, at room temperature
$\frac{1}{2}$ cup granulated sugar
$\frac{1}{3}$ cup plus 1 tablespoon unbleached
     all-purpose flour
Confectioners' sugar, for dusting
Brandied Sour Cherries
     (recipe follows)
Chantilly Cream
     (page 411) or
     vanilla ice cream
     (optional)

1. Combine the dried cherries with the brandy in a small saucepan and bring to a simmer over medium heat. Remove from the heat, cover, and let sit while you prepare the cake batter.

2. Adjust an oven rack to the middle shelf and preheat the oven to 325°F. Butter and flour a 9-inch springform pan.

USEFUL CHOCOLATE TIPS

*H*ere are a few things to keep in mind when you are working with chocolate:

✦ Chocolate melts most easily if it is grated or chopped first.

✦ When grating chocolate, hold it with a paper towel to insulate it from the heat of your hand.

✦ When you need a large quantity of grated chocolate, coarsely chop the chocolate, place it in a food processor, and pulse until it is finely ground.

✦ Melting chocolate at a very low temperature is critical to the final texture. It should be melted gradually in a warm water bath or chocolate warmer until the temperature reaches approximately 86 °F. If over- or underheated, the chocolate will turn gray and lose its gloss. Temperatures over 115 °F will make the chocolate thick and coarse.

✦ Make sure that the water in the bottom of the dou-ble boiler barely simmers and doesn't boil. Do not let the hot water touch the bottom of the pan containing the chocolate, because too much heat will scorch the chocolate.

✦ While the chocolate is melting, it must be protected from any contact with water or any other liquid, as liquids tend to cause the chocolate to stiffen and "seize." If that happens, stir in 1 teaspoon cold unsalted butter for each ounce of chocolate to smooth out the chocolate.

✦ For the smoothest melted chocolate, stir it constantly; never leave it unattended.

✦ Chocolate can also be melted in a microwave. Put the grated chocolate in a glass bowl. Cover with plastic wrap and microwave on high power for 30 seconds and stir. Continue to microwave and stir at 30 second intervals until the chocolate is completely melted and smooth.

3. Place the chocolate and butter in a metal bowl or the top of a double boiler, and place it over a pan of simmering water (it should not touch the water). Stir until the mixture is melted and very smooth. Remove the bowl from the heat and let the chocolate cool.

4. Combine the whole eggs, egg yolks, and granulated sugar in another bowl, and place the bowl over the pan of simmering water. Stir just until the egg mixture feels warm and the sugar is dissolved. Remove the bowl from the heat. Using the whisk attachment of your mixer, beat the warm egg mix-ture at high speed until the batter is pale, thick, and tripled in volume, about 8 minutes, depending on the power of your mixer. Reduce the speed to low, and gradually stir in $1/3$ cup of the flour.

5. Off the heat, using a long spatula or wooden spoon, gradually stir the cooled chocolate mixture into the egg batter. As you stir, make sure to lift the batter gently from the bottom rather than stirring it in a circular motion. Mix just until the color is uniform, no more.

6. Drain the cherries, then toss to coat

them with the remaining 1 tablespoon flour. Gently stir the cherries into the batter, the same way you mixed in the chocolate, being careful not to overmix.

7. Scrape the batter into the prepared cake pan. Bake until the cake is set and a bamboo skewer inserted into the center comes out clean, about 1 hour. Cool slightly in the pan on a rack.

8. Run a sharp knife around the edges of the cake, then unmold it onto a cake plate. Sprinkle the cake lightly with confectioners' sugar, top with Brandied Sour Cherries, and serve with Chantilly Cream, if desired.

Brandied Sour Cherries

YIELD: 1 PINT

Green grapes, plums, apricots, figs, raspberries, or kumquats can be preserved the same way. As a bonus, the fruit-infused brandy may be served by itself as an after-dinner digestif. Spoon the fruit and its syrup over warm cake or ice cream. It's potent but delicious! The macerated fruit will be ready in 1 week and it will keep for up to 1 year. As you use the cherries, add more

fruit, spirit, and sugar so that you have a steady supply. Allow the fruit to macerate for 1 week after each addition. Instead of Cognac, you may want to try grappa, an Italian brandy, or vodka.

1½ cups fresh sour cherries, stems removed
½ cup sugar
½ cup Cognac

1. Pack the cherries into a clean pint jar, layering them with the sugar until the jar is about three-quarters full.

2. Add the Cognac to cover, and seal the jar. Gently shake the jar several times to distribute and dissolve the sugar. Refrigerate for at least 1 week before using.

HAWAIIAN SHORTCAKES

YIELD: 6 SERVINGS

Most of us associate shortcake with strawberries, but there's no rule that prevents us from using any fruit we fancy. Here, I have given shortcakes a Hawaiian twist by dressing them up with fresh pineapple and roasted macadamia nuts, all bathed in gingered, amber maple syrup. Similar shortcakes could be made with mango, papaya, or peaches.

SHORTCAKES

1 cup cake flour (not self-rising)

1 cup unbleached all-purpose flour

2 tablespoons granulated sugar

2 teaspoons cream of tartar

1 teaspoon baking soda

½ teaspoon salt

⅛ teaspoon ground ginger

8 tablespoons (1 stick) unsalted butter,
  cut into small pieces, well chilled

¾ cup plus 1 teaspoon light cream or
  half-and-half

PINEAPPLE FILLING

1 medium ripe fresh pineapple

⅔ cup maple syrup

1½ teaspoons finely grated peeled fresh ginger

1 cup well-chilled heavy (or whipping) cream

¼ cup sour cream

1 tablespoon granulated sugar

1 cup honey-roasted macadamia nuts,
  coarsely chopped

Confectioners' sugar, for dusting (optional)

A WORD ABOUT CAKE FLOUR

Cake flour is a soft-wheat flour that contains more starch and less gluten than all-purpose flour. It makes a cake or biscuit dough lighter and more delicate. Do not confuse cake flour with self-rising flour, which is all-purpose flour premixed with salt, baking powder, and baking soda. You may substitute 1 cup minus 2 tablespoons sifted all-purpose flour for each cup of cake flour called for in a recipe.

1. Adjust an oven rack to the middle shelf and preheat the oven to 400°F.

2. To make the shortcakes, sift together the flours, granulated sugar, cream of tartar, baking soda, salt, and ground ginger into a medium-size bowl. Using a pastry blender, fork, or your fingers, cut in the butter until the mixture resembles coarse meal. Make a well in the center. Add the light cream and stir with a spoon just until blended. The mixture should be soft and tender, similar to biscuit dough. Do not overmix.

3. Turn the dough out onto a well-floured board. Gather the dough and gently knead 2 or 3 times until it is well formed. Do not overwork. Pat the dough 5 or 6 times, into a disk about ¾ inch thick. Dip a 3-inch round cookie cutter in flour and cut out as many circles as possible. Gather the scraps into a ball, pat it into a circle, and cut out more rounds. (You should have a total of 6 biscuits.)

4. Place the biscuits on a baking sheet and bake until they are golden, 15 to 20 minutes. Transfer the biscuits to a rack to cool. (This can be made up to 4 hours ahead.)

5. To make the pineapple filling, peel, quarter, and core the pineapple. Halve each quarter lengthwise, then cut acrosswise into ½-inch-thick slices.

6. Combine the maple syrup and ginger in a medium-size saucepan. Bring to a simmer over low heat and cook for 2 to 3 minutes. Strain the sauce through a fine sieve into a medium-size bowl and add the pineapple

pieces. Discard the ginger. Let the mixture sit for 15 minutes, then strain, reserving the pineapple and the syrup. (This can be made 2 hours before serving.)

7. Ten minutes before serving, chill a large mixing bowl and the beaters of an electric mixer in the freezer. Combine the heavy cream, sour cream, and sugar in the chilled bowl and whip with the chilled beaters until soft peaks form.

8. Split the shortcakes horizontally. Place the bottom half of a shortcake on each of 6 dessert plates. Moisten each shortcake half with a tablespoon of the gingered syrup, then top with a generous spoonful of whipped cream. Scatter some pineapple and macadamia nuts over the whipped cream, then top the fruit with more whipped cream. Replace the biscuit tops. Drizzle with 1 tablespoon syrup. Dust the shortcakes with confectioners' sugar, if desired.

NOTE: Shortcakes should be assembled just before you are ready to serve them. Assembly ahead of time and refrigeration will make the biscuits too soggy. Also, room-temperature fruit is much more flavorful than cold fruit. If you wish, you may wrap and freeze unbaked shortcakes, and bake them as needed. Don't defrost them; just take them directly from the freezer to a preheated oven, but reduce the heat slightly and let them bake a few minutes longer.

VARIATION
ROASTED PEAR SHORTCAKES WITH BOURBON SAUCE: Prepare the shortcakes as directed above. As a filling, use the Roasted Pears with Bourbon Sauce (page 416, doubling the amounts for the Bourbon Sauce). Cut each roasted pear lengthwise into thin wedges and assemble the shortcakes as directed above, omitting the macadamia nuts.

TRIPLE STRAWBERRY SHORTCAKES

YIELD: 6 TO 7 SERVINGS

If you love strawberries as much as I do, this recipe is for you. As delicious as it is uncomplicated, this variation of strawberry shortcake has a rich concentrated strawberry flavor. I dub it "triple strawberry shortcake" because there are strawberries everywhere: in the biscuits, in the sauce, and in the ice cream. If that's more berry than you can take, use Chantilly Cream (see Index) instead of strawberry ice cream.

½ recipe Hot Strawberry Biscuits (page 301; see step 1 below)
2 pints (4 cups) fresh strawberries, hulled and sliced
¼ cup granulated sugar
Juice of 1 lemon
2 pints strawberry ice cream
Confectioners' sugar, for dusting (optional)

1. Prepare the biscuits as directed, but omit the rosemary and the glaze. Increase the grated lemon zest to 2 teaspoons.

2. Mix the strawberries with the granulated sugar and lemon juice in a medium-size bowl. Cover and let the mixture sit for 10 minutes, then mash with a potato masher.

3. Split the biscuits horizontally. Place the bottom half of a biscuit on each dessert plate. Top with a scoop of strawberry ice cream. Spoon some crushed strawberries over the ice cream, then replace the biscuit top. Spoon some more crushed strawberries over the shortcakes and dust with confectioners' sugar, if desired.

ORANGE-PINEAPPLE CHEESECAKE

YIELD: 10 TO 12 SERVINGS

To my mind, nothing is more inviting than a good, creamy piece of cheesecake. Since this comforting dessert lends itself to almost any fruit topping, I've given you one of my favorites—fresh pineapple chunks and bitter orange marmalade—in the main recipe, and followed it up with some wonderful variations.

The cheesecake itself is velvety smooth and light, and the topping is less sweet than tradition usually dictates. (I do not recommend using canned crushed pineapple, because it lacks the tanginess required to balance the sweet marmalade.) I sent a big piece to my husband's office for an approval rating. It became an instant hit! This cheesecake is ideal for entertaining, as it can be prepared up to 2 days ahead, covered, and refrigerated.

CHEESECAKE
1½ cups crushed vanilla wafers
4 tablespoons (½ stick) unsalted butter, melted
2 packages Neufchâtel or cream cheese
(1 pound total), at room temperature
⅓ cup sugar
Finely grated zest and juice of 1 lemon
2 large egg yolks

TOPPING
½ cup Seville orange marmalade
1 tablespoon dark rum
½ fresh ripe pineapple, peeled, cored,
and diced (about 2 cups)

1. Adjust 1 oven rack to the middle shelf and position a second rack just below it. Preheat the oven to 350°F. Butter a 9-inch springform pan.

2. To make the cake, mix the crushed vanilla wafers and the butter in a medium-size bowl. Press the mixture into the

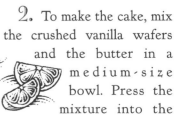

bottom and 2½ inches up the sides of the buttered pan to make a crust. Refrigerate.

3. Beat the Neufchâtel and sugar in a large mixing bowl until very smooth, using an electric mixer at medium speed. Add the lemon zest and juice and beat until smooth. Beat in the yolks, one at a time, until smooth, stopping occasionally to scrape down the sides of the bowl with a rubber spatula.

4. Scrape the filling into the prepared crust and place the pan in the center of the oven. Fill a roasting pan halfway with hot water and place it on the rack below the cake pan. This will produce steam during baking, resulting in a moist, smooth cheesecake. Bake until the cake is set around the edges but still slightly soft in the center, about 40 minutes. Transfer the cheesecake to a rack and cool completely. Cover and refrigerate at least 8 hours or overnight.

5. To make the topping, combine the marmalade and rum in a small saucepan, and heat over medium heat, stirring frequently, until just melted. Remove from the heat, and cool slightly. Transfer the pineapple to a colander and gently squeeze to remove excess moisture. Mix the pineapple with the orange marmalade.

6. Remove the cheesecake from the pan and set it on a large platter. Spread the fruit mixture evenly onto the cheesecake. Chill until ready to serve.

VARIATIONS

BLACK CHERRY TOPPING: Drain 1 cup syrup from 1 can (16 ounces) black cherries into a small saucepan. Stir 2 teaspoons cornstarch into the syrup. Bring the liquid to a simmer over medium heat, stirring frequently, and cook until the mixture is thickened, about 2 minutes. Stir in the cherries, 2 teaspoons fresh lemon juice, and 1 tablespoon kirsch, if desired. Cool the mixture before spooning it over the cheesecake. Refrigerate until the topping is set.

CRANBERRY TOPPING: Prepare one recipe of Light Cranberry Sauce (see Index), using only 4 teaspoons cornstarch. Cool the sauce before spooning it over the cheesecake. Refrigerate until the topping is set.

MANGO AND PASSION FRUIT TOPPING: Combine 3 tablespoons sugar and 2 teaspoons cornstarch with ¼ cup orange juice in a small saucepan. Stir to dissolve the cornstarch. Halve 6 passion fruits and scoop their contents into the saucepan. Bring the liquid to a simmer over medium heat, stirring frequently, and cook until the mixture thickens, about 2 minutes. Cool the sauce slightly. Spoon half the sauce onto the cheesecake. Peel 1 large mango and cut the fleshy cheeks into thin, long slices. Arrange the mango slices over the cheesecake, overlapping them slightly. Spoon the remaining sauce over the fruit. Refrigerate until the topping is set.

TRIPLE BERRY TOPPING: Combine 1½ cups sour cream with 3 tablespoons sugar. Five minutes before the cheesecake has finished baking, spoon the sour cream mixture over the cake, and return it to the oven to complete baking. Cool the cake and refrigerate it overnight. Heat ⅓ cup seedless raspberry preserves in a large skillet over medium heat until melted. Off the heat, toss in 1 cup each fresh blueberries, raspberries, and sliced strawberries with 1 tablespoon kirsch or framboise. Mound the berries on the cheesecake. Refrigerate 30 minutes before serving.

BLANCHING ALMONDS

*T*o blanch almonds, drop unpeeled whole almonds into boiling water for about 30 seconds. Drain, and slip the skins off with your fingers and discard. Dry with paper towels before using.

TUTTI FRUTTICAKE

YIELD: 1 LARGE FRUIT CAKE, OR 8 SMALL CAKES

I am not really fond of those commercial fruitcakes that are ubiquitous around the Christmas holidays. They are typically too dense—loaded with cloying candied fruit—dry, and flavorless. Come the holidays, I make my own fruitcake for fun. It's not too sweet and it's light, spirited (in at least two senses of the word!), and moist, with extra moisture provided by the addition of a fresh apple. For best results, make sure your dried fruits are soft to begin with. This long-lasting cake can be prepared 1 week in advance and stored in the refrigerator up to 2 months. For lovely holiday gifts, bake several cakes in small pans, seal them in foil, wrap with colored cellophane or tissue paper and tie with a handsome ribbon.

2 cups chopped dried peaches or apricots

2 cups golden raisins

1 cup chopped dried pears

1 cup chopped dried pineapple

1 large Granny Smith apple, peeled, cored, and coarsely chopped

1¾ cups bourbon or dark rum

¾ cup fresh orange juice

2½ cups unbleached all-purpose flour

¾ teaspoon ground cloves

¾ teaspoon freshly grated nutmeg

½ teaspoon salt

½ teaspoon baking soda

1 cup blanched slivered almonds, toasted (for blanching instructions, see box, above; for toasting instructions, see page 64), and coarsely chopped

12 tablespoons (1½ sticks) unsalted butter, at room temperature

½ cup sugar

4 large eggs

⅔ cup heavy (or whipping) cream or buttermilk

¼ cup honey

1. In a large mixing bowl, combine the dried fruits, apple, and 1¼ cups of the bourbon. Heat the orange juice in a small saucepan over low heat until warmed through. Pour it over the fruits. Cover and let stand at room temperature, tossing frequently, until the liquid has been absorbed, about 2 hours, or refrigerate overnight.

2. Adjust an oven rack to the middle shelf and preheat the oven to 325°F. Generously butter a 10-cup Bundt pan. Dust the pan with flour, shaking off any excess.

3. Sift 1 cup of the flour with the cloves, nutmeg, salt, and baking soda into a small bowl. Set aside. Add the remaining 1½ cups flour and the toasted almonds to the fruits, and toss thoroughly. Set aside.

4. With an electric mixer at medium speed, beat the butter and sugar in another large mixing bowl until light and fluffy. Add the eggs, one at a time, beating well after each addition. Add the sifted flour mixture in 3 parts, alternating with the cream, mixing well after each addition. Fold the batter into the fruit mixture, mixing well.

5. Scrape the mixture into the prepared pan. Smooth the top. Bake until a bamboo skewer inserted in the center of the cake comes out clean, about 1 hour 20 minutes. Cool the cake in the pan for 10 minutes, then turn it out onto a rack.

6. Combine the honey and the remaining ½ cup bourbon in a small saucepan, and cook over low heat, stirring, until the honey

has dissolved, about 2 minutes. Brush half of the hot glaze over the top and sides of the cake. Gently turn the cake over, and brush the remaining glaze over the top. Let the cake cool thoroughly.

7. Wrap the cake tightly in plastic wrap, then in heavy-duty aluminum foil. Let the cake mellow a couple of days at room temperature before serving.

VARIATION

MINIATURE FRUITCAKES: Use eight individual loaf pans, 5 ¾ × 3¼ × 2-inches deep, instead of the Bundt pan. Butter and flour the pans. Fill each with 1⅓ cups of batter, and smooth the tops. Bake for 45 minutes, then glaze as directed above.

A STAR IS BORN

Nobody knows for sure the origin of brownies, but it is said that a recipe for them first appeared in print in the 1897 Sears, Roebuck catalog. One story has it that they owe their humble beginnings to a baking "accident." Apparently, a cook's chocolate cake failed to rise. Since the cook couldn't bear throwing away the expensive chocolate confection, she (or maybe he) decided to serve it anyway, cutting the rather flat-looking cake into squares. When she served her unsuspecting guests the rich, moist, and slightly chewy sweet, they went absolutely wild. Encouraged by their enthusiastic response, the cook repeated her baking "failure," and a new culinary sensation was born. All of our baking disasters should have such splendid results!

HEAVENLY RASPBERRY BROWNIES

YIELD: 16 BROWNIES

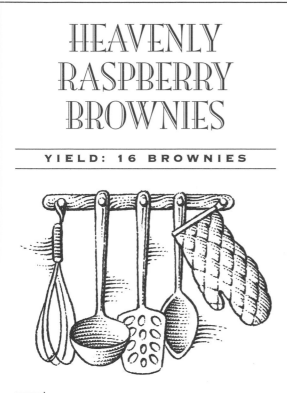

For nearly a century, brownies have tempted Americans, even those who are indifferent to chocolate. Brownies can vary from softly moist to fudgy to thick and cakey. The idea of adding raspberries to brownies came to me one day when my certified-chocoholic husband ordered a chocolate cake at a restaurant. The fudgy, dark dessert came in a pool of raspberry sauce with fresh raspberries strewn around it. From that moment on, I was determined to come up with a perfect recipe for brownies that paired bitter dark chocolate with sweet raspberries. And, here it is! Well wrapped, these luscious brownies will keep moist and fresh for at least a week in the refrigerator. They would also make a most seductive Valentine's Day gift!

5 squares (5 ounces) unsweetened chocolate, preferably Baker's, coarsely chopped

4 tablespoons ($\frac{1}{2}$ stick) unsalted butter

3 large eggs, at room temperature

$1\frac{1}{4}$ cups sugar

1 teaspoon vanilla extract

$\frac{1}{4}$ cup unbleached all-purpose flour

2 tablespoons unsweetened cocoa, plus 2 teaspoons, for dusting

1 teaspoon baking powder

$\frac{1}{2}$ teaspoon salt

$1\frac{1}{2}$ cups raspberries, thawed and drained, if frozen

1. Adjust an oven rack to the middle shelf and preheat the oven to 325°F. Butter and flour a 9-inch square pan.

2. Place the chocolate and butter in a metal bowl or top of a double boiler and melt the mixture over a pan of barely simmering water, stirring with a wooden spoon until smooth. Remove from the heat and let the mixture cool.

3. In a bowl with an electric mixer, beat the eggs, sugar, and vanilla extract at high speed until light and fluffy, 2 to 3 minutes. Sift in the flour, 2 tablespoons of the cocoa, the baking powder, and salt. Mix on low speed to combine, stopping once or twice to scrape the sides of the bowl with a rubber spatula.

4. Fold in the raspberries with a rubber spatula, then scrape the batter into the prepared baking pan. Bake for 40 to 45 minutes, or until a bamboo skewer inserted in the

center comes out with some crumbs adhering to it.

5. Cool the brownies in the pan on a wire rack. Cut the brownies into 16 squares and sprinkle with the remaining 2 teaspoons cocoa.

LEMON-STRAWBERRY SQUARES

YIELD: 16 SQUARES

These cookies have a satisfying melt-in-your mouth consistency, an agreeable sweet, tart, and fruity taste, and a homey character with lots of charm. They are perfect to make in early June, when fresh strawberries are at their peak. After they have cooled, cover and store them in the refrigerator; that is, if they are not gone already!

1 cup plus 3 tablespoons unbleached all-purpose flour
$^{1}/_{3}$ cup confectioners' sugar, plus extra for dusting
8 tablespoons (1 stick) unsalted butter, cut into small pieces, well chilled
2 tablespoons sour cream
$^{1}/_{2}$ teaspoon vanilla extract
$^{1}/_{2}$ cup granulated sugar
$^{1}/_{4}$ teaspoon salt
$^{1}/_{2}$ cup milk
3 large egg yolks
$^{1}/_{4}$ cup fresh lemon juice
Grated zest of 1 lemon
$^{3}/_{4}$ cup sliced fresh strawberries

1. Adjust an oven rack to the lowest shelf and preheat the oven to 350°F.

2. Place 1 cup of the flour, the confectioners' sugar, and butter in a food processor. Pulse until the mixture resembles coarse meal. Add the sour cream and vanilla extract. Process briefly, 2 to 3 seconds, or until the dough is just moistened.

3. Transfer the dough to a lightly floured surface, and press it together to form a rough square. Press the block of dough evenly into the bottom and $^{1}/_{2}$ inch up the sides of a 9-inch square baking pan.

4. Bake the crust until it is pale golden, about 20 minutes.

5. Mix the granulated sugar, the remaining 3 tablespoons flour, and salt in a small saucepan. Whisk in the milk, egg yolks, lemon juice, and lemon zest.

USEFUL COOKIE TIPS

*F*or maximum taste and minimum effort, follow these tips when making cookies:

✦ Unless you avoid animal fats, do not substitute shortening, margarine, or other vegetable-fat-based spreads for butter. Because these shortenings don't have as fine a taste or texture as butter and do not hold up as well in baking, your cookies will not turn out satisfactorily.

✦ When using an electric mixer, start mixing the ingredients at low speed to prevent them from flying out of the bowl. Take the same precaution when mixing flour into wet ingredients.

✦ Whenever a cookie dough mixture seems too soft to handle, simply chill it in the freezer until it's just firm enough, 20 to 30 minutes. Chilling makes the dough easier to shape or to roll, and results in more tender cookies.

✦ Drop-cookie doughs tend to spread more than other cookie doughs do. So to keep these doughs from spreading too much, chill them after mixing, then drop them onto cool cookie sheets and bake. If you are reusing cookie sheets that are straight from the oven, be sure to let them cool completely before baking your next batch of cookies.

✦ Cookie dough can be rolled up in waxed paper or aluminum foil, sealed in freezer bags, and stored either in the refrigerator for up to 1 week or in the freezer for up to 3 months. When ready to bake, bring the stiff dough to room temperature before shaping and baking.

✦ Baked cookies also keep well in the freezer. Remove them from the container or bag before thawing, so they will retain their crispness. If they should become too soft, arrange them in a single layer on a baking sheet and place in a pre-heated 325°F oven about 5 to 10 minutes to recrisp them.

---

6. Cook the mixture over medium heat, stirring, until it thickens, 5 to 7 minutes. Remove the pan from the heat, then stir in the strawberries. Place the pan in a large bowl of ice water and stir the custard until it is cool.

7. Spread the cooled custard over the crust. Bake until the custard is set, about 30 minutes.

8. Remove the pan from the oven and let cool on a rack. Dust with confectioners' sugar and cut it into 16 squares.

BANANA-CHOCOLATE CHIP COOKIES

YIELD: ABOUT 6 DOZEN COOKIES

---

*T*he first banana arrived in Boston harbor with Captain Lorenzo Baker in 1870, and the fruit quickly became popular with American cooks. It's now ubiquitous, having found its way into numerous confections, like breads, pies, cakes, and even cookies. A delicious variation on traditional chocolate chip cookies results when bananas are added to the batter. Banana is a great compliment to the chocolate and makes the cookies soft and fluffy.

2¼ cups unbleached all-purpose flour
½ teaspoon baking powder
½ teaspoon baking soda
1 teaspoon salt
2 large ripe bananas
2 teaspoons banana extract (available in health food stores) or vanilla extract
1 cup vegetable shortening, preferably Crisco, at room temperature
½ cup granulated sugar
½ cup (firmly packed) light brown sugar
2 large eggs
1 cup semisweet chocolate chips
1 cup coarsely chopped walnuts

1. Adjust an oven rack to the middle shelf and preheat the oven to 400°F.

2. Sift together the flour, baking powder, baking soda, and salt. Set aside.

3. Mash the bananas with the banana extract, making about 1 cup. Set aside.

4. In the bowl of an electric mixer, beat the shortening and sugars at medium speed until light and fluffy, then blend in the mashed bananas. Add the eggs, one at a time, beating well after each addition. The mixture will look curdled. At low speed, blend in the flour mixture, stopping once or twice to scrape down the sides of the bowl with a rubber spatula. Fold in the chips and nuts.

5. Drop the dough by heaping teaspoonfuls 1½ inches apart onto ungreased baking sheets.

6. Bake until the cookies are golden brown, about 12 minutes, then remove to racks to cool. Store in a cookie jar for up to 1 week.

OATMEAL CRANBERRY COOKIES

YIELD: 2 DOZEN COOKIES

I never used to have much luck with oatmeal cookies. After several experiments, however, I came up with this recipe, which I think comes closest to what I like in a cookie. It has crunch, nutty flavors, and chewiness, and it is

not overly sweet. These oatmeal cookies also depart from the ordinary ones with the addition of dried cranberries, coconut flakes, and roasted peanuts. My husband and his colleagues, all of whom claim to be cookie experts, gave thumbs up to these fruity little confections.

½ cup cranberry juice cocktail

⅓ cup dried cranberries

⅓ cup raisins

1 cup unbleached all-purpose flour

½ teaspoon baking soda

½ teaspoon baking powder

½ teaspoon salt

8 tablespoons (1 stick) unsalted butter, at room temperature

½ cup (firmly packed) dark brown sugar

1 large egg

1 teaspoon vanilla extract

1 cup rolled oats

⅓ cup toasted shredded coconut (for toasting instructions, see page 64)

¾ cup unsalted dry-roasted peanuts, coarsely chopped

1. Adjust the oven rack to the middle shelf. Preheat the oven to 375°F. Butter 1 large baking sheet or two smaller ones.

2. In a small saucepan, bring the cranberry juice, cranberries, and raisins to a boil over medium heat and cook until the fruits start to plump and soften, about 1 minute, stirring once or twice. Strain the mixture through a sieve, reserving the liquid.

3. Sift together the flour, baking soda, baking powder, and salt into a medium-size bowl.

4. In the bowl of an electric mixer, beat the butter and sugar at medium speed until creamy. Add the egg and vanilla extract, and beat until smooth, stopping occasionally to scrape the sides of the bowl with a rubber spatula. Beat in 2½ tablespoons of the reserved cranberry liquid. The mixture will look curdled.

5. On low speed, gradually add the flour mixture, stopping to scrape the sides of the bowl with a rubber spatula. Mix in the oats, coconut, peanuts, cranberries, and raisins.

6. Drop the dough by heaping tablespoonfuls 1½ inches apart onto the baking sheet. Press each mound of dough lightly with wet fingers to form smooth 2½-inch rounds.

7. Bake until the cookies are lightly browned around the edges, about 12 minutes. Do not overbake. Using a wide metal spatula, transfer the cookies onto wire racks to cool.

SEASONAL FRUIT CHART

The table below shows the availability of fruits throughout the year. Orange dots indicate the months when each fruit is at its best and should be least expensive. Fruits like bananas, kiwis, lemons, limes, pineapples, and plantains are plentiful all year.

	JAN	FEB	MAR	APR	MAY	JUNE	JULY	AUG	SEPT	OCT	NOV	DEC
APPLES	●	●	●	●	●	●	●	●	●	●	●	●
APRICOTS					●	●	●	●				
AVOCADOS	●	●	●	●	●	●	●	●	●	●	●	●
BANANAS	●	●	●	●	●	●	●	●	●	●	●	●
BLACKBERRIES			●	●	●	●	●	●	●			
BLOOD ORANGES	●	●	●								●	●
BLUEBERRIES	●	●	●		●	●	●	●	●	●	●	●
CHERRIES	●	●			●	●	●	●				●
CLEMENTINES	●										●	●
CRANBERRIES	●								●	●	●	●
CURRANTS	●	●					●	●				●
DATES	●	●	●	●	●				●	●	●	●
FIGS								●	●	●		
GOOSEBERRIES								●	●	●		
GRAPEFRUITS	●	●	●	●	●	●	●	●	●	●	●	●
GRAPES	●	●	●	●	●	●	●	●	●	●	●	●
HUCKLEBERRIES								●	●			
KIWIS	●	●	●	●	●	●	●	●	●	●	●	●

	JAN	FEB	MAR	APR	MAY	JUNE	JULY	AUG	SEPT	OCT	NOV	DEC
KUMQUATS	●	●								●	●	●
LEMONS	●	●	●	●	●	●	●	●	●	●	●	●
LIMES	●	●	●	●	●	●	●	●	●	●	●	●
MANGOES	●	●	●	●	●	●	●	●	●	●	●	●
MELONS (Including Watermelon)	●	●	●	●	●	●	●	●	●	●	●	●
NECTARINES	●	●	●	●	●	●	●	●	●	●	●	●
ORANGES	●	●	●	●	●	●	●	●	●	●	●	●
PASSION FRUITS	●	●	●	●	●			●	●	●	●	●
PAPAYAS	●	●	●	●		●		●	●	●	●	●
PEACHES	●	●	●	●	●	●	●	●	●	●	●	●
PEARS	●	●	●	●	●	●	●	●	●	●	●	●
PERSIMMONS	●	●								●	●	●
PINEAPPLES	●	●	●	●	●	●	●	●	●	●	●	●
PLANTAINS	●	●	●	●	●	●	●	●	●	●	●	●
PLUMS	●	●	●	●	●	●	●	●	●	●	●	●
POMEGRANATES										●	●	●
RASPBERRIES		●	●	●		●	●	●	●	●		
STAR FRUITS	●	●	●					●	●	●	●	●
STRAWBERRIES	●	●	●	●	●	●	●	●	●	●	●	●
TANGERINES	●	●	●	●	●						●	●

C O N V E R S I O N   C H A R T

U.S. WEIGHTS AND MEASURES

1 pinch = less than $\frac{1}{8}$ teaspoon (dry)

1 dash = 3 drops to $\frac{1}{4}$ teaspoon (liquid)

3 teaspoons = 1 tablespoon = $\frac{1}{2}$ ounce (liquid and dry)

2 tablespoons = 1 ounce (liquid and dry)

4 tablespoons = 2 ounces (liquid and dry) = $\frac{1}{4}$ cup

$5\frac{1}{3}$ tablespoons = $\frac{1}{3}$ cup

16 tablespoons = 8 ounces = 1 cup = $\frac{1}{2}$ pound

16 tablespoons = 48 teaspoons

32 tablespoons = 16 ounces = 2 cups = 1 pound

64 tablespoons = 32 ounces = 1 quart = 2 pounds

1 cup = 8 ounces (liquid) = $\frac{1}{2}$ pint

2 cups = 16 ounces (liquid) = 1 pint

4 cups = 32 ounces (liquid) = 2 pints = 1 quart

16 cups = 128 ounces (liquid) = 4 quarts = 1 gallon

1 quart = 2 pints (dry)

8 quarts = 1 peck (dry)

4 pecks = 1 bushel (dry)

TEMPERATURES: FAHRENHEIT (F) to CELSIUS (C)

-10°F = -23.3°C (freezer storage)	300°F = 148.8°C
0°F = -17.7°C	325°F = 162.8°C
32°F = 0°C (water freezes)	350°F = 177°C (baking)
50°F = 10°C	375°F = 190.5°C
68°F = 20°C (room temperature)	400°F = 204.4°C (hot oven)
100°F = 37.7°C	425°F = 218.3°C
150°F = 65.5°C	450°F = 232°C (very hot oven)
205°F = 96.1°C (water simmers)	475°F = 246.1°C
212°F = 100°C (water boils)	500°F = 260°C (broiling)

APPROXIMATE EQUIVALENTS

1 quart (liquid) = about 1 liter

8 tablespoons = 4 ounces = $\frac{1}{2}$ cup = 1 stick butter

1 cup all-purpose presifted flour = 5 ounces

1 cup stone-ground yellow cornmeal = $4\frac{1}{2}$ ounces

1 cup granulated sugar = 8 ounces

1 cup brown sugar = 6 ounces

1 cup confectioners' sugar = $4\frac{1}{2}$ ounces

1 large egg = 2 ounces = $\frac{1}{4}$ cup = 4 tablespoons

1 egg yolk = 1 tablespoon + 1 teaspoon

1 egg white = 2 tablespoons + 2 teaspoons

CONVERSION FACTORS

If you need to convert measurements into their equivalents in another system, here's how to do it.

OUNCES TO GRAMS: multiply ounce figure by 28.3 to get number of grams

GRAMS TO OUNCES: multiply gram figure by 0.0353 to get number of ounces

POUNDS TO GRAMS: multiply pound figure by 453.59 to get number of grams

POUNDS TO KILOGRAMS: multiply pound figure by 0.45 to get number of kilograms

OUNCES TO MILLILITERS: multiply ounce figure by 30 to get number of milliliters

CUPS TO LITERS: multiply cup figure by 0.24 to get number of liters

FAHRENHEIT TO CELSIUS: subtract 32 from the Fahrenheit figure, multiply by 5, then divide by 9 to get Celsius figure

CELSIUS TO FAHRENHEIT: multiply Celsius figure by 9, divide by 5, then add 32 to get Fahrenheit figure

INCHES TO CENTIMETERS: multiply inch figure by 2.54 to get number of centimeters

CENTIMETERS TO INCHES: multiply centimeter figure by 0.39 to get number of inches

BIBLIOGRAPHY

Ackart, Robert. *Fruits in Cooking*. New York: Macmillan, 1973.

Bacon, Josephine. *Exotic Fruits A–Z*. Topsfield, Mass.: Salem House Publishers, 1989.

Beard, James. *Beard on Food*. New York: Alfred A. Knopf, 1974.

Beck, Bruce. *Produce: A Fruit and Vegetable Lover's Guide*. New York: Friendly Press, 1984.

Blanc, Georges. *The Natural Cuisine of Georges Blanc*. New York: Stewart, Tabori & Chang, 1987.

Brillat-Savarin, Jean Anthelme. *The Physiology of Taste*. Translated by M. F. K. Fisher. New York: North Point Press, 1986.

Colwin, Laurie. *Home Cooking*. New York: Alfred A. Knopf, 1988.

Cost, Bruce. *Bruce Cost's Asian Ingredients*. New York: William Morrow, 1988.

Courtine, Robert, ed. *Larousse Gastronomique*. Paris: Librairie Larousse, 1984.

Dumas, Alexandre. *Le Grand Dictionnaire de Cuisine*. Translated by Loris Colman. New York: Simon & Schuster, 1958.

Kirchner, Bharti. *The Healthy Cuisine of India*. Los Angeles: Lowell House, 1992.

Lee, Kay, and Marshall Lee, eds. *America's Favorites*. New York: Putnam, 1980.

Marcus, George, and Nancy Marcus. *Forbidden Fruits and Forgotten Vegetables: A Guide to Cooking with Ethnic, Exotic, and Neglected Produce*. New York: St. Martin's Press, 1982.

Mariani, John. *The Dictionary of American Food and Drink*. New York: Hearst Books, 1994.

McCully, Helen, and Eleanor Noderer, eds. *The American Heritage Cookbook*. New York: American Heritage Publishing Co./Bonanza Books, 1980.

Murdich, Jack. *Buying Produce: The Greengrocer's Guide to Selecting and Storing Fresh Fruits and Vegetables*. New York: William Morrow, 1980.

Root, Waverely. *Food: An Informal Dictionary*. New York: Simon & Schuster, 1980.

Rosso, Julee, and Sheila Lukins. *The New Basics*. New York: Workman Publishing, 1989.

Schlesinger, Chris, and John Willoughby. *Salsa, Sambals, Chutneys and Chowchows*. New York: William Morrow, 1993.

Schneider, Elizabeth. *Uncommon Fruits and Vegetables: A Commonsense Guide*. New York: Harper & Row, 1986.

Von Welanetz, Diana, and Paul Von Welanetz. *The Von Welanetz Guide to Ethnic Ingredients*. New York: Warner Books, 1987.

Woolfok, Margaret. *Cooking with Berries*. New York: Clarkson N. Potter, 1979.

INDEX

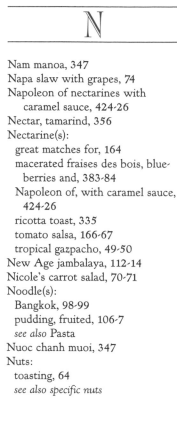

Q

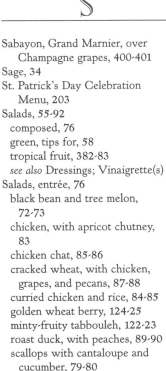

T